T0130705

Get the eBook FREE!

(PDF, ePub, Kindle, and liveBook all included)

We believe that once you buy a book from us, you should be able to read it in any format we have available. To get electronic versions of this book at no additional cost to you, purchase and then register this book at the Manning website.

Go to https://www.manning.com/freebook and follow the instructions to complete your pBook registration.

That's it!
Thanks from Manning!

Software Telemetry

RELIABLE LOGGING AND MONITORING

JAMIE RIEDESEL

MANNING

SHELTER ISLAND

Manning Publications Co.
20 Baldwin Road
PO Box 761
Shelter Island, NY 11964

Development editor:	Marina Michaels
Technical development editor:	Miloš Todorović
Review editor:	Aleksandar Dragosavljević
Production editor:	Deirdre S. Hiam
Copy editor:	Keir Simpson
Proofreader:	Keri Hales
Technical proofreader:	Serge Simon
Typesetter:	Gordan Salinovic
Cover designer:	Marija Tudor

ISBN 9781617298141
Printed in the United States of America

To my wife, Amy. We've been together over half our lives, from when we really met while you were avoiding a long walk in subzero Minnesota winter weather by hanging out in my dorm hall to everything we've done since. I love you.

brief contents

v

contents

preface

I came to software telemetry the way most of us do: as a producer through the use of print statements in my code and as a consumer by reading the logs and metrics produced by the code I was using. In spite of my computer science degree, I did not go into software engineering right out of college. No, I went into what was then called IT or operations, and I stayed there until I had clocked 14 years of experience. That brought me to 2011, which was a new era in a lot of ways.

That year, I left my job in higher education to join a 20-person legal technology startup as its only operations person. That year also was in the middle of a revolution in software telemetry, when the monitoring systems long used by operations teams and systems administrators started to be extended for use directly by software. The *metrics* style of telemetry was born. Over the next decade, we saw two more styles of telemetry emerge as databases became featured enough to support them: *observability* (which did not last long on its own) and *distributed tracing*.

When I had the idea for this book in 2019, I had watched the feedback software engineers use evolve over two and a half decades. In the beginning, it was common for developers to watch log files inside a telnet session directly in production, and by 2019, all that telemetry was instead accessed through browser-based applications. *Telemetry*—the feedback engineers use to understand their environments—was an understood concept centering on the three Pillars of Observability: logs, metrics, and traces. And I, who was still on the systems or platform side of the infrastructure, realized that all these new telemetry methods had the same core concepts—and the same core vulnerabilities. I looked for, and I found, plenty of resources on specific technologies such as Kafka,

Prometheus, application monitoring, and how to do centralized logging. But no resources discussed the *ecosystem* of telemetry systems that were available.

That lack is terrible. Telemetry systems underpin the efficient functioning of software development organizations, because these systems tell you how your code (and the systems that run your code) is operating. There are so many competing demands on our telemetry systems now. I set out to write a book to help you navigate these competing concerns, improve cost management, and get better at *operating* these mission-critical systems. This book is about improving what you're already doing and better adapting to new telemetry technologies as they emerge.

This book is about improving what you already have, because every software ecosystem has at least some telemetry at its core. Whether you're working on a planet-scale Software as a Service (SaaS) application that deploys to wider percentages of your global *data centers* as part of your canary deploy process, or a time-card entry system for your city government that you update every couple of months, you're using telemetry. *This book is both for companies in which software is the business and organizations in which software merely enables the mission.*

If your ecosystem is a fleet of serverless functions running in your cloud provider's platform, or if you're running a VMware ESX cluster down the hall, you need software telemetry in much the same ways, even if the tools you use are quite different. Telemetry is a vast topic, with no one product (or even technique) suiting everyone's needs. After reading this book, I want you to better understand what your needs are and how to go about meeting them.

As an industry, we've come a long way from the beginning of the digital age, when a blinking indicator light on the room-size computer was our only feedback that it was

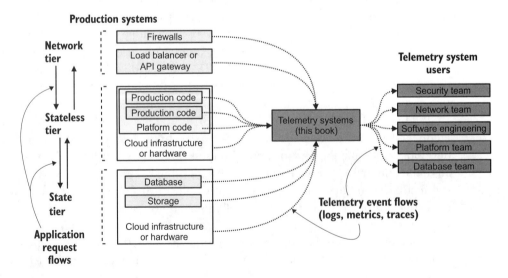

Figure 1 Where telemetry systems fit alongside production systems. All production systems emit telemetry; telemetry is how we know they're working right. This book is about the systems that handle that telemetry and transform it so that people can view it.

actually processing something. (Blinking too fast or too slow meant something was wrong.) The figure shows where telemetry systems fit into a modern web development stack, which is connected to everything.

We're not done innovating our feedback systems—not by a long shot. Expect fun and interesting things to come onto the market over the next 10 years. This book should set you up to operate those systems when they arrive.

acknowledgments

This book would have taken far longer to write without the sacrifices of my wife, Amy. Writing is a solitary job, especially when it isn't your main gig. Her contribution to this work was accepting many lonely evenings and weekends when I was there only for chores and meals, and she deserves recognition. Thank you so much. We've been together for more than 20 years; I think we can keep going.

Thanks to Josh for suggesting that I put in a proposal for this book. You had a kid coming and didn't have time for a big project, but you suspected that I might have the time. It turns out I did. You gave me the push I needed to bring this book to life.

Thanks to Alex, Corrine, and Jake for teaching me how enterprise IT works with Apple hardware. The Apple revolution happened after my time in IT, so I needed the example!

Thanks to my development editor, Marina, who certainly had to do some developing. The first versions of chapters 1–5 were quite different from what you see now. You stuck with me, and we made a book.

Further acknowledgements must go to the first-round reviewers, who gave me the feedback I needed to see all the problems with those first chapters. I got the hang of things by the time the third round of reviews came about.

Thanks to my technical development editor, Miloš, and my technical proofer, Serge, who together kept me honest in all things code. I may have a CompSci degree, but that doesn't make me a *software engineer*. Your actual software engineering points of view made my code samples far more useful to readers than they would have been otherwise. Most of them actually run!

I would also like to thank the rest of the staff at Manning: Deirdre Hiam, my project editor; Keir Simpson, my copy editor; and Keri Hales, my proofreader.

Thanks to all the reviewers: Aleksandr Novomlinov, Andres Sacco, Andrew Bovill, Clifford Thurber, Conor Redmond, Frederick Price, Joel Holmes, Karthik Sirasanagandla, Krishna Aerabati, Lokesh Kumar, Matthew Farwell, Mike Jensen, Milorad Imbra, Richard Vaughan, Rob Pacheco, Sander Zegveld, Serge Simon, Sergiu Raducu, Steven K. Makunzva, Sushant Bhadkamkar, Tim Wooldridge, and Warren Myers. Your suggestions helped make this book better.

I must also acknowledge the millions who died of COVID-19. This book is a pandemic book. I signed the deal to write it just as the world was hearing about Wuhan, China, and the problem there, and I finished writing while vaccine distribution was ramping up to truly heartening levels. Because 2020 and early 2021 were horrific times, I feel that any work put together in that time must pay homage to the dead. All the closures and lockdowns certainly gave me more time to write, and this book is not a small one, so it owes a debt to those we've lost and those who are still suffering.

about this book

Software Telemetry teaches you the general architecture of all telemetry systems while giving you many examples of real-world telemetry system designs as inspiration. Although every organization uses telemetry differently, telemetry still supports the same *decisions* in every organization. This book presents a systematic approach to operating these key decision-support systems.

Architecture is one thing, but telemetry system operators need to be familiar with certain techniques to reduce costs and better accomplish the mission of the organization. When your organization grows enough that *everyone can see all telemetry* is no longer a good idea, you need to adopt multitenancy concepts. When you are using a lot of regular expressions in your telemetry system, making those expressions more efficient will improve telemetry system performance. When your production code is running on platforms where local file access is problematic, such as containers or Function as a Service (FaaS), you need different ways to ship your telemetry. This book covers these techniques—and more.

Data regulations worldwide increasingly require special handling procedures for privacy- and health-related information—information that all too easily leaks into our telemetry systems. A decade ago, we mostly didn't care except for health information, but regulations like the European Union's General Data Protection Regulation (GDPR) are forcing us to care. Our telemetry systems need to deal with these changes the same way that our production systems do. This book details techniques you can use to defend against leaking protected data and to make cleaning up after leaks easier.

By the end of part 1, you should have a solid mental model of the architecture of telemetry systems, which will help you reason about new systems and improve the ones you already have. Part 2 helps you cement what you learned in part 1 by giving you 11 real-world examples of telemetry architectures in three different styles of organizations. By the end of part 3, you will have a suite of techniques you can use to solve problems in your current telemetry systems and make them easier to operate overall.

> **NOTE** This book is intended to help organizations that use containers exclusively, organizations that use containers merely as part of their operations, and organizations where containers haven't yet made their presence felt. As the author William Gibson said, "The future is already here—it's just not evenly distributed." So it is with containers and serverless techniques. The *abstract principles* I talk about apply to all computing types, container-based or not, whereas the *specific examples* I use to teach those principles draw from diverse computing styles. If I'm not covering your style as completely as you want, know that another reader is having their *Aha!* moment.

Who should read this book

This book is for people who are looking to improve their existing telemetry systems or are considering redesigning the ones that are already in use—systems engineers supporting centralized logging systems, software engineers writing observability systems for internal use, security engineers seeking to improve compliance, and more. This book is not code-centric, but I do use code to illustrate examples.

I assume that you have a basic ability to write code, which includes common data structures and conditional logic as well as reading and writing files, and that you understand what a stack dump is telling you. You also should have some familiarity with writing searches, either directly (as with SQL) or indirectly (through query builders). I don't assume that you have detailed database knowledge, but you should know the differences between tables, columns, and rows, and you should know in broad terms how relational databases like MS-SQL and PostgreSQL differ from NoSQL systems like Elasticsearch and MongoDB.

You will get more from this book if you have used or maintained telemetry systems such as these:

- SaaS providers like Datadog, New Relic, Splunk, Sumo Logic, and Honeycomb.io
- Dedicated log-shipping systems like Fluentd, Fluentbit, and Logstash
- Telemetry review platforms like Grafana, Kibana, and Jaeger
- Telemetry storage platforms like KairosDB, Elasticsearch, MongoDB, Cassandra, Loki, and Prometheus

How this book is organized: A road map

This book is divided into three parts. Part 1 gives you the general architecture that all telemetry systems follow, and you should read it before the other two parts.

- Chapter 1 introduces telemetry systems and provides definitions of the four styles of telemetry I cover in this book: centralized logging, security information event management, metrics, and distributed tracing. Even if you're working with this stuff every day, this chapter gives you the nomenclature I use throughout the book.
- Chapters 2–5 describe the three major stages of a telemetry pipeline—emitting, shipping, and presentation—and the techniques you use to move telemetry in each stage.
- Chapter 6 is about the types of transformations and markup you perform on telemetry in each of the three stages.
- Chapter 7 describes multitenancy concepts, why you sometimes need multitenancy, and how it changes telemetry system design.

Part 2 looks at three different types of organizations and follows how their telemetry use changes. Feel free to skip the chapters on organizations that you're not familiar with; they're here to give you more examples to chew through if you want.

- Chapter 8 follows the evolution of telemetry in a sample cloud-based company writing a SaaS application. This chapter starts at the small stage, when telemetry is entirely contained in the cloud provider's dashboards, and ends at the enterprise stage, when the company has brought most telemetry in-house.
- Chapter 9 follows how telemetry is used in organizations that write software only for internal use—if they write software at all. This chapter shows more about how telemetry is used in office IT contexts, which changes significantly as organization size increases, and how telemetry use expands when in-house development arrives.
- Chapter 10 follows how telemetry is used in legacy computing environments: mainframes. Don't be scared off; mainframes are merely components of an infrastructure, and their telemetry use will feel familiar.

Part 3 contains specific techniques that are useful for optimizing and improving telemetry system operation, and the chapters are written to be read individually.

- Chapter 11 walks through optimizing your use of regular expressions. Many telemetry systems rely on regular expressions to extract and transform telemetry, so optimizing them will give you performance boosts.
- Chapter 12 discusses standardized telemetry formats and walks you through building a structured logger. Structured loggers are key components of telemetry systems that involve in-house code.
- Chapter 13 dives into nonfile telemetry emitting techniques and provides a close look at how telemetry is used in container and FaaS environments.

- Chapter 14 digs into the issue of cardinality and shows how managing cardinality forces changes in telemetry systems.
- Chapter 15 covers telemetry integrity and ways to ensure that telemetry is not changed, even in environments that can't tolerate immutability.
- Chapter 16 addresses handling regulated information (toxic data) in your telemetry pipelines through redacting toxic-data spills both in real time and after the fact. The chapter also covers reprocessing—reingesting telemetry—to handle storage system upgrades or migrations to new platforms.
- Chapter 17 describes how to build retention policies to determine how long you store telemetry online and offline, how to create a metrics aggregation policy that maintains statistical validity, and how sampling improves the retention period for distributed tracing.
- Chapter 18 walks you through the impacts of legal discovery processes on telemetry and the early steps you can take to reduce the panic if you ever have to deal with discovery.
- Appendix A talks about seven telemetry storage systems, showing where each excels and where its use could be challenging.
- Appendix B is a reference for all the recommendation checklists I've built in the chapters.
- Appendix C contains answers and guidance for the exercises included throughout the book.

About the code

Telemetry systems cover a vast range of software, so no single code framework is suitable for a book about software telemetry. For examples written in general-purpose languages, I use Python 3 for its relative ubiquity. To a lesser extent, I use Ruby due to its better handling of certain edge cases and because two major telemetry shipping systems (Fluentd and Logstash) are written in Ruby, which is their extension language.

> **NOTE** For a thorough guide to Fluentd (part of the Cloud Native Computing Foundation), see *Logging in Action,* by Phil Wilkins (Manning, 2021; http://mng.bz/VGlW).

This book also includes configuration file examples from several frameworks. I don't expect you to run these files, but they are there to illustrate points and provide concrete examples. The configuration file format I most commonly use is Logstash (http://mng.bz/xGvg).

> **NOTE** The Gitlab repository for this book includes Java versions of most of the Python listings. You can find the GitLab repository at http://mng.bz/RKxv.

This book contains many examples of source code, both in numbered listings and inline with normal text. In both cases, source code is formatted in a `fixed-width font like this` to separate it from ordinary text. Sometimes, code is also **in bold** to highlight code that has changed from previous steps in the chapter, such as when a new feature adds to an existing line of code.

In many cases, the original source code has been reformatted; we've added line breaks and reworked indentation to accommodate the available page width in the book. In rare cases, even this was not enough, and listings include line-continuation markers (➥). Additionally, comments in the source code have been removed from the listings when the code is described in the text. Code annotations accompany many of the listings, highlighting important concepts.

liveBook discussion forum

Purchase of *Software Telemetry* includes free access to a private web forum run by Manning Publications where you can make comments about the book, ask technical questions, and receive help from the author and from other users. To access the forum, go to http://mng.bz/2zDa. You can also learn more about Manning's forums and the rules of conduct at https://livebook.manning.com/#!/discussion.

Manning's commitment to our readers is to provide a venue where a meaningful dialogue between individual readers and between readers and the author can take place. It is not a commitment to any specific amount of participation on the part of the author, whose contribution to the forum remains voluntary (and unpaid). We suggest that you try asking the author some challenging questions lest their interest stray! The forum and the archives of previous discussions will be accessible from the publisher's website as long as the book is in print.

Other online resources

Not every telemetry system uses regular expressions (*regexes*), but if yours does, you will be well served by https://regex101.com and its careful breakdown of how regexes perform. Each language processes regexes differently in small ways, but if your language is not on regex101, it will still help you reason through writing regexes in general.

The major public cloud providers, such as AWS and Azure, are starting to offer managed versions of telemetry systems, so now their documentation covers maintenance and operation of these telemetry styles. If your production systems are in a public cloud provider, the managed telemetry systems and their documentation are worth a look.

The video archives of the Monitorama conference (https://monitorama.com) contain presentations on metrics, distributed tracing, and system observability in general. Vendor conferences by telemetry SaaS providers such as o11ycon from Honeycomb.io (https://o11ycon-hnycon.io; *o11y* is a numeronym for *observability*, which has 11 characters between the beginning *o* and ending *y*) and {Future}Stack from New Relic (https://newrelic.com/futurestack) are additional sources of presentations and talks on the subjects I talk about in this book. More important, these conferences give you "how to use telemetry" guidance that deserves a book beyond this one.

about the author

JAMIE RIEDESEL is a staff engineer at Dropbox, working on the HelloSign product. She has more than 20 years of experience in the technical field, starting with office IT, moving to systems administration and engineering, and most recently working in DevOps. She has been presenting at technical conferences since 2015 on topics such as Logstash optimization, monitoring system refactoring, and getting over workplace-induced traumas. You can find her blog at https://sysadmin1138.net/mt/blog.

about the cover illustration

The figure on the cover of Software Telemetry is captioned "Catalanne," or a woman from Catalonia. I chose this image because it shows a woman between two places: market and home. This book is about the space between our production systems (market) and where we make our decisions (home). Someone had to build and maintain that road, just as someone has to build and maintain the systems that let us learn how our production systems are operating.

The illustration is taken from a collection of dress costumes from various countries by Jacques Grasset de Saint-Sauveur (1757–1810), titled *Costumes de Différents Pays*, published in France in 1797. Each illustration is finely drawn and colored by hand. The rich variety of Grasset de Saint-Sauveur's collection reminds us vividly of how culturally apart the world's towns and regions were just 200 years ago. Isolated from each other, people spoke different dialects and languages. In the streets or in the countryside, it was easy to identify where they lived and what their trade or station in life was just by their dress.

The way we dress has changed since then and the diversity by region, so rich at the time, has faded away. It is now hard to tell apart the inhabitants of different continents, let alone different towns, regions, or countries. Perhaps we have traded cultural diversity for a more varied personal life—certainly for a more varied and fast-paced technological life.

At a time when it is hard to tell one computer book from another, Manning celebrates the inventiveness and initiative of the computer business with book covers based on the rich diversity of regional life of two centuries ago, brought back to life by Grasset de Saint-Sauveur's pictures.

Introduction 1

This chapter covers

- What telemetry systems are
- What telemetry means to different technical groups
- Challenges unique to telemetry systems

Telemetry is the feedback you get from your production systems that tells you what's going on in there—feedback that improves your ability to make decisions about your production systems. For NASA, the production system might be a rover on Mars, but most of the rest of us have our production systems right here on Earth (and sometimes in orbit around Earth). Whether it's the amount of power left in a rover's batteries or the number of containers live in production right now, everything is telemetry. Modern computing systems, especially those operating at scale, live and breathe telemetry, which is how we can manage systems that large at all. Telemetry is ubiquitous in our industry:

- If you've ever looked at a graph describing site hits over time, you've used telemetry.
- If you've ever written a logging statement in code and later looked up those statements in a log-searching tool such as Kibana or Loggly, you've used telemetry.
- If you've ever researched application performance in Datadog, you've used telemetry.

1

- If you've ever configured the Apache web server to send logs to a relational database, you've used telemetry.
- If you've ever written a Jenkinsfile to send continuous integration test results to another system that could display it better, you've used telemetry.
- If you've ever configured GitHub to send webhooks for repository events, you've used telemetry.

As figure 1.1 shows, *Software Telemetry* is about the systems that bring you telemetry and display it in a way that will help you make decisions. Telemetry comes from all kinds of things, from the power distribution units your servers (or your cloud provider's servers) are plugged into to your running code at the top of the technical pyramid. Taking that telemetry from whatever emitted it and transforming it so that your telemetry can be displayed usefully is the job of the telemetry system. *Software Telemetry* is all about that system and how to make it durable.

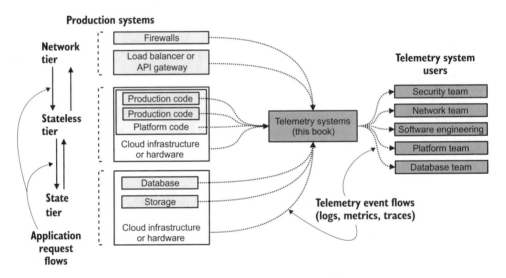

Figure 1.1   Where telemetry systems fit inside your overall technical infrastructure. Everything we run gives us some indication of how it is running. Those indications (dotted lines here) are telemetry, and this book is about handling that telemetry.

Telemetry is a broad topic and one that is rapidly changing. Between 2010 and 2020, our industry saw the emergence of metrics (adding to the monitoring that operations groups were already doing) and distributed tracing, which combined with logs into the three Pillars of Observability. We saw two new styles of telemetry systems in the past decade; who knows what we will see between 2020 and 2030? This book will teach you the fundamentals of how all telemetry systems operate, including ones you haven't seen yet, which will prepare you to modernize your current systems and adapt to new styles of telemetry. Any time you teach information passing and translation, which is what telemetry systems do, you unavoidably have to cover how *people* pass information. This book will teach you both the technical details of maintaining and upgrading telemetry systems and the conversations you need to have with your co-workers while you revise and refine your telemetry systems.

All telemetry systems have a similar architecture. Figure 1.2 is an architecture you will see often as you move through parts 1 and 2 of this book.

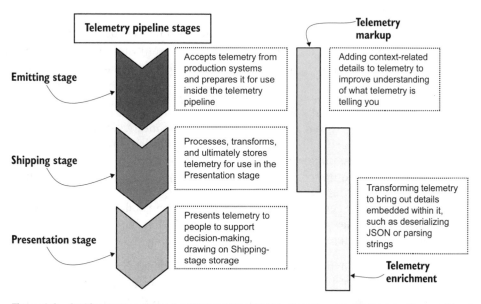

Figure 1.2 **Architecture common to all telemetry systems, though some stages are often combined in smaller architectures. The Emitting stage receives telemetry from your production systems and delivers it to the Shipping stage. The Shipping stage processes and ultimately stores telemetry. The Presentation stage is where people search and work with telemetry. The Emitting and Shipping stages can apply context-related markup to telemetry; the Shipping and Presentation stages can further enrich telemetry by pulling out the details encoded within.**

Telemetry is data that production systems emit to provide feedback about what is happening inside. Telemetry *systems* are the systems that handle, transform, store, and present telemetry data. This book is all about the systems, so let's take a look at the four major telemetry styles in use today:

- *Centralized logging*—The first telemetry system created, which happened in the early 1980s. This style takes text-based logging output from production systems and centralizes it to ease searching. Note that this technique is the only one widely supported by hardware.
- *Metrics*—Grew out of the monitoring systems used by Operations teams and was renamed metrics when software engineers adopted the technique. This system, which emerged in the early 2010s, focuses on numbers rather than text to describe what is happening. Metrics allow much longer timeframes to be kept online and searchable compared to centralized logging.

- *Distributed tracing*—Focuses directly on tracking events across many components of a distributed system. (Large monoliths count as a large distributed system, by the way.) This style emerged in the late 2010s and is undergoing rapid development.
- *Security Information Event Management* (SIEM)—A specialized telemetry system for use by Security and Compliance teams, and a specialization of centralized logging and metrics. The technique was in use long before the term was formalized in the mid-2000s.

These telemetry styles are used throughout this book, so you will see them mentioned a lot. Section 1.1 provides you longer definitions and histories of these telemetry styles and shows how each style conforms to the architecture in figure 1.1.

> **NOTE**   In the past couple of years, the concept of *Pillars of Observability* has emerged. The word *observability* was first used to define a specific style of telemetry and evolved as a sophistication of the metrics style. Today, however, *observability* is generally considered to be a practice rather than a telemetry style. The three pillars are logs, metrics, and traces. If you use all three styles, you are best equipped to observe how your system is operating. This book is about supporting the systems that provide your observability. The SIEM systems used by Security teams are a form of observability, telling you who did what, when they did it, how they did it, and what happened when they did, just like the Pillars.

Because people matter as much as the telemetry data being handled by our telemetry systems, section 1.2 breaks down the many teams inside a technical organization as well as the telemetry systems each team prefers to use. These teams are referenced frequently in the rest of this book.

Finally, telemetry systems face more disasters than production systems do. Section 1.3 covers some of these disasters in brief. Part 3 of this book has several chapters that are useful for making your telemetry systems durable.

1.1   Defining the styles of telemetry

The list of telemetry styles provided in the introduction to this chapter provides a nice thumbnail of what each style of telemetry does and will be a good reference for you as you move through this book. This section provides far more detailed definitions of the four telemetry styles and gives real-world examples of them.

1.1.1   Defining centralized logging

Centralized logging brings logging data generated by production systems to a central place where people can query it. Figure 1.3 shows an example of such a system in use today.

Centralized logging supports not just software telemetry, but hardware telemetry as well! The Syslog Server box in figure 1.3 represents the modern version of a system that was first written around 1980 as a dedicated logging system for the venerable

Example of a centralized logging system

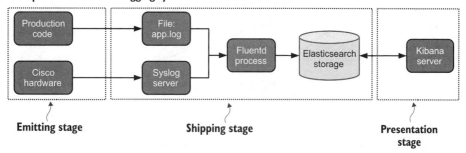

Emitting stage   Shipping stage   Presentation
                                                stage

Figure 1.3 A centralized logging system using Fluentd, Elasticsearch, and Kibana as major components. Telemetry is emitted from both production code and Cisco hardware. Then this telemetry is received by Shipping-stage components, centralized in Fluentd, and stored in Elasticsearch. Kibana uses Elasticsearch storage to provide a single interface for people to search all logs.

`sendmail` program from the Berkley Software Distribution 3BSD. By 2000, Syslog was in near-universal use across UNIX and UNIX-like operating systems. A standardization effort in 2001 resulted in a series of requests for comment (RFCs) that defined the Syslog format for both transmission protocol and data format. Making Syslog a standard gave hardware makers one option for emitting telemetry that wasn't likely to change over the decade lifespan of most hardware. The other option is Simple Network Management Protocol (SNMP), which is covered in chapter 2.

I bring up Syslog because the concepts it brought to the table influenced much of how we think about logging from software. If you've ever heard the phrase *Turn on debug logging*, you've heard a concept introduced by Syslog. The concept of log levels originated in Syslog, which defined the eight levels listed in table 1.1.

Table 1.1 Syslog standard log levels

ID	Severity	Keyword
0	Emergency	`emerg, panic`
1	Alert	`alert`
2	Critical	`crit`
3	Error	`err, error`
4	Warning	`warn, warning`
5	Notice	`notice`
6	Info	`info`
7	Debug	`debug`

Syslog's biggest influence is on the keywords in table 1.1. Not every software logger builds all eight levels; a few add more to this table, such as `fatal` and `trace` from Java. But nearly all loggers have some concept of debug, info, warning, and error:

```
logger.debug("Entering Dangerous::Function with #{args.count} params.")
logger.info("Dangerous::Function finished in #{timer.to_seconds} seconds.")
logger.warn("FIXME: Dangerous::Function was not passed a CSRF token.")
logger.err("Dangerous::Function failed with ArgumentError::InvalidType")
```

If you've written software, chances are good that you've used these levels at some point in your career. The concept of log levels also introduces the idea that all logging has some context: a log level indicates how severe the event is, and the text of the event describes what happened. Logging from software can include considerably more context than simply priority and a message; section 6.1 describes this markup process in much more detail.

The middle stage of centralized logging, represented in figure 1.3 as the Fluentd server, takes telemetry in the emitted format (Syslog for the Cisco hardware, whatever the log file format is for the production code) and reformats it into the format needed by Elasticsearch. Elasticsearch needs a hash data structure (an array, but with names for each element instead of numbers), so Fluentd rewrites the Syslog format in Elasticsearch's format before storing it in Elasticsearch. This reformatting process, called *enrichment*, is covered in chapter 4.

The end of the pipeline, represented in figure 1.3 as the Kibana server, uses Elastic-search as a database for queries. Section 5.2 goes into greater detail about what constitutes a good Presentation-stage system for centralized logging. Here, Kibana is used to access telemetry and assist with analysis.

1.1.2   *Defining metrics*

Metrics-style telemetry is about using numbers (counters, timers, rates, and the like) to get feedback about what's going on in your production systems. Whereas a centralized logging system often uses plain language to suggest how long something took, as in

```
logger.info("Dangerous::Function finished in #{timer.to_seconds} seconds.")
```

metrics systems encode the same information by encoding a number and some additional fields to provide context. In this example, a function name is added for context and a timer is used for the number:

```
metrics.timer("Dangerous_Function_runtime", timer.to_seconds)
```

Figure 1.4 is an example of a real-world metrics pipeline.

Figure 1.4 shows a metrics system being used for both software metrics and system metrics. The system metrics are gathered by a monitoring tool called collectd, which has the capability to push metrics into a Graphite API. Prometheus is a database custom built for storing data over time, or *time-series data.* Such time-series databases are

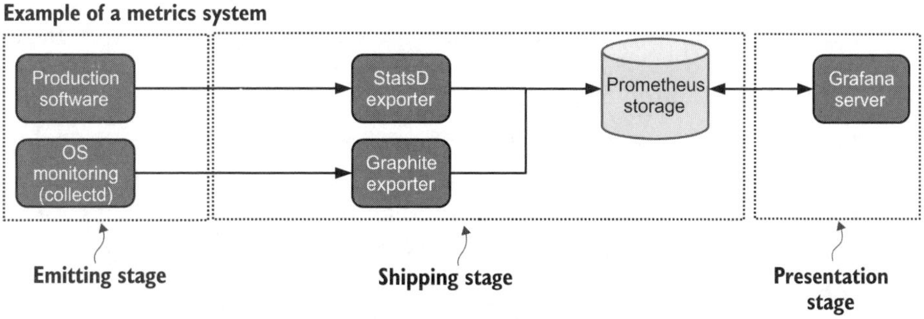

Example of a metrics system

Emitting stage   Shipping stage   Presentation stage

Figure 1.4 **A metrics system in which the production software emits metrics from code into a Prometheus StatsD exporter process; the operating system has a monitoring package called collectd that collects system metrics and reports directly to a Prometheus Graphite exporter. These exporters submit summarized metrics to Prometheus. A Grafana server acts as the interface point for all users of this metrics system.**

the foundation of many metrics systems, though other database styles can certainly be used successfully. Grafana is a widely used open source dashboarding system, in this case being used by both the Operations team running the infrastructure and the Software Engineering team managing the production software.

Like centralized logging telemetry, metrics telemetry is almost always marked up with additional details to go with the number. In the case of the statement before figure 1.4, we are adding a single field with `Dangerous_Function_runtime` as the value. Additional fields can be added, though doing so introduces complexity to the metrics database. This complexity is known as *cardinality*.

> **DEFINITION** *Cardinality* is the term for index complexity—specifically, the number of unique combinations the fields in the index may produce. If you have fields A and B, where A has two possible values and B has three possible values, the cardinality of that index is A * B, or 2 * 3 = 6. Cardinality significantly affects search performance no matter what data storage system is being used.

Cardinality is a big part of how metrics came to be its own discrete telemetry style. Centralized logging, with all the data it encodes, has the highest cardinality of the four telemetry styles I talk about in this book; it also takes up the most resources by far. Due to the combination of those two factors, centralized logging requires the most complex databases and the largest volume of data of any style. Because of budget constraints, however, centralized logging systems can rarely keep data online and searchable for long. Compare centralized logging with metrics, with its low cardinality, and focus on easy-to-store numbers, and you have a telemetry system that can keep years' worth of telemetry online and searchable for a fraction of the cost of a centralized logging system!

In the 2009–2012 era, when metrics began to be known as a software telemetry style (it had long been used on the operations side as a monitoring system), its lower cost versus centralized logging was one of the biggest drivers for adoption. Centralized logging was still used, but a specialized telemetry flow designed for the decision type was a revolution—one that set up the next telemetry style to come on the scene.

1.1.3   *Defining distributed tracing*

Distributed tracing is a strange union of metrics and logging—the cardinality of logging with the analytical power of metrics. Tracing enables explicit automation to add entire execution flows (figure 1.5 shows one such flow) to the presented context when you look to see what happened during an execution. Logging shows specific events as they happened, with some attributes to provide context around the event. Metrics gives you a broad overview of how the system is performing. Tracing uses the extra context you should have on your logged events to create a linked view of executions, as you see in figure 1.5. This visualization makes it easier for people to quickly isolate interesting places to investigate. Figure 1.5 presents the kind of display of execution flow that a distributed tracing system can provide.

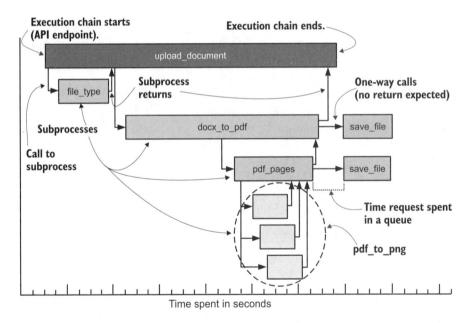

Figure 1.5   An example of a distributed tracing system's display, following the flow of execution similar to a stack trace. Here, we see a call to `upload_document` and all the other processes that `upload_document` called during its execution. When tracing a fault in a `pdf_to_png` process, you will be presented the full context of events leading up to that specific execution.

Tracing is useful not only in microservices environments, but also in the following:

- *Large monolithic codebases to which many teams contribute code*—The traces produced don't respect political boundaries, thereby reducing barriers to troubleshooting.

- *Micromonolith environments with a few large applications working together*—Such environments often have separate teams working on the larger applications, so tracing across all applications breaks down silos between teams.
- *Monoliths that are in the process of being chipped apart and have only a few additional microservices so far*—This telemetry style often is the best choice for providing shared context between separate systems.

Tracing also came on the scene in the late 2010s and is undergoing rapid development. The OpenTelemetry project (https://opentelemetry.io) is an effort by major players in the U.S. tech industry to provide standards for communication and data format for tracing telemetry. Programming languages that are well established and mostly overlooked by the big names in the U.S. tech industry—languages such as PHP, COBOL, and Perl—often lack a software development kit (SDK) for tracing. Frustration among software engineers is a prime driver of innovation, so I expect that these underserved languages will get the support they need before long.

In spite of the newness of distributed tracing, we have real-world examples to look at today. Figure 1.6 shows one such example.

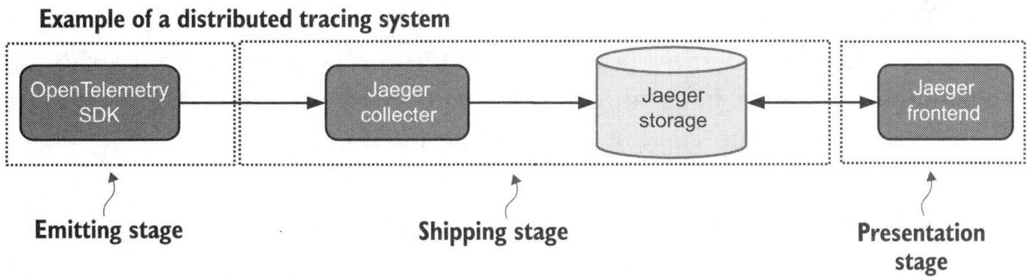

Example of a distributed tracing system

Figure 1.6   An example of a distributed tracing system circa 2021. Production code is running an OpenTelemetry SDK, which sends events to a system running the Jaeger open source tracing system. Then the Jaeger collector stores the event in a database. The Jaeger frontend provides a place to search and display traces from production systems.

What about Application Performance Monitoring?

Application Performance Monitoring (APM) is a term that has been used in industry since the early 2010s. APM began as a form of metrics but has evolved into rather more through use of steadily increasing amounts of context—much like distributed tracing systems do today. APM systems were around before the industry started getting excited about observability; as a result, APM systems moved hard into that space. Today, APM systems from New Relic and Datadog are one-stop-shopping systems that provide all three Pillars of Observability. In other words, APM systems unite centralized logging, metrics, and distributed tracing. These big companies have been around for a long time, so expect them to keep up with changes in the software telemetry marketplace of ideas.

In this book, whenever I refer to the Pillars of Observability, know that I'm also talking about APM systems.

1.1.4   *Defining SIEM*

Many companies and organizations operate with constraints imposed on them from outside, such as mandatory stock market reporting, industry-specific regulation in the banking industry, and optional compliance frameworks such as those defined by ISO standards. These standards, regulations, and compliance frameworks have been with us for decades and have grown up along with the technical industry. Most of these external controls require a common set of monitoring techniques inside technical organizations, including the following:

- Track all login, logout, and account lockout events.
- Track all use of administrative privileges.
- Track all access to sensitive files and records.
- Track compliance with password complexity and age requirements.

Because these requirements are so common, and tracking and later correlating them is so complex, they have given rise to a separate telemetry style known as the Security Information Event Management system (SIEM). Due to the complexity of the task, SIEMs are almost always paid-for software; few, if any, open source projects do this work. As a telemetry style operator, you will spend more time connecting sources of telemetry to a system that knows how to interpret the data. Figure 1.7 shows one possible architecture for integrating a SIEM into a larger telemetry system, branching off the centralized logging system shown in figure 1.3.

Example of a SIEM system paired with a centralized logging system

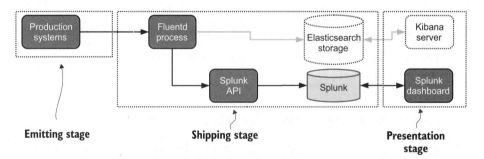

Figure 1.7   One possible SIEM system. Because SIEM systems are often derived from centralized logging systems, this figure shows an identical source for the centralized logging flow and SIEM flow. When telemetry enters the Fluentd process, it produces two feeds; one feed goes into Elasticsearch for centralized logging, and a second feed is submitted to the Splunk SaaS API. Splunk is acting as a SIEM in this case.

There are many architectures; figure 1.7 shows only one. In another architecture, Security has installable agents running on host servers, which emit in a completely different way from the centralized logging flows, making for a fully separate system. Both approaches are viable.

1.2   How telemetry is consumed by different teams

Because telemetry is used to support decision-making about production systems, you unavoidably have to consider how the people who make decisions are organized and how that affects their use of telemetry. This section defines the major teams in a technical organization for use later in the book. Your role is likely to be in this list somewhere, and if you've been in the industry for a long time, you may have been on more than one team. In my career, for example, I've been in customer support, operations, DevOps, and site reliability engineering (SRE), and have done close work with Security teams.

> **NOTE**   I use the term *organization* instead of *company* to be inclusive of noncorporate organizations that create technology, such as government entities and not-for-profit organizations. The teams listed here are broad categories, and when you see team names in capitals, such as Software Engineering, know that I am referring to definitions in this chapter.

1.2.1   Telemetry use by Operations, DevOps, and SRE teams

For all that they cover somewhat different areas, Operations, DevOps, and SRE teams share a lot of background. (SREs will be mentioned again in section 1.2.3 because they share background with Software Engineering teams.)

Operations teams were the first of these three teams to emerge (in the 1970s). Today, teams with *Operations* in the title are likely in long-standing organizations that computerized during the 1960s and 1970s, though sometimes these teams add the word *Infrastructure* to create the term *Infrastructure Operations* or use the term *Platform Engineering*. In this book, I use *Operations*. Teams with this name typically are in charge of keeping the machinery running and the production code operating—cloud or hardware, including operating systems.

DevOps teams emerged in the first decade of the 2000s to fight the silos that had grown up between Operations and Software Engineering teams. These days, DevOps teams often stand in for Operations teams while maintaining the systems that ensure that code meets minimum quality standards (*continuous integration*) and getting it into production (*continuous deploy*). Using DevOps in a job title is controversial—DevOps is a philosophy, not a job title—but that doesn't stop it from being common practice anyway.

SRE emerged in rough parallel to DevOps in some of the biggest tech companies on the planet. Originally, SRE was the team in charge of making sure that your (web-based) software was available to customers, the way your customers needed it to be. The term means somewhat different things to each organization that has an SRE team, but all these organizations care about your (usually web-based) software being available to customers.

Operations teams have been caring about uptime since the beginning. DevOps cares about software quality as a way to defend uptime. SRE teams are explicitly charged with availability. All these converging needs mean that these three teams have common telemetry requirements, as shown in figure 1.8.

Figure 1.8   The preferred telemetry styles for Operations, DevOps, and SRE teams. Centralized logging is used because the infrastructure these teams manage emits there by preference, and metrics is used because it is the basis for tracking site availability and general monitoring. Use of the other two styles is possible, but centralized logging and metrics are most common.

1.2.2   *Telemetry use by Security and Compliance teams*

Security is charged with defense of your overall organization from outside threats. *Compliance* is charged with ensuring that your organization complies with legislated regulations and optional compliance frameworks, such as the Service and Organization Controls (SOC 2) standard. Security and Compliance teams are often the same team until an organization decides that separating these concerns is a good idea. Not every organization has a Security team, though many that do not should. These teams are unavoidable in certain industries, however, especially those involving finance and health. Supporting both Security and Compliance missions requires setting several policies and procedures, such as the following (not an exhaustive list):

- A vulnerability management program to ensure that software used in production and telemetry systems is kept up to date
- Procedures for regular reviews of who has access to production and telemetry systems
- Procedures for ensuring that terminated employees' access is swiftly revoked from production and telemetry systems
- Reporting to identify failed logins to production and telemetry systems
- Reporting to track the use of administrative privileges for a period of years
- A password-complexity and authentication policy to provide sufficient defense against password-guessing and other credential-theft threats

Their charge is not only setting policies, but also *ensuring that those policies are followed* by Security and Compliance teams. This task is where telemetry comes into play, because it allows external auditors to determine whether these policies are effective. When these teams are not ensuring compliance with policies, Security teams also have the hard job of responding to security incidents. Figure 1.9 shows the relationship of Security and Compliance teams with telemetry.

Figure 1.9   The relationship of Security and Compliance teams to telemetry systems. The primary system is SIEM, but centralized logging provides much of the proof that policies are being followed.

Security incidents are special cases, so when they happen, every source of telemetry is potentially useful during the investigation. If you are on a different team, be ready to support incident responders by providing information about how to use and search the telemetry under your care. Security is everyone's job.

Compliance with regulation and voluntary frameworks invariably requires keeping certain kinds of telemetry around for years (often seven, a number inherited from the accounting industry). This default long-term-retention requirement is unique among the telemetry styles here, with metrics being the only other style that approaches SIEM systems' retention period. (Chapter 17 addresses retention policies in detail.)

1.2.3　Telemetry use by Software Engineering and SRE teams

Software Engineering teams are responsible for writing the software in your production environment. I mention SRE again because the mission of an SRE team is to ensure that the availability of your software extends to both the infrastructure the code runs on (section 1.2.1) and the code itself (this section). Some organizations split systems-oriented SRE from software-oriented SRE as well. Software Engineering brought about the metrics and distributed tracing styles of telemetry to better track what code was doing, so figure 1.10 should be no surprise.

Figure 1.10　Telemetry systems used by Software Engineering teams (almost all of them). All three Pillars of Observability are used.

Whereas Software Engineering teams focus on how their code is performing in production, SRE teams focus on whether the code is meeting promised performance and availability targets. This task is related to what Software Engineering desires, but the difference matters. Software Engineering is concerned with failures and how they affect everything, whereas SRE is concerned with overall aggregated performance.

1.2.4　Telemetry use by Customer Support teams

Customer Support teams have a variety of other titles, including Technical Support, Customer Success, Customer Services, and Support Account Management. These teams are charged with working with your customers (or users or employees) and resolving problems. They have the best information about how your production system works for people, so if your Software Engineering and SRE teams are not talking to them, something has gone horribly wrong in your organization. This communication needs to go both ways, because when Customer Support teams are skilled in using the telemetry systems used by Software Engineering, the quality of problem reporting increases significantly. In an organization where Customer Support has no access to telemetry systems, problem reports come in sounding like this:

> *Account 11213 had a failed transaction on February 19, 2023 at 18:02 UTC. They say they've had this happen before, but can't tell us when. They're a churn risk, $21K annual contract at risk.*

Compare this report with the kind of report your Customer Support teams can make if they have access to query telemetry systems:

> *Account 11213 has had several failed transactions. The reported transaction was ID e69aed5a-0dfc-47e2-abca-8c11374b626f, which had a failure in it when I looked it up. That failure was found four more times with this account. I also saw it happening for five other accounts and reached out to all five. Two have gotten back to me and thanked us for proactively notifying them of the problem. It looks like accounts with billing-code Q are affected.*

This second problem report is objectively far better because the work of isolating where the problem may be hiding has mostly been done. You want to empower your Customer Support teams. Figure 1.11 demonstrates the sort of telemetry systems of which Customer Support makes the best use.

Figure 1.11   The telemetry systems best suited to Customer Support teams. Because these teams are most interested in specific failures, telemetry styles that rely on aggregation (metrics) are not as useful. Note that when Customer Support is more of a help desk for internal users, SIEM access is often also granted and useful.

Customer Support teams work with customers to figure out what went wrong, which means that they are most interested in events that happened recently. Telemetry systems that rely on aggregation (metrics) are not useful because the single interesting event is not visible. Telemetry systems that rely on statistical sampling (distributed tracing; see section 17.3) can be somewhat useful, but the interesting error needs to be in the sample. You can get around this problem by persisting error events outside the statistical sample, perhaps in a second errors database. (See chapter 17 for more on this technique.)

1.2.5   *Telemetry use by business intelligence*

Business intelligence (BI) teams are sneaky; they work on the telemetry of the business rather than the telemetry of the technical organization. Their versions of telemetry include data such as marketing conversion rates, rate of account upgrade/downgrade, signup rate, feature use, and click rates in email marketing campaigns. Although BI teams often aren't considered to be part of the technical organization, I mention them here for two reasons:

- People inside BI teams often have training in statistical methods, so they represent an internal resource for you when you start applying statistical methods to your technical telemetry.
- If you are building a SaaS platform, BI teams are likely to approach you to engineer telemetry flows into their systems alongside the ones you already have for your technical organization.

If your organization already has people who are skilled in handling and manipulating data, you need to talk to them when you are building or upgrading data handling systems. They will tell you when your plan for aggregating data won't return valid results (getting the MAX value of a series of data that was averaged will not give you the true MAX value in the source data, for example). It can feel strange to ask people in a radically different department for help, but you will build better systems if you do.

1.3 Challenges facing telemetry systems

Telemetry systems face the same disasters that production systems do: fire, flood, equipment failure, unexpected credit-card expiration, labor actions, bankruptcies, pandemics, civil unrest, and many more. Telemetry systems in particular are vulnerable to disasters specific to telemetry, which is what this section introduces. The four major problems derive from three points:

- Telemetry systems aren't revenue systems (see section 1.3.1).
- Different teams need different things from the telemetry they use (see section 1.3.2).
- Telemetry is still data, even if it isn't production data, and many people and organizations have an interest in data (see sections 1.3.3 and 1.3.4).

1.3.1 Chronic underinvestment harms decision-making

By far the biggest threat to your telemetry systems is insufficient investment of resources. Telemetry systems are decision support tools; they present the feedback you send out of your production environment in a way that helps you figure out what to do next. Maybe you focus on technical debt for the next couple of sprints because your availability metrics are failing your service-level agreement targets. Or maybe handling 12,000 connections a second is when your load-balancer nodes start responding badly, and it's time to buy more for your cluster. Whatever you're looking for, these systems will help you find it. Underinvestment can be caused by many factors:

- *Telemetry systems aren't revenue systems.* "If they don't make money, they're overhead, so cut overhead to make profit; QED." This argument shows that business management has an incorrect understanding of the value that telemetry systems provide the overall organization.
- *Don't fix what ain't broke.* "What you have now works fine; why bother changing?" This argument shows a disconnect between the people who would get the most value from well-designed telemetry systems and the people who would authorize the time and money to be spent for a well-designed telemetry system.

- *Centralized logging is all we need.* "Why do you need a tracing system when we can do the same with our current system in only six searches?" Centralized logging is a powerful tool, as decades of computer management have shown. Centralized logging can also be forced to do the jobs of SIEM, metrics, and even distributed tracing, but it does them much more poorly than the systems designed for those tasks. You will find yourself spending so much time writing glue automation to make this square peg fit the hexagonal hole than setting up a new specialized system would likely save in time and money.
- *Features! Features! Features!* "We don't have time for that; we need to ship this next set of features to enable sales!" More of a pathology in growing SaaS companies, this argument is another example of business management misunderstanding the value that telemetry systems bring to an organization.

The broad trends boil down to not understanding what telemetry does and a disconnect between those who feel the pain and those who would approve fixing the pain. None of these problems is an easy fix for a simple technician on a team. Depending on your organizational culture, fixing either problem may be impossible for the managers who feel the pain because approving major updates like a telemetry system needs to happen so far up the chain of command that it doesn't matter.

When you're facing these headwinds, you still have a chance to make a change. If the organizational culture is otherwise good, underinvestment is largely a problem of ignorance. You can fix ignorance, as follows:

- Explain the kinds of decisions that improved telemetry systems will enable. Managers get that sort of language.
- Explain how paying for a SaaS provider now will improve everyone's ability to make decisions faster than spending 24 months building your own systems (and will likely result in much better features than a DIY system could offer).
- Explain how a new telemetry style works differently than the current systems, provide a framework showing how it would operate in your existing production systems, and point out how it would improve identification of problems and prioritization of work.

I spent 14 years in the public sector, 7 of them during recessions when spending new money had to wait for the economy to turn around. Many organizations are at the mercy of an annual or biannual budgeting process in which a group of rarely technical elected officials decide whether you will get your expensive new system. Fighting chronic underinvestment is hard work, but it can be done. Make the case, do it well, and plan far enough in advance (months, if not years) that you won't be in a panic if the answer comes down to "Not this year."

1.3.2 *Diverse needs resist standardization*

As you read section 1.2, which described the teams in a technical organization and their telemetry needs, you may have noticed some different goals. Here are some of the top-level differences:

- Customer Support teams need recent (within a few weeks) telemetry, and they need all of it (no aggregation or summarization) in case what a customer is talking about is in there.
- Security teams need their SIEM systems to keep seven or more years' worth of telemetry.
- To be affordable, distributed tracing systems need to sample their data statistically.
- Centralized logging systems are the most expensive to operate (on an expense per day of telemetry basis), so keeping years' worth of telemetry online is prohibitively expensive. Sometimes, weeks' worth of telemetry is too expensive for an organization.

Figure 1.12 provides a view of the diverse storage and retention needs of the four telemetry styles talked about here.

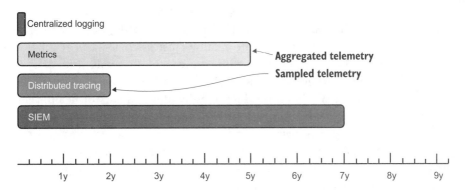

Figure 1.12   The four telemetry styles charted for their preferred online availability periods. SIEM systems have the longest retention due to external requirements. Distributed tracing achieves retention through statistical sampling. Metrics achieves its duration through aggregations of the numbers stored inside. Centralized logging is just plain expensive, so it gets the smallest online retention period.

A "one policy applies to all" approach simply will not work for a telemetry system. Your retention policies need to be written in ways that accommodate the diverse needs of your teams and telemetry systems. (Chapter 17 is dedicated to this topic.) There is also diversity in the shape of your telemetry data itself:

- Hardware emits in two standardized formats: Syslog or SNMP. If you can't handle the standard formats, you're not going to get that telemetry.
- Telemetry SaaS provider SDKs might not have support for emitting telemetry through HTTP proxies—a required feature in many production environments.

- Platform services such as VMWare vCenter have their own telemetry handling systems.
- Infrastructure providers such as Amazon Web Services (AWS) and Digital Ocean provide telemetry in their own formats and in their own locations, leaving it up to you to fetch and process it.
- Operating system components (Windows, Linux, FreeBSD, AIX, HP-UX, z/OS, and so on) emit in their own formats, such as Syslog and Windows Event Log. If you want that telemetry, you need to handle those formats.
- The programming languages in which your production systems are written and their ages can prevent you from having access to SDKs for distributed tracing.

Challenges like these increase the complexity of your telemetry system but are not insurmountable. I cover methods of moving telemetry in chapter 3 and transforming formats in chapter 4. If you happen to be using a language or platform that is unloved by the hot-new-now tech industry, you're likely used to building support for new things yourself. I'm sorry (she says, having run Tomcat apps on NetWare successfully).

1.3.3   *Information spills and cleaning them up to avoid legal problems*

Information spills and their consequences are a direct result of increasing legislation regarding privacy (personally identifiable information [PII]) and health-related (personal health information [PHI]) information. Just as toxic-waste regulation largely didn't exist until the last half of the 20th century, the first half of the 21st century is seeing information start getting classified as toxic. Telemetry systems receive feedback from production systems, but if production is handling privacy or health-related data, it is possible that the telemetry stream will include such toxic data as well.

You never want to see privacy- or health-related data in your telemetry systems, because access to telemetry data will have to follow all the rigorous (and tedious) access control and use policies that accessing production data requires. Making access to your telemetry data more difficult reduces the overall utility of your telemetry system in general. Few organizations are culturally and technically equipped to easily handle data of this type, and they're all healthcare or finance companies. For the rest of us, keeping privacy and health-related data out of the telemetry stream is a never-ending battle. There are three major sources of information leaks:

- *The biggest leak source: exception logging with parameters*—Parameters are incredibly useful for debugging but can include privacy and health-related data, so they are by far the largest sources of leaks I've seen in my own systems. This situation is made worse by the fact that many logger modules don't have redaction concepts baked into them (see chapter 16 for more on redaction), and software engineers aren't used to thinking of exceptions as needing in-code redaction before emission. Use of a structured logger (see chapter 12) gives you ways to redact exceptions.

- *Unthinking inclusion of IP address and email addresses in logging statements*—IP and email addresses are useful for fighting fraud and isolating which account a statement is about. Unfortunately, IP address and email addresses are protected by many privacy regulations. If you must include these details, consider hashing them instead to provide correlation without providing the direct values. Section 14.2.1 provides another method to limit allowed values in telemetry.
- *Inclusion of any user-submitted data of any kind in logging statements*—Users will stuff all kinds of things they shouldn't into fields. Unfortunately for you, many privacy and health-data regulations require you to detect and respond to leaks of this type. If you are in a place subjected to that kind of law (ask your lawyers) and have a bug-bounty program, expect to pay bounties to bug-hunters who find ways to display user-supplied input on unprotected dashboards. But it's best not to emit user-submitted data in your telemetry stream in the first place.

As deeply annoying as this fact is, you must have policies and procedures in place to retroactively remove mistakenly stored privacy and health-related information. Legislation that makes these types of data toxic hasn't been around long enough for telemetry handling modules to include in-flight redaction as a standard feature alongside log levels. I hope that this situation will change in the future. Until then, we have to know how to clean up toxic spills. Chapter 16 covers this topic extensively.

1.3.4 Court orders break your assumptions

Nearly every country on the planet has judicial rules that allow each party in a lawsuit to request relevant business records from the opposing party or parties. Email and Slack messages are famously business records, but telemetry data is as well. If your organization is party to a lawsuit, opposing counsel (the other side's lawyers) can request telemetry data. What happens between the time the request is made and the time you take action on it will be decided by your organization's lawyers, opposing counsel, and the judge overseeing the case, as shown in figure 1.13.

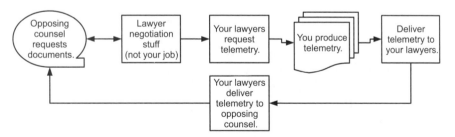

Figure 1.13 A greatly simplified flow of the document-discovery process as it relates to telemetry data. Your lawyers will be fighting on your organization's behalf to reduce the telemetry you have to give to the other side. You can help this process by teaching your lawyers what technically can and can't be produced by your telemetry system. Lying to your organization's lawyers about what you are able to produce will get you fired. Let the lawyers do their jobs; you're there only as a technical consultant.

Two court processes force you to change how you handle, store, and grant access to telemetry:

- *Request to produce documents*—This flow, illustrated in figure 1.13, requires you to create an extract of telemetry. The format you need to create will be negotiated by the lawyers, so you are likely to be pulled in to consult on the capabilities of your telemetry systems.
- *Request to hold documents*—Of the two demands, this one has the greater effect on you, the telemetry system operator. A request to hold documents means that you have to exempt certain telemetry from your aggregation, summarization, and deletion policies. Because legal matters sometimes take years to resolve, in bad cases you can end up storing many multiples of your usual telemetry volumes.

Not every organization has to prepare for lawsuits to such a degree that they need well-tested procedures for producing and holding telemetry, but certain industries are prone to lawsuits, such as finance, drug manufacturing, and patent law. Also, certain kinds of lawsuits, such as those filed for leaks of toxic data and insider sabotage, are far more likely to dive into telemetry data. You should have at least a whiteboard plan of what to do when you face a court order. Chapter 18 covers this topic.

1.4 *What you will learn*

This book is a guide to help any team operate telemetry systems in a technical organization. It focuses on optimizing the operation of systems involved in handling and displaying telemetry, rather than optimizing your overall use of telemetry. To benefit from this book, you should have worked with telemetry systems in some capacity, such as making searches in dashboards or writing logging statements in code. You should also have manipulated and searched strings by using code and built queries in graphical applications. In this book, you will learn

- The architecture of telemetry systems and how your current telemetry systems follow the architecture
- How to optimize your telemetry handling to reduce costs and increase the online searchable period
- How to ensure the integrity of your telemetry systems to support regulation and compliance frameworks, as well as security investigations
- Techniques to use to support court orders as part of legal processes
- Procedures to safely handle and dispose of regulated information, such as PII and PHI

To help you learn these skills, I will be using examples drawn from three styles of technical organization. Know that what I teach here is applicable to a growing startup, to companies with a founding date in the 1700s, and to organizations in which writing and running software supports the business but is not the reason for the business.

Summary

- Telemetry is the feedback you get from your production systems.
- Telemetry is how modern computing works, because it tells us what our production systems are up to.
- Telemetry ultimately supports the decisions you have to make about your production systems. If your telemetry systems are poor, you will make poor decisions.
- Centralized logging, which was the first telemetry style to emerge (in the mid-1980s), brings all logging produced by your production systems to a central location.
- Logging format standards such as as Syslog ensure that hardware systems emit in standard formats, so you need to support those formats as well if you want telemetry from hardware systems.
- Syslog introduced the concept of log levels (debug, info, warn, and error among others) to the industry.
- Metrics (which emerged in the early 2010s) focuses on aggregatable numbers to describe what is happening in your production systems.
- *Cardinality* is the term for index complexity in databases. The more fields a table has, the higher its cardinality. Centralized logging is a high-cardinality system; metrics systems generally are low-cardinality.
- Distributed tracing emerged in the late 2010s and focused on tracing events across an execution flow crossing system boundaries.
- Distributed tracing provides the context of the entire execution flow when investigating an interesting event, which further improves your ability to isolate where a problem started.
- SaaS companies dominate the distributed tracing space due to the complexity of distributed tracing systems.
- SIEM systems are specialist telemetry systems for Security and Compliance teams; they store information relating to the security use case.
- SIEM systems store consistent information because regulation and voluntary compliance frameworks largely track the same kinds of data and often require such data to be stored for years.
- Operations and DevOps teams use telemetry to track how their infrastructure systems are operating, focusing on centralized logging and metrics styles.
- Security and Compliance teams focus on both centralized logging and SIEM systems because SIEM systems share a lot of history with centralized logging, and centralized logging is useful during audits for compliance with regulation and external compliance frameworks.
- Software Engineering teams use every telemetry system except SIEM systems in an effort to understand how their code is behaving in production.

- The Pillars of Observability is a software engineering concept describing the telemetry that allows a system to be *observable*: logs, metrics, and traces.
- SRE teams use every telemetry system except SIEM in their mission to ensure that the organization's software is available.
- Customer Support teams use the centralized logging and distributed tracing styles to better isolate problems reported by customers and to improve the quality of bug reports sent to engineering.
- Business intelligence teams are rarely part of the technical organization but are responsible for building systems for business telemetry. BI people are valuable resources when you're deploying a new telemetry style due to their familiarity with statistical methods.
- A chronic threat to telemetry system is underinvestment, which can stem from a misunderstanding of the value that telemetry systems bring to the organization and a disconnect between decision-makers and those who feel the pain of a bad telemetry system.
- Different teams need different things from telemetry, and different telemetry styles benefit from different retention periods. Your telemetry system needs to accommodate these differences to be a good telemetry system.
- Hardware, SaaS providers, infrastructure providers, third-party software, and operating systems all emit telemetry in relatively fixed formats. Your telemetry system needs to handle these formats if you want their telemetry.
- Privacy information (PII) and health information (PHI) require special handling, and most telemetry systems aren't built for that purpose. Do what you can to keep PII and PHI out of your telemetry systems.
- The largest source of toxic information spills are exception logs that include parameters; do what you can to redact them before they enter the telemetry pipeline.
- Telemetry systems are subject to court orders the same way your production systems are, so you may be called upon to produce telemetry by your lawyers for a legal matter.
- A court order to hold data means that the affected data is no longer subjected to your retention policy, which can be quite expensive if the legal matter drags on for years.

Part 1

Telemetry system architecture

Each of the telemetry systems described in chapter 1 follows the same general architecture. Every production system *emits* telemetry data. Then this data is *shipped* into a data store of some form, which could be a relational database, a NoSQL document store, a SaaS provider, or even an object store, if not more than one. From there, it is *presented* in such a way that people can use the processed telemetry data to support decisions, which could be in the form of reports or on-demand charting. Along the way, telemetry is *marked up* with context-related details and then *enriched* to pull out details encoded in the telemetry. Figure 1 describes this architecture.

Chapter 1 discussed four styles of telemetry:

- *Centralized logging*—Bringing all logging output from hardware, cloud providers, and software into a single searchable system. Often the first telemetry system built, this style has high cardinality and high costs.
- *Metrics*—Bringing numbers-based telemetry (such as rates, counts, and sets) into a central system, tagged with fields to provide the basis for charts and analysis. This style has low cardinality and low costs.
- *Security Information Event Management* (SIEM)—A form of centralized logging specific to Security and Compliance team needs. This style needs to support storage over many years due to external constraints.
- *Distributed tracing*—Using new databases and presentation time processing, tracing is designed to enable following execution chains through functions, microservices, macroservices, and different tenants. This style has high cardinality, but statistical methods help keep costs down.

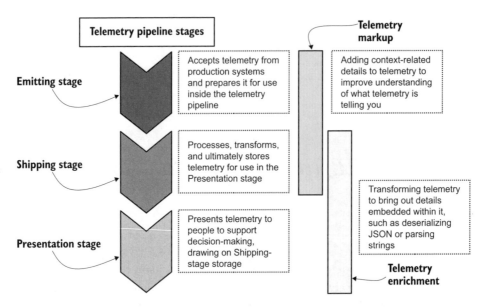

Figure 1 Telemetry system pipeline stages with their definitions. The Emitting stage packages telemetry for the Shipping stage, which processes, transforms, and stores telemetry to be consumed by the Presentation stage. Markup adds context-related telemetry during the Emitting and Shipping stages, where enrichment transforms telemetry to improve its usefulness during the Shipping and Presentation stages.

Each of the telemetry styles discussed in chapter 1 has its telemetry follow the stages in figure 1. Figure 2 provides three real-world examples of telemetry pipelines for metrics, centralized logging, and distributed tracing (also known as the Pillars of Observability).

All telemetry has an emitting system that prepares telemetry for use inside your Shipping stage (chapter 2). The systems that receive emissions—the Shipping-stage systems—process and transform telemetry to prepare it for storage (chapters 3 and 4). Finally, Presentation-stage systems use telemetry stored by the Shipping stage to provide the visualizations and analysis needed to support decision-making (chapter 5). Chapter 6 describes the markup and enrichment that telemetry systems apply at all three stages of your pipeline. Finally, chapter 7, which introduces multitenancy, describes the changes to telemetry systems that happen when more than one owner is involved.

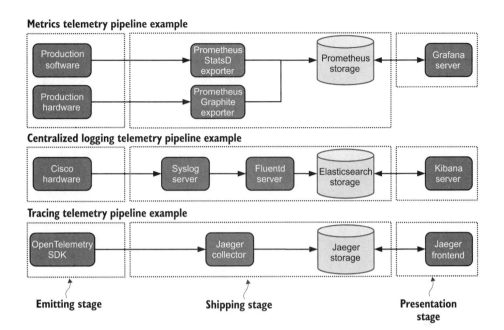

Metrics telemetry pipeline example

Centralized logging telemetry pipeline example

Tracing telemetry pipeline example

Emitting stage   Shipping stage   Presentation stage

Figure 2 Example telemetry pipelines for three telemetry styles, with metrics at the top, centralized logging in the middle, and tracing at the bottom. Black directional lines indicate telemetry flow. Each pipeline is broken into three stages: Emitting, Shipping, and Presentation. These technologies are different, but the same flow of data handling shows the similarities of these telemetry styles.

The Emitting stage: Creating and submitting telemetry

This chapter covers

- Understanding what the Emitting stage does
- Emitting telemetry from software you're developing
- Emitting telemetry from hardware and third-party software
- Emitting telemetry from SaaS and IaaS platforms

The Emitting stage, shown in figure 2.1, is the first stage in your pipeline, where telemetry generated by a production system enters the pipeline. This first stage can be many things:

- Your production code itself. A logging class inside the production code provides the needed formatting and telemetry delivery (section 2.1). You can use several techniques when emitting this way.

- A hardware system like Cisco networking gear or Dell servers that you configure to emit telemetry (section 2.2).
- A Software as a Service (SaaS) or Infrastructure as a Service (IaaS) platform such as Amazon Web Services (AWS), Azure, Atlassian products, or GitHub that is able to provide a telemetry stream (section 2.3).

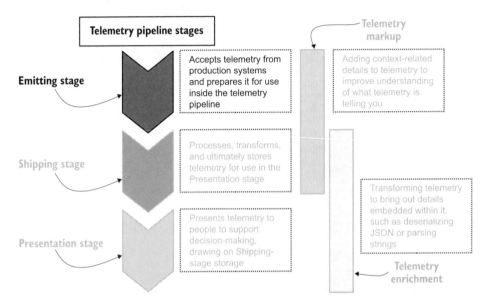

Figure 2.1   Telemetry system pipeline stages with the Emitting stage shown first, illustrating where it fits in the overall telemetry pipeline. The Emitting stage is where telemetry enters the pipeline from the production systems. Production systems can be code, whereas the Emitting stage is often inside the production system itself, or hardware and Software-as-a-Service systems.

When this telemetry is emitted from the Emitting stage, it is handled by the Shipping stage, where telemetry is transformed into a format for storage used by the Presentation stage. Because emitting telemetry requires knowledge of the Shipping stage, we cover some of the inputs of Shipping stages in this chapter. To help explain the real-world uses of these emitting types, we use examples drawn from three types of technical organizations:

- A 100-person startup building an API-driven application running in AWS. This example demonstrates emitting from software you develop.
- A global logistics company founded in 1848 that computerized its business processes in the late 1960s. This example demonstrates emitting from hardware infrastructure.
- A 200-person company providing in-person continuing education courses, with strong seasonality in its hiring. This example demonstrates emitting telemetry from SaaS platforms.

2.1 *Emitting from production code*

In this section, we talk about a 100-person startup that wants to start emitting metrics from its production systems and discuss three ways of accomplishing this goal. Although we are talking about metrics in the examples, you can use the same techniques to emit logging data.

In the Emitting stage, the big difference between metrics and logging is the format of the data: numbers and some extra details in the case of metrics versus strings for logging. Figure 2.2 describes the company's production system.

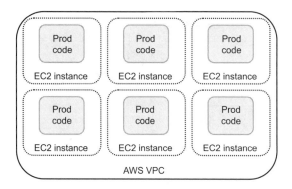

Figure 2.2 The production system for the 100-person startup, running in AWS. Production code is deployed to EC2 virtual machines running in a Virtual Private Cloud. This architecture allows us to examine several techniques for emitting telemetry from production code.

This startup is running code in AWS and has elected to run that code on EC2 virtual machines. Although Lambda or either of AWS's container services (Elastic Container Service and Elastic Kubernetes Service) may be more appropriate for a company of this type, using EC2 virtual machines allows me to demonstrate more telemetry emission methods. This section talks about Emitting-stage techniques that are pure emitters—that deliver telemetry to the same system the code is running on. Emitting stages that send telemetry to a different system, perhaps to a queue or a database, are Emitter/Shipper stages, which we will cover in detail in section 3.1. The top half of figure 2.3 describes the differences between these two types of emitters.

The bottom half of figure 2.3 demonstrates the components of a structured logger and how it relates to the emitter and emitter/shipper concepts. (For a full examination of structured loggers, see chapter 12.) Most programming frameworks have one or more structured logging options available. Structured loggers have three components:

- A *logger* that acts as the callable item for structured loggers. For telemetry pipelines, the logger is how telemetry enters the Emitting stage. The name of this component differs depending on the programming language.
- A *formatter* that reformats received telemetry in the format needed by the Emitting- and Shipping-stage systems. There can be more than one formatter.
- A *writer* that sends the reformatted telemetry to the next step. In some logging frameworks, you may be able to send only to the console or a file. Other frameworks have many more delivery options, if not extensible, allowing sending to databases, queues, streams, SaaS providers, and many more destinations.

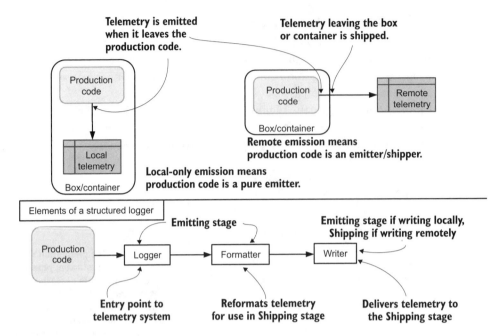

Figure 2.3   **Two styles of emitting telemetry directly from production code, showing how these concepts relate to a structured logger. The pure emitter at top left (described in section 2.1) emits telemetry in the same box, container, or function as the production code, and the emitter/shipper at top right (described in section 3.1) emits telemetry to an external system.**

Pure emitters require a Shipping-stage component (see section 4.1) to move (ship) telemetry farther down the telemetry pipeline. In this section, we cover three methods of emitting locally:

- Emitting into a log file
- Emitting into the system logger
- Emitting into standard out

NOTE   Emitter/shipper functions emit to telemetry on systems remote from the production code and are covered as part of the Shipping stage in section 3.1.

The three methods this section covers are among the oldest methods for getting feedback from what your program is doing. There is a reason why the "Hello world!" program is using a print function to echo back `Hello world!`

The code samples in this chapter use Python 3 and the default Python logger to demonstrate telemetry emission concepts. Although Python 3 is used in my code examples, several other loggers behave in similar ways for different programming languages:

- *Python*—The structlog module (https://www.structlog.org/en/stable)
- *Ruby*—The twp/logging gem (https://github.com/twp/logging)
- *PHP*—The Monolog module (https://github.com/Seldaek/monolog)

- *NodeJS*—The Winston (https://github.com/winstonjs/winston) and Bunyan (https://github.com/trentm/node-bunyan) modules
- *Java*—The log4j 2 framework (https://logging.apache.org/log4j/2.x)
- *Go*—The Zerolog (https://github.com/rs/zerolog) and Zap (https://github.com/uber-go/zap) modules
- *.NET Core*—The built-in ILogger (http://mng.bz/ZYz5)
- *Rust*—The Slog module (https://docs.rs/crate/slog)

2.1.1 Emitting telemetry into a log file

The 100-person startup wants to create a metrics-emitting function in its code. This section covers how to create this function by using log files, which can be created in a couple of ways:

- Using the programming-language's file read/write features to write directly to files
- Using an add-on module (such as an egg, gem, NuGet, npm, jar dependency, or PECL) to provide a fully featured logging library to abstract away file I/O and provide a higher-level interface for logging

Most programs of any size opt for the second bullet option: using a built-in or add-on logging library. You may be asking, "Why would I use a logging library for metrics?" The answer is given in the intro to section 2.1: Emitting-stage systems are all about preparing telemetry for the Shipping stage, and there is little difference between logging output and metrics output when you plan to send your telemetry to a file.

Our first version of this startup's metrics logger in listing 2.1 is written in Python 3 and makes use of the `logging` Python module to give us a high-level interface for sending telemetry into log files. Figure 2.4 depicts the overall flow of execution leading up to the writing of a log file entry.

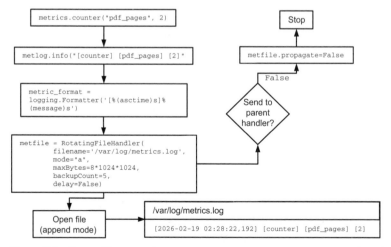

Figure 2.4 How calling `metrics.counter("pdf_page", 2)` gets written into a logfile at /var/log/ metrics.log. After passing into the metrics.counter function, the formatted string is sent into the predefined logger at the info priority. The string is reformatted by the formatter to add a timestamp. Then the Handler decides to not propagate the event to a different handler and outputs the formatted line to /var/log/metrics.log.

In listing 2.1, we see the full metrics module.

Listing 2.1 metrics.py: Using the Python logger to send telemetry to a log file

```
import logging
from logging.handlers import RotatingFileHandler

metlog  = logging.getLogger('metlog')          ◁──── Creates the metric logger

metfile = RotatingFileHandler(
  filename='/var/log/metrics.log',
  mode="a",                                     Creates the logging
  maxBytes=8*1024*1024,                         handler, rotating the
  backupCount=5,                                log file after 8MB
  delay=False)

metlog.setLevel(logging.DEBUG)      ◁────  Sets the minimum log level handled by this facility

metfile.propagate=False   ◁────  Ensures that events handled by this facility
                                  will not also be sent to the root facility

metric_format = logging.Formatter(
  '[%(asctime)s] %(message)s',                  Creates the log format
  )

metfile.setFormatter(metric_format)    ◁────  Assigns the formatter to the handler

metlog.addHandler(metfile)   ◁────  Assigns the handler to the logger
                                    and completes logger setup

def counter(msg, count=1):                     ◁─
    """Emits a metric intended to be counted or summarized.

    Example: counter("pages", "15")            Creates the 'metrics.counter' method:
    """                                        'metrics.counter("executions", "2")'
    metlog.info("[counter] [%s] [%s]", msg, count)

def timer(msg, time=0.0):                      ◁─
    """Emits a metric for tracking run-times.   Creates the 'metrics.timer' method:
                                                'metrics.timer("run_time", "3.8")'
    Example: timer("convert_worker_runtime", "2.7")
    """
    metlog.info("[timer] [%s] [%s]", msg, time)
```

When listing 2.1 is called through the counter function, it starts a chain of events, shown in figure 2.4:

1 The Python logging facility is set up and named metlog.
2 The counter function inside the metrics class calls the info method of metlog, submitting [counter] [pdf_pages] [2] to the metlog facility.
3 The formatter reformats the string to add a timestamp, making it [2026-02-19 02:28:22,192] [counter] [pdf_pages] [2].
4 The handler defined with RotatingFileHandler does not send the event to any other handlers because propagate was set to False.
5 The handler opens /var/log/metrics.log.

This library is brought into another Python program through `import metrics`, allowing this startup's software engineers to emit metrics through function calls like these:

- `metrics.counter("profile_image_uploaded")` to increment the count of uploaded profile images by 1
- `metrics.counter("pdf_pages", 2)` to indicate that the number of pdf_pages encountered was 2
- `metrics.timer("profile_image_convert_time", 0.9)` to indicate that converting the uploaded profile image to an appropriate image dimension took 0.9 seconds

Function calls like these will create the following entries in the /var/log/metrics.log file:

```
[2026-02-19 02:27:26,396] [counter] [profile_image_upload] [1]
[2026-02-19 02:28:22,192] [counter] [pdf_pages] [2]
[2026-02-19 02:28:27,921] [timer] [profile_image_convert_time] [0.9]
```

What happens after this log file is created depends on the Shipping telemetry stage, which is discussed in section 4.1. If only a single EC2 instance ever runs this code, a software engineer could watch the metrics roll in by watching that one file from an SSH session, but we know from the architecture diagram that this startup has at least six instances running. Instead, software implementing the Shipping stage reads this file and transmits, converts, and ultimately stores events in a database that allows queries as part of the Presentation stage.

What happens next? The /var/log/metrics.log is read by a Shipping-stage component (see section 4.1.1).

2.1.2 *Emitting telemetry into the system log*

Suppose that our 100-person startup wanted to send its metrics into the system log rather than a log file; this section covers how it would make this change. The system log is managed by the operating system. On UNIX-like systems, the system log is almost definitely running something compatible with IETF standardized Syslog. On Linux systems, Syslog interfaces are present, but the Systemd logging component named journald is likely to be running the system log. On Windows systems, the system log is the Event Log. Most modern languages intended be executed on servers include some simple way to send events to the system log.

> **System loggers and Linux systems**
>
> Ask any BSD user what they think of Linux, and they will shake their head. One of the biggest reasons for the pressed lips and quiet (or, if pressed, the rant) has been the adoption of a framework called Systemd by every major Linux distribution. Systemd is a replacement for several long-standing (meaning stable and therefore reliable) UNIX subsystems:

(continued)

- Replacing the long-standing and widely understood script-based on-boot startup sequence with a vastly more complicated service framework that is hard to reason about and equally hard to tune. A service framework that has far better dependency management that can react to service failures with more certainty and start services way faster.
- Replacing the long-standing and battle-tested set of utilities needed to turn Domain Name System (DNS) names into IP addresses (and other resolver actions) with a brand-new utility that needed a decade to shake the bugs out (and isn't done shaking them yet).
- Abstracting the long-standing system logger, Syslog, with a new system named journald that radically upended decades-long assumptions about where system log files end up and how they are stored. This type of system has far better ability to review the logs from specific services versus the older pure Syslog solutions, provides much more detailed metadata, and has an actual access control system.

Systemd ends up being a nice parable of the Paradox of Maturity:

I use only mature systems in my production environment.
Systemd is not yet mature.
Therefore, I will not use Systemd in production.
Therefore, Systemd will never get the testing it needs to become
mature. QED.

Systemd is bringing a lot of new features to the Linux ecosystem, much as it pains old hands to admit. The Systemd project is heading in the right direction, in my opinion, but we still have at least another five to seven years of grumbling and bug-fixing to match the maturity of the systems it replaced.

Fortunately for us, journald listens to the operating system the same way Syslog did, so for programs running on Linux systems, it seems that nothing has changed with respect to the system logger. For humans, on the other hand, it's radically different. For all the advances Systemd brought to the table, it deliberately left one feature unbuilt: the ability to send system log data somewhere off the server it's running on. This lacking feature, weirdly enough, is why Systemd still allows sending system log data to an actual local Syslog server.

Yes, this means that on many Linux systems, you have two ways to look at the system logger telemetry. Simplicity means different things to different people; let's leave it at that.

Because of the three tiers of structured logging (logger, formatter, and writer), updating the metrics.py function that was sending logs to a file to send them to the system log instead is a matter of changing three lines: importing a new module and updating the formatter and handler. Figure 2.5 shows the changed flow of telemetry.

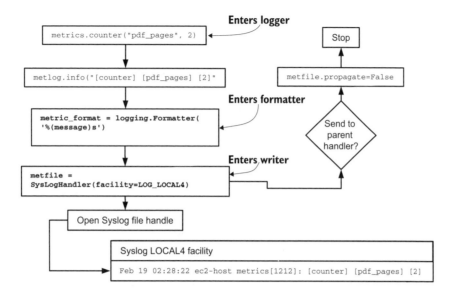

Figure 2.5 How calling `metrics.counter("pdf_page", 2)` gets written into the local system log. Inside the `metrics.counter` function, the logger is invoked through the `info` method, passing in a formatted string. Then the formatter reformats the telemetry. Next, the writer, a `SysLogHandler` in this case, decides to not send the telemetry to another facility; instead, it sends the telemetry into the local Syslog, using the LOCAL4 facility.

Listing 2.2 shows the locations of those two changed lines in the metrics.py file.

Listing 2.2   metrics.py: Using the Python logger to send telemetry to the system log

```
import logging
from syslog import LOG_LOCAL4
from logging.handlers import SysLogHandler

metlog  = logging.getLogger('metlog')

metfile = SysLogHandler(facility=LOG_LOCAL4)        Creates a handler to send logs to
                                                    Syslog on the LOCAL4 Syslog facility

metlog.setLevel(logging.DEBUG)

metfile.propagate=False

metric_format = logging.Formatter(
    '%(message)s',                   Removes the date/time stamp because
    )                                Syslog will insert it automatically

metfile.setFormatter(metric_format)

metlog.addHandler(metfile)

[...]
```

Listing 2.2 is substantially the same as the log file version in listing 2.1, but with three changes:

- We import the LOG_LOCAL4 facility from the Syslog modules.
- The handler is changed to the Syslog handler, using the LOCAL4 facility.
- The format of emitted metrics is changed to remove the timestamp because Syslog will automatically date- and timestamp everything it receives anyway.

Using this revised metrics library, the emitted telemetry would look like this for the three examples used with the log file version:

```
Feb 19 02:26:26 ec2-host metrics[1212]: [counter] [profile_image_upload] [1]
Feb 19 02:28:22 ec2-host metrics[1212]: [counter] [pdf_pages] [2]
Feb 19 02:28:27 ec2-host metrics[1212]: [timer] [profile_image_convert_time]
⇒ [0.9]
```

Note that the log file version of these metrics includes millisecond resolution, whereas Syslog resolves to the second. If you are building a telemetry system that uses Syslog and need subsecond resolution of timestamps, you will need to include your own timestamp in your emitted telemetry. But if your data will only be aggregated, second-level resolution can be completely fine.

This example function goes to a Syslog facility on the box it is running on. Functionally, the address= attribute is using the default value of localhost. If we had a centralized Syslog server that we wanted to talk to directly, we would update the handler creation line like so:

```
metfile = SysLogHandler(facility=LOG_LOCAL4, address=("syslog.prod.internal",
⇒ 514))
```

Figure 2.6 demonstrates how this update alters the flow of telemetry.

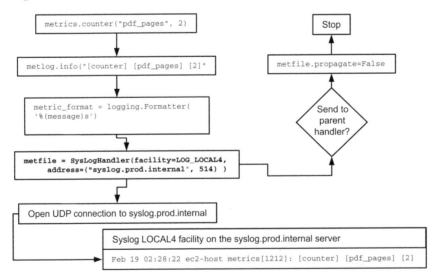

Figure 2.6   A version of figure 2.6 in which the Syslog event is sent to a remote Syslog server over UDP/514. This figure is an example of an emitter/shipper function using Syslog.

The rest of the file would be identical. When the file is set up this way, any metrics received result in the sending of a User Datagram Protocol (UDP) packet to the `syslog.prod.internal` host over UDP port 514. (For another look at using UDP to send telemetry, see section 13.2.) With the metrics library configured this way, the running code no longer needs to create files or interact with a service running on the same box, which makes this library much more capable of running inside a container or serverless framework such as AWS Lambda. This function is an emitter/shipper function (section 3.1), but all we need to do is add a single line to the Emitter function. *The concept of emitting directly to a centralized Syslog server is core to integrating hardware-generated telemetry.*

What happens next? A Shipping-stage component reads the system log (see section 4.1.2).

2.1.3 *Emitting telemetry into standard output*

In this section, we cover emitting telemetry to the standard output (stdout), or the console. If you run the program in a terminal, stdout is what you see printed back. `10 PRINT("Hello world!")` emits in the standard output. Emitting telemetry in the standard output means that your production code expects something executing the code to handle that stream of telemetry. If your production code is running on a Linux system, the system logger (journald) will happily capture all your output and give you a convenient place to page through it. Function as a Service (FaaS) providers such as AWS Lambda and Azure Functions, as well as container platforms such as Docker and Kubernetes, have ways to trap stdout for display and further shipping. (For more on containers and FaaS, see chapter 13.)

Standard output is a single channel. If several different threads are emitting telemetry through stdout, you must take steps to ensure that they don't collide; otherwise, your output may be quite garbled. Using a logging library as we did in the preceding two sections will help greatly, as those libraries (mostly) have been written so that at least each line of output is emitted individually.

There is a second standard output: the error channel known as standard error (stderr). The idea of a discrete channel for reporting error messages came in the 1970s and has been used in UNIX-like systems ever since. Task execution, command execution, and Platform as a Service (PaaS) frameworks like Windows Task Manager, Linux Systemd, Docker, and Kubernetes all monitor both streams.

stdout, stderr, and file handles: The ghost of POSIX

When you open a file from a program on a UNIX-like system, you are granted a file handle by the operating system. All your operations on that file are done through that handle. By convention, this value is a numeric value.

The standard outputs, stdout and stderr, are assigned the handle IDs 1 and 2, respectively. These assignments are made by convention and unlikely to change.

(continued)

If you've ever wondered what the bit of shell programming `my-program 2>&1` means, it's telling the shell to send the contents of file handle 2 (stderr) into the stream for file handle 1 (stdout) to provide a single stream of all output on either handle. This shell recipe is particularly handy when the process that executes a program, such as cron, considers any data on stderr to be a problem that must be reported. This invocation also works on Windows systems, in both command-shell and PowerShell.

If we wanted to revise the metrics library from the previous two subsections to emit to standard output instead, we would need to change three lines from listing 2.2, once again updating the formatter and handler. Figure 2.7 shows the changed flow.

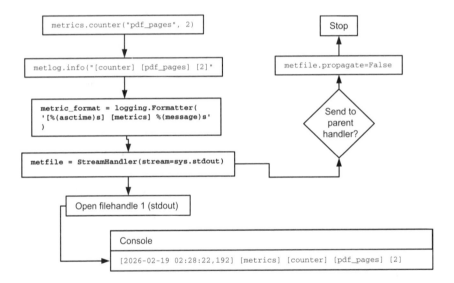

Figure 2.7   The counter is invoked the same way as in figures 2.4–2.6. The logger is called with the `info` method and passed a string. The formatter reformats the telemetry for the Shipping stage, adding a `[metrics]` tag. Finally, the writer emits the telemetry to standard out. The emitted telemetry will be gathered by a Shipping-stage system that monitors the standard output.

Listing 2.3 shows where in the function the changes are made. It uses `StreamHandler` to send telemetry to a file handle, which is stdout:

Listing 2.3   metrics.py: Using the Python logger to send telemetry to the console

```
import sys
import logging
from logging import StreamHandler

metlog  = logging.getLogger('metlog')
```

```
metfile = StreamHandler(stream=sys.stdout)
```
Creates a handler to
send logs to stdout

```
metfile.setLevel(logging.DEBUG)

metfile.propagate=False

metric_format = logging.Formatter(
    '[%(asctime)s] [metrics] %(message)s',
    )
```
Adds a timestamp and a field
to provide disambiguation

```
metfile.setFormatter(metric_format)

metlog.addHandler(metfile)

[...]
def counter(msg, count=1):
    """Emits a metric intended to be counted or summarized.

    Example: counter("pages", "15")
    """
    metlog.info("[counter] [%s] [%s]", msg, count)
    metfile.flush()
```
Adds an explicit stream flush
to ensure that the metrics are
emitted, which is useful during
shutdowns

The key changes between this version of metrics.py and the ones in listings 2.1 and 2.2 are the location to which the logging is sent (standard out) and the format of the emitted string. We're inserting [metrics] to disambiguate the output from this function from other streams that also use stdout. The output from this function is similar to the output from the log file emitting version, but with the second field added:

```
[2026-02-19 02:27:26,396] [metrics] [counter] [profile_image_upload] [1]
[2026-02-19 02:28:22,192] [metrics] [counter] [pdf_pages] [2]
[2026-02-19 02:28:27,921] [metrics] [timer] [profile_image_convert_time] [0.9]
```

The stdout/stderr split matters to whatever is executing our production code. For Linux and journald, the journalctl command is used to view the output from a service, and any output from stderr is both in another color and boldfaced to visually separate stderr output from regular stdout output. PowerShell on Windows operates similarly, with stderr displayed differently.

Colors and stderr

Increasingly, shells and utilities are starting to color-code output from standard error to allow visual separation between the stdout and stderr streams. This same convention holds for many other programs that handle and display the two streams.

The default color picked by the systems is overwhelmingly red—a color that many color-blind people perceive as being a shade of gray. (Also, red is a United States–centric color to use for an error message.) Many of these systems provide methods for changing the color, but the default color remains the problematic one. If you find yourself color-coding output, consider using other colors or boldface instead.

If our example library had been run on a Linux system running journald, we could access our log-stream through

```
journalctl --unit my-program --lines=100
```

which would allow us to look at the most recent 100 lines sent to stdout for our program.

What happens next? Software engineers who write production code that emits telemetry into standard out do so knowing that the system that receives that telemetry—the framework that runs the production code—is able to do something with it (see section 4.1.3). That problem is a Shipping-stage problem.

2.1.4   Formatting telemetry for emissions

The examples in the preceding three sections used a simple format for their emissions, though how the timestamp was handled changed somewhat depending on what we were emitting into. For a metrics logger, a simple delimited format such as [metric-type] [metric-name] [metric-value] is an easy-to-parse format in the Shipping stage. But what if you want to encode telemetry more complex than metrics? Or what if you want a format that can emit more than one metric in a given emission of telemetry? This section covers those topics.

When you are writing your own emitter, you have the luxury of owning the format. Hardware, installed third-party software, and SaaS and IaaS providers impose a format on you—overwhelmingly Syslog for hardware and HTTP + JSON for SaaS providers. But in your own software, you can make the telemetry format fit your specific needs.

Knowing your telemetry pipeline helps you decide on a format. Understanding the constraints in your Shipping stage allows you to reduce the load of handling your telemetry. The Shipping stage itself may transform emissions into something else entirely, as covered in section 4.2.1.

The code in the preceding sections formats the emissions in two lines of code. The first formatting happens immediately after the function is called,

```
metlog.info("[counter] [%s] [%s]", msg, count)
```

which is where the [metric-type] [metric-name] [metric-value] format is set. If we want to revise our class to accept a hash of metrics, we need to change the code around the metlog.info line. Given the input

```
pdf_metrics = { "pdf_pages": 2, "pdf_size" : 2.9 }
metrics.counters(pdf_metrics)
```

we would rewrite the def counters function as shown in the following listing.

Listing 2.4   metrics.py: multivalued `counter` function

```
import json
[...]

def counter(msg):
    """Emits metrics intended to be counted or summarized.

    Example: counter( { "pages": 15, "words": 16272 } )
    """
    counter_metrics = {                                    Builds
        "counters": msg                                    metrics hash
    }
    counter_emission = json.dumps(counter_metrics)         Converts Python
    metlog.info(counter_emission)                          dict to JSON string
```

Emits the JSON string [annotation pointing to `metlog.info(counter_emission)`]

With no other changes except to this function, the Syslog version of this metrics emitter would return a line that would read

```
Feb 19 02:26:26 ec2-host metrics[1212]: { "counters": { "pdf_pages": 2,
➥ "pdf_size" : 2.9 } }
```

Two metrics, one emission. The Shipping stage is responsible for taking this string and turning it into two entries in the metrics database.

> **WARNING**   Input validation applies to logging-library functions such as this one as much as it does for any function that accepts untrusted user input. People stuff the strangest things into their logging function calls (including untrusted user input; don't do that). The example here does not include input validation for clarity of teaching. The full function would ensure that the hash contained no nested values and that all values were of a numeric type, and it would reject any invalid types.

JSON is used in this example, but it isn't the only way to encode an object. The reason why the single-metric versions of this function used a delimited format instead of JSON is that the human eye parses delimited formats far more easily than it does JSON-encoded formats. JSON is the data transaction format of much of the modern web, so a lot of effort has been put into making JSON encoding/decoding operations extremely fast, even though delimited formats are simpler algorithms. (For more discussion of telemetry formats, see section 4.2.1, which examines string formats in the Shipping stage and goes into more detail than I do here.) The Shipping stage has to translate any emission into a format that's acceptable to the storage system, and you can help speed that process by making sure that your emissions format is efficient to parse. Here are three tips for easing the parsing burden of the Shipping stage:

- Remember that software engineers likely need to read their emissions locally in their development environment. The human eye parses telemetry quite differently from the algorithms in the Shipping stage, so consider emitting telemetry in a human-readable format in development environments and a machine-readable format everywhere else.
- Use object-encoding formats (JSON, YAML, XML) to encode complex objects. If you find yourself using these formats for simple key-value pairs, know that you're sacrificing readability for speed.
- Delimited formats are more flexible than you might think.

The following lines are different ways to share the same telemetry in different delimited formats. First is the comma-separated-values (CSV) list,

```
"2026-02-26T17:52:01.002+0:00","pdf_pages exited with a fatal exception",
➥ "ip-172-16-0-12"
```

with three fields, and the parser needs to understand what position each field describes. This technique is fast. Next up is a series of key-value pairs:

```
timestamp="2026-02-26T17:52:01.002+0:00" message="pdf_pages exited with a
➥ fatal exception" host="ip-172-16-0-12"
```

The key-value format encodes the field names as part of the string, so the parser doesn't have to know what fields to expect. This format is more flexible than CSV, if longer as a result; it's slightly slower than CSV but still blazingly fast.

This next format is a bit different in that it is a combination of formats:

```
[timestamp="2026-02-26T17:52:01.002+0:00" host="ip-172-16-0-12"] [pdf_pages
➥ exited with a fatal exception]
```

A format like this one is expected to be parsed in more than one pass. The first position is always host details and context (context-related details; see chapter 6). The second position is the message. Then the first position is further reparsed as key-value to get those fields. Parsing efficiency is more of a Shipping-stage problem (see section 4.2 for details), but the Emitting stage is where the problem starts being solved.

Exercise 2.1

You're developing a program by using Docker. When you review telemetry as you develop, you're using the `docker logs` command to see what has been emitted. What style of telemetry emission is this?

    a Emitting into a log file

    b Emitting into the system log

    c Emitting into standard output

> **Exercise 2.2**
> Match the three structured logging components from column A with their role in the structured logger in column B.
>
> | Column A: | Column B: |
> |---|---|
> | Logger | Delivers telemetry to the Shipping stage |
> | Formatter | Entry point into the structured logger |
> | Writer | Rewrites telemetry to fit the Shipping stage |

2.2 Emitting from hardware

For this section, we change what kind of organization we're working with. Here, the organization is a global logistics company founded in 1848, and unlike the 100-person startup, this company has been using computers since the 1960s. If this global logistics company has one thing that the startup doesn't have, it's extensive hardware in its data centers. Whereas with software you write, anything goes with regard to telemetry, for hardware systems, you're stuck with whatever the hardware system speaks.

Hardware systems emit telemetry for the same reason that software systems do: humans want feedback about what's happening. This situation is especially true for hardware, because hardware is true black boxes (or beige, charcoal, or pretty teal), and the only clues we have regarding what's going on in there are vendor documentation and whatever telemetry the hardware can spit out. For physical infrastructures of any size, getting this telemetry into a single place is a major convenience for that infrastructure's operators. Overwhelmingly, hardware makers choose a standards-based emission method, mostly Syslog, but systems based on Simple Network Management Protocol (SNMP) are often used in networking equipment.

2.2.1 Explaining SNMP

SNMP is neither simple nor solely for network management. SNMP is simple in the sense that there isn't much to configure, leaving all the complexity of the protocol in how it is used. The use of SNMP was widespread once, but these days, you rarely encounter it outside legacy infrastructures and networking systems. I discuss it in this section because you need to know about it in case your telemetry maintenance duties bring you into contact with SNMP.

Like Syslog, SNMP is a UDP-based protocol. SNMP has two modes of operation, shown in figure 2.8:

- A *polling* mode, in which a network management station polls SNMP-enabled devices and either requests information or sets configuration. Polling mode is used for distributing configuration and gathering metrics telemetry (often described as *monitoring* in network management circles). Similarly to the GET and PUT verbs used for HTTP, SNMP uses GET and SET.
- A *trap* mode, in which SNMP-enabled devices notify a network management station of significant events—a form of centralized logging and SIEM telemetry.

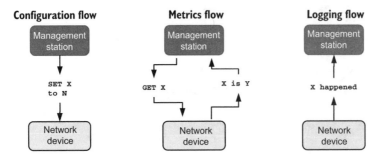

Figure 2.8   The three SNMP styles of operation; configuration, metrics, and logging. Configuration uses the SET verb to push configuration. Metrics uses the GET (and GETNEXT, not pictured) verb to fetch metrics data. Logging uses SNMP traps issued by devices to capture events.

In the modern era, SNMP is used almost solely by networking infrastructures, though you may still encounter non-networking use in old, long-established infrastructures like the global logistics company we're talking about in this section. Historically, operating systems such as Windows, NetWare, and Linux had SNMP services that allowed management stations to poll for system state as part of a monitoring system. Old and established systems sometimes decide to keep a perfectly functional metrics system in place and upgrade their SNMP based metrics systems to keep working, but few new companies elect to do so. This OS monitoring use has largely migrated to agents dedicated to specific platforms, such as the CollectD system of monitors and WMI for Windows. Networking systems in specific, however, maintain SNMP capabilities. Version 3 of the protocol introduced cryptographic communication and much-improved authentication capabilities.

My first telemetry script

In 1998, I was two years into my postcollege career and was a member of a group of system administrators in charge of a set of Novell NetWare servers. The organization we belonged to also had Windows NT and Solaris, but management of WinNT and Solaris wasn't our job (yet), so it didn't matter to us.

One day, I noticed that all discussions about disk provisioning were gut checks and thought it would be nice to have charts of this stuff. So I embarked on my longest programming challenge after graduating with a CompSci degree and wrote a disk-space poller in Perl. This script used the SNMP agent running on NetWare to extract out the total space and free space, and it computed space metrics for each of our network volumes. It polled twice a day, morning and evening, and not on weekends. It used an Oracle database to store data because the Oracle database administrator had the cube across from mine, and a tablespace that got 28 rows inserted a day was met with the reaction "Let the new kid have their toy."

It took a while before the database had enough data to be impressive, but when the Excel charts produced trendlines with the number of days until we intercepted the zero-free-space mark, the power of metrics was proved. Data from that script drove many resourcing decisions at that job.

I took the script with me to my next job, which was jointly managing NetWare and Windows 2000 systems. I added Windows support (it also had an SNMP OID to poll for space) and converted to MS-SQL for a backend. That approach was fine until the day our largest volume was extended to 2.3 TB, and I found out that the NetWare SNMP agent had returned a negative number for the space details. A 32-bit signed integer had overflowed. I dutifully updated the script to convert the number to an unsigned int.

I never found out what happened when the volume crossed 4 TB; we got rid of NetWare and moved all of our file serving to Windows 2008 before then. But I did find out that the Windows SNMP agent also returned a signed int for disk space details. This discovery drove me to rewrite the script from Perl using SNMP to PowerShell and WMI, which was properly 64-bit. That script is the longest-running piece of telemetry infrastructure I've written.

2.2.2 Ingesting telemetry from a Cisco ASA firewall

Now that I've explained SNMP, I'll go back to the old global logistics company. This company has been operating data centers for decades and has a large installed base of networking hardware to support those data centers. It is adding a new set of Cisco ASA firewalls to its infrastructure, and the security teams want the events that these firewalls generate. The network operations team already has the events thanks to SNMP, but the events are in a proprietary system that the team doesn't want to share.

To solve this problem, the network operations team decides to enable the Cisco ASA's Syslog output. Figure 2.9 demonstrates the process.

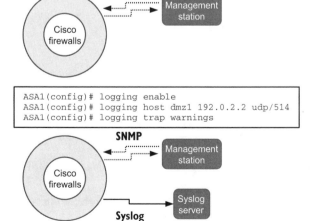

```
ASA1(config)# logging enable
ASA1(config)# logging host dmz1 192.0.2.2 udp/514
ASA1(config)# logging trap warnings
```

Figure 2.9 Configuring a Cisco ASA to emit logging using Syslog to a specific server. Dotted directional lines are UDP SNMP traffic; solid directional lines are UDP Syslog traffic. The top is the before state; the middle is the commands used to enable the after state (bottom). Dual emission allows multiple teams to receive event flow from the Cisco ASA firewalls.

There are three commands we need to issue on the Cisco ASA to enable the Syslog output, and send telemetry to our Syslog server:

```
ASA1(config)# logging enable
ASA1(config)# logging host dmz1 192.0.2.2 udp/514
ASA1(config)# logging trap warnings
```

First, we enable logging. Next, we configure where the Syslog server is—in this case, the IP address 192.0.2.2, reachable by using the dmz1 interface. Finally, we configure the ASA to send warnings and higher-level events to the Syslog server. (For more on the log levels available in Syslog, see table 1.1.) When it's set this way, the firewall forwards events to a central Syslog host, similar to the metrics script in listing 2.2. After we enable forwarding, events flow into the Syslog host, are formatted following the Syslog standards, and look similar to this record of a DNS request:

```
Feb 19 02:26:26 asa1.net.prod.internal %ASA1: Teardown of UDP connection
162121 for outside:1.1.0.0/53 to dmz1:192.0.2.19/59232 duration 0:00:00
bytes 136
```

The management framework for this hardware platform also shows these events, because they are still being sent through SNMP to the management station, but forwarding them to a central system allows more teams than network operations team to access the event stream. Such a split also enables data enrichment possibilities beyond what the management system offers natively. Chapters 5 and 6 cover data enrichment generally.

The technique demonstrated in figure 2.9—using device configuration to emit to a Syslog server—is common to most hardware systems. This example uses Cisco ASA, but many other hardware systems allow such configuration. The following list is not exhaustive, merely suggestive of how widespread the emit-to-Syslog feature is:

- Cisco hardware generally
- Hewlett Packard Enterprise ProCurve network hardware
- Dell servers with iDRAC Enterprise
- HP servers with iLO
- Supermicro servers with licensed OOB/IPMI
- Hitachi storage systems running Vantara
- APC Metered Power Distribution Units (also supports SNMP)

As figure 2.9 demonstrated, for hardware systems, the procedure is simple:

1 Enable the Syslog output.
2 Configure the Syslog server to send output to (generally, an IP address or DNS name plus a port number).
3 Configure the types of events that need to be sent through Syslog.

> **Exercise 2.3**
>
> Both SNMP and Syslog emit over what network protocol?
>
>   a   TCP
>   b   UDP
>   c   A mix of TCP and UDP

2.3   *Emitting from as-a-Service systems*

For this section, we are focusing on the 200-person continuing education company to describe how telemetry works when using SaaS and IaaS systems. Unlike the companies in the previous two examples, the startup company and the long established logistics company, this company develops as little software as possible and delegates as much of the burden of operating software to outside companies, which allows the company to focus on what it does best. SaaS and IaaS platforms allow this company to focus on the business of teaching rather than the business of writing software. This section covers two cases:

- Emitting events from a SaaS system
- Emitting events from an IaaS system

2.3.1   *Emitting events from SaaS systems*

Our continuing education company uses a variety of SaaS products in its business. Because of the highly seasonal nature of their business, the company does extensive recruiting of instructors for their courses in the many metro areas where it does business. It uses an applicant-tracking SaaS provider to manage the life cycle of a potential instructor's application. Because of the number of people moving through the applicant system, our company wants to get a feed of events from the applicant-tracking system to another SaaS provider that it's using for centralizing events. This SaaS provider for telemetry is similar to SumoLogic, Splunk, and SolarWinds Loggly. For SaaS systems, these products allow access to a telemetry feed in two main ways:

- Offering an API endpoint that, when accessed with the HTTP GET verb, returns a list of events, requiring you to build a system to poll that endpoint regularly. This method is asynchronous.
- Offering an interface that calls a configured URL to be hit every time an event needs to be emitted, requiring you to accept HTTP POST requests. This method is called a *webhook* and is synchronous.

As with the hardware systems in section 2.2, you are not in control of the format of the emissions coming from the SaaS system. Handling those emissions is a problem for the Shipping stage, which we'll get to in chapters 3, 4, and 6. But this company has delegated that problem to the telemetry SaaS provider, so it doesn't have to worry. The SaaS telemetry provider offers an HTTP endpoint for cases like this one, in which the client needs to receive webhook telemetry from any number of sources. Their webhook endpoint looks like this:

```
https://api.example.com/v3/submit-logs
```

When attempting to POST data to this URL, the sender (in this case, the applicant-tracking system) needs to authenticate itself so that the SaaS telemetry provider knows which of its many accounts to send the telemetry to. There are several valid ways of providing this authentication:

- Add a URL parameter such as `?token=secretText` to the URL when POSTing.
- Use HTTP Basic authentication with the POST request, such as `https://acccount:secretPW@api.example.com/v3/submit-logs`.
- Use an HTTP Header with the POST request, with the header containing the signature and a secret key. This method requires both sides of the connection to support the header. In the case of our continuing education company, the telemetry SaaS provider would need to support the applicant-tracking SaaS provider's telemetry.

As it happens, the telemetry SaaS provider does not have prebuilt integration for the applicant-tracking provider, so it has to use one of the other authentication methods. Now that we know this, we know that the URL that will receive the webhook will be

```
https://api.example.com/v3/submit-logs?token=atvhwpqxncrutndjfbtdf
```

Next, we configure the applicant-tracking system to send the webhook. For that purpose, look at the configuration page in figure 2.10.

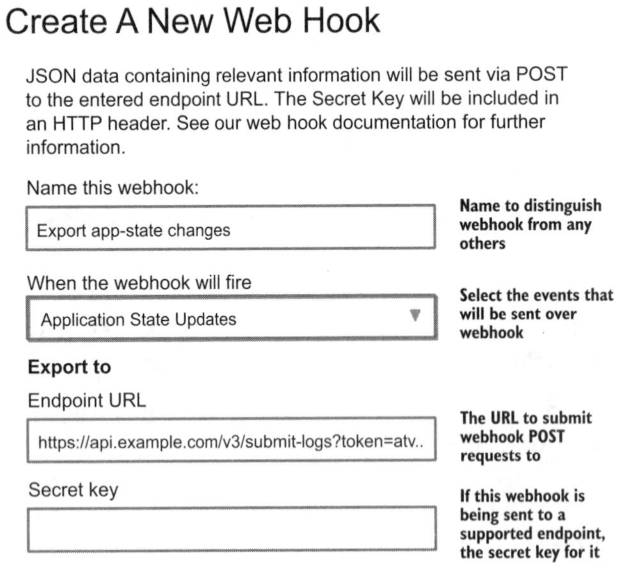

Create A New Web Hook

JSON data containing relevant information will be sent via POST to the entered endpoint URL. The Secret Key will be included in an HTTP header. See our web hook documentation for further information.

Name this webhook:

```
Export app-state changes
```

Name to distinguish webhook from any others

When the webhook will fire

```
Application State Updates                          ▼
```

Select the events that will be sent over webhook

Export to

Endpoint URL

```
https://api.example.com/v3/submit-logs?token=atv..
```

The URL to submit webhook POST requests to

Secret key

```

```

If this webhook is being sent to a supported endpoint, the secret key for it

Figure 2.10   The outbound webhook configuration page for the applicant-tracking SaaS provider used by our continuing education company. Because the system receiving the webhook does not have an explicit integration with this SaaS provider, the secret key is left blank; instead, a URL parameter is used to provide authentication.

Because the format is decided by the SaaS provider, configuration is almost as simple as configuring a Cisco ASA firewall to send telemetry to another system. You need the name of the webhook so that you can tell it apart from others, the URL to POST to, and what kind of telemetry to send. That's it.

At this point, the telemetry SaaS vendor will start receiving a steady flow of events from the applicant-tracking SaaS provider. When the events show up in the telemetry provider, the Emitting stage's work is done.

2.3.2 *Emitting events from IaaS systems*

Our 200-person continuing education company couldn't avoid running some servers, so it elected to run the few it needs in AWS, an IaaS provider that operates a little differently from SaaS providers like the applicant-tracking system when it comes to telemetry. Rather than offering webhooks and API endpoints, IaaS providers such as Microsoft Azure and Digital Ocean often have unique ways to expose their telemetry streams, because their users have the technical skill needed to accommodate each IaaS provider's distinctiveness.

Our company needs to pull the audit log for its AWS account into its telemetry SaaS provider so that the events can be easily searched. The pertinent feature in AWS is CloudTrail, which allows files with audit information to be sent to an object storage system known as an S3 bucket. Figure 2.11 shows the AWS architecture.

Figure 2.11 CloudTrail configured to send all audit logs to a specific S3 bucket. Fetching the audit logs from the bucket for ingestion by a Shipping-stage component is left for another day.

To tell AWS to send audit logs to a bucket, our company needs to complete two steps in the AWS command-line interface, as shown in listing 2.5:

1 Create the S3 bucket.
2 Configure CloudTrail.

Listing 2.5 Configuring CloudTrail to emit into an S3 bucket

```
aws s3api create-bucket --bucket ********* \
  --create-bucket-configuration \            Creates a bucket, name-obscured,
  LocationConstraint=eu-central-1      ◁───── in the eu-central-1 region

aws cloudtrail create-trail --name whole-audit-log \    Creates the CloudTrail
  --s3-bucket-name ********* \                           configuration to store all
  --include-global-service-events \                      events from everywhere
  --is-multi-region-trail
```

This is good; the audit logs are being generated. The audit logs are not yet somewhere useful, however, because the telemetry SaaS provider can't fetch them. More important, the telemetry SaaS provider *doesn't know that the logs need to be fetched.*

Fortunately for this company, AWS provides a way to configure notices to be sent through a service called Simple Notification Service (SNS). The telemetry SaaS provider has explicit support for AWS CloudTrail, so the desired architecture looks like figure 2.12. The company modifies its CloudTrail configuration to send notices of new audit logs to an SNS topic (listing 2.6).

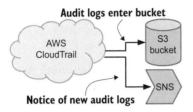

Figure 2.12   AWS CloudTrail configured to emit audit logs to an S3 bucket and emit notices of new audit logs to an SNS topic. When the SNS topic is defined and sending notices of new audit logs, you can configure a shipping system to subscribe to the topic so that it knows to fetch new audit logs from the S3 bucket.

Listing 2.6   Configuring CloudTrail to notify an SNS topic of new telemetry

```
aws sns create-topic --name eu-audit-logs \      ⟵──── Creates an SNS topic
  --region eu-central-1

aws cloudtrail update-trail --name whole-audit-log \   | Modifies CloudTrail to
  --sns-topic-name eu-audit-logs                       | use the SNS service
```

Now that audit logs are being generated and notices are being published, the last step is subscribing the Shipping-stage systems to the SNS topic, which can be done with a single command:

```
aws sns subscribe --topic-arn arn:aws:sns::*****:eu-audit-logs \
  --protocol https \
  --notification-endpoint \
  https://api.example.com/v3/cloud-trail-data?token=*****
```

The telemetry SaaS provider automates the subscription confirmation process. Then CloudTrail telemetry flows into the telemetry SaaS provider! Figure 2.13 shows the final architecture of how CloudTrail data flows. AWS CloudWatch logs are now visible inside the telemetry SaaS provider's dashboards.

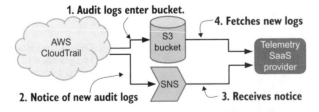

Figure 2.13   The order of audit-log flow for ingesting AWS CloudWatch audit logs into a telemetry SaaS provider. Logs first publish to an S3 bucket; then notice is posted to an SNS topic. The telemetry SaaS provider subscribes to the topic and gets that notice, triggering its retrieval of the new audit log. When this process is complete, the CloudWatch logs will be visible in the SaaS provider's dashboards.

Summary

- Programming languages often provide sophisticated methods for sending telemetry to the system log, files, or other endpoints. This function is called a Logger and may be an extension rather than built in.
- Logging methods may be extended for other purposes, such as creating a metrics system for tracking and aggregating numbers-based telemetry.
- Logging methods may include the ability to emit to a wide variety of targets, such as files, Syslog, Windows Event Log, queues, streams, and SaaS providers.
- Telemetry emissions from logging functions can be plain-language statements; delimited emissions such as CSV, XML, and key-value pairs; and object-encoding emissions such as JSON, YAML, and XML.
- When you're building an Emitting stage from code, consider the developer use case. A single engineer will be viewing logs directly, whereas in production, the logs will be machine-parsed. Using different formats for development and production will make everyone happier.
- Networking hardware largely supports SNMP, often with proprietary vendor-specific management frameworks that make integration with a larger telemetry pipeline more difficult.
- Most hardware systems support emitting to Syslog because Syslog is a format defined by RFCs and therefore is unlikely to change fast. For organizations that want to build a telemetry pipeline that integrates hardware and software, supporting Syslog is highly recommended.
- SaaS systems do not support Syslog; instead, they rely on HTTP methods for telemetry handling.
- SaaS systems may provide API endpoints to poll for their telemetry or webhook systems to send telemetry to a shipper.
- IaaS systems are often subject to compliance and regulatory frameworks, so they have detailed telemetry emissions.
- IaaS systems have notification methods to ease the work of Shipping stages in ingesting emissions from the IaaS provider.

The Shipping stage: Moving and storing telemetry

This chapter covers

- The role of the shipping stage in a telemetry pipeline
- The emitter/shipper function in production code
- Ways of moving telemetry through the Shipping stage

The Shipping stage in a telemetry pipeline is the second stage of the pipeline, as shown in figure 3.1. The Shipping stage receives telemetry from the Emitting stage, optionally marks up and enriches it (see chapter 6), and stores it for use in the Presentation stage. When the Emitting stage is entirely within your production code, the Shipping stage can be combined directly with the Emitting stage to make an emitter/shipper, or the Shipping stage might be a whole multisystem infrastructure handling the telemetry needs of your incredibly diverse production system. Both approaches are valid, and hybrid approaches are equally so.

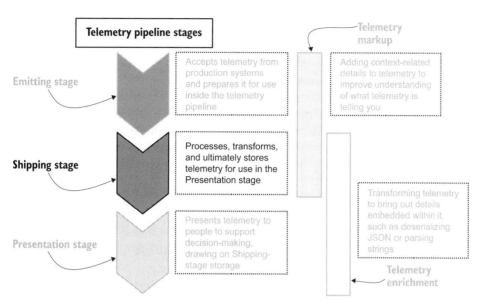

Figure 3.1 Telemetry pipeline stages, with the Shipping stage second. The Shipping stage receives telemetry prepared by the Emitting stage and then processes and transforms it for storage. The Shipping stage is the only stage that performs both markup and enrichment (chapter 6).

The Shipping stage must perform two major roles:

- Move telemetry between components of the Shipping stage and ultimately into storage (chapters 3 and 4)
- Transform telemetry through both markup and enrichment to add context (markup) and bring out details (enrichment) (chapter 6)

The markup and enrichment role also happens during all three stages of the telemetry pipeline, which is why I cover it after discussing the Presentation stage in chapter 5. Moving and storing telemetry is a big job, because your Shipping stage needs to handle whatever formats the Emitting stages in your telemetry system emit as. Emitting stages, especially hardware systems, are often inconveniently opinionated in the formats they emit.

The Shipping stage is a big topic, which is why I'm covering the Shipping stage across two chapters:

- Chapter 3 covers moving telemetry around, including new techniques for emitting telemetry (the emitter/shipper functions promised in chapter 2) and a discussion of tipping points that push for Shipping-stage changes.
- Chapter 4 covers formats: emitting formats, transforming formats to meet standards, figuring out your standard formats, and getting telemetry ready for storage.

Chapter 6 goes into more depth about enriching and transforming telemetry, which often happens in the Shipping stage but doesn't have to. To help with explaining Shipping-stage architectures, I will use the example organizations from chapter 2 again:

- A 100-person startup building an API-driven application, running in AWS. This example demonstrates shipping in fully cloud environments where the telemetry emitting format is entirely controlled by the organization.
- A global logistics company founded in 1848 that computerized its business processes in the late 1960s. This example demonstrates Shipping stages in physical data centers where the emitting format is variable and in some cases inflexible.
- A 200-person company providing in-person continuing education courses, with strong seasonality in its hiring. This example demonstrates shipping between SaaS applications.

3.1   *Emitter/shipper functions, telemetry from production code*

Section 2.1 covered emitting telemetry directly from production code to somewhere on the same system as the production code. This section covers emitting and shipping telemetry to somewhere off the system, such as into a queue. You have a trade-off to make when deciding whether to emit to a file and have something else move telemetry off the system (section 4.1) or to have your production code do the moving (this section):

- By emitting to a file or the system log (section 2.1), a dedicated shipper program can handle the complexity of moving telemetry so your production systems don't have to, and will be simpler for your production systems. Also, emitting telemetry to somewhere off the system won't block production code-paths if the queue or stream is temporarily down.
- By emitting directly from production code to somewhere off the system, your telemetry spends the least amount of time on the production system possible. Also, you don't need to configure an additional shipper to move telemetry, so your overall telemetry system is simpler.

Section 3.1.1 covers shipping directly into storage from your production code. The same techniques can be used later in the shipping pipeline to move telemetry into storage. Section 3.1.2 covers shipping into queues and streams from your production code.

3.1.1   *Shipping directly into storage*

This section covers the simplest Shipping stage, in which your Emitting-stage emitter sends telemetry directly into storage. Section 2.1.1 described the simplest possible way to do this: sending your telemetry to a file. Sending to a file is centralized logging only if your production code is running in only one place. (When you're writing software, writing to a file may be all you need during development.) This chapter is about shipping your telemetry off the system, so we will be looking at sending telemetry to a database of some kind.

Our 100-person startup is facing a problem. The company has grown enough that keeping logs inside the Kubernetes cluster isn't scaling, so it wants to send its logs to an Elasticsearch cluster maintained by their cloud provider instead. Figure 3.2 illustrates the desired architecture.

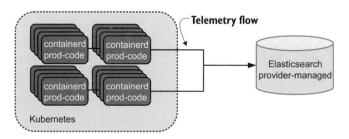

Figure 3.2 The desired flow of telemetry from the startup's container-based production code to a cloud-provider-managed Elasticsearch. Emitter functions in the production code will be rewritten to send telemetry directly to Elasticsearch, so telemetry is no longer taking up space in the Kubernetes cluster.

To get to the desired architecture, we need to rewrite the metrics function to send to Elasticsearch. Figure 3.3 shows how the metric data will be transformed and written to Elasticsearch.

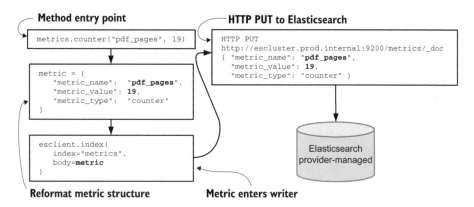

Figure 3.3 metrics.py rewritten to insert into an Elasticsearch cluster. The function is called the same way as the functions in chapter 2. Next, the function creates a hash with the supplied values and passes it to the `esclient` object to index it into the cluster. Then the `index` method makes an HTTP PUT on an Elasticsearch specific indexing URL, passing the hash as data.

The rewritten metrics.py function is simpler than the versions in chapter 2. This simplicity is in large part due to the fact that we are not using the structured logging library for Python; instead, we are embracing the Formatter/Writer aspects directly. Listing 3.1 shows the rewritten method.

NOTE This listing requires the Python 3 `elasticsearch` module to run. Install it with `pip3 install elasticsearch`.

Listing 3.1   metrics.py: Emitting into Elasticsearch

```
from elasticsearch import Elasticsearch

esclient = Elasticsearch (
  hosts=[
    {"host": "escluster.prod.internal", "port" : 9200}
  ],
  sniff_on_start=False,
  sniffer_timeout=60
  )
```
Defines a client class for Elasticsearch

```
def counter(msg, count=1):
```
Defines a counter class
```
  """Emits a metric intended to be counted or summarized.

  Example: counter("pages", "15")
  """
  metric = {
      "metric_name": msg,
      "metric_value": count,
      "metric_type": "counter"
  }
```
Builds a hash with the metric document we will insert for the counter
```
  esclient.index(
      index="metrics",
      body=metric
  )
```
Inserts the metric hash into the 'metrics' index

```
def timer(msg, time=0.0):
```
Defines a timer class
```
  """Emits a metric for tracking run-times.

  Example: timer("convert_worker_runtime", "2.7")
  """
  metric = {
      "metric_name": msg,
      "metric_value": time,
      "metric_type": "timer"
  }
```
Builds a hash with the metric document we will insert for the timer
```
  esclient.index(
      index="metrics",
      body=metric
  )
```
Inserts the metric hash into the 'metrics' index

The function in listing 3.1 is much shorter than the ones in listing 2.1 but is called the same way in code:

- `metrics.counter("profile_image_uploaded")` to increment the count of uploaded profile images by 1
- `metrics.counter("pdf_pages", 19)` to indicate that the number of `pdf_pages` encountered was 19
- `metrics.timer("profile_image_convert_time", 0.9)` to indicate that converting the uploaded profile image to an appropriate image dimension took 0.9 seconds

Instead of emitting lines into a file or lines into Syslog, this code injects JSON-formatted documents into an Elasticsearch index. Elasticsearch, which is the storage for this particular Shipping stage, indexes the document for searchability. A Presentation-stage system using Elasticsearch as storage could retrieve this telemetry through a search like

```
metric_name:"pdf_pages"
```

which will return all the metrics telemetry with that value in `metric_name`. When combined with a date-range search—the timestamp on our JSON documents is created automatically by Elasticsearch when they are indexed—the searcher can narrow to a small window of time. The presentation system will handle converting and aggregating the `metric_value` field. (See section 5.1 for more about aggregating metrics.) Elasticsearch is used in this example, but you can use many databases for metrics. Here are a few:

- *Prometheus*—A dedicated time-series database that is open source and a component of the Cloud Native Computing Foundation stack
- *InfluxDB*—Another dedicated time-series database and open-core (open source for basic features, pay for extended features such as clustering)
- *KairosDB*—A dedicated time-series database built on top of Cassandra
- *Any relational database*—Such as MySQL, Postrgres, and MS-SQL

Although the example here uses metrics, the same direct-insert method is useful for centralized logging as well.

3.1.2 *Shipping through queues and streams*

Not all emitter/shipper functions ship directly to storage; often, telemetry data needs more transformation before it is ultimately stored. Also, having the vast majority of your production systems writing to a database individually can be woefully inefficient (not to mention hard on the database). This section is about centralizing the flow of telemetry to allow downstream Shipping-stage components to bulk-insert into your storage systems. The most popular ways to accomplish this task are to use queues and a related technology called *streams* (also known as *event buses*):

- A *queue* is a basic structure. Data is pushed onto the bottom of the queue, and data at the top is serviced by the next system requesting data. The flow is first in, first out (FIFO).
- A *stream* adds the concept of a *consumer group*—systems that act together and see the same FIFO behavior. Different consumer groups see the same data, but the FIFO behavior is kept inside each consumer group. To accomplish this task, the stream system needs to keep each item of data in a stream until all consumer groups have seen it. This system is quite powerful, and we'll get into more on this topic later in this section (with more concepts in chapter 7 on multitenancy).

In the previous section, our 100-person startup had a Kubernetes cluster and wanted its production code to send telemetry directly into Elasticsearch. But what if the example startup had not a single Kubernetes cluster, but 100 of them? It isn't hard to imagine that Elasticsearch would be dealing with 10,000 containerd instances, each submitting telemetry. Figure 3.4 provides two views of this problem, one with all 10,000 containerd instances writing to Elasticsearch and a second with those instances instead writing to a queue or stream.

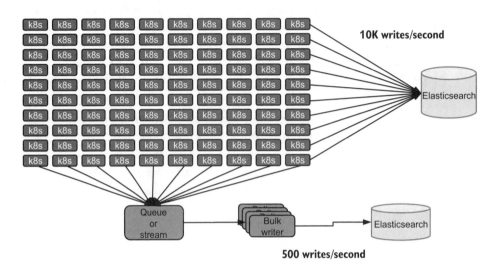

Figure 3.4   Two views of the 100 Kubernetes/10,000 containerd instances problem. To the right, all 10,000 containerd instances are writing directly to Elasticsearch. Below, the instances write to a queue or stream. A group of bulk writer systems service the queue or stream and bulk-insert into Elasticsearch. Write transactions are reduced by 95% compared with the direct-insert model.

Although it is entirely possible to engineer Elasticsearch to accept 10,000 small writes a second, Elasticsearch requires fewer resources (and has an easier time with consistency) when dealing with fewer, larger writes. Most databases generally behave this way, in fact. By extending our telemetry pipeline to add more stages, we take load off of the database.

USING QUEUES IN A SHIPPING PIPELINE

To start talking about how to use queues, this section provides an example of using a queue to take load off a storage system. Let's focus on modifying the emitter demonstrated in listing 3.1 to emit to a Redis list instead of an Elasticsearch database. We will examine the bulk writers later. Redis is an in-memory data-structure store that allows storing lists, hashes, sets, and other types of data. For our purposes, we will be using a list, because a list can be made to function like a queue. Our data transformation flow from figure 3.3 is revised into what you see in figure 3.5.

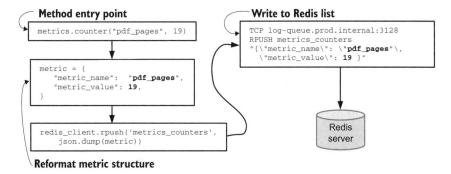

Figure 3.5   The metrics logger revised to send to a Redis list instead. Flow through the logger program is similar to figure 3.3, with fewer details encoded in the hash. The `rpush` method is called on the `redis_client` to submit the telemetry. The Redis `RPUSH` command is called, inserting our telemetry into the end of the list named `metrics_counters`.

We follow the same number of steps but instead are writing to a new destination. Listing 3.2 provides a view of the changes to our metrics.py method.

> **NOTE** This listing needs the `redis` module installed. Install it with `pip3 install redis`.

Listing 3.2   metrics.py: Emitting to a Redis queue/list

```
import redis
import json

redis_client = redis.Redis(
  host='log-queue.prod.internal'        ⟵ Creates an interface to a Redis
)                                          server on log-queue.prod.internal

def counter(msg, count=1):             ⟵ The counter class, same
  """Emits a metric intended to be counted or summarized.    as in previous examples

  Example: counter("pages", "15")
  """
  metric = {
    "metric_name" : msg,
    "metric_value" : count
  }
  redis_client.rpush('metrics_counters',   ⟵ Pushes the generated hash into
  ➥ json.dump(metric))                       the list named metrics_counters

def timer(msg, time=0.0):              ⟵ The timer class, same as
  """Emits a metric for tracking run-times.    in previous examples

  Example: timer("convert_worker_runtime", "2.7")
  """
  metric = {
    "metric_name": msg,
    "metric_value": time,
  }
  redis_client.rpush('metrics_timers',   ⟵ Pushes the generated hash into
  ➥ json.dump(metric))                     the list named metrics_timers
```

The revised metrics logger in listing 3.2 is called the same way as in previous examples. The change is how telemetry is moved into the Shipping stage. When metrics.timer or metrics.counter is called, this function generates a structured hash. Then this hash is injected into Redis by the RPUSH command, which adds the hash to the bottom of a list structure in Redis and makes the list work like a queue.

Our bulk writer systems would use the BLPOP (Blocking List POP) command to fetch the first element of the named list while blocking to ensure that no other system would fetch the same values. Then it would inject this hash into the storage system of the Shipping stage for display by the Presentation stage. Making sure that telemetry doesn't linger in the pipeline too long is a concern, however, so the bulk-writer-counter.py program needs to flush writes early in certain cases. Figure 3.6 shows the flow.

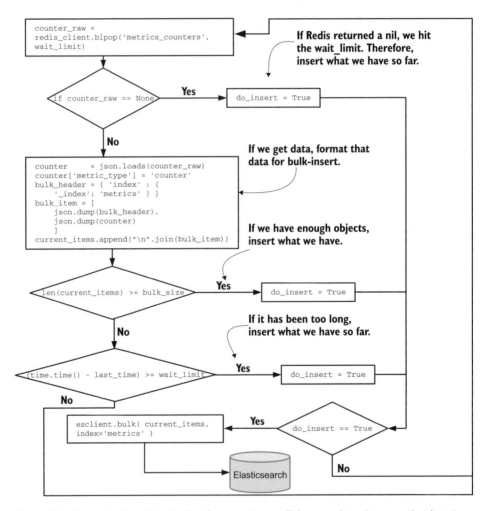

Figure 3.6   Execution flow during bulk-writer-counters.py. This example makes sure that inserts into Elasticsearch have enough items to be worthwhile except when too much time has elapsed since an insert.

One possible version of the bulk writer script is shown in listing 3.3.

> **NOTE** This listing needs both the `elasticsearch` and `redis` Python 3 modules installed.

Listing 3.3 bulk-writer-counters.py: Watching Redis and shipping to Elasticsearch

```
import json
import redis
import time
from elasticsearch import Elasticsearch

redis_client = redis.Redis(host='log-queue.prod.internal' )
esclient = Elasticsearch (
  hosts=[{"host": "escluster.prod.internal", "port" : 9200}],
  sniff_on_start=False,
  sniffer_timeout=60                    Sets the maximum time in
  )                                     seconds we will wait to insert
wait_limit = 5

bulk_size  = 200                        Sets the maximum number
                                        of items we will insert

last_time    = time.time()
current_size  = 0                       Sets defaults for the
current_items = []                      loop before we enter it
do_insert    = False

while True:
    counter_raw = redis_client.blpop(           Fetches a value from the named
 'metrics_counters', wait_limit)                list, waiting up to wait_limit
  if counter_raw == None:
    do_insert = True                    If the timeout expired, forces an insert;
  else:                                 otherwise, processes the value
    counter      = json.loads(counter_raw)       Updates the hash to add the metric_type field
    counter['metric_type'] = 'counter'
    bulk_header = { 'index' : {
      '_index': 'metrics' } }
    bulk_item = [                       Formats a hash for
      json.dump(bulk_header),           Elasticsearch bulk insert
      json.dump(counter)
      ]                                                 Newline delimits the
    current_items.append("\n".join(bulk_item))         bulk_items array as
    if len(current_items) >= bulk_size:               it is appended.
      do_insert = True
    elif (time.time() - last_time) >= wait_limit:      Checks whether we're
      do_insert = True                                 ready to insert

  if do_insert:
    esclient.bulk( current_items, index='metrics' )
    last_time = time.time()                            Performs the bulk
    do_insert = False                                  insert to Elasticsearch
      current_items = []
```

Decodes the JSON into a native hash

The bulk-writer-counters.py script would need small tweaks to turn it into a bulk-writer-timers.py script supporting timers; change the name of the Redis list to `metrics_timers` and adjust the value of `metric_value` to `timers`. When the script is written this way, we ensure that up to 200 metrics are inserted into Elasticsearch each time we insert. But we are also using timeouts to make sure that our metrics data is recent enough, so we can insert fewer than 200 metrics if we've waited too long to insert. Whereas we were individually writing 10,000 metrics per second, now we are writing 10,000 per second in 500 batches. The end-to-end flow is shown in figure 3.7.

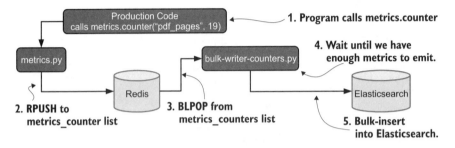

Figure 3.7   The flow of counter metrics, starting in the production code and ending in Elasticsearch. Along the way, writes are collated in the bulk-writer-counters.py script and bulk-inserted into Elasticsearch. This example greatly reduces the number of write transactions Elasticsearch has to handle per second versus the direct-write model in section 3.1.

Figure 3.7 describes how this script would sit in a shipping pipeline for metrics. The flow of telemetry would be as follows:

1 The program calls `counter('pdf_pages', 19)`.
2 The `metrics` function injects a JSON document into the `metrics_counters` list in the Redis server, using the `RPUSH` command.
3 The bulk-writer-counters.py script issues a `BLPOP` command for the `metrics_counters` list, which will receive the JSON document when it is injected.
4 The bulk-writer-counters.py script decodes the hash to add a field and waits until enough metrics are ready to go before attempting to write.
5 The bulk-writer-counters.py script bulk inserts the collated metrics into the `metrics` index of the Elasticsearch cluster.

Other than performance, there are several reasons why you might prefer to send telemetry to storage in a later part of the shipping pipeline when you could go there directly:

- A different team may own the storage and won't let systems write directly to it without lots of negotiation.
- Submit-to-queue may be part of the standard metrics library used by all code, including systems that don't have the ability to write directly to storage.

- The storage may lack appropriate access-control lists, so granting write to emitting systems also grants delete, allowing attackers who gain control of emitting systems to modify storage. Using a queue breaks this chain and preserves the integrity of the storage system.
- Handling storage system outages may be too complex for emitting systems, so it is best to use the queue as a buffer.

Generally speaking, as telemetry ecosystems increase in size, the need to queue or otherwise batch updates to storage grows. The telemetry generation rate may force certain architectural compromises to maintain performance; queues help with this task. Queues also allow buffering between emitting and storage, increasing the ability of the telemetry system to survive storage outages. If the emitting system can't buffer updates internally, the performance of the production system may be harmed, as emitting functions block until service is restored.

USING STREAMS IN A SHIPPING PIPELINE

Streams (also known as *event buses*) are modifications of the queue idea, but the items in the stream aren't removed after they're serviced. Multiple consumers of a stream can be servicing different parts of the stream. Stream implementations vary, but the concept of multiple consumers following their own place in the list is common to all stream implementations. How long telemetry remains in the stream also depends on the implementation of the stream.

> **NOTE** Every streaming service supports multiple defined streams. Redis calls its streaming objects a *stream*, for example, but Apache Kafka, which originated the concept of streaming, calls its streaming objects *topics*.

To demonstrate how streams are used, let's go back to the global logistics company. In section 2.2.2, we described how to configure their Cisco firewalls to emit telemetry into a Syslog system. Because the company has a global footprint and is operating data centers, it has many systems emitting telemetry. Being a global company, it has many teams that consume telemetry, some of which is needed by multiple teams. The firewall data is useful for the security/compliance and network operations team. Both teams need the same telemetry but have their own infrastructures for handling it. Streams are how we satisfy both teams' needs.

Figure 3.8 illustrates the architecture in use:

1 The Cisco firewall emits a Syslog line, sending it to the Syslog server at `syslog .prod.internal`.
2 The Syslog server sends that line to a stream service, in a topic named `syslog_ stream`. This newline is the head of the stream.
3 The security/compliance team's shipper listens to the topic, pulls lines, and stores them in a SIEM system.
4 The network operations team's shipper does so as well and stores them in Elasticsearch.

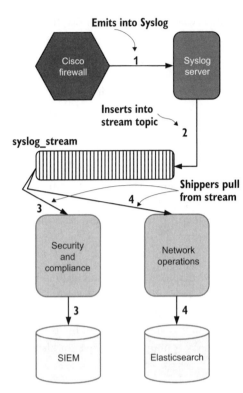

Figure 3.8   **Shipping pipeline using a stream to split telemetry flow to two consumers. The stream allows two later Shipping-stage systems to get an identical feed of telemetry, facilitating forking a stream, which is useful for multitenant systems (chapter 7).**

We've already shown the commands needed to send telemetry to the Syslog server in section 2.2.2. Now let's look at how to configure the Syslog server to send telemetry to the stream. This task requires two bits of code: code for the Syslog server and a shipping script running on the Syslog server. First, we need to configure the Syslog server to send telemetry to a named pipe, which is a one-line addition to the rsyslog configuration file:

```
# Config file for rsyslog

[...]
local07.*   | /dev/syslog_stream
[...]
```

This code tells rsyslog to send telemetry coming on the local07 Syslog facility to a named pipe at `/dev/syslog_stream`. This named pipe is created by a service script written by the operations team that runs as part of bootup of the Syslog server. This code is short; it creates the named pipe (FIFO) and then sits in a `while` loop waiting for lines.

> **NOTE**   If you want to run this code, it should run on UNIX-like systems, but you need a Redis server to execute it successfully.

Listing 3.4   stream_shipper.py: On-boot service to make a FIFO and ship to Redis

```python
import os
import redis

os.mkfifo('/dev/syslog_stream')

redis_client = redis.Redis( host='log-stream.prod.internal')

rsyslog_stream = open('/dev/syslog_stream', "r")
while True:
    for line in rsyslog_stream:
        redis_client.xadd(
            'syslog_stream',
            '*',
            line )
```

Creates a FIFO device, a named pipe, at /dev/syslog_stream

Opens the named pipe

Waits for each line to come in on the pipe and act on it

For each line, adds it to the 'syslog_stream' stream on Redis through the XADD command.

For each line that is sent to the pipe by the Rsyslog server, the script submits that line directly to a Redis-based stream. Figure 3.9 shows this flow.

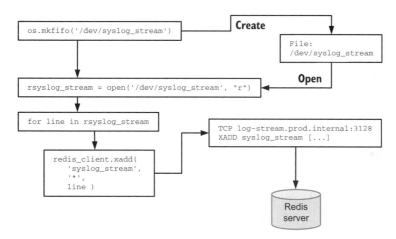

Figure 3.9   The flow of execution for stream_shipper.py. First, this script creates an operating system structure called a FIFO at /dev/syslog_stream; then it opens the stream and starts listening to lines. For each received line of text, it inserts the text into a Redis stream hosted at log-stream.prod.internal on the syslog_stream topic. Use of a stream allows more than one downstream system to get a full copy of events.

Using the Redis stream feature, listing 3.4 uses a stream named `syslog_stream`. Telemetry is appended to the stream by this shipper script. We're using an OS-level queue called a FIFO, or a named pipe, to pass data between rsyslog and the shipper script. The shipper doesn't care about the consumers; all it cares about is appending data to the stream.

At the global logistics company, two teams consume the firewall feed: security/ compliance and network operations. Consuming items from the stream requires a few steps in Redis. The following listing is the beginning of a script used by the network operations team to consume telemetry from the stream. The script creates a connection to the stream and then sits in a `while` loop waiting for telemetry.

NOTE If you want to run this code successfully, you need a Redis server to talk to.

Listing 3.5 consume_syslog.py: Consuming the Redis stream from listing 3.4

```
import redis

redis_client = redis.Redis( host='log-stream.prod.internal' )
redis_client.xgroup_create('syslog_stream',
    'noc_team', '$')                          ◁────── Creates the consumer group

while True:
    line = redis_client.xreadgroup(  ◁────── Reads from the consumer group
        'noc_team',
        'noc_ingest',        ◁────── Name of the individual consumer
        'syslog_stream',     ◁────── Name of the stream to consume
        '>')                 ◁────── Indicates 'give me events that no one else has seen before'
    do_something(line)
```

The important line of code is the one that reads from the stream. This code has a lot going on. Figure 3.10 breaks out what each part does.

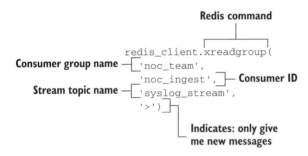

Figure 3.10 Diagram of the key command in consume_syslog.py, the Redis command that pulls information from the stream topic. We need to create five configuration items to set up a subscriber for the `syslog_stream` topic. Then this loop will get only new items that no other members of the consumer group (named `noc_team`) have seen.

The script used by the security/compliance team would look similar but use `sec_team` instead of `noc_team` for the name of its consumer group. This way, both teams get a full stream of telemetry emitted by the Syslog server and the shipper script, but if the network operations team's script happened to be much faster than the security/compliance team's shipper, the `sec_team` shipper would not miss telemetry.

The Syslog server configured here was configured to send Syslog `local07` facility telemetry to the stream. The same Syslog server can handle multiple facilities, so it could send `local06` facility telemetry to a different stream and `local05` facility telemetry to a queuing system. At the same time, a fleet of database servers could emit telemetry from their local Syslog servers to a `database_syslog` stream. Chapter 7 goes into complex architectures like this database fleet.

3.1.3   *Shipping to SaaS systems*

So far, we've talked about organizations keeping their entire telemetry systems internally, but not all organizations do so. Small startups, for example, have too much going on to waste time building a telemetry system, so paying someone else to do the work makes all kinds of sense. For telemetry styles such as distributed tracing, paying someone else is by far the best option until your production systems are truly large.

Let's take another look at the 100-person startup. The company had a metrics service (which we built in the previous two sections) but wants a deeper look at how its system is evolving. That system is no longer the four containers in Amazon Elastic Container Service it started as! The company has decided to get into distributed tracing and picked Honeycomb.io as its SaaS provider. To use Honeycomb, the company needs to add the Honeycomb SDK to its codebase, and start instrumenting its functions.

The company has taken a microservices approach to its system, with lots of small container images doing work. As we've seen so far, they have a function called `pdf_pages` that we've seen metrics from. This small function does two things:

- Counts the number of pages in a supplied PDF file
- Calls out to another function called `pdf_to_png`, one for each page, to request that PNG images be created from each page in the PDF

Figure 3.11 shows the flow of telemetry from when the SDK is initialized through doing the work of `pdf_pages`, ending in telemetry being sent to Honeycomb.io.

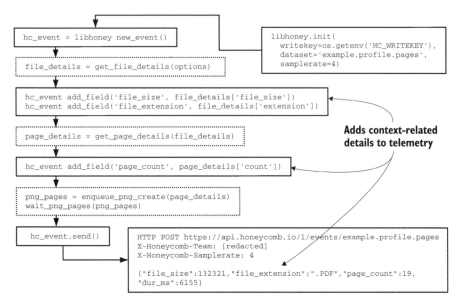

Figure 3.11   Flow of execution during a single instance of `pdf_pages`. Dotted boxes are function work; solid boxes are distributed tracing actions leading up to a POST to the Honeycomb Events API. Note that context-related telemetry is gathered at multiple places during this flow. The `.send()` event is nonblocking, sending to a not-pictured queuing system, to reduce the impact of telemetry operations on the production code.

Listing 3.6 is our `pdf_pages` function, highlighting telemetry operations. This program is not intended to be fully functional; it demonstrates how to mark up a function with a tracing system's functions.

Listing 3.6   pdf_pages.py, instrumented with tracing

```
# This is not intended to be executable
import libhoney                              ⟵——— Loads the Honeycomb SDK
import [lots of other things]

libhoney.init(
  writekey=os.getenv('HC_WRITEKEY'),          Initializes the
  dataset='example.profile.pages',            Honeycomb connection
  sample_rate=4)

def get_file_details(options):
  [...]

def get_page_details(file_details):
  [...]

def enqueue_pdf_create(page_details):
  [...]

def wait_png_pages(png_pages):
  [...]

# Main event hook.
def do_work(options):
  hc_event     = libhoney.new_event()    ⟵——┐  Creates new event and begins tracking
  file_details = get_file_details(options)  ⟵——— Fetches file-specific details
  hc_event.add_field('file_size',
  ➥ file_details['file_size'])              Adds file-specific context
  hc_event.add_field('file_extension',     details to the event
  ➥ file_details['extension'])

  page_details = get_page_details(file_details) ⟵——— Fetches pdf-specific details
  hc_event.add_field('page_count',
  ➥ page_details['count'])              ⟵——— Adds pdf-specific details to the event

  png_pages = enqueue_png_create(page_details)  │ Calls out and waits for
  wait_png_pages(png_pages)                      │ pdf_to_png processes to return

  hc_event.send()    ⟵——— Finalizes the event and sends to Honeycomb
```

The `pdf_pages` function here leaves out all the code that does the work of `pdf_pages`, instead showing how the Honeycomb SDK is used to track context-related details. Note that we are capturing a `page_count` metric as part of this work, which will be associated with this event in the Honeycomb dashboards. Two more pieces of explicit context are also being gathered:

- `file_size`—Captures the size of the source file
- `file_extension`—Captures the extension of the file, which isn't always .pdf

You may be wondering why we capture the extension when presumably, we already know that this file is a PDF. The answer is that bugs in the past have caused certain extensions to fool our PDF page-counting code, so the software engineers want to track file extensions in case a similar bug happens. If you look at the final HTTP POST in figure 3.11, however, you will notice an extra bit of telemetry we didn't specify:

```
dur_ms: 6155
```

This value, captured by the Honeycomb SDK directly, represents the time between the `libhoney new_event()` call and the `hc_event.send()` call. Because these calls bracket all the functions that do the work of `pdf_pages`, `dur_ms` captures how long this `do_work()` function took to perform. In figure 3.11, the function took 6.155 seconds to count pages in the supplied PDF and wait for individual PNG images of each page to be created.

One final thing to note is the parameter `sample_rate=4`, which we gave when we initialized the libhoney library. This value, which ended up being a header to the HTTP POST to the Honeycomb API, indicates what percentage of events of this type to keep—25 in this case (the true sample rate, 1, divided by the `sample_rate` value). Because all telemetry SaaS vendors charge on volume in some way, using a sample rate is among the best tools at your disposal for keeping costs down.

Because 25% is a large sample, software engineering teams should learn how the `pdf_pages` function operates in the context of the overall system without the costs associated with keeping every event. When software engineering has a solid understanding of how this function works, the sample rate can be reduced even further, bringing costs down as well.

Exercise 3.1

Your company provides a standard library for moving logs and metrics telemetry out of application code and into the centralized telemetry systems. When a log or metric needs to be emitted, this standard library sends that data to Kafka. Which type of style of emitter/shipper is this library using?

    a Direct-to-storage
    b Shipping through a queue or stream
    c Shipping to a SaaS application

3.2 Shipping between SaaS systems

Section 3.1 focused on software-oriented organizations, but not all organizations are in the business of writing software. The 200-person continuing education company uses software—quite a lot of it—but writes as little of it as possible. It may appear that a company such as this one has no need for telemetry systems, but it does. The company's telemetry systems look different from the telemetry that a SaaS provider organization would build, but those systems are still telemetry systems. Our continuing education company uses a lot of SaaS products, and its telemetry system is no different. This section is about shipping telemetry between SaaS systems.

When you don't control the emitting system, such as hardware, you're stuck with whatever format your emitting systems use. For organizations like our continuing education company, the constraints are imposed by the SaaS systems themselves. As discussed in section 2.3.1, most SaaS systems handle telemetry emissions through a polling method, in which the shipping system fetches telemetry, or a push system, in which the SaaS product makes an HTTP call to a configured endpoint whenever telemetry needs to be shipped. These two telemetry emission methods are a marked difference between the direct, queue, and stream-based approaches discussed in section 3.1.

Some SaaS platforms can provide all your Shipping- and Presentation-stage needs. Services such as SumoLogic, Loggly, and Splunk offer diverse methods of getting emissions into their system to allow you to query and learn about what is going on in your technical infrastructure. All three services permit setting up HTTP endpoints to receive webhooks from other SaaS products and may even be able to poll a SaaS provider's endpoint if a direct integration is available.

The continuing education provider we talked about in section 2.3.1 set up a webhook in a product that manages the whole workflow of job postings and interviewing, tracking all the job applicants and their progress through the hiring process (an applicant-tracking system). This webhook is configured to hit to an HTTP endpoint configured in a telemetry service provider. When this endpoint is in place, telemetry flows from the SaaS provider to the telemetry service provider, enabling business decisions and tracking. Figure 3.12 shows how this architecture looks after several of the company's providers are connected to the telemetry SaaS provider.

The telemetry styles that aim at understanding software systems—metrics and distributed tracing—do not show up in this company's telemetry system. Centralized logging is the style displayed in figure 3.12. Section 1.2.5 talked about business

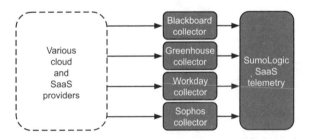

Figure 3.12   A view of the Shipping-stage components for a continuing education company that relies heavily on SaaS and cloud-based offerings. The company picked SumoLogic as its telemetry provider. Using the procedure from section 2.3.1, the company configured telemetry to flow into SumoLogic from four SaaS and cloud providers: Blackboard Learning Systems for classroom interactions, Greenhouse for managing teacher applicant flow, Workday for handling human resources, and Sophos for handling antivirus telemetry coming from the desktop fleet.

intelligence teams and how they work on telemetry for the business. For our non-software-producing company, software telemetry and telemetry for the business are close friends. In this company, both telemetry styles—software and business—can be handled by the same team.

3.3　*Tipping points in Shipping-stage architecture*

This section covers events that can force change in a Shipping stage. Change is unavoidable, and major events like these can force significant change in a shipping pipeline:

- Introduction of a new compliance framework that requires separation of certain types of telemetry, such as making separate telemetry flows for telemetry that might contain personally identifiable information and telemetry that definitely will not
- Infrastructure growth that makes the current telemetry methods infeasible for cost or latency reasons, forcing time to be spent on optimization, buffers, and reorganization
- Team growth that forces the adoption of telemetry routing (chapter 7) so that multiple teams can have their own telemetry storage and presentation systems (multitenancy)
- A merger with another organization that forces reconciliation of the organizations' telemetry handling procedures
- Internal pressure to adopt a new telemetry system style, such as distributed tracing
- Onerous upgrade and maintenance workflows that call for a redesign to reduce operational overhead

Few telemetry systems are truly unchanging. Software end-of-life, patches to fix vulnerabilities, and other keep-the-lights-on activities can force changes that otherwise wouldn't happen. Sometimes, these forced changes can be profound, such as when your preferred data store updates to a new version that requires extensive rebuilding and new software libraries, and the old version goes out of support.

Standards such as Syslog make certain types of telemetry emission unchanging, which is why hardware vendors support it so strongly. For everything else, such as the distributed tracing systems used by software engineering teams, change is a constant. It could be that by 2026, distributed tracing tools will be considered to be kind of old and inflexible, and a hot new thing is where people should be focusing their efforts, but we can't see that future from 2021.

> **WARNING**　Telemetry systems follow one big rule: *telemetry system outages should not cause production system outages.* Your telemetry system design should be built in a way that outages in the pipeline will not materially affect your production systems. If you find that production systems get slow when telemetry systems get slow, you should seriously think about redesigning your telemetry systems.

Synchronous vs. asynchronous

One area in which telemetry system design can affect production systems is how tightly coupled the two systems are. In listing 3.1, we wrote a logging function that emitted directly from the production code into Elasticsearch. In this operation, which is *synchronous*, execution in that processing thread paused while the telemetry was shipped and persisted. If the Elasticsearch cluster is having problems and can't accept writes as fast as it needs to, the blocking write operation in our logging function will cause the production system to block as well, slowing performance of the production system.

In listing 3.2 in section 3.1.2, we rewrote that blocking logging function to emit directly into Redis, an in-memory cache system, instead of Elasticsearch. Should the Elasticsearch cluster have ingestion problems, the production systems can continue to emit telemetry into Redis and not slow down. Writes to Elasticsearch are asynchronous. If the Redis system is at maximum memory and rejecting writes, of course, the production systems will still be affected. There are no perfect solutions—only less-bad ones that fit your needs better than the even-worse ones.

Exercise 3.2

Look at how telemetry is handled at your organization. In the next five or ten years, are any of the listed tipping points likely to happen? How will your organization react?

Summary

- The Shipping stage in a telemetry pipeline is the stage that receives telemetry from the Emitting stage, optionally modifies the telemetry, and stores it for later presentation in the Presentation stage.
- The Shipping stage often acts as a translator between the telemetry format received from the Emitting stage and the telemetry format used by the Presentation stage.
- A Shipping stage may be anything from a single function in the code to an entire multisystem infrastructure with dedicated engineers.
- Having the Emitting stage ship directly to storage used by the Presentation stage is a valid Shipping stage, called an emitter/shipper, and is quite powerful.
- Having the Emitting stage send telemetry to a queue or stream allows the Emitting stage to handle fewer service-interruption cases than it would if the telemetry were sent directly to storage.
- Streams operate somewhat like queues, with FIFO behavior, but allow trivial forking in the form of consumer groups. A consumer group receives the stream in a FIFO way, but a second consumer group would see the same items in their own FIFO presentation.

- Streams are powerful in telemetry systems because they allow systems pushing data into the stream to have no knowledge of any system consuming their data. This power enables you to reconfigure your telemetry data flows without touching your emitting systems.
- Using SaaS vendors for your telemetry allows you to focus on what you do best rather than on building and maintaining the full telemetry pipeline.
- Most SaaS telemetry vendors charge based on volume of data received, so statistical sampling methods can be used to reduce cost while maintaining the validity of your analysis.
- Queues and streams inside a Shipping stage allow complex Shipping-stage architectures, allowing separate teams to own pieces of the telemetry pipeline.
- Organizations that use SaaS offerings exclusively still need to handle telemetry, and platforms such as Splunk, Loggly, and SumoLogic are dedicated to filling that need.
- Changes in Shipping-stage architecture can be forced by several external factors, including a merger with another organization, a key component of the Shipping stage going out of support, infrastructure growth that makes maintaining the Shipping stage too expensive, and new telemetry techniques that gain internal advocates for adoption.

The Shipping stage: Unifying diverse telemetry formats

This chapter covers

- Shipping locally emitted telemetry
- Interacting with emitting stages with flexible and inflexible formats
- Picking formats for shipping telemetry

This chapter is the second chapter covering the Shipping stage. Whereas chapter 3 covered moving telemetry around and preparing it for storage, this chapter covers the format (and format transformations) of telemetry data in the Shipping stage. A lot happens in the Shipping stage, which is why this stage is taking me a few chapters to describe:

- Telemetry moves around (chapter 3). In larger systems, moving telemetry around can be quite complex, involving telemetry systems owned and controlled by different teams (multitenancy; chapter 7).

- The Shipping stage needs to deal with whatever formats the Emitting stage can handle and in diverse environments (hardware and software), many formats (section 4.1).
- The Shipping stage needs to not only move telemetry around, but also support any markup and enrichment (chapter 6) that happens during the Shipping stage and the formats those components need (section 4.2).

A common misconception among many people who are new to telemetry is that the Shipping stage is where all markup and enrichment happen. Although the Shipping stage does perform quite a lot of both, markup can happen during both the Emitting and Shipping stages, and enrichment can happen in the Shipping and Presentation stages. The end-to-end nature of markup and enrichment is why that topic gets its own chapter (chapter 6).

This chapter focuses on two topics:

- Receiving telemetry from Emitting stages such as local log files and the system logger, and moving them down the pipeline (section 4.1).
- Determining the telemetry data formats supported by your Shipping-stage systems. This process is both technical and political; there will be meetings, so be warned (section 4.2).

To help with these concepts, I use the same example organizations from chapters 2 and 3:

- A 100-person startup building an API-driven application, running in AWS, with a technical organization that is entirely software-driven.
- A global logistics company founded in 1848 that computerized its business processes in the late 1960s. This example demonstrates Shipping stages in physical data centers where the emitting format is variable and, in some cases, inflexible. Also, this example is be where the nontechnical (political) discussion is focused; big companies have big people problems.
- A 200-person company providing in-person continuing education courses, with strong seasonality in hiring. This company uses software rather than producing it.

4.1 *Shipping locally-emitted telemetry*

Section 2.1 described several ways of emitting telemetry locally:

- Emitting into a log file (section 2.1.1)
- Emitting into the system logger (section 2.1.2)
- Emitting into standard output (section 2.1.3)

This section is about moving locally stored telemetry into the broader Shipping-stage pipeline. Chapter 3 was all about moving telemetry around, from shipping directly to storage (section 3.1.1), to shipping into queues and streams (section 3.1.2), to shipping directly to SaaS providers (section 3.1.3). We will use the techniques from chapter 3 to move telemetry that we pick up locally:

- Section 4.1.1 describes shipping telemetry from a log file and into a stream.
- Section 4.1.2 describes shipping telemetry from a Windows-based system logger and into a SaaS provider.
- Section 4.1.3 describes shipping telemetry sent to standard out and then directly into Elasticsearch-based storage.

4.1.1   Shipping telemetry from a log file

Section 2.1.1 described sending telemetry to a log file. This section describes getting telemetry out of that locally stored log file and into a Kafka-based stream (section 3.1.2). To help explain these concepts, we're going back to the global logistics company that computerized in the 1960s. Its telemetry systems are mature, but even old companies try new things once in a while.

The networking operations group finally updated the infrastructure managing the company's extensive Cisco install base and wants to send the log data produced by Cisco Prime (the Cisco framework for managing Cisco installs) to centralized logging. This company has been writing Java software since the late 1990s, so the software engineering teams have long experience with centralized logging. Also, being a large company means that the centralized logging system is already set up for multitenancy, so adding a telemetry feed from the network operations group is not hard for the system to deal with. The problem is getting the log-file-based data into the system. Figure 4.1 shows the planned architecture.

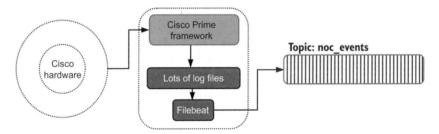

Figure 4.1   The planned Shipping-stage components of the network operations teams. These components are filled-in boxes. This Shipping-stage pipeline inserts events into a stream on the noc_events topic. Telemetry flows out of the Cisco hardware (the production system, in this case), and into the proprietary Cisco Prime framework. Then Cisco Prime generates a variety of log files. Filebeat ships telemetry from the log files and into the stream. Use of agents such as this one is common for moving file- and system-logger-based telemetry to more advanced systems.

The network operations group at our logistics company intends to use the Filebeat program, made by Elastic.co, to move telemetry from the log files into an Apache Kafka-based stream. Filebeat uses YAML as a configuration format. The simple format has two sections:

```
filebeat.inputs:
output.kafka:
```

The inputs section is where you define what files Filebeat should pay attention to. The outputs section defines where Filebeat sends telemetry it processes.

> **NOTE** Listing 4.1 is not intended to be executed, but if you want to execute it, you will need a Kafka cluster to talk to.

Listing 4.1   noc_beats.yml: Filebeat config for the network operations shipper

Input block defines what Filebeat tracks.

Type set to log for log files.

```
filebeat.inputs:
- type: log
  paths:
    - /opt/CSCOlumos/logs/**
  fields:
    environment: "production"
    data_center: "EUC1"
output.kafka:
  hosts: ["k7-euc1-1:9092", "k7-euc1-2:9092",
    "k7-euc1-3:9092"]
  topic: "noc_events"
  username: "nocevents_euc1"
  password: *****
  client_id: "cisco_prime"
```

Array of paths to watch, with wildcard

Context-related fields to add to all events

Output block defines where telemetry is sent (Kafka).

Defines the array of Kafka hosts to connect to and the topic

Defines a unique client identifier

Defines authentication for Kafka

The Filebeat configuration in noc_beats.yml will have Filebeat monitor all the files in /opt/CSCOlumos/logs and send all log lines to the Kafka topic named noc_events. Figure 4.2 provides more context on what each part of the configuration does.

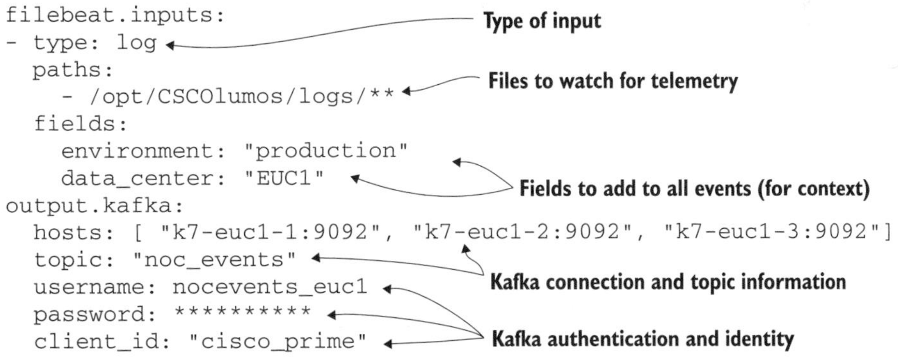

```
filebeat.inputs:
- type: log
  paths:
    - /opt/CSCOlumos/logs/**
  fields:
    environment: "production"
    data_center: "EUC1"
output.kafka:
  hosts: [ "k7-euc1-1:9092", "k7-euc1-2:9092", "k7-euc1-3:9092"]
  topic: "noc_events"
  username: nocevents_euc1
  password: *********
  client_id: "cisco_prime"
```

Type of input

Files to watch for telemetry

Fields to add to all events (for context)

Kafka connection and topic information

Kafka authentication and identity

Figure 4.2   The configuration file for Filebeats on the Cisco Prime server. This configuration pulls telemetry out of all the log files in the Cisco Prime logging location and sends it on to a Kafka cluster, injecting telemetry into the nocevents_euc1 topic. The centralized logging platform operated by the software engineering teams will eventually consume the nocevents_euc1 topic and store this telemetry in the centralized logging database.

The pattern shown here—using a third-party shipper to move telemetry data out of log files to somewhere more useful—is a common one. I use Filebeat in this example because it is a Go binary, so it's small and relatively cross-platform, and it does the two things I needed it to do. Here's a list of several packages that fill the need to move file-based data somewhere else:

- *Filebeat*—This Go-based binary produced by Elastic.co is built to pull log data out of log files, containers, and a few other sources. It can also send data to queues, streams, and Elasticsearch directly (no surprise).
- *Fluentd/Fluentbit*—A fully open source product and member of the Cloud Native Computing Foundation, these Ruby-based (Fluentd) and C-based (Fluentbit) multipurpose log shippers can pull from many frameworks and ship into queues, streams, and a variety of databases.
- *Logstash*—Another Elastic.co product, this JVM-based framework is a fully featured telemetry transporting system. It can read from files but is far more capable with respect to where it can send data. You can build an entire Shipping stage with Logstash, which makes it overkill for simply shipping files to a queue or stream.
- *Splunk Forwarder*—This Splunk product, which ships as a precompiled binary, is the entry point for telemetry into a Splunk-based telemetry ecosystem. It can ship into the Splunk Cloud product as well a locally hosted Splunk servers. Splunk is famous as an off-the-shelf (and now SaaS-based) centralized logging, metrics, and SIEM provider.
- *Telegraf*—An InfluxData product, this Go-based multipurpose log and metrics shipper can send logs to Syslog and Kafka streams. It can talk natively to the InfluxDB time-series database for metrics, but for text-based logs, it is better as a telemetry mover.

Filebeat and its friends

Filebeat is one of several open source agents that Elastic.co offers for moving data into its Elasticsearch database. Filebeat is customized to move strings from files. But there are several other specialized agents:

- *Metricbeat*—Pulls system-level metrics in a manner similar to how the collectd, telegraf, and nagios agents collect and ship metrics
- *Auditbeat*—Pulls security-related information such as the audit.log on Linux systems
- *Winlogbeat*—Pulls Windows Event Log data, including the Security log, and ships it
- *Journalbeat*—Pulls telemetry out of journald (part of the Linux Systemd utilities) and ships it
- *Packetbeat*—Monitors and ships network flow telemetry

Other agents are available, and more come out every year. Elastic.co makes its money selling enterprise plans, so if these open source shippers fit your needs out of the box (without an enterprise plan), they can stand alone quite well. For many telemetry product vendors, the hard problem (also known as the problem you can make money solving) is analyzing telemetry (the combination of Elasticsearch and Kibana for Elastic.co) rather than shipping it (Filebeat and friends), so these products are loss leaders for their real revenue-generating products.

Log files are in many ways the default shipping method for off-the-shelf production systems designed to run on servers. Containers and FaaS platforms prefer standard output (see section 4.1.3). Building skill in handling log files will set you up for success. This area is one in which the problem of getting the telemetry off your system is already solved, for the most part, so you shouldn't need to write much code. Using agents to handle this part is much faster.

4.1.2 *Shipping telemetry from the system logger*

Section 2.1.2 described emitting telemetry into the system logger; this section covers pulling telemetry out of the system logger and into a SaaS system (section 3.1.3). To illustrate this process, we're going back to our continuing education company that doesn't produce software if it can help it. Figure 3.12, reproduced here as figure 4.3, illustrates the company's current approach to software telemetry.

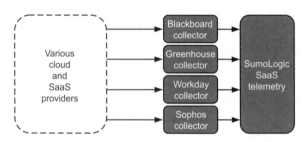

Figure 4.3 **The Shipping stage for our continuing education company. Its complete reliance on cloud and SaaS vendors for both production and Shipping-stage systems is intentional; not everyone runs servers, or wants to.**

The company has a problem. The U.S. state in which its headquarters are based has released new requirements for education companies, so this company needs to audit far more activities on educator laptops. Until now, the company has taken a kind of benign neglect approach to educator laptops, letting their teachers do what they need to do while forcing minimal security services such as antivirus and endpoint protection. It's simply not doing the kind of end-to-end employee surveillance that larger intellectual-property-based companies do, so addressing this regulation requires new processes.

This company is using Windows laptops because it has been in business for two decades and Windows laptops are what it's always used. Because not all the teachers teach in a single facility, instead teaching all over their registered states, the company can't rely on adding every laptop to an Active Directory domain and configuring event forwarding; the laptops simply aren't on the enterprise network often enough.

The planned approach is to install a SumoLogic collector on each of the traveling laptops and configure that collector to send events to the company's SumoLogic account. Figure 4.4 describes the intended architecture.

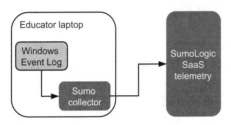

Figure 4.4   The telemetry collection design that our continuing education company intends to build. The state requires certain events captured in the Windows Event Log to be centralized, so the company installs a SumoLogic collector on each laptop and configures that collector to send events to the existing SumoLogic cloud. This setup doesn't require connection to the enterprise network via virtual private nework (VPN), making it well-suited to a highly mobile teaching organization.

First, our continuing education company needs to install the collector everywhere, which is a two-step process:

1 Install the software.
2 Configure it.

The installation process is a single command-line command:

```
SumoCollector.exe -console -q "-Vsumo.accessid=[redacted]" \
  -"Vsumo.accesskey=[redacted]" \
  -"Vsources=C:\\HQ_Data\\sumo_sources.json"
```

This command triggers the following behavior:

1 Sends all output to the console (`-console`)
2 Installs in quiet mode (`-q`)
3 Configures the login credentials needed for the SumoLogic cloud (`sumo.accessid` and `sumo.accesskey`)
4 Points the installer to a configuration file that defines what telemetry this collector will ship into the SumoLogic cloud (`C:\HQ_Data\sumo_sources.json`)

The contents of this file are shown in listing 4.2.

Listing 4.2   sumo_sources.json: Defining Windows telemetry collection

```
{
    "api.version": "v1",        ◁──┤ Sets the SumoLogic API version
    "sources": [
        {
                                                   Defines the type of source,
            "sourceType": "LocalWindowsEventLog",  ◁──┘ gathering local Windows events
```

When set to true, gathers all metadata from Windows events

```
      "name": "TeacherLaptop",      ◁──── A name for this source (unique per collector)
 ┌─▷ "renderMessages": true,
      "logNames": [
        "Security",                         Defines which Event Logs to
        "ApplicationBestClassroom"          gather, including a special app
      ]
    }
  ]
}
```

With this configuration, our continuing education company is sending the contents of two system logs to the SumoLogic cloud:

- The built-in Security log, which includes all security events configured for the teacher laptops. This flow of events includes logins, logouts, changes to security policy, and many other details. Depending on the security policy pushed from corporate, this flow of events can be massive.
- A special application log called ApplicationBestClassroom, which is an event log produced directly by the off-the-shelf classroom software. This event log is produced by software, not by the system, using the Windows Event Log feature.

If we tweak figure 4.4 just a bit, we can see the two types of event streams that this company is interested in (figure 4.5).

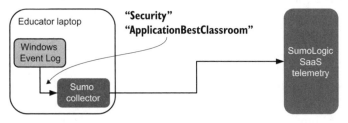

Figure 4.5 Configured telemetry collection for our continuing education company. Here we see that the SumoLogic collector pulls Security and ApplicationBestClassroom Event Log data and injects it into the SumoLogic cloud.

For a company that's handling a fleet of highly mobile computers, using installed local agents to send to a SaaS provider makes a lot of sense. Although this case shows collecting telemetry on desktop systems, it also applies to Windows servers. Inside an Active Directory domain, you have even more options, because remote Event Log collection is possible (unlike in our example here), which reduces the number of collectors that need to run in your organization.

4.1.3 *Shipping telemetry from standard output*

Section 2.1.3 described emitting telemetry to the standard output (stdout), the console or default output for a print statement, trusting that whatever program launched our production software would be listening to that output. This section covers processing that kind of output and sending it directly to storage (section 3.1.1). To help with this process, we're going back to our 100-person startup.

In section 3.1, we looked at this startup's architecture, which is running Kubernetes clusters in a public cloud provider, and saw the company rewrite its emitting functions to send telemetry directly into Elasticsearch. In section 3.2, we rewrote the functions to send to a queue or stream to allow a downstream process to bulk-write into Elasticsearch. Now we're going to look at a third way to reduce write-loading on the Elasticsearch cluster: have the Kubernetes cluster machines handle the writes. Figure 4.6 describes the intended architecture.

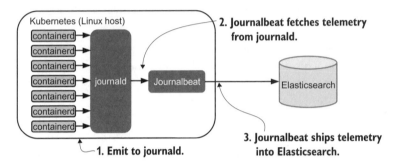

Figure 4.6   Getting telemetry out of Kubernetes and containerd for our 100-person startup. The containerd containers (not the software inside the containers) is configured to emit stdout to journald of the Kubernetes host. From there, Journalbeat ships telemetry into Elasticsearch. Because Journalbeat batches writes, the Elasticsearch cluster faces reduced write transactions versus the containerd confined software writing directly.

Our 100-person startup runs Linux-based Kubernetes clusters. As a result, Kubernetes automatically sends the stdout from containerd into the systemd system called journald. (If you're running Docker outside Kubernetes, `--log-driver=journald` in the Docker config does the same thing.) To get telemetry out of the journal on the Kubernetes hosts and into Elasticsearch, the company installs and configures Journalbeat from Elastic.co. (See the end of section 4.1.1 for a list of other Beats.) By default, Journalbeat pulls the entire system's journal and sends it on, but Journalbeat needs to be told where to put the journal; we want to send it into Elasticsearch. Listing 4.3 shows the configuration file. As with Filebeat earlier, we see an input section and an output section.

NOTE   This listing is not intended to be executed, but if you want to run it, you need to run it on a Linux system and have an Elasticsearch cluster to talk to.

Listing 4.3   kate_beat.yml: Shipping journald telemetry to Elasticsearch

```
journalbeat.inputs:           Fetching from the default
  - paths: []          ◁──┘   journald location
output.elasticsearch:
  hosts: [ "http://log-es.prod.internal:9200" ]   ◁──┘ Specifies what Elasticsearch
                                                        server to connect to
  index: "kates-%{+yyyy.MM.dd}"   ◁──
                                        Specifies which Elasticsearch
                                        Index to send data into
```

The coding on the index name is special. `kates-%{+yyyy.MM.dd}` appends a date stamp to the index name, such as `kates-2023.02.19` for February 19, 2023. This code will create one index per day automatically. Creating an index a day this way allows our company to set retention policies quite easily. To keep 90 days' worth of indices online, once a day, delete any index older than that.

Section 3.1.2 asked what would happen if instead of one Kubernetes cluster, the company had 100. Whereas the code we wrote in section 3.2 had the production code sending telemetry to a single queue or stream, Journalbeat can be configured to send telemetry to a Redis-based queue or a Kafka-based stream. We saw an example of a Kafka output as part of the code in section 4.1.1:

```
output.kafka:
  hosts: [ "k7-eucl-1:9092", "k7-eucl-2:9092", "k7-eucl-3:9092"]
  topic: "noc_events"
  username: "nocevents_eucl"
  password: *****
  client_id: "cisco_prime"
```

The same settings will work for Journalbeat. Outputting to Redis is simpler, because Redis is a simpler system:

```
output.redis:
  hosts: [ "prod-logs.prod.internal:6379" ]
  key: "kates"
```

Specify a hostname to send telemetry to and the key to write everything to. A system servicing this queue will pop events off the `kates` key for further processing.

> **Exercise 4.1**
> For off-the-shelf software (download and install), what is the most common telemetry emission format you will have to handle?
>
>   a Log files
>   b The system logger, such as Syslog, or Windows Events
>   c Standard output

4.2 Unifying diverse emitting formats

This section covers the technical and political challenge of selecting telemetry formats. The sheer diversity of Emitting-stage systems means that no standard emitting format exists. Most Emitting-stage systems do so in strings, but as with human languages, the format of those strings is as variable as the humans who write the strings. Ultimately, telemetry needs to get stored somewhere, and that location also has opinions about what format telemetry will be in. In a telemetry pipeline, the Shipping stage is often charged with unifying telemetry formats for storage, especially in pipelines that involve hardware and SaaS systems with inflexible emission formats.

Because most telemetry systems use strings to pass data, there are many ways to encode complex data structures into strings. For simple telemetry systems with one or two emitters and only one system storing telemetry, you don't need to pay much attention to this problem. For complex telemetry systems with a wide variety of emitters (hardware, many kinds of software, feeds coming from SaaS systems, and so on), the problem of unifying formats is real. The following sections help us address these problems:

- Section 4.2.1 examines many ways to encode telemetry into strings for shipping.
- Section 4.2.2 covers the process of selecting shipping formats for a telemetry system with diverse needs.
- Section 4.2.3 is an example of translating telemetry emitted in Syslog into an object-encoding format better suited for use in the Shipping stage.
- Section 4.2.4 provides guidance on selecting shipping formats with an eye on reducing database cardinalities to keep costs low and search performance high.

4.2.1 Encoding telemetry into strings

We have already worked through several examples of encoding telemetry into strings for shipping, but this section covers the variety of widely available string formats available to you. These formats are not plain-language formats, but ways to encode (serialize) structured data in ways that are easy to translate back into structured data (deserialize). We need the ability to transmit data structures, because the act of marking up and enriching telemetry (see chapter 6) in the Emitting and Shipping stages sets up the Presentation stage for success. We examine two types of formats:

- Delimited formats that encode relatively simple structures that are more human-readable, and tend to be very fast to serialize and deserialize
- Object-encoding formats that allow encoding complex structures

ENCODING INTO DELIMITED FORMATS

This section covers the most common delimited formats, the most famous of which is the comma-separated values (CSV) list. Delimited formats work by using a character (or a string) to mark separate fields. Think of them as a way to encode an array or a simple one-level hash. Building a parser for these formats is relatively easy, and for common formats like CSV, general programming languages often have a built-in function for parsing. (Even the ancient COBOL has a native way to read CSV.) The general-purpose Shipping-stage platforms—Elastic's Logstash and the open source Fluentd, both Ruby-based—have parsers that can handle these formats, so you don't have to write a parser. Here are three delimited formats to examine:

- *Comma- or tab-separated value lists,* in which each position is assigned a field name, and this assignment has to be preshared to both the emitter and parsing side. The delimiter can also be other characters; I've seen the semicolon and pipe characters used as well.

Example:

```
"2023-02-19T23:04:55.293+0:00",pdf_pages,2
```

- *Key-value pairs,* allowing flexible field mapping but a flat field structure (no sub-keys). This format allows encoding a simple one-level hash without preknowledge of the fields.
  Example:

```
time="2023-02-19 23:04:55.293" metric_name="pdf_pages" metric_value=2
```

- *Positional-delimited,* a variant of the separated value list, most commonly using square brackets. This format is often used as a wrapper (or container) format for others, expecting that the string will be parsed more than one time.
  Example:

```
[2023-02-19T23:04:55.293+0:00] [pdf_pages=2]
```

Here, the first bracket statement is the timestamp; the second bracket statement is a key-value pair that will be run through a key-value parser in a second pass.

Delimited formats generally are computationally cheap to parse, making them desirable for optimizing a parsing step in a telemetry pipeline. They're often just expressive enough, and human-readable enough, that the format can be looked at raw by humans doing development in a virtual machine or Docker, and they're also easily parsable by machines for display in a Presentation-stage system with production-system telemetry.

Delimited formats aren't expressive enough, however, if complex data structures such as multilevel hashes need to be handled. For cases in which delimited formats are too constraining, you can use any of three object-encoding formats:

- JSON
- XML
- YAML

Parsing speed can be surprising

Although the algorithms behind parsing a key-value stream are simpler than the algorithm needed to parse an object-encoding format like JSON, they're not necessarily faster. To demonstrate, here are the results of a parsing-speed test I ran using Logstash to test the performance of the key-value, CSV, JSON, and XML parsers. The same 10-element hash was encoded in each format and then decoded. I tracked how long (in milliseconds) the decoder took to handle 1 million hashes:

(continued)
- *JSON*—0.011 ms per 10-element hash
- *Key-value*—0.069 ms per 10-element hash
- *CSV*—0.198 ms per 10-element hash
- *XML*—3.700 ms per 10-element hash

How can performance for the two complex object-encoding parsers, JSON and XML, be three orders of magnitude apart? And why does JSON blow everything else out of the water? The answers have to do with how Logstash is written. Logstash is written in JRuby, which is Ruby running on top of Java. For JSON, Logstash uses the native Java JSON engine, but for the other three formats, raw Ruby constructs are used. Because JSON parsing doesn't have to recompile from Ruby into Java and back to Ruby, instead staying in Java the whole time, the parsing process is more efficient. Given that fact, it makes sense that the simple-to-parse key-value set performs best of the raw Ruby parsers.

When you're building a parsing stage for your Shipping stage, it's worth your while to test parsing speeds in various formats. Your assumptions may be wrong; mine certainly were.

ENCODING INTO JSON

JSON (JavaScript Object Notation) began in the JavaScript ecosystem and has been embraced by many other systems. JSON provides easy encoding of string and number types with complex subkey structures in hashes and arrays. NodeJS, being a JavaScript language, assumes JSON format for all data structures natively. Most new web-based APIs consume JSON as the transaction format. Logstash, the Shipping-stage engine built by Elastic, uses JSON objects as part of its internal queuing system.

The ability to encode complex data structures makes JSON valuable when your telemetry system needs to pass around highly enriched telemetry data. Going back to our metrics examples, here is a JSON-encoded version of our metrics that passes two separate metrics values in the same telemetry instead of a single value:

```
{
    "metrics" : [
      { "metric_name" : "pdf_pages", "metric_value" : 2 },
      { "metric_name" : "file_size", "metric_value" : 292.5 }
    ]
}
```

This example encodes two separate metrics, `pdf_page` and `file_size`, in a single emission. Such a format would be challenging in a tab or CSV list, is easier with a key-value system expecting multiple metrics per line, and relies on a second parser for the positional-delimited method.

ENCODING INTO XML

XML (eXtensible Markup Language) provides a sophisticated format for moving data. Before JSON stole its thunder, XML was the data-interchange format of choice for APIs. Because of this history, many (usually older) systems still produce XML preferentially. Unlike JSON, XML was not built explicitly to encode data structures but to be a multipurpose way to encode data of any kind.

For telemetry purposes, XML's lack of focus on rendering data structures makes it both more powerful and harder to use than JSON. This extra power also make XML prone to parser-specific assumptions about how data structures are defined. You can encode the same pair of metrics that you did with JSON:

```
<MetricsEmission>
  <DateTime>2023-02-19T23:04:55.293+0:00</DateTime>
  <MetricsItems>
    <MetricItem>
      <MetricName>pdf_pages</MetricName>
      <MetricValue>2</MetricValue>
    </MetricItem>
    <MetricItem>
      <MetricName>file_size</MetricName>
      <MetricValue>292.5</MetricValue>
    </MetricItem>
  </MetricsItems>
</MetricsEmission>
```

This example encodes both the `pdf_pages` and `file_size` metrics as the JSON example. The two `<MetricItem>` entries form an array of hashes. `<MetricsEmission>` forms a hash. Unlike JSON, XML is more visually explicit about what each component is named.

ENCODING INTO YAML

YAML (Yet Another Markup Language) is the newest of these three formats. (In the tech industry, the third of a thing often gets prefixed by *yet another*, *tradition!*) YAML allows the encoding of more-sophisticated structures than JSON does and has mechanisms for passing strings without the need for JSON-style escaping, making it a safer format if your data includes lots of special characters, double quotes, or slashes. YAML has some of XML's ability to render not just data structures, but also complex data. YAML is most commonly seen as a configuration language and a data-transaction language.

Although it's not useful for telemetry, YAML allows comments to be put into its structure, which is why you see it used a lot as a configuration language. YAML's ability to support data types beyond what JSON does makes it more expressive than JSON. Once more, let's see the YAML version of the pair of metrics we encoded in JSON and XML:

```
---
metric_emission:
  time: "2023-02-19T23:04:55.293+0:00"
  metrics:
    - metric_name: "pdf_pages"
```

```
  metric_value: 2
- metric_name: "file_size"
  metric_value: 292.5
```

This formatting feels more compact than JSON and is certainly shorter than XML. The value for pdf_pages is detected as an integer because there is no decimal in the value, whereas the value for file_size is detected as float because it does have a decimal in the value. To explicitly cast the value of pdf_pages as a float, simply add .0 to the number or prefix the number with !!float, as in metric_value: !!float 2. YAML represents a middle ground between the expressiveness of XML and the rigid simplicity of JSON.

All three object-encoding formats allow encoding complex data structures without line breaks or unneeded whitespace on a single line—a format known as *minified*. Such minified lines generally are not human-readable, so I'm not going to render an example here, but they do save considerable space when humans aren't expected to parse them visually. Minified or not, object-encoding formats are algorithmically more complex to parse than delimited strings—a fact that can be quite significant if your Shipping pipeline is handling thousands or hundreds of thousands of emissions a second.

That said, using a format as ubiquitous as JSON is on the modern web means that JSON parsers have seen a lot of optimization since 2010. When making the decision between JSON or another object-encoding format, definitely test your pipeline to verify that performance is as you expect. Delimited formats are visually easy to parse, easy to create, and easy to write, but that ease does not guarantee performance advantages.

The problem of protobufs

The protocol buffer (*protobuf*) is a concept that originated at Google. The company wanted a way to serialize/deserialize data that was faster than XML, so in classic Google fashion, it invented its own way. Unlike JSON, XML, and YAML, all of which serialize into strings, protobufs are not string-based when serialized; protobufs are binary-based.

Being a binary format truly does make protobuf pretty darned fast for serialize/deserialize operations. But it does mean that whatever technique you use to pass protobufs around needs to support binaries too.

Protobufs are like the comma-/tab-separated value lists in that the schema of the message needs to be preshared before communication will work. This sharing speeds protobufs but makes them unlike JSON, XML, and YAML, which can't encode arbitrary data structures. If your telemetry pipeline creates arbitrary data structures, protobufs will be a difficult fit for you. But if you can work with a binary format and use a static schema, protobufs are among the most efficient ways to transact data (so long as you can ship the format at all).

Protobufs can be excellent in telemetry pipelines, but the need to define the object format on both sides makes the format somewhat inflexible—great for metrics and tracing, but not so great for centralized logging. In spite of the pains of using protobufs, expect to see more of them in future telemetry systems.

4.2.2   *Picking a shipping format*

This section covers the process of picking telemetry shipping formats. The fewer shipping formats you have to support, the easier it is overall to maintain your Shipping-stage systems, so it is worth your time to try to focus telemetry formats down to a few. To help with this process, we will examine a complex telemetry Shipping stage for the global logistics company mentioned in this chapter's introduction and section 4.1.1. As the introduction warned, the process is both technical and political.

The first thing to understand about picking a shipping format is that you are permitted to use more than one. *It is more important for your telemetry to get into storage than it is for the telemetry be shipped in the one true format.* If shipping your telemetry into storage requires a mix of JSON and key-value, so be it. Your choice of format has as much to do with the politics of your technical organization as it does with the abilities of your production systems; you need to accommodate both.

The Shipping stage, especially in large technical organizations, forces telemetry system operators to interact with many teams in the technical organization. Figure 4.7 shows the sort of large organization you would find in the global logistics company we've used for a few chapters now.

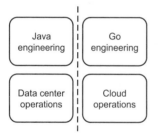

Figure 4.7   The four teams of interest in our global logistics company as they work to pick a shipping format for their telemetry systems. We see that the Java software is running in actual data centers, whereas the Go software is running in a public cloud. Bridging this divide is a key part of the negotiation process.

In this example, we see four teams: two operations-like teams and two software engineering teams building on completely different platforms. This separation was intentional on the part of senior technical management (the reasons for which we'll get into later), and the teams have reached the point where they need to unify their approaches. To help set the scene, figure 4.8 illustrates both architectures.

In a telemetry shipping pipeline like this example, we have the physical data center components (VMware and Cisco) emitting into Syslog. The Java Spring Boot applications are also emitting into Syslog. The Syslog server has been configured to ship into two kinds of centralized logging and also sends events to a metrics shipper that stores metrics data in a third database. Meanwhile, a different group is building in AWS. The CloudOps team ingests infrastructure logs into a database maintained by the operations team in the physical data center, while a software engineering team is building Go-based applications in Elastic Kubernetes Services, shipping directly from code into both metrics and distributed tracing systems. The system they want to get to is described in figure 4.9, which is a pretty significant change!

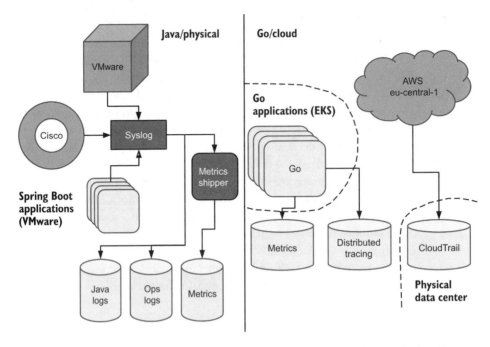

Figure 4.8   The existing telemetry systems for the Java-on-data-center and Go-on-cloud environments. On the left are the Java systems; on the right are the Go systems based in AWS, which ships directly to metrics and distributed tracing. Additionally, the AWS logs themselves are shipped to a CloudTrail repository in the physical data center. Global-scale companies often have nearly completely separated computing systems like this example. (For more on that style of computing, see section 10.3.)

In figure 4.9, we see a shipping pipeline with several components:

- The stream service acts as a unified event stream for the entire telemetry system in both the physical and cloud production systems.
- The Syslog server for the physical data center acts as a centralized shipping point for everything in the data center, sending telemetry into the stream.
- Emitter/Shipper functions in the Go applications ship directly into the stream.
- A dedicated shipper maintained by the CloudOps team moves AWS events into the stream.
- Four dedicated shipping systems consume telemetry from the stream, each operated by a different team.

This figure also shows five telemetry storage systems:

- Three log repositories, one shared between the operations and CloudOps teams, and dedicated log repositories for the Java engineering and Go engineering teams
- A metrics repository, shared between the Java and Go engineering teams
- A distributed tracing repository, used by the Go engineering team

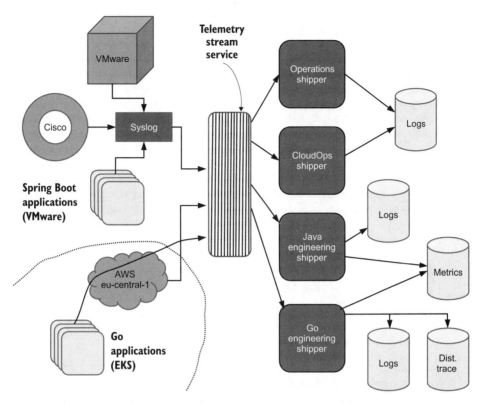

Figure 4.9   The unified telemetry system for our global logistics company, which centers on the use of a stream system to act as a unified data pipeline. Team-specific Shipping-stage components subscribe to stream topics to handle each team's telemetry and ultimately store it in databases.

This complex example demonstrates the technical and political trade-offs that need to be made when settling on supported shipping formats. For this example, the event that triggered the need for a unified format was deciding to implement the telemetry stream service. To start the process of determining a supported or supportable list of formats, we first look at three areas:

- The emitting and shipping capabilities of each component
- The existing shipping pipeline
- Which teams manage which emitting and shipping components, and how the *teams* (not components) already interface

Using the information we gather here, we move to the next stage: negotiation. This last stage is where the trade-offs between a singular format versus ease of integration are made.

The fractured nature of global companies

Truly global companies are often a bunch of smaller companies in a trenchcoat, with the various smaller companies operating somewhat to totally independently. One business unit may be all in on public cloud and serverless architectures, whereas another unit is 60 years into its mainframe story and has no plans to stop. Being part of a single company does not guarantee a common technical base everywhere inside that company! The global logistics company in this section is no different, but it's trying to get better. You will see another couple of cases like this one in part 2.

DETERMINE THE EMITTING CAPABILITIES OF EXISTING SYSTEMS TO PROVIDE THE BASELINE

This section covers the first area of identifying telemetry shipping formats: identifying the emission capabilities of each production system. We need this information to provide the technical basis for our later format negotiation. For the infrastructure described in figure 4.8, we can see several main emitting components:

- The Cisco and VMware systems, which emit only in Syslog
- The Java Spring Boot software, which can emit in anything but is currently emitting in Syslog
- The AWS CloudTrail infrastructure logs, which emits as JSON files
- The Go software, which can emit in anything

Although Java Spring Boot can emit in anything, in this specific case the Java applications themselves were first written in 1999 and have been maintained with the occasional significant rewrite ever since. The early Java applications were wired to emit to the same Syslog used by the operations team around 2000, a capability that every maintenance and upgrade effort has ensured will continue. The Syslog history here is deep and long; it is a well-understood and above all *comfortable* format for the teams using it.

The Go software running in Elastic Kubernetes Services is brand-new, less than a year old. The decision to deploy in AWS was made by senior engineering management as an experiment for this company—one that appears to be quite promising. This company is looking to integrate these new software and deployment platforms into the existing telemetry systems. We're left with three main constraints:

- The hardware that requires Syslog and supports nothing else
- The deep Syslog integration in the Spring Boot applications
- The JSON emitted by the AWS CloudTrail service

The Go applications don't contribute a constraint at this stage! Next, we look at the existing shipping pipeline.

EXAMINE SHIPPING-STAGE CAPABILITIES TO NARROW THE CHANGE SCOPE

This section covers the second area of identifying telemetry shipping formats: determining what kind of telemetry handling is in place. This information will tell us how much effort we need to spend to make updates, depending on the changes agreed to in the negotiation stage. The most mature shipping pipeline in this company is in the physical data center for the Java environment. As discussed in the section on identifying emission capabilities, this pipeline is strongly Syslog-based, thanks to two decades of history and the presence of opinionated hardware. All the hardware and software systems emit to Syslog. Then the Syslog servers emit into three separate storage systems, as shown in figure 4.10:

- A centralized-logs repository for the operations team
- A centralized-logs repository for the Spring Boot software
- A metrics repository used by the Spring Boot software

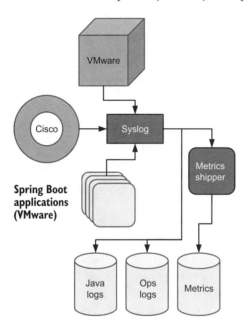

Figure 4.10   The existing Syslog-based telemetry pipeline used by the data-center-based Java teams. Everything emits into Syslog. The Syslog server ships into two separate logging databases (one for ops and one for the Java apps), and to a metrics shipper built by the Java team that sends telemetry into a metrics database. This example demonstrates close integration between the operations and Java teams.

The pipeline in the AWS environment isn't nearly as detailed because it hasn't been released into production yet, but it does have some shipping elements, as shown in figure 4.11:

- An S3 bucket full of JSON files emitted by CloudTrail that is pulled into the physical data center
- A metrics repository used by the Go software
- A distributed tracing repository used by the Go software
- Go logs viewed through the AWS EKS console (because the Go engineering team is attempting to use the tracing logs for centralized logging wherever possible)

With analysis, we can tell that there will be a lot of inertia involved with any change to the Java Spring Boot telemetry pipeline. The Java pipeline has been in place for more

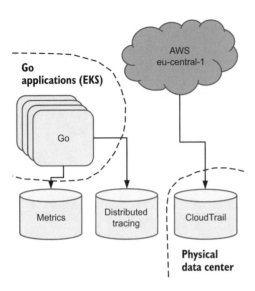

Figure 4.11 The premerger telemetry pipeline for the AWS-based engineering teams. The Go-based software emits directly into two telemetry systems. Meanwhile, the CloudOps team emits the AWS telemetry into a database in the physical data center. The integration between the CloudOps and Go engineering teams isn't as strong as with the Java/data center environment.

than two decades and has been custom-fitted over the years to that specific use case. The combined Syslog platform supports large parts of the business, so making changes there is somewhat risky, but that process is part of our next analysis.

IDENTIFYING TEAM COMMUNICATION LINKS TO PROVIDE SCOPE FOR THE POLITICAL NEGOTIATION

This section covers the third area of identifying telemetry shipping formats: identifying which teams will be involved in the telemetry pipeline and how the teams communicate. This information tells us which telemetry passing will be easy (because it replicates existing communication links) and which will be hard (because it requires establishing new communication links). Looking at figure 4.8, we can identify four teams involved in this telemetry discussion:

- The software engineering team writing the Java Spring Boot software
- The software engineering team writing the Go software
- The operations team supporting the physical data center hardware underlying the Spring Boot software
- The CloudOps team supporting the AWS infrastructure underlying the Go software

When we dig deeper into the organization, we learn a few more things:

- The Spring Boot software team develops software on two continents and deploys its software in three data centers on three continents.
- The operations team is spread across three continents to support the data centers where the Java Spring Boot software is deployed.
- The Go software team is 30 engineers working out of the office in Hamburg, Germany.
- The CloudOps team is across the hall from the Go team, with three remote team members working out of the Singapore office.

It's important to this discussion of team communication that half of the Go team consists of former Java engineers tapped to work on this new project. The other half of the Go team consists of engineers who were hired specifically for that team and had no previous experience with the company. The injection of perspectives that aren't shaded by the history of the company is already sparking heated conversations (debates) about best practices and the next targets for refactoring/rewriting.

Software developed by both teams supports the business of being a global logistics company. The teams write sales-enablement software, to permit shippers and receivers in different countries to handle manifests and paperwork. They write inventory-tracking software to keep track of everything in transit, waiting in customs, or waiting transshipment. They write software to predict future demand so the company can improve routing of carrier assets to meet those demands.

The Java software drives most of these development cases, which grants the Java Spring Boot software engineering teams a lot of political weight in management meetings. Meanwhile, the Go engineering teams are seeing a greenfield in which to radically update this company's software practices. Everyone agrees that having a single telemetry pipeline enables many business decisions, but there are strong disagreements on how best to make that so. Enter negotiation.

NEGOTIATING STANDARD FORMATS TO MAKE A PLAN FOR CHANGE

This section talks about bringing together the elements from the preceding three sections to decide on the official telemetry formats. Because we need to make a decision, it's time to start the negotiation process. Technical requirements are only part of how this decision is made; negotiations between business units and teams are how the standards documentation is approved. This process is where Conway's Law (http://www.melconway.com/Home/Conways_Law.html) comes into play:

> *Any organization that designs a system (defined broadly) will produce a design whose structure is a copy of the organization's communication structure.*

A telemetry system seeking to connect diverse parts of an organization will likely mirror the communication structure of the organization. A technical organization with two teams that don't talk to each other is unlikely to share a telemetry system. Conversely, someone seeking to create a telemetry system for teams that don't communicate will also have to create those interteam communication links as part of the process. Where you get new communication links, you also need to negotiate how the teams relate.

When you're going into a negotiation like this one, which can involve a couple of emails with a co-worker or months of hour-long meetings between product groups, remember a few key points:

- *The goal is to get people using the new telemetry systems.* Wrong use is generally better than no use. Wrong can be corrected later.
- *Simple is relative to the observer.* What is simple for you can be quite complex for another team, and the converse is also true. Have empathy for everyone involved.

- *Shared understanding of goals and constraints helps everyone toward consensus.* Teach, guide, and then direct the conversation.
- *You're allowed to use more than one telemetry shipping format.* You want people using the standards, and allowing more than one format lowers the barrier to adoption facing telemetry producers.

Our global logistics company that's seeking to add a stream-based pipeline to its telemetry systems and get the AWS-based Go systems into the pipeline faces a few problems:

- The Java Spring Boot software engineering teams are large, distributed, and have the weight of history.
- The Go software engineering teams are in a true greenfield, allowed to try new things in the hope of spurring innovation.
- Although some members of the Go teams came from the Java side, many have no experience with the Java side or with much of the rest of the company; therefore, they have no attachment to the way things have always been done.

Already, we can see a probable communication issue between the two software engineering teams. Part of this problem comes from the deliberate isolation surrounding the Go teams, put there from the start to avoid biasing team members through exposure to existing processes. Another part of the problem is the emergence of radically different approaches to developing software.

At the same time, forces are working in favor of a unified telemetry pipeline. The Go team was not set up in a vacuum; people were specifically hired to be on that team, so an executive somewhere had the budget approved to try this new idea. The use of new infrastructure, AWS Cloud instead of physical data centers, also represents approved budget and executive buy-in. Although the Java teams are large and have a lot of political sway, management has shown clear, obvious intent to explore new ways of achieving the goals of the business. To start, let's look at the Java team's existing telemetry pipeline in figure 4.12:

1. Ships from code into a Syslog process running on the same host.
2. The host Syslog forwards to a central Syslog, with the Spring Boot telemetry emissions encoded in the message part of Syslog. For Cisco and VMware, vendor-defined telemetry is encoded as the message part.
3. The central Syslog, far more complex than the host-based Syslog processes, takes Syslog-encoded telemetry and sends it into an Elasticsearch cluster.

   One index is used by the Operations team, and the Spring Boot application development teams use a second index.
4. A metrics shipper utility consumes a stream of metrics and sends them into a time-series database (InfluxDB).

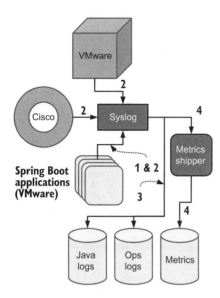

Figure 4.12   Java Spring Boot shipping pipeline, showing how telemetry moves through to storage. This architecture demonstrates extensive collaboration between the Java and operations teams.

This example contains a lot of sophistication, for all that the emission from code is simple. Now look at the telemetry pipeline that emerged in the Go engineering team and at figure 4.11 again (reproduced here as figure 4.13):

- The Go application emits and ships directly into a distributed tracing repository based on Jaeger; logs are viewed from AWS consoles.
- The Go application also emits and ships directly into a metrics system based on Prometheus, which (like Kubernetes) is a member of the Cloud Native Computing Foundation, so the two systems work together easily.
- The cloud operations team has written a shipper to send AWS CloudTrail logs into the Elasticsearch instance operated by the physical data center's operations team.

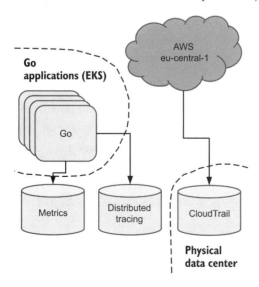

Figure 4.13   The premerger telemetry pipeline for the AWS-based engineering teams. Centralized logging is not centralized, with the software and operations teams sending their logs to different places. The software team uses metrics and distributed tracing, shipping directly to storage from the Go software.

In some ways, the Go application team's telemetry pipeline is both simpler and more complex than the Java team's. The pipeline is simpler in that the pipeline is definitely shorter; the Go application is emitting directly into the repositories. It's more complex in that the Go team is using a new telemetry technique, distributed tracing.

With the goal of unifying these two systems and modernizing their telemetry handling overall, the Java and Go teams begin negotiating. During architectural analysis, the central Syslog service for the Java environment is identified as a key player in a future architecture because it already centralizes the emissions of the Java and hardware-driven environment. Also, both teams are taking a similar approach to metrics even though they're using different platforms for the same goal (InfluxDB and Prometheus).

Given the desire of management to modernize, both teams look at their overall telemetry handing architectures and consider how to handle their different operational patterns. They settle on a stream-based system, as described in section 3.1.2 (and section 4.1.1), as a capable way of handling these different use cases. The proposal requires a few changes:

- The Go applications will ship directly into a topic on the stream dedicated to the Go environment.
- The Java teams will continue to emit into Syslog, with a plan to move the Java applications slowly to emitting directly into a topic on the stream.
- The central Syslog server for the operations and Java Spring Boot teams will emit into two separate topics: one for the Java application and one for the use of the physical operations team.
- The cloud operations team will create a shipper that sends CloudTrail events into the same topic used by the operations team.
- All four teams—Java engineering, Go engineering, operations, and cloud operations—will create shippers that consume events from their topics and send processed events into the storage of their choice.
- Both the Go and Java team's shippers will emit metrics into the same metrics system based on the time-series database InfluxDB, due to the fact that InfluxDB has already been scaled up to handle the Java team's much larger load. InfluxDB will run with the Prometheus connector to support the Go team. (Sorry, fully open source Prometheus.)
- The Jaeger distributed tracing tool used by the Go team will remain in place but will be fed by the Go team's shipper rather than directly from the Go applications.

Along the way, the teams had much discussion about telemetry formats. Because the architecture allows dedicated topics to support dedicated shippers for each team, the Java and Go architecture teams *do not need to have the same format*. Both teams support the same metrics system, so both shippers need to send telemetry in the same format to InfluxDB.

Due to their extensive existing logic for parsing Syslog-encoded messages, the telemetry format used by the Java and operations teams will continue to be Syslog-encoded strings on the topic. But excitement about future ability to customize the format has energized the Java team to rewrite its logging functions to emit directly into the topic and experiment with object-encoding formats such as JSON.

On the Go team, there is some resistance to shipping to a stream rather than continuing to ship directly to storage. But when it is pointed out that the stream architecture makes for far more resilient telemetry systems in the event of a hack, grumbling subsides to mere background levels. The telemetry encoding format for the stream was driven by the telemetry format of the distributed tracing tool, which is JSON; for simplicity, the Go team elected to pass all telemetry as JSON on the stream topic.

When the implementation is done, the logistics company's business intelligence unit notices the new data stream and asks to get a feed of metrics. Perhaps both teams would consider emitting new metrics to ease the BI team's number-crunching. The goal of enabling better business decisions has been accomplished. Figure 4.14 shows the final architecture and the shipping formats.

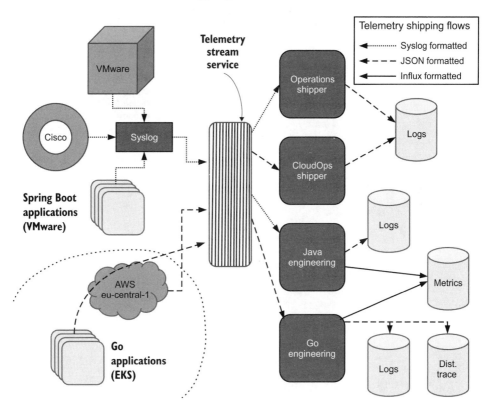

Figure 4.14 A large unified telemetry pipeline with four teams participating, using three telemetry shipping formats. Using multiple formats allows this telemetry system to support differing needs and survive future demands.

4.2.3   *Converting Syslog to JSON or other object-encoding formats*

This section addresses the need to convert standards-based Syslog to JSON or other object-encoding formats. Syslog is an ancient format by the standards of Internet time. (Being born around 1980 has that effect.) But that stability means that Syslog is the one format that most infrastructures that aren't 100% public cloud provider services have at least some capability of handling. Like the logistics company in section 4.2.2, many companies that use hardware need to transform Syslog into something else as part of the shipping pipeline.

Listing 4.4 demonstrates a minimal config file for Syslog-ng, using a method that the logistics company from section 4.2.1 used to connect its Syslog server to the Apache Kafka-based stream.

Listing 4.4   Syslog-ng shipper for JSON to Kafka

```
@module mod-java          These two are required to
@include scl.conf         use the Kafka exporter.

source s_syslog {
  syslog(
    ip(fdb5:48de:c615:15::192)
    transport(tls)
    tls(                            Sets up a Syslog
      peer-verify(require-trusted)  listener using TCP
      ca-dir('/etc/pki/home-ca/')   over IPv6 and TLS
      key-file('/etc/pki/syslog.key')
      cert-file('/etc/pki/syslog.pem')
    )
  );
};

destination d_kafka {
  kafka (
    client-lib-dir("/opt/syslog-ng/lib/syslog-ng/java-modules:
    ⇒ /[path to kafka libs]")
    kafka-bootstrap-servers(
    ⇒ "[fdb5:48de:c615:15::42]:9092,    Hints on where to find the Kakfa servers
    ⇒ [fdb5::48de:c615:b2::42]:9092") ◁
    topic("${PROGRAM}")                 ◁──── Topic is the channel to publish events to.
    template("$(format-json --scope rfc5424
    ⇒ --exclude DATE --key ISODATE)") ◁──── Reformats log lines into JSON-encoded strings
  );
};
```

Listing 4.4 configures a single input and a single destination. The use of the ${PRO-GRAM} macro in the topic configuration allows events to be sent to different channels/topics based on the content of the Syslog PROGRAM field. In the context of the example of section 4.2.2, the Java Spring Boot team's new shipper would listen to the topics with their program names. The template parameter in the d_kafka section re-encodes the standard Syslog format into one parsable by something expecting JSON. Figure 4.15 demonstrates this telemetry flow.

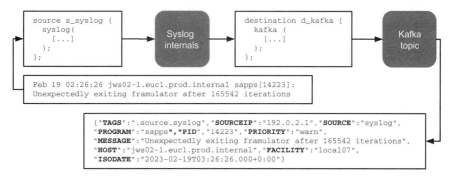

Figure 4.15   **The process of translating a Syslog-formatted message sent by a Java web host into a JSON-formatted message sent to the Kafka topic. This example translates a software-issued Syslog line, but the same process applies to hardware-issued Syslog lines.**

Another method for making this translation involves using a separate utility. Elastic's Filebeat and Logstash utilities both allow reading files generated by Syslog and transforming them into other formats, such as JSON. The format that Filebeat uses will be similar to the format produced by Syslog-ng, in that the message component of Syslog will also be in a JSON field labeled `"message"`. Logstash has the ability to further transform and parse the Syslog files before passing them on to the next stage in the pipeline. The following listing is a minimal Logstash pipeline configuration that ingests a single Syslog-formatted file, parses it, conditionally reparses the `message` field if the `program` field is right, and sends it to the same Kafka topic as listing 4.4. Because this code involves parsing strings, here is an example of Syslog output to keep in mind when reading the code:

```
Feb 19 02:28:22 ec2-host java_metrics[1212]: {"metric_name": "pdf_pages",
 "metric_value" : "2" }
```

Listing 4.5   Logstash translating Syslog to JSON and shipping to Kafka

```
input {
  file {
    path => "/var/log/syslog"          'tail' to follow updates to the file
    mode => "tail"             ◁
    type => "syslog"           ◁
  }                                     Used in conditionals later
}

filter {
  if [type] == "syslog" {
    dissect {
      mapping => {
        "message" => "%{time} %{+time} %{+time}
           %{host} %{program}[%{pid}]: %{syslog_message}"
      convert_datatype => {
        "pid" => "int"          ◁——— Process Identifier (PID) is always integer.
      }
    }
```

```
    date {
      match => [                          Extracts the timestamp of
        "time", "MMM dd HH:mm:ss"         the event from the event
      ]
    }

    if [program] == "java_metrics" {
      json {
        source           => syslog_message
        tag_on_failure => "_bad_java_metrics"       Drop syslog_message after
        remove_field    => [ "syslog_message" ]      we've extracted from it.
      }
    }
  }
}

output {
  if [program] == "java_metrics" and
    "_bad_java_metrics" not in [tags] {
    kafka {
      topic_id           => "%{program}"          Ensures that the event is JSON-
      codec              => "json"                  coded when sent to Kafka
      bootstrap_servers =>
      ➥ "[fdb5:48de:c615:15::42]:9092,
      ➥ [fdb5::48de:c615:b2::42]:9092"
    }
  }
}
```

Logstash config files have three stages in their internal pipeline: Inputs > Filters > Outputs. Inputs receive emitted telemetry. Filters transform telemetry. Outputs ship telemetry. Filters run in the order in which they appear in the file, so our `dissect {}` block parses and extracts several fields that are used later:

- `time`—Used by the `date {}` filter to set the event's timestamp to match that of the Syslog line
- `program`—Used in conditionals to determine which fields get further processing
- `syslog_message`—Used inside a conditional, where it is parsed for JSON data

A `date {}` filter is extremely useful in cases where the timestamps in the data coming into the filter are significantly different from now. In the case of the shipper used by the global logistics company, the timestamps usually are close to now. But when the Logstash process was restarted and Syslog continued to send data to the file, Logstash would set correct timestamps on the events coming in.

The next block is a conditional, applying the `json {}` filter only if the parsed program field is the right value. With the Syslog parser right before the code, after this filter is run, the event would have the `metric_name` and `metric_value` fields populated. Then the `syslog_message` field is dropped from the event, because it contains only the JSON string and isn't useful otherwise. If JSON parsing fails, Logstash sets a specific tag on the event. To demonstrate how parsing works, figure 4.16 walks us through the parsing stages.

```
Feb 19 02:28:22 ec2-host java_metrics[1212]: {"metric_name": "pdf_pages", "metric_value" :
"2" }
```

```
input {
  file {
    path => "/var/log/syslog"
    mode => "tail"
    type => "syslog"
  }
}
```

Internally creates a hash structure but does not yet JSON-parse our log line

```
{"message":"Feb 19 02:28:22 ec2-host java_metrics[1212]: \{\"metric_name\": \"pdf_pages\",
\"metric_value\" : \"2\" \}","type","syslog" }
```

```
if [type] == "syslog"
```

Breaks apart Syslog-formatted log line to create more fields on our event

```
dissect {
  mapping => {
    "message" => "%{time} %{+time} %{+time} %{host} %{program}[%{pid}]: %{syslog_message}"
  convert_datatype => {
    "pid" => "int"
  }
}
```

```
{"message":"Feb 19 02:28:22 ec2-host java_metrics[1212]: \{\"metric_name\": \"pdf_pages\",
\"metric_value\" : \"2\" \}","type":"syslog","time":"Feb 19 02:28:22","host":"ec2-host",
"program":"java_metrics","pid":"1212","syslog_message":"\
{\"metric_name\": \"pdf_pages\", \"metric_value\" : \"2\" \}" }
```

```
date {
  match => [
    "time", "MMM dd HH:mm:ss"
  ]
}
```

Adds year to timestamp because the Syslog protocol does not have a year in the format

```
{"@timestamp":"2023-02-19T02:28:22.00","message":"Feb 19 02:28:22 ec2-host
java_metrics[1212]: \
{\"metric_name\": \"pdf_pages\", \"metric_value\" : \"2\" \}","type":"syslog",
"time":"Feb 19 02:28:22","host":"ec2-host","program":"java_metrics","pid":"1212",
"syslog_message":"\{\"metric_name\": \"pdf_pages\", \"metric_value\" : \"2\" \}" }
```

```
if [program] == "java_metrics"
```

```
json {
  source       => syslog_message
  tag_on_failure => "_bad_java_metrics"
  remove_field   => [ "syslog_message" ]
}
```

Adds metric_name and metric_value to our event and drops syslog_message

```
{"@timestamp":"2023-02-19T02:28:22.00","message":"Feb 19 02:28:22 ec2-host
java_metrics[1212]: \
{\"metric_name\": \"pdf_pages\", \"metric_value\" : \"2\" \}","type":"syslog",
"time":"Feb 19 02:28:22","host":"ec2-host","program":"java_metrics","pid":"1212",
"metric_name":"pdf_pages","metric_value":2 }
```

```
output {
  kafka { }
}
```

Figure 4.16 Parsing flow for the Logstash config in listing 4.5. The final JSON block is sent into a Kafka topic, which will be parsed by a later Shipping-stage system and eventually inserted into a database. This example illustrates enrichment (extracting details from telemetry), which will be covered in detail in chapter 6.

The output block uses both the program field and the tag set by the json {} filter to determine whether the event will be sent on to Kafka. Like the Syslog-ng example before, the Kafka topic_id is set to the value of the program field.

4.2.4   *Designing with cardinality in mind*

This section discusses the trade-offs between rich telemetry and maintainability. *Cardinality* specifically, the number of unique combinations the fields in the index may produce. If there are two fields A and B, where A has two possible values and B has three possible values, the cardinality of that index is A * B, or 2 * 3 = 6. Cardinality has a significant impact on search performance no matter what data storage system is being used. Chapter 14 goes in depth about cardinality, but the topic needs to be considered in selecting telemetry formats. The Syslog file format has five fields, one optional, as shown in figure 4.17.

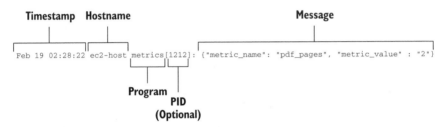

Figure 4.17   The five fields of a Syslog-formatted string. The process identifier (PID) is optionally encoded in brackets attached to the Program field to enable you to tell emissions apart from multiple executions of the same program.

Of these five fields, two are going to be unique: the timestamp and the message. Syslog messages, with their five fields, create quite high cardinalities, so the data storage system holding Syslog messages will need to handle high cardinalities. Some databases, such as Elasticsearch, are designed for this sort of full-text searching. Others, such as time-series databases like InfluxDB and Prometheus, end up being terrible at handling such high cardinalities.

Elasticsearch encounters a different but related problem when the *number of fields in an index* grows large or when most events don't have all available fields. The problem comes from how Elasticsearch works; every event in an index gets every field on it, but empty fields hold a null value. If you have an event with 15 fields, but 15,000 fields are available in the index, that event will have 15 fields with defined values, and 14,985 fields with null values. It is entirely possible that the null fields will take up more storage space than the 15 fields with defined values.

If you have an Elasticsearch index storing Syslog-formatted data, every event in the index will have all five fields defined. The Elasticsearch index with events like that will likely store compactly, at the cost of having to rely on string searches within the message field to find details about what happened. In the metrics example in section 4.2.3, looking for metric_name and metric_value in such a Syslog-formatted Elasticsearch index would rely on string searching, which is relatively inefficient compared with looking for a metric_name field directly in events.

The Logstash example shown in listing 4.5 and figure 4.17 potentially adds metric_name and metric_value to the event as it passes through the filter stage of the Logstash pipeline. But not every event passing through is a metric or will get those values, so an Elasticsearch index containing everything that passes through that pipeline will have events with and without those two fields. Balancing the slight cost of null-valued fields against the tremendous performance improvement in searching is a decision you will need to make, but here are a few pointers to help you:

- If your traffic is dominated by a single generator of telemetry, such as more than half your overall events, your telemetry storage systems will likely behave better if telemetry emitted by that generator is sent to a separate index that's not shared with other telemetry. (See section 14.2.2 for more on this method.) Telemetry will be stored efficiently for both the high-rate system and the rest, and you will save money and space.
- If you have the ability to modify telemetry fields within the Shipping stage, taking steps to ensure that different telemetry formats overlap on fields will create some efficiencies. (See section 14.2.1 for more on this method.) Many logging formats have a field for priority, so if you can get all the priority fields into the same data type, you will save field counts.
- If you have a telemetry generator that produces huge numbers of fields, perhaps because it emits in an object-encoding format, sending that telemetry to a single index will isolate the performance hit to that specific production system. (See section 14.2.2.)
- If your large telemetry-producing systems are software that your organization develops, taking the time to work with the software engineering teams for your organization's software to teach them how to optimize their telemetry systems can help reduce field sprawl. (Chapter 12 and section 14.2.1 address this topic in detail.)

Summary

- The Shipping stage in a telemetry pipeline is the stage that receives telemetry from the Emitting stage, optionally modifies the telemetry, and stores it for later presentation in the Presentation stage.
- The Shipping stage often acts as a translator between the telemetry format received from the Emitting stage and the telemetry format used by the Presentation stage.
- A Shipping stage can be anything from a single function in the code to an entire multisystem infrastructure with dedicated engineers.
- Collecting telemetry from log files is one of the oldest telemetry system problems, and as a result, there are a lot of off-the-shelf ways to solve it.

- Several open source and open core agents will move telemetry from log files into something more useful, if not into storage.
- Among the hardest problems in telemetry systems are the analysis and presentation of telemetry, so companies can afford to provide log shippers for free.
- Organizations that don't write software still use telemetry systems, making them look more like business telemetry. Such organizations often use SaaS platforms by preference because they're not in the business of running data centers or managing software.
- Most Shipping-stage infrastructures pass telemetry around as strings, which may be encoded in any of several formats, including delimited formats (such as CSV lists and key-value pairs) and object-encoding formats (such as JSON, XML, and YAML).
- Using protocol buffers (protobufs) is another way to encode (serialize) complexly formatted telemetry. This format differs from JSON, XML, and YAML in that it is a binary format. Unlike string-based formats, protobufs require both the encode and decode systems to know the format of a protobuf.
- Picking a telemetry format requires understanding the technical capabilities of the production systems and existing telemetry systems, as well as the communication capabilities of the teams that maintain every component.
- You are allowed to support more than one telemetry format. The goal is to have the telemetry used; being prescriptive about format can cause some teams not to use the telemetry systems and build their own instead.
- The Syslog format is defined by RFC and is considered to be stable. Hardware vendors allow telemetry emissions in Syslog format because that format is standardized.
- Converting Syslog-formatted telemetry to other formats is often done in the Shipping stage.
- Cardinality is the measure of database index complexity, computed by multiplying the number of unique values in a field by the number of unique values in other fields.
- Certain telemetry storage systems, such as Elasticsearch, are built to handle high-cardinality data and are well-suited to centralized logging systems.
- Other telemetry storage systems, such as the metrics time-series databases InfluxDB and Prometheus, handle high cardinality poorly.
- When you're using a high-cardinality system, you must make trade-offs between the number of available fields, the size of the index, and search performance. Fewer fields perform better.
- If your telemetry system involves data generated by software that your organization built, teaching the software engineers how to reduce field sprawl will help the organization save telemetry handling costs.

The Presentation stage: Displaying telemetry

This chapter covers

- The function of the Presentation stage
- How to aggregate and display metrics data
- Features needed in centralized logging and security systems
- How correlation drives distributed tracing

The Presentation stage is the last stage of the telemetry pipeline and the one that most people in the technical organization (and outside it) use to interact with telemetry. For telemetry SaaS companies, the Presentation stage is what sells their products. This chapter teaches how telemetry is presented in each of the four telemetry system styles covered in previous chapters:

- Section 5.1 covers metrics systems and how charts and aggregations are produced.
- Section 5.2 covers centralized logging systems and what features a good presentation system for centralized logging should have.

- Section 5.3 covers security systems and their specialized presentation needs.
- Section 5.4 covers distributed tracing systems and how correlation drives the value it provides.

By the time telemetry has reached a Presentation-stage system, it has already flowed through the Emitting and Shipping stages of the telemetry pipeline, shown in figure 5.1. Production systems first send telemetry through the Emitting stage, which performs the initial formatting of telemetry for processing (chapter 2). Telemetry flows through the Shipping stage, which optionally further transforms it for storage in the Shipping-stage storage systems (chapters 3 and 4). Finally, people looking to support decision-making use Presentation-stage systems, pull telemetry from Shipping-stage storage, and display it.

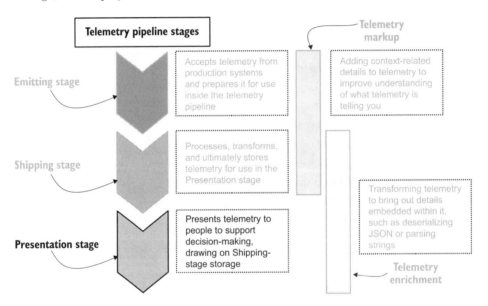

Figure 5.1   The telemetry pipeline stages with the Presentation stage last. The Presentation stage consumes storage from the Shipping stage and presents it to people to support decisions. The Presentation stage has access to all the Shipping-stage storage, allowing it to enrich telemetry beyond what the previous two stages were able to provide

The job of Presentation-stage systems is to filter, transform, aggregate, and optionally provide complex analysis on Shipping-stage data, all to produce the tables, charts, dashboards, and reports that people need to make decisions. Increasingly, Presentation-stage systems are gaining the ability to define real-time alarms, which are used to notify on-call rotations of critical events as they happen. When a table, chart, dashboard, or report is requested, most of the transformation work happens while the person waits. For this reason, the engineering behind Presentation-stage systems is among the most complex in the entire telemetry pipeline—so complex, especially in the case of distributed tracing, that open core (open source software that requires a paid support plan and licensing to enable most of the features) and SaaS providers dominate the space.

Because the Presentation stage is how humans consume telemetry, having the right presentation systems for the decisions that need to be made is important. For many people in a technical organization, the Presentation-stage systems will be the only place they will interact with the telemetry pipeline. In many ways, the Presentation-stage systems are the deliverable "service" of the telemetry ecosystem. This chapter covers the major use cases of telemetry, the sort of presentation systems each telemetry style commonly uses, and the desirable Presentation-stage features to look for in each style.

The Pillars of Observability (logs, metrics, and traces) are made useful through these Presentation-stage systems. When all three Pillars are used together, using presentation systems that are well-suited to their task, your technical organization will be best positioned to learn how your system is operating.

The perils of Presentation-stage perceptions

For better or worse, most people in a technical organization consider your Presentation-stage systems to be the entire telemetry system because those systems are where they interact with the telemetry system as a whole. This perception is great for most people, but it does have some unfortunate side effects for operators.

You see, when management is happy with how the Presentation-stage systems are working, it's harder to get resources to fix problems in the Emitting and Shipping stages. If the volume of telemetry you're handing has increased due to growth (a great "problem" to have), the utter heroics you're doing to keep the Shipping-stage systems running can go unseen so long as the Presentation systems are still behaving.

As with any platform or largely hidden service, you have to do more work to make decision-makers aware of how problems cascade into the revenue-driving systems. I've spent a career in platform-like systems, so I have long experience with this problem.

5.1 Displaying telemetry in metrics systems

This section provides an overview of displaying metrics-style telemetry. Metrics systems are dominated by numbers, their primary data type, and use a small number of text fields to provide searchability. The use of an easily compressible form of data—numbers—makes metrics-style telemetry among the cheapest to store for long periods. In organizations that have been operating metrics-based telemetry systems for a long time, you are often able to search years into the past.

Metrics systems are close cousins (if not directly part of) the monitoring systems used for real-time alerting of on-call rotations. Alerts are typically set with a threshold value, beyond which (or below which) a person is paged to deal with a problem. Where charts and graphs are used for tracking behavior over time, alerting uses the same calculations to come up with a *right now* metric that will be compared with the threshold. The statistical techniques I cover in this section apply equally to alerts:

- Section 5.1.1 gives an overview of producing graphs and charts from metrics telemetry and the common features of successful metrics presentation systems.
- Section 5.1.2 delves into the telemetry transformation technique that most metrics display systems use: the aggregation functions.
- Section 5.1.3 ties the concepts from the earlier two sections with the pdf_pages metrics function written in various styles in chapters 2–4.

For more information about on-call and alerting in general, see *Operations Anti-Patterns, DevOps Solutions,* by Jeffrey D. Smith (Manning, 2020; http://mng.bz/RKED).

5.1.1   *Making pretty pictures with telemetry*

This section covers the most charismatic display of metrics: the graph, as shown in figure 5.2. Squiggly lines in a box have been in business reports since before the invention of the computer, and computers certainly made them easier to generate. When you look at a graph, your brain will plot (possibly inaccurate) trends and identify patterns in your data. In the absence of any other kind of advanced analytics, a graph can stand alone and be quite informative.

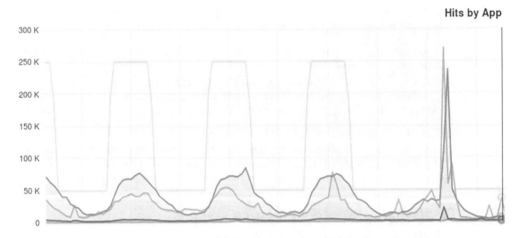

Figure 5.2   An example of charted metrics displaying the HTTP hit-rate split by application and an unusual event that deserves investigation. Showing telemetry often reveals features that would be hidden in another format, such as a report. Here, the spike is obvious at a glance. Displaying data graphically allows the human analytic system to take some of the load away from the display automation.

The ability to create graphs is required for any metrics system. If your telemetry system does not provide that ability, people will find a way to make the charts anyway. Perhaps your engineers will export the numbers from the telemetry system, import them into Microsoft Excel (or Google Docs), and make a graph there. Excel has been the numerical Presentation stage of business processes going back decades; do not imagine that software engineers are any different if Excel is the only tool that will give them what they need.

For hardware systems, access to the Emitting stage is limited to operations and other hardware-maintenance teams. For software systems, software engineering teams are the only ones with access. For Shipping-stage systems, the teams that interact with them are again limited to the operations and software engineering teams maintaining the pipeline. Anyone in the technical organization is likely to interact with Presentation-stage systems, however. This broad use provides constraints for metrics-style presentation systems. The most successful metrics presentation systems have common features:

- *They allow a wide variety of users to create charts and graphs,* enabling decision support or troubleshooting for any team that needs it.
- *They have guided user interfaces for building the queries behind charts and graphs,* so users don't have to memorize query syntax and can build complex queries easily.
- *They have the ability to organize collections of charts and graphs,* often called dashboards, to provide at-a-glance views of a decision point that a team needs.
- *They have the ability to organize dashboards,* making locating the right ones easy. Otherwise, you get a big pile of dashboards that's hard to work with.
- *They allow the creation of ad hoc dashboards without saving,* permitting a user to investigate something immediately without having to clutter the dashboard listings with a dashboard that will be used once.

Dashboards that a single person uses can take any form and be successful so long as that person gets what they were looking for. Dashboards that are used by more than one person, or that are part of routine reporting and review supporting engineering and support goals, need to be usable by all users. Here are a few guidelines for building dashboards that support multiple users:

- *Beware of how dark-/light-mode themes affect contrast.* If the presentation system supports changing background colors, pick colors so that users with dark and light backgrounds will be able to see the lines. Yellow pops on black but is nearly invisible on white, for example, and dark blues show up beautifully on white but disappear on black.
- *For dashboards with multiple charts, put the most important charts at the top.* People don't like to scroll.
- *Beware of information density.* If you have too many charts on a page, users who are unfamiliar with what the dashboard is displaying won't know what to look at.

If you're interested in building beautiful, informative dashboards, here are a few resources that will help:

- For a focus on operations, DevOps, and SRE dashboards, see chapter 4, "Data instead of information," in Jeffrey D. Smith's *Operations Anti-Patterns, DevOps Solutions* (Manning, 2020; http://mng.bz/2zj9).

- For information on using graphs and visualizations to find trouble spots, see section 3.2, "Spotting problems using graphics and visualization," in Nina Zumel and John Mount's *Practical Data Science with R*, 2nd ed. (Manning, 2019; http://mng.bz/1Ajy).
- For a deep dive into the theory of visualizations in general, see Corey L. Lanum's *Visualizing Graph Data* (Manning, 2016; http://mng.bz/PaWg).
- For advice on how to approach metrics and charting in the context of managing an agile team, see chapter 7, "Working with the data you're collecting: The sum of the parts," in Christopher W. H. Davis's *Agile Metrics in Action* (Manning, 2015; http://mng.bz/Jv1P).

5.1.2   *Feeding the graphs with aggregation functions*

This section covers the techniques metrics systems use to enable simple statistical analysis over sets of data, allowing people to identify trends that may be hidden in the raw data. For time-series data, you pick a period of time and select an aggregation function to be run on the resulting metrics to yield a number. An *aggregation function* is a mathematical function that returns a single number when run on a set of numbers. Presentation-stage systems use aggregation functions when each pixel in the graph would otherwise represent more than one item of collected data. Aggregation functions yield an aggregated value that can be graphed or used in other analysis. Here are some simple aggregation functions that most metrics display systems can support, several of which are used in section 5.1.3:

- *minimum*—The smallest number in the period is returned by `minimum`.
- *maximum*—The largest number in the period is returned by `maximum`.
- *mean*—The average number (arithmatic mean) in the period is returned by `mean`.
- *median*—The exact middle of a sorted list if all the numbers in the period are sorted from lowest to highest.
- *mode*—The most common value in the period is returned by `mode`.
- *sum*—All the numbers in the period added together represent the `sum`.
- *count*—The number of events in the period is returned by `count`.
- *percentile*—If all the numbers in the period are sorted from lowest to highest, and that list is divided into equal parts, a percentile is a specific equal part of that group. The median is the 50th percentile.

Each of these aggregation functions tells you something a little different about the telemetry it is aggregating. You can also use aggregation functions to smooth telemetry that is noisy, such as turning a set of telemetry containing processing time for a function from unchartable noise to a smooth line. Figure 5.3 demonstrates smoothing, with the dark line being a running mean, the average of a consistent period of time before each pixel of the line, of the noisier light line. Shading indicates the area below the graph and provides contrast to enable users to pick out more details.

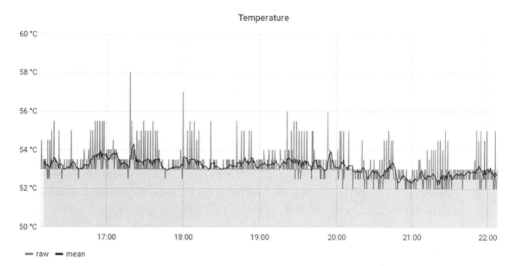

Figure 5.3   Example of using aggregation functions to smooth lines, with the dark line being a smoothed version of the light line, showing the overall trend in temperature. Pairing noisy data with smoothed data gives the viewer more context as to what is happening and the overall trends. If you've ever added a trend line in Excel, you've provided a form of smoothed line.

Beyond providing simple smoothing, each aggregation function tells you different things about your telemetry:

- The mean and median are different ways to find the middle of your telemetry in a given period.
- The 50th percentile is equivalent to the median in the same way that the 0th percentile is equivalent to the minimum and the 100th percentile is equivalent to the maximum.
- If the telemetry has a long tail—such as a response-time metric in which most values are between 0.5 and 1.5 but a tiny number of events oozes out to 30—the maximum value may not be useful, but the 95th percentile may better capture the top edge of the interesting telemetry.
- Displaying the 5th, 50th, and 95th percentiles gives you a better feel for the shape of your telemetry than a simple mean/median line.

WARNING   Beware of further aggregating aggregated data, because that technique almost always leads to lies. Wherever possible, work on raw values, because they will tell you accurate information. If the data you're working with has already been aggregated once, unless you take care to pick an appropriate function, subsequent functions turn what you see into lies. A sum function on data that has already had a sum run on it will be accurate, but running a sum on data that has been run through a mean function will be lies. If you are working with preaggregated data, a least-harm approach is to use the same aggregation function for data that has already been through an aggregation function. Summing your sums is safe, but anything else will be lies—lies that will look kind of like your data but won't be statistically valid. I've lost count of the number of charts I've had to fix because they used a `mean` function on a `sum`, and the person who asked for help wondered why expanding the chart to one month from one week didn't increase the charted numbers. Section 17.2 covers this problem in more detail.

Some presentation systems also offer additional functions that can provide predictions of the future or handle special types of data. These additional functions vary with presentation systems, but two deserve a closer look: `derivative` and `spread`.

Derivative gives you the rate of change between two points on the graph. Derivative is most useful for telemetry such as disk space, where the reported value is a high number every time it is polled or a metric that accumulates value over time. For metrics such as disk space, a graph showing how much space is left on a volume is interesting on its own, but a derivative function will allow you to produce a graph showing how fast that volume is filling. A graph displaying the rate of change will help make spikes far more visible.

Spread gives you the difference between the `minimum` and `maximum` values in a given period. Functionally, spread is the `minimum` aggregate subtracted from the `maximum` aggregate. Spread is a useful function for telemetry that normally flows within a narrow range, when you want to draw attention to events for which that narrow range doesn't hold true.

Aggregation functions aren't useful only in the Presentation stage; they're also useful during the Shipping stage as part of an aggregation policy. Section 17.2 covers building an aggregation policy in a way that will retain statistical validity when used in Presentation-stage systems.

5.1.3   Using aggregations with pdf_pages

In chapters 2–4, we built Emitting and Shipping stage components to handle metrics coming from a function with the name `pdf_pages`. The production systems use the Emitting-stage component from listing 2.3 to write to the standard output (stdout) indicating the number of pages that a function named `pdf_pages` processed. A Shipping-stage component reads this file and the metric (see section 4.1.1), and sends it to a database. Figure 4.6 demonstrates this architecture, which is reproduced here as figure 5.4.

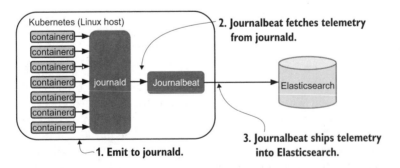

Figure 5.4   Emitting and shipping architecture producing the telemetry behind the `pdf_pages` metrics charts. Telemetry is emitted from the containerized production code into the standard out. Kubernetes sends this telemetry to journald. The Elastic.co program Journalbeat is installed and configured to ship journald telemetry directly into Elasticsearch. With our metrics in Elasticsearch, a Presentation-stage system will be used to make the next series of figures.

**Figure 5.5 Demonstrating the sum aggregation function over 60 minutes of `pdf_pages`
telemetry, revealing many peaks and valleys. The sum aggregation for a raw count yields the
total count of pages in this period. By extending the summarization period to 60 seconds,
we can smooth noisy data as well as show trends over longer time scales.**

This section shows you how a group of `pdf_pages` metrics looks when aggregated with
various functions. Figure 5.5 shows the value of all of our `pdf_pages` metrics aggregated with a simple sum.

Figure 5.5 demonstrates a noisy set of data. The number of PDF pages being handled over the graphed hour is highly variable, going from a low point of 134 pages in
one minute to a high point of 418 pages. Showing the total number of pages handled
is interesting, but if we want to know more about the range of pages handled for each
function call, we need to use a different approach. Figure 5.6 shows the same data
with the mean/average function run on it.

**Figure 5.6 Demonstrating the `mean` or average aggregation function over 60 minutes of `pdf_pages`
telemetry, revealing one version of the middle of the data. There are different versions of "middle" for
data; mean/average is merely one version. Use `mean` when you want the numerical average case.**

The mean of PDF pages tells us more about what kind of traffic our pdf_pages function—which calls our metrics function to emit its telemetry—is dealing with. Average page counts are between 4 and 5 for the most part. To explore further, let's look at what the median, or middle-value, aggregation function tells us in figure 5.7.

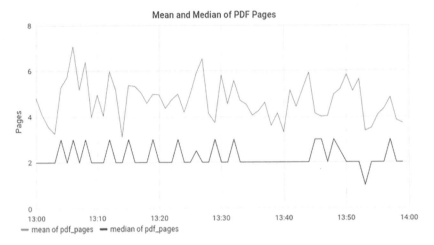

Figure 5.7   Comparing the mean and median aggregation functions over 60 minutes of pdf_pages telemetry, with median being the darker line. When the median is lower than the mean/average, you know that the data contains some high values.

Figure 5.7 shows the mean as the light upper line and the median as the darker lower line. The median line is significantly lower than the mean! The median value is mostly 2, but it sometimes pops up to 3, and there's a single 1 at 13:52. Because the median shows us the middle value, having the mean be higher tells us two big things:

- Most of the page counts are between 1 and 2.
- A large population of page counts is rather higher, drawing the mean higher with them.

To get a better feel for the shape of the pdf_pages data overall, let's use the percentiles function on the data to generate figure 5.8.

Figure 5.8 shows four percentiles of pdf_pages, where the 50th percentile line matches the line from figure 5.7 showing the median. The 95th percentile on this graph approximates the top end of the page counts handled by our function and shows that we're dealing with some high page counts. A common feature of all three graphs is a low point about 13:52. The sum graph shows a low point then, the mean showed a low value, the median was a 1 for the only time in the period, but the 95th percentile was low at that point. We can see how the higher value page counts affect the graph overall.

To finish our exploration of the pdf_pages data, let's introduce a new type of graph: the heat map. Imagine figure 5.8 without colored lines but with the axis. This

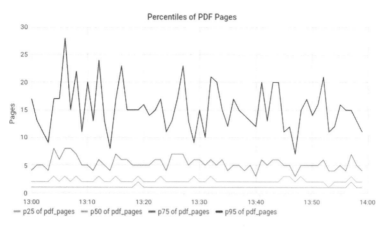

Figure 5.8 Demonstrating the 25th, 50th, 75th, and 95th `percentiles` aggregation function over 60 minutes of `pdf_pages` telemetry, revealing the rough shape of the data. If in each time slice the data is ordered, percentiles show us how that part of the ordered list moves over time. When we're charting multiple percentiles, the change in lines tells us how the shape of the data altered over the period displayed.

bare graph with only the light guidelines breaks the rectangular graph into blocks. A heat map colors each of those blocks based on the amount of telemetry in that block. Larger counts get darker colors, and smaller counts get lighter colors. A heat map based on the `pdf_pages` data would give us an even better feeling for the shape of the data. Figure 5.9 demonstrates a heat map for `pdf_pages` data.

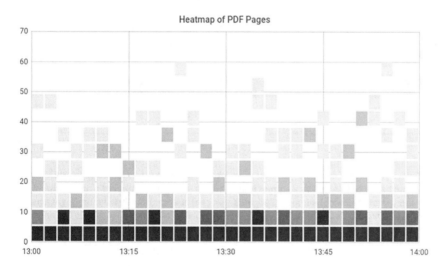

Figure 5.9 Demonstrating a heat map of 60 minutes of `pdf_pages` telemetry, showing the shape and distribution of the data. Heat maps chart the density of data in each given box, bounded by time on the X-axis and in this case count on the Y-axis. Similar to the percentiles example in figure 5.8, this example provides a detailed look at the shape of the data during the charted period.

The line of dark boxes at the bottom of figure 5.9 tells us that the large majority of metrics generated by our function fits into the smallest page counts. The fact that `median` and `mode` are different, the way they are in figure 5.7, tells us that this result is likely. The `percentiles` in figure 5.8 told us that there was a population of high page-count metrics in the hour, shown by the 95th percentile line. The heat map shows page counts higher than 50!

5.2   *Displaying telemetry in centralized logging systems*

In this section, we handle the problem of displaying telemetry in centralized logging systems. Unlike metrics telemetry, which is mostly numbers, centralized logging telemetry is mostly strings. You can definitely produce graphs based on centralized logging telemetry, which is especially useful for tracking the rates of occurrence for certain emissions, as I will show you in this section. Most interactions with centralized logging systems, however, involve digging into context about an event, which requires looking at strings.

Centralized logging is the most storage-intensive telemetry system of the systems presented in this book, and often the most expensive style to use to maintain long periods of searchable history. Because of this cost, centralized logging systems often maintain a short period of time in online searchable format—a time most frequently measured in weeks and days, not months and years. Figure 1.12, reproduced here as figure 5.10, demonstrates this problem.

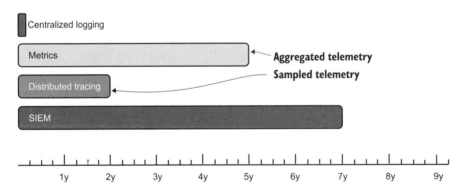

Figure 5.10   The four telemetry types and their preferred online retention periods. SIEM systems have the longest retention due to external requirements. Distributed tracing achieves its retention through the use of statistical sampling. Metrics achieves its duration through aggregations on the numbers stored inside. Centralized logging . . . well, it's just plain expensive, so it gets the smallest online retention period.

Metrics and distributed tracing achieve their long retention times through the use of aggregation and sampling, and SIEM achieves their retention times by being selective in what it stores and not being allowed to keep data offline. Whereas other styles of telemetry, such as metrics and distributed tracing, sacrifice flexibility to focus and optimize for a specific aspect of telemetry, *centralized logging is in many ways the catch-all system that everything flows to if something better isn't available.*

In spite of storing so much telemetry, it is incredibly unlikely that each individual item of telemetry will ever be looked at directly. If such telemetry is referenced, it is most often accessed indirectly in aggregate as part of a trend line of similar events. In rare cases, one datum among billions contains the key to an investigation, so you'll be glad you saved it. Most telemetry that lands in a centralized logging system is sent there in case it might be needed later. *Just in case* makes centralized logging incredibly powerful, but also resource-hungry.

Being primarily string-based, display systems for centralized logging require assistance from three major sources:

- Additional markup and enrichment in the Emitting and Shipping stages (see chapter 6)
- Search optimizations found in the databases used for centralized logging (see appendix A)
- Regular-expression engines in the Presentation-stage system

Listing 4.5 in section 4.2.2 is a basic example of marking up and parsing as part of the Shipping stage, in that example enriching and parsing Syslog-formatted telemetry to produce additional fields. You can use the same technique for telemetry that follows other formats. Chapter 6 goes into detail about that sort of enrichment. In this section, we assume that those fields are already present. I cover creating those fields in chapter 6. The next two subsections help you identify a good presentation system for centralized logging:

- Section 5.2.1 explains features you want to see in the display system for centralized logging.
- Section 5.2.2 provides a walk-through of a full-featured display system.

5.2.1 Selecting needed features in a display system for centralized logging

Display systems for centralized logging systems have a common set of features that have emerged from both the necessity of using any centralized logging system and from how many organizations use centralized logging as a catch-all system for telemetry of all kinds.

To do metrics, display systems need to create visualizations. To do distributed tracing work, display systems must be able to build data tables based on varied and possibly unique search criteria. Centralized logging display systems can be minimally good enough for those cases, but specialized systems dedicated to metrics and distributed-tracing use cases will be far more functional. Many technical organizations that want to diversify their telemetry pipelines will look to their existing centralized logging systems to fill those roles initially.

Selecting a centralized logging display system to fill all the needs of centralized logging means picking a display system that supports diverse needs. Software engineering teams need features to help them drill down to failing code and isolate fault paths. Support teams need to pick specific failures to draw engineering attention to them. Operations teams look for infrastructure events that will require their attention. Each of these different use patterns means that a good display system for centralized logging must have these features:

- *Ability to search by field contents*—All centralized logging systems I've interacted with have the concept of fields and allow users to build queries by using those fields. Use of field (searching for `priority:"high"` versus `"high"`) content will greatly speed the performance of searches.

- *Ability to support complex search logic*—Sometimes, all you need is a single string. At other times, getting what you need requires a complex "If this, then that, except for these other things, but do include this one thing" kind of statement.

- *Ability to customize field display*—Events in centralized logging systems may include tens or even hundreds of fields, displaying each one in a table that often shows information the searcher doesn't care about. The ability to customize a result table to show specific fields allows the searcher to scan the table for interesting events.

- *Ability to save searches and table layouts for later*—If you wanted to know something enough to build a search and table layout, chances are good that you might need it again. The ability to save the layout for later will save you work in the future.

- *Ability to share saved searches/layouts between users*—Sharing searches among users of the telemetry system allows sharing analysis tools to improve the organization's ability to respond to problems instead of relying on a few skilled searchers to do the work.

- *Ability to share URLs of searches and have the same search and layout come up*—Related to sharing saved searches, sharing improvised or ad hoc searches is critical during problem response. If the URL of the telemetry display system doesn't re-create the search, other responders will have to do more work to see the interesting results. A good display system will ease this effort.

- *Require a login to use*—Centralized logging systems often contain company-sensitive information and sometimes contain regulated information such as personally identifiable information (PII). The absolute minimum requirement is to require authentication and authorization before using the display system. Chapter 15 covers this security topic in detail.

5.2.2 Demonstrating centralized logging display

In this section, we take a look at a Presentation-stage system that meets all the criteria listed in section 5.2.1 for the features of a centralized logging display system. Kibana (version 7 is shown here), published by Elastic.co as part of its Elasticstack series of tools, provides these features. The example data used here is drawn from section 2.2, involving a Cisco ASA firewall's emissions. This example telemetry line is emitted from the firewall:

```
Feb 19 02:26:26 asa1.net.prod.internal %ASA1: Teardown of UDP connection
162121 for outside:1.1.0.0/53 to dmz1:192.0.2.19/59232 duration 0:00:00
bytes 136
```

Figure 3.8, reproduced here as figure 5.11, demonstrates the Shipping stage that delivered events from the Cisco firewall into storage. This section shows how that Cisco firewall telemetry might be displayed in Kibana, a Presentation-stage system.

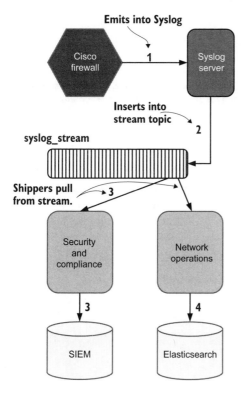

Figure 5.11 Shipping pipeline sending firewall data to Syslog for eventual display in a Presentation-stage system drawing from Elasticsearch, from which data is displayed. This example demonstrates multitenancy, because two separate teams consume the same telemetry for their own needs. The security team uses it to populate a SIEM; the network operations team uses it for a centralized logging system stored in Elasticsearch.

Figure 5.12 demonstrates searching firewall data in Kibana and shows a range of events that happened on March 22, 2025. All these events are various DNS lookups to a pair of DNS servers managed by CloudFlare, 1.1.0.0 and 1.1.1.1. Let's take a closer look at how this dashboard was created and what else it tells us.

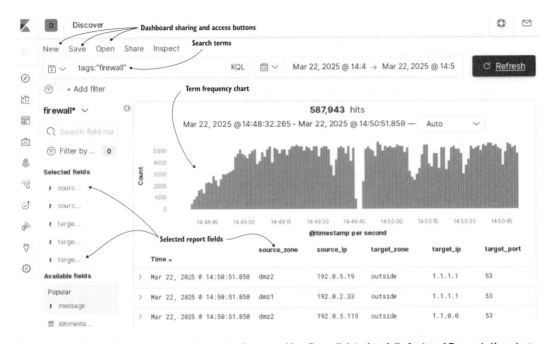

Figure 5.12   Kibana 7 discovery page demonstrating searching firewall data in a fully featured Presentation-stage system for centralized logging. We can select which fields to include in the report, as well as search telemetry, select the time scale to search within, and choose buttons for saving and opening dashboards. All these features are listed in section 5.2.1 as being desirable.

Figure 5.13 points out the search being used here. This example uses a field called `tags` created as part of the Shipping stage. Our Shipping-stage systems add a value of `firewall` to the `tags` field for telemetry coming from the Cisco ASA firewalls. Adding this field and value permits us to look at all our firewall traffic by using a single search in our Presentation-stage system. Let's look at what kind of data we get.

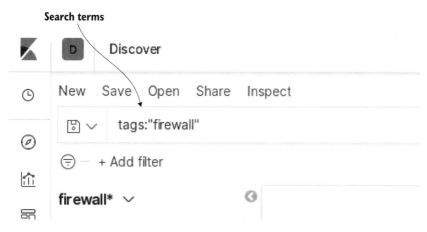

Figure 5.13 Searching Kibana, using fields to discover firewall-specific telemetry. Kibana uses Lucene syntax for searching, demonstrated here. Far more complex queries can be produced. The Add Filter button provides an additional method of building search queries.

Figure 5.14 gives us an example of the kinds of fields that our Shipping stage puts in the events. The initial log line ingested from the Cisco side is stored in the message field, which is truncated for space in figure 5.12. Parsing the message field (enrichment) gives us several new fields:

- conn_bytes—The number of bytes transacted in this connection
- conn_duration—How many hours, minutes, and seconds this connection took
- firewall_action—The Cisco log line extracted from the wrapping format
- firewall_conn—A number for this connection
- firewall_proto—The protocol used for the connection (UDP in this case)
- host—The host generating the event
- source_ip—The IP address of the internal resource opening the connection
- source_port—The IP port on the source_ip side of the connection
- source_zone—The firewall zone the internal asset belonged to
- target_ip—The IP address the internal resource opened a connection to
- target_port—The IP port the internal resource connected to
- target_zone—The firewall zone the source_ip belongs in

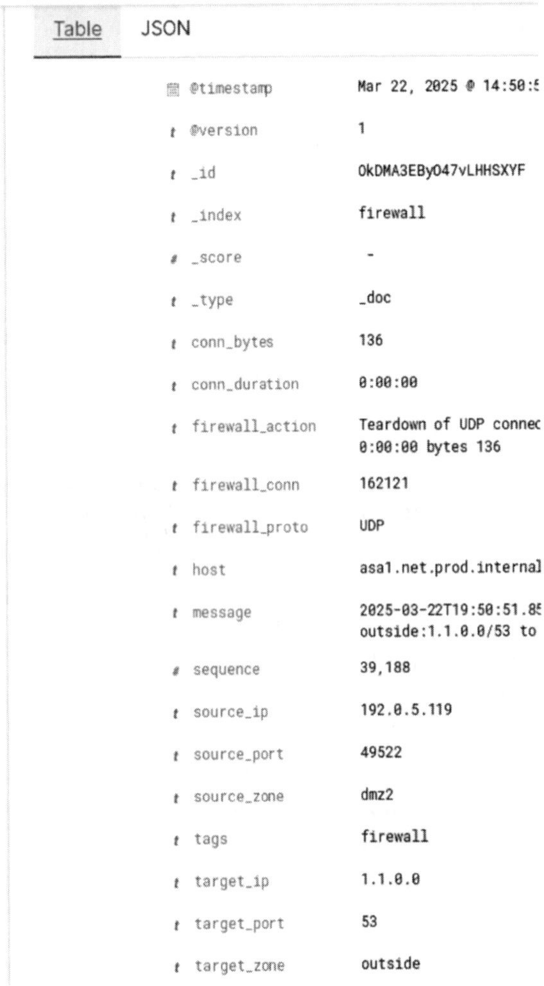

Table	JSON

🗓	@timestamp	Mar 22, 2025 @ 14:50:5
t	@version	1
t	_id	OkDMA3EByO47vLHHSXYF
t	_index	firewall
#	_score	-
t	_type	_doc
t	conn_bytes	136
t	conn_duration	0:00:00
t	firewall_action	Teardown of UDP connec 0:00:00 bytes 136
t	firewall_conn	162121
t	firewall_proto	UDP
t	host	asa1.net.prod.internal
t	message	2025-03-22T19:50:51.85 outside:1.1.0.0/53 to
#	sequence	39,188
t	source_ip	192.0.5.119
t	source_port	49522
t	source_zone	dmz2
t	tags	firewall
t	target_ip	1.1.0.0
t	target_port	53
t	target_zone	outside

Figure 5.14   Returned fields for a firewall event demonstrating Shipping-stage enrichment, shown when you expand a table line in Kibana. The fields here were generated by the Shipping stage, which allows our Presentation stage to use any of these fields in searches. tags: firewall is highlighted because it is the current search term.

The value of the tags field is highlighted because our search field references it. Kibana provides highlights as a visual cue for the information that was requested from the search itself. If we want a specific field to be visible in the overall report—as figure 5.12 shows with the source_name, source_ip, target_zone, target_ip, and target_port fields—we need to add them from the field sidebar, as shown in figure 5.15.

Next, we refine our search terms to locate unusual DNS activity. Because we have a field for target_ip, we can exclude known-good IPs. As we saw in figure 5.12, most of our traffic was to two different IP addresses. Figure 5.16 demonstrates excluding those two addresses to get at the interesting events.

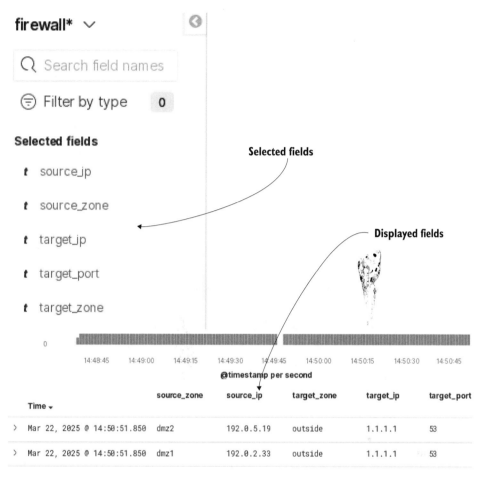

Figure 5.15 Selecting fields in the Kibana sidebar makes them columns in the results panel. Columns can also be moved right to left and clicked to sort. In this view, the current sort is by Time, but any field shown can be used as a sort.

Figure 5.16 Kibana search excluding two well-known IPs to narrow the search to interesting results. This example demonstrates using filters to extend an existing search—in this case, excluding two IP addresses. With the vast majority of events removed, we are left with the ones that deserve our attention.

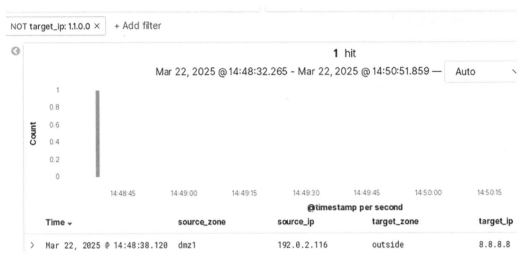

Figure 5.17   Demonstrating the results from the search in figure 5.16: a single event. Drilling down to a lone interesting event is a core feature of Presentation-stage systems for centralized logging.

With the exclusions in place, figure 5.17 shows a single event that is unusual! Someone hit the Google-managed DNS servers instead of our usual ones. This event might deserve investigation, so we save this chart for later.

To save this chart for use by our co-workers, we click the highlighted Save button in figure 5.12. Clicking Save brings up a dialog box that allows us to name the chart, as shown in figure 5.18.

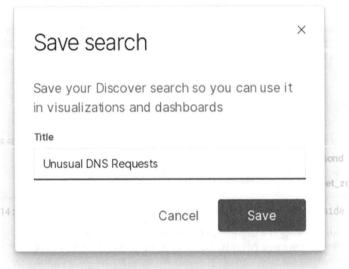

Figure 5.18   The Kibana Save dialog, allowing this chart to be used by co-workers. The ability to save and open dashboards and charts is a key feature of Presentation-stage systems that support centralized logging.

After this dashboard is saved, a co-worker can click the Open button (figure 5.12), bringing up another dialog that allows them to search for the dashboard we created. When many searches have been saved, Kibana allows users to search the list of saved searches. After you find what you are looking for, click the item, and the saved search will load, including the search terms, the two exclusions, and all the selected fields to display.

Other solutions offer features similar to those of Kibana. The SaaS systems Splunk and Sumo Logic both have dashboards similar to Kibana's that interact with the Shipping-stage storage systems they maintain. When you're looking at Presentation-stage systems to display your centralized logging data, remember the feature list in section 5.2.1.

An emerging trend: Making the Presentation stage do most of the enrichment work

Grafana Labs' Loki centralized logging solution is new (2018), and doesn't need lots of preprocessing the way Kibana does. Loki is a far more cloud-native solution, relying on cloud provider data stores such as S3 and databases such as DynamoDB. Kibana assumes that the data it is searching has already been fully enriched—all the fields we just looked at. Loki, on the other hand, does enrichment at query time. So long as the telemetry being ingested is already in an easy-to-parse format like JSON, Loki will deserialize and query in real time.

This trend is part of a long-term trend in telemetry as computing has improved. When Kibana emerged in the early 2010s, storage was still mostly on magnetic disk and therefore slow, so it benefited from ingestion-time preprocessing to speed query-time access. Ten years later, that calculus has changed: now it's economical to do minimal preprocessing and rely on query-time processing.

Also, relying on cloud providers for storage and trusting in query-time processing greatly reduce the costs of keeping telemetry data online and searchable. In systems such as Loki, keeping a year of telemetry online is much cheaper than in the older style of telemetry system. It will be fascinating to see how this situation evolves over the 2020s!

5.3 *Displaying telemetry in security systems*

In this section, we go over displaying telemetry in the telemetry systems used by security teams. Security teams will use centralized logging, as discussed in section 5.2, but the telemetry system unique to security teams is Security Information Event Management (SIEM). SIEM systems are designed for the use case of security teams investigating incidents and verifying compliance with external regulation. The telemetry that SIEM systems contain is often mandated (directly or indirectly) by regulations, which include the General Data Protection Regulation (GDPR) and Health Insurance Portability Accountability Act (HIPAA) for personal privacy and personal health information. Also, compliance frameworks such as Sarbanes-Oxley (SOX) and Service

Organizational Controls 2 (SOC 2) set minimum standards for organizations' overall technical practices.

SIEM systems share many features of the centralized logging systems discussed in section 5.2 but differ from them in key ways, as shown in table 5.1.

Table 5.1   **Differences between centralized logging and SIEM systems**

	Centralized logging	**SIEM**
What is the main data type?	Strings (also numbers, but mostly strings)	Strings (numbers show up a lot, but strings are the main type)
Who are the main users?	Everyone	Security teams and external auditors
What is the mission?	Helps people isolate problems and learn about the production systems	Helps security-incident responders trace actions taken within the overall system and prove to external auditors that such capabilities exist
Who decides what events get added?	Anyone who writes a logging statement in a production system that is hooked up to the centralized logging system	Regulation and compliance frameworks provide minimum event coverage; Security and compliance teams drive additional events.
How long is telemetry online and searchable?	Days to weeks, driven mostly by the cost of keeping that much data online	Years, as required by regulation and compliance frameworks

SIEM systems and centralized logging systems work primarily in strings, at least at the emitting end of the pipeline. Both systems potentially handle large quantities of telemetry compared with metrics and distributed tracing systems. Centralized logging handles large quantities of telemetry because of its role as a catch-all telemetry system; SIEM systems handle large quantities because tracing what happened in an incident requires extensive telemetry. You definitely can build a rudimentary SIEM out of your existing centralized logging system, but a system built for the role will serve your needs better.

Although most of the telemetry sent into a centralized logging system is emitted just in case someone needs something, SIEM systems ingest data that is specifically asked for to support certain workflows that the security team needs to perform. Some of those common workflows are

- Proving to auditors that the actions of users with elevated privileges are tracked
- Tracking authentication and account lockout events in the production systems
- Assessing compliance with data-retention policies
- Assessing compliance with user activation and deactivation policies
- Identifying changes not performed with an appropriate change request
- Tracking an intruder's path through the production systems
- Identifying production data that was accessed by people without authorization

Telemetry systems sold as SIEM systems have a feature that many centralized logging systems don't have: a robust way to correlate events from different parts of the production system. SIEM systems should be able to correlate a login event with a user's process-execution history, for example. Correlation engines need to handle a wide variety of inputs, which creates a large opportunity to make money providing that value, meaning that few open source SIEM systems do this work. In many ways, SIEM systems provide the Pillars of Observability to security teams, letting them trace, track, and monitor users of the technical system.

Because SIEM systems share the centralized logging system problem of having to maintain potentially large stores of data, SIEM system operators have to weigh how long telemetry can remain online and searchable against the cost of providing that online search capability. The nature of security team work incentivizes longer online periods than centralized logging, so security teams spend correspondingly more time curating what telemetry is sent into the SIEM system.

Displaying telemetry in SIEM systems has similar requirements to centralized logging systems like the one described in section 5.2. The list of features needed for centralized logging systems in section 5.2.1 also applies to SIEM systems, but SIEM systems add several more items:

- *Ability to define alerts*—Whereas centralized logging systems are about asking questions you may not have thought to ask before, SIEM systems function as part of a monitoring system. Therefore, the ability to create alerts to notify humans of problems is a critical feature, whereas in centralized logging systems, it is merely optional.
- *Ability to define alert priorities*—Automatically triaging alarms by priority levels allows responding humans to defer lower-priority alarms safely, leading to better sleep and greater workplace enjoyment.

In addition to SIEM systems, security teams work with vulnerabilities in the production system. *Vulnerability management programs*, called for by most regulatory and compliance frameworks, are policies and procedures in place to handle bugs in first- and third-party software. The primary source of vulnerability notifications is the Common Vulnerabilities and Exposures (CVE) list operated by Mitre (https://cve.mitre.org), but these notifications also come from vendors such as Microsoft, Adobe, and VMware.

Part of a vulnerability management program is software that analyzes production systems for CVEs, known as *vulnerability scanning*. After a vulnerability list is generated, each vulnerability finding needs to be addressed, typically by operations and DevOps teams for operating system and hardware vulnerabilities, but an increasing number of software engineering teams are getting this work as part of software module maintenance. Managing vulnerabilities requires specialized tools, and these presentation systems have common features:

- *Ability to track vulnerabilities*—These vulnerabilities mostly come from the CVE list but may include vendor-specific announcements such as those from Adobe and Microsoft. A vulnerability management program is a common requirement for regulatory and compliance frameworks, so vulnerability management systems must support that role.
- *Ability to track accepted risks and false positives*—Related to tracking vulnerabilities, a vulnerability management system must track vulnerabilities (risks) that have been accepted by the organization, as well as vulnerabilities that show up as being applicable but are considered to be false-positive detections. This tracking allows for an ongoing vulnerability management program.

Software modules in vulnerability management programs

Each software development platform has some way of importing externally developed modules or libraries:

- Eggs for Python
- Gems for Ruby
- NuGets for .NET
- NPMs for NodeJS
- Modules for Perl, Go, and Java
- Pecls for PHP
- Packages for Elixir

Although most vulnerability-scanning software focuses on the software packages used in the operating system, newer scanners can scan software module lists to identify which modules have open CVEs on them. Whereas fixing and remediating vulnerabilities used to be entirely the domain of operations teams, now software engineering teams often have to force updates to modules they otherwise would prefer to keep set at a specific version.

As more software is deployed in containerized format, which greatly reduces the impact of operating-system-level packages, vulnerability management programs by necessity focus on the software module ecosystem. Ideally, your continuous integration environment includes a scanner for new vulnerabilities in software modules and will fail a build until those vulnerabilities are addressed. We are all in this together!

A SIEM and a vulnerability management programs are rarely found in the same software. An example of a suite of products that addresses both needs is Nessus Cloud used in combination with Splunk. Nessus Cloud provides vulnerability management features and has some ability to set alarms, whereas Splunk provides the centralized logging and alarming features needed as part of a SIEM. Together, both products provide base telemetry needs for security teams. Other combinations exist, such as AWS Inspector for vulnerability management and Sumo Logic for SIEM and centralized logging functions. As time moves forward, other options will emerge; look for them.

5.4   *Displaying telemetry distributed tracing systems*

Distributed tracing provides a more formalized framework for emitting telemetry from software with the intent of overcoming some of the limitations of centralized logging. One of the chief limitations of centralized logging is its built-in assumption that telemetry events will be correlated; in distributed tracing systems, events are linked in an easy-to-discover way. For centralized logging systems, that work is left as a tedious manual exercise by the person who asked questions. Distributed tracing systems overcome this limitation by automatically creating links between production code events in the Shipping and Presentation stages, allowing the Presentation-stage systems to display linked events easily and cheaply.

Let's look at someone investigating why a Microsoft Office .docx file failed to convert to PDF after being uploaded by a user of the system. Our person is using a centralized logging system for troubleshooting. The steps in their research look like this:

1. Searches for and finds the process exception where the `docx_to_pdf` process failed.
2. Uses the file identifier passed to the `docx_to_pdf` process to locate what code sent the job to the `docx_to_pdf` process that failed, and finds an `upload_document` process that sent the job.
3. Searches logging for the `upload_document` process for something interesting, finds that it timed out waiting for the file conversion, and sent the same file identifier to a `file_type` process.
4. Searches for `file_type` processes that picked up a job with that queue identifier, and finds one.
5. Searches for logging in that `file_type` process for anything interesting, discovering an exception and an identified type of .docx.
6. Reads the code for `file_type` and discovers that it has a bug: it shows a file's type as .docx for anything it can't identify.

Although the search may be a thrilling ride of revealing interesting details over the course of half an hour, your eyes likely glazed over the list and skipped to the end. The reality is that someone doing this research with only centralized logging needs to understand enough about the schema of their telemetry systems to know how to phrase the right queries. For someone who is unfamiliar with what sort of telemetry is available in the centralized logging system, moving from step 1 to step 2 might require waiting several hours for the right person to answer a question about how to find step 2.

Distributed tracing systems simplify this process by doing all the linking before anyone looks at it. The same person doing the same research in a distributed tracing system would have fewer steps:

1. Opens the user's stream of traces and looks for traces with exceptions, finding one trace with five separate exceptions in it, four from `docx_to_pdf`.
2. Opens the trace with the exceptions, giving us figure 5.19, showing exceptions in both `file_type` and four different `docx_to_pdf` executions. Also, `upload_document` fails due to exhausting retries in file-conversion.

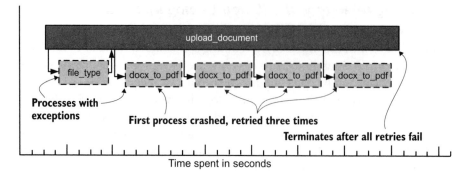

Figure 5.19 A trace showing exceptions (dashed boxes) in both `file_type` and `docx_to_pdf`, with three retries of `docs_to_pdf` also failing. The `upload_document` process detected the failure in the first `docs_to_pdf` process and retried the process three times before giving up. This pattern tells us that the crash in `docx_to_pdf` is likely not related to random chance but to the specific document being converted.

3 The exception in `file_type` is interesting, because it threw an exception and still returned a file type.

4 Reads the code for `file_type` and discovers that it has a bug: it shows a file's type as .docx for anything it can't identify.

With a distributed tracing system in place, the person doing the searching needs much less awareness of what telemetry looks like to get to the problem area—a misbehaving `file_type`—quickly. For comparison's sake, figure 5.20 shows a normal, unexceptional execution of this workflow.

Figure 5.20 is rather different from figure 5.19, with `docx_to_pdf` taking longer to run, itself calling a new process named `pdf_pages` (a process that creates the graphs shown in section 5.1.3), which further calls `pdf_to_png` processes to build per-page images of the PDF created by `docx_to_pdf`. In spite of all this extra activity, `upload_document` takes less time to run because it isn't having to handle a retry cascade.

Generating a chart like this one requires each process involved in the chain of execution to track and pass correlation identifiers whenever it accepts an API call, pops a job off a queue, pushes a job onto a queue, or makes an API call. A *correlation identifier* is a string or number that uniquely identifies that specific execution or workflow. Shipping-stage components for a distributed tracing system link events with the same correlation identifiers, allowing the Presentation-stage system to easily produce the charts shown in figures 5.19 and 5.20. Correlation identifiers can be created explicitly or abstracted as part of a tracing library used by the production code. The OpenTelemetry project is building vendor-agnostic libraries for this kind of work. These tracing libraries function as the Emitting-stage components of the telemetry pipeline, similar to the various metrics.py functions we wrote in chapters 2–4.

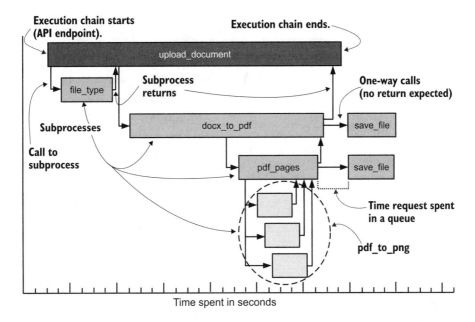

Figure 5.20   A normal (no exceptions) example of a distributed trace showing conversion of a .docx file that resulted in three pages. This example demonstrates the call stack in the form of services, not functions or classes, for this particular execution. Two functions, `docx_to_pdf` and `pdf_pages`, make second calls to a `save_file` function in addition to returning results to their parent service. A chart formatted like this one provides extensive context for someone who's looking to troubleshoot problems, and context speeds resolution.

When you select a specific process in figure 5.20, most Presentation systems for tracing provides a window showing specific telemetry for the given process. Figure 5.21 shows an example of the sort of telemetry that can be displayed.

All the correlation identifiers in figure 5.21 make it possible for software engineering teams to ask a variety of questions:

- *How do documents converted from .docx differ in convert times from native PDFs for generating page images?* Compare the `avg_convert_wait_time` metrics between events with `source_doc_type` of .docx and .pdf.
- *What percentage of page conversions takes longer than 1,000 ms for account 12497714?* Count the total `pdf_page` executions for `account_id` 12497714; then count executions for `account_id` 12497714 with `avg_convert_wait_time` longer than 1,000 ms.
- *What processes had errors for account 12497714 during a specific login session?* Get processes for `account_id` 12497714 and `session_id` sassqnrfoploqje with `errors` greater than zero.

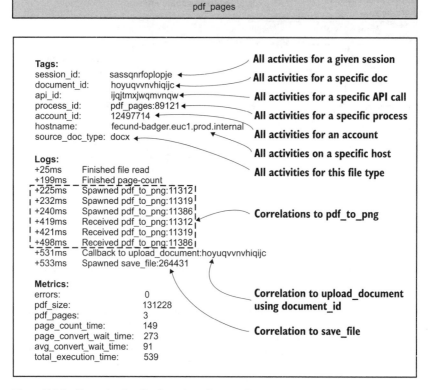

Figure 5.21   Example of a distributed tracing detail page, showing the many correlation identifiers used to create the chart in figure 5.20 and process-specific telemetry. A wide variety of correlation identifiers is being used here, each permitting a separate correlation to be investigated.

Tracing and user-supplied data

The name of the file that the user uploaded never shows up in any of the fields for figure 5.20. I did this intentionally. Even though the filename is a value being passed to and from the processes in the execution chain, there is too much risk in logging it because privacy regulations are increasingly strict about PII and health information. Logging user-supplied data can expose you to legal risk. Although the product may say *Do not submit private information in these fields* in bold letters on every field title, there will be one user who submits a scan of their Social Security card and uses their Social Security number as the filename. It's better to not log user-supplied fields. If you don't have a choice in whether to log user-supplied data, chapters 15 and 16 address safely handling data of this kind and cleaning up data spills.

The process execution in figure 5.20 is an example of what distributed tracing provides to a software engineering team. The questions that figure 5.21 answers are examples of what modern SaaS tracing systems and the Jaeger open source tracing system can provide a software engineering team. When used in combination with logs and metrics, traces greatly refine the power of collected telemetry.

Section 5.1 (metrics systems) and section 5.2 (centralized logging systems) discussed the cost trade-off between being able to search for long periods of time and economics of storage:

- Metrics systems store telemetry cheaply but lack much detail, whereas centralized logging systems are stuffed full of detail but are expensive to store.
- Distributed tracing systems share some of the problems of centralized logging in that they're also stuffed full of detail and suffer the same storage-cost problem as centralized logging systems.
- The use of correlation identifiers allows distributed tracing systems to benefit from statistical sampling to reduce costs.

Chapter 16 covers sampling in more detail, but sampling is storing a small but representative group of events from which you can draw valid conclusions. In its broadest form, distributed tracing systems work best when execution chains are sampled.

5.5 *Displaying telemetry in large organizations*

Large organizations have many discrete teams within each functional group, such as nine software engineering teams working on their own pieces of a product. When telemetry handling is a large enough problem to have dedicated teams for the telemetry pipeline, the definition of *affordable* changes in key ways. To offload the effort of building a telemetry pipeline, small organizations will by necessity use off-the-shelf or SaaS systems by default. When organizations become larger, the economics begins to shift in favor of bespoke, or in-house, solutions.

Developing something in-house starts looking like a good idea when

- The cost of a key SaaS or purchased off-the-shelf presentation system becomes large enough to force the question.
- The organization's telemetry needs shift in ways that further adaptation of the existing off-the-shelf solutions raises questions about their fitness.
- Dissatisfaction with telemetry presentation forces an organizational reassessment of telemetry handling.

Looking like a good idea and being a good idea are different things, so here is some advice on telling the difference. In most cases, the prerequisite for being a good idea is a pool of software engineers available to develop the product and DevOps/operations/SRE people able to support the product. Without that dedicated pool, creating *and maintaining* a new system from scratch are going to decrease overall satisfaction with telemetry presentation systems.

As mentioned in the introduction to this chapter, the presentation systems are most people's only interaction with the telemetry pipeline. Being the only interaction point makes presentation systems seem to be the only component that matters. When you're deciding to make your own presentation systems, consider what improved user experience a new bespoke presentation system will provide over the current ones. Degrading user experience with a new bespoke system will seem like a step down for people who were not feeling the pain and pushing for the change in the first place, which will lead to organizational strife.

If cost is a driving factor in the push for a bespoke system, consider the main role of telemetry systems: decision support for management and engineering. Moving to a bespoke system may save direct costs, but a poorly-built presentation system will reduce the ability of the technical organization to make decisions. The cost impacts of poor decisions are hard to quantify but are still present and need to be accounted for in the decision.

Summary

- The Presentation stage in a telemetry pipeline is the stage humans use to interact with telemetry.
- The Presentation stage's role is to consume the storage prepared by the Shipping stage and translate it for humans.
- For many people in a technical organization, the Presentation-stage systems are the only places they will interact with the telemetry pipeline, so a wider selection of users will interact with Presentation-stage systems than those in any other stage.
- Metrics systems are designed to take numbers, which are far more efficient to store than strings, and store them for long periods.
- The graph or chart is a telemetry format that humans desire. Be thoughtful about what you display, and make it possible for people to build their own charts and graphs.
- If people aren't allowed to build their own graphs or charts, you may find them building their own with whatever is available (such as Excel).
- Aggregation functions summarize data over a given period, allowing graphs to be built that smooth the source data or reveal patterns in the raw data.
- When graphing telemetry that has already been run through an aggregation function, perhaps in the Shipping stage, running a second aggregation function over the telemetry will give you distorted results (also known as *lies*). Using the same aggregation function a second time (mean your means, min your mins) will give you a sense of the shape of data, but don't think that you're getting the true shape; for that result, you need to work on the raw values.
- Metrics display systems need certain features, listed in section 5.1.1, to fully serve your needs.

- Centralized logging systems are designed around string handling, which makes them the most expensive systems for keeping telemetry online and searchable for long timeframes.
- Centralized logging systems are often the catch-all system that everything flows to if something better isn't available.
- Telemetry sent to centralized logging systems usually is sent there in case it is ever needed, which makes centralized logging systems incredibly powerful tools (though resource-hungry).
- Centralized logging display systems need certain features, listed in section 5.2.1, to fully serve the needs of users.
- Security teams use SIEM systems, which function similarly to centralized logging systems.
- Centralized logging systems focus on just-in-case information, whereas SIEM systems focus on data explicitly needed by teams, enabling the longer retention periods required by regulatory and compliance frameworks.
- Security teams also need telemetry systems to support a vulnerability management program, called for by most regulatory and compliance frameworks.
- Distributed tracing tools operate on correlation identifiers, allowing presentation systems to display execution chains spanning many systems.
- Logging user-supplied data of any kind puts you at risk of failing to comply with regulatory frameworks surrounding private information.
- When reaching a tipping point between using adapted or off-the-shelf presentation systems and building your own, ensure that the new system's user experience is at least close to the old one. If you don't, the decision to change will be seen as a step backward by many people.

Marking up and enriching telemetry

This chapter covers

- The difference between markup and enrichment
- Where markup and enrichment happen
- How each telemetry style handles markup and enrichment

Much of the power of a telemetry pipeline derives from the transformation of telemetry between when the Emitting stage receives it from the production systems and when telemetry is displayed to a human by the Presentation stage. Each of the three stages of the telemetry pipeline—Emitting (chapter 2), Shipping (chapters 3 and 4), and Presentation (chapter 5)—has the opportunity to enhance telemetry. The two biggest forms of added value are the right side of figure 6.1:

- *Marking up* telemetry by adding context regarding where it originated, providing clues to people asking questions about where and when certain events happened. This context can include execution details such as the browser session, server identifier, and software version that produced a piece of telemetry, as well as business details such as payment level, user type, and team identifier.

- *Enriching* telemetry by transforming the format to improve the ability of the Presentation stage to answer questions and providing correlations between events, such as taking a phrase like *processed 2 pages* and parsing it to produce a database field named pages with a value of 2.

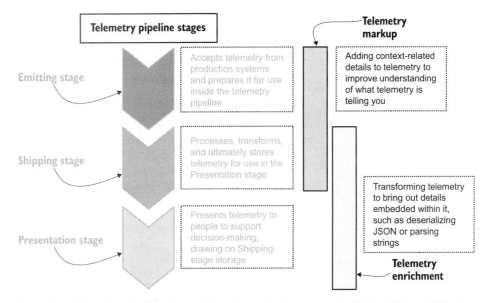

Figure 6.1 Telemetry pipeline stages. Telemetry markup happens during the Emitting and Shipping stages, whereas telemetry enrichment happens during the Shipping and Presentation stages. Markup and enrichment happen in all pipeline stages, which is the focus of this chapter.

We saw a great example of enrichment in chapter 5 while talking about Presentation-stage systems for centralized logging. Figure 5.14 gave us a long list of fields that the telemetry pipeline was able to extract from this emission from a Cisco firewall:

```
Mar 22 19:50:51 asa1.net.prod.internal %ASA1: Teardown of UDP connection
➥ 162121 for outside:1.1.0.0/53 to dmz2:192.0.5.119/49522 duration 0:00:00
➥ bytes 136
```

Figure 6.2 shows the wide array of details that our telemetry pipeline was able to extract from this one log line.

After this thorough enrichment, the Cisco-generated log line gives us an event with lots of detail—and, more important, lots of searchable and indexed detail that will make it far easier to perform research involving firewall data. This chapter is about the additional value that our telemetry pipeline produces:

- Section 6.1 dives into the sort of markup applied by the Emitting stage.
- Section 6.2 describes the markup and enrichment techniques of the Shipping stage.
- Section 6.3 covers the enrichment provided by the Presentation stage.
- Section 6.4 covers each of the four telemetry styles and describes in brief how each style prefers markup and enrichment to happen.

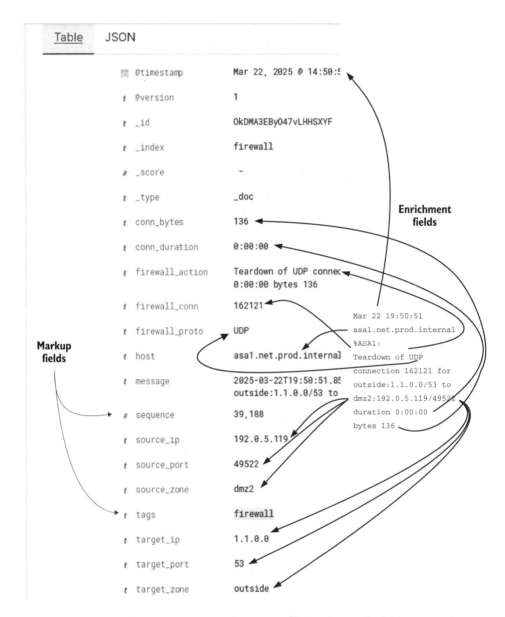

Figure 6.2 After running through the whole telemetry pipeline, the Cisco ASA log line (on the right, in the middle of all the arrows) turns into all the fields displayed here. Arrows point from source text to the enriched fields displayed on the left. To the left of the list of fields are arrows pointing to two fields that are markup—context details created by telemetry pipeline components. This figure is a typical example of enrichment of telemetry coming from hardware systems.

6.1   *Markup in the Emitting stage*

In this section, we cover the sorts of markup and enrichment that can be done in the first stage of the telemetry pipeline: the Emitting stage. The Emitting stage is where telemetry generated by a production system enters the telemetry pipeline, which it can do from any number of sources. Telemetry generated by software is among the most diverse telemetry, whereas telemetry emitted by hardware systems is the most standardized (almost always using Syslog, though some hardware systems prefer SNMP). Figure 6.3 zooms figure 6.1 into the focus of this section.

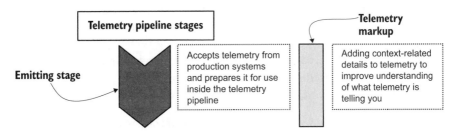

Figure 6.3   The Emitting stage and telemetry markup. The Emitting stage is the best place to apply markup because it is closest to the production systems and their context.

The Emitting stage is the best place for you to apply *markup*—clues to the context of the emitted event—because the emitter has the most available context surrounding what is being emitted. The absolute best place to apply markup is *inside the production system itself,* such as the emitter and emitter/shipper functions we looked at in sections 2.1, 3.1, and 4.1. When you are adding context for software systems, useful context items can include the class, method, and function call the code was in when the telemetry was emitted, as well as useful or interesting parameters (so long as they're not privacy- or health-related). For hardware systems, useful context is likely applied by the Syslog server that receives the telemetry, which is more a function of the Shipping stage (covered in detail in section 6.2). For SaaS platforms, emissions format and telemetry are likely set by the platform, and you have to adapt; again, the Shipping stage is likely your most useful injection point for markup and enrichment. This section covers mostly software systems and marking up their emissions.

In section 3.1.2, we looked at a Python module implementing a metrics logger that ships into a Redis-based list structure (listing 3.2). The code in that section produces entries in the list that look like this JSON structure:

```
{
  "metric_name": "pdf_pages",
  "metric_value": 3
}
```

This JSON is inserted into a Redis list (a form of queue) named `counters`. The JSON and the list name gives us three points of telemetry produced by listing 3.2:

- The list name (counters)
- The name of the metric (pdf_pages)
- The value of the metric (3)

Three items make for a minimal list of telemetry; the only context regarding where the code execution happened is encoded in the name of the metric. At the Presentation stage, someone investigating execution couldn't drill down to the code running on the specific host that generated the example JSON. To drill down to the host running the code, we need to add hostname (at minimum) to the telemetry emitted by our metrics logger. If we want to drill even deeper, we can add the process identifier (pid) to tell the person asking questions which process on which host emitted our metric. If the code has that information, it would be nice to know what version or release of our software emitted the metric (version_id). Listing 6.1 rewrites listing 3.2 to add the three new pieces of context-related telemetry and consumes a program-specific data structure called metadata that contains context about the specific user interaction.

> **NOTE** This listing needs the redis module installed before it will execute. Create a file named version.py in your directory, and define __version__ in it.

Listing 6.1 metrics.py: Emitting to `redis`, with context-related telemetry

```
import redis
import json
import socket                         Imports modules needed to
import os                             fetch context-related telemetry
from version import __version__

redis_client = redis.Redis( host='log-queue.prod.internal')

def __context_telemetry(metadata):        Private method to generate
  context = {                              context-related telemetry
    "hostname" : socket.gethostname(),
    "pid" : os.getpid(),
    "version_id" : __version__,
    "payment_plan" : metadata['payment_plan']
  }
  return context

def counter(msg, metadata, count=1):
  """Emits a metric intended to be counted or summarized.

  Example: counter("pages", metadata, "15")
  """
  base_metric = {
    "metric_name" : msg,                    Fetches context-related telemetry
    "metric_value" : count
  }                                          Merges both hashes to create
  context = __context_telemetry(metadata)    unified hash with context telemetry
  metric = { **base_metric, **context }
  redis_client.rpush('metrics_counters', json.dump(metric))
```

```
def timer(msg, metadata, count=1):
    """Emits a metric for tracking run-times.

    Example: timer("convert_worker_runtime", metadata, "2.7")
    """
    base_metric = {
        "metric_name" : msg,
        "metric_value" : time
    }
    context = __context_telemetry(metadata)
    metric = { **base_metric, **context }
    redis_client.rpush('metrics_timers', json.dump(metric))
```

Fetches context-related telemetry

Merges both hashes to create unified hash with context telemetry

Listing 6.1 produces a JSON document with more telemetry than the one produced by listing 3.2:

```
{ "hostname": "ebulent-gnu.euc1.prod.internal",
  "pid": 13221,
  "version_id": "2025.02.19.8cd321b9",
  "payment_plan": "2023a1cdb4",
  "metric_name": "pdf_pages",
  "metric_value": 3 }
```

Figure 6.4 describes how this hash was built.

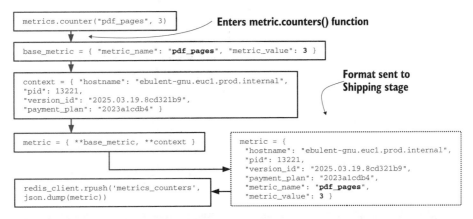

Figure 6.4 **How the metrics emission is built with additional context-related details (markup). The `metrics.counters()` function adds a standard set of details (hostname, process identifier, software version number, and payment-plan identifier) to all calls to the function. Then the marked-up hash is sent to the Shipping stage (`redis` in this case). We are able to add these details in large part because this function is running inside the production software itself.**

The JSON produced here includes far more details regarding *what* produced the metric, which makes this telemetry far more useful than the version produced by listing 3.2. What's more, adding the extra context is cheap in terms of CPU or RAM cost:

- `hostname` is fetched by a single system call, which retrieves a (mostly) static value from the operating system kernel. In most cases, there is no disk access for this call.
- `pid` is a piece of telemetry that all running processes have in the environment and counts as a static identifier.
- `version_id` is statically defined in code. Taking the extra time to add context when writing this metrics logger greatly improves the utility of the metrics produced.
- `payment_plan` was set well before the metrics were emitted and is a simple hash lookup by the time of the metrics emission.

This technique, adding context-related telemetry, is one of the secrets behind how distributed tracing provides the value it does. Let's take another look at figure 5.20, reproduced here as figure 6.5.

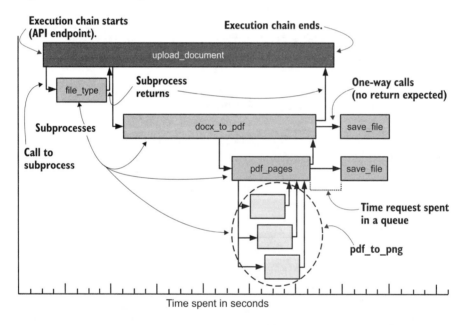

Figure 6.5   Example distributed tracing chart showing the flow of execution including `pdf_pages`, producing three page images in .png format. This chart is made possible through the use of correlation identifiers applied as part of the software libraries for distributed tracing. These correlation identifiers often include user-added context-related telemetry such as a `process-id` (to correlate telemetry coming from a specific running instance) and browser `session-id` (to correlate all telemetry from a specific login session).

The chart in figure 6.5 shows, from beginning to end, a single process flow of an API call to `upload_document`. The execution flow ran through several stages before `upload_document` finished execution. We can display this chain because we tracked context-related telemetry at emission time as part of the context telemetry that the distributed tracing system applied. Emission-stage markup allows the Presentation stage chart to be built. Listing 6.2 shows how OpenTelemetry (http://mng.bz/gxJ8), an open source framework for tracing, would mark up the `perform()` function of pdf_pages. Use `pip install opentelemetry` to install that module.

Listing 6.2 pdf_pages: OpenTelemetry example

```
import os
import socket
from opentelemetry import trace

tracer   = trace.get_tracer(__name__)     ←  Instantiates the
hostname = socket.gethostname()               tracing infrastructure
pid      = os.getpid()

# Called by queue system        Sets our correlation
def perform(options)            identifiers and context
  attributes = {          ←
    "session_id" : options[session_id],
    "document_id" : options[document_id],
    "process_id" : pid,
    "account_id" : options[account_id],
    "host" : hostname
  }
  with tracer.start_as_current_span("pdf_pages",   |  Starts the tracing, known as
  ⮕ attributes=attributes):                         |  a span, using our attributes
    pages = convertPages(options)
    metrics.counter("pdf_pages", pages)
  # end trace          ←
# end perform()              Causes the span to close
                             and telemetry to emit
```

In listing 6.2, we have the `perform()` function of a larger piece of code that is pulling jobs off a queue. The jobs arrive with a payload: a hash named `options`. When the `perform()` method is entered, we first set our correlation identifiers in an `attributes` hash and put some local context in the tracing method. Next, we open a *span*, a distributed tracing term used to define a segment of code whose start and stop times will be tracked. Then we do the work of pdf_pages by calling `convertPages()`. Although execution leaves the scope of the `perform()` method, it is still considered to be part of the span. In `convertPages()`, as shown in figure 6.5, pdf_to_png is called three times. When `convertPages()` returns a number of pages, we use that number to emit a metric value, using our metric function from listing 6.1. When execution leaves the `with` statement, the span is closed, and two forms of telemetry are reported to the Shipping stage:

- The span and attributes are reported to the distributed tracing Shipping stage.
- The count of pages metrics is reported by way of the `metrics.counter` function from listing 6.1.

Figure 6.6 illustrates which telemetry is context-related and when it is applied.

```
def perform(options)
  attributes = {
    "session_id" : options[session_id],
    "document_id" : options[document_id],
    "process_id" : pid,
    "account_id" : options[account_id],
    "host" : hostname
  }
  with tracer.start_as_current_span("pdf_pages",
                        attributes=attributes):
  pages = convertPages(options)
  metrics.counter("pdf_pages", pages)
```

Context-related telemetry passed in from the process that submitted the queue job

Add context telemetry to the span.

Pass context telemetry to next stage.

Figure 6.6   How context-related metadata moves through listing 6.2. Here, we are using context-related telemetry passed into the function from a parent function and adding one of our own (`process_id`). This hash of attributes is used to associate with the span (a distributed tracing concept noting a traced context). Note that we also pass the same options hash to another function. In the grand scheme of things, waiting for child processes to finish gets recursive fast, allowing figure 6.5 to be built.

The technique demonstrated here is passing correlation identifiers along with the payload of jobs in a queue. You could build this same technique of passing identifiers and waiting for a return by using Remote Procedure Call patterns, or using them as part of an API. If you don't have a distributed tracing system, passing correlation identifiers with your request for work (queues, procedure calls, API calls, and so on) will still allow you to ask deeper questions of your telemetry systems.

Exercise 6.1

Examine some of the telemetry coming out of a program you work with.

What markup is being applied by the program?

What additional markup would make this telemetry more useful?

6.2 Markup and enrichment in the Shipping stage

The Shipping stage, the second stage in the telemetry pipeline, accepts telemetry from the Emitting stage. (See chapters 3 and 4 for details about what the Shipping stage does.) This section covers both the markup that can be added in the Shipping stage and the sort of enrichment that the Shipping stage may apply. The Shipping stage is especially important when the Emitting stage isn't software under your control, such as with hardware emissions or emissions coming from SaaS platforms. The other major function of the Shipping stage is to reformat telemetry for storage in the storage systems used by the Presentation stage. Figure 6.7 illustrates the overlapping nature of markup and enrichment in the Shipping stage.

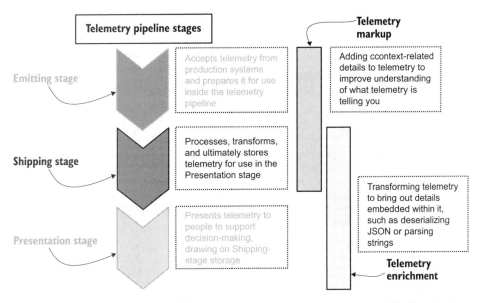

Figure 6.7 The Shipping stage is responsible for both markup and telemetry, and is the only stage that does both things. Transforming telemetry into a format that can be stored is a form of enrichment, which is why format transformation happens alongside extracting details from telemetry.

This section covers these topics:

- Section 6.2.1 covers adding telemetry relating to the context that generated it, greatly enhancing the ability of someone to find related events.
- Section 6.2.2 covers decoding and extracting meaning in telemetry to create fields to improve searchability.
- Section 6.2.3 covers converting types of telemetry from the format in which it was emitted to the format needed by the Shipping-stage storage systems. These conversion operations improve the Presentation-stage system's ability to analyze telemetry.

6.2.1 *Applying context-related telemetry in the Shipping stage*

The Emitting stage is best suited to applying context-related telemetry. But Shipping-stage components that receive directly from the Emitting stage can apply some context-related telemetry even if the emitting system is not capable of adding it. Adding context to telemetry generated by hardware and SaaS can be done by the first Shipping-stage system. This section shows how a Shipping stage can apply context-related telemetry. Let's look at some Shipping-stage architecture. Figure 4.1 demonstrates components of a Shipping pipeline that exist on a server, reproduced here as figure 6.8.

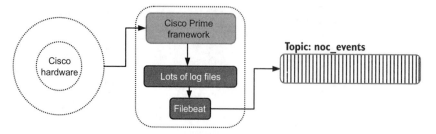

Figure 6.8   Shipping log files from production software that can't do anything else. Cisco Prime creates log files and leaves it to local administrators to do something with them. Here, the Elastic.co program called Filebeat is configured to ingest the log files and send telemetry into a Kafka-based stream on a topic called `noc_events`. This configuration allows the local network operations team to view Cisco Prime telemetry from the centralized logging system.

Figure 6.8 shows Cisco Prime, the proprietary software package for administering Cisco networking gear, emitting telemetry into a set of log files. These emitted log files are consumed by Filebeat, which sends the telemetry into a Kafka stream on the `noc_events` topic. Looking at the context-related telemetry we produce in listing 6.1, we find hostname, process identifier, software version, and payment plan. Filebeat is in a place to provide most of these items of context even though the emitting program cannot to do so itself:

- *hostname*—Filebeat is running on the same host, so adding this field to the telemetry received from Cisco Prime is trivial. In fact, Filebeat adds it by default.
- *process identifier*—This telemetry is the hardest because it requires Filebeat to poll running processes to determine the process ID of the program.
- *version*—Filebeat is running on the same host as Cisco Prime, so fetching the version of the program is possible. If the version doesn't change often, Filebeat could be statically configured to apply version telemetry. Alternately, the production software deploy process can update the Filebeat configuration file to add static values like this one.
- *payment_plan*—Unlike the emitter-shipper function in listing 6.1, Filebeat is not in a place to directly receive a data structure from the production software, the way that listing 6.2 did. Of the four types of context-related telemetry, this one is the one that Filebeat can't provide by itself. (As it happens, Cisco Prime does not produce this telemetry, even internally.)

Having the production program apply these items of context-related telemetry would be better, but if the program is incapable of producing this telemetry, or if updates that would allow this function are prohibited, the Shipping stage can get most of this list. Shipping-stage components that are custom-written for the use case, unlike the off-the-shelf Filebeat, may apply quite detailed context-related telemetry for programs that can't handle adding context details themselves. The effort is truly justified only if your unmodifiable program is central to the function of your production systems, as maintaining the software of the custom shipping component is a maintenance cost that will have to be paid continually.

Dealing with inflexible log file formats from software

To engineers who are looking to provide as much local context as possible for their telemetry emissions, off-the-shelf software *that simply doesn't provide it* is a constant vexation. If you are dealing with such software, a few techniques may allow you to get what you're looking for:

- *Set logging to debug mode.* Often, off-the-shelf software has the ability to enable verbose and debug modes, with debug modes giving hints as to what internal function the software was in when something was emitted. The trade-off here is that debug mode can slow software performance, and you will have to handle a possibly vastly higher volume of log data.
- *Use systemd and journal on Linux hosts.* If you can direct the log stream into standard out, the logs will be handled by journald on modern Linux hosts. journald will provide a PID value because its format is very similar to Syslog format.
- *Use Syslog on UNIX hosts.* As with journald, if you can direct the log stream to Syslog somehow, you will get hostname and PID for free.
- *Run the program as a service through* `sc create` *on Windows hosts.* The sc program will direct stdout to the Application event log, which will add several other pieces of telemetry, such as the timestamp of the event, the user who ran it, and the name of the computer that generated it.
- *Run the program under Docker.* This approach works best if you're already using Docker and are familiar with it, but Docker is built to capture standard out and send that stream to several places, including the system logger (even in Windows).

For hardware systems, having a shipping component on the same hardware as the emitter is rarely possible; this approach reduces the amount of context-aware telemetry that the Shipping stage may glean from the Emitting stage. Figure 6.9 demonstrates a basic shipping architecture, with a Cisco firewall emitting to a Syslog server. The standardized nature of Syslog makes it an attractive shipping format for hardware makers (when they aren't making bespoke telemetry systems as part of their add-on management platforms, such as Cisco Prime). Taking standardized, string-based telemetry and turning it into something that modern Presentation-stage systems can consume is the job of the Shipping stage.

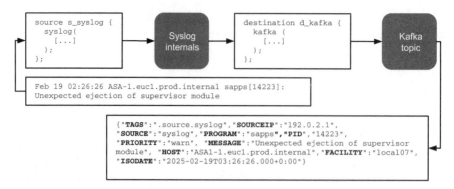

Figure 6.9   A Cisco firewall emitting directly to a Syslog server, part of the Shipping stage, and the Syslog server reformatting the received telemetry to send on to a Kafka topic. The transformation here is from the Syslog format defined by RFC to a JSON-encoded format that another Shipping-stage system subscribed to the topic will consume and further process. All the attributes in the hash came from the Syslog server itself or the UDP packet that contained the emission.

At the point where the Syslog event is received by the Syslog server, having been emitted by the Cisco firewall in figure 6.9, the Syslog server already has many pieces of telemetry defined by the Syslog standard:

- `date`—The month, day, hour, minute, and second when the event was created
- `facility`—A Syslog identifier, statically set when setting up Syslog forwarding on the Cisco firewalls
- `host`—The IP of the firewall device that generated the event
- `message`—The full text of the emission

The `date` and `host` are valuable pieces of context-related telemetry built into the protocol. The Syslog protocol itself encodes several fields, should devices be configured to use them. For devices with more complete Syslog support, we could also get `severity` (a ranking of how urgent the event is), `process-id` (the same as emitted in listing 6.1), and `program tag` (to identify which of the many processes on the box emitted the event). The contents of the `message` field are important, though. Programs and hardware that emit through Syslog know Syslog's limitations and often insert context-related telemetry into the plain-text part of the Syslog event. To decode such embedded telemetry, we need to talk about enrichment.

6.2.2   *Extracting and enriching telemetry in-flight*

Part of the job of the Shipping stage is to extract interesting telemetry from less-well-formatted telemetry and enrich each item of telemetry to improve its utility in the Presentation stage. This section covers the techniques needed to provide extraction and enrichment in the Shipping stage. In most cases, we parse an existing telemetry field to populate more fields, though some systems have the ability to enrich telemetry based on data held in multiple events. To start, let's use an example from chapter 2, the sample output for a Cisco ASA firewall:

```
Teardown of UDP connection 162121 for outside:1.1.0.0/53 to
➡ dmz1:192.0.2.19/59232 duration 0:00:00 bytes 136
```

We can see several items of interest in this string:

- `Teardown of UDP connection` gives us an event string.
- `UDP connection` gives us the protocol used (UDP).
- `connection 162121` gives us a connection number, 162121, which is possibly useful for correlation.
- `outside:1.1.0.0/53` gives us several details:
  - The interface used (outside)
  - The IP address connected to (1.1.0.0)
  - The port connected to (53)
- `dmz1:192.0.2.19/59232` gives us similar details for the inside identity.
- `duration 0:00:00` tells us how long the connection took (not long at all).
- `bytes 136` tells us how much data was transacted (136 bytes).

That's quite a bit of information crammed into a short space! Fetching telemetry out of a long string like this is the bread and butter of centralized logging shipping systems, and there are a couple of main methods for doing so. The first method is to use regular expressions and capture groups. Listing 6.3 shows an example Logstash filter configuration that will pull out all these details. (Logstash is an Elastic program built to be a dedicated Shipping-stage system.)

Listing 6.3   Extracting firewall fields with Logstash `grok{}`

```
filter {                                    Conditionals to try parsing only the right lines

  if [facility] == 'local07' and [syslogmessage] =~ "^Teardown" {    ⬦─────
    grok {
      match => {
        "syslogmessage" => "^%{DATA:firewall_action} %{NUMBER:conn_id} for
        ➡ %{NOTSPACE:target} to %{NOTSPACE:source} duration %{TIME:duration}
        ➡ bytes %{NUMBER:bytes}$"
      }
    }
  }

  grok {        ⬦───── Second-pass parsing
    match => {
```

First-pass parsing ➝ `grok {`

```
          "source" =>
      ➡    "^%{WORD:source_int}:%{IP:source_ip}:%{NUMBER:source_port}$"
          "target" =>
      ➡    "^%{WORD:target_int}:%{IP:target_ip}:%{NUMBER:target_port}$"
          "firewall_action" => "for %{WORD:protocol} connection"
        }
      }
    }
  }
```

Use the Logstash `grok {}` filter plugin (http://mng.bz/5W17) when you need to apply regular expressions to text and extract fields. Like all regular expression engines, match patterns can become incomprehensibly complex, even to those who supposedly maintain them (like me). Chapter 11 covers optimizing the use of regular expressions at scale, and section 11.3 covers optimizing for this telemetry specifically. The two `grok {}` statements here parse out many fields and could be combined into a single `grok {}` statement but would turn already-long lines into even longer ones (which you'll see in chapter 11; it's a doozy). The first statement takes a first pass at the data, capturing several fields. Figure 6.10 shows how it works.

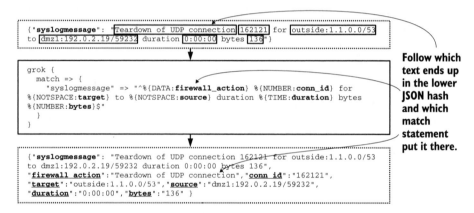

Figure 6.10 How our firewall emission is transformed by the first `grok{}` statement into a hash with far more explicit details. Text in the original hash that is matched by `grok{}` is boxed; new attributes in the final hash are underlined.

That first `grok {}` statement gives us six new fields: `firewall_action`, `conn_id`, `source`, `target`, `duration`, and `bytes`. Then processing moves to the second `grok {}` statement, which adds even more fields (figure 6.11).

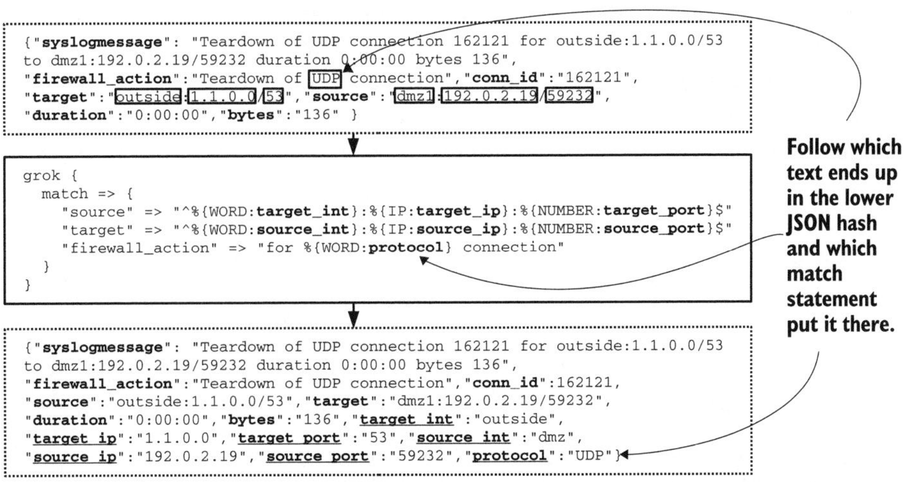

```
{"syslogmessage": "Teardown of UDP connection 162121 for outside:1.1.0.0/53
to dmz1:192.0.2.19/59232 duration 0:00:00 bytes 136",
"firewall_action":"Teardown of UDP connection","conn_id":"162121",
"target":"outside:1.1.0.0/53", "source": "dmz1:192.0.2.19/59232",
"duration":"0:00:00", "bytes":"136" }
```

```
grok {
  match => {
    "source" => "^%{WORD:target_int}:%{IP:target_ip}:%{NUMBER:target_port}$"
    "target" => "^%{WORD:source_int}:%{IP:source_ip}:%{NUMBER:source_port}$"
    "firewall_action" => "for %{WORD:protocol} connection"
  }
}
```

Follow which text ends up in the lower JSON hash and which match statement put it there.

```
{"syslogmessage": "Teardown of UDP connection 162121 for outside:1.1.0.0/53
to dmz1:192.0.2.19/59232 duration 0:00:00 bytes 136",
"firewall_action":"Teardown of UDP connection","conn_id":162121,
"source":"outside:1.1.0.0/53","target":"dmz1:192.0.2.19/59232",
"duration":"0:00:00", "bytes":"136", "target int":"outside",
"target ip":"1.1.0.0", "target port":"53", "source int":"dmz",
"source ip":"192.0.2.19", "source port":"59232", "protocol":"UDP" }
```

Figure 6.11 How our firewall emission is further transformed by the second `grok{}` statement. Text in the original hash that is captured by the `grok{}` statement is boxed. New fields in the final statement are underlined. Seven new fields are added, derived from fields parsed from the first `grok{}` statement. All 13 fields could be derived from a single, huge, mostly incomprehensible `grok{}` statement, but splitting them up makes the flow easier to follow (if slower to process).

After these two grok {} statements, we've added 13 new fields to the telemetry:

- firewall_action—Teardown of UDP connection
- conn_id—162121
- target—outside:1.1.0.0:53
- source—dmz:192.0.2.19:59232
- duration—0:00:0
- bytes—136
- source_int—dmz
- source_ip—192.0.2.19
- source_port—59232
- target_int—outside
- target_ip—1.1.0.0
- target_port—53
- protocol—UDP

Because of how Logstash's grok {} filter works, all these fields will be of the string data type. If we wanted to convert the numbers to integers, we could do so by modifying the capture statements, such as this one capturing conn_id:

```
%{NUMBER:conn_id:int}
```

After all these fields are put in storage, the Presentation-stage systems will be able to build visualizations and reports using the enriched data. For a feed of firewall events, being able to exclude events that you already know is helpful for isolating the *interesting* events. Figure 5.16, reproduced here as figure 6.12, demonstrates excluding known DNS servers to help find internal users touching unknown DNS servers.

Figure 6.12   Excluding known DNS servers to find interesting events. The base filter finds all firewall events (`tags:"firewall"`). Then the search is modified with two explicit excludes, removing events with `target_ip` set to 1.1.1.1 or 1.1.0.0. Thereafter, only events with `target_ip` addresses that aren't the two well-known values will be visible and worth investigating.

Although regular expressions are powerful, they have a reputation for being somewhat slow. In cases such as firewall emissions, in which the format is well-known and unchanging, we have other ways to generate these fields efficiently. Logstash has another filter called `dissect {}` that does not rely on regular expressions; instead, it relies on a simpler capture expression. Listing 6.4 rewrites the Logstash config to use `dissect` instead of `grok`.

Listing 6.4   Extracting firewall fields with `dissect`

```
filter {

  if [facility] == 'local07' and [syslogmessage] =~ "^Teardown" {
    dissect {
      mapping => {
        "syslogmessage" => "Teardown of %{protocol} connection %{conn_id}
        ➡ %{source} to %{target} duration %{duration} bytes %{bytes}"
      }
    }

    dissect {
      mapping => {
        "source" => "%{source_int}:%{source_ip}:%{source_port}"
        "target" => "%{target_int}:%{target_ip}:%{target_port}"
      }
    }
  }
}
```

Listing 6.4 is simpler to read than listing 6.3, which improves maintainability and performs faster. The performance improvements come from how `dissect` parses the Syslog string. Everything that's not inside a curly brace is considered to be a delimiter, and strings between delimiters are fields; that's it. `dissect` is a not a one-to-one equivalent to `grok`, though; we're missing the `firewall_action` field. We're missing that field because this string does not have a way to separate (delimit) that part of the string from the rest. `dissect` is simpler and easier to maintain, but with some cost in flexibility.

> ## Writing for maintainability is good; you should do it
>
> A *maintainable* system is one with low barriers to understanding what a system is doing. Regular expressions have a decades-long reputation for being gibberish to those who don't know what every symbol means, and they can still be gibberish to those of us who do know those meanings. It takes time to diagram what's going on in there. Regular expressions can be incredibly powerful, but using that power limits who can fix an expression when something goes wrong. If you can solve a string-parsing problem without using complicated regular expressions, you have likely improved the maintainability of the overall system.
>
> This concept applies to software systems in general. Any old codebase almost definitely has one function/class/method that is way too long, is doing way too much, and has a comment at the top of it saying
>
> ```
> # Number of people who tried to refactor this and gave up: 7
> ```
>
> Such code is almost always the result of years of accumulated scar tissue relating to edge cases. Code like this survives style refactors because the dark calculus of maintainability means having all that code in one place is the least-bad option versus hiding it all in eight one-use functions scattered across the entire codebase that would require a whiteboard and lots of sticky notes to trace the logic flow. Least-bad is not good, but sometimes, reality means that least-bad is the best you can do. Here are two points to consider when facing code that might be unmaintainably complex:
>
> - If you have to choose between stylish and maintainable, lean toward maintainable. Intellectual purity isn't worth the maintenance headaches.
> - What you, the expert, consider to be maintainable often isn't maintainable to someone who doesn't have all your context (see also: writing this book). Let someone else make the maintainability decisions (see also: all the editors and proofers involved in making this book work at all). Your code will survive after you're gone; plan for it.

`dissect` also lacks a way to convert fields to specific data types the way `grok` does, but Logstash provides a way to convert arbitrary fields to specific types. Data types are important for storage and Presentation-stage systems because of the limits that each data type imposes. Many systems will be happy to add the string `"12"` to the string

"13" to produce a sum of "1213", but the integer 12 can be added to the integer 13 to get 25.

Exercise 6.2

Given the following telemetry sample, identify as much enrichable telemetry as you can.

```
2025-02-19T00:59:26.142  INFO  9202 --- [expl-http-api]
➡ c.a.s.s.t.CallbackWorker : API callback triggered for account
➡ 3671 using APPID 9285861, response 403
```

6.2.3   *Converting field types during the Shipping stage*

In this section, we cover the places in a Shipping stage that may perform type conversions and discuss why you want to convert types. Adding strings together produces inconsistent results, as discussed at the end of section 6.2.2, so converting a string representation of a number to a number will make math operations easier later in the pipeline. Listing 6.5 gives us an example that converts the dissected string values from listing 6.4 to their appropriate data type.

Listing 6.5   Converting `dissected` fields to their correct data type

```
filter {
  if [facility] == 'local07' and [syslogmessage] =~ "^Teardown" {
    dissect {
    [... Listing 6.4 code ...]
    }

    mutate {
      convert => {
        "conn_id"     => "integer"
        "bytes"       => "integer"
        "source_port" => "integer"
        "target_port" => "integer"
      }
    }
  }
}
```

Let's see what this `mutate {}` statement does to the JSON hash from figure 6.11. With our telemetry data now in the correct type, as shown in figure 6.13, the analysis we can perform on this telemetry has been magnified. Creating a step in the Shipping pipeline to ensure that field data types are what the storage expects is a good idea, and you should implement it if Shipping-stage technology allows.

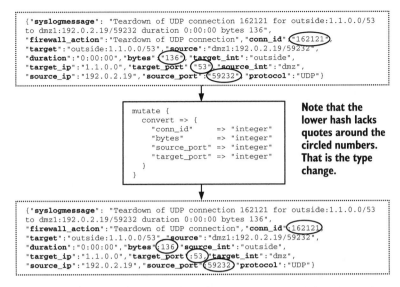

Figure 6.13   Typecasting our firewall telemetry to turn important values into numbers instead of strings. This `mutate {}` statement is converting four values to integers. Due to how JSON formats numbers, it seems that all this code is doing is removing the quotes around the numbers. When this retyped telemetry reaches Shipping-stage storage, the difference will be profound; you can perform different analysis on number-based data instead of string-based data. Converting telemetry data to the correct type is powerful.

A classic reason why rationalizing data types is a good idea can be explained by looking at Boolean values and how they convert. A Boolean value is either `true` or `false`. Representing that truth value as a string or number has several conventions, however. All these values are equivalent to `true` in some cases (but critically, not all):

- The integer 1
- The integer 0 (uncommon)
- An integer or float value greater than zero
- An integer or float value not equal to zero (may be negative)
- The string `'t'`
- The string `'true'`
- The string `'y'`
- The string `'yes'`
- A string of any length greater than zero

One of the main roles of a Shipping stage is to convert data types to something that the storage systems can handle, so be sure to convert types out of string wherever feasible. When you're converting into a storage system that has a Boolean type, *it is better to do the type conversion in the shipping pipeline and not rely on the storage system's Boolean conversion logic*. Doing the type conversion in the pipeline makes the conversion explicit and puts the conversion logic where it will be more maintainable (see sidebar in section 6.2.2).

Section 2.1.4 introduces the concept of using object-encoding formats such as JSON and YAML as part of emissions, and section 4.2 covers the decision process for selecting telemetry emissions formats generally. The Shipping stage is one of the main places where that format is converted from the negotiated standardized formats (section 4.2) to the format needed by storage systems. Generally speaking, object-encoding formats such as JSON, YAML, and XML (for a discussion of protobufs, see sidebar in section 4.2) are good at representing several data types:

- Strings
- Numbers
- Arrays
- Hashes

Although strings are a simple type, numbers are not. Integers are different from floating-point numbers, and some storage systems treat the two types differently. Whether that storage difference matters to you depends on your data, but you should be aware that the difference is possible. The Boolean type is not represented uniquely in these object-encoding formats, so if storage uses Boolean, something—possibly the storage system itself—will need to convert the strings and numbers to their appropriate `true` and `false` values.

Data types and numbers

Integer (number without a decimal) and floating-point (number with a decimal) types are the basic computing number types, going back before even the vacuum-tube era. Performing math operations on integers requires different logic from performing them on floating-point numbers, so CPUs can be better or worse at one task versus the other. The Intel 8088 CPU that launched the IBM PC was good with integers, but doing floating-point computations fast required an extra chip: the math coprocessor known as the 8087. These days, a regular Intel or AMD CPU can do extensive floating-point math on chip, but the math coprocessor's role has moved to Graphics Processing Units, such as those produced by NVidia. The IEEE 794 standard (1985) defines how floating-point mathematics happens inside hardware.

Two others concepts that are familiar to programmers are *precision* and *overflow*, which relate to the number of bits assigned to hold a number. An 8-bit-wide integer can hold a value of 2 to the eighth power or 2 to the seventh power if that value needs to include positive and negative numbers. Attempting to store a number that can't be held in eight bits *overflows* the integer. The year 2038 problem exists because that's when the UNIX Epoch counter will overflow a 32-bit signed integer and turn negative.

Precision applies to floating-point numbers. Floating-point numbers are not as prone to overflow as integers are; they merely become less precise. The bit width of a floating-point number determines the number of decimal places to which the number is accurate.

When it comes to telemetry, numbers take on a different meaning. Some makers of telemetry systems have noticed that when humans chart numbers, especially floating-point numbers, they rarely look past the seventh digit. The operations performed on telemetry system numbers are rarely the complex multistage analysis functions that precision problems magnify and compound, but simple methods in which imprecision is hidden by the digits not shown.

The idea of a scaled float is starting to emerge in telemetry storage systems as a result of this observation. A *scaled float* is an integer with a second integer to record the decimal place. As a true format for performing complex math functions, a scaled float is terribly imprecise, but it's definitely good enough for dashboarding. Scaled floats store more efficiently than true floating-point numbers do, which matters when it comes to resource provisioning. If you store a lot of floating-point numbers, using scaled floats wherever possible will save you money.

You can convert data types in several places, and some (larger, longer, rather complex) pipelines convert data several times before it is finally stored. Listing 6.5 demonstrated a conversion in the middle of the pipeline. But type conversion can also happen at the beginning of the Shipping stage, when the emitted telemetry enters the Shipping system. In listing 6.6, we are using Logstash to ingest a file produced by an older Arabic-language Windows system running codepage 1256, which is not Unicode.

Listing 6.6   Converting old Windows Arabic to UTF-8 by using Logstash

```
input {
  file {
    path => "C:/Program Data/AppLog/output.txt"      ⟵—— The path of files to ingest
    codec => plain {
      charset => "Windows-1256"      ⟵┐
    }                                    │ Tells Logstash what character
  }                                      │ set string will be encoded as
}
```

The file is produced by the production systems, where Logstash ingests it. The `file {}` plugin tells Logstash to expect the file to be in the Windows codepage `Windows-1256`. Logstash always converts strings internally to UTF-8; because it knows the format in which strings are entering the pipeline, Logstash will know how to translate text into UTF-8. Any later `filter {}` and `output {}` plugins will be working on UTF-8 data.

WARNING   Not everyone is blessed enough to work solely with UTF-8 strings. Java programmers see UTF-16 strings more often than those who work in other programming languages, and Windows used a dialect of UTF-16 by preference for much of its post-Windows-NT history. Mainframes and other systems running code that was first written in the 1960s and 1970s and continually updated often don't emit in Unicode at all (EBCDIC). Knowing how to convert string encodings will allow you to build a telemetry pipeline to support more of your production systems.

Type conversion often also happens at the interface between the Shipping-stage storage system and the systems that send it data. The adapter that inserts telemetry into a storage system can convert types, and the storage system itself can convert types. In listing 6.7, we have a Logstash output adapter sending telemetry into the InfluxDB time-series database, where we are converting types as part of the adapter rather than trusting InfluxDB to convert types correctly.

Listing 6.7   Using the `influxdb` output adapter to perform type conversions of numbers

```
output {
    influxdb {
        host => "influxdb.euc1.prod.internal"      ◁── Hostname of the InfluxDB server
        db => "app_metrics"          ◁
        measurement => "java_metrics"        The database to send metrics into
        data_points => {
            "host" => "%{host}",
            "pid" => "%{pid}",
            "version_id" => "%{version_id}",      The list of fields to
            "name" => "%{counter_name},            send into influx
            "value" => "%{counter_value},
            "type" => "counter"
        }
        send_as_tags => [
            "host",
            "pid",
            "version_id",           The list of
            "name",                 fields to treat as
            "type"                  indexed values
        ]

        coerce_values => {
            "value" => "float",        Fields to type-convert into
            "pid"   => "string"        specific InfluxDB types.
        }
    }
}
```

The measurement (table) to send metrics into → `measurement => "java_metrics"`

The `coerce_values` section in listing 6.7 is forcing the data type of the `value` field to be float and `pid` to string. Although a process identifier is a number, its value in this database system is to act as an identifier, so converting it to string will make it more powerful. Figure 6.14 shows this transformation process.

To see an example of a storage system itself doing the type conversion, let's look at Elasticsearch, which provides a method for converting types in the form of index templates that predefine field types. In listing 6.8, we're setting the `priority` field to the keyword type and the `percent_cpu` field to a special type.

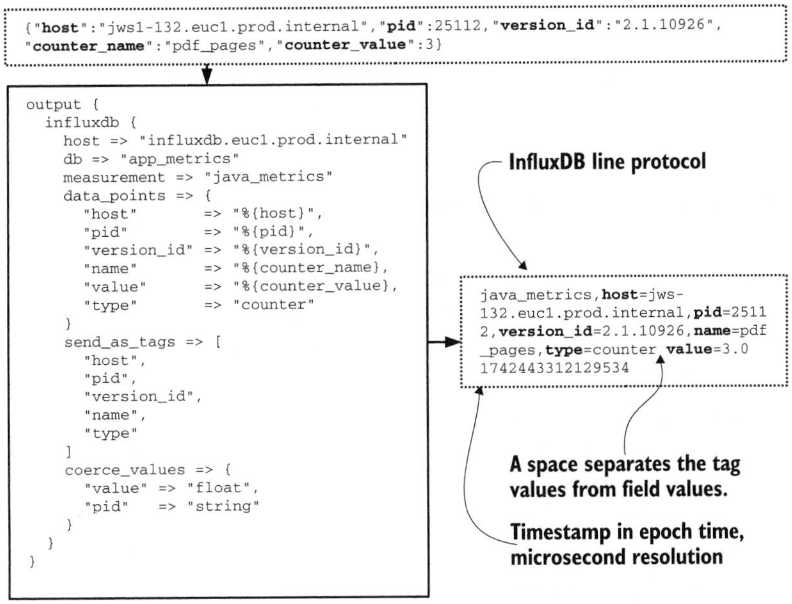

{"**host**":"jws1-132.euc1.prod.internal","**pid**":25112,"**version_id**":"2.1.10926", "**counter_name**":"pdf_pages","**counter_value**":3}

```
output {
  influxdb {
    host => "influxdb.euc1.prod.internal"
    db => "app_metrics"
    measurement => "java_metrics"
    data_points => {
      "host"       => "%{host}",
      "pid"        => "%{pid}",
      "version_id" => "%{version_id}",
      "name"       => "%{counter_name},
      "value"      => "%{counter_value},
      "type"       => "counter"
    }
    send_as_tags => [
      "host",
      "pid",
      "version_id",
      "name",
      "type"
    ]
    coerce_values => {
      "value" => "float",
      "pid"   => "string"
    }
  }
}
```

InfluxDB line protocol

```
java_metrics,host=jws-
132.euc1.prod.internal,pid=2511
2,version_id=2.1.10926,name=pdf
_pages,type=counter value=3.0
1742443312129534
```

A space separates the tag values from field values.

Timestamp in epoch time, microsecond resolution

Figure 6.14 **The type conversion performed as part of the `influxdb` output adapter. We see the incoming data in the JSON hash at the top, with `pid` and `counter_value` set to a number type. To the right, we see how the `output {}` block transforms this data structure into the InfluxDB line protocol. `value` is typecast to float as part of the adapter. If it were specified as an integer, `value` would be represented as 3 with no decimal point.**

Listing 6.8   Elasticsearch template defining types and type conversion behavior

```
{
  "mappings": {
    "_doc": {
      "properties": {
        "percent_cpu": {
          "type": "scaled_float",
          "scaling_factor": 1000
        },
        "priority": {
          "type": "keyword"
        }
      }
    }
  }
}
```

The `keyword` type is a special form of string that gets less indexing but is more efficient in producing your visualizations. The `scaled_float` type is a custom form of floating-point number that is stored as an integer but allows decimal values; in this case, it is set to include three places past the decimal. In Elasticsearch, the data type is converted when a new event is inserted into the database. In the case of percent_cpu, the Shipping stage converts the source metric from the string it started life as to a double-precision floating-point value. When the metric is ingested into Elasticsearch, it is further converted to a scaled float.

6.3   *Enrichment in the Presentation stage*

The Presentation stage of a telemetry pipeline is the stage that displays telemetry for humans and is the public face of the telemetry system. Chapter 5 covers the Presentation stage in detail, but this section focuses on the sorts of markup and enrichment the Presentation stage can provide. Being the last stage in the telemetry pipeline, the Presentation stage uses telemetry that has been marked up and enriched by the Emitting and Shipping stages to provide even more detail.

The distributed tracing style of telemetry makes the most use of Presentation-stage enrichment of telemetry because it focuses on using correlation identifiers to link telemetry. Depending on the technical details, the linkage of telemetry might happen in the Shipping stage as part of storage, but it is the Presentation stage that takes those correlations and displays them to improve decision-making and troubleshooting by people. Figure 6.5, which gave the context for the work done by listing 6.2, is an example of the sort of display a distributed tracing system can generate based on correlation data, and most of this enrichment is happening in the Presentation stage. Figure 6.5 is reproduced here as figure 6.15.

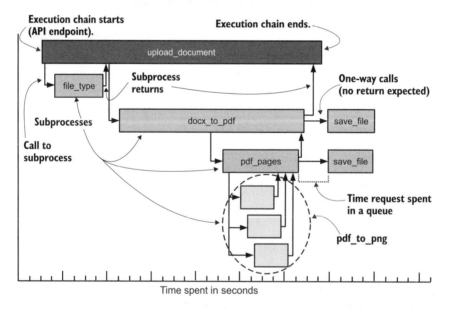

Figure 6.15   A normal, no-exception example of a distributed trace showing conversion of a .docx file that resulted in three pages. This figure demonstrates the call stack—in the form of services, not functions or classes—for this particular execution. A chart formatted like this one provides extensive context for someone who's looking to troubleshoot problems, and context speeds resolution.

Enrichment in the Presentation stage is less about modifying telemetry for better performance and more about creating visual displays that are useful for humans. Charts and graphs are visual displays as much as tables with curated columns. Trend lines on graphs and forecasting columns for reports built from telemetry are another form of enrichment that Presentation-stage systems produce.

Section 5.1.3 provides a series of charts exploring the enrichment possibilities available through the use of aggregation functions when you're manipulating metrics data produced by the `pdf_pages` function by way of the metrics.py file from listing 6.1. Each aggregation function provides a different view into a set of telemetry, allowing the person doing the research to learn about the shape of the data and what patterns may be present. The enrichment here is provided by the system displaying the metrics data.

For centralized logging data, which is mostly strings enriched and marked up by the Emitting and Shipping stages, different forms of enrichment are possible. Given a set of centralized logging telemetry, here are some example charts and reports that you can make:

- Chart the occurrence of a specific error message over time to determine whether the error is increasing or decreasing after a recent software release.
- Chart the occurrence of messages with a priority of `CRITICAL` for a specific application to identify spike patterns.
- Chart the ratio of `INFO` to `CRITICAL` messages coming from a specific function to isolate periods when failure rates are higher.
- Chart the count of API calls from a specific customer to learn what their request patterns are.
- Chart the code classes making the highest number of `CRITICAL` messages to determine areas to focus technical debt work on.
- Report the hosts making connections to the public Ruby Gems servers to identify software not configured to use the proxy systems.
- Chart the number of internal hosts making network connections to a malware command-and-control server to determine how many infected hosts there are.
- Report sudo use by the Operations team to ensure that change-control procedures are being followed.

Figure 5.12, reproduced here as figure 6.16, gives us one example of enriched data in a Presentation-stage system.

Figure 6.16 gives us a view of DNS requests made over a couple of minutes, using telemetry enriched by the Shipping stage (see section 6.2.2 for a description) to provide the fields we see in the report. The emitted string had no markup or enrichment, so the Shipping stage extracted and enriched the telemetry as new events flowed through the pipeline. Each field in the report can be used in the search query to restrict the graph to the interesting telemetry.

A technique used by the big SaaS vendors for centralized logging, such as Splunk and Sumo Logic, puts in place more explicit Presentation-stage enrichment. When

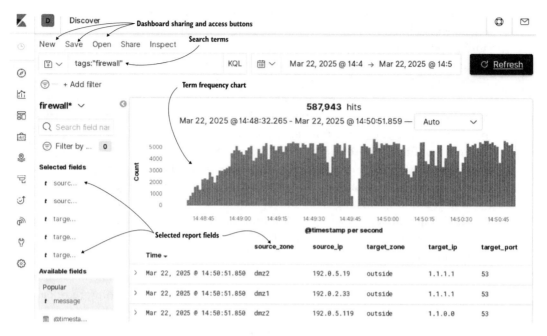

Figure 6.16   **Providing an enriched view of telemetry, displaying a frequency chart and a report of findings. This dashboard software (Kibana 7 from Elastic.co) provides all the features needed for a good Presentation-stage system for centralized logging.**

you're operating large distributed systems with the goal of providing centralized logging services to large numbers of customers, certain problems of scale start showing up, such as cardinality. (See chapter 14 for more about that problem in your systems.) One method that is economical at a SaaS provider's scale is to handle decoding of object-encoding formats like JSON during the presentation process rather than as part of the Shipping stage. You provide a query that broadly selects the data you need; as part of a second stage of the query, a field containing JSON data is converted to fields (deserialized). The fields produced by this pass can be used in later queries or made part of a report. Listing 6.9 provides an example query for Sumo Logic.

Listing 6.9   Using Shipping-stage markup in Sumo Logic

```
(_collector="FrankfurtDC")                          ◁——— Selects dataset to operate with
| json field=_raw "syslog.severity" as severity
| json field=_raw "syslog.facility" as facility      Adds fields to dataset
| json field=_raw "syslog.hostname" as host          by parsing JSON
| where severity = "WARN"        ◁—
                                    └— Uses added field as conditional
                                       to reduce dataset returned
```

The first line selects which dataset we are interested in, and a time range is selected in the user interface (not pictured here). The second, third, and fourth lines use the pipe operator to parse the JSON blob in the _raw field to pull out three fields and make them part of the event being displayed. The fifth line is a conditional using one of the created fields. All three of the extracted fields are available for reporting.

Presentation-stage enrichment of this kind can be powerful, but the more transformation work the Presentation-stage systems have to do, the slower they seem to be for the people who are asking questions. SaaS providers allow this sort of system because their presentation systems sell their product, so they put years of engineering into making that experience fast. A feature such as this one is not yet widely available in open source solutions, but that situation is changing; GrafanaLabs' relatively young Loki product is already built to use exactly this style of Presentation-stage enrichment!

6.4 *How telemetry style affects markup and enrichment*

Sections 6.1 through 6.3 teach how markup and enrichment happen at each stage of the telemetry pipeline. This section focuses on the four telemetry styles and their preferences for where markup and enrichment happen. The styles we're focusing on are

- *Centralized logging*—The first telemetry system to emerge from multicomputer infrastructures
- *Security Information Event Management* (SIEM) —A form of centralized logging specialized for security-team workloads involving incident response and compliance
- *Metrics*—A way to store information online and searchable longer by focusing on numbers and a few tags to search them
- *Distributed tracing*—Specialized for tracing execution flows across distributed systems and associated telemetry events

We will go over each of these styles in turn and explain why they enrich and markup where they do. The state of the art is constantly changing, so by the time you read this book, there might be new styles that are not in this list. If you find yourself wondering where a new style might fit, read the next few sections to discover the trends.

Why timestamp format and correct time matter

Telemetry systems have a simple rule: *all clocks generating timestamps must be synchronized to the same source to ensure that telemetry from all systems can be ordered correctly by your presentation systems.*

There is a corollary to this rule: *Timestamp formats must be as precise as possible (to the millisecond, microsecond, or nanosecond, if required) to improve ordering by your presentation systems.*

The Syslog RFC 3164 specified a timestamp format that is accurate to the second and leaves off the year. Anything that parses these timestamps has to guess what year the telemetry was emitted in—not a good choice for high-resolution telemetry systems in which milliseconds matter.

Syslog RFC 5424 clarifies the Syslog timestamp format to allow far more accurate timestamps, such as those conforming with ISO8601.

(continued)

ISO8601 is the format responsible for timestamps like 2025-02-19T19:57:18.922-01:00, indicating Feb 19 in the year 2025, at 19:57, 18 seconds, 922 milliseconds in a time zone offset −1 from UTC.

ISO8601 is a convenient format for timestamps because it uses fixed widths for each digit, allowing parsers to take shortcuts to speed parsing. This format is a highly machine-parsable format, and you should use it wherever you are allowed to do so.

Be warned: the more precise your timestamps are, the more visible clock drift will be. The NTP protocol is pretty good at keeping servers synchronized, but there is a lower bound to how precise it is. When you have microsecond or nanosecond resolution, you will start seeing events happening a bit out of order from how they actually occurred, and you won't have a way to tell that this is the case.

6.4.1 Markup and enrichment with centralized logging

Centralized logging is the modern descendant of the first programs that emitted a stream of output meant for operators and developers rather than program users. Centralized logging systems take the log output of programs across the production systems and bring them into one place for operators, engineers, and managers to search and ask questions. It is the oldest telemetry style, dating from the Berkeley Software Distribution around 1980.

Syslog, Windows Event Log, and Systemd's journald are operating-system-based platforms designed for collecting logs on a given server and electively sending them somewhere else. Applications have the option of building their own telemetry delivery systems; perhaps they send telemetry into a queue or a stream, or directly into a database. A common factor in all of these delivery methods is that centralized logging is about shipping, manipulating, and searching strings. Figure 6.17 provides an example drawn from figure 1.3.

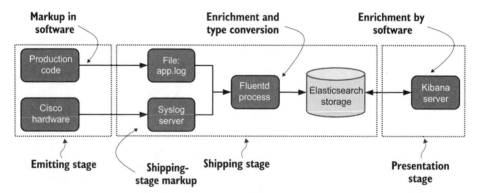

Figure 6.17 Figure 1.3 with pointers to where centralized logging prefers to do its markup and enrichment. We see both software- and hardware-produced telemetry in this pipeline. Software performs its own markup, whereas the Cisco hardware relies on Shipping-stage components to do that work. Enrichment is handled mainly as part of the Shipping stage, with the Presentation-stage software providing the rest. Centralized logging relies more on Shipping-stage enrichment than metrics.

For centralized logging systems, here are a few guidelines on when and where to enrich and mark up your telemetry:

- If the Emitting stage can't do context-related markup (see section 6.2.1), such as for hardware systems, the Shipping stage may be used to extract and enrich telemetry based on the logged strings, as demonstrated in listings 6.4 and 6.5.
- If software is emitting telemetry, it has the best context for adding context-related markup right at the time telemetry is emitted, just before or during the Emitting stage. Markup can be added directly to the event right at emission.
- If hardware is emitting telemetry, it often includes context-related telemetry in the logged string. The Shipping stage can extract the context-related telemetry and enrich the telemetry event for the Presentation stage, as was done in section 6.2.2.
- Timestamps and other date/time structures are critical for making centralized logging systems work well. The Shipping stage should transform various date/time strings from their source format to the format that the Presentation-stage systems need.
- Syslog's protocol deliberately leaves the year off its timestamp because it should be obvious when a line was emitted. If you are dealing with Syslog-formatted telemetry in any capacity, consider adding a timestamp in the logged line if possible, or making rules for how to add a year.
- Regular expressions may be needed to extract interesting telemetry from strings—a function done mostly by the Shipping stage.
- Object-encoding formats such as JSON, YAML, and XML are one way to ship telemetry objects in strings, to be converted back to objects (enriched) by the Shipping stage.

Centralized logging systems are almost definitely in place in your environment; they emerge naturally in any multisystem environment. Centralized logging is the most resource-intensive of the telemetry system styles, so taking time to optimize your pipelines will save money and improve everyone's experience.

6.4.2   Markup and enrichment with SIEM systems

SIEMs are specialized versions of centralized logging focused on the workflows that security teams encounter during incident response, compliance, and regulatory-related activities. Where centralized logging systems handle telemetry that's interesting to software engineering and operations teams, security teams focus on specific well-known types of telemetry. SIEM systems are built to enable those workflows, and this section describes where SIEM systems prefer markup and enrichment to happen.

SIEM systems are almost always purchased software, including cloud options, because of the scale of the problem. The amount of engineering needed to deliver a viable solution for diverse needs makes this an added value you can use to finance a company. A poor SIEM can be cobbled together out of a centralized logging system, but when the organization reaches the level of having compliance or regulatory requirements, a full-featured SIEM becomes necessary. The purchased constraint limits the effectiveness of markup and enrichment in the Emitting and Shipping stages because the SIEM itself may be the Shipping stage. Paying for add-ons to enhance correlation is a valuable option that you should consider. Figure 6.18 is figure 1.7 with the areas of markup and enrichment that SIEM systems prefer.

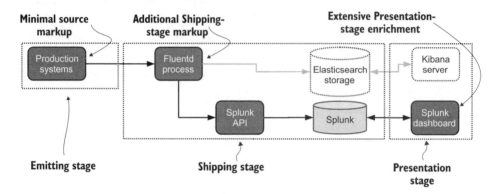

Figure 6.18   The example SIEM system from chapter 1, with pointers to where markup and enrichment happen. The Emitting stage has some markup, but the Shipping stage completes it. Because this example uses a SaaS system, telemetry data is sent to the SaaS provider, where extensive enrichment happens. Dashboards for SIEM systems are backed by complex analysis systems.

There is a distinction between security and anomaly detection inside the production system using production data written in production-system code and security and anomaly detection using telemetry. The former is more a product feature. The latter is a telemetry system charged with tracking the old standby security concerns: making sure that users with elevated privileges are using them correctly, tracking logins to the production environment, and catching excessive login attempts at external access points. Traditionally, SIEM telemetry systems are the second kind of security system.

For larger companies that can afford full-time software engineers to write an in-house SIEM system, the calculus changes considerably. For companies at that scale, the volume of data entering the SIEM may be large enough that the annual salaries of a couple of software engineers can be cheaper than the cost of relicensing a purchased solution. When the SIEM is an in-house-developed product, markup in the Emitting stage can be incredibly powerful. Generally, for security-incident response, more context is never bad. The real engineering challenge exists in the Shipping and Presentation stages, where correlation and display happen.

6.4.3   *Markup and enrichment with metrics*

Metrics grew out of the union between monitoring systems run by operations teams and the desire of software engineering teams to track how their code was performing. Early metrics systems used outright monitoring systems such as Nagios and Xenoss. Around 2010, mindshare began to shift into calling this pattern *metrics*, and the first dedicated time-series databases began to be released. This section covers where and when metrics systems like to have markup and enrichment.

Metrics was an improvement on centralized logging because numbers compress well, allowing much longer timescales to be online and searchable for a similar cost— years versus weeks for centralized logging. Metrics in this era contained only a few nuggets of context-related telemetry because the databases backing metrics systems weren't built for infinite cardinalities. Metrics were often summarized to further improve their storage efficiency, which by necessity lost context.

The monitoring systems used in the early years are still present, and modern equivalents, such as Telegraf from InfluxData, can emit directly into storage—*push-based monitoring*, to use the old term. (For a closer look at monitoring-system choices for pull versus push, see section 9.3.) Systems like these often exist in parallel to software-based metrics. The union between systems metrics and program metrics can enable deep understanding of the impact of code changes on an environment. Figure 1.4 showed the union of system and software metrics, reproduced here as figure 6.19 with the markup and enrichment points described.

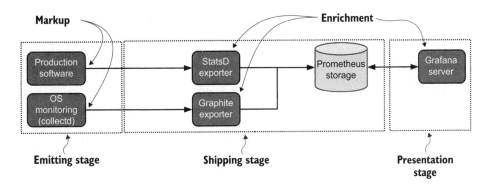

Figure 6.19   The example metrics pipeline from chapter 1, with the markup and emitting points highlighted. Metrics and monitoring rely extensively on markup during the Emitting stage. Here, we see the production software being aggregated (enriched) by a Prometheus StatsD exporter, and the OS monitoring software is talking to the Prometheus Graphite exporter. The Grafana server in the Presentation stage provides extensive enrichment for both monitoring and metrics systems.

Sections 2.1 and 3.1 use metrics as a teaching pattern for Emitting- and Shipping-stage architectures because of their ease of use. The metrics.py listing variants presented in section 2.1 demonstrate several ways of emitting metrics into a centralized logging system; listing 6.1 is a version that adds context-related telemetry; and section 6.2

describes how to turn those metrics into numbers. Then the Shipping stage inserts the numbers into a time-series database, the same as the one used for systems metrics. For metrics-style telemetry systems, here are a few guidelines on when and where markup and enrichment should happen:

- Emitting-stage systems add context-related telemetry, such as a class path, hostname, program name, or other broad details, as shown in listing 6.1.
- Shipping-stage systems transform emitted telemetry into numbers and deliver them to a metrics database, as shown in listing 6.7.
- Shipping-stage systems may generate metrics on their own, based on telemetry observed in the pipeline, such as a count of telemetry with priority set to WARN.
- Emitter/shipper functions, the direct-to-storage pattern from section 3.1.1, do all these things in one place.
- Metrics databases often have limits on cardinality, so be selective when picking context-related telemetry.
- Presentation systems use aggregation functions to enrich displayed telemetry, as covered in-depth in section 5.1.

6.4.4 *Markup and enrichment with distributed tracing systems*

Distributed tracing systems slowly emerged during the mid-2010s as databases began to catch up with unmet cardinality demands and storage systems became SSD by default. The first tracing systems, confusingly called observability systems, simply added correlation identifiers to metrics and used Presentation-stage analysis to make sophisticated charts. By the late 2010s, the name *distributed tracing* was cemented, and tracing became the third Pillar of Observability (the other two being logs and metrics). Tracing systems allow correlating events across an entire system—microservice, monolith, or variants; it doesn't matter—greatly expanding the technical organization's ability to understand complete workflows. Figure 6.20 provides a view of where markup and enrichment happen for this style.

Distributed tracing relies heavily on context-related telemetry, specifically in the form of correlation identifiers added during the Emitting stage. The SDKs for distributed tracing systems add their own correlation identifiers as part of the protocol, but

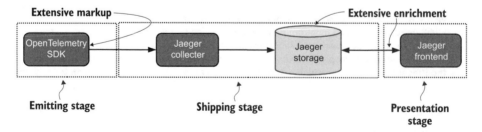

Figure 6.20   Markup and enrichment points for distributed tracing, here using the Jaeger tracing platform. These telemetry styles rely heavily on markup set on telemetry at the time it is emitted. Presentation-stage systems perform deep analysis of data and provide most of the enrichment.

they also allow emitting additional telemetry. In fact, tracing encourages emitting additional telemetry during the Emitting stage to improve an operator's ability to understand (observe) production systems.

The distributed tracing platforms available at the dawn of the 2020s don't rely on general Shipping-stage platforms the way that centralized logging and metrics can. Distributed tracing platforms quite often emit directly into a dedicated tracing service without having to pass through queues or streams first. But the Shipping stage plays a large role in one architecture: programming languages like COBOL that don't have an SDK for a distributed tracing platform.

For software that lacks an SDK for a tracing platform, you can use the Shipping stage to transform a telemetry event from such a software platform into an event that can be ingested by a tracing platform. Figure 6.21 demonstrates an architecture in which a software platform that lacks an SDK can still emit into a tracing system.

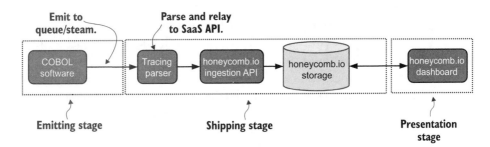

Figure 6.21 Tracing from a non-SDK software platform and ingesting into a SaaS provider of tracing. This example relies on extending the production software to provide tracing data, which is then shipped through a queue/stream. A tracing parser reads this tracing data and relays it up to the SaaS API. From there, the pipeline looks the same as with a supported platform. An architecture like this one allows tracing systems that otherwise couldn't be traced.

Instrumenting COBOL software for distributed tracing, which does not directly support a distributed tracing SDK, can still be done through a few steps:

1 COBOL emits telemetry into a stream, as in section 3.1.2.
2 A tracing parser running a supported platform reads the tracing data, marks it up appropriately, and relays it to the SaaS provider's API.

Supporting an architecture like this one requires you to design a shipping format that the tracing parser can use to create an event compatible with the tracing platform you are using. You can use an approach like this one when a distributed tracing SDK isn't permitted directly inside the production environment. Some production systems working in highly secure environments are not permitted to make the network connections required for current tracing SDKs, so proxying those connections by way of a queue or stream makes sense.

Summary

- Most of the analytical power of a telemetry pipeline comes from the transformation of telemetry between when it is sent out of the production systems and when a person views it as part of the Presentation stage, greatly simplifying the effort a person needs to go through to answer questions and gain insights.

- Markup adds context to telemetry about when and where an event occurred. When you add markup, you improve people's ability to understand the environment around a specific item of telemetry.

- Enrichment is transforming the format of telemetry to make details inside telemetry more searchable. When you enrich, you also improve the ability of people to understand what a specific item of telemetry is saying.

- The Emitting stage is the best place to apply markup, because the Emitting stage is closest to the context of the production system at the time telemetry was emitted.

- For hardware systems, which rely predominantly on Syslog, the Emitting stage is not under your control, so you should handle markup as part of the Shipping stage, which is under your control.

- Common added context for telemetry, known as markup, includes the class, module, or function that generated the event; the process identifier; and the version of the software that generated the event. These extra context-related details help people isolate which code or specific execution is responsible for a given event.

- The Shipping stage is especially important in enriching telemetry coming from Emitting stages you don't control, such as from hardware or SaaS platforms, allowing you to extract meaning to ease understanding what happened.

- The Shipping stage is responsible for transforming the format telemetry was emitted in to the format used by Shipping-stage storage, which means that the Shipping stage performs most of the enrichment in a telemetry pipeline.

- Converting data types in the Shipping stage, usually from a string to some form of number, is one of the main enrichment functions that a Shipping stage performs. When it's converted to numbers, number-based telemetry is far more powerful than the string format it began as.

- It is better to do Boolean type conversions in the Shipping stage than to rely on automatic type conversion in storage systems. Doing so makes the type conversion explicit and more maintainable.

- Converting data types as they are injected into storage by the adapter makes the type conversions explicit and more maintainable.

- The Presentation stage takes advantage of all the markup and enrichment done by the Emitting and Shipping stages to provide visualizations and reporting.

- Converting string-based timestamps to a dedicated date/time format allows you to build time-based reporting in the Presentation stage.
- For metrics-style telemetry, the Presentation stage provides extensive enrichment through the use of aggregation functions enabled by type conversions performed by the Shipping stage.

Handling multitenancy

This chapter covers

- How multitenant systems came into being
- How queues and streams are used to move telemetry
- What Presentation-stage features you need

A system with *multitenancy* is one in which different owners control, or have rights to, different parts of the overall system. A system like Digital Ocean is an example of a multitenant system, in which each account owner operates certain assets inside Digital Ocean's infrastructure. For telemetry ecosystems, multitenancy can be as simple as having a robust access control framework on the dashboarding system, or it may involve complicated event routing infrastructure to deliver telemetry events to storage and presentation systems owned and operated by different teams.

The core multitenant feature is the ability to hide telemetry from other tenants and data owners. Because telemetry data can be concealed in many ways, a multitenant telemetry ecosystem means different things to different technical organizations. This chapter will help you figure out what it means for you:

- Section 7.1 covers how organizations transform into multitenant architectures.
- Section 7.2 covers designing for multitenant telemetry systems.
- Section 7.2.1 covers Shipping stages that use two different techniques to deliver telemetry to owners: queues and streaming systems.
- Section 7.2.2 covers multitenant Presentation-stage systems and the features you want to have when implementing systems in the Presentation stage.

7.1 How multitenant architectures come about

All telemetry systems evolve over time, accommodating production-system changes, adding new telemetry systems, upgrading or removing old ones, and adapting to changing regulatory environments. Changes such as these can force a telemetry system into multitenancy where it wasn't before. This section covers several ways this change comes about. For some systems, multitenancy shows up overnight, such as when a corporate merger is announced. For other systems, multitenancy creeps in on silent cat feet, and how the current system is different from what came before is visible only to old-timers if they sit and think about it. To understand how the evolution happens, we need to look at a few single-owner systems and what their telemetry systems look like:

- An early-stage startup, with only software engineers in the technical organization (one of whom is possibly a founder)
- An organization with a culture of free sharing of telemetry
- An organization inside a much older company that maintains strong separation between member teams of the technical organization

7.1.1 Evolving multitenancy in an early-stage startup

For an early-stage startup, the entire technical organization is almost always made up of software engineers, fewer than 10 of them. A technical organization this small is incredibly nimble because little organizational inertia provides incentives to stay the course. A startup, especially in the modern era, is all but guaranteed to be running its infrastructure in a public cloud of some form, such as AWS, Digital Ocean, or Azure. This section shows how a company like this one, small enough that everyone knows everyone else, can evolve into multitenancy.

The software stack that this early-stage startup is running can be almost anything, which has some bearing on the implementation details of what the telemetry systems look like. Perhaps the company is running everything in a monolithic Ruby on Rails application to get a viable product to market as fast as possible. Or maybe it's running in a serverless platform such as AWS Lambda or Azure Functions to provide easy scaling. Whatever the production system looks like, the important fact is that *a single team is operating, maintaining, and building the production system.*

Figure 7.1 demonstrates that both production and telemetry systems are controlled by a single team. In fact, an early-stage startup simply has no other teams. The concept here is that small organizations generally don't bother with multitenancy.

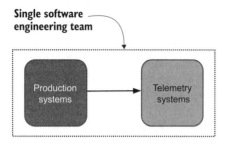

Single software engineering team

Figure 7.1   An early-stage startup's production and telemetry systems, managed by a single team. A single team can share context across the entire organization (the team), and everyone has access to everything. When more teams are added, this simplicity goes away.

They don't yet have the need to provide separation to accommodate different owners; there is only one owner, and that owner is "us."

For the early-stage startup, the most likely driver of multitenancy is growth. Startups need to grow or die, so you can predict where the problems are going to be. Although this example startup had fewer than 10 software engineers during the early stage, by the time it becomes a mid-stage startup and is starting to pursue big contracts, it may have five to seven software engineering teams, in addition to picking up a DevOps or SRE team along the way, as well as an early security team. The simple telemetry system from figure 7.1 is no more. For more on how growth in a startup affects telemetry systems, see chapter 8.

7.1.2   *Evolving multitenancy in a culture of free sharing*

This section covers the next organization we're looking at: an organization with a culture of free sharing of telemetry. This organization is different from the early-stage startup in section 7.1.1, in that it is both larger and more complex. We saw an example of a free-sharing organization like this one in section 4.2, which discussed telemetry shipping formats. In that discussion, the older software development group had been shipping Java software since the 1990s and had worked cooperatively with an operations team ever since. Figure 4.10, reproduced here as figure 7.2, demonstrates the environment.

Here, we have a telemetry system that joins the operations team's hardware—both Cisco and VMware infrastructure—

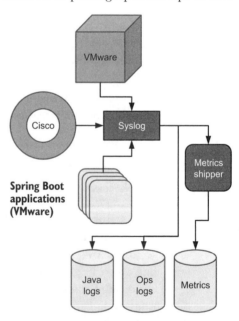

Figure 7.2   A telemetry system shared by software and operations teams, with telemetry event flow represented by directional arrows and ending in storage systems (cylinders). The software team maintains the Spring Boot application software, with the operations team maintaining most of the rest. This shared system is open to all participants even though multiple teams are involved.

with the software engineering team's application telemetry. In this case, the architecture came about because the two systems grew up together hand in hand. Using the same Syslog-based telemetry pipeline gave this organization efficiencies in its centralized logging telemetry system, and the teams share a metrics system. Although logs are stored in different systems, nothing is stopping a software engineer from poking their nose into virtual-machine start/stop events or an operations engineer from looking into errors coming from the Java environment. Although two quite different teams are interacting with this telemetry pipeline, their culture of sharing has grown up with them. Figure 7.3 demonstrates how joint the telemetry system is.

The software engineering team manages the metrics shipper and part of the data storage for metrics; the operations team manages Syslog and both of the centralized log repositories. The operations team uses the metrics system and provides consulting on ways to make the metrics system more durable. This technical organization can be quite large.

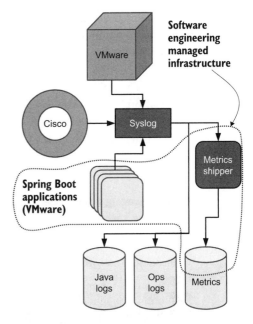

Figure 7.3   A telemetry system shared by operations and software engineering, with the systems managed by software engineering marked, demonstrating the extent of the shared system. Arrows indicate the direction and flow of events, which end up stored in one of three storage systems. Software engineering is maintaining and operating the metrics shipper used by both the software and operations teams, and both teams jointly operate the metrics storage system. This system is shared, not multitenant.

For the organization with a culture of free sharing, the conversion to multitenant can come from several sources. One possible way was described in section 4.2, which discussed picking a shipping format. In that discussion, we found out that management created a new software engineering team using a different software platform (Go instead of Java) and hired a different operations team to run on a different infrastructure (AWS instead of physical data centers), all in a bid to spark innovation inside the company. The experiment worked out, and the two separate infrastructures negotiated a shared telemetry system that could support the long-standing Java environment and the new Go-based one.

A second way that organization with a culture of sharing can convert to multitenancy can happen when this organization decided to move into the healthcare market and took on all the regulation governing handling of health information. Most laws governing access to health information take an understandably exclusive approach to who can access what and where they can do it. If there is any possibility that health information could show up in the telemetry pipeline, that pipeline needs to be locked down. There is a lot of work to be done in general when moving into a regulated market, and telemetry systems are not excluded from that work.

A third way that a culture of sharing can turn into a culture of asking for permission is as a result of a merger. Suddenly having to integrate with another technical organization is a great way to discover the limits of your own; more important, two different technical *cultures* create a huge incentive to provide some separation between owners. Integration activities between the two parts of the company can take years to resolve.

> **Living through a merger, part 1**
>
> The single-tenant telemetry systems I built and maintained for HelloSign looked much like this organization; application and operational telemetry were in the same system, and everyone could see everything. This arrangement worked great right up until we got purchased by Dropbox.
>
> We didn't immediately merge our telemetry systems with Dropbox because there were much bigger merger-related problems to solve than deduplicating our telemetry infrastructure. In the immediate aftermath of the merger, Dropbox had two islands of telemetry systems: their stuff and our stuff. We looked more like the section 7.1.3 organizations!

7.1.3   *Evolving multitenancy in a culture of strong separation*

This section is about our third organization, which maintains strong separation between teams and their supporting telemetry infrastructure. This organization is in many ways the opposite of the shared infrastructure described in section 7.1.2. The software engineering teams manage centralized logging, metrics, and distributed tracing infrastructure that the operations team has no visibility into. The operations teams manage centralized logging and a metrics system (called a monitoring system). Additionally, the security team is consuming a feed of events from the operations infrastructure that is handled by a SIEM system managed by the security team. Figure 7.4 demonstrates this split infrastructure.

With two separate centralized logging systems in figure 7.4, it is easy to challenge the assertion that either system is centralized. Words mean different things to different people, however, and in this particular technical organization, which shows little cooperation between teams, the software engineering and operations teams separately consider their centralized logging system to be centralized.

For our organization with minimal sharing, change is not likely to happen organically. This company is long-standing and well-established, which in turn means that a lot of organizational inertia is preventing such a move. A move to multitenancy has to be imposed externally somehow.

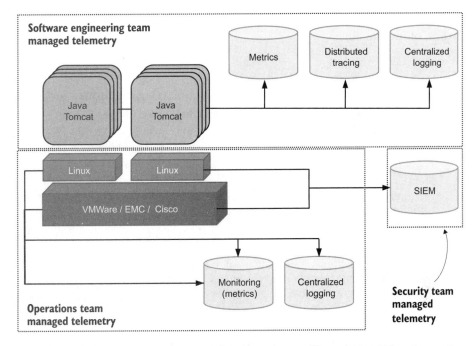

Figure 7.4 Three teams, three separate telemetry systems, with no sharing. Telemetry event flow is directional arrows indicating where the telemetry will be stored. Metrics and centralized logging are duplicated between the software engineering and operations teams because they don't share, and neither system is multitenant. The teams don't want to share; each thinks that the other team is icky.

One method of imposition is for management to push for a DevOps transformation in an effort to bring agility into the technical organization. DevOps transformations come in many types, but one of the core concepts of DevOps is to get different parts of the technical organization talking to one another. Don't have just the managers of each team talk to one another; get the engineers talking as well. As people start talking, learning about what everyone else is working on, getting used to helping others without having to be told by their boss that help is allowed, some questions start to get asked. One such question might be "We have two metrics and centralized logging systems. Why do we need two? I bet we can save money if we consolidate to one!"

Multitenancy is born. At this point, the company starts looking to consolidate its systems, leading to discussions on format (section 4.2) and cross-team telemetry standards (chapter 12).

The other method for imposing multitenancy externally is the same as that for the sharing culture: a merger with a larger organization. This organization is already all about separation, so keeping the technical organization separate from the parent organization is second nature. But what happens if the parent organization wants to merge the two? Breaking culture like that one is fraught with peril, but if the breakup is done with empathy and concern for all sides, it can be brought about with a minimum of rage-quitting engineers and engineering managers. The result is some form of multitenancy.

> **Living through a merger, part 2**
>
> The Dropbox and HelloSign telemetry systems started as islands for the understandable reason that they had never worked together before. Two years later, our systems are very separate. The reason is not the cultural example I've described; Dropbox and HelloSign engineering (and platform engineering) get along well. The problem is technical.
>
> Dropbox and HelloSign built their products on different platforms and assumptions. The much larger Dropbox had written telemetry libraries for engineers to use to ease getting telemetry into the central systems—libraries that were not written in any language HelloSign used. HelloSign's approach to telemetry was based more on stock APIs instead of libraries that abstracted away API/RPC management.
>
> In time, some degree of unification will be inevitable, and that's fine. Also, I mentioned before that truly global companies are often many smaller companies in a trenchcoat. Mergers are big drivers of that sort of thing.

You likely recognize one of these three systems from your own history; the patterns are common. The paths to multitenancy are different for every organization. You may think that multitenancy is inevitable, which isn't all that wrong. For small technical organizations, multitenancy isn't worth the effort. For larger ones, you can avoid multitenancy for a long time by maintaining common telemetry systems for everyone. But market constraints, regulation, and sheer stubborn politics often force technical organizations to adopt multitenancy in their telemetry systems.

7.2 *Designing multitenant telemetry systems*

Multitenant telemetry systems have two major design points that you need to consider when designing systems:

- Build the Shipping stage to handle telemetry from different owners and systems.
- Build the Presentation stage to handle separating access to telemetry.

Building fully separated telemetry systems like those shown in figure 7.4 is not multitenancy—that is, silos of access do not cross boundaries. Figure 7.4 can be uncharitably rewritten as figure 7.5.

A true multitenant system has Shipping or Presentation stages that allow (and separate) access to more than one type of team. Allowing software engineers from different products to review metrics for their separate systems from the same interface is one version; another is a centralized logging system that has a single ingestion point but can deliver logs to many storage systems supporting separate Presentation-stage systems.

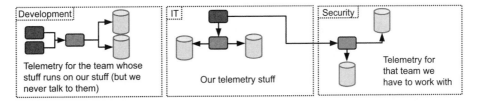

Figure 7.5 Editorially rewriting figure 7.4, demonstrating communication problems among the three teams represented here. The darkest boxes are queues or streams; the lighter boxes are telemetry parsers; cylinders are telemetry storage. Although this figure shows some slight multitenancy, it is clearly grudging, and strict boundaries are maintained whenever possible.

In some organizations, a group like operations or DevOps might maintain the unified Shipping stage. In others, a team may be dedicated to maintaining the telemetry pipeline. Individual approaches will vary, and that's fine.

The following two sections address multitenancy in the Shipping (section 7.2.1) and Presentation (section 7.2.2) stages.

7.2.1 *Multitenancy in the Shipping stage*

This section covers the effects of multitenancy on the Shipping stage. As mentioned in previous chapters, the Shipping stage is responsible for a large part of the transformation of telemetry from when the production systems send it to the Emitting stage and when humans review telemetry as part of the Presentation stage. *In multitenant systems, the Shipping stage is often charged with delivering telemetry to the correct storage system.*

Shipping stages must be able to perform two tasks in a multitenant system, illustrated in figure 7.6:

- Route telemetry to the correct storage systems
- *Fork* telemetry to allow delivery of the same telemetry to multiple recipients

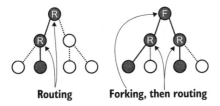

Routing   **Forking, then routing**

Figure 7.6 Two example telemetry systems. Dotted lines represent possible paths that telemetry can take; solid lines are paths that are selected; filled circles pass through or store telemetry. The left side performs routing, sending telemetry to a single location across one or more hops. The right side performs forking to create two streams and then routes both forks in a second hop.

Routing telemetry seems to be obvious, but forking isn't. Think of the case of the security team and the telemetry it is interested in. Security teams care deeply about events that describe account logins and logouts, use of privileges, and who accessed what when. Often, telemetry including this list of events is bundled inside telemetry that operations or DevOps teams maintain as part of the stream of events coming out of operating systems. Both teams have interest in those events, so both teams need to be able to receive them. A multitenant shipping system will enable dual delivery of telemetry.

Routing of telemetry applies to most of the telemetry system styles discussed in this book. Centralized logging and metrics both benefit strongly from multitenant systems. The SIEM systems used by security are often the first multitenant system a telemetry system has to accommodate. The distributed tracing systems currently available (early 2021) requires a direct connection to dedicated Shipping-stage components; this situation is likely to change as the OpenTelemetry project and its supporting ecosystem mature.

Two technologies allow routing and forking to take place: queues (point-to-point message passing) and streams (decoupled publisher/subscriber message passing). The next two sections address Shipping-stage architecture that uses both of these systems. Hybrid Shipping stages that use both are definitely possible; as you read the sections, consider how the concepts can be mixed and might apply to your own telemetry system.

NOTE   For more examples of multitenant shipping systems beyond the descriptions here, see the three part 2 chapters. Each chapter in part 2 includes examples of large telemetry systems. Such systems almost always have some aspect of multitenancy.

Designing architectures with queues

Multitenant shipping stages use queues to buffer the event stream and provide isolation between event producers and consumers. Also, queuing systems are somewhat easier to build and maintain than common streaming systems, so they are an attractive technology for routing telemetry. Because queues are a FIFO system, the ability of a queue to support forking seems to be suspect, but this attitude overlooks the true architecture. Figure 7.7 is one version of a queue-based routing system.

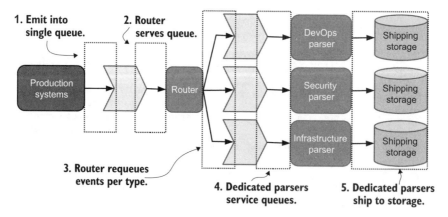

Figure 7.7   A queue-based telemetry routing system, including a routing tier and multiple parsers allowing routing and forking. Telemetry flow is described with directional arrows. An architecture like this one reduces the need for sophistication in the Emitting stage.

In figure 7.7, telemetry leaving the production systems follows this path through the telemetry pipeline:

1 All telemetry from all sources is emitted into a single queue.

2 A dedicated telemetry routing system, which can be a horizontally scaling group of systems, pulls telemetry off the routing queue and makes routing decisions.

3 The dedicated routing system pushes telemetry into the correct queue based on what kind of telemetry it is.

4 Dedicated parsers for each team pull telemetry from their queues.

5 Dedicated parsers for each team parse, transform, reformat, and submit the finalized telemetry to storage.

An important note is that a fork can happen in step 2 of this process. An SSH login event recorded by the production systems will be routed to both the DevOps parser and the security parser. This system is simple but still powerful. The design presented in figure 7.7 makes several assumptions:

- Emitting-stage systems are written with the eventual routing stage in mind, adding context-related telemetry wherever possible (section 6.1) to ease the routing-decision stage.

- All Emitting-stage systems emit directly into a queue (section 3.1.2), or helper shipping programs on the production systems pull from what the Emitting stages can produce and inject telemetry into the routing queue (section 4.1.1).

- The routing system expects to receive telemetry in a predictable format, so Emitting-stage and helper programs need to generate/transform telemetry into that format (section 4.2).

- The routing system performs minimal markup and enrichment (section 6.2), preferring to let the dedicated parsing systems handle that task, which lets the routing system handle more events per second.

- Dedicated parsing systems and the storage they send telemetry into are controlled by their respective teams.

Figure 7.8 shows another architecture that brings routing decision-making closer to the production systems.

Figure 7.8 brings the router to the production system directly. In this architecture, the routing system collects telemetry from the production system in the form of log files or one of the nonfile techniques from chapter 13, and then directly ships collected telemetry to the dedicated queues. In this architecture, only the dedicated router needs to emit to a queue; all the other Emitting- stage components can emit however works best for them. This system is a simpler one in the sense that each item

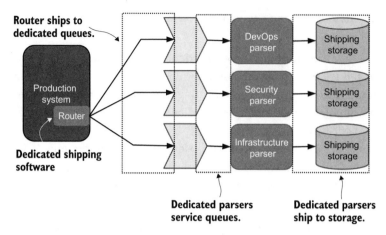

Figure 7.8 **A queue-based telemetry routing system, including routing software in the production system, that directly reduces the time telemetry takes to reach storage. Telemetry flow is solid lines, ending in dedicated storage systems. This architecture puts the routing decision into competition with production software—a potentially undesirable parasitic load.**

of telemetry has to take fewer hops to reach its storage destination. This simplicity has a few costs, though:

- The routing software on the production system is competing with production software for CPU and RAM resources—a parasitic load that can be quite significant if the production systems are prolific telemetry generators.
- An attacker gaining access to the production system will have a good idea what the telemetry system looks like by examining the configuration of the routing software.
- Pushing configuration changes to the routing software is a far more complex task when the routing software is on every production system versus on a dedicated tier of systems.

How parasitic is that parasitic load?

Determining how parasitic telemetry operations are on a production node takes some analysis. There are three areas where telemetry operations could make your production systems slower:

- *CPU costs*—If the only thing you're doing with your telemetry is reshipping it, with no other changes, this area is not likely to be significant. If you do perform changes, however (perhaps one of the chapter 15 techniques to ensure telemetry integrity), this charge can be significant. In large hardware instances, you may not notice these costs. But in container or FaaS environments, the increased run time of the container or function can be noticeable.

- *RAM costs*—Depending on how your shipping software works, you need RAM to perform your change operations and to batch up events for sending downstream. On large hardware instances or virtual machines, this change may not be significant. For containers or FaaS, where RAM usage is metered, these effects can be noticeable.
- *I/O costs*—Writing a whole bunch of telemetry to disk is an I/O charge; so is reading it by your telemetry software. If your storage is slow, telemetry I/O absolutely will compete with production I/O. If you're running slow storage, you will be better off if you put your logs on separate disks from your production operations. Or maybe you can redesign your telemetry systems to use one of the chapter 13 techniques and avoid files altogether. In my career, I've seen cases in which telemetry I/O dwarfs I/O generated by production operations!

In reality, the best way to determine the impact of your telemetry operations on your production systems is to run experiments. Play with different ways to emit telemetry (avoiding files) or the amount of enrichment you're providing inside the production environment, and see what happens.

Queue-based systems can do away with the routing tier altogether. Figure 7.9 demonstrates one system in which the parsing and routing tiers are combined.

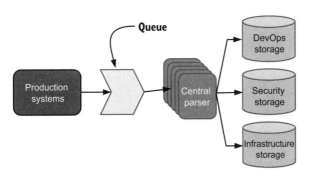

Figure 7.9 A queue-based telemetry routing system in which the routing and parsing tier are merged. Telemetry event flow is directional arrows ending in storage systems. All telemetry continues to be emitted into a single queue serviced by a group of centralized parser nodes. This parser group routes telemetry to dedicated storage based on what kind of telemetry is being processed.

Figure 7.9 shows the same central queue as figure 7.7. Unlike the architecture in the earlier figure, however, the routing system in figure 7.9 is also doing all the parsing. This architecture is similar to the architectures discussed in section 3.1.2. With parsing centralized in this way, all telemetry parsing needs to be done by a single tier of systems. If the technical organization has a dedicated telemetry engineering team, such a system is likely to be maintained by that team.

The architecture in figure 7.9 can be one step in the evolution from a shared ecosystem to one with owners. The process begins like figure 7.1, with production systems shipping into a telemetry system owned by a single team. As that telemetry system evolves, new storage systems are added. Then, as the technical organization grows and new teams are added, dedicated Presentation-stage systems are created while the existing Shipping stage is retained. From there, the telemetry system can further evolve into the one in figure 7.7, with separate teams taking over some parsing duties from the central parser.

> **NOTE**   One central idea behind sending all telemetry to a queue and parsing it at a later stage rather than on the production systems is to get the telemetry off the production systems as fast as possible. This idea has nothing to do with multitenancy and everything to do with making it harder for an attacker to manipulate telemetry before it enters the pipeline. Doing minimal markup and enrichment on the production system and shipping it to a queue in a timely way will make your production systems more defensible in the event of an attack. Should you be lucky enough to bring a prosecution to court (chapter 18 is all about helping your legal team), the validity of your telemetry will be easier to prove because of how little time the attacker had to fiddle with it. Chapter 15 provides more guidance on making your telemetry systems defensible.

DESIGNING ARCHITECTURES WITH STREAMING SYSTEMS

Multitenant telemetry ecosystems that use streams have options beyond what queues provide, which we cover in this section. Streams are a relatively recent innovation made popular by the Kafka project (https://kafka.apache.org). The base concept behind a stream is that a publisher sends data into a topic in the stream and has no awareness of any consumers of the data, who subscribe to the topic. The important distinction is that each consumer independently tracks where in the stream topic it has gotten to. Queues work as a FIFO system; when a piece of data reaches the front of the queue, the first system to request data will get that data. Most streaming systems allow consumer groups to enable queue-like behavior within that group, while allowing other consumer groups to do likewise. Whereas a queue-based system might require a producer to push data into multiple queues to deal with different consumers, in a stream-based system, the producer has to push only once. In multitenant telemetry systems, streams provide real power. Figure 7.10 shows the differences between a queue-based and a stream-based system.

In both the telemetry systems shown in figure 7.10, we see the SSHD process generating events, where they are picked up by Syslog and shipped onward. In the queue-based system, Syslog injects telemetry into two separate queues: one for operations and a second for security. In the stream-based system, Syslog injects telemetry only once, to a stream topic called ssh_events. The security and operations parsers subscribe to that topic, and both receive a complete flow of events. Because Syslog doesn't have to know what downstream parsers will need events, the Syslog configuration is simpler in the stream version versus the queue version.

One problem with streams is that the technology is relatively new, so not all telemetry emitting systems support them. For telemetry ecosystems that need to accommodate emitters that don't support streams, such as Syslog-emitting hardware and third-party software that can ship only to a log file, using a better-supported queue as a temporary

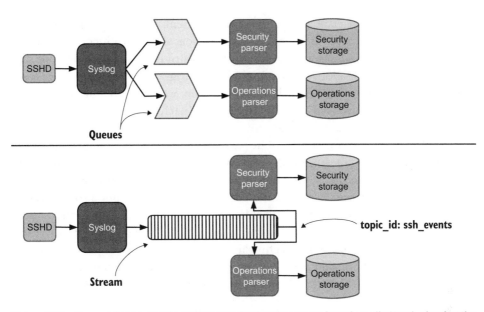

Figure 7.10   A queue-based multitenant system (top) and a stream-based one (bottom), showing the different approaches to shipping telemetry. Solid directional lines indicate telemetry flow. Forking in a queue-based system requires awareness of the need to fork in the enqueing system, whereas in the stream-based system, the forking decision is made by the consumer side of the stream rather than the producer side.

way-station is quite permissible. Figure 7.11 demonstrates a hybrid infrastructure with hardware emitting through Syslog and programs that don't have stream support.

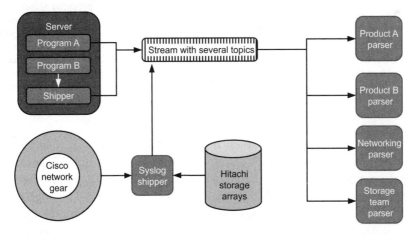

Figure 7.11   A stream-based multitenant telemetry system with support for hardware and software emitters, showing how less-capable emitters can ship into a stream. Solid directional lines indicate telemetry flow. The hardware systems (Cisco and Hitachi) emit to a Syslog system acting as an entry point for telemetry, which then injects received telemetry into the stream on various topics. Whereas Program A emits directly to the stream through emitter/shipper functions in the code, Program B emits into a log file and relies on a shipper program to move telemetry into the stream.

In figure 7.11, we have several production systems with two programs: Cisco networking gear and Hitachi storage arrays. Only one of the production systems—Program A—has direct stream support. Program B is third-party software that has support only for emitting into a log file, which a shipper program on the server ingests and injects into the stream's topic. On the hardware side, we have a Syslog shipping system that receives emissions from both the Cisco and Hitachi hardware and then resubmits it to the stream under appropriate `topic_id` settings for the hardware. On the other side of the stream system, we have four parsers, one for each of the production systems on the left. This architecture is the stream version of the queue-based architecture in figure 7.8, in which the routing decisions are made on the emitting side.

Figures 7.10 and 7.11 show the power of streams, but they also are architectures in which the stream system is accessible from the front-line production systems, which in turn means that they are accessible to an attacker who gains access to the front-line production systems. Some technical organizations consider this risk to be perfectly acceptable; others will need a buffer between the stream systems and the emitters. Figure 7.12 shows a hybrid architecture combining queues and streams.

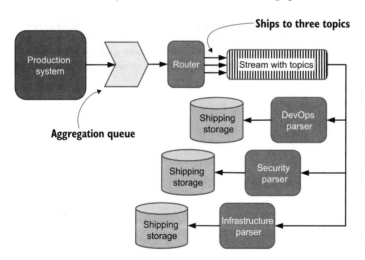

Figure 7.12 A telemetry system using a queue-based router to shield the streaming system from potential attackers. Solid directional lines indicate telemetry flow. Production systems emit all telemetry into a single queue, which is serviced by a router before getting moved to the stream.

There are a lot of similarities between figure 7.12 and figure 7.7, which is the fully queue-based version of this shipping architecture. Whereas figure 7.7 had the router sending telemetry to individual queues, with streams, the router is sending telemetry to individual topics that are picked up by the dedicated parsers. The approach in figure 7.12 merges the protection of queue-based systems when getting telemetry off the production systems with the flexibility of streams for handling parsing tasks. In the figure 7.12 architecture, if the security team wanted to parse all telemetry going to both DevOps and infrastructure, it is easy to set a consumer group in each topic and ingest everything. There's no need to update the router to fork events so that security can get a combined feed!

One difference between queues and streams comes down to who can suck down what telemetry. With streams, it is easy to set up additional consumer groups to fork a telemetry feed without having to bother any upstream development teams to add that support. When you're managing a stream system in a multitenant ecosystem, managing access control lists and users is paramount. The security team in the previous paragraph could consume two topics because the user on the stream system permitted that activity. The DevOps parser, on the other hand, is permitted access to only the one topic. Multitenant systems require managing access control, often inside the pipeline itself. (Section 15.2 covers ACL management inside Shipping stages as a defense against attackers.)

7.2.2 *Multitenancy in the Presentation stage*

This section covers how multitenancy manifests in the Presentation stage, which is the stage that most telemetry-consuming people consider to be *the* telemetry system. For telemetry systems such as centralized logging and metrics, the Presentation stage can be all you need for true multitenancy. Currently, open source distributed tracing systems lack the access-control features needed to provide true multitenancy, but this situation is likely to change across the 2020s, as the SaaS distributed tracing vendors already provide these features.

Multitenancy in the Presentation stage happens when you have a display technology, such as Grafana for metrics or Kibana for centralized logging, that has access to telemetry storage systems owned by different teams but allows denying access to a storage system if the user isn't on the right teams. Rather than run multiple versions of the same software, if the Presentation-stage software offers features enabling multitenancy, you can save maintenance overhead by running a single system. You want to see certain features in a Presentation-stage system that supports multitenancy, which extends the feature lists provided for metrics in section 5.1, centralized logging in section 5.2, and SIEM in section 5.3:

- *Ability to define roles*—The core of any access control system is the ability to define roles or groups with permissions.
- *Ability to use single-sign-on* (SSO) *frameworks such as SAML and OpenID Connect* (OIDC)—The Presentation system can hook into an existing authentication framework maintained by the technical organization.
- *Ability to restrict access to data sources by role*—You can keep members of different roles from accessing databases they shouldn't, which reduces the cleanup area of leaks of regulated data.
- *Ability to assign users to multiple roles*—Users should be able to serve in multiple roles, such as engineering managers who need to be in several team roles.
- *Ability to restrict access to dashboards by role*—Not every dashboard is intended for use by every member of the system, so limiting access applies to accessing dashboards, making for a less-crowded experience for everyone.

- *Ability to restrict who can create or modify dashboards by role*—View-only users can find existing dashboards to be quite powerful, and restricting edit access reduces dashboard sprawl.

One thing to keep in mind is that the open source dashboard vendors, such as Kibana (Elastic.co) and Grafana (GrafanaLabs), consider extensive access control and single-sign-on support to be paid add-ons; projects need to make money somehow, and organizations that are big enough to need these features are big enough to afford to pay for them. For Kibana, basic authentication is supported in the open source version, but the ability to tie authentication to an SSO system such as SAML or LDAP requires a paid add-on. Grafana also supports basic and SSO authentication in the open source version, but restricting access to specific data sources requires a paid add-on. The requirements of running a SaaS system mean that these features are present by default for SaaS vendors, but full richness in open source, especially SSO support, may be bought only at enterprise price levels.

The realities of how software works for Presentation systems forces certain choices in multitenant architecture. Figure 7.13 demonstrates the difference between using free and low-cost systems versus systems with paid enterprise features.

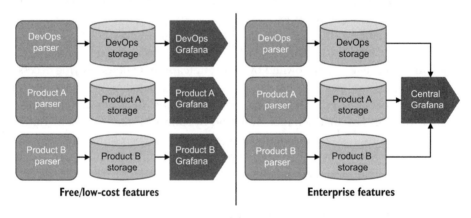

Figure 7.13   Two different Presentation-stage designs based on the cost of features. Telemetry is parsed and sent to storage, and that storage is consumed by Grafana.

On the left side is a free version of the Grafana metrics presentation system (https://grafana.com). Each of the interested teams operates its own Grafana installation to maintain separation between its telemetry and that of other teams. This separated version is not multitenant in the Presentation stage, because multitenancy was handled in the Shipping stage alone.

On the right side is an enterprise (paid) version of Grafana, which comes with features that enable separation of telemetry through the use of access control rules on data sources, allowing only one Grafana installation to be required. The central version is multitenant, because several tenants share an access system.

For large telemetry systems with many tenants, multitenancy in the Presentation stage can make the overall telemetry system easier to maintain. Politically, central systems are likely to be managed by a dedicated telemetry team, but they can also be managed by DevOps or SRE teams as part of their developer enablement and availability missions.

For an example, let's look at figure 7.14, which shows four Presentation-stage systems for all four telemetry styles: metrics, logging, tracing, and SIEM. There are two SaaS providers in this mix. SaaS providers use multitenant features as a key part of their service. The other two Presentation-stage systems, Kibana and Grafana, need enterprise plans to provide the multitenancy features required by the company. Grafana can also display logging data alongside metrics data, so it pulls from the logging data storage systems. By having four systems fronting a large telemetry system, this company saves money and staff time by having to manage Presentation-stage systems only once. The alternative, as with the highly siloed system we saw in figure 7.5, is to maintain many of the same Presentation-stage systems in different places serving from different storage systems, likely in different software versions, which magnifies the cost of managing Presentation-stage systems for the technical organization as a whole.

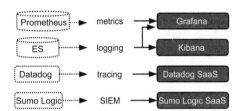

Figure 7.14   Presentation-stage systems for a large cloud-based startup, with Shipping-stage items in dotted lines and Presentation-stage systems in solid lines. This type of architecture is likely centrally managed to serve many teams and to be using enterprise-support plans for Grafana and Kibana.

Summary

- A system with multitenancy is one in which different owners control or have rights to different parts of the overall system.
- Telemetry systems often start as single-tenant and evolve into multitenant as the organization grows and changes. This history is important when you try to make changes in a telemetry system that's new to you.
- Small organizations generally don't bother with multitenancy because they don't need it yet.
- Medium-size and even large technical organizations can stay single-tenant if they have a culture of open sharing among teams. Sharing is often a sign of healthy communication within the organization.
- External forces, such as new regulation or compliance frameworks and mergers, can force a single-tenant telemetry system to adopt multitenancy.
- Some technical organizations operate separate telemetry systems rather than share them among teams. This arrangement is single-tenancy.
- Organizations that have strict separation between teams can be forced into multitenancy after external events such as a DevOps transformation or a corporate merger.

- Multitenant telemetry systems need to consider how to design the Shipping stage to handle telemetry destined for multiple owners and how to separate access in Presentation-stage systems.
- To support diverse teams, multitenancy in the Shipping stage needs to support the ability to route telemetry to correct storage systems and fork telemetry to allow multiple delivery of telemetry.
- Forking in the Shipping stage is the ability to send the same telemetry to multiple owners, possibly undergoing separate transformations along the way.
- Shipping telemetry off a production system to a dedicated routing queue or stream topic makes the Emitting stages on the production systems easier to maintain and provides isolation to defend against attackers.
- Putting a Shipping-stage system that performs routing decisions on production systems means that the router is competing for CPU and RAM with the production software.
- Stream systems were popularized by the Apache Kafka project and provide more telemetry system flexibility than queue-based Shipping-stage systems.
- Consumer groups in a stream system allow queuelike behavior within the consumer group while still providing all events to all consumer groups.
- Streams are relatively new technology, so support for them in software isn't as robust as it is with queues.
- Using a queue in front of a stream is an effective way of getting telemetry into a stream from systems that support only queues.
- Managing multitenancy in a Shipping stage often requires some degree of access-control management by separate owners.
- Multitenancy in the Presentation stage happens when you have more than one owner accessing telemetry through a common system while preventing one owner from seeing the telemetry of another owner. This arrangement is similar to how SaaS providers operate.
- Presentation-stage systems that support multitenancy require features for defining and enforcing user roles, accessing data sources, and restricting access to defined dashboards.
- SSO support, such as SAML or OIDC, is quite often an enterprise feature requiring a higher-level paid plan for many Presentation-stage software platforms. Elastic.co and Grafana Labs both use this model as their primary revenue stream.
- Large technical organizations find that using centralized multitenant Presentation-stage systems offers favorable costs and a higher level of overall features, compared with having each team manage its own system independently of the rest of the technical organization.

Part 2

Use cases revisited: Applying architecture concepts

Whereas part 1 described the overall architecture for telemetry systems, focusing on techniques, technology, and some of the people aspects of operating telemetry systems, part 2 gives you a catalog of examples of how different organizations design their telemetry systems. Every organization approaches the problem of telemetry differently, so we will be covering three quite different example organizations. The cases here are merely examples to describe differences; they're not intended to be paragons you must meet. I hope that at least one of these examples will be familiar to you.

The software industry is vast, and the concrete examples I used throughout part 1 had to be equally diverse. If you had trouble connecting the lessons from part 1 to your own experience, the chapters here should get you closer to making that connection:

- Chapter 8 covers a technology startup, beginning from the early stage with a small handful of engineers and ending after the initial public offering as the company moves into enterprise dominance, with a technology organization of well over 1,000 employees and a global presence.
- Chapter 9 covers companies in which software merely gets the job done; it isn't what they're selling. This chapter covers companies with small offices of a few people all the way up to enterprise-size with significant internal software development.

- Chapter 10 covers long-established companies, the kind that incorporated during the paper-and-ink era and computerized well before the IBM PC era. If you ever wondered how telemetry operations work with mainframes, this chapter is yours. It covers organizations up to true multinational companies.

Each chapter includes organizations of different sizes and addresses the reasons behind changes in their telemetry systems as organizations grow. Long-established organizations may have already been enterprise or multinational when they first adopted computers. The 2010s were a time of rapid improvement of telemetry system options. All organizations had to adapt. The 2020s and 2030s undoubtedly will bring about even more options. Understanding how different organizations react to change will position you to handle the coming transformations.

NOTE These chapters are intended to provide you more examples of telemetry systems as they exist in different sizes and types of organizations. If you feel that you have a solid grasp of the concepts from part 1, it is entirely safe for you to skip these chapters and move on to part 3.

Growing cloud-based startup

This chapter covers

- Startup telemetry architecture at many stages of growth
- Forces that drive change at different growth stages
- How telemetry architecture changes with rapid growth

This chapter is about how telemetry system design changes over the life cycle of a cloud-based technology startup. This company is building everything from scratch—a blank canvas to develop its big idea. For teaching purposes, this company is stuck in a moment. It became a small company now; its growth to enterprise is all now. In truth, by the time a technology company moves from three people with a big idea to one that built its own headquarters building, it is accommodating a decade or more of technology decisions every time a new decision is made.

NOTE All the part 2 chapters are written to tell telemetry stories using the techniques from part 1, as a means of providing more concrete examples of integrated telemetry systems. If you feel that you need more real-world examples to understand how these systems work, these chapters are for you. If you feel that you already have a good grasp of the concepts, skipping these chapters and moving on to part 3 is fine.

A cloud-based technology startup has several distinguishing features:

- *It is young.* This company is less than 10 years old. If it's much older than 10, it begins to look more like the organizations in chapter 9.
- *Nothing came before.* This company is building from scratch; there is no *before* to work past or refactor.
- *It moves fast, at least at the start.* When you have no history, history can't force you to stay the course, so you can change direction quickly. This advantage goes away as the company ages, though.
- *The tech industry loves it.* This fact has many effects, such as easing finances and improving the company's ability to hire technical talent. Popularity has its benefits, which is why this chapter is the first in part 2.

From the point of view of telemetry systems, the key difference among startups, non-software organizations (chapter 9), and long-established computing organizations (chapter 10) is the existence of a group of technical employees who need to use telemetry to do their work—a group that has been there from day one. For a nonsoftware company, such a group doesn't show up until the company is a certain size (see section 9.3). For a long-established company, this group of technical employees has been around since the 1970s, which was long after the company's founding. For a startup, telemetry handling is among the long list of things to be addressed before the product is brought to market.

Each section in this chapter has two subsections:

- A description of the example organization's production and telemetry systems to highlight changes among companies of different sizes
- An analysis of the telemetry techniques the telemetry systems are using, drawn from chapters 2–7, to demonstrate how these techniques fit together in a complete telemetry system

This chapter is all about showing how the skills you learned in chapters 2–7 are used in an organization of these sizes and types. As you read about each type of company, ask yourself a few questions:

- What is the telemetry architecture on display?
- What incentives are in place to make the described telemetry architecture the one that was picked?
- What elements of how the *technical organization* is structured drove the telemetry architecture design?

The answers to these questions will teach you what to expect when your career takes you to organizations of this type. When you are asked to integrate a new telemetry system, you will be able to place it correctly within the context of the existing telemetry systems and business drivers. Remember: *the politics of the humans has as much to do with telemetry system design as the realities of the technology you are using.*

8.1 Telemetry at the small-company stage

A small cloud-based startup is one that hasn't released a product yet or that has a small number of people supporting its product. This section covers how the problem of telemetry is approached by an organization of this size that also has dedicated software engineers. This organization might have been started by three software engineers who had other jobs, but they have a big idea and started working on it in their free time. At some point, the big idea looked like something with some market potential, so the three people decided to take the plunge and incorporated to start selling the big idea to investors.

When investors decide that the big idea has some market legs, a seed round (initial investment) allows the three founders to start growing their new company without immediate fear of running out of money. More engineers are hired to help build the big idea; some customer account managers are hired to maintain relationships with customers and close deals.

The business challenge of a company in this phase is looking for market fit—any market fit, wherever they can find it. Concepts such as *minimally viable product* (MVP, the simplest product that will be accepted by the market) are mentioned a lot, and MVP models are tweaked based on feedback from sales and support. Every closed deal is celebrated, and when high-contract-value customers get cranky, everyone pays attention. The biggest risk to the business is running out of money.

Minimally viable product

Much of the effort in a small startup is spent on figuring out what the MVP is. Some companies get lucky and figure it out on the first shot; others have to tweak their product to adapt to what their target market is saying, or react to an unexpected market deciding that their product fits quite well. In case the point made earlier wasn't clear, a small startup is in constant fear of running out of money before it finds the MVP.

But that's not all. The MVP concept also applies to any market the company tries to get into. It could be that the first market it did well in was one- to three-person real estate offices. Multioffice real estate agencies, however, have rather more advanced requirements that need satisfaction, which means that the MVP for those companies is more challenging. The MVP concept never goes away with startup-style companies. Even companies that are comfortably selling to Fortune 500 companies still talk about MVP products when they are bringing something new to market to diversify what they sell.

The fear of running out of money and the drive to find market fit are strong incentives to the small but growing technical organization to focus all its efforts on the production system. Everything else needs to be delegated to third parties if at all possible, which is why companies of this size almost always host their production systems in a public cloud of some form. Their telemetry systems will either be the native option that comes with the public cloud or a third-party option that manages as much of the telemetry pipeline as possible. Figure 8.1 shows an example of this fully delegated approach to telemetry.

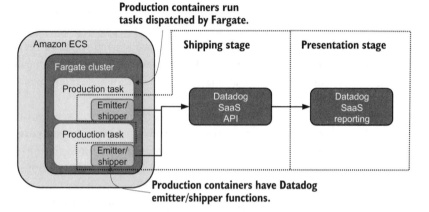

Figure 8.1   An early-stage startup production/telemetry architecture, based on the AWS Elastic Container Services (AWS ECS) offering. By delegating the Shipping and Presentation stages to a SaaS provider, our startup's software engineering team can focus entirely on producing the production systems and get to profitability faster.

8.1.1   *Describing the small company's telemetry system*

In figure 8.1, we see an example architecture that a small startup might use for its production and telemetry systems. This company picked the telemetry SaaS vendor Datadog to provide its telemetry ecosystem. The company is running its code in AWS ECS and using an emitter/shipper function (see section 3.1.3) inside its production code to emit telemetry to a Datadog API. When people want to interact with telemetry, they use the SaaS platform Datadog to do so. This architecture allows the software engineering teams to worry only about being compatible with the Datadog API—not about building and maintaining an entire telemetry ecosystem themselves.

An architecture of this shape, with telemetry delegated, allows the technical organization to focus its efforts on the production code. Being in a public cloud, especially for a highly managed service such as AWS ECS and Fargate, frees the technical organization from bothering with managing the operating system and the networking components of the production system. Although telemetry service providers like Datadog often base their prices on the amount of data ingested, a small startup likely doesn't have enough traffic for such costs to be a major problem yet.

For telemetry styles, the ECS consoles are likely to be the sole sources of centralized logging. Datadog provides metrics and optionally distributed tracing. A company of this size and age might be relying entirely on distributed tracing for its centralized logging needs and using AWS consoles for AWS-specific telemetry.

Companies of this size often have only software engineers in their technical organization because everything else has been delegated to third parties. An operations team isn't needed because the cloud provider is doing almost everything; what is left can be handled by software engineers. A DevOps team might be present, but it's likely made up of software engineers who focus more on testing and deploy tooling than on the production software and may not consider themselves to be a separate team yet. Security teams are present only if the market the company is attempting to sell to requires high-security solutions. The technical org chart is as pared down as the production/telemetry system architecture: a single box.

8.1.2 Analyzing the small company's telemetry system

Let's take a look at how telemetry is handled at the Emitting, Shipping, and Presentation stages of the telemetry pipeline of this small startup. We see from figure 8.1 that the company is using two telemetry styles:

- Metrics, from the software itself
- Centralized logging, from AWS itself and whatever gets emitted by the software to standard out

EMITTING STAGE

This section focuses on the Emitting stage for our small startup's telemetry pipeline. Small products have small footprints, as we see in figure 8.2.

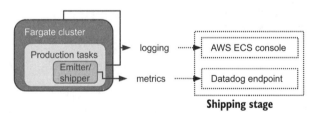

Figure 8.2 Emitting stage for the small cloud-based startup, with two telemetry styles (metrics and logging) shipping to SaaS providers. Emitting-stage components are filled boxes and solid lines. The Fargate cluster ships to the AWS console, and any output from the production tasks also ships to the AWS console. A Datadog function in the production tasks ships metrics to the Datadog SaaS cloud. The lone component that our startup is maintaining directly is the emitter/shipper function for metrics inside the production code. Maintain as little of the Emitting stage as possible to maximize focus on the production code.

There are exactly two sources of emissions in this architecture:

- Metrics issued by the production system
- Anything that shows up in the AWS ECS consoles, including AWS- and Fargate-specific telemetry and output from the production software

Their production software uses an emitter/shipper function inside the code, which is the technique from section 3.1.3. This code uses the Datadog SDK, which is running in the production software, to emit into a Datadog API endpoint. Although Datadog supports tracing, this company's production systems aren't complex enough for that feature.

Centralized logging is handled end-to-end entirely by AWS. Section 2.1.3 describes how you can use standard output for a way to emit telemetry, which this company is doing with AWS ECS and Fargate. AWS ECS itself is using techniques from section 4.1.3 to capture the output, which leads us to the Shipping stage.

SHIPPING STAGE

This section focuses on the Shipping stage for our small startup. Because the telemetry pipelines are highly delegated to third parties, this section focusses mostly on how telemetry moves into the Datadog and AWS systems. Figure 8.3 demonstrates the Shipping-stage components of its systems.

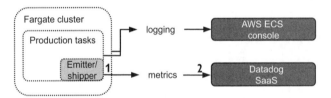

Figure 8.3   Shipping stage for the small cloud-based startup. Filled boxes are Shipping-stage components; dotted boxes are Emitting-stage components. SaaS providers and their code make up the entire Shipping stage, leaving our small startup to focus entirely on getting its product to profitability.

For the metrics telemetry, the emitter/shipper function is still part of the shipping system. The emitter/shipper code sends metrics to the Datadog cloud. The metrics shipping pipeline is

1. Emitted from the emitter/shipper function in the production software
2. Received by the Datadog agent in the production code and then shipped to the Datadog cloud

For centralized logging, when telemetry is emitted into the standard output, it enters the AWS platform, and that's all we care about right now. This system is deliberately simple because our company is more focused on reaching profitability than on making sure that its software is fully instrumented with logging, metrics, and tracing.

PRESENTATION STAGE

This section covers the Presentation stage for our small startup, which has a pretty small system. This company has delegated the Presentation stage to third parties, so its Presentation-stage systems are outside systems. For metrics, the Datadog SaaS portal provides all the metrics needed for the Presentation stage. For centralized logging, the AWS ECS console fills all Presentation-stage logging needs.

8.2 *Telemetry at the medium-size company stage*

A medium-size cloud-based startup is one that has figured out how to sell to at least one market and is established. This company has enough incoming revenue to quiet the small-stage fear of running out of money. Money fears aren't entirely gone—they never are in a startup—but the prospect of corporate death is now years in the future instead of months. The bigger fears of insiders are layoffs to get expenses back under revenue. This section is about a company that has figured out its market and is looking to expand its share of that market.

This company has grown a lot since the small-company stage. Whereas it used to have a single big team of software engineers, now it has enough people in the technical organization to have multiple teams. At this stage, a DevOps team has likely gained independence and is an official team. (Whether their team name includes the word *DevOps* depends on the people in the technical organization.). This team focuses on improving development workflows and making software deploys as easy as possible. This stage is the first one in which an SRE team might show up, possibly instead of a DevOps team, to make the product stable from the point of view of customers. A separate security team remains unlikely, but you'll see one if the market requires such a team to be present.

Although it has continuing revenue, the company has likely run out of the money provided in the initial investment by outside investors. Companies at this stage often seek a second or third round of investment (the A and B series of investments) to continue living beyond their means and supercharge development of their product. Generally speaking, if a company isn't a superstar, the more outside investment it needs to keep operating, the more influence investors have on its operations. This influence sometimes guides the way that the technical infrastructure grows.

This company has had several years to build, refine, and enhance its product. More features mean more code and more complexity in the production systems. Figure 8.4 shows how the architecture has changed from figure 8.1.

8.2.1 *Describing the medium-size company's telemetry system*

When comparing figure 8.4 and figure 8.1, we see that the company has expanded its use of AWS ECS and added a second telemetry SaaS product in the form of Sumo Logic, and it is now using more than one Fargate cluster to host production code. The company added a new Fargate cluster dedicated to its continuous integration and deployment services, used to test code for quality before deploy (continuous integration [CI])

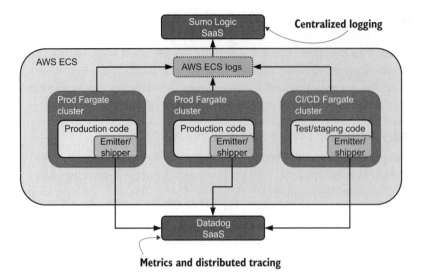

Figure 8.4   Example production and telemetry system architecture for a midsize cloud-based startup. Two external providers for telemetry services are present instead of one. (Sumo Logic is new.) We also see a dedicated continuous integration/deploy Fargate cluster. SaaS providers remain the sole telemetry system to allow software engineering to continue focusing solely on product.

and to automate the deployment process (continuous deployment [CD]). Whereas the small company used the AWS ECS console for centralized logging, the midsize company has realized the limitations of that system and subscribed to the Sumo Logic SaaS product to provide centralized logging for both the production systems and CI/CD systems. It retained Datadog to continue providing metrics and now distributed tracing services. As with the small company, nearly all the telemetry pipeline is contracted to external parties rather than owned.

The company continues its practice of using emitter/shipper functions in production systems. These functions now emit into two separate pipelines, one for each of the SaaS companies that handle telemetry. The CI/CD cluster emits into Datadog because it uses the metrics and tracing data to verify that new code does not introduce performance regressions.

At this stage, reliance on external parties for telemetry services begins to show up in the corporate bottom line. Until now, using third parties for telemetry services has allowed the company to focus on what really matters: making the product that will make money. Now that the product is making money, improving profitability by reducing operating costs starts looking attractive. Every company is different and faces different forces, but if our midsize startup begins to run out of investment money and has to live on direct earnings, bringing those delegated telemetry services in-house starts to make sense.

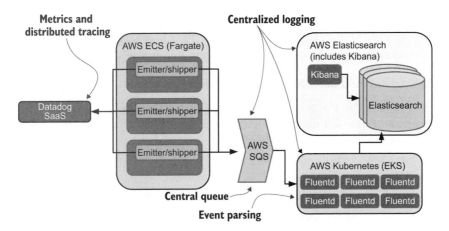

Figure 8.5   A variation on the midsize cloud-based startup, with centralized logging handled in AWS instead of another SaaS application. Moving centralized logging in-house signals cost sensitivity to using a SaaS service for the most expensive telemetry style (centralized logging).

Figure 8.5 presents a different architecture for this shift of telemetry. Facilitating this change are those DevOps or SRE teams, which often have infrastructure management experience.

In figure 8.5, we see that the centralized logging role played by Sumo Logic in figure 8.4 has been replaced by a different system hosted in a combination of AWS (SQS), AWS Elastic Kubernetes Services (EKS), and AWS Elasticsearch. Here, the emitter/shipper functions in the production ECS tasks have been updated to emit directly into SQS, an architecture similar to the one presented in section 3.1.2. From there, Fluentd has been configured to pull items off of the SQS queue. After Fluentd is done processing and transforming events, it stores them in Elasticsearch. Kibana, provided as part of the AWS Elasticseach offering, is used as the Presentation stage for the centralized logging system.

Finally, seeing EKS in the figure is a sign that this company is beginning to feel the constraints of the AWS ECS platform. ECS is opinionated; it makes a specific type of application design easy, and varying from that pattern makes for a lot of work. This arrangement is great for a company that's just starting out, because it doesn't have to waste time building deploy automation or spend meetings deciding on application design patterns. Going outside the ECS box while still using containers, however, generally means adopting EKS to provide that extra flexibility. EKS requires more maintenance than ECS does, which is where those DevOps and SRE teams come into play. To summarize, the changes from small to medium-size company include

- A much larger technical organization is broken into multiple teams.
- The production systems are much more complicated and now include CI/CD systems.

- Telemetry systems have added a third telemetry style: tracing.
- The cost of SaaS-based telemetry systems is now large enough to be a concern and can trigger moving a telemetry system in-house.

8.2.2 *Analyzing the medium-size company's telemetry system*

Let's take a look at how telemetry is handled in each of the three stages of the telemetry pipeline. Complicating matters somewhat is the shift this company made partway through its medium-size stage, where centralized logging started as part of a SaaS solution (the early medium stage) but was moved in-house on a different public cloud container management offering (the late medium stage).

EMITTING STAGE

This section covers the Emitting stage for our medium-size startup and the drivers that forced changes here. Emissions continue to focus more on emitter/shipper functions, but those functions are now getting more complex in how they work. Figure 8.6 shows how the Emitting stage changed partway through.

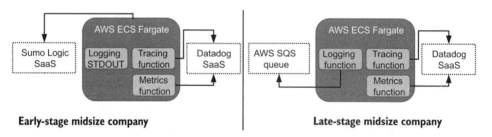

Figure 8.6   Emitting-stage components for a midsize cloud-based startup. Emitting-stage components have a solid fill. This figure shows an early/late split in telemetry handling; the early midsize company used a SaaS provider for centralized logging but moved to an in-house solution for cost reasons late in the midsize period. The late stage is the first time this company has taken on the burden of directly creating and maintaining a telemetry system.

The early-stage systems look much as they did in the small company, with production software using emitter/shipper functions inside the code to send metrics and now logging telemetry to SaaS providers. But now there are three separate emitter/shipper functions:

- Using the Datadog SDK, the company wrote a specific metrics-emitting function that sends to the Datadog agent.
- Also using the Datadog SDK, it instrumented their code for tracing, used for distributed tracing, that also sends to the Datadog agent.
- After configuring AWS ECS logs to go directly to Sumo Logic, the company wrote specific loggers sending events to the standard output (see section 2.1.3).

After the company moved to the late stage as a medium company, centralized logging was moved in-house. Doing so required changing the third emitter/shipper function away from shoveling everything into stdout and instead sending directly to a SQS in AWS—the direct-to-queue pattern from section 3.1.2.

SHIPPING STAGE

This section covers the Shipping-stage portion of our medium-size startup as it transforms through growth. Unlike the small version of this company, the late-period midsize company starts maintaining part of the Shipping stage (figure 8.7).

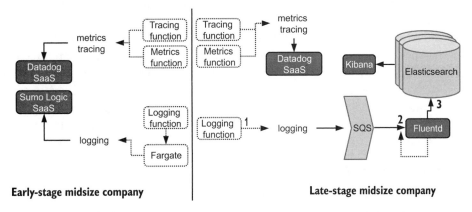

Early-stage midsize company | **Late-stage midsize company**

Figure 8.7 Shipping-stage components for the midsize cloud-based startup in both its early and late periods. Dotted lines and boxes are Emitting-stage components and event flow; solid lines and filled boxes are Shipping-stage components and event flow. The company's move to maintain its own telemetry system and Shipping-stage components is made possible by financial security and improving skill in the technical organization.

As in the Emitting stage, there are significant differences between the early- and late-stage telemetry architectures. The early-stage architecture is much like the small-company architecture, with metrics, distributed tracing, and centralized logging pipelines looking like this:

1 Metrics, tracing, and logging emit from emitter/shipper functions.
   a Tracing and metrics emit directly to the SaaS provider.
   b Logging emits through the standard output and is captured by Fargate logging.
   c Sumo Logic polls Fargate logging.
2 Metrics, tracing, and logging are ingested by the SaaS provider cloud.

Bringing centralized logging in-house marks the first real change in this company's Shipping stage. The new pipeline involves self-managing the markup and enrichment (chapter 6) end to end. The pipeline stages are

1 An emitter function in the production code adds context-related telemetry (see section 6.1) and sends telemetry to an AWS SQS queue (see section 3.1.2).
2 Fluentd, running in EKS on AWS, is configured to pull events from the queue.
3 Fluentd enriches the telemetry (see section 6.2.2) and converts data types as needed (see section 6.2.3) before sending the telemetry to storage in Elasticsearch.

If you look at figure 8.7 closely, you will see dotted lines (Emitting-stage event flow) coming from Fluentd and going to the SQS queue. This dotted-line event flow represents telemetry emitted by the telemetry systems themselves that will be ingested. The Elasticsearch and Kibana components don't have this dotted line because they're part of the managed AWS Elasticsearch service.

PRESENTATION STAGE

This section covers the Presentation stage of the telemetry system used by our medium-size startup and shows how it changed with the move of part of the Shipping stage to an internally manage system. The early- and late-stage medium-size company architecture has a key difference in that for the first time, the late-stage architecture has a presentation system managed by the company rather than a SaaS provider. The early-stage company used two SaaS providers for its Presentation stage systems: Datadog for metrics and tracing, and Sumo Logic for centralized logging. The late-stage company, however, uses the feature list from section 5.2 to develop a Presentation-stage system for centralized logging, using the Kibana provided by AWS Elasticsearch.

8.3   *Telemetry at the large-company stage*

A large cloud-based startup is one that is well-established in small to medium-size business markets and is looking to move upmarket to gain contracts from the likes of the Fortune 500. Small and medium-size businesses are not picky about who they select for providers, but large companies often require vendor assessments to be completed by any new vendor to ensure that the newcomer is safe to do business with. What was a quite viable product in the small and medium-size business market is not even minimally viable in the big companies. MVP has changed, so to move upmarket, the product has to change again. This section is about the changes that being a large company brings to the production and telemetry architectures.

This company has grown from a middle-size company, with revenue now in the high tens of millions (if not more). The technical organization has also grown in complexity as the company has consolidated its place in the small/medium-size business space. There are now enough software engineers that all-hands meetings require an auditorium, and everyone doesn't know everyone else. SRE is created as a new team if it didn't arrive during the medium-size stage, bringing technical discipline to product development. The move to enterprise and all the vendor assessments that come with it spurred the creation of a security team for the first time, if one wasn't already in place. DevOps or operations teams now exist because maintaining the platform on which the production systems run is a big enough job to call for full teams.

This stage is also the first big off-ramp from public cloud to running actual computers in a data center. The decision to make this shift, even for a partial chunk of the production systems, is a major shift in focus, so isn't done lightly. If the product involves lots of storage, running a data center full of storage systems provides enough efficiency of scale to beat public cloud options. Or maybe the market benefits from specialist hardware that public clouds simply don't provide. Whatever the cause, the move to physical hardware can happen at this point, bringing a true operations team into the technical organization.

Use of public cloud options can also shift at this stage, as economies of scale begin to factor into platform decisions. AWS ECS is fabulous for bringing code to market fast, and its fully managed systems allow technical organizations to focus on what they do best: write code. The cost calculus changes when a technical organization has more than 250 people, because some of those people could be quite skilled at building and maintaining the kind of systems that were previously contracted out. Or maybe the managed options are merely pretty good, and the company needs *awesome*, so it builds its own version in a generalist cloud such as AWS or Azure.

The production systems at this point are fully featured for the small/medium-size business space and aim to challenge the big players. This system has a beautiful web UI, an API for interacting with the system programmatically, and a mobile experience. There are likely several databases backing different features.

Codewise, the choices made when the company was small are coming back to haunt the large company, making for a creeping tech-debt problem. The cutting-edge technology that was picked when the company was three people with a big idea now borders on mainstream, and this company may even be one of the drivers behind that push. All these factors considered alongside the growth in customers add up to a significant redesign of the product to change design assumptions. Monoliths are broken apart; microservices are merged; the technical organization is reorganized; databases are split or merged; and telemetry systems are looked at anew.

The final driver of organizational change is the desire to land contracts with Fortune 500 companies. The vendor assessments that such companies require is an extended interview process to ensure that a prospective vendor has safe data-handling processes, is likely to survive common disasters, and is likely to still be in business in five or ten years. This interview process can be shortened considerably, and sometimes eliminated, by achieving compliance with frameworks like the Service Operational Controls 2 (SOC 2) framework from the American Institute of CPAs.

Compliance frameworks like SOC 2 require an organization to meet certain standards of internal processes, procedures, and data-handling policies, and are audited by third-party auditors on a schedule. Presenting a prospective customer with a report issued by a third party detailing your company's compliance with safe operating procedures greatly improves the speed of landing big sales deals. This situation is wonderful, but getting to that point is a huge project that often takes years.

SOC 2 and other compliance frameworks force a technical organization to a specific minimum level of organizational maturity that likely hasn't existed before (or hasn't existed uniformly). Whereas the small company with five engineers allowed each engineer to push code to production directly and directly probe how production systems are working, a company that's subject to compliance frameworks has to greatly reduce or eliminate the ability of the people who write the code to modify production systems directly. A process must be in place to ensure that code moving to production has been tested and approved for deployment and that changes to production systems have been similarly vetted. This process is a change management process.

NOTE   Telemetry systems are central to assessing procedure compliance by third-party auditors. When you go through your project to achieve compliance, your telemetry systems will see a lot of updates. You'll find that you need to add much more to your telemetry streams than you did before. Be prepared.

Whereas the infrastructure charts of the small and medium-size companies were similar enough to be recognizable, the one for the large company is radically different because of all the changes needed to push into the enterprise market. Figure 8.8 shows the production systems.

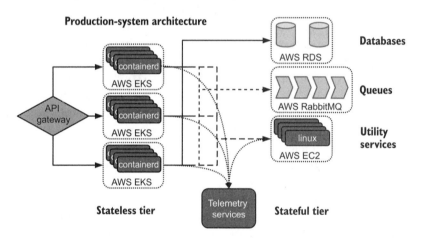

Figure 8.8   Production-system architecture for the large cloud-based startup, showing extensive use of AWS managed services (AWS EKS, RDS, and RabbitMQ) and new use of general purpose systems (AWS EC2 using Linux). The use of RabbitMQ replaces SQS, used in the medium-size company architecture. Containers in EKS and instances in EC2 communicate with telemetry services (figure 8.9). This figure demonstrates the increasing sophistication of the production environment and improving skill with operating a large system.

We see that company has expanded its use of AWS since its midsize days, extending its use of EKS and adding both AWS Relational Database Services (RDS) databases and AWS RabbitMQ queues. The company is running an API gateway that points to the EKS resources. Not shown here for space reasons are the CI/CD systems that now run in AWS EKS, same as the production systems.

Significant changes in the production systems are small compared with what happened to the telemetry systems. Figure 8.9 shows the telemetry changes.

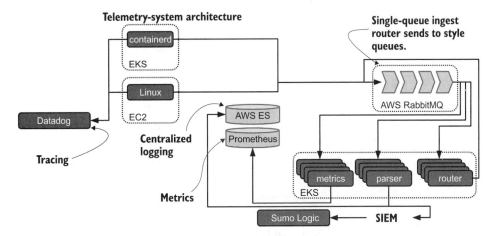

Figure 8.9 Telemetry system architecture for the large cloud-based startup, showing four telemetry styles in use and event flow from the production systems. SaaS providers now provide only distributed tracing and SIEM services; centralized logging and metrics have been brought inside. The fact that metrics has been brought inside is a sign that this company needed more complexity in its metrics telemetry than the SaaS provider could support.

8.3.1 Describing the large company's telemetry system

Sumo Logic used to be the centralized logging service back in the early stage of the medium-size company, but the company removed it due to cost pressure by the late stages. Why is it back? The new security team needed a SIEM, and Sumo Logic has features that make it work for that team, giving Sumo Logic a highly filtered stream of telemetry from the centralized logging flow, handled here as part of the router service.

The company also removed Datadog as a metrics service but kept it for the more expensive distributed tracing telemetry style. This change is a sign that the company thought that the Datadog metrics service, which had served it well in the small and medium-size stages, wasn't featured enough for what it now wanted and decided to build its own. The new metrics service is built on the foundation of the Prometheus time-series database with custom-built automation to provide aggregation and reporting.

Another difference between the medium-size and large telemetry architecture is what is serving as the queue. The medium-size architecture used Amazon's SQSas the central point of shipping, yet in the large architecture, that role is being filled by Amazon's managed RabbitMQ service. What caused the change? Features. SQS is a simple queue, but the company needed a true message broker and chose RabbitMQ because of its use of the well-supported Advanced Message Queuing Protocol (AMQP) and ability to support distributed architectures.

This new telemetry architecture also demonstrates multitenancy for the first time, with a security team being all by itself in Sumo Logic. The use of a router is a multi-tenant technique, talked about more in section 7.2.1, though here it is used more to direct telemetry to style-specific queues. That said, the seeds are planted for supporting fuller multitenancy.

Not displayed here is the sheer volume of telemetry flowing through this ecosystem. Compliance frameworks have clear mandates to be able to trace (and prove that they can trace) who did what, when, where, and how; satisfying this mandate requires capturing far more system-level telemetry than was captured before. Handling all this tracing telemetry requires dedicated security software: the SIEM.

That's a lot of change! Here are some quick hits that drove most of that change:

- The need for a passing audit report for a compliance framework is driving significant changes to both the production and telemetry systems.
- Message routing complexity is becoming a driver of telemetry system changes.
- Increasing the size of the technical organization also increases the capabilities of the organization, allowing the company to handle directly tasks that used to be contracted out.
- Increasing technical sophistication in production systems is beginning to drive the company from its original cloud provider in favor of providers that allow the level of customization it needs.

8.3.2 Analyzing the large company's telemetry system

In this section, we take a look at how the three telemetry pipeline stages evolved between the medium-size and large company stages. We saw the beginning of the process of moving telemetry services inside as part of the medium-size stage, and this process moved farther along at the large stage.

EMITTING STAGE

This section covers the Emitting-stage components of our large startup and shows how it changed to support a new computing platform. These components (figure 8.10) are familiar from the late-stage medium-size company, as the company continues to use emitter/shipper functions wherever possible.

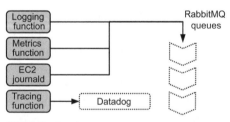

Figure 8.10   Emitting-stage components of the large cloud-based company, now running code in two public clouds

The biggest evolution in the Emitting stage is the addition of EC2-based Linux servers as a deployed platform in the production system, but even the container code is continuing to follow the pattern of emitter/shipper functions inside the production code. Whereas the company was still using Datadog for metrics at the medium-size stage, now it's brought metrics inside and built internally maintained SDKs for software engineers to use to provide metrics emissions from their code. With metrics moving to self-hosted and the queue changing from SQS to RabbitMQ, however, the emitter/shipper functions have changed subtly:

- For code running in AWS EKS, all centralized logging and metrics emissions are submitted to a RabbitMQ-based queue instead of the SQS queue.
- For telemetry coming from the EC2-based Linux servers themselves, Fluentd is installed locally to send system telemetry from journald into RabbitMQ.
- Telemetry systems running on EC2 instances are new and also emit centralized logging to the RabbitMQ-based queue.
- Datadog continues to be used by both EKS- and EC2-based production systems.

The large stage is when security and compliance concerns start biting for real: the system log that comes with managing operating systems now *has* to be included in the telemetry stream because the new security team needs that telemetry. What happens to the system log telemetry—be it Syslog or Windows Event Log—is a story for the Shipping stage.

SHIPPING STAGE

This section covers the Shipping-stage components for our large cloud-based startup and shows how it adapted to a new platform and compliance requirements. Sophistication has increased significantly from the medium-size system as our company further refines how it uses telemetry. Figure 8.11 shows the Shipping-stage components.

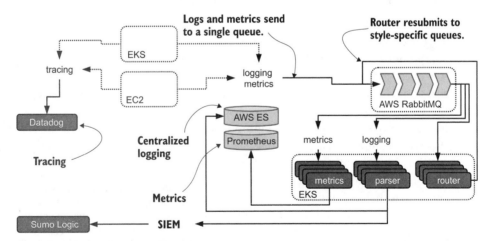

Figure 8.11 Shipping-stage components of the large cloud-based startup. Emitting-stage components and event flows use dotted lines, Shipping-stage components are filled, and event flows use solid lines. All telemetry sources continue to use Datadog for tracing. This system demonstrates multitenancy in the form of the SIEM system.

The Shipping stage for the large company is quite a bit more complex than the one for the medium-size company. Whereas the medium-size company had a centralized logging system using SQS for shipping telemetry, the large system

- Moved the queue to RabbitMQ instead of SQS to save money and increase flexibility. (Unlike SQS, RabbitMQ allows complexity.)
- Embraced the router concept from section 7.2.1, with containers dedicated to deciding which telemetry system, or owner, needs to be the next one to process each item of telemetry. The router uses dedicated queues for the logging and metrics telemetry styles. Queue-based routing allows simplifying the SDKs needed in the production code. (Ship everything to the queue, and let the router sort it out.)
- Forked logging telemetry at the new parser. The security team also needs this feed, so the parser sends security-relevant telemetry to two places.
- Diversified its parser system, adding dedicated container groups for logging and metrics to scale with the size of its infrastructure.

The use of a combined stream for centralized logging and metrics, to be split at a router, is a multitenancy concept from chapter 7. Although this company has only two political owners—security and everyone else—each telemetry style's system (metrics and centralized logging, in this case) are functional owners. This telemetry system demonstrates multitenancy in the Shipping stage. The metrics pipeline functions similarly to the centralized logging one, with a dedicated metrics parser. The tracing pipeline remains the same. (Ship telemetry directly to Datadog.)

PRESENTATION STAGE

This section covers the Presentation-stage components for our large cloud-based startup and the addition of a new style of telemetry. Unlike the medium-size company, the large company manages many systems for presenting its telemetry. Figure 8.12 shows the components.

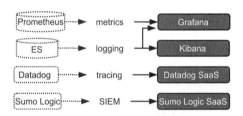

With the move of metrics from Datadog to an internal system, this company had to come up with Presentation-stage software for its metrics. (See section 5.1 for a discussion of presentation systems for metrics telemetry.) It picked the Grafana (https://grafana.com) dashboard system to act as the Presentation stage for metrics. Grafana has robust support for the company's metrics database, Prometheus, which allows the creation of dash-

Figure 8.12   Presentation-stage components for the large cloud-based startup. Presentation-stage components are filled, and their data sources (part of the Shipping stage) are dotted. SaaS providers are supplying the tracing and SIEM presentation stages, whereas internally managed telemetry systems are using Grafana for metrics and logging, and Kibana for logging. Unlike the organizations you will see in chapters 9 and 10, this company has managed to centralize telemetry into one system for each telemetry style.

boards and has an access control system. Grafana also supports pulling logging data to pair with metrics in dashboards, so that system also pulls from Elasticsearch.

Centralized logging continues to use the Kibana that comes with the managed AWS Elasticsearch service, as it did with the late-stage medium-size company. The addition of compliance requirements pushed this company to adopt SAML-based SSO and access controls into Kibana to be able to trace who viewed what telemetry and when. Using presentation systems supporting ACLs allows the company to separate application telemetry from the growing operating system telemetry managed by the DevOps/SRE teams, demonstrating multitenancy in the Presentation stage. (See section 7.2.2 for a discussion of multitenancy in the Presentation stage.)

Tracing data continues to be served by Datadog, though the volume of tracing data is becoming a budgetary concern. SIEM functionality for the security teams is being supplied by Sumo Logic.

8.4 Telemetry at the enterprise stage

The enterprise stage of our cloud-based startup is the end stage. A company that makes it to this stage—and few companies do—has not only figured out how to sell to Fortune 500 companies, but also is doing well in that market segment. This company is an established name in the big-company space, while also serving its small and medium-size business roots. There are few markets left to enter, such as government and international sales.

This company has grown a lot since its large-company days, and not only financially. The technical organization alone numbers in the high hundreds to thousands of people, making a product framework far larger than any one person could hold in their head. The technical organization is spread across multiple offices and might even have expanded internationally; time zones are now major barriers to cross-team cooperation.

This company is no longer a startup, but one of the established players in the field. It has taken the founders a decade or longer to climb from three people with a big idea to chief executive officer, chief information officer, and chief operating officer of a company with revenue pushing $1 billion U.S. The company isn't a startup anymore, but a *unicorn* (a one-in-a-million shot that paid off).

The enterprise stage is when a company's production systems are big enough that building data centers to run them is a perfectly reasonable stance to take. The public cloud goes far, but there comes a time when the cost of paying a provider like AWS or Azure to run data centers for you is less attractive than running those data centers yourself. Some companies gleefully jump at the savings; others are quite happy to keep paying the professionals at their public cloud provider. Regardless of the cloud state, the production systems are big enough that hard work has gone into making sure that a regional disaster (such as a massive earthquake or a hurricane) can no longer take everything down.

The telemetry systems have transformed as much as the production systems. The scale of enterprise-stage telemetry means that any SaaS providers are likely to be either niche players or full strategic partners; there is no in-between stage. Telemetry systems are now built to handle the same regional disaster tolerance that the production systems are, which requires as much service mirroring and replication as in the production systems—a requirement that smokes out telemetry service components that don't support that level of availability. More of the telemetry ecosystem is developed and maintained internally than at any previous stage. This stage is where companies consider open-sourcing their internal telemetry tooling to help the broader community.

The three major drivers of change since the large-company days and the big compliance push are

- Pushing into international markets, exposing the company to different regulatory frameworks, contract, and labor laws
- Surviving regional disasters (a requirement for doing business with some companies)
- Scaling everything up to handle a global user base

The product is rather more complex than it was in the large-company days, with autoscaling pools, complex network routing to handle failovers, failover logic in the code itself, and the existence of actual hardware in production systems. New hires have no idea how the product ever ran in a single ECS Fargate cluster.

Figure 8.13 shows that our enterprise-size company is operating three physical data centers: two in the United States and one in Germany. It is still making extensive use of AWS. The two U.S. data centers and two AWS regions are on the East and West coasts and are configured to replicate to each other. The data centers are hot standbys, meaning that failing over to the other data center is a fast process, but a brief outage still occurs. Bringing failover to Europe is in the process of being built out. Customers are provisioned in the U.S. or EU data centers, and fancy networking is used to route customers to the United States or European Union as appropriate.

Figure 8.13   Data centers and AWS regions in use by the enterprise-size cloud-based startup. Physical data centers are used for the first time, and U.S. systems are configured for replication. AWS is still supported. Telemetry systems are also replicated—the first time we've seen replication in a telemetry system.

The telemetry systems follow the same general architecture, with a few differences:

- Due to the legal penalties for mistakenly transmitting private user data, the European Union and United States operate fully separate centralized logging systems. Logging data recorded in the European Union stays in the European Union, whereas data recorded in the United States is replicated to the other U.S. data centers but not sent to the European Union.
- Metrics are replicated between the U.S. and EU data centers and may be accessed from either, with a replication delay when viewing metrics from the remote data center.
- Distributed tracing is no longer being handled by a SaaS provider.

To begin our investigation of their telemetry systems, let's take a look at the Emitting-stage (and early-Shipping-stage) components in figure 8.14.

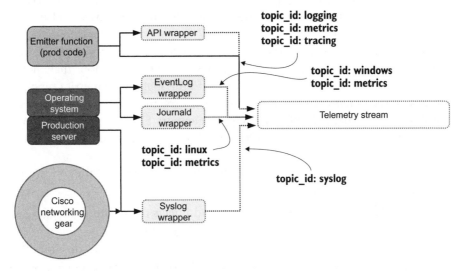

Figure 8.14   Emitting (solid lines, dark boxes) and early Shipping-stage (dotted lines, light boxes) components for the enterprise-size company, showing three emitting techniques (emit to stream from code, emit to API, and emit to Syslog), sending telemetry into a stream, demonstrating a partial emitter-based routing architecture in the form of which stream `topic_id` telemetry is written to.

EMITTING AND EARLY SHIPPING STAGE

This section covers the Emitting and early Shipping stages of our enterprise-size cloud-based startup, which includes hardware for the first time. Everything eventually ends up in a streaming system with topics. (See section 7.2.2 for a discussion of stream-based Shipping stages.) This telemetry system has several features:

- All production code includes an emitter function for emitting logging and metrics telemetry to an API wrapper for code that doesn't support streams or directly to a topic in a telemetry stream system (see section 3.1.2 for a discussion of this style of emitting) for code running in AWS or on hardware.

- All production code also includes tracing libraries based on the OpenTelemetry SDK, which emits tracing telemetry to an API wrapper for code that doesn't support streams or directly to a telemetry stream for code that does.
- Cisco networking gear in the data centers is configured to emit to a Syslog server. (See section 2.2 for a discussion of emitting telemetry from hardware.)
- Production servers are configured to emit their IPMI events—telemetry that emits directly from server hardware—to Syslog, similar to the Cisco hardware.
- Four wrappers are configured to accept telemetry and inject it into the telemetry stream system: an API wrapper for telemetry coming from production code, a EventLog wrapper for events coming from Windows systems, a journald wrapper for events coming from Systemd, and a Syslog wrapper for events coming from hardware systems.

The journald wrapper is installed on all Linux systems and ships to the stream directly from a process in the operating system. Any Windows systems would have a similar wrapper for Event Log.

Standardized logging libraries have been created for every software framework in use at this company. This logging library includes helper functions that allow software engineers writing code to emit telemetry into the logging or metrics pipelines easily. Because this company has dropped Datadog for tracing, it's become a corporate sponsor of OpenTelemetry and is using OpenTelemetry SDKs to provide tracing instead. Part of the logging library includes functions to emit tracing telemetry into the stream.

Production code emits directly into the stream, but each of the four wrappers also emits into dedicated topics:

- The API-wrapper accepts API calls and injects them into the logging stream as part of the `logging`, `metrics`, and `tracing` topics.
- The EventLog wrapper running on all the Windows hosts consumes the system, application, security, and any configured additional event-log streams and injects events, with appropriate context-related markup (see chapter 6), into the logging stream as part of the `windows` or `metrics` topic.
- The journald wrapper running on all the Linux hosts consumes the local system log and injects events, with appropriate context-related markup, into the logging stream as part of the `linux` or `metrics` topic.
- The Syslog wrapper accepts events from hardware systems, marks it up with context-related telemetry, enriches the format to the one supported by downstream shippers, and injects them into the logging stream as part of the `syslog` topic.

The stream is handling six topics:

- A `logging` topic containing application logging
- A `metrics` topic containing both application and operating system metrics

- A `tracing` topic containing OpenTelemetry telemetry
- A `linux` topic containing Linux operating system logging
- A `windows` topic containing Windows Event Log telemetry
- A `syslog` topic containing logging coming from hardware systems

WHOLE SHIPPING STAGE

This section covers the Shipping stage of our enterprise-size cloud-based startup—specifically, the part of the Shipping stage after the central stream system—and shows how it meets the mission of cross-region high availability. Now that we have examined the telemetry deep enough to see how it is funneled into a single pipeline system, let's take a look at the whole Shipping stage after telemetry is centralized into the stream system. This stage is where the international architecture begins to be visible. First, let's look at figure 8.15, which shows how centralized logging is handled.

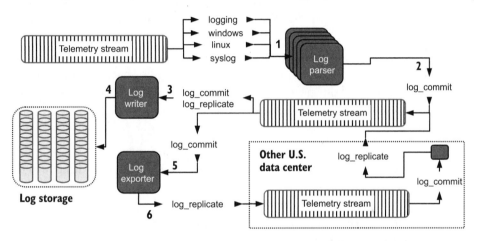

Figure 8.15 Log parsing and storage components of the centralized logging Shipping stage, including replication to a remote data center. Events enter the telemetry stream on any of four topics and in the United States are eventually shipped to a remote data center for replication. This centralized logging system demonstrates both dedicated systems for bulk-writing efficiently into storage and high-availability replication.

As we saw with the Emitting- and early-Shipping-stage architecture, this company makes extensive use of streams. Let's follow the path that centralized logging telemetry takes from the four centralized logging topics (`logging`, `syslog`, `windows`, and `linux`):

1. A large group of machines performing log parsing is in a consumer group and subscribes to the `syslog`, `linux`, `windows`, and `logging` topics of the telemetry stream.
2. The log parsers further enrich telemetry unifying the format and send it back into the stream under the `log_commit` topic.

3   A smaller group of machines dedicated to storing telemetry is in a consumer group and subscribes to both the `log_commit` and `log_replicate` topics, where `log_replicate` is the stream of events coming from the remote data center (United States only).

4   The log-writer group stores telemetry in many storage targets based on telemetry encoded by the log parsers, functioning as a router (see section 6.2.1).

5   In the United States, and planned for the European Union, another group of machines dedicated to log exporting is in a consumer group and also subscribes to the `log_commit` topic, giving it only the telemetry that was generated by the local log parsers.

6   The log-exporting machines send data across wide-area networking (WAN) links to a stream in the remote U.S. data center in the `log_replicate` topic.

7   (not pictured) The log writers in the remote U.S. data center, which are subscribed to the `log_replicate` topic, also store telemetry from the first U.S. data center.

Centralized logging telemetry follows many steps, but the design here allows the remote data center to have a (mostly) complete record of what happened in both data centers. When we look at the Shipping stage as a whole, we see that each bit of generated telemetry takes three or four hops before getting stored locally, as shown in figure 8.16:

1   Emission from code, operating system, or hardware is sent to a wrapper (except code that is able to emit directly to a stream, which emits directly to the stream and skips step 2).

2   The wrapper ships telemetry into the stream.

3   The log-parser machines enrich and transform the telemetry, shipping it back to the stream in a new topic.

4   The log writer writes telemetry to storage based on details in the telemetry.

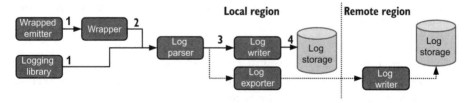

Figure 8.16   The flow of centralized logging events from emission to storage, including the replication flow. This architecture provides a (mostly) complete mirror of logging storage between the two regions.

With the centralized logging system out of the way, let's take a look at the metrics system and its Shipping stage. Unlike centralized logging, metrics telemetry is allowed to replicate outside the U.S./EU regions, so there is a central system for metrics

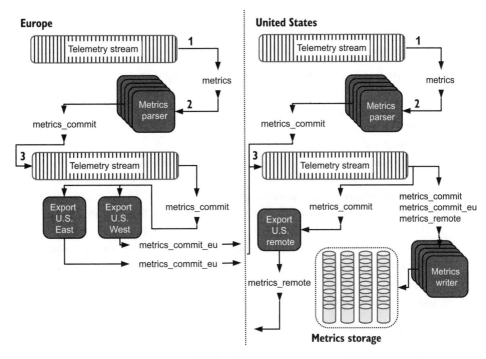

Figure 8.17 Metrics parsing and storage components of the metrics Shipping stage. This example centralizes writes into the United States, with replication between U.S. East/West data centers for high availability.

operated from the U.S. data centers. Figure 8.17 shows the metrics architecture in two regions.

The early life of a metrics emissions is common in both the European Union and United States:

1. Metrics ship into the `metrics` topic in the telemetry stream.
2. Metrics parsers in a consumer group that subscribes to the `metrics` topic receive the telemetry stream.
3. The metrics parsers enrich and transform the telemetry, and submit the telemetry to the `metrics_commit` topic.

When the metrics telemetry is in the `metrics_commit` topic, we start to see different handling between the United States and European Union:

- In both the the United States and European Union, dedicated exporters subscribe to `metrics_commit` to ship received metrics to streams in different regions. There are two exporters for the European Union and one for each of the U.S. data centers. The United States has a single exporter, exporting to the other U.S. data center.

- Both U.S. data centers have a group of metrics writer machines that subscribe to all three of the `metrics_commit`, `metrics_commit_eu`, and `metrics_remote` topics to store telemetry from all regions.

This company chose to store metrics data in a single location for a couple of reasons. First and most important, metrics data is small and cheap to store (and to transmit across the Atlantic Ocean), making a single big repository viable. Second, metrics data is far less likely to contain the sorts of information that is subject to export controls—information such as PII and health information.

Tracing data for this company hasn't been sent to Datadog since the company joined the development effort for OpenTelemetry. Not sending tracing data to a SaaS provider ended up being a significant savings, but joining in an industry effort to standardize tracing techniques pays dividends for the whole industry.

Unlike logging and metrics, this company's tracing data is not replicated between data centers. The reason is part of the development effort: the company is helping to write the components that will enable such ocean-spanning architectures and hold high volumes of tracing data. The replication isn't production-ready yet. Figure 8.18 shows the tracing architecture in each region.

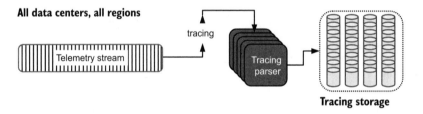

Figure 8.18   Tracing parsing and storage components of the Shipping stage. Support for replication and bulking writes through dedicated writers is still being developed as part of the OpenTelemetry development effort. Use of a relatively immature technology by a company of this size can radically speed maturity of that technology.

Compared with the centralized logging and metrics architectures, tracing is simpler. Not having to build replication topologies greatly simplifies the flow of telemetry. There is another reason why this company hasn't pushed hard to get replication in place, and that reason has to do with the nature of distributed tracing telemetry. Tracing is most useful for software engineers, enabling them to analyze what broke in a specific workflow and to see how performance changed across software versions. Troubleshooting is most commonly done on recent data (less than a few weeks old). Software-version analysis needs telemetry that goes back months or possibly years but does not need every single workflow that happened; it needs only telemetry that has been statistically sampled. (See section 17.3 for more on sampling.)

In the future, the plan is to provide a single access point for tracing data for software engineers, but that plan is waiting for better maturity in the software that handles replication. Until then, engineers need to remember which data center their stuff is running in and hitting that tracing endpoint.

The next telemetry system we need to look at is how security's SIEM evolved in the enterprise era of this company. In the large stage, the SIEM was an appendix to the centralized logging system, accepting a feed of telemetry from centralized logging before it was parsed and persisting it in Sumo Logic. In the enterprise stage, forking is still happening, though a sizable amount of SIEM data is now being held internally (figure 8.19).

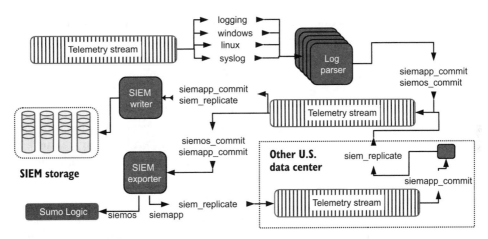

Figure 8.19 SIEM architecture for the enterprise organization. Telemetry destined for storage in the SIEM enters the pipeline the same way as the logging data, at the log parsers. The parsers fork SIEM-related events to two new topics. Eventually, SIEM data lands in both replicated self-hosted storage and Sumo Logic. This split use shows that our enterprise-size company is beginning to bring some SIEM components inside. SIEM is the last telemetry style at the enterprise-size company to continue using a SaaS provider.

This architecture is quite similar to the centralized logging architecture in figure 8.15. In fact, the first steps of the SIEM telemetry pipeline are identical right up to when telemetry enters the log parser. Then the log parser routes telemetry, with centralized logging reentering the stream on the log_commit topic ID, and security telemetry on the siemapp_commit and siemos_commit topics. From there, SIEM telemetry follows a similar path, but through different components, as the centralized logging telemetry. The big difference is that Sumo Logic is also receiving a feed of telemetry: the siemos_commit topic, the last SaaS product remaining in this telemetry system.

The reason why Sumo Logic is still there has to do with the nature of SIEM systems in general. Compliance and regulatory frameworks require certain common types of telemetry to be persisted in SIEM systems—telemetry such as login, logout, lockout, privilege use, elevated command use, and other relevant details commonly gathered by operating systems. The problem of correlating all those events and displaying them in a useful way is a complex one, and one you can build a company around. Therefore, our enterprise-size company is using an outside vendor to provide correlation and presentation for common security-related telemetry generated by operating systems and hardware.

The security team, however, has extended its monitoring of security events to inside the main application. Unlike OS and hardware events, the application generates events unique to this company, so it makes sense for the company to handle those events directly, which is where the `siemapp_commit` stream topic comes into play. The software engineering teams have built in support for emitting SIEM-related events, which are emitted as part of the logging streams. The log parser routes those events into the SIEM pipeline. Dedicated software engineers with the security team have built Presentation-layer systems for this extra, internal feed of telemetry.

If it feels like there was a universe of change between the large and enterprise sizes of the company, you're not far wrong. The dual problems of increasing complexity in the production systems *as well as the technical organization itself* made the transition from medium-size to large significant and was even more profound here. With a technical organization as large as the enterprise one, the prospect of building your own telemetry system from scratch becomes cost-advantageous. Additionally, the technical complications of running in both multiple data centers and on different continents provides strong pressure toward bespoke systems.

PRESENTATION STAGE

This section covers the Presentation-stage components of our enterprise-size cloud-based startup (no longer a startup by any means except historical). The sheer scale of enterprise telemetry has left its mark on this company's presentation systems. Let's take a look at each telemetry style in turn. This system is not a clean one; you don't get this big without bringing along some of your past.

For centralized logging, the company has mostly moved away from Kibana; annual renewal costs are high enough to fund dedicated software engineers to build their own presentation systems, which they have started to do. Kibana is still around in some areas, but the use is considered to be deprecated. The Kibana-based system is kept around as a restore target for old data to support restore requests coming from external auditors as part of annual compliance work. (See section 17.1 for more on retention policies and how supporting no-longer-used telemetry systems affects such policies.)

For metrics, there has been a large fracturing of databases as different product owners built their own. The enterprise-size company's shipping pipeline allows multitenancy of this sort and even provides replication. The presence of multitenancy and replication, however, means that the company's presentation systems need to deal with them. Grafana is still in wide use, with multitenant features. But other metrics presentation systems, including one built by the company, are also in use.

For SIEM work, Sumo Logic continues to be the main access point for security events related to common operating system and public cloud systems. For security events that come from the production code itself, new presentation systems have been written by this company and stored entirely internally.

For distributed tracing, the company is actively developing Presentation-stage open source software as part of the wider OpenTelemetry project and ecosystem. These systems are hosted in each data center, with region-specific URLs for access. A grand unified access point is on the road map for the future, with an eye toward releasing it as open source software.

8.5　*Looking back at all this growth*

The cloud-based startup has to grow or die, which makes it a great example of how telemetry systems evolve over the course of the new tech-company life cycle. If you get hired in the small stage and stick around until the enterprise stage, you can see all the changes in telemetry handling firsthand. Few companies go from three people with a big idea and day jobs to a name that everyone recognizes within a decade.

The guiding principle for telemetry at the start was to do as little work with it as possible, because getting the production systems built was far more important. Use your cloud provider's tools for everything as long as you can so that you don't waste effort on stuff that doesn't lead directly to revenue. The biggest risk to the business is running out of money to operate, so polish such as having a nice telemetry system is a problem to solve later.

When revenue has advanced far enough, or when not having a nice telemetry system hurts enough, don't invent the system yourself; instead, use a third-party provider. Yes, it costs money, but at the small-company stage, the lowest developer price plan can be all you need. You get a professionally polished presentation system without having to write it yourself.

The "Have other people do it" principle holds into the medium-size stage, even though revenue is less of a concern. Engineering resources are scarce, and building it yourself takes people away from product development. Even so, this stage is the first one where the cost of third-party solutions can start forcing some telemetry systems inside. The highest-cost telemetry style, centralized logging, is often the first to be brought inside.

The medium-size stage is when production systems often start getting dedicated emitter/shipper components, such as dedicated logging libraries. These emitter/shipper components aren't commonly perceived as being part of a telemetry system, but they are the home-built interface between the production systems and third-party telemetry systems. Such components are a sign that telemetry operation is getting attention from software engineering.

The large-company stage is when changes start to truly bloom in telemetry systems. At this point the company is well-established, and the technical organization is growing large. The cost of paying other people to do telemetry system handling is now a serious part of the budget. Centralized logging could have been brought inside at the medium-size stage, but the large stage is where that decision is made part of the strategy. The large stage is also where the costs of other telemetry styles, such as metrics and distributed tracing, are reassessed.

Business needs at the large stage often trigger the creation of a security team as part of a move into the enterprise market segment, which incentivizes the adoption of compliance frameworks to ease selling into that market. Whereas a company may not have bothered with a SIEM before, doing compliance work guarantees that it will have to do something about SIEM functionality. This stage also represents the first major instance of multitenancy in a telemetry system, as the security team needs to have assurances that any infrastructure teams that maintain the existing telemetry systems can't alter telemetry residing inside the SIEM systems.

The enterprise stage brings far more fundamental changes to telemetry systems because, at this stage, there is enough internal technical prowess to bring all telemetry operations inside. Additionally, organizational complexity has reached the point where the telemetry system has no choice but to handle multitenancy at multiple levels. Use of third parties for telemetry systems can certainly be done, but doing so is a strategic choice rather than what happened because no one thought to change things.

As a side effect of doing telemetry at the enterprise stage, the company is big enough and doing enough complex things to consider open-sourcing its techniques. LinkedIn adopted Kafka, a streaming technology and turned it into a tool that our example enterprise company made extensive use of. Etsy released the StatsD program for metrics. The OpenTSDB time-series database came out of StumbleUpon to solve a metrics problem. Not every company chooses to open-source a technique, but those that get here have the opportunity to do so. Or if releasing the project themselves is not possible, companies can join in industry efforts—such as the OpenTelemetry effort to provide a broad standard for distributed tracing—to advance existing projects in useful ways.

Summary

- Cloud-based startups are young, building from scratch, and moving fast. Not having any technical legacy to bring forward allows these companies to use the latest technology right away.
- Production systems for the small cloud-based startup are based in a public cloud to speed development, which frees the startup from having to worry about operating its compute platform and allows it to focus on building a revenue-producing product.
- Telemetry handling for the small cloud-based startup is delegated to SaaS providers so that the company can focus on making a revenue-producing product.
- The biggest risk for a small cloud-based startup is running out of money, so a lot of tech debt is taken on at this stage of growth.
- The small cloud-based startup uses SaaS SDKs to write metrics libraries—emitter-shipper functions (section 3.1.3) that talk directly to SaaS providers.
- Logging for the small cloud-based startup is handled by a public cloud provider and is not well built out yet.

- The medium-size cloud-based startup has a more complex production system and introduces concepts including CI/CD telemetry, causing the company to add a new SaaS provider for its centralized logging needs.
- The medium-size cloud-based startup is the stage at which costs associated with SaaS-based telemetry systems can start to be significant, so the company opts to bring centralized logging (the most expensive telemetry style) inside and self-manage it,
- Also at the medium-size stage, dedicated DevOps or SRE teams become discrete teams, adding to the software engineering teams already present. These new teams drive different use cases for telemetry systems and enable self-hosting of telemetry systems.
- The biggest driver of change for the large cloud-based startup is the need to achieve compliance, such as with SOC2, to land contracts with the largest companies.
- Compliance requires the presence of a security team, which in turn requires the presence of a SIEM system.
- Telemetry systems are central to assessing procedure compliance by auditors, which drives significant telemetry change, often over the course of years.
- The large cloud-based startup has enough internal technical knowledge to manage multiple telemetry systems, reducing its reliance on expensive SaaS providers.
- The enterprise stage of a cloud-based startup is the end stage. The company is one that you recognize. Almost no startups make it this far on their own.
- The enterprise stage is where concepts such as multiregion serving and international hosting start showing up in the production and telemetry systems.
- Being international also exposes the company to different data-handling laws, which forces them to keep logging telemetry centralized per legal boundary rather than globally.
- The enterprise-stage company uses SaaS products only for niche or specialized use cases, such as providing a SIEM system for security. Use of a SaaS product at this stage is a deliberate choice.
- Presentation-stage systems at the enterprise stage are fractured due to how long it takes to move to a new presentation system and incomplete adoption of internal standards.
- Technical skill in the enterprise stage is high enough that the company is able to sign on to industry-wide open source efforts and make significant contributions.

Nonsoftware business

This chapter covers

- Telemetry use in companies that don't sell software
- How business size changes telemetry use
- How business IT uses telemetry techniques

NOTE All the part 2 chapters are written to tell telemetry stories using the techniques from part 1, as a means of providing more concrete examples of integrated telemetry systems. If you feel that you need more real-world examples to understand how these systems work, these chapters are for you. If you feel that you already have a good grasp of the concepts, skipping these chapters and moving on to part 3 is fine.

Whereas chapter 8 covered telemetry use in a software-producing startup, following the changes in telemetry use at each stage of the startup's growth from three people with a big idea to a name-you-recognize unicorn, this chapter is about a much larger part of the technical industry: organizations that consume software but produce it only for internal use. You know these organizations; they're everywhere. Here are a few examples:

- The locally-owned pizza shop, with its point-of-sale systems for managing orders, a fleet of delivery drivers, and marketing
- The veterinarian you take your pets to, with animal-oriented patient tracking systems and pharmaceutical and lab ordering platforms
- The design studio you contracted to rebuild your main bathroom, with its architectural software, digital filing, and customer communication systems
- The construction firm contracted by the state to rebuild the highway interchange near you—a project that will take three years—and all the project management, vendor management, subcontractor management, and human resources systems needed to pull it off
- The keyless-entry locksmith, famous for a century for providing keyed locks, you chose to replace the keyed lock on your front door, with all the embedded programming, server infrastructure, and API systems needed to support a mobile-oriented keyless-entry system.

The smallest of these software-consuming organizations may not care one little bit about telemetry, and that's fine. We're interested in those organizations that do have an interest because they're more likely to employ people like us to keep their telemetry systems organized. The larger these organizations are, the more likely they are to create software to support the business; the keyless-entry locksmith is a prime example in the preceding list. As a broad rule of thumb:

- Small and medium-size organizations are most concerned with business telemetry (think office IT crossed with business intelligence), which for our purposes is the same as software telemetry. Sections 9.1 and 9.2 cover organizations of this size.
- Large and enterprise organizations still care about business telemetry but are likely to do telemetry relating to software development as well. Sections 9.3 and 9.4 cover organizations of this size.

Unlike chapter 8, which followed one company from inception to global dominance, this chapter focuses on four organizations to highlight how each one uses telemetry. The "Grow or die" imperative of startups doesn't apply here; these organizations are already profitable and happy where they are.

One last word before we dig in: more companies employ people to manage desktop and laptop fleets than there are companies that employ software engineers. In fact, for small and medium-size organizations that consume software, office IT is a larger department than software engineering (if software engineering exists). The telemetry concepts we covered in part 1 apply to those organizations, too.

9.1 *Telemetry use in small organizations*

Small organizations are those with 20 people or fewer. They're delivering a service or product that is enabled by software, but they're not making the software themselves. A software-consuming organization of this size has a few attributes we are interested in:

- It uses SaaS products for everything it can.
- It is not likely to be managing its desktop or laptop fleets, letting each person do what they need to on their computer so long as they have a browser that supports all their SaaS apps.
- Specialist-installed software, such as accounting or numerical analysis software, is installed on only a few computers.
- It is not managing servers in any way—not if it can avoid doing so, that is. If the company has to run a server, that server is in a closet next to the copier/printer; gets upgraded every eight years or so; and is run by Brent, who has been with the company (as an employee, spouse of an employee, or long-term volunteer) for 20 years.

The SaaS revolution made its biggest changes in organizations of this size, which means that the telemetry ecosystem for this organization is full of SaaS platforms. Figure 9.1 gives us a taste of one version.

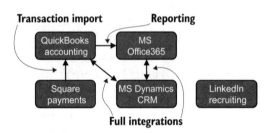

Figure 9.1   The production (and telemetry) ecosystem of one small organization. This organization uses SaaS products for nearly all its operations.

Figure 9.1 shows five SaaS systems used by our small organization, managing accounting (QuickBooks), payment processing (Square), customer relations (Microsoft Dynamics CRM), office operations (Office 365), and recruiting (LinkedIn). What little management of laptops and desktops is being done (endpoint management) is being handled by Office 365, and the company isn't doing much of that management yet. As suggested earlier in this section, desktop/laptop management involves ordering a new computer online when one is needed and letting the person who gets the computer do pretty much whatever they want with it.

The closest thing this organization has to any of the four telemetry styles mentioned in part 1 is QuickBooks, which receives a feed of payments from Square, integrates with the customer relationship management (CRM) system, and exports reports in the form of Excel spreadsheets to Office 365. Even so, LinkedIn is an island that doesn't integrate with anything else, and frankly, this organization doesn't need it to.

This organization doesn't have centralized logging. Its metrics are contained entirely within the walled garden of each SaaS vendor. Not doing endpoint management means that the company has no need for a SIEM, and it's not developing software, so it doesn't need distributed tracing. So why are we talking about this organization at all?

TIP Small organizations sometimes turn into bigger ones, and you need to understand what came before when you help these organizations adapt to growth.

Now let's look at a different kind of small organization in an industry that requires telemetry use: a small-town doctors' office. This office has two doctors, three nurses, and six support staffers of various types. A coffee shop has as many employees as this office, but healthcare regulations require far more computerization than the coffee shop does. Figure 9.2 gives us a feel for the practice's production systems.

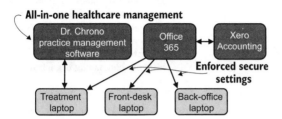

Figure 9.2 The production environment of an 11-person small-town doctors' office, which uses SaaS applications for everything. We see three SaaS products in use, but unlike in figure 9.1, computers are managed centrally. The practice management software provides all healthcare-related needs in a single product, including all telemetry needs. Office 365 is used to enforce settings that protect health-information privacy on all laptops used in this office.

When you're running a business in a highly regulated market such as healthcare, external forces often require practices that an organization of this size wouldn't bother with otherwise. The doctors' office in figure 9.2 is doing three things that the more casual business across the street doesn't do:

- *Enforcing laptop settings*—Protecting health information requires minimum settings. If a doctor forgets and leaves a treatment machine alone with a patient, that patient shouldn't be able to view any other records. Settings such as an annoyingly short screen-lock timeout are key here.
- *Enforcing endpoint protection software*—Health information requires software to defend against malware attacks. Because these laptops (endpoints) run Windows, a lot of malware is written for them.
- *Reviewing access logs*—Access to health information is regulated in most countries, so the practice management software tracks and reports which users accessed which records that might be required during any audits. Also, the Office 365 management system tracks logins on all laptops.

We're seeing some telemetry use here! The use is centralized logging, but it's recognizable, unlike in the organization depicted in figure 9.1. Figure 9.3 describes the two uses of centralized logging.

The primary telemetry store for our doctors' office is the one provided by its practice management software, which manages the repository of private health information.

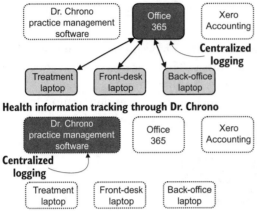

Endpoint management through Office 365

Health information tracking through Dr. Chrono

Figure 9.3   **Uses of centralized logging in our small-town doctors' office. Office 365 and the practice management software do internal reporting of events. This use isn't truly centralized, but it represents the first consistent use of telemetry techniques for software-consuming organizations.**

Telemetry use in an organization of this size, when it happens at all, often happens inside all-in-one products such as the one we see here. Centralization happens because organizations of this size rarely have the need or skill to design and build a centralized logging system that pulls feeds from multiple SaaS products. (There are always exceptions, though.)

The last thing I need to mention about organizations of this size is that they're the most responsive to changes in the industry. Small organizations of this type may have been around for 50 years, but they use SaaS products because there isn't enough inertia to keep maintaining servers in the copier room. You'll run into servers like those from time to time, but they're almost always old and running equally old software.

9.2   *Telemetry use in medium-size organizations*

Medium-size organizations are those that range between about 30 and 500 employees. (This definition doesn't overlap with the definition of small organizations; these boundaries are squishy.) Organizations of this size face complications that smaller organizations rarely face, which affects how they use telemetry. We'll cover these complications in this section. Medium-size architectures have a few drivers of change compared with small architectures:

- *The presence of professional IT*—Enough people are having problems with their computers now that a specific person or a department to solve problems becomes a core business need. (Goodbye, Brent.) This need *radically* changes how endpoint management is done and drives telemetry adoption and maturity.
- *The presence of human resources*—An organization of fewer than 30 people can avoid having professional human resources department, but the more people you have, the harder the problems of benefits management and managing people become. Human resources complicates the number of business systems in use, as dedicated Human Resources Information Systems (HRIS) start showing up.

- *Changing business rules*—Laws vary by country, but there is often a threshold of employee count at which businesses start getting treated differently by regulations and laws. In some countries, if you have fewer than a certain number of employees, you don't have to offer health insurance, for example.

Software-consuming organizations of this size have several attributes that affect their use of telemetry techniques:

- Professional IT is managing endpoints, which opens the door to centralized logging and SIEM systems.
- SaaS application use is still the primary means of getting things done.
- Specialist-installed software is still avoided wherever possible, but the presence of professional IT makes this challenge less severe.
- Software development, if present, is likely limited to support scripting built by professional IT.
- Managed servers appear at this level. There are few of these servers, they are run in the cloud if possible, and they support endpoint management and other systems managed by professional IT.

The small organization had software-focused telemetry buried inside all its business telemetry, but here, we have the chance of seeing systems that are more like those I spent all of part 1 explaining. Professional IT really makes a difference! Figure 9.4 gives us a view of the production systems that contribute to telemetry systems.

All the endpoint management systems shown in figure 9.4 focus on the employee's computer, and every component in the system reports log data to the Sumo Logic cloud. This system is the kind of software telemetry system we looked at in part 1, one

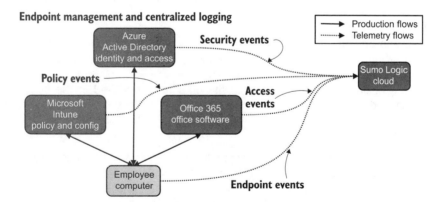

Figure 9.4 Production systems that contribute to telemetry for our medium-size software-consuming organization. The endpoint (employee computer) management framework is quite comprehensive versus that of the small organization. Professional IT also introduces centralized logging in the form of the Sumo Logic Cloud SaaS product, which centralizes logs from Azure Active Directory (login, logout, and other security details), Microsoft Intune (policy enforcement actions), Office 365 (use of documents), and the employee's computer itself. Software professionals (IT) introduce telemetry in a real way.

that came in with the professional IT department. At first, centralized logging remains the domain of the IT department and endpoint management, but having a single place to trace who did what is a capability that managers across the company will realize has great power. After IT has made some demonstrations, it won't be long until many more SaaS systems are wired in (figure 9.5).

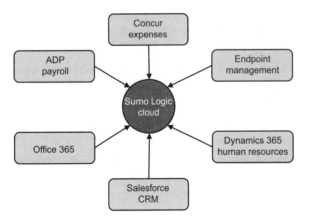

Figure 9.5   The medium-size organization has configured each of its SaaS products to send telemetry to the Sumo Logic cloud as part of a centralized logging system. This centralized logging system is used by both professional IT and business operations, extending well beyond the endpoint management system shown in figure 9.4. This system is a true centralized logging system.

Telemetry systems like the one depicted in figure 9.5 are quite unlike the software-development driven telemetry systems we looked at in chapter 8, which examined telemetry use in a growing startup company. Our medium-size software-consuming company has centralized the feeds provided by many SaaS vendors to provide managers the support they need to make decisions and make investigations. This telemetry system is all about business operations, and much software is involved in this architecture.

Business operations and professional IT matter for startups, too

It should be obvious by now that this chapter focuses our telemetry story on the business operations part of the organization. As you read this chapter, think about how the business operations side of the organization worked in the startup-style organizations examined in chapter 8. The software engineers in a software-creating company are the rock stars, the talent that makes the business do what it needs to do, and they earn a lot of attention.

But business operations matters in medium-size, large, and enterprise-size startup-style companies too. The professional IT departments that maintain them may not ever talk to the software engineering department or its managers, but IT has as many telemetry needs as software engineering does. In a software-producing organization, the chance that professional IT includes significant internal software development is higher than in purely software-consuming organizations, but whether that internal development is permitted to use the same telemetry systems as software engineering is determined by the culture of the organization.

> If it helps, think of each company described in this chapter as the telemetry story of the nonengineering part of a startup-style business. Large and enterprise-size startup-style businesses still need to worry about payroll processing, expense management, and HRIS.

9.3 *Telemetry use in large organizations*

Large organizations start at about 500 employees and become hard to separate from enterprise-size organizations. For our purposes, large organizations focus on a single large office or region, whereas enterprise-size organizations have offices in multiple regions, if not multiple countries. To split hairs even further, this section covers large organizations that began life after 1981 (the year when the IBM PC was released, launching the Intel revolution in offices worldwide). Section 10.2 covers large organizations that began before 1981.

Organizations of this size rarely grow up overnight all by themselves, so we're looking at an organization that likely was at least medium-size in the 2000–10 era. This era came before the SaaS explosion, so companies of this size most often ran servers somewhere to support business operations. These companies probably run fewer of those servers now than they did in previous decades, as tasks that used to require server-installed software (such as email) moved into the cloud and SaaS, but the organizational history still exists. The big drivers of change in a large organization are

- *The company has experience managing servers and likely still has facilities for hosting them.* If not, the company is operating in a public cloud after a "lift and shift" operation to bring all its physical servers into a public cloud like AWS or Azure and still maintain its server-operating fluency.
- *Professional IT is long established.* The company has history with professional IT, and chances are good that some employees are 20-year veterans. That kind of organizational history is both a blessing (deep organizational context) and a curse (it worked 10 years ago; it'll keep working now).
- *The servers were on-premises before they were in the cloud.* Having server management in the organizational history has a lot of subtle effects, the most important one being an unshakable assumption that every endpoint touches the internal network—something that COVID-19 taught the world is definitely not the case. Expect to see a lot of virtual private network (VPN) requirements in organizations of this type.
- *It has a lot more devices that need management.* Larger employee counts mean more endpoints to manage. But not just that, more diversity in those endpoints such as Apple and Google hardware in addition to the computers running Windows.

Age and presence in the pre-SaaS era have a lot of effects, as we'll find out. When it comes to telemetry use, here are the major organizational attributes that drive telemetry use by this large company:

- The company has been managing servers for decades at this point, so it has a monitoring system (also known as a metrics system, but probably not called that).
- Managing servers for decades means that the company already has some skill in centralized logging.
- Age and size mean that the company has faced its share of security incidents, so it has a security team and a SIEM system.
- The company deployed Microsoft Active Directory (AD) in the early 2000s and has spent the past decade tying SaaS services to AD authentication by way of Security Assertion Markup Language (SAML) integrations.
- Development of internal software is common at this size of company, so we will see software-development style telemetry for the first time.

The large organization has a mature IT organization that's used to managing servers and the telemetry systems that go with them, and is doing internal software development with those telemetry requirements. Whether those two telemetry systems are unified depends on the culture of the technical organization. If the systems aren't unified, you end up with telemetry systems that look like figure 7.5, reproduced here as figure 9.6.

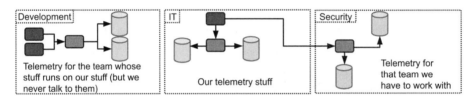

Figure 9.6   An uncharitable look at telemetry systems for a large organization with a culture of strong separation between IT and development teams. Our professional IT team is the middle panel; the software development team the left panel; and security is the right panel. This example is a viable way to do telemetry, but it leads to significant duplication of effort.

Large software-consuming organizations are far more likely not to have gone through the DevOps transformation than their software-producing counterparts, making them much more likely to have strong to insurmountable barriers between telemetry systems maintained by software development (Dev) and professional IT (Ops). First, we will look at the professional IT telemetry system, followed by the software development telemetry system. Then we'll talk about how a unified environment would look.

Figure 9.7 shows a fairly traditional telemetry ecosystem for the kinds of in-house machine rooms operated in the 2000–10 era (I spent the entire decade with systems like these), brought forward to the 2020s. We see that centralized logging is in use, focusing on Splunk software installed locally and Splunk's Syslog integration for everything else. We see a monitoring system in use (also known as a metrics system to developers) built on the SolarWinds monitoring product. Although Emitting-stage components are not

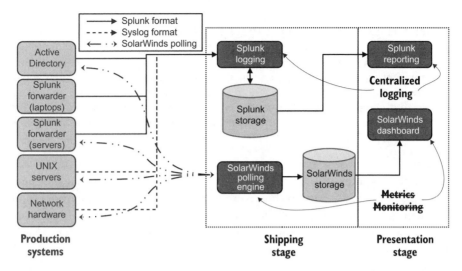

Figure 9.7   The telemetry ecosystem of our professional IT department for the large software-consuming organization. This figure shows two telemetry styles in use: centralized logging and metrics. Centralized logging centralizes events from both the employee computer fleet and the servers the department is managing.

in the figure for space reasons, the Shipping and Presentation stages are marked. This ecosystem gives the overall organization quite a lot of value:

- Due to the use of SAML for all of the SaaS products, the access logs coming from AD provide broad-level access tracing for the entire production system.
- With full AD and Splunk forwarders installed on employee computers, the organization has high-resolution tracing data for what happens on employee computers.
- Faults in server hardware are centralized, allowing correlation with other events to discover fault chains and speed root-cause analysis.
- Server metrics are centralized, allowing correlation between resource use and loads running on hardware.

This kind of full-resolution telemetry is common in organizations that have a high level of maturity in server and data center operations. Next, we need to look at the telemetry systems used by the in-house software development team, which is charged with writing software to speed the business but will always be run by internal teams. This software can be used by customers or other people who interact with the company, such as in vendor management portals or building-permit filing systems (in the case of a county clerk's office). Most company web pages qualify as internally developed software and are often the biggest developed pieces of software a company has.

SolarWinds? Didn't they get mega-hacked?

Yes, indeed, SolarWinds (specifically, SolarWinds Orion) was the target of a highly publicized nation-state attack. Why am I including it in examples? SolarWinds definitely lost a lot of business as a result of the intrusion, but it did not disappear. Its network monitoring platform is a dominant player in the market, and an organization like that doesn't get toppled easily. You will see SolarWinds products in telemetry stacks for years to come. What doesn't kill you (or put you out of business) makes you stronger.

Although this internal software development team could look like the medium-size startup in section 8.2, with exclusive use of public cloud and SaaS products, our internal team is working with an IT department that knows how to run things on servers. So for variety, figure 9.8 demonstrates how an internal development team can use telemetry that isn't exclusively SaaS-based.

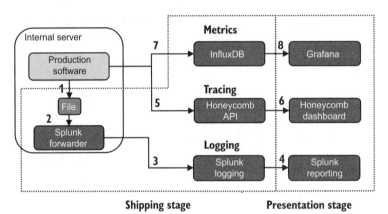

Figure 9.8   Telemetry system for our internal development team in a large software-consuming company. Unlike the architecture in the startup example, this architecture uses internally managed serving facilities to host the production system. Logging, metrics, and tracing are used here, but only tracing uses a SaaS provider; logging uses the existing Splunk logging pipeline, and metrics is managed internally.

We see the three Pillars of Observability (logs, metrics, and traces) hooked into the production software. First is centralized logging, which uses the same Splunk-based flow as the IT systems and even uses the same storage and presentation systems. The flow of telemetry for logging is

1 Logging telemetry is emitted from an emitter function in the production code into a file. (See section 2.1.1 for this pattern.)
2 The Splunk forwarder ingests log lines from the file. (See section 4.1.1 for this pattern.)

3 The Splunk forwarder ships the ingested log lines to the internally running Splunk Logging server.

4 Splunk reporting uses storage in the logging system to provide a Presentation stage for centralized logging.

The tracing pipeline's steps are shorter because it uses a SaaS API:

5 Tracing telemetry is emitted directly from the Honeycomb SDK integrated into the production software and sends telemetry to the Honeycomb API SaaS end-point.

6 Tracing telemetry is searched from the Honeycomb dashboard to provide a Presentation stage for tracing.

Metrics telemetry is hosted on internally managed software similar to Splunk, but instead, the software is open source. This metrics system is only for software development, not for IT. Even though it is internally hosted, the number of steps matches the SaaS pipeline used for tracing:

7 Metrics telemetry is emitted directly from metrics functions in the production software, an example of an emitter/shipper function (see section 3.1.1 for this pattern), shipping directly into the InfluxDB open source time-series database.

8 The presentation system for metrics telemetry is the Grafana open source dashboarding system.

We have two groups that share one telemetry system (centralized logging) but nothing else. How could these two groups improve their telemetry system sharing? The most obvious point is finding a way to get the current split between SolarWinds (monitoring system for the IT department) and InfluxDB/Grafana (metrics system for software development) unified into something new. Although software development is using the metrics system extensively, IT management, always on the lookout to cut costs, asks a key question: "Can InfluxDB and Grafana cut down on our annual licensing renewal for SolarWinds?" IT points out that SolarWinds and InfluxDB/Grafana use separate methods for gathering metrics:

- *Pull-based metrics*—SolarWinds maintains a list of everything it is tracking and polls the list on a schedule. The SolarWinds polling engine needs to be told explicitly what to look for, where to look for it, and how often to look for it.

- *Push-based metrics*—InfluxDB/Grafana has no awareness of what it is tracking; instead, it relies on systems to send metrics directly into InfluxDB. This style relies on the systems generating metrics to know where to send them.

Although the production software has been written to push (ship) metrics into InfluxDB, the Windows and UNIX operating systems managed by IT don't have that capability yet. After doing research, IT discovers the Telegraf series of agents offered by InfluxData, which provides installable software that knows how to extract system-level metrics from operating systems, databases, caches, and other components of infrastructure and send those collected metrics to InfluxDB. These agents aren't as convenient to use as the ones produced by SolarWinds—free open source generally costs more time—but the cost in money is hard to argue with. Figure 9.9 demonstrates one way to get system metrics out of Windows and into InfluxDB.

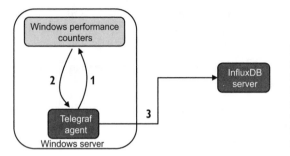

Figure 9.9   **Using Telegraf agents to fetch system metrics from Windows servers and send the metrics to InfluxDB. IT configures the Telegraf agent to poll metrics on a schedule and push metrics into InfluxDB, which provides push-based metrics support for a system (Windows, in this case) that assumes a poll-based metrics approach.**

Figure 9.9 shows a three-step process for moving Windows system metrics into InfluxDB:

1 On a schedule (every 10 seconds by default, but this setting is configurable), poll Windows Performance Counters for metrics.
2 Receive metrics from the perf subsystem.
3 Repackage and ship metrics to InfluxDB.

Ultimately, our company determines that Telegraf/InfluxDB/Grafana is not a complete replacement for its existing system, but it does provide some cost benefits versus SolarWinds. SolarWinds is kept for network operations—the network engineers aren't willing to give up all those nice features just to save money—but the role of Solar-Winds in application and system monitoring is significantly scaled back. Then professional IT takes over management of the InfluxDB system, which results in a lot of high-availability engineering work to make InfluxDB and Grafana reliable enough to bet the company on. The result is that software development and professional IT are using the same telemetry components for centralized logging and (most) metrics.

Figure 9.10 shows the unified telemetry system our large software-consuming organization built as part of the metrics/monitoring unification effort. We see that the network teams continue to use SolarWinds because that platform suited the company's needs better than the savings would justify, a political decision made by the people in the company. If you face this choice, you may decide differently, which is fine. The software developed by the internal software development team remains the only system using tracing, which is not surprising because tracing (at least in its early-2020s form) is a software-only concept.

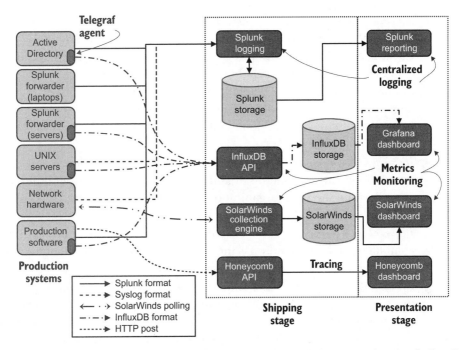

Figure 9.10 The unified telemetry ecosystem for our large software-consuming organization. Software development manages the production software box and is the sole emitter to the Honeycomb API. Network Hardware remains on SolarWinds, a political decision made by this organization during the metrics/monitoring unification efforts. Unlike the systems used by the startup-style companies in chapter 8, this telemetry system involves hardware at a much earlier stage.

9.4 *Telemetry use in enterprise organizations*

Enterprise organizations are the largest, most sprawling of the software-consuming organizations we're looking at in this chapter. These organizations have major presences in multiple regions, maybe having big offices in Chicago and Atlanta, or operate internationally. The organizations in this section are different from the ones described in section 10.3 in that they came to computers after 1981, the year the IBM PC was released.

Like the large organizations in section 9.3, companies don't get to this size overnight, so we're looking at organizations that automated their business operations in the late 1980s to early 2000s. Automating during this time made these companies ones that grew to enterprise size while operating servers in employee break rooms, copier closets, machine rooms, and small data centers. Unlike the large organizations in section 9.3, these organizations did all those things while handling business operations (and computing) in diverse regions. The big drivers of change between large and enterprise-size organizations are

- *An enterprise-size company is used to operating with wide-area networks (WANs).* Because the business is multiregional, so is its approach to computing. It's likely to have been handling multiregion operations back when WAN links were expensive and slow, and brought those approaches forward.
- *Multiregional means multicultural.* Different regions, even different regions in a large country like the United States, have different cultures. This organization has come to terms with regional holidays, differing standards of vacation time, and different labor markets.
- *It's used to operating under different labor laws.* Being multiregional, and especially international, means that this organization has to operate under different labor laws all within the same organization. Being international means accommodating different state holidays and still continuing operations.
- *It uses at least some public cloud for operations.* The company's history is in running computers, and it definitely has those skills. But the benefits of public cloud are obvious enough that the company has made some headway moving into it.
- *It's developing large amounts of software for internal use.* A company doesn't get to this size without having some need to create bespoke solutions. Software complexity certainly can rival the complexity we examined in the enterprise-size software producing organization in section 8.4, if not quite to the same horizontal scale.

The first three points of this list add up to one of the major cultural differences between enterprise companies and the others: internal divisions are far more apparent, leading to islands of software telemetry built in ignorance of (or in objection to; never underestimate the driver of innovation known as spite) other systems in the organization. Public cloud, the fourth point, makes these islands of telemetry far easier to bring about than they were back when you needed to put servers in your copier room or a spare cubicle. These telemetry islands look a lot like the medium-size (section 8.2) and large (section 8.3) telemetry systems we examined in chapter 8.

Figure 9.11 depicts a worst-case scenario for a global enterprise organization, showing 12 telemetry islands that share little, if anything—three for Office IT based on regions and nine for different business functions. This legacy of separation also means that the organization may manage far more diverse technology internally as a result of the same problem getting solved many ways by many people. Organizations this size are often lots of smaller organizations in a trenchcoat; they look like one big organization but are in truth a bunch of smaller organizations that work closely together. Some of the diversity this organization can experience includes

- Maybe the website engineering department follows modern software development practices drawn from Bay Area companies, where warehouse operations continues to use IBM AIX-based terminal systems because that's what it started using in the 1990s and hasn't bothered to get off them.

- Maybe office IT (Americas) is managing an employee computer fleet that is 70% Apple computers, but office IT (Europe/Middle East/Africa) is 100% Windows.
- Maybe business intelligence and website engineering operate large databases doing heavy transactional loads but share zero infrastructure or administrative support.

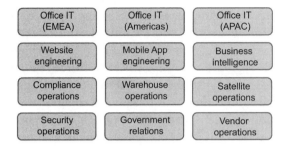

Figure 9.11   An example of telemetry islands in an enterprise-size software-consuming organization. This example is a severe case of isolation, but most enterprise-size software-consuming companies have islands of some kind.

Many organizations come to realize that they're split into pieces and decide to attempt to unify things, or at least provide some standards to prevent further fragmentation. In this section, we will examine that environment: a set of prebuilt telemetry services offered by the organization to allow software developers to add telemetry fast, and nudge them to use centralized services rather than reinventing the telemetry wheel.

We'll call this effort the *Paved Roads Project*, giving software developers easy-to-access paved roads to hook into telemetry in an effort to keep them from building new roads from scratch. Developers like easy; it lets them focus on what they want to be doing. We already know which roads we need to pave:

- *Centralized logging for applications*—Provide an emissions standard for applications that can emit directly, provide wrapper-format standards for applications that have to emit indirectly (such as those that have to emit through Syslog), and provide easy-to-access ingestion points and an interface to get at them.
- *Centralized logging for systems*—Physical data centers are easier to control, so provide hardware standards and configuration runbooks to ensure that hardware is emitting where it should. For operating systems, which can run on hardware or public clouds, provide software and endpoints to send events. Wire public cloud telemetry into these systems as well.
- *Metrics for applications and systems*—Provide an emissions standard for applications that can emit directly and wrapper formats for those that can emit only indirectly. Also provide agents for operating systems and a dashboarding system to chart metrics, as well as alert functionality to enable the metrics system to work as a monitoring system.
- *Tracing for applications*—Operating systems and hardware don't need these features, so these features are only for developed software. The best path here requires creating and deploying libraries for every supported programming language in the organization (which is probably too many)—a lot of work, but it pays off in the long run.

Much of this work focuses on building Shipping- and Presentation-stage components that can handle a wide variety of telemetry coming from the production systems. Emitting-stage components are, for the most part, not under the control of the department that builds the unified telemetry offering. Our telemetry operators need to provide easy-to-use building blocks and hope that people use them. (Please use them.) So long as developers building software decide to use these building blocks, they will get a high level of telemetry maturity for a low cost of effort. Unlike the software-producing enterprise organization from section 8.4, this organization isn't worried about replicating telemetry into multiple regions, so it keeps telemetry inside regions.

Figure 9.12 shows what a paved road looks like in the abstract. The Shipping- and Presentation-stage systems are managed centrally and sized to accommodate the scale of handling everything. The Emitting stage is where the politics happens; because we need to provide encouragement to software development groups to use our systems, we need those SDKs and libraries to be mature. Not all production systems can use SDKs or libraries; hardware and operating systems have their own emitting formats that aren't flexible. For these inflexible emitters, we need proxies, such as Syslog servers, that can accept telemetry in the format our inflexible emitters can emit and then translate the telemetry into our Shipping-stage format (section 4.2). For flexibility, we use a streaming system, in which a group of systems subscribes to stream topics to enrich telemetry and injects it into storage. Finally, a reporting interface consumes storage for people asking questions.

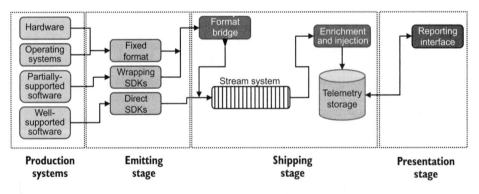

Figure 9.12   An abstract rendering of a paved road for telemetry. The Shipping and Presentation stages are centrally managed. Emitting-stage SDKs are provided to the creators of the production system. For production systems that are unable to talk directly to the stream, a format bridge system (or group of systems) is provided to proxy connections in a format the production system is able to use. This paved road accommodates both well-supported and partially-supported software, as well as hardware and operating system emitters that have fixed emission formats.

Let's look at a real implementation, this time for metrics (figure 9.13).

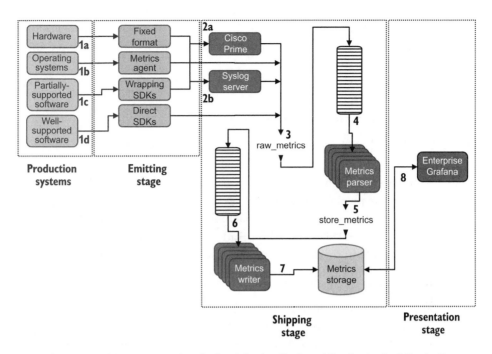

Figure 9.13 The eight-stage metrics pipeline following the Paved Roads standard. Production systems emit in the formats they are capable of emitting in. This pipeline provides many ways to get metrics into a centralized system and should reduce the number of metrics telemetry islands in the organization.

Figure 9.13 shows the Paved Roads architecture for metrics telemetry in this organization. Let's walk through it:

1 Metrics is emitted by production systems.
   a Hardware systems emit in their fixed formats.
   b Operating systems have a metrics agent installed, and the agent emits in its own format.
   c Partially-supported software submits telemetry in a wrapped format, going to Syslog.
   d Well-supported software emits directly to the stream.
2 Fixed formatted telemetry is run through proxy systems to unwrap metrics.
   a Cisco Prime is used to translate telemetry coming from the networking infrastructure.
   b Syslog is used for everything else that emits in a fixed format, including partially-supported software.
3 Proxies and well-supported software emit into the stream on the raw_metrics topic.
4 A group of metrics parsers subscribes to the raw_metrics topic and parses the metrics format into its final form.

5 The metrics parsers submit finalized metrics to the `store_metrics` topic.

6 A group of metrics writers subscribes to the `store_metrics` topic and prepares metrics for storage.

7 The metrics writers store metrics into metrics storage (which is OpenTSDB, based on Hadoop).

8 The Enterprise Grafana system uses metrics storage to present metrics.

The metrics system here includes several features for scalability and use by many departments:

- Streams buffer metrics so processing-rate problems won't block metrics coming from the production systems.
- The metrics-parser group of machines is horizontally scalable to handle bursts.
- Use of OpenTSDB (based on Hadoop) uses in-house experience with Hadoop to provide horizontal scalability of the time-series database.
- Enrichment during the metrics-parser stage of the pipeline encodes attributes used for multitenancy.
- The metrics writers use attributes created by the metrics parsers to write metrics telemetry to different OpenTSDB databases to support multitenancy.
- Grafana is running with a paid subscription to enhance its multitenant support.

Multitenancy—the ability of a system to separate access to parts of the system based on roles and groups (see chapter 7)—is a foundational feature of the Paved Roads Project. Multitenancy is needed for political reasons, because not every department gets along well with each other, making strong isolation between departmental data a firm requirement. Once again, the "many smaller organizations in a trenchcoat" nature of enterprise organizations affects telemetry design.

Now let's take a look at the Paved Roads architecture for tracing. Unlike metrics, tracing is intended to support only software, so the need to support hardware and operating systems is dropped. Complexity isn't reduced all that much, though, as we see in figure 9.14. The architecture is similar to the one for metrics, using separated enrichment and writing stages to improve overall throughput.

Because sections 9.1–9.3 spoke a lot about office IT style telemetry, it's only fair that we cover how office IT handles telemetry in an organization of this size. Every organization does telemetry in a different way. If your global company isn't doing it this way, that's fine. We saw this example for a medium-size organization in figure 9.4. Figure 9.15 is more complex, because our enterprise-size organization is running more than Windows on its employee computers and is running physical servers instead of cloud servers in Azure.

The Azure-only Microsoft Intune in the medium-size organization is replaced by Microsoft Endpoint Manager (EM) in the enterprise-size organization because EM runs on servers you manage. New to this chart is JAMF Pro, which is a highly featured management framework for Apple OSX systems. In this enterprise-size organization, Apple endpoints can be managed by either EM or JAMF Pro, depending on the

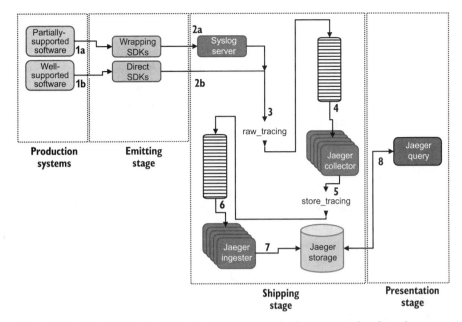

Figure 9.14 The eight-stage pipeline for distributed tracing in our enterprise-size software-consuming organization. This architecture uses the Jaeger project to provide tracing functionality internally. Well-supported software (which has a native Jaeger SDK) emits telemetry directly into the stream on the `raw_metrics` topic. Partially-supported software (which needs to wrap tracing data in another format) emits to Syslog, where the Syslog server will unwrap the tracing telemetry and send it into the `raw_metrics` stream. From there, the Jaeger collector transforms tracing data from the stream and submits it back to the stream on the `store_tracing` topic for the Jaeger ingester to insert into storage. Jaeger query is used to pull up traces. In the only example of reduced complexity from the metrics version, this system accepts inputs from fewer systems.

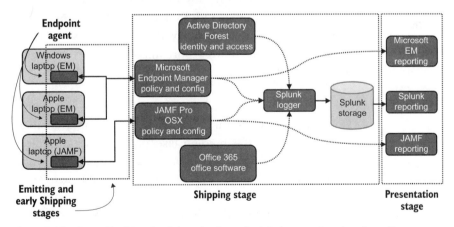

Figure 9.15 Centralized logging telemetry for endpoints in our enterprise-size software-consuming organization. This design supports both Apple and Microsoft endpoints, and provides two management frameworks for the Apple endpoints to increase the chance that departments will use the centralized system. Agents installed on endpoints ship telemetry to servers, which repackage telemetry for shipping to a Splunk-based centralized logging system. Both JAMF and Microsoft Endpoint Management provide reporting facilities inside their software offering in addition to the logging sent through to Splunk.

preferences of the local office IT department. This system is still a Paved Roads system because management flexibility is built-in.

The high degree of diversity inside a software-consuming organization of this size makes it quite a different thing from the software-producing organization we looked at in section 8.4. Telemetry systems are more of a marketed service than in the software-producing organization, whereas in the other organization, telemetry is driven by the needs of the software being produced. Both organizations value software engineer speed, though their approaches are different.

Summary

- Business operations dominate telemetry growth in small and medium-size organizations; software development becomes a factor only in large and enterprise-size organizations.
- Small software-consuming organizations try to use SaaS products exclusively wherever possible, to avoid having to manage software.
- Small organizations avoid having to install software wherever possible, or on only a few computers.
- Small organizations often don't bother managing employee computers (endpoints), letting each person do their own thing so long as they have a browser that works with the SaaS products.
- Small organizations working in certain industries, such as healthcare, often have external requirements that force them to care about telemetry, such as the ability to produce audit logs of health-record accesses.
- Small organizations are the most responsive to changes in the industry. The SaaS revolution benefited them the most of all the organizations in this chapter.
- Medium organizations are big enough to need someone to answer "Why is my computer broken?" questions, which is why they have professional IT groups.
- Professional IT groups in medium-size organizations often introduce the first recognizable telemetry system: centralized logging, generally of endpoint events.
- Medium-size organizations try to use SaaS software wherever possible, but professional IT reduces the pain if using installed software is unavoidable.
- Endpoint management in the medium-size organization is likely driven by cloud options (Azure and Office 365 for Windows-dominated organizations, JAMF for Apple-dominated ones), all to avoid having to manage servers.
- Unlike small and medium-size organizations, large organizations managed servers before the SaaS revolution and likely still manage them somewhere. This experience gives them far more comfort with server-based solutions than medium-size organizations have.
- Large organizations commonly produce software internally, unlike small and medium-size organizations.

- Large organizations have more endpoints, but also more endpoint diversity; Apple and Google hardware often joins the Windows endpoints, which complicates endpoint management.
- Large organizations are the first to have a security team and a SIEM system. Smaller organizations would have them only if outside forces such as regulation required them to do so.
- Office IT and software development don't always share telemetry systems in large organizations because the software telemetry system often grows up independently of the one used by office IT, leading to duplicated efforts.
- Enterprise software-consuming organizations are the largest organizations and have a major presence in multiple regions, if not multiple countries.
- Enterprise-size organizations are used to doing computing across wide areas because they did so back when networking was slow.
- Enterprise-size organizations are unavoidably multicultural in the sense of differing regional traditions, holidays, and labor laws. These cultural differences increase the sense of separation from other parts of the organization, which affects the level of cross-organization coordination that happens.
- Enterprise-size organizations are developing large amounts of software for internal use, so have full software engineering teams and their telemetry systems.
- Being large and with a history of separation between departments makes for far more internal diversity of technology than in the software-producing organization of the same size in section 8.4.
- Enterprise-size organizations are often a bunch of smaller organizations in an enterprise-size trenchcoat, which makes centralized telemetry standards harder to bring about.
- Building a centralized set of telemetry systems in an enterprise-size organization requires building a system that can compete with SaaS-based systems in terms of ease of use, nudging software developers to use the central systems when they can.
- Multitenancy is a core feature of any centralized telemetry system in a software-consuming enterprise organization because it allows the separation between departments that builds trust in the overall system.

Long-established
business IT

This chapter covers

- Telemetry use in organizations that started with paper and ink
- How adopting modern telemetry systems works in mature organizations
- The role of mainframes in modern infrastructures

In this chapter, we cover a slightly different type of organization: one that started operating in the paper-and-ink era and later computerized before the IBM PC revolution. *Organization* in this case can mean governments, and some governments have been operating for centuries. Some companies in Europe have founding dates in the 1600s, which long predates the typewriter, much less any electronic computing devices. Computerizing your business operations in an era where the organization had a single computer, which occupied a whole room and required a crew of eight to operate, leaves an indelible mark on an organization's approach to technology. Where you get changes in computerization, you get changes in approaches to telemetry.

NOTE All the part 2 chapters are written to tell telemetry stories using the techniques from part 1, intending to provide more concrete examples of integrated telemetry systems. If you feel you need more real-world examples to understand how these systems work, these are your chapters. If you feel you already have a good grasp of the concepts, skipping these chapters and moving to part 3 is fine.

Unlike in chapters 8 and 9, we won't be looking at a small version of this organization type. As mentioned in chapter 9, small organizations are the most responsive to changes in computerization because they have the least organizational inertia to overcome when adopting changes. A 30-person firm that incorporated in France in 1951 likely didn't bother computerizing until the 1980s anyway, which would make it more of a fit for section 9.1. A small firm that adopted a few computers in the mid-1970s likely did away with them in favor of much-cheaper-to-operate Intel-based computers during the rise in office automation in the late 1980s and 1990s.

The 1960s and 1970s were a career ago now in the industry, so the memory of what computing in that era was like is beginning to fade. It certainly predates me, but I spent the first seven years of my career around people who grew up then. These are the attributes of computing Back When:

- Every organization that had a computer or three operated a machine room to keep it in, with special cooling, power, and likely plumbing. (Several computer systems of the era were water-cooled.)
- It was the era before TCP/IP, so talking to the computer required a lot of serial connections (specifically, the RS-232 standard).
- Computers operated in batch mode, which required computer operators to mount and dismount tapes to load data and store results, as well as make sure the batch jobs executed on time and without problems.
- Some computers could switch between online and batch mode. Online mode was used during the day when the system had to handle lots of transactions, such as those from a room full of data-entry clerks typing in yesterday's parking tickets. Batch mode was used for running reports. This mode switch was scheduled, and you couldn't do both at the same time.
- Computer operators also worked the night shift, because that's when most batch jobs ran. Your Cron daemon was named Kathy, and you saw her some mornings if you got in early.
- Computer operators kept the computer fed with tapes (for loading programs, reading input, and recording output from programs). Kathy, the night operator, was also your auxiliary I/O controller.
- System programmers wrote batch jobs that computer operators ran, and computer operators often had a list of system programmers to call on the phone if anything went wrong. Kathy, the night operator, was also your alerting system.

- System programmers also provided documentation about what kind of output to expect from each job. Kathy, the night operator, was also your monitoring system.
- Systems analysts managed system programmers and kept track of how the batch jobs interacted. The systems analyst likely met Kathy, the night operator, a few times but otherwise didn't know her.

It turns out that no one likes working the overnight shift, so the computing industry has spent every year since the .com boom took off trying to put Kathy, the night operator, out of a job and has mostly succeeded. We now automate our batch jobs, track their telemetry, and automate callouts should something go wrong, and the ~~system programmer EDP analyst developer~~ software engineer who wrote the code can look up job output themselves without bothering anyone else. It's a nice world now, and almost no one has to work overnight anymore.

Except in the organizations that computerized back when, the ghost of Kathy and the world she worked in remains in everything they do (including job titles like senior systems analyst III). Although Kathy may now be a director of IT on the edge of retirement, exorcising the ghost of Kathy, the night operator, requires a deliberate lift-and-shift operation to destroy the past and rebuild on a new platform. Many organizations did this in the 1990s and 2000s and got rid of their mainframes, minicomputers, and batch systems to build new ones on Solaris, AIX, or even Windows. Or they waited until the early 2010s and lifted and shifted to the early public cloud offerings, like AWS. But the legacy computing operational patterns remain, which we will see in the next three sections. That said, *all* these organizations have been writing software for internal use for more than 40 years. This chapter walks through the stories of three different sizes of organization:

- Section 10.1 talks about telemetry use in medium-size organizations.
- Section 10.2 talks about telemetry use in national organizations.
- Section 10.3 talks about telemetry use in global organizations.

10.1 *Telemetry use in medium-size organizations*

For the purposes of this section, medium organizations are similar to the ones described in section 9.2 except that they start closer to 150 people instead of 50 and run to about 500. Of the three sizes of organizations in this chapter, the medium-size organization is the one most likely to have forgotten its past and moved on. Organizations that have forgotten look like the organizations from section 9.2; those that haven't quite done so are what we talk about in this section. Organizations that continue the mainframe pattern have the resources of a medium-size organization, so they are less able to keep up with the latest trends in mainframe-style computing. When you look at the larger organizations in sections 10.2 and 10.3, you will see how constrained operating mainframes can feel at this size of organization.

Unlike the medium-size software-consuming organizations in section 9.2, these legacy computing organizations definitely still have software development going on inside them. For that reason, our examination of the use of software telemetry will focus on two big use cases:

- Telemetry use in office IT
- Telemetry use in production systems

Our example organization is the unemployment insurance office of a U.S. state. This government agency is responsible for managing income from paycheck unemployment premiums and payments to the unemployed. Like all U.S. social support systems, it has complex and ever-changing rules regarding who gets what, when they get it, what people need to do to get it, how often they get it, and under which conditions they can be denied benefits ever again. The COVID-19 recession of 2020–21 forced more changes as certain rules were suddenly relaxed and benefits were increased (until they weren't). Any unemployment insurance system needs to respond rapidly to changing legislation, which requires programmers and a software distribution system.

Benefits systems such as this one computerized early due to the sheer scale of the problem and the need to do accounting of a statewide money disbursement system in a reasonable time. Early batch-mode computers were a good fit, so many U.S. states adopted mainframes and minicomputers (smaller than mainframes, bigger than toy computers) to automate their benefits management systems. The time being the 1970s, benefits applications were done on paper and keypunched (by data-entry clerks) into the computer, and benefits were batched to check printers and mailed or held at will-call windows. In the 2020s, paper applications have been replaced by web portals, and paper checks have (for the most part) been replaced by electronic funds transfers or reloadable debit cards. In many cases, the mainframe/minicomputer model is still being used today rather than moving to clusters of autoscaling microservices and horizontally scaling, sharded databases. That said, both computing styles faced different scaling problems when 20% of the workforce suddenly became unemployed due to a pandemic and the corresponding 7× increase in benefits workload.

10.1.1 Telemetry use in office IT

This section discusses the use of software telemetry in our hypothetical unemployment insurance agency for a U.S. state, which is subject to the IT guidelines of the state government. Such guidelines tend to be liberal due to the diverse nature of government agencies. Our unemployment insurance agency has office operations like those of any other organization, including both software development and what in other organizations would be called customer service representatives. We will be looking at how this organization manages its office operation automation. This organization differs from the one we examined in section 9.2 in several ways:

- It's developing software and using mature, reliable technology to do it.
- It has had computers in the office directly on desks, or indirectly in the form of serial terminals to the computer in the data center, since the 1970s.

- It's continuing to manage servers.
- It's quite willing to install specialist software on employees' machines and has been doing so for 30-plus years.
- It's a government employer, so employees tend to stick around for a long time.
- It's had in-house human resources, accounting, and other business processes since long, long before the SaaS revolution, so it uses much less SaaS than other organizations of its size. (It's hard to give up a bespoke system that does exactly what you need it to for a system that does most of what you need and requires you to change how you do things for the rest.)
- Their workforce is not at all mobile, and any remote access is done through VPN.

This workforce looks like organizations in the 1995–2010 era: server-focused, using Microsoft file servers for sharing documents, centralized login for employee Windows desktop machines, grudging adoption of laptops and mobile devices, and the all-seeing eye of the employer surveillance panopticon.

Figure 10.1 shows the office IT telemetry ecosystem. This figure looks somewhat like figure 9.15 (an enterprise-size software-consuming organization), but it depicts a medium-size organization. Our unemployment insurance department has been running servers for decades, so when new telemetry needs emerged, it reached first for the infrastructure it already had: servers. There is one odd similarity to the enterprise-size organizations self-hosting their centralized logging system; the larger organization wrote its own software for this role, but the medium-size organization is using off-the-shelf software (Splunk) installed on its own servers. Even so, we see some differences between that larger organization and this one:

- The presence of SharePoint and file serving, which are two different ways to save and share files when not using a cloud service. There are likely two and a half decades of files in these servers that don't exist in the Office 365 storage.
- A new telemetry system used for tracking employee web browsing, which requires installing an agent on employee endpoints and provides a dedicated reporting interface for use by managers.
- No Apple hardware. This unemployment insurance department clearly wants extensive control of employee endpoints. Smaller organizations that desire as much control over endpoints rarely have the organizational bandwidth to support more than one operating system. If support for Apple hardware exists at all, it is half-baked and for special trusted employees such as executives.

As we've seen with all the office IT telemetry systems, this organization's telemetry focuses most on centralized logging systems. The reporting systems can also derive metrics-like charts from logging data, but that still isn't *metrics* the way we talked about through all of part 1; that's centralized logging standing in for metrics which it can do, if not nearly as good. How does this centralized logging focus translate to the software-development side of the house?

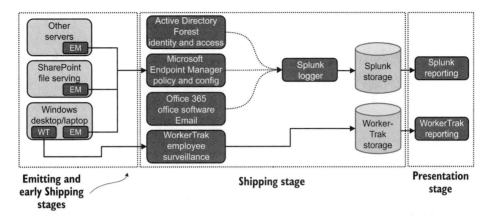

Figure 10.1 Our office IT telemetry ecosystem for our medium-size legacy computing organization. This IT ecosystem collects event-log telemetry from all Windows systems (servers and employee endpoints) and uses Endpoint Manager for pushing configuration and policy. Employee surveillance is new in this organization, which stores web-browsing telemetry for review in a reporting interface in the Presentation stage. Such detailed and SaaS-free telemetry is a result of this organization's decades-long history of running servers internally.

My experience with a medium-size organization

My first job out of college was with a city government. Although I was hired to help with desktop support for a Windows-based office (with NetWare file servers), the system driving payroll and human resources was a minicomputer. This minicomputer was made by Pr1me Systems (anyone born after 1970 has likely never heard of it), was purchased in 1978 and upgraded a few times in the 1980s, and was still doing work in 1999. It ran Oracle 4 (released in 1984).

What ultimately killed the Pr1me system was the year-2000 problem. The city knew that the deadline was coming and spent 1997 and 1998 attempting to convert the payroll and human resources systems to an off-the-shelf solution. That project was abandoned after the feasibility study determined that the project could be brought in at the top of the budget for the bottom of the requested features. The city council caught all kinds of grief for making the decision to stop ("You're throwing all that money away! It's a waste of taxpayer resources!"), but it was the right decision.

The city spent 1998 and 1999 rewriting the Pr1me-based payroll and human resources systems, written in COBOL and Oracle 4, as something that would run on a Windows machine. Helping this process was the fact the original programmer, who wrote it in 1978, was still on staff and led the rewrite effort. I helped specify the hardware that would host the rewritten software, which was still running COBOL, but with Oracle 8i.

We didn't hit the ship deadline (January 1, 2000), so the Pr1me had to have its clock turned back to 1973 because the calendar that year was the same as for the year 2000. Don't worry—our paychecks still had the right year on them. (I checked.) But when the payroll department ran its first payroll on the new system, everyone was ecstatic.

(continued)

When the data entry was done, generating the payroll took 15 minutes, whereas it used to take four hours.

Twenty years later, I would not be at all surprised if that bespoke system first written in 1978 is still running.

10.1.2 *Telemetry use in production systems*

Office IT in section 10.1.1 showed a lot of self-hosted solutions, using centralized logging as the only telemetry system in use. The production software side of our unemployment insurance department is definitely using telemetry. This section shows how telemetry works in an organization as focused on self-hosting as this one is and that started computer operations in the 1970s. Figure 10.2 illustrates the production software environment for our government agency.

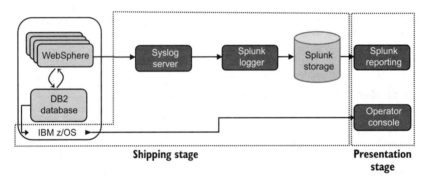

Figure 10.2   The telemetry system for the production software for our unemployment insurance department. Web serving and database operate on an IBM mainframe running z/OS. The WebSphere software has a familiar telemetry feed to Splunk, but the z/OS is new: an operator console.

Our unemployment insurance department is using a single IBM mainframe running z/OS to process transactions. This mainframe is running a cluster of web and application servers (IBM WebSphere) and using the IBM DB2 database for storage. Not pictured are the batch jobs specified in Job Control Language (JCL) that distribute benefits. We see that the WebSphere servers (functionally virtual machines) are following a familiar pattern by emitting into a Syslog server, ultimately into Splunk for centralized logging. The DB2 and z/OS telemetry, on the other hand, follows a new process: it gets sent to an operator console.

The operator console, which is straight out of the pre-PC era, traditionally was a printer that spat out system events as they happened or a monitor that displayed events. More modern versions can color-code events so operators can quickly tell which ones are important. (Think of it as a kind of monitoring and alerting system for mainframes with logging functionality.) In our unemployment insurance case, the operator console is where telemetry related to the database and JCL (business automation running inside z/OS) events can be viewed. This viewing can be done physically in the data center by an operator or through the right kind of remote terminal connection.

What we see here is a system in a box. It's a big box, called a mainframe for a reason, but it's a box that's also supporting a whole state's unemployment insurance system. This department is still relatively small, so it's using vendor components for everything it can to try to save money. Also, being a government department in the United States means chronic underfunding, so operations aren't quite up to the state of the art for mainframes. (We'll see what state of the art looks like in section 10.3.) Like office IT, all the telemetry operations are variations on centralized logging.

Their lone point of convergence between their production software and office IT is the Splunk infrastructure. We see here that the agency's experience with running servers has it doing just that for office automation, as well as the production systems. The agency is doing only centralized logging for office IT and production system telemetry; its development patterns don't provide incentives to look deeply into metrics or tracing.

10.2 *Telemetry use in large organizations*

We cover large organizations in this section—the legacy computing type that have one central office and lots of branch offices or other small nodes of access. Think a regional bank with a central headquarters but branches scattered across five states or an auto-parts maker with factories in three states. Whereas the medium-size organization has a single location that does a lot of work, the large organization works in many places. More important, the large organization has more resources for developing software than the medium-size organization does. This section shows how a large organization mixes mainframe-style computing with more conventional computing.

Here are some major differences between medium-size organizations and large ones in the legacy computing space:

- Large organizations have more development resources, so their production software environments are correspondingly more complex.
- They are managing employees in multiple locations remote from where all the servers are.
- They are managing both legacy computing and more conventional computing at the same time.
- They have more people in general, so they are able to keep up with best practices better.

In this chapter, we are going to look at an auto-parts maker operating factories in three states that sends auto parts to both automakers and retail chains. It may seem that not much software is involved in these processes, but there is quite a lot of it.

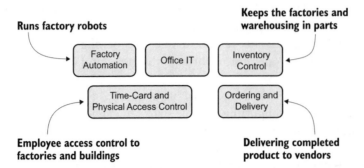

Figure 10.3   The five areas of software use and development our auto-parts maker is managing. Factory Automation is for the software controlling the machines involved in the factory. Office IT is for business office automation. Inventory Control is for managing supplies for the factory and storage of completed product. Ordering and Delivery is for managing the process of shipping completed product. Time Card and Physical Access Control (PACS) is for tracking access to facilities and managing hourly employee timekeeping. Multiple zones such as these are common in companies involved with making things.

Figure 10.3 shows the various zones of software use and development that our auto-parts maker is managing.

The unique box in figure 10.3 is Factory Automation; this box is all about Supervisory Control and Data Acquisition (SCADA) systems and how they interact with both humans and other computer systems in the company. SCADA systems control *hardware*; they handle and display the telemetry generated by the hardware components, such as like welding robots, coolant pumps, and assembly-line motors. Because this is book is about *software* telemetry, we will be looking at the telemetry provided by the supervisor computer running the SCADA system rather than the telemetry from the eight enframulators on the factory floor, as demonstrated in figure 10.4.

The history of our auto-parts maker matters in how the rest of the infrastructure is put together. This company came into existence in the 1950s and has been serving the Big Three U.S. automakers ever since. The first systems to computerize were inventory, ordering, and delivery in the mid 1960s. Factory Automation began to adopt robotics in the early 1970s. The time-card system computerized in the early 1980s, which is when office IT started to emerge. Factory robots got more complex in the 1980s, so the first SCADA systems were introduced. The late 1980s saw access to the factories change from a key-and-watchman system to proximity cards, which allowed the merger of the time-card system with the PACS. In the 1990s, ordering and delivery were split from inventory control as part of an internal reorganization at the company.

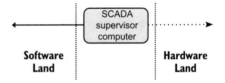

Figure 10.4   SCADA systems and the separation between the hardware and software sides. Hardware Land is where the supervisor computer controls all the hardware systems and manages telemetry coming from the hardware. Software Land is where non-SCADA software communicates with the SCADA system. We will be focusing on the left side of this chart.

Figure 10.5 demonstrates how these five software zones connect and where each zone exists between the head office, factories, and warehouse. It also shows two different CPU architectures: mainframe-style IBM POWER9 and commodity hardware amd64-based systems. Unlike our medium-size organization, this organization is managing diverse hardware in its production systems. To start looking at software telemetry use, let's look at the Factory Automation group.

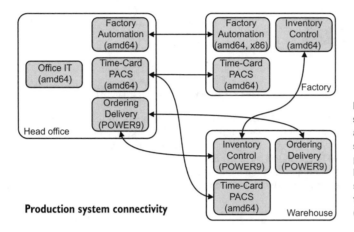

Production system connectivity

Figure 10.5 Production system connectivity (and CPU architecture) between the five software zones for our auto-parts maker. Although we do have five separate zones and software stacks, they talk to one another quite a bit (macroservices, if you will).

Which is it: amd64 or x86? And what about x86_64?

What you call the CPU architecture that Intel and AMD produce chips for depends on who you ask. If you ask Debian what CPU architecture its running, you'll get variations on amd64. Ask SuSE, and you get x86_64. The mainframe world calls CPUs from Intel and AMD x86 exclusively, and has done so for decades in spite of the change of terms in the rest of the industry. I'm using amd64 for these figures because readers of this book will likely be more familiar with that term. However, it's called amd64 because AMD built the first widely adopted 64-bit specification for the PC market.

Intel had a 64-bit architecture (called Itanium, or IA64) that never saw widespread marketplace acceptance. Intel licensed AMD's 64-bit architecture because it seemed that the marketplace liked it better. In areas where you see universal use of Intel and AMD CPUs, x86 is still sometimes used as a generic term, but for the most part, CPU architecture doesn't come up. Sometimes, x86 is used to refer to 32-bit Intel/AMD CPUs if a distinction is needed.

With Apple releasing hardware running on ARM CPUs, not Intel, however, CPU architecture discussions are once again starting to happen even in stalwart Intel environments. By the time a second edition of this book is called for, I imagine that there will be far more dual-architecture (amd64 plus ARM) environments out there.

To start, let's focus in on the Factory Automation group. Figure 10.6 lays out its telemetry systems, split between the head office and factory locations.

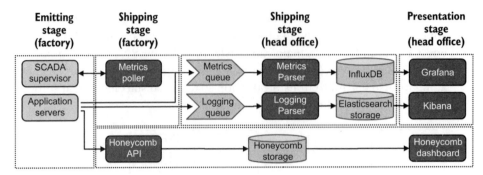

Figure 10.6   Telemetry system flows for the Factory Automation group at our auto-parts maker. We see three telemetry systems in use here: metrics, centralized logging, and tracing. Metrics are extracted from the SCADA systems through a metrics poller the group has written. Metrics are submitted across the WAN to a queue in the head office. Logging follows a similar path, with log lines submitted across the WAN to a queue in the head office. Tracing is using the Honeycomb.io SaaS product. Centralizing telemetry in one location is common in organizations working with branch offices.

The telemetry pipeline for our Factory Automation group is surprisingly similar to what we saw in chapter 8 with the software-producing companies, all in spite of having SCADA to work with. The SCADA supervisor in their case is running on 32-bit hardware (x86 instead of amd64) and communicates with 16- and 8-bit hardware as part of its duties. It offers interfaces for the auto-parts maker to request metrics, however, which allows our auto-parts maker to integrate telemetry from the factory floor into its overall management framework. The head-office metrics and logging infrastructure are interesting for us because this infrastructure is shared among teams. Now let's look at the other amd64-based group: Time Card/PACS.

Telemetry for the Time Card/PACS group, as shown in figure 10.7, is significantly different than the telemetry used for the Factory Automation group. Although both groups are using the centralized metrics and logging pipelines, how telemetry moves into those pipelines is different. Both the employee time-card system and the PACS system are purchased software frameworks, meaning that the Time Card/PACS group is mostly managing software it didn't write. The group did create a logging poller for use with the PACS system; this poller queries API endpoints on the PACS in each remote facility to fetch events and then repackages those events for submission to the logging queue. The time-card systems in the head office are part off-the-shelf software and part in-house-developed software, which is why that system is able to emit metrics and logging directly to the queues. Unlike the Factory Automation group, this group isn't using Honeycomb.io for tracing; most of what it works on is purchased software, so tracing wasn't a big enough need to bother building out.

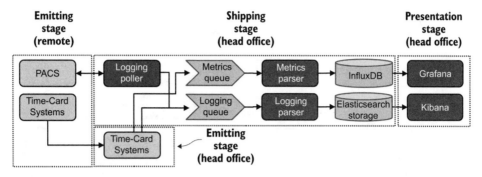

Figure 10.7 **Telemetry system flow for the Time Card/PACS group.** *Remote* **refers to both warehouse and factory locations. We see the time-card systems rolling up inside the production software to the head office, where metrics and logging are emitted into the same infrastructure our Factory Automation group used. The PACS systems require a dedicated logging poller running in the head office to fetch logging data, which is then sent into the centralized systems. Unlike the Factory Automation group, the Time Card/PACS group is not using tracing. As both the PACS and time-card systems are purchased software, the ability to use tracing is greatly reduced.**

We'll look at the architectures of the Inventory Control and Ordering and Delivery groups together. Although the two groups split apart in the 1990s as part of a reorganization, both groups continue to follow mainframe-centered development patterns. The inventory software used by our auto-parts maker is purchased software that is licensed by the CPU, which is why the Inventory Control group has a small mainframe of its own to reduce overall costs to the company. The Ordering and Delivery group operates its mainframe in the head office, and the Inventory Control group operates its directly at the warehouse. Ordering and Delivery uses a small partition of the Inventory Control group's mainframe for warehouse-local operations, isolating the partition so it doesn't increase software license costs. (This sort of partitioning is a core feature of mainframes.) Inventory Control operates a small group of amd4 machines at each factory to act as interfaces to its system.

Figure 10.8 shows the telemetry architectures of the Inventory Control and Ordering and Delivery groups. This figure is the first time we've seen a mainframe emit to a logging queue, which is accomplished by running Linux in partitions (logical partition, or LPAR) on the Ordering and Delivery mainframe. These Linux partitions run software developed by our auto-parts maker that interfaces with the software running in z/OS and also acts as the web frontend for vendors and customers. By using more conventionally built software—in modern languages more common on amd64 systems—the Ordering and Delivery group is able to use the full range of telemetry, but it has chosen to use only logging due to a long history on mainframes that biases the group toward that method alone.

Meanwhile, the Inventory Control group has taken a slightly different approach. Its purchased software emits only to the console, true, but it has built wrapper automation

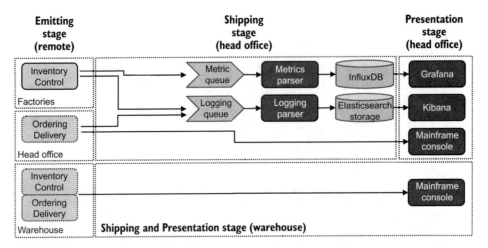

Figure 10.8   The telemetry architecture for the Inventory Control and Ordering and Delivery groups. Solid boxes on the left are amd64-based production systems; dot-filled boxes on the left are IBM POWER9-based production systems. Each POWER9 system emits to the mainframe console. The head office Ordering and Delivery system also emits to the logging queue through a Linux partition on the mainframe. The Inventory Control systems running in each factory continue to emit metrics and logging data to queues hosted in the head office. Again, we see that mainframe operations has a strong preference for using the console for all telemetry.

around the purchased inventory-management software to take some of the sharp edges off the interfaces. This group is operating amd64-based systems in each of the three factories that interface across the WAN with the mainframe back at the warehouse. The amd64-based systems emit into centralized logging and also the metrics pipelines in the head office.

Which brings us around to Office IT. This company has had computers or serial terminals (often both in the 1980s and 1990s) on the desks at the head office going back to the 1970s, and also had a machine room to put servers in. The Office IT telemetry system we saw for the medium-size organization in section 10.1.1 was heavy on locally hosted server-based solutions for the same reason, and the large organization isn't any different. The difference is that Office IT for the large organization also has three factories and a warehouse to manage, whereas the medium-size organization has a single office.

The first thing that stands out in figure 10.9 is that it shares no infrastructure with the software telemetry designs we've seen so far for our auto-parts maker. The reason for this separation is historical. Back in the 1980s, when the PC revolution kicked off, this company already had mainframes. The IBM PC was considered to be a microcomputer in those days (this name has been dropped), with no clear business use beyond replacing typewriters, so the existing software and hardware operations groups for our auto-parts maker didn't bother to manage the new computers popping up on desks

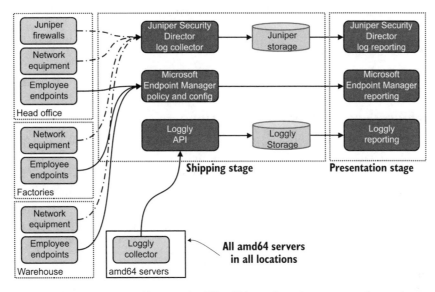

Figure 10.9 Telemetry architecture for Office IT in our large legacy computing environment. This design accounts for multiple office locations, unlike the medium-size organization's version in figure 10.1. We see network telemetry being gathered in a vendor-specific framework, and endpoint telemetry moving through Microsoft Endpoint Manager. We also see that all amd64 servers (Windows and Linux) have a SaaS vendor's collector installed, which ships logging data to the Loggly cloud. This architecture has no metrics telemetry, but it has three different ways of handling centralized logging!

here and there. Eventually, the company learned that PCs could replace serial terminals and that when PCs were networked together, sharing electronic files was more efficient than sharing paper files. The office hired someone to manage these new networked computers, which led to the creation of a different department. That separation has been maintained for more than 30 years.

Unlike the large software producing organization we saw in section 8.4, which phased out its use of SaaS providers for logging, this company is still embracing it. Our auto-parts maker is using the Loggly cloud platform for centralized logging, but only for Office IT. It can get away with doing this, unlike the large software-producing organization, because making parts for automobiles requires fewer computers overall than running a SaaS provider. Scale is still working in the company's favor, so it's embracing scale—and is almost the only group in this company doing so. (The other is the Factory Automation group, with Honeycomb for tracing.)

All in all, the telemetry system for our large organization is quite a bit more complex than the one we examined for the medium-size provider. More people makes for more departments, which in turn leads to more software being written and more telemetry systems being used. The decades-long history of computing in this company certainly makes a significant difference in how it approaches telemetry compared with the software-producing organizations in chapter 8:

- Far more use of centralized logging
- Almost no use of tracing
- Continued use of SaaS products

10.3 *Telemetry use in global organizations*

Much like the enterprise organizations we talked about in section 9.4, the global organizations we talk about in this section operate in many legal jurisdictions. This chapter is on large organizations that computerized before 1981, so they achieved wide adoption of computers before Intel dominated the CPU market. Chances are good that these organizations helped set the standard for computerization in their markets (think banking, airlines, and insurance) and have been living that legacy ever since. Organizations of this size still make extensive use of amd64-based computing, as we will see. Here are the major differences between global organizations and the large organizations we talked about in section 10.2:

- Global organizations operate internationally, so they have different legal entities in each country, are subject to different laws, and have different workplace cultures.
- They were big before computerization, so they were able to go big on computers in the era when having more than one was kind of a big deal.
- Like the enterprise organizations in section 9.4, they produce a lot of software. Unlike the section 9.4 organizations, they've been producing and refining the same software for several decades.
- Whereas the large organization had branch offices, the global organization has branch offices all over the world.

The organization we'll focus on here is a European airline that began flying in the 1950s and survived seven decades of regulation, deregulation, mergers with rivals, strikes, and the ever-increasing security apparatus surrounding air travel. The airline has not only survived business environment changes, but also weathered the explosion of computerized reservation systems, computerized flight-plan submissions to aviation authorities, GPS flight tracking, introduction of Internet connectivity in flight, and deployment of mobile applications so passengers can access in-flight entertainment from their own devices. Airlines have gone deep into technology, and they did it early.

Although the airline's mobile and web-application development looks much like that of the software-creating organizations from chapter 8, the reservation, inventory, and aviation-authority systems were among the first to get computerized. Because our company started in the 1950s, these first computerized systems were put on the same kind of mainframes as the organizations from sections 10.1 and 10.2. Those mainframes are still there and form the (deeply buried) foundation of all the online, mobile, and travel agent reservation systems. To understand how this works, let's look at the hypothetical path followed by a query of available flights in figure 10.10:

1 The user submits the request to an edge web service.
2 The edge web service sends an API call to the internal capacity API.
3 The internal capacity API sends the request to a capacity querent for fulfillment.
4 The capacity querent queries the Db2 database for matching records.
5 The Db2 database returns records to the capacity querent.
6 The capacity querent returns results by way of the internal capacity API.
7 The internal capacity API returns the call to the edge web.
8 The edge web service starts rendering results for the user.

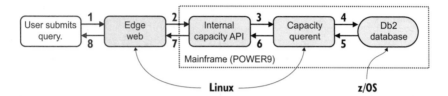

Figure 10.10 The flow of requests (a trace, if you will) that happens when a user submits a query for available flights. The frontend web service is a modern autoscaling pool of servers, but the capacity API it uses to fulfill the request from the user is on a mainframe. Note that this mainframe is running both Linux and z/OS applications.

The edge web box in figure 10.10 could be a geographically distributed set of machines (to be closer to end users), each of which sends queries to the same Db2 database housed in France. The mainframe in this architecture is the central transaction-handling system. Historically, mainframes have been extremely good at handling high transaction rates. In section 10.1, we saw a system that was contained on a single mainframe. In section 10.2, we saw an ecosystem with multiple mainframes and amd64-based systems working together. In this section, the mainframe is merely another part of a large, complex software ecosystem. Like the enterprise-size software-consuming organization we looked at in section 9.4, however, our airline is made up of many parts that consume and use software, as shown in figure 10.11.

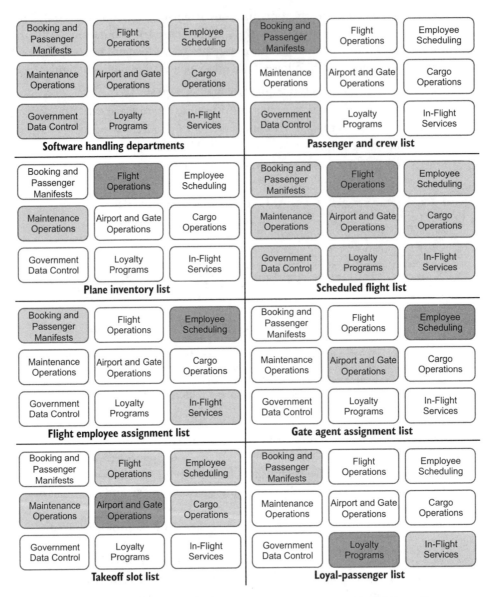

Figure 10.11 Software-consuming and -producing departments for our global airline, with seven examples of data produced and consumed within the airline. Producing departments are darker boxes; consuming departments are lighter boxes.

Each department in figure 10.11 owns certain kinds of data and provides it to others, much like a group of smaller companies operating inside a bigger one. Here are some examples from figure 10.11:

- Booking and Passenger Manifests owns the list of which passengers and crew are on each flight, which is consumed by government data control to maintain compliance with transportation security laws in relevant countries.
- Flight Operations owns the plane inventory list, which is consumed by Maintenance and Cargo Operations.
- Flight Operations also owns the list of scheduled flights, which is consumed by everything else.
- Employee Scheduling owns the list of which employees are assigned to flights, which is consumed by Booking and Passenger Manifests and In-Flight Services.
- Employee Scheduling also owns the list of gate agents, which is consumed by Airport and Gate Operations to staff gates.
- Airport and Gate Operations owns the list of takeoff slots and assigned gates, which is consumed by Flight Operations, Cargo Operations, Maintenance Operations, and Employee Scheduling.
- Loyalty Programs owns the list of which passengers are enrolled, which is consumed by Booking and Passenger Manifests and In-Flight Services.

We're going to take a close look at the software telemetry used in two departments:

- Section 10.3.1 examines the telemetry ecosystem for the Booking and Passenger Manifest department, which computerized operations in the 1970s.
- Section 10.3.2 examines the telemetry ecosystem for Loyalty Programs, which computerized much later.

10.3.1 Telemetry use in the Booking and Passenger Manifest department

The Booking and Passenger Manifest department for our European airline is charged with maintaining passenger data, including reservations, as well as flight manifests that also include the flight crew. This department handles truly worldwide operations, accepting transfers from other airlines, getting check-in data from every gate as it happens worldwide, automates the fare structure for the entire airline's operations, and so much more. This department has a lot going on, and this section covers how it keeps track of its automation. This department uses a mix of mainframe and conventional approaches to computing. Unlike the medium-size organization, this department takes a state-of-the-art approach to computing and telemetry.

Before we can dig into the telemetry architecture, we need to look at the production systems. We'll be looking at two primary workflows. The first is the reservation workflow, which is a (mostly) conventional web application with a mainframe as the database. The second is the gate-check flow, where boarding passes are scanned and a passenger manifest is built.

Figure 10.12 shows both of the workflows, which interact with three API systems running on an IBM mainframe. The regional web clusters support the airline's reservation systems. The gate computers at each airport gate that loads passengers is responsible for supplying the data that will build the flight manifest that will ultimately ship with the

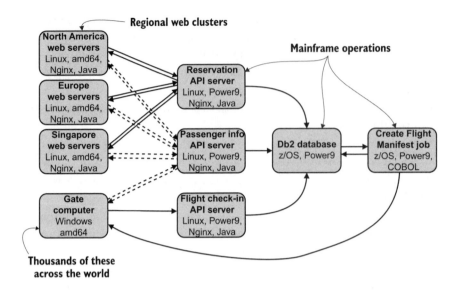

Figure 10.12   Two workflows for our Booking and Passenger Manifest department: one for accepting reservations and a second for checking in passengers to generate a flight manifest. This airline operates three regional clusters of web servers supporting reservations in North America, Europe, and Singapore. There is a gate computer at each airport gate loading passengers. The reservation servers and the gate computer talk to up to three APIs hosted on a central mainframe in Europe. The flight manifest is created as a batch job after all passengers are checked in. We will be looking at this production environment in later figures.

plane itself for the in-flight staff, be sent to civil aviation authorities for flight tracking, and be delivered to other government security entities that are required by law to receive such data.

Figure 10.13 gives us the flow of logging data out of the Booking and Passenger Manifest department's production servers and into the telemetry pipeline. A lot is going on here, so let's step through it:

1   Events are emitted by the three production systems.

  a   Globally located reservation web servers ship events by way of webhook to webhook receivers hosted in the Paris data center, using emitter/shipper functions in the backend application code. (See section 3.1.3 for an example of sending telemetry by way of HTTP POSTs.)

  b   API servers running in LPARs on the Paris mainframe ship events directly into a Kafka-based stream on the logging_raw topic, also using emitter/shipper functions. (See section 3.1.2 for an example of sending telemetry into streams.)

  c   The Create Flight Manifest batch job on the Paris mainframe emits job output into the mainframe system's console.

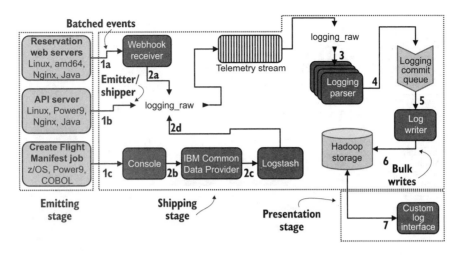

Figure 10.13 Centralized logging telemetry flow for our global European airline example, showing both the reservation/booking system telemetry (reservation web servers and API servers) and the flight check-in telemetry flow (API servers and create flight manifest batch job). Three emission and shipping techniques are used here. This figure demonstrates how mainframe batch jobs can contribute logging data to telemetry pipelines.

2 Events from the web servers and the batch job ship into the stream.

   a The webhook receiver reformats telemetry from the reservation web servers and injects them into the logging_raw stream topic (similar to how section 3.1.2 describes sending into streams).

   b Data from the mainframe console ships into the IBM Common Data Provider.

   c The Common Data Provider sends console telemetry into Logstash, running in a partition on the mainframe.

   d Logstash sends events into the logging_raw stream topic.

3 Logging parsers subscribe to the logging_raw stream topic and enrich events. (See "Using streams in a shipping pipeline" in section 3.1.2 and section 6.1 for enrichment during the Shipping stage.)

4 Logging parsers send enriched telemetry onto a queue called logging commit queue.

5 Logging writers pop events off of the logging commit queue.

6 Logging writers aggregate and bulk insert events into a Hadoop cluster.

7 Logging data can be reviewed through a custom logging interface the airline has written.

The metrics pipeline looks similar.

Figure 10.14 shows a metrics telemetry flow that looks almost identical to the logging flow in figure 10.13, but with some of the names changed. Here, metrics data is stored in OpenTSDB instead of Hadoop, which is a bit of a lie because OpenTSDB sits on top of Hadoop. Having the metrics pipeline be so similar to the logging pipeline

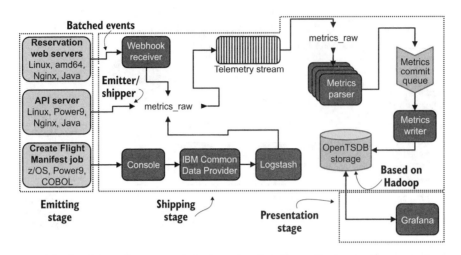

Figure 10.14   The metrics telemetry flow for our global European airline. The flow is identical in steps to the logging flow but instead flows into OpenTSDB instead of Hadoop. But OpenTSDB is based on Hadoop and is optimized for time-series data. The similarity in telemetry flows with logging eases maintenance burdens by being easier to comprehend by the teams supporting both.

(in fact, the webhook receiver functions the same in both pipelines, with different endpoints based on the type of telemetry) makes comprehending the entire pipeline ecosystem easier for everyone and eases maintenance burdens.

Our Booking and Passenger Manifest department is doing modern web development, so it is also using distributed tracing techniques. Their COBOL components don't play a role in the key booking workflows, but the API servers running on the mainframe are critical to the process. Figure 10.15 shows the tracing telemetry flows.

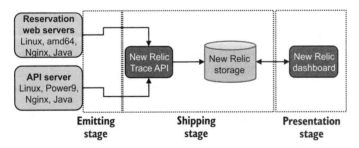

Figure 10.15   Distributed tracing flows for the Booking systems for our European airline. The department picked the New Relic SaaS platform to provide tracing. Use of SaaS providers at this scale is a deliberate choice. Our airline has the technical skill to host a tracing pipeline internally but has elected not to.

Figure 10.15 shows something unexpected for a company this size: use of a SaaS product! Why use SaaS at this scale; when the software-producing company at this size was actively getting rid of any SaaS use? First, that company was still using SaaS for its

SIEM systems, which is an example of a *strategic* use of SaaS products when you have enough traffic for a seven- to eight-figure annual renewal cost. Second, both this airline and the company from section 8.4 chose to use SaaS in a given place because they believed that they got better value from paying someone else to build and maintain the system than from doing it themselves. The software-producing company in section 8.4 had so many software engineers around that it could handle distributed tracing internally, whereas this legacy computing airline felt that the role best outsourced to a long-standing partner.

> ### Mainframes are for more than batch jobs
>
> Section 10.3.1 shows Linux servers running on the mainframe. The old standard role of mainframes was batch-job engine, where jobs were scheduled to run (written in Job Control Language) that ran queries against the database and returned results. Mainframes are far more these days, however. One of the key selling points is reliability; mainframes are engineered to provide years between restarts. Mainframe systems allow you to hot-swap a CPU with a spare without dropping computing load, and that's only one reliability feature.
>
> As we see in section 10.3, organizations that use mainframes still need to coexist with systems that provide reliability as a distributed system instead of one highly reliable (and large) box. Not every workload can be distributed; it needs to have that one box not go down but still needs to talk to systems that can be distributed. To help, mainframes offer built-in ways to talk to z/OS components fast (in-memory networking and similarly optimized paths) and also provide interfaces for external systems to the mainframe ones. Logical partitions are virtualized environments similar to what VMware ESX provides; they allow running other operating systems, which in turn allows moving traditional software systems into the mainframe's high-availability zone.
>
> Where you get Linux, you also get other open source products. Mainframe is among the last environments supported by open source products, but supported it is. Both Kubernetes and containerd can run on mainframe, which means that you can do microservices on a mainframe! Hosting ephemeral containers seems to be the opposite of what mainframes are about, but the reason why so much of the rest of the industry has moved to containers is the same reason why mainframe shops move to it. Mainframes are only components—highly available ones—of an organization's technical ecosystem.

10.3.2 *Telemetry use in the Loyalty Programs department*

The Loyalty Programs department of our European airline is charged with managing this airline's frequent-flyer and awards programs for all its brands. This role requires tracking the spending patterns of loyal customers using branded credit cards, points or miles earned during flights, and arranging award use of points or miles. Frequent-flyer programs are more recent innovations than commercial air travel, coming into existence between 1972 and 1982, making this story look like the software-consuming organizations of chapter 9. This section shows how this department's telemetry use differs from what we examined with the Booking and Passenger Manifests department in section 10.3.1.

The main customer interfaces are a subsite on the airline's main site and the airline's mobile application. Although the Booking and Passenger Manifest department maintains the website, leaving the Loyalty Program department as a tenant, the roles are reversed in the mobile application. This organization isn't terribly efficient, but politics makes for seemingly strange choices. Strange organizational structures always are there for a reason, but that reason doesn't have to be a good one.

To start, we need to look at the Loyalty Programs department's production systems. Unlike the Booking and Passenger Manifest department, which has to supply data to civil aviation and government security services, the Loyalty Programs department shares only with other airlines and financial institutions. As part of this data interchange agreement with other airlines, it supplies APIs for looking up loyalty details for internal and external alliance use.

Figure 10.16 shows a multilayered production system with application, API, database, and batch tiers. Although this system is not microservices strictly speaking, it does show a tendency to split roles into different code bases. We also see two different software stacks in use, with Java being used on the reservation web servers and credit card interfaces, and .NET Core being used for all the API tier systems. We also see mobile development for the first time. Let's take a look at what that means for the telemetry systems. First up is logging flows.

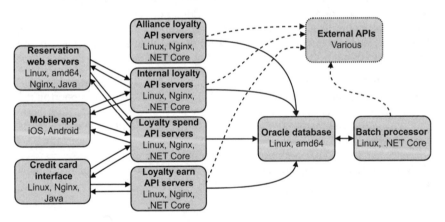

Figure 10.16 The production systems for our Loyalty Programs department. The main applications supported are a subapplication on the Java-based Reservation Web Servers, mobile apps in the Google and Apple app stores, and a credit-card interface system. These applications consume four APIs, which use an Oracle database. A batch processor runs scheduled jobs and is not a mainframe app. The batch processor and various APIs also communicate with APIs not managed by this department; some are internal and others are external, such as the Loyalty Program APIs for allied airlines. This architecture, which uses modern software practices, can emerge in even century-old companies.

Figure 10.17 shows the logging telemetry system, which uses three delivery methods. The Reservation Web Servers use the same delivery method the Booking and Passenger Manifest systems did in figure 10.13, sending events to a webhook receiver. Meanwhile, the API servers running in Azure and on .NET Core submit telemetry directly to an Azure-managed stream service called an Event Hub. Mobile apps don't log from the application, but a crash-reporting service sends application-crash data to a Crash Report API. They are also running a set of log parsing instances that service both the logging Event Hub and the crash Event Hub to enrich telemetry before inserting it into an Elasticsearch cluster maintained by Azure.

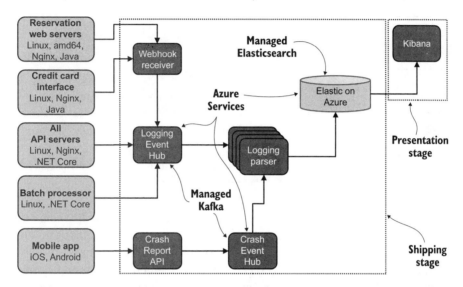

Figure 10.17 Logging telemetry flows for the production systems of the Loyalty Programs department for our European airline. Although the production systems may not be all hosted in the public cloud, this department's telemetry system certainly is, demonstrating that even old companies use public cloud systems in some cases.

This architecture represents a radical difference from any we've seen so far in this chapter in that *the telemetry systems are all in the public cloud (Azure)*. Organizations the size of our European airline are big enough that islands of computing can spawn that draw little from the history of the organization as a whole. In this case, rather than hosting everything in one of the long-standing data centers the airline operates, it is hosting everything in the public cloud. So far, we've seen that this airline is API-driven internally, which allows different parts of the company to operate on radically different stacks so long as API support is maintained.

Figure 10.18 shows the distributed tracing system used by the Loyalty Programs department, and we see diversity here. Remember that Loyalty Programs is running a subsite on the Reservation Web Servers managed by the Booking and Passenger Manifests department. Because of that subsite, the department has no choice but to use the

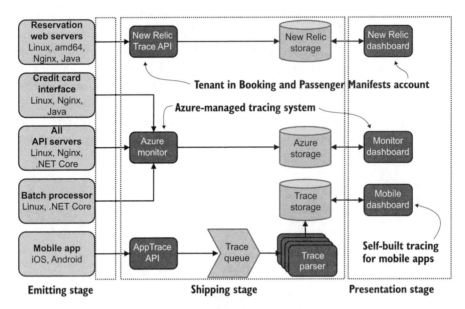

Figure 10.18   Tracing telemetry flow for the Loyalty Programs department of our European airline. We see three separate tracing systems here! As nice as it is to have everything flow into one bucket and have one place to look at things, it isn't always possible.

New Relic tracing system as a tenant in the account managed by Booking and Passenger Manifests. For the credit-card, API, and batch-processing systems, it uses the Azure-managed tracing service known as Azure Monitor. Finally, for mobile applications, it built an AppTrace API system to receive tracing telemetry generated by mobile applications, which feeds into a custom-built parsing, storage, and presentation system.

This system is absolutely not the converged tracing system we saw with the enterprise-size software-producing organization in section 8.4! Convergence is not always possible; the trick is to know when splitting your telemetry is a good idea. Loyalty Programs decided to split their tracing infrastructure up for a few reasons:

- The tracing system for the website was set by another department, so it had no choice.
- Tracing from mobile applications has different constraints from tracing from an application running on your own networks, such as dodgy networking, privacy settings or filters blocking certain kinds of telemetry from reaching home, and operating system updates that break functions.
- The department wanted to trace user actions in addition to software flow inside the mobile applications, so writing a converged tracing stream required a customized solution.

Also, this department doesn't have a metrics telemetry system; it decided a while ago that tracing gave it everything it needed, so it never bothered to build one. System metrics are visible in the Azure dashboards if anyone needs to look at them, but the department is doing nothing special to gather, collate, and enrich metrics telemetry.

Summary

- Small firms are the most responsive to changes in computing, so small, long-established IT companies are more likely to follow the pattern discussed in section 9.1.
- Computers before the IBM PC era were different from what we're used to now, which makes reasoning about how they were used (and their impact on technology use in companies 40 years later) harder to predict.
- Early computers often operated in batch mode, running predefined jobs on a schedule with no interactivity. Mainframes are the descendants of those early computers and are still some of the best systems for running large batch jobs on large datasets.
- Organizations that computerized in the 1960s and 1970s often still have a small data center (sometimes called a machine room) because of this legacy.
- Breaking the habit of local computing requires a deliberate decision by management to break with the past, which we saw in the 1990s and early 2000s as people moved to UNIX or Windows platforms, and in the 2010s as they moved to public cloud computing.
- Organizations that computerized early also got into the habit of writing custom software early, so all the organizations in this chapter are writing software.
- Medium-size organizations computerized early because they had a problem that required fast resolution of financial accounting, so batch-mode mainframes made a lot of sense. Organizations of this size are often still running mainframe-style because they lack the organizational talent for a lift and shift to a new platform.
- Medium-size organizations automated business processes such as human resources and accounting long before the SaaS revolution, so they are using fewer SaaS platforms than the medium-size organizations in sections 9.2 and 8.2.
- Office IT telemetry use in the medium-size organization follows the pattern we saw in chapter 9, focusing mostly on centralized logging.
- The system log for mainframes is the operator console, which stands in for centralized logging.
- Large organizations are those with a single central office and a lot of branch offices, which is a contrast to the medium-size organization that was hosted in a single location. Being bigger and having to deal with WANs change how large organizations approach telemetry use.
- Large organizations have more people to develop software than medium-size organizations do, so their sophistication in telemetry use tends to be higher as a result.

- SCADA systems control industrial processes and handle detailed physical telemetry from robots and sensors throughout a facility. Software telemetry interfaces with SCADA systems at the supervisory computer, which can expose APIs for metrics polling.

- The modern CPU architecture used in mainframes is POWER, instead of amd64/x86_64 or x86, which matters quiet a lot if you are running Linux on a mainframe. Your Linux distribution (and any software you write) needs to be compiled for POWER.

- Organizations operating in the head office-plus-branch office pattern often roll their telemetry up to the head office from the branch location, simplifying their computing footprint in the branch locations.

- The large organization still uses SaaS products in telemetry systems, unlike the large software-producing organization in section 8.3. Although the large organization is still producing software, it's not to the scale of the section 8.3 organization, so the economics of SaaS are still in favor of use.

- Global organizations operate internationally, unlike the large organizations, making them subject to many legal environments.

- Global organizations computerized in a big way before the IBM PC revolution, so they have the most inertia to overcome if they want to do away with mainframes.

- The largest global organizations are in heavily regulated industries such as finance, air travel, and insurance, which makes changing business practices harder to bring about.

- Modern web development can still use mainframe-based databases as part of their architecture, which makes mainframes harder to identify when looking at how a site works.

- Mainframes allow creating LPARs that allow running different operating systems, similar to how VMWare ESX works for virtualization. It is actually possible to run Kubernetes on a mainframe through use of Linux in an LPAR!

- IBM makes a Common Data Provider that enables shipping of mainframe console data into other places, such as streams and queues, allowing it to participate in centralized logging and metrics pipelines.

- Global organizations are big enough that islands of computing can exist independently and grow unaware of the greater organization's history in early computing practices. This is how one department can be mainframes and some Linux, where another department is hosting the entire infrastructure in Azure.

- Mobile application development has very different constraints when it comes to tracing, with dodgy networking, privacy filters blocking actions, and Google or Apple changing the operating system in ways that break your telemetry. For these reasons, tracing for mobile looks different from tracing for server-deployed software.

Part 3

Techniques for handling telemetry

Part 1 taught you the overall architecture of telemetry systems, and part 2 gave many examples of real-world telemetry systems in a variety of settings. I hope that you found some familiar ground in part 2. Part 3 is all about specific techniques. This part is a toolbox; each chapter solves a problem facing telemetry systems.

> **NOTE** These chapters can be read selectively, though the structured logging concepts in chapter 12 show up again in chapters 13–16. For this reason, you should consider reading chapter 12 regardless of what else you plan to read.

Chapter 11 dives into the performance bane of telemetry systems: regular expressions. Powerful but slow, regular expressions are hard to avoid if your telemetry systems have to deal with telemetry data coming from hardware systems. This chapter provides several easy techniques to speed the regular expressions you can't avoid. Not everyone needs to optimize regular expressions, but if you do, you *really* do.

Chapter 12 covers standardized logging formats and how to build them. When you have the luxury of controlling the format your telemetry emits as, such as with production code your organization writes, great gains in maintainability and performance can be realized. Getting there takes some work (see section 4.2 for that story), but this chapter is about the technical details of making standards happen.

Chapter 13 provides methods of avoiding files altogether when emitting (and receiving) telemetry. Sending telemetry over TCP sockets or UDP datagrams avoids potentially expensive disk I/O. Sometimes, you need to build an additional emitting method beyond what you're already doing to handle a special need, such as emitting distributed tracing telemetry. Kubernetes and FaaS technologies need to emit telemetry too, and sometimes, their built-in methods aren't quite good enough.

Chapter 14 digs into the technical problem of index cardinality in your telemetry data-stores. Paying attention to cardinality as part of your overall telemetry system design sets you up for successful scaling. This chapter presents several techniques for tackling the cardinality problem.

Chapter 15 addresses telemetry system security, because telemetry systems are critical systems supporting your organization's regulatory and compliance efforts. Attackers (internal and external) love to modify telemetry to hide their tracks, so this chapter will discuss ways to prevent such tampering, or make such tampering evident. Telemetry data can support legal actions, so if that is a concern for you, pay attention to this chapter.

Chapter 16 covers procedures that far too few telemetry system operators think about until it's too late: how to clean up after data spills. Privacy legislation worldwide is slowly making certain types of data toxic to handle—such as health information, personally identifiable information (PII), and financial details—so your telemetry system must be prepared to clean up after spills. If your production systems handle any kind of regulated information, your telemetry systems may end up accidentally storing some of it in the form of exception traces with parameters and other logging data.

Chapter 17 dives into one of the bigger drivers of telemetry system cost: sprawling data-storage costs. Data aggregation and retention policies let you save storage costs at the cost of not having full-resolution data for as long. This chapter covers how to set aggregation and retention policies, and shows how they intersect with regulatory and compliance frameworks.

Chapter 18 gives you guidance on surviving one of the scariest things to happen to a telemetry system operator: court orders to produce or preserve data. Certain industries are more prone to receiving such judicial demands than others, but if your organization receives them, you will thank yourself for having at least some sketched-out procedures in place for handling the demands. This chapter is not legal advice; it sets you up to help your organization's legal team. You will not get a subpoena directly; it will pass through your own lawyers first.

Optimizing for regular expressions at scale

This chapter covers

- Knowing where regular expressions are used in telemetry
- Optimizing your regular-expression use
- Changing your emissions to speed regular expressions

The best way to optimize regular expressions (*regexes*) at scale is to not use regular expressions. But the telemetry tooling we have available sometimes doesn't give us the option of avoiding regular expressions, and we have to deal with them anyway. This chapter is about making the regexes you must use perform the best they can. Much like programming, regexes are used for two reasons in a telemetry pipeline:

- *Control program flow*—If a string matches a regex, do something, such as attempt parsing a certain way.
- *Extract fields from strings*—Using regex, you can capture expressions to add fields to telemetry being processed, known as enrichment. (See chapter 6 for more on enrichment in general.)

277

Section 6.2.2 provides examples of both of these uses, including code, so if you haven't already used regular expressions in telemetry systems, I recommend reading that section before moving on here. Regexes are incredibly powerful tools, but with great power comes greatly hidden complexity that will hurt your performance in many ways. Like many powerful tools, simple expressions that are easy to understand often perform worse than a far more complex but more tightly scoped expression. Regular expressions are terrible when it comes to building maintainable code because the code that performs best is the hardest for someone unfamiliar with the specific use case to reason about. To prove the point, the following regex matches any IPv4 address, such as 192.0.2.241:

```
(?<![0-9])(?:(?:[0-1]?[0-9]{1,2}|2[0-4][0-9]|25[0-5])[.](?:[0-1]
➥  ?[0-9]{1,2}|2[0-4][0-9]|25[0-5])[.](?:[0-1]?[0-9]{1,2}|2[0-4][0-9]
➥  |25[0-5])[.](?:[0-1]?[0-9]{1,2}|2[0-4][0-9]|25[0-5]))(?![0-9])
```

Believe it or not, this three-line monstrosity performs better and handles more edge cases than this vastly more readable one-liner:

```
[0-9]{1,3}.[0-9]{1,3}.[0-9]{1,3}.[0-9]{1,3}
```

Even though I work with stuff like this, I rub my forehead when trying to dive into a regex as complex as the first one. I certainly can do it, but I don't enjoy doing so, and you are unlikely to need to build patterns as unreadable as that one. My goal for this chapter is to show you enough of the power of regexes to build expressions that perform well and have a hope of being readable.

> **NOTE** The biggest reason for not being able to avoid regular expressions is handling telemetry emissions from sources such as hardware, third-party software, and SaaS platforms. These sources emit telemetry in their own formats and leave it up to you to turn those generated strings into enriched telemetry. Section 11.3 provides a detailed look at parsing one example of this type of telemetry. If your telemetry enrichment engine has regular expressions only, this chapter is for you.

The way you make regexes perform fast is to build them so that the regular-expression engine knows to stop trying to find a match as fast as possible. For badly optimized expressions, a match failure can be far more expensive in resources than a full match. I cover three techniques for making regular expressions perform better:

- Section 11.1 describes a simple trick known as anchoring to make your regular expressions perform faster.
- Section 11.2 goes into a less simple trick for giving hints to the regex engine to get it to stop matching.
- Section 11.3 applies what you learned in sections 11.1 and 11.2 to dig into a familiar piece of telemetry—that coming from a Cisco ASA firewall.

- Section 11.4 talks about changing your emissions (for code you control) to make them easier to perform regular expressions on and make your expressions easier for more people to understand.

WARNING The regular expressions in this chapter use Ruby-flavored regex because the two major Shipping-stage engines, Fluentd and Logstash, are written in Ruby. I know that this is a change from the Python used until now, but if you end up using either platform, you'll likely need to produce at least some Ruby.

11.1 *Anchoring expressions for speed*

This section shows you how a simple technique called anchoring can make your existing regexes perform better. When I deployed anchoring in my telemetry pipelines, I saw a 12% improvement in overall throughput per node parsing telemetry, and 12% matters a lot when you're handling 20,000 events a second. When you're handling 100,000 events a second, a 12% increase saves money. Not everyone will see 12%—that increase had more to do with how our regexes were already written—but you will see some improvement.

DEFINITION *Anchoring* is the use of the beginning-of-string marker (^ or caret) and the end-of-string marker ($ or dollar sign) as part of your regular expression.

To explain how anchoring works, we need to look at a set of plain-language logging statements of the kind software engineers write when they're not using a highly sophisticated logging framework inside their applications. If you have five engineers working in the same codebase, especially in English, you will have seven ways of phrasing the same idea. Here is the list we will be working with:

```
Added account 1141 in zone 42 with email twitterbot@example.com
Account 1141 deleted from zone 37
Suspended zone 42 account 1141 for excessive email volume
Created new zone: 99
Zone 98 deleted
```

These five log lines tell slightly different things in different ways, added over the course of three years. To start, let us look at the regex that matches the first line.

Figure 11.1 shows a regular expression that will parse the first line in the list of five lines. This regex is using Ruby regular expressions because the two big open source log shippers in the market, Fluend and Logstash, are Ruby projects. The Logstash Grok plugin uses Oniguruma Regex (http://mng.bz/6N1R), which is Ruby but with support for a regex-pattern library added to it (among other things, which we don't need to go into here). The figure shows the core concept of regular expressions in enrichment: the named capture group. We have four capture groups that populate four fields in our telemetry as it moves through the Shipping and Presentation stages.

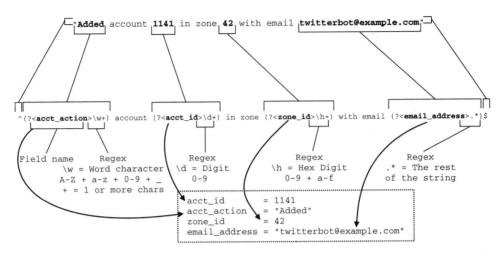

Figure 11.1   A regular expression matching the first of the example log entries. This expression contains four separate capture groups (fields, for enrichment) named `acct_action`, `acct_id`, `zone_id`, and `email_address`.

> **TIP**   The examples in the listings in this chapter are written in Ruby. If you don't have Ruby installed locally, the online Ruby regex tester at https://rubular.com will be quite helpful for testing capturing and other concepts.

Figure 11.2 gives us an expression that matches the second of our example log entries. Because this log entry has one fewer piece of useful context-related telemetry encoded within it (it lacks the `email_address` field from the first log line), the expression is shorter. We also see three reused capture groups from the first expression.

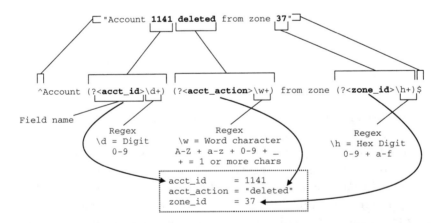

Figure 11.2   Regular expression matching the second of the example log entries. This log entry has three capturable pieces of information; all three were in the first expression in figure 11.1. Because of the natural-language nature of the original log lines, the only ways to tell this set of fields apart from the ones in figure 11.1 are the lack of an email address and the contents of `acct_action`. This sort of differentiation is common in software with lots of natural-language logging.

Figure 11.3 provides the match expressions for the other three log lines, completing the listing of matching regular expressions for our sample log lines. We see two new fields: `suspension_reason` and `zone_action`. But the regex patterns used to capture these new fields are the same as we've seen in others; `email_address` is the same as `suspension_reason`, and `acct_action` is the same as `zone_action`.

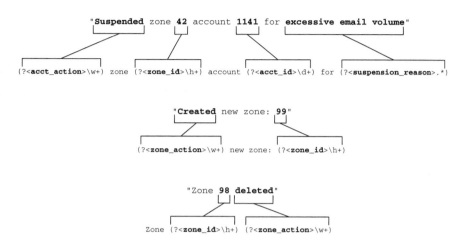

Figure 11.3   Matching regular expressions for the remaining three log lines of our example set. This sort of natural-language logging is easy to parse visually but leaves much to be desired when we're attempting to parse it by computer.

Now that we have all five expressions, let's put them to work in some code. Listing 11.1 is a benchmarking script I'll use to describe how anchoring our regexes improved throughput for my company's Shipping stage by 12%. The benchmark script in listing 11.1 has four test cases, which we'll look at in pieces:

- *Unanchored regular expressions*, matching directly to their log line with no failures.
- *Anchored regular expressions*, matching directly to their log line with no failures.
- *Unanchored regular expressions*, where each log line is matched to all five regex patterns. A dictionary pattern has a lot of match failures.
- *Anchored regular expressions*, following the dictionary pattern from the unanchored expression test case.

Listing 11.1   Benchmarking regexes with anchoring and dictionaries

```ruby
#!/usr/bin/env ruby
require 'benchmark'

log_examples = [
  'Added account 1141 in zone 42 with email
➥ twitterbot@example.com',
  'Account 1141 deleted from zone 37',
```

Our example
log lines

```
    'Suspended zone 42 account 1141 for excessive email volume',
    'Created new zone: 99',
    'Zone 98 deleted',
  ]
iter = 1000000
rbase = [
  Regexp.new('(?<acct_action>\w+) account (?<acct_id>\d+) in zone
   ➥ (?<zone_id>\h+)with email (?<email_address>.*)'),
  Regexp.new('Account (?<acct_id>\d+)
   ➥ (?<acct_action>\w+) from zone (?<zone_id>\h+)'),
  Regexp.new('(?<acct_action>\w+) zone (?<zone_id>\h+) account
   ➥ (?<acct_id>\d+)for (?<suspension_reason>.*)'),
  Regexp.new('(?<zone_action>\w+) new zone: (?<zone_id>\h+)'),
  Regexp.new('Zone (?<zone_id>\h+) (?<zone_action>\w+)')
]

ranchor = [
  Regexp.new('^(?<acct_action>\w+) account (?<acct_id>\d+) in
   ➥ zone (?<zone_id>\h+) with email (?<email_address>.*)$'),
  Regexp.new('^Account (?<acct_id>\d+)
   ➥ (?<acct_action>\w+) from zone (?<zone_id>\h+)$'),
  Regexp.new('^(?<acct_action>\w+) zone
(?<zone_id>\h+) account (?<acct_id>\d+) for
   ➥ (?<suspension_reason>.*)$'),
  Regexp.new('^(?<zone_action>\w+) new zone:
   ➥ (?<zone_id>\h+)$'),
  Regexp.new('^Zone (?<zone_id>\h+)
   ➥ (?<zone_action>\w+)$')
]
Benchmark.bmbm do |rep|
  rep.report("Plain Regex-match") {
    for m in 1..iter
      for q in 0..4
        log_examples[q].match?(rbase[q])
      end
    end
  }
  rep.report("Anchored Regex-match") {
    for m in 1..iter
      for q in 0..4
        log_examples[q].match?(ranchor[q])
      end
    end
  }
  rep.report("Plain Regex-dictionary") {
    log_examples.each do |sl|
      for m in 1..iter
        rbase.each do |relist|
          sl.match?(relist)
        end
      end
    end
  }
```

Our example log lines

Number of iterations to loop through in runs

Unanchored regexes for testing, precompiling to ensure that we don't compile during tests

Anchored regexes for testing, also precompiling

Test case 1: Unanchored direct matches

Test case 2: Anchored direct matches

Test case 3: Unanchored regexes in a dictionary

```
rep.report("Anchored Regex-dictionary") {
  log_examples.each do |sl|
    for m in 1..iter
      ranchor.each do |relist|
        sl.match?(relist)
      end
    end
  end
}
end
```

Test case 4: Anchored regexes in a dictionary

Anchoring is the simple act of putting the beginning-of-string (^) and end-of-string ($) markers in your pattern. Put two characters at the beginning and end of your patterns, and you can see serious speed improvements. This change is the simplest you can make to your regexes to get speedups.

NOTE Anchoring works only when you are *matching the whole string.* If your patterns are matching substrings, anchoring will be much less helpful. If your substring is always at the beginning (^) or end ($) of your string, using one of the anchors will still help.

Two of our four test cases mention a dictionary pattern, in which each known regular expression is matched against each log line coming through for enrichment. In our case, with five log lines and five expressions, test cases 3 and 4 loop through the benchmark and will result in 25 attempts at matching. Figure 11.4 illustrates this dictionary-pattern process.

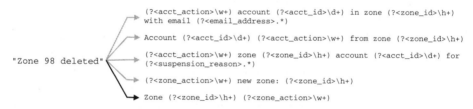

Figure 11.4 The dictionary pattern of regex matching. Each incoming piece of telemetry is compared with the set of regexes. Here, we see that the last regex matches (darker arrow) after four failures. When using the dictionary pattern, you want to put your regexes with the highest likelihood of matches at the top and your regexes with the lowest likelihood of matches lower.

The dictionary pattern in figure 11.4 seems to be horribly inefficient, and it is. But if your enrichment tooling can't filter strings before attempting to match them against their exact regex, this technique will get you the enrichment you want. There are better ways to do this, ways that take a lot more work, and section 11.4 provides the best way to use regexes on emissions from code you manage (if you have to use regexes).

Now let's look at some benchmarking results that show how anchoring affects performance. Figure 11.5 compares the performance of the direct-match and dictionary-match patterns using Ruby 3.0 and shows how anchoring changes both patterns.

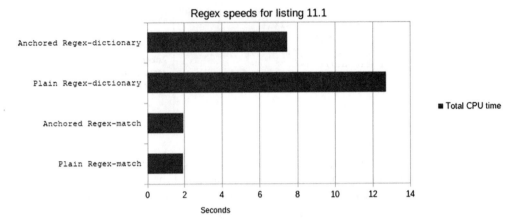

Figure 11.5   Benchmarking results from listing 11.1 showing speed results for four different tests. We see that for the Ruby regular-expression engine, anchoring provides radical speed improvements versus unanchoring when using a regex dictionary and for straight matches, a negligible difference in performance.

Remember that the regex-*match* tests are comparing each log line directly with its matching regex, so they will have no failed matches. This scenario represents the best case, and we can see that anchoring provides no significant benefit. This benchmark uses the Ruby regular-expression engine, but regex engines in other languages perform a bit differently. If you're building a custom Shipping-stage parser, definitely test your platform's regex engine to see how performance differs.

The regex-*dictionary* tests follow the pattern shown in figure 11.4. Each log line is compared with all five regexes, so each log line will cause four match failures and one match success. This scenario represents the worst case, and we see a radical speedup when anchors are used, making for 41.2% faster performance! When we performed this optimization, we saw 12% improvement because we ordered our dictionary of regexes so that the most common log lines were at the top of the list, and our entire dictionary didn't need to be parsed for each line nearly as often. The difference between

```
Zone (?<zone_id>\h+) (?<zone_action>\w+)
```

and

```
^Zone (?<zone_id>\h+) (?<zone_action>\w+)$
```

makes for significant performance increases and is a small change. This speed increase is entirely attributable to the anchors, because they tell the regex engine to start matching at the beginning of the string instead of walking through the string looking for anything that matches. Fast failures make for a faster telemetry pipeline. We have other ways to achieve faster failures, which we talk about in section 11.2.

Isn't `email_address` technically personally identifiable information? Why are we looking at that?

Under European privacy regulations, email addresses are now considered to be PII and therefore are subject to special handling procedures, so you should stop using email addresses in your logging statements. Chapter 16 covers the topic of handling regulated data like email addresses, but handling regulated data well requires you *to know that it's there.*

The regular-expression parsing you did in this section will leave you with a field called `email_address`. Then your Shipping stage can directly handle redacting or masking this field as appropriate. It's better to not emit this data, but if you're cleaning up after bad habits, the techniques here set you up to do better.

Exercise 11.1

Using https://regex101.com, build a regular expression that will match the following two lines. Copy both lines into the test-string field, and build your regular expression in the regular-expression field. The match-information field will tell you what your matches are, and the site will colorize your matched strings. Use named capture groups to grab the action, the application ID, response code, and the log level.

```
[INFO] Sent API callback to APPID 1141, response 200
[WARN] Sent API callback to APPID 96821, response 503
```

On the left is a regex debugger that will show you the steps that your expression takes to reach a match.

11.2 Building expressions to fail fast

A *fast regular expression* is one that tells the regex engine to stop trying to match a bad string as fast as possible. More speed is found by reducing the options the regex engine has to work through. Using string anchors like the beginning-of-string (^) and end-of-string ($) markers, as discussed in section 11.1, is a powerful way to get a fast failure. This section is about more ways to make your regex engine stop match attempts faster.

Before I go into specific techniques, I need to talk a little about how matching works with a regex engine. These engines try hard to find any match in a given string and will backtrack across the string to find matches if that's what it takes. Let's look at a simple regular expression and see how it handles the matching process for a string. Here are the regular expression and the string it will match in figure 11.6:

```
.*Account: (?<acct_id>\d+?).*Zone: (?<zone_id>\h+?)
2028-02-19T14:08.232 Account: 1121 Region: EMEA Zone: 42
```

Figure 11.6 shows the 49 attempts the regex engine made to make a match with our example string. We also see that most of the attempts were caused by the `.*` at the beginning of the string, because this part of the expression matched the whole string, and the regex engine had to back through the string one character at a time before finding a match for the next part of the expression. This example illustrates *greediness*; it grabs everything and slowly gives characters back until the next match happens.

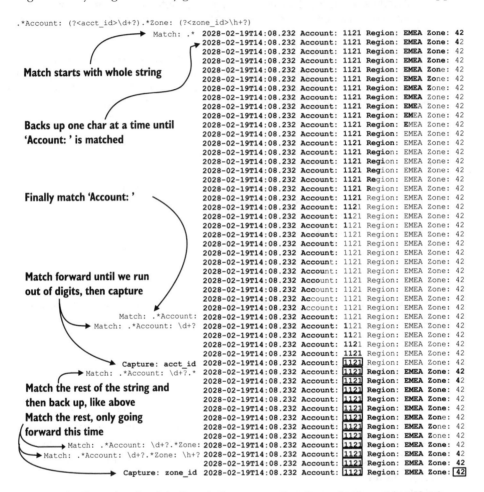

Figure 11.6 The series of match attempts for our example regex and a given string. Match attempts are boldfaced; captured fields have squares around them. We see that `.*` matches the whole string immediately, and the regex engine backs the match up one character at a time until it finds `'Account: '`. The process is repeated with the second `.*` until it matches `'Zone: '`.

Also note what happened with the `\d+?` expression as part of the `acct_id` capture. This matches base-10 digits, and the `?` modifier makes it step *forward* one character at a time until it runs out of digits. The plus operator is also greedy, but adding the question-mark operator makes it *lazy*; it takes one additional character at a time until the next match happens.

> **WARNING** Using greedy operators like .* (dot-star) and .+ (dot-plus) is quite dangerous for performance. If you are building regular expressions for telemetry enrichment, use only .* (or any other format, such as \d* or \w*) if you mean "Match everything past this point." Even better, use .*$ or .+?, pairing .* or .+ with the end of string marker ($) to further hint to the regex engine that you intend to match everything else. Using .* or .+ anywhere in the middle of an expression will slow performance in most cases. Consider using .+? (dot-plus with question-mark) instead; this operator is lazy, so it will step forward in the string until it finds the next match.

Believe it or not, figure 11.6 is a simplified view of what happens! When you give a character range for matching, such as \d for 0-9 and \h for 0-9 & a-f, the regex engine will attempt to match the next character with each character in the range until it finds a match. Figure 11.7 visualizes this for matching \h+? with Zone: 42.

Test: `Zone: 4`	==	`Zone: 1`	Fail
Test: `Zone: 4`	==	`Zone: 2`	Fail
Test: `Zone: 4`	==	`Zone: 3`	Fail
Test: `Zone: 4`	==	`Zone: 4`	**Pass**
Test: `Zone: 42`	==	`Zone: 41`	Fail
Test: `Zone: 42`	==	`Zone: 42`	**Pass**

We see in figure 11.7 that the example regex engine took six tries to match 42. If we combine using greedy and lazy operators with taking care to limit the character set, we can give the regex engine many clues that it should stop trying to find a match for a string that won't ever match. We can do more to help so long as we know what kind of telemetry data

Figure 11.7 Regular-expression matching for ranges, here using \h to match base-16 numbers. We see the regex engine iterating through the numbers until it matches the string before moving on to the next character. Overly large character ranges will harm regex-engine performance, so use narrow ranges to speed your performance.

we will be operating with. The string our examples were matching, Account: 1121 Region: EMEA Zone: 42, had a Region: entry in the middle of our two capture statements for acct_id and zone_id. The regex we tested in figure 11.6 had a greedy .* to skip this telemetry we don't care about, which resulted in match failures before finding Zone:. If we know what values Region: will have, we can tune the regex engine to match faster (changes in boldface):

.+?Account: (?<acct_id>\d+?) **Region: .{2,4}** Zone: (?<zone_id>\h+?)

The .{2,4} construct tells the regex engine to accept any group of two to four characters, and we don't capture the characters. Placed this way, the engine will match any characters between the space characters. With this regex, figure 11.6 turns into figure 11.8.

Figure 11.6 required 49 match attempts before matching the entire string, whereas our revised regex in figure 11.8 needs only 35. Most of the savings came from starting the expression with .+? (dot-plus question-mark) instead of .* (dot-star), with the rest coming from our optimization with Region:. This regex is well optimized for the

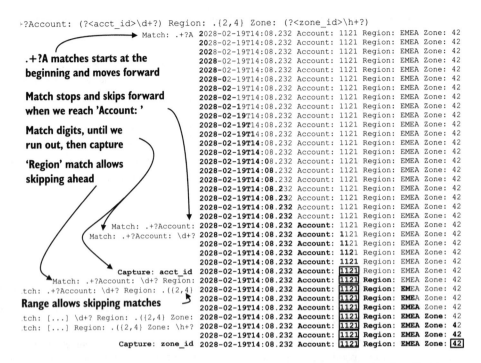

Figure 11.8   Regex matching attempts for our better-optimized regular expression. Matches are boldfaced; field captures have boxes. Unlike in figure 11.6, we see no evidence that the regex engine backtracked in the string during processing; progress is always forward. By handling the `Region:` data in the regex, we reduce the number of attempts the regex engine has to make to confirm a match.

successful case, but if we wanted to optimize it to fail fast we would embrace the timestamp at the front of the string and apply anchoring:

```
^2.+?Account: (?<acct_id>\d+?) Region: .{2,4} Zone: (?<zone_id>\h+?)$
```

When we add `^2` to the beginning of the string, our regex engine can tell within two tries whether it is worthwhile to match this string. That's failing fast, all right! If a Java stack dump is in the telemetry stream, starting with a tab character or other whitespace, adding `^2` to the beginning of our regex will make those lines fail extremely fast.

This method is highly useful when using the dictionary pattern. Match each telemetry line with a list of regexes, described in section 11.1. Because the *beginning-of-string marker followed by 2* is extremely simple and fast to test, you can use it as a filter for the more complex dictionary regexes. Listing 11.2 presents a mockup of how this works in Logstash, with the regex plugin Grok.

Listing 11.2   Example Grok statement gated by a regex-using filter

```
filter {
  if [message] =~ "^2" {          ◁───┐   This regex test must succeed
    grok {                              │   for the grok {} block to run.
      match => {
        "message" => [
          "regex1"
          "regex2"             │   The dictionary
          "regex3"             │   pattern
        ]
      }                                     ┌   Tagging failures eases improving
      tag_on_failure => "_regex_fail"  ◁──┘   the regexes and filter.
    }
  }
}
```

The grok {} block, which is the Logstash regex plugin, will run only if the string being tested begins with the digit 2. Grok operates in order, so each regex will be tested until one matches; the rest of the patterns will be not tested. Rather than have three regexes each test and fail, by applying the filter before the Grok block, we ensure that the string is tested only once, and fails, and execution moves on to other things. Figure 11.9 shows this conditional in action.

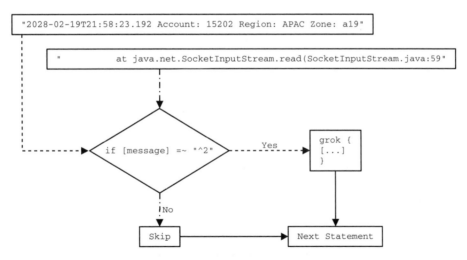

Figure 11.9   Two strings being tested by our Logstash config: one regular log statement (dashed line) and one component of a Java stack dump (dotted-dashed line). Because our regular log statement begins the string with a 2, it is sent to Grok for parsing. Our Java stack-dump component does not begin with a 2, so Logstash skips Grok for this statement. The conditional prevented running rather more complex regular expressions on our stack dump and speeded the logging pipeline.

TIP   Using a simple, fast regular expression to test whether to try a far more complex regex is an effective method for reducing the performance hit of using regular expressions.

11.3   *Digging into the Cisco ASA firewall telemetry*

Now that we have anchoring (section 11.1) and failing fast (section 11.2) down, this section examines using regular expressions with some telemetry we worked with during part 1: the telemetry coming from Cisco ASA firewalls. (For a look at what this enrichment work enables, see section 5.2.) We will look at three ways to parse this telemetry, including the method from section 6.2.2. This section will show the difference in performance between easy regular expressions and complex optimized ones, and discuss why overoptimization doesn't always pay off in improvements.

> **WARNING**   This section will show you why you want to benchmark your regular expressions. Optimizing your expressions so that the regular-expression engine can find (or fail to find) a match in the fewest steps is useful, but sometimes, overhead in your programming language is more expensive.

Our Cisco ASA firewall telemetry enters the pipeline through Syslog, which is what Cisco ASA speaks. Here is an example string (the colon after %ASA is the delimiter between the Syslog telemetry and the Cisco telemetry):

```
Feb 19 02:26:26 asa1.net.prod.internal %ASA1: Teardown of UDP connection
➡ 162121 for outside:1.1.0.0/53 to dmz1:192.0.2.19/59232 duration 0:00:00
➡ bytes 136
```

Listing 6.3 in section 6.2.2 provided an example of grok {} parsing of this string. (Section 6.2.2 also gave a much faster nonregex method of parsing the string.). But that regular expression was inefficient to fit the page and teach, so we're going to look at how to change the regular expression matching this example string, using what we learned earlier in this chapter. Table 11.1 shows three regular expressions that extract the same number of fields but are written in increasingly optimized ways.

- *3-pass*—Matches the method used in section 6.2.2, where the regex engine does a first matching pass and then performs a second and third pass on fields extracted in the first pass. This expression is the simplest to understand and the worst-performing.
- *1-pass*—This expression gathers all the fields that 3-pass did, using the same regex capture groups, in a single expression and a single pass.
- *1-pass slimmed*—The 1-pass version, with lengths specified for each regex component to further guide the regex engine on what kind of strings to expect. This expression is the most complex statement and should be the best-performing (but isn't).

Table 11.1 Three regex variations matching Cisco ASA telemetry

String to match	3-pass (first pass)	3-pass (second and third passes)	1-pass	1-pass slimmed
`Teardown of `	`Teardown of `		`Teardown of `	`Teardown of `
UDP	`(?<protocol>\w+?)`		`(?<protocol>\w+?)`	`(<protocol>[A-Z]{3})`
` connection `	` connection `		` connection `	` connection `
162121	`(?<conn_id>\d+?)`		`(?<conn_id>\d+?)`	`(?<conn_id)\d+?)`
` for ``	` for `		` for `	` for `
outside:1.1.0.0/53	`(?<source>\S+?)`			
outside		`(?<source_int>\w+?)`	`(?<source_int>\w+?)`	`(?<source_int>\w{1,8}`
1.1.0.0		`(<source_ip>\S+?)`	`(<source_ip>\S+?)`	`(?<source_ip>\S{7,15})`
53		`(?<source_port>\d+)`	`(?<source_port>\d+)`	`(?<source_port>\d{1,5})`
` to `	` to `		` to `	` to `
dmz1:192.0.2.19/59232	`(?<target>\S+?)`			
dmz1		`(?<target_int>\w+?)`	`(?<target_int>\w+?)`	`(?<target_int>\w{4,8})`
192.0.2.19		`(?<target_ip>\S+?)`	`(?<target_ip>\S+?)`	`(?<target_ip>\S{7,15})`
59232		`(?<target_port>\d+?)`	`(?<target_port>\d+)`	`(<target_port>\d{1,5})`
` duration `	` duration `		` duration `	` duration `
0:00:00	`(?<duration>\S+?)`		`(?<duration>\S+?)`	`(?<duration>\d{1,2}:\d{2}:\d{2})`
` bytes `	` bytes `		` bytes `	` bytes `
136	`(?<bytes>\d+)`		`(?<bytes>\d+)`	`(?<bytes>\d+)`

To show how these three regexes perform, we're going to compare them with four strings:

- *hardfail*—Obvious failing match
- *halfmatch*—Teardown of TCP connection 113121 SYNTAX ERROR
- *substringmatch*—Feb 19 02:26:26 asa1.net.prod.internal %ASA1: Teardown of UDP connection 162121 for outside:1.1.0.0/53 to dmz1:192.0.2.19/59232 duration 0:00:00 bytes 136
- *fullmatch*—Teardown of UDP connection 162121 for outside: 1.1.0.0/53 to dmz1:192.0.2.19/59232 duration 0:00:00 bytes 136

We will also be comparing anchored versions of each regex (see section 11.1 for a description) to demonstrate how anchoring works with the optimizations here. As mentioned in section 11.1, anchoring is most useful for getting the regular-expression engine to stop attempting to match a string that won't match but makes matching against a true match slightly slower.

Figures 11.10–11.13 are generated from data from the cisco-regex.rb script in the CH11 folder of the Git repository for this book (http://mng.bz/oGJD). This script is similar in form to what you saw in listing 11.1 but made for the case we are testing in this chapter. It tests all three regex patterns against the four strings described earlier.

Figure 11.10 shows how the three regexes, including two more to test anchoring, perform against the hardfail string. The 3-pass variant used in section 6.2.2 performs worst of the bunch by quite a bit. The extra code (nonregex) conditionals needed to test whether to try to perform the second and third passes take enough extra time to make matching more than twice as slow. The difference between the anchored versions and unanchored versions is visible, if slight. When I run this test with an older version of Ruby, the differences go away.

But the 1-pass-slim variant—the one that uses range expressions like \w{2,6} instead of the lazy operator like \w+?— performed worse than the 1-pass variant. The effect is slight, about 4.8%, but there. Explaining why requires looking into what happens during matching.

All the 1-pass regex variants start with either the letter T or the anchored expression ^T. The anchored versions will look for the beginning of string, followed by a T, which "Obvious failing match" doesn't have; the match fails after two steps. The unanchored version will start at the beginning of "Obvious failing match", step forward one letter at a time, and not find a T anywhere. Because we're not seeing a 23× difference in performance, this benchmark clearly is including some form of overhead from the language (Ruby). The longer and more complex 1-pass-slimmed regular expression adds more overhead than it saves, at least in the hardfail case. Definitely test your regex engine to see how it performs! Let's see whether this problem continues.

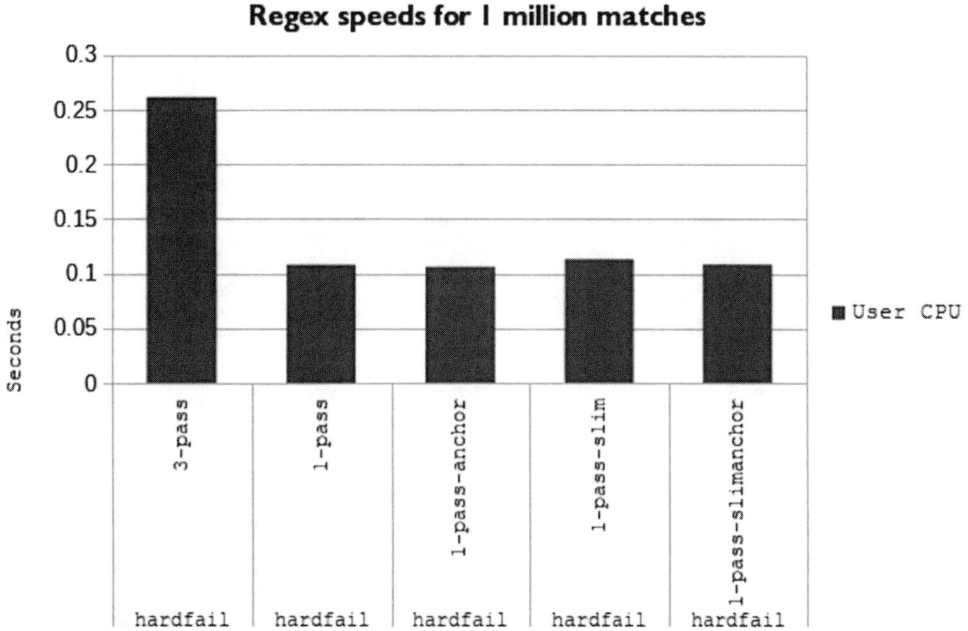

Regex speeds for 1 million matches

Figure 11.10   Regex timings for the `hardfail` string. This example tests how efficient each regex is at failing fast. We see that the 3-pass regex is terrible at that task. Different regular-expression engines behave differently, so definitely test yours.

Figure 11.11 shows how each of our three regexes performs against the `halfmatch` string, which includes the first part of the full string. This test is a different match-failure case, in which the string being tested conforms to the regex expectations (to a point). We don't expect anchoring to help with this test, because the beginning of the string matches for a few components in the regex, and we see that the anchored expressions perform a bit slower than the unanchored versions (about 2.1%, which is slightly above the margin of error).

Did we see the same performance regression for the slimmed versions? You can't see it in figure 11.11, but the 1-pass-slimmed version was 1.4% slower than the simpler 1-pass, which is right on the margin of error. The "More complex regexes slow match speed" hypothesis, however, finds new data in the anchored expressions. Here, anchoring merely adds a single step to the beginning, so the impact should be minimal, but that's not what we see. The 2.1% performance regression versus the unanchored versions can be explained by the overhead of the longer regex itself.

The next string is our `substringmatch`. Figure 11.12 shows the performance of each regex versus the `substringmatch` string, where the tested string contains our telemetry but the whole string does not match. Anchoring will not help here, because we're not expecting a whole-string match for the regex, so the anchoring variants should perform similarly to the failure patterns in previous figures. As we see, that's the case here.

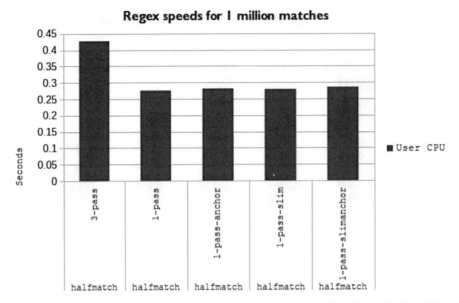

Figure 11.11   Regex speeds for the `halfmatch` that includes a portion of the full string. This example tests how efficient each regex is about failing fast in a string that has some, but not all, matches. Once again, the 3-pass regex is the slowest by far. The anchored expressions performed slightly worse than the unanchored versions.

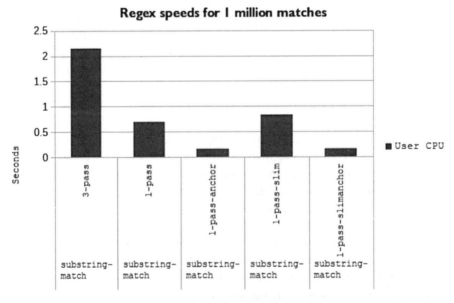

Figure 11.12   Regex speeds for the `substringmatch`, where the string contains what the unanchored regexes expect but not the anchored versions. This example tests performance of partial string matches. Anchored versions should fail because anchoring implies a full-string match. We see that the most-optimized expression, 1-pass-slim, doesn't perform better than the 1-pass version!

We also see an unexpected spread in performance for the variants that did match. 3-pass remains the slowest of the bunch but is now extremely slow, coming in at three times as slow as the 1-pass variant. The optimization we spent on character expectations in the 1-pass-slimmed variant hurt overall performance; that version performed 19% slower than 1-pass. Clearly, the time we spent optimizing the 1-pass-slim variant wasn't worthwhile for the substring match case; the variant slows everything.

Finally, let's look at whole-string match performance, which is the happy path of all five versions. Figure 11.13 shows how each regex performs against a string that will fully match it. We see the same general pattern we saw in figure 11.11 and the sub-stringmatch, but this time the anchored expressions are performing equivalently to their unanchored versions. The easy-to-understand 3-pass version performs abysmally compared with the others. Once again, 1-pass-slimmed performs worse than 1-pass (about 22% worse).

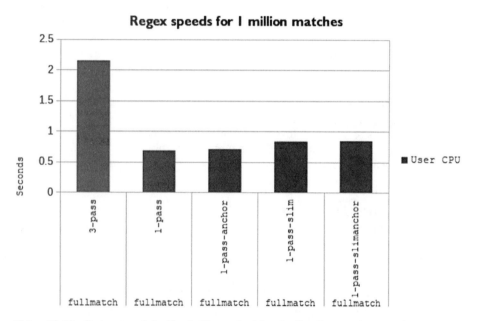

Figure 11.13 Regex speeds for the `fullmatch` string, testing the complete-match case. All regexes succeed in this test.

The performance I show here is Ruby, which is what both Fluentd and Logstash are written in. For Ruby, shorter regular expressions perform better than longer but more tightly scoped ones. As you build your own telemetry systems, absolutely benchmark how your programming language performs under these conditions! Assumptions can be wrong, and overoptimizing can make things worse.

Given what we've seen here, we've learned a few things:

- The more optimized the regular expression, the harder it is to understand what it is doing.
- When you're using chained regexes, the 3-pass regex pattern is terrible for performance. It's better to merge the patterns into a single one (the 1-pass pattern) if you value speed over maintainability.
- Supplying length expectations in your regex (such as [a-z]{3,8} for three to eight lowercase characters) means that the regular-expression engine takes fewer steps to find a match versus the lazy operators (+?; start at 1 and move forward).
- Anchoring is extremely effective when a *portion* of the string being tested would otherwise match the regex; it turns a soft failure into a full failure faster. If you intend to match only full strings, anchoring will speed things markedly.
- The size of the regular expression factors into overall performance, so benchmark your system to determine how big a problem this is. For Ruby at least, shortness matters more than fewer regex steps.

Exercise 11.2

The regular-expression visualizer at https://regex101.com is quite useful for optimizing expressions. Use it to see for yourself how the four 1-pass variants perform against the four test strings. *Tip:* Change the delimiter from forward slash (/) to tilde (~) to avoid having to escape the forward slashes in your regexes.

Test strings

- *hardfail*—Obvious failing match
- *halfmatch*—Teardown of TCP connection 113121 SYNTAX ERROR
- *substringmatch*—Feb 19 02:26:26 asa1.net.prod.internal %ASA1: Teardown of UDP connection 162121 for outside:1.1.0.0/53 to dmz1:192.0.2.19/59232 duration 0:00:00 bytes 136
- *fullmatch*—Teardown of UDP connection 162121 for outside: 1.1.0.0/53 to dmz1:192.0.2.19/59232 duration 0:00:00 bytes 136

Regular expressions

- *1-pass*—Teardown of (?<protocol>\w+?) connection (?<conn_id>\d+?) for (?<source_int>\w+?):(?<source_ip>\S+?)/(?<source_port>\d+?) to (?<target_int>\w+?):(?<target_ip>\S+?)/(?<target_port>\d+?) duration (?<duration>\S+?) bytes (?<bytes>\d+)
- *1-pass-anchored*—^Teardown of (?<protocol>\w+?) connection (?<conn_id>\d+?) for (?<source_int>\w+?):(?<source_ip>\S+?)/ (?<source_port>\d+?) to (?<target_int>\w+?):(?<target_ip>\S+?)/ (?<target_port>\d+?) duration (?<duration>\S+?) bytes (?<bytes>\d+)$

- *1-pass-slimmed*—Teardown of `(?<protocol>[A-Z]{3})` connection
  `(?<conn_id>\d+?)` for `(?<source_int>\w{1,8})`:`(?<source_ip>\`
  `S{7,15})`/`(?<source_port>\d{1,5})` to `(?<target_int>\w{4,8})`:
  `(?<target_ip>\S{7,15})`/`(?<target_port>\d{1,5})` duration
  `(?<duration>\d{1,2}:\d{2}:\d{2})` bytes `(?<bytes>\d+)`
- *1-pass-slimmed-anchored*—`^`Teardown of `(?<protocol>[A-Z]{3})`
  connection `(?<conn_id>\d+)` for `(?<source_int>\w{1,8})`:
  `(?<source_ip>\S{7,15})`/`(?<source_port>\d{1,5})` to
  `(?<target_int>\w{4,8})`:`(?<target_ip>\S{7,15})`/
  `(?<target_port>\d{1,5})` duration `(?<duration>\d{1,2}:`
  `\d{2}:\d{2})` bytes `(?<bytes>\d+)$`

On the left side of Regex101 is a link to a Regex debugger that will let you walk through all the match steps each expression follows while attempting a match. Regex101 uses Perl-flavored regex by default, which is close enough to Ruby-flavored that these expressions should not need translation.

11.4 Refining emissions to speed regular-expression performance

The best way to speed regular-expression performance is to get rid of the regular expressions and use a different method of enriching your telemetry. Unfortunately, not everyone works where replacing a major part of the telemetry system is viable. This section talks about making the best use of what you have, giving you time to work on the far harder problem of changing how you handle centralized logging in your production code. The techniques here are for code you manage, so you control the emission format.

Sections 11.1–11.3 gave us several techniques to speed regular-expression performance:

- If you are matching entire strings, using the beginning-of-string (^) and end-of-string ($) markers can seriously accelerate performance when using a regex dictionary.
- Using the greedy operators (* and +) at the end of a string prevents a major performance regression. Instead, use the lazy operator (+? for one or more matches; *? for zero or more matches) for midstring matches.
- Specifying lengths in your regular expressions (such as `\d{3,7}` for three to seven base-10 digits) will shorten the number of match attempts the regex engine makes. This advantage is balanced by the cost of the longer regex string itself; overoptimization can reduce speed, benchmarking is the only way to judge you've found the correct balance.
- Pretesting strings with an easy regex (such as `^20[2-3][0-9]` for matching only lines beginning with a timestamp with year) before applying your complex, optimized regex dictionary reduces expensive match failures.

Section 11.1 also gave us a set of five example log emissions that I used to talk about how anchoring speeded things:

```
Added account 1141 in zone 42 with email twitterbot@example.com
Account 1141 deleted from zone 37
Suspended zone 42 account 1141 for excessive email volume
Created new zone: 99
Zone 98 deleted
```

If the only telemetry components you control are the emissions themselves and the regular expressions that match them, what can you do to improve your event throughput? These five samples came into being when five software engineers found the need to write a log statement and wrote their statements on the spot, using the grammar that popped into their heads at the moment. There are no standards here beyond natural language. Looking at the five log lines, we see that the top three involve actions on accounts:

```
Added account 1141 in zone 42 with email twitterbot@example.com
Account 1141 deleted from zone 37
Suspended zone 42 account 1141 for excessive email volume
```

The bottom two involve actions on zones:

```
Created new zone: 99
Zone 98 deleted
```

What if we prepended a string to indicate account or zone and then pretested each log line against those strings?

```
[account] Added account 1141 in zone 42 with email twitterbot@example.com
[account] Account 1141 deleted from zone 37
[account] Suspended zone 42 account 1141 for excessive email volume
[zone] Created new zone: 99
[zone] Zone 98 deleted
```

We could place the account regexes under a conditional that tests for `^\[account\]` and the zone regexes under a conditional that tests for `^\[zone\]`, which would mean the log lines about zone actions would never be compared with the account regexes. When we test for exact strings, not ranges, and use the beginning-of-string marker (`^`), we make these pretests extremely fast.

Listing 11.3 is an excerpt from another benchmarking script that I'll use to show the difference in performance between what we saw back in section 11.1 and what happens after we pretest the string against two regex dictionaries. Listing 11.3 provides the key code for the benchmark test case of the split version.

Listing 11.3   Excerpt of [appendix script] showing account/zone split

```
[...]
split_examples = [
  '[account] Added account 1141 in zone 42 with email
  ➥ twitterbot@example.com',
  '[account] Account 1141 deleted from zone 37',
  '[account] Suspended zone 42 account 1141 for excessive email volume',
  '[zone] Created new zone: 99',
  '[zone] Zone 98 deleted',
]


raccount = [
  Regexp.new('^\[account\] (?<acct_action>\w+) account
  ➥ account (?<acct_id>\d+?) in zone (?<zone_id>\h+?) with email
  ➥ (?<email_address>.*)$'),
  Regexp.new('^\[account\] Account (?<acct_id>\d+?)
  ➥ (?<acct_action>\w+?) from zone (?<zone_id>\h+?)$')
  Regexp.new('^\[account\] (?<acct_action>\w+?) zone
  ➥ (?<zone_id>\h+?) account (?<acct_id>\d+?) for
  ➥ (?<suspension_reason>.*)$'),
]


rzone = [
  Regexp.new('^\[zone\] (?<zone_action>\w+?) new zone:
  ➥ (?<zone_id>\h+)$'),
  Regexp.new('^\[zone\] Zone (?<zone_id>\h+?)
  ➥ (?<zone_action>\w+)$')
]

isaccount = Regexp.new('^\[account\]')
iszone    = Regexp.new('^\[zone\]')

[...]

  rep.report("Account/Zone split regexes") {
    split_examples.each do |sl|
      for m in 1..iter
        if sl.match?(isaccount)
          raccount.each do |relist|
            sl.match?(relist)
          end
        elsif sl.match?(iszone)
          rzone.each do |relist|
            sl.match?(relist)
          end
        end
      end
    end
  }
```

Dictionary of Account regexes

Dictionary of Zone regexes

Pretest conditional to determine which regex set gets tested.

Now let's see how performance differs! Figure 11.14 provides the comparison from testing all five regexes versus testing them in groups based on the prepended string.

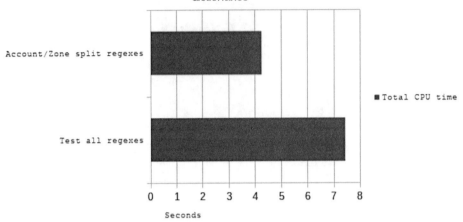

Performance differences between a single dictionary, and pre-tested dictionaries

Figure 11.14 Two techniques for applying regular expressions to a list of five example log items. The top bar is performing a beginning-of-string test for either [account] or [zone] before attempting to capture telemetry from the log data. The lower bar is testing all regular expressions against each log line. We see a radical improvement in the time it takes to process our example log lines by pretesting and splitting the regular expressions.

Simply splitting our dictionaries by prepending a string took 57% of the time of running every log line with every anchored regex. A performance improvement like this one is enough to justify changes to both the log-emitting and log-enrichment systems. But we can eke even more performance out of this set of log lines. Prepending the string got us a lot, but our language is still natural language and made by many software engineers. Our three account log lines

```
[account] Added account 1141 in zone 42 with email twitterbot@example.com
[account] Account 1141 deleted from zone 37
[account] Suspended zone 42 account 1141 for excessive email volume
```

flow cleanly from an English-language point of view, but they convey similar information. We have account and zone IDs in each of them, and for two of them, we have some extra information. If we re-word our log lines with an eye to improving regex performance, we get

```
[account] Added account 1141 in zone 42 with email domain example.com
[account] Deleted account 1141 in zone 37
[account] Suspended account 1141 in zone 42 for excessive email volume
```

This step is a great place to look at what you are logging and make changes. Here, we are no longer logging the email address used to create an account because email addresses are now private information. This is still natural language, but it is also far easier to parse with regular expressions.

```
^\[account\] (?<acct_action>\w+?) account (?<acct_id>\d+?) in zone
➡ (?<zone_id>\h+?)\S?(?<acct_extra>.*)$
```

This code is somewhat complex, but note that \S? means "Match zero or more whitespace characters," and the final (?<acct_extra>.*$) means "Match everything else in the string." This construction allows the Deleted log line, which has no extra text, to be matched while also matching the Added and Suspended cases. Depending on your regex engine's specifics, acct_extra will be null, undefined, or an empty string if it isn't matched, as in the Deleted case. Table 11.2 provides a side-by-side look at this unified regex and shows how it matches all three log lines.

Table 11.2   Unified account regex capturing all three log lines

Log line 1	Log line 2	Log line 3	Regex
`'[account] '`	`'[account] '`	`'[account] '`	`'^\[account\] '`
`'Added'`	`'Deleted'`	`'Suspended'`	`(?<acct_action>\w+?)`
`' account '`	`' account '`	`' account '`	`' account '`
`'1141'`	`'1141'`	`'1141'`	`(?<acct_id>\d+?)`
`' in zone '`	`' in zone '`	`' in zone '`	`' in zone '`
`'42'`	`'37'`	`'42'`	`(?<zone_id>\h+?)`
`' '`	`' '`	`' '`	`\S?`
`'with email domain example.com'`	`''`	`'for excessive email volume'`	`(?<acct_extra>.*)$`

Now let's do the same for the pair of zone log lines:

```
[zone] Created new zone: 99
[zone] Zone 98 deleted
```

These lines can easily be turned into

```
[zone] Created zone 99
[zone] Deleted zone 98
```

which makes for a nicely simple regex:

```
^\[zone\] (?<zone_action>\w+?) zone (?<zone_id>\h+)$
```

If we update our benchmarking script to add a third case, using these singular unified regexes in place of the prepended one, we can compare how all three cases work. Listing 11.4 shows the additions to the code in listing 11.3 that adds our new test case.

Listing 11.4   Excerpt of benchmarking script adding the unified regex case

```
[...]
unified_examples = [
  '[account] Added account 1141 in zone 42 with eamil
➥ domain example.com',
  '[account] Deleted account 1141 in zone 37',
  '[account] Suspended account 1141 in zone 42 for
➥ excessive email volume',
  '[zone] Created zone 99',
  '[zone] Deleted zone 98'
]
```
Example log lines to test

```
[...]
```

```
eaccount = Regexp.new('^\[account\]
(?<acct_action>\w+) account (?<) in zone
➥ (?<zone_id>\h+?)\S?(?<acct_extra>.*)$')
```
Regex for account-style log lines

```
ezone    = Regexp.new('^\[zone\] (?<zone_action>\w+?)
➥ zone (?<zone_id>\h+?)$')
```
Regex for zone-style log lines

```
isaccount = Regexp.new('^\[account\]')
iszone    = Regexp.new('^\[zone\]')
```

```
[...]
```

```
  rep.report("Account/Zone unified regexes") {
    unified_examples.each do |sl|
      for m in 1..iter
        if sl.match?(isaccount)
          sl.match?(eaccount)
        elsif sl.match?(iszone)
          sl.match?(ezone)
        end
      end
    end
  }
```

First, each log line will be pretested to see whether it is an account- or zone-style log line; then it is compared with the single unified regular expression for that type. This example should perform better because it isn't trying multiple regexes for each log line. Let's see how different it is. Figure 11.15 provides a breakdown of performance for the three test cases.

Performance has improved markedly once more! Using the unified regular expressions performed in 56% of the time versus simply prepending a string and splitting the tests. Also, the unified regex performed in 32% of the time versus the dictionary pattern of testing each log line against all five regexes. If your production code and telemetry systems are using regular expressions to this degree, it is well worth your time to do the optimizations listed here.

Getting to the most-improved state is a project that spans many phases. The size and age of your codebase are (sadly) going to determine how much work you have to

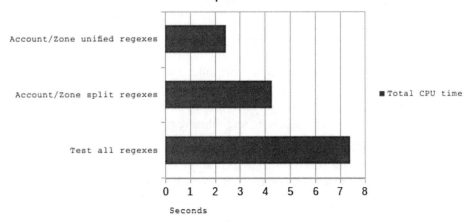

Figure 11.15 **Three techniques for testing an example set of five log lines against their matching regular expressions. The top bar is the most efficient, using a pretest check for [account] or [zone] at the beginning of the string before attempting to capture using a singular regular expression tuned to capture all account or zone telemetry. The bottom bar is the worst case, where each log line is tested against each regular expression.**

do. The longer a code base has been in existence and the more engineers contributed to it, the more subtle differences in natural-language logging you will have to investigate. The major project phases are

1 Agree to a set of prepended strings.
2 Agree to a regexable grammar with your team.
3 Update your telemetry system to handle prepended and not-prepended log data.
4 Add your unified regexes for each prepend string to your telemetry system.
5 Convert existing log emissions to the new grammar.
6 When all log emissions are converted, remove support for the old grammar from your telemetry system.

Let us dig into each phase a bit more.

PHASE 1: AGREE TO A SET OF PREPENDED STRINGS

The prepended strings are the [account] and [zone] in the above example, but you will need to look at your current logging statements (the ones that are examined by regex) to determine what common sets you have. If your software product is large, this analysis will be a cross-team activity. If your organization uses a design review process, absolutely use that process for this work.

PHASE 2: AGREE TO A REGEXABLE GRAMMAR WITH YOUR TEAM

Now that you have your logging groups (the prepend strings from the first phase), examine each group to see how you can re-word each statement to allow a single regex statement. Look at re-wording both the log statement text and your regex sophistication. It is possible that you will find some log statements that need to be split (or combined) to work under the proposed grammar, which is fine and will be fixed in a later phase.

PHASE 3: UPDATE YOUR TELEMETRY SYSTEM TO HANDLE PREPENDED AND NOT-PREPENDED LOG DATA
Your telemetry system will need to handle both cases for a while, so this phase sets the stage for handling the migration. You will be moving entirely to prepend-only in a later phase. While you are at it, now is a great time to assess where you're sending private data such as email addresses into your logging stream and to stop doing that. (See chapter 16 for more about private and other regulated data.)

PHASE 4: ADD YOUR UNIFIED REGEXES FOR EACH PREPEND STRING TO YOUR TELEMETRY SYSTEM
Depending on your project, this phase can be combined with phase 3. Log data that has a prepended string will get matched against one of the unified regexes; the unprepended strings will get matched against the current (inefficient) handling.

PHASE 5: CONVERT EXISTING LOG EMISSIONS TO THE NEW GRAMMAR
Start converting your existing log statements to the new grammar. You can make this conversion one prepend string at a time, one class at a time—whatever works for you. You will likely discover during this process that your grammar isn't sophisticated enough. That's fine; update your telemetry system regexes as needed, and keep moving.

PHASE 6: WHEN ALL LOG EMISSIONS ARE CONVERTED, REMOVE SUPPORT FOR THE OLD GRAMMAR FROM YOUR TELEMETRY SYSTEM
This phase is the last step of the migration process. When all your logging data is converted to the new grammar, remove support for the old grammar from your telemetry system. This phase makes the telemetry system slightly more efficient because it will have one fewer compare to perform when processing telemetry data.

When this project is done and your telemetry is flowing faster, I hope that this efficiency project will earn you enough reputation in your organization to allow you to push for adopting new telemetry patterns. Organizations that use regex to enrich centralized logging telemetry data, as we've done in this section, are working around a limitation in their telemetry systems. Rather than pass a single string that you later have to parse, a better approach is to provide a string and a hash of attributes (correlation identifiers, to use the distributed tracing term), taking the burden of parsing away from your telemetry systems. The string

```
"Added account 1411 to zone 42"
```

turns into

```
"Added account -- acct_id=1141 zone_id=42"
```

In this case, a logging string is separated from a string of key-value pairs by a double dash. (Chapter 12 covers this sort of encoding of standards, if you want to read more.)

This string is quite easy to split into logging data and enrichment data, much easier than regular expressions, and with more flexibility. Good luck!

> **Exercise 11.3**
> Rewrite the following three log lines into a regexable grammar and provide a regular expression that will match all three:
>
> ```
> Converted 0.192 MB pdf file in 0.89 seconds
> Took 1.2 seconds to digitally sign a 0.192 MB pdf file
> Successfully uploaded type:pdf size:0.192 time:0.019
> ```

11.5 *Additional regular-expression resources*

This section points you to tools you can use to explore regular expressions in general. Many online tools are available for testing regular expressions. Although all the examples in this chapter use Ruby, there is no guarantee that you will be working with Ruby when you start fixing the regexes in your telemetry systems.

- https://regex101.com provides a browser-based experience for PHP/Perl, JavaScript, Golang, and Python-flavored regular expressions. This website also provides a visual guide to matching expressions and explains the components of a regex you paste in.
- https://rubular.com provides a browser-based experience for Ruby-flavored regular expressions. If you don't have Ruby installed locally and want to see how the regex in my listings works, this website will be a great help.
- http://www.regexplanet.com provides a wide variety of languages not shown on Regex101, such as .NET, Java, and Haskel.

If you are looking to get deep into regular expressions, these books will help:

- *An Introduction to Regular Expressions*, by Thomas Nield (O'Reilly Media, 2019)
- *Mastering Regular Expressions*, 3rd ed., by Jeffrey Friedl (O'Reilly Media, 2016)
- *JavaScript Regular Expressions*, by Loiane Groner and Gabriel Manricks (Packt Publishing, 2015)
- *Java 9 Regular Expressions*, by Anubhava Srivastava (Packt Publishing, 2017)

Summary

- The best way to optimize your regular expressions is to stop using regular expressions, because regexes are the slowest method of enriching your telemetry.
- Sometimes, you don't have a choice about using regexes, such as when you're re-enriching telemetry coming from hardware and SaaS platforms.
- In telemetry systems, regexes are used for both control flow (determining which processing and routing events will receive) and enrichment flow (extracting useful fields from telemetry data).

- Regular expressions are difficult to maintain because tightly scoped expressions that perform well are often vastly more complex than simple expressions, reducing the number of people who can maintain them.

- The goal of optimizing regular expressions is to get the regex engine to stop attempting to match a string that won't match. You want the attempt to fail fast. The performance improvements between badly optimized regex and well-optimized ones is highly significant.

- For badly optimized regexes, the regex engine will take more time with a failing match than with a successful match. You want to avoid this case wherever you can.

- Logstash and Fluentd are open source telemetry shipping platforms that have regular-expression support. Both use Ruby (and Ruby's regex library) as their foundation, though Logstash is slowly moving to straight Java.

- If you are doing whole-string matches, adding anchors—the beginning-of-string (^) and end-of-string ($) markers—to your expression will give you significant performance improvements when you are testing multiple regexes for each event.

- If you always compare a string with its exact matching expression, anchors will slow you slightly.

- The greedy regex operators (* and +) will match to the end of the string and step back one character at a time until it finds what it is looking for. Use the greedy operator (such as .*) only when you intend to match the rest of the string. In that case, .*$ makes that intention explicit.

- The lazy operator (?) modifies a greedy operator to instead add characters until it runs out of matches. An expression like .*? will match zero or more characters, adding one at a time. This operator often performs better than the greedy versions when used in the middle of a regex.

- Using a simple regular expression to test for fitness before trying a far more complex regex is an effective way to prevent the complex regexes (and the test failures they bring) from being executed against strings that won't match.

- Providing explicit length guidance in your capture expressions, such as [a-z]{3,8} for three to eight lowercase characters, reduces the match attempts that a regex engine makes but potentially makes matches slower by making the regex itself more complex.

- Re-wording your logging statements to reduce the number of regexes you need to use also provides large increases in performance.

Standardized logging and event formats

This chapter covers

- The components of a structured logger
- Building support for a telemetry emissions format in your code
- Parsing the telemetry emissions format in your Shipping stage

This chapter focuses on emitting (and parsing) events from your production code. Chapter 2 was all about the Emitting stage in general, and if you haven't read it, this chapter will make less sense. Standardizing the format of telemetry for centralized logging and metrics emissions makes your telemetry system easier to maintain overall. There is a clear up-front cost to building standards—especially if you are retrofitting standards into an existing group of software—but the results should provide room to grow.

Figure 12.1 should be familiar if you've read part 1; it describes the various pipeline stages for telemetry and the roles each stage plays. The standards we're talking about in this chapter are encoded in the Emitting stage and decoded in the Shipping

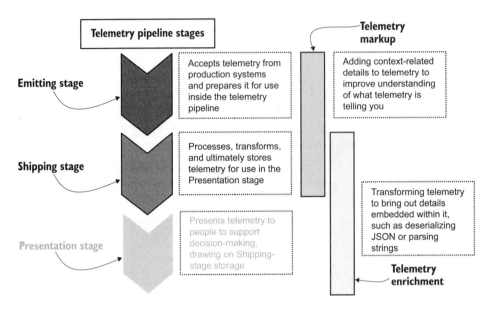

Figure 12.1   The Telemetry pipeline stages touched by logging and event standards. The Emitting and Shipping stages are deeply connected by standards, because that is where the standards are encoded (Emitting) and decoded (Shipping). Also, the concepts of telemetry markup (context-specific telemetry) and telemetry enrichment (extracting details from existing telemetry) play a key role in event-standard building and implementation. The Presentation stage merely consumes the results of all this standards work.

stage. This encode/decode process also provides a great chance to add context-specific details (telemetry markup) as part of the Emitting-stage work and to make the process of extracting additional telemetry from existing telemetry (telemetry enrichment) far more efficient in the Shipping and Presentation stages. The Presentation stage plays a minor role in all this standards work, as it passively consumes the finished product.

Standardizing your emitting formats provides many benefits:

- A well-written set of standards reduces your need to include regular expressions in your Shipping-stage systems, which will make your telemetry system more efficient overall. (See chapter 11 for the impact of regular-expression use.)
- Embracing structured logging techniques—mentioned in part in chapter 2 but explored in depth in section 12.1—gives your Emitting stage far more options regarding where it sends telemetry data and enables multiple streams of telemetry. Structured logging emitters allow sending data over novel channels like TCP sockets directly, as discussed in chapter 13.
- Taking a systematic look at logging standards gives you tools to fight the problem of index cardinality in your centralized logging and metrics data stores. Chapter 14 is your deep dive into managing the cardinality problem.

- Structured logging formatters (more on this topic in section 12.1) are where you can start making your telemetry tamper-evident, providing resistance to attackers meddling with telemetry. Chapter 15 examines more of the topic of making telemetry durable in the face of attack.
- By providing a systematic way to add context-related details (markup) as part of the Emitting stage, telemetry in your Presentation stage will be far more detailed about *when and how* an event happened, improving your ability to plug leaks of regulated information. (See chapter 16 for more on cleaning up after data spills.)

Standardized logging formats are part of the foundation of a truly robust and efficient telemetry pipeline. To cover this foundational topic, this chapter is split into three sections:

- Section 12.1 covers what structured logging is, the components of it, and how to build a structured logger.
- Section 12.2 covers using structured logging to implement two example logging standards.
- Section 12.3 covers decoding the two example logging standards in the Shipping stage, using both a dedicated Shipping-stage product (Logstash) and general-purpose programming.

12.1 Implementing structured logging in your code

This section covers creating standard emitting formats for your production code and using structured logging to support the standard. *Structured logging* is the name for a systematic approach to handling logging data coming out of an application. Logging data can be centralized logging, part of a metrics system, and even support tracing. Chapter 2 covered structured logging in brief. In fact, figure 2.3 broke down the components of a structured logger. Part of that figure is reproduced here as figure 12.2.

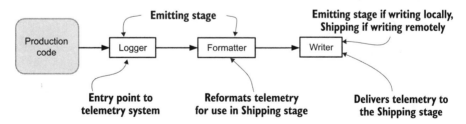

Figure 12.2   The components of a structured logger: logger, formatter, and writer. Structured logging is a built-in feature of most modern programming languages; if it isn't, support is easily added through a module.

A structured logger has three components:

- A *logger*, which is where telemetry enters the logging system. This object or function is called by the production code when it needs to emit telemetry.
- *Formatters* take the telemetry received from the logger and transform it into whatever format is needed later in the telemetry system. This is the first place where telemetry standards are built.
- *Writers* send formatted telemetry to the next stage in the telemetry pipeline, which might even be directly to the final storage used by the Presentation-stage systems.

The three names—logger, formatter, and writer—are general names for the main roles of a structured logger; each structured logging framework can call these roles different names. The important concept here is the three components. Although we looked at some logging examples in chapters 2 and 3, let's take a look at a new Python listing. Listing 12.1 gives us a Python-based structured logger using the structlog module.

NOTE   To run listing 12.1, you need to install the structlog module (pip3 install structlog), written for Python 3. The structlog module is used for many of the listings in this chapter.

Listing 12.1   A Python example of structured logging using the structlog module

```
import logging
import datetime
import sys                        Modules supporting
import socket                     context-related telemetry
import os
from structlog import (
  get_logger,
  configure,
)
from structlog.stdlib import (
  LoggerFactory,
  BoundLogger,
  add_log_level
)
from structlog.processors import (
  KeyValueRenderer,
  JSONRenderer,
  UnicodeDecoder,
  TimeStamper
)

logging.basicConfig(
  format="%(message)s",          Configures the default Python
  stream=sys.stdout,             logger to send to stdout
  level=logging.INFO,
)

__release__ = "0.7.1"
__commit__ = "f0d00b1"
```

```
configure(
  processors=[
    TimeStamper(fmt="iso"),
    UnicodeDecoder(),
    add_log_level,
    KeyValueRenderer(key_order=[
      'timestamp', 'metric_name',
      'metric_type', 'metric_value'])
  ],
  context_class=dict,
  logger_factory=LoggerFactory(),
  wrapper_class=BoundLogger,
  cache_logger_on_first_use=False
)
logger = get_logger()

def __add_context(event):
  event = event.bind(
    hostname=socket.gethostname(),
    pid=os.getpid(),
    release_id=__release__,
    commit=__commit__
    )
  return event

def __do_metric(metric, value, mtype, metadata):
  event = logger.bind(
    payment_plan=metadata['payment_plan'],
    metric_name=metric,
    metric_value=value,
    metric_type=mtype)
  event = __add_context(event)
  return event

def counter(msg, value, metadata):
  event = __do_metric(msg, value, 'c', metadata)
  event.info()

def timer(msg, value, metadata):
  event = __do_metric(msg, value, 't', metadata)
  event.info()

counter('pdf_pages', 3, {'payment_plan': "alpha"})
counter('pdf_pages', 19, {'payment_plan': "thunderdome"})
timer('page_convert_time', 0.92, {'payment_plan': "alpha"})
```

Tells structlog to use the basic logger defined earlier for writing

Formatters for structlog, adding timestamps and ending in key-value formatting

Tells structlog to use basic logger classes

Instantiates the structlog; runs the configure block

Internal function to add generic context-related telemetry

Base metrics function called by counter and timer

The counter class, called from code

Creates a new logger object from the instantiated object, adding context

Injects static context-related telemetry into the event

Causes logging data to emit

Listing 12.1 will send to standard out (the console) and will generate the following:

```
timestamp='2023-02-19T17:47:30.712266Z' metric_name='pdf_pages'
➥ metric_type='c' metric_value=3 payment_plan='alpha' hostname='k8s-
➥ 14.euc1.prod.internal' pid=32595 release_id='0.7.1' commit='f0d00b1'
➥ level='info'
timestamp='2023-02-19T17:47:30.712449Z' metric_name='pdf_pages'
➥ metric_type='c' metric_value=19 payment_plan='thunderdome' hostname='k8s-
➥ 14.euc1.prod.internal' pid=32595 release_id='0.7.1' commit='f0d00b1'
➥ level='info'
timestamp='2023-02-19T17:47:30.712591Z' metric_name='page_convert_time'
```

```
➥ metric_type='t' metric_value=0.92 payment_plan='alpha' hostname='k8s-
➥ 14.euc1.prod.internal' pid=32595 release_id='0.7.1' commit='f0d00b1'
➥ level='info'
```

To understand how we go from counter('pdf_pages', 3, {'payment_plan': "alpha"}) to the first of the log lines above, we have to look at how we added context-related telemetry and what happens in that stack of processors in the configure () block. Each time we call .bind(key=value), we are eventually adding another key-value pair to the output.

Figure 12.3 charts the flow of execution between when we called counter() to the created log line. Along the way, we add key-value pairs to the logger in two spots, capturing both the values that were submitted as part of the counter() call and static information added to all telemetry. When the logger is told to write information, execution moves into structlog. Four different processors (formatters) modify the event hash, the last of which, KeyValueRenderer(), turns everything into a single string value full of key-value pairs. Finally, this string value is sent to LoggerFactory (the writer), where the string value is emitted to the console.

Now, if we replace the KeyValueRenderer() line with JSONRenderer(), a one-line change, our output changes to

```
{"payment_plan": "alpha", "metric_name": "pdf_pages", "metric_value": 3,
➥ "metric_type": "c", "hostname": "k8s-14.euc1.prod.internal", "pid": 2371,
➥ "release_id": "0.7.1", "commit": "f0d00b1", "timestamp": "2023-02-
➥ 19T17:47:30.712266Z", "level": "info"}
```

The structlog module for Python supports both key-value and JSON out of the box. Building your own processors (formatters) is supported by structlog, and we will be digging into that process as part of section 12.2. This code emits directly to the console, but it doesn't have to; using the built-in Python logger as the log emitter means we can send to Syslog, the Windows Event Log, and a number of other places.

Although I use Python as a concrete example here to teach the concepts, remember that other programming languages have support for structured logging. The git repository for this book includes Java versions of my Python listings. Some languages have multiple extensions to support structured logging! Here is a nonexhaustive list of languages and their structured-logging options:

- *Python*—The structlog module (https://www.structlog.org/en/stable)
- *Ruby*—The twp/logging gem (https://github.com/twp/logging)
- *PHP*—The Monolog module (https://github.com/Seldaek/monolog)
- *NodeJS*—The Winston (https://github.com/winstonjs/winston) and Bunyan (https://github.com/trentm/node-bunyan) modules
- *Java*—The log4j 2 framework (https://logging.apache.org/log4j/2.x)
- *Go*—The Zerolog (https://github.com/rs/zerolog) and Zap (https://github .com/uber-go/zap) modules
- *.NET Core*—The built-in ILogger (chapter 17 of http://mng.bz/n2Jd)
- *Rust*—The Slog module (https://docs.rs/crate/slog)

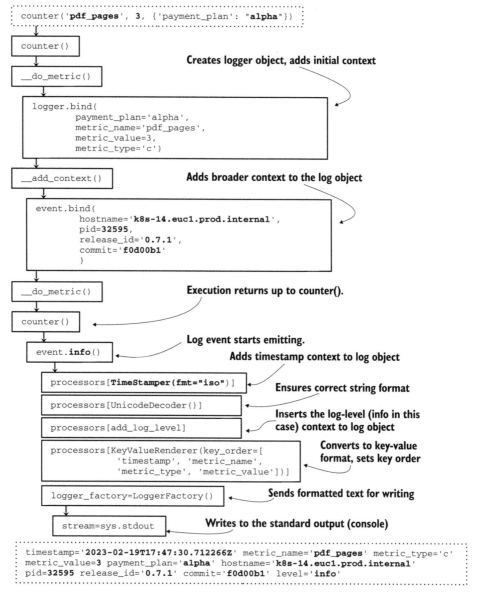

Figure 12.3 How the final log entry (bottom dotted box) was created from the initial function call (top dotted box). The execution stack runs from top to bottom. The logger object is created in `__do_metric()` and is passed into `__add_context()` as an object, where the function adds more context. Execution returns to `counter()`, where the `.info` method is called on the logger object (returned from `__do_metric()`. From there, the log object passes through three formatters (call processors here), which add an ISO8601-formatted timestamp, ensure that the string handles Unicode correctly, and is formatted as a list of key-value pairs with certain keys at the front of the string. Finally, this formatted string is passed to `LoggerFactory`, which writes the string to the console.

12.2   *Implementing standards in your code*

Whereas section 12.1 introduced structured logging, this section is about writing your telemetry standards into your structured logging system. I talked about negotiating the standards within the technical organization in section 4.2, so I recommend looking there for a longer discussion of how to go about selecting a standard. Telemetry format standards aren't required, but they make your job as a telemetry system operator far easier. In brief:

- You are allowed to support more than one telemetry standard; it is more important that people use *a* standard than to use only the one true standard. Also, certain formats are easier than others to implement in specific programming languages, so having more than one standard to choose among will keep people from improvising in hard-to-support ways.
- Object-encoding formats (JSON, YAML, and XML) are amazingly versatile, and JSON parsing has seen radical optimization since 2010. Even so, delimited formats such as CSV and key-value are algorithmically simpler. Definitely test parsing speeds when selecting a format to verify your performance assumptions.
- The process of selecting the telemetry format standard has as much to do with the humans supporting the production technical systems as with the actual technical systems themselves. Sometimes; the optimal technical solution isn't the optimal political solution. This negotiation process is why I encourage supporting more than one format.

When you have your standards, it's time to build support for them in your production code (and also your Shipping stage, but we'll get to that in section 12.3). We will be expanding on the structured logger we built in listing 12.1 to discuss these concepts. Listing 12.1 emits key-value pairs to the standard output as part of a metrics logger, but we will also look at revising that base to be part of centralized logging. To start, we need to examine the role of the processors from listing 12.1.

```
processors=[
  TimeStamper(fmt="iso"),
  UnicodeDecoder(),
  add_log_level,
  KeyValueRenderer(key_order=[
    'timestamp', 'metric_name',
    'metric_type', 'metric_value'])
],
```

As we saw in figure 12.3, this ordered list describes the order of transformations our metrics telemetry went through:

1 TimeStamper—Adds a timestamp value to the telemetry, using an ISO format (ISO8601)
2 UnicodeDecoder—Transforms the strings in the telemetry to be unified
3 add_log_level—Adds the logging level (debug, info, warn, err, critical, and so on) to the telemetry

4 KeyValueRenderer—Transforms the one-dimensional hash of telemetry into a single string, formatted in key-value, with four keys ordered at the beginning of the string

The last value here, KeyValueRenderer, encodes the metrics standard this function was written against:

```
timestamp='2023-02-19T17:47:30.712266Z' metric_name='pdf_pages'
➡ metric_type='c' metric_value=3 payment_plan='alpha' hostname='k8s-
➡ 14.euc1.prod.internal' pid=32595 release_id='0.7.1' commit='f0d00b1'
➡ level='info'
```

Replacing that one line with JSONRenderer gives us JSON-encoded telemetry:

```
{"payment_plan": "alpha", "metric_name": "pdf_pages", "metric_value": 3,
➡ "metric_type": "c", "hostname": "k8s-14.euc1.prod.internal", "pid": 32595,
➡ "release_id": "0.7.1", "commit": "f0d00b1", "timestamp": "2023-02-
➡ 19T17:47:30.712266Z", "level": "info"}
```

For a metrics emitter, either of these formats is pretty complete. It has a metrics name with value, and context-related details are packaged with the metrics. The context-related details are static, however. How would we update listing 12.1 to accommodate an optional hash of context to also emit with the metrics? Right now, metrics are emitted with a call like this:

```
counter('pdf_pages', 3, {'payment_plan': "alpha",'account_id': "1121"})
```

A hash of metadata is the third parameter, which is consumed by logging functions such as the one from listing 12.1. In the listing 12.1 case, only payment_plan is extracted from the metadata hash and emitted; the others, like release_id, are a static set of details that gets emitted for everything. Let's rewrite listing 12.1 so that people calling our metrics function can specify which fields in the metadata hash to include with their metrics, as follows:

```
context_fields = ['payment_plan', 'account_id', 'region', 'datacenter']
counter('pdf_pages', 3, metadata, context_fields)
```

To start with, our counter() function's define will need to be rewritten from

```
def counter(msg, value, metadata):
```

to a version that can handle the extra parameter and the idea that metadata is optional (it's mandatory in listing 12.1):

```
def counter(msg, value, metadata = [], fields = []):
```

Also, because counter() is a wrapper for __do_metric(), we need to rewrite that function's define as well, from

```
def __do_metric(metric, value, mtype, metadata):
```

to

```
def __do_metric(metric, value, mtype, metadata = [], fields = []):
```

Now that we're inside __do_metric(), we need to update the logic inside it to handle variable fields. The original version only statically assigned a single value from the metadata hash:

```
def __do_metric(metric, value, mtype, metadata):
  event = logger.bind(
    payment_plan=metadata['payment_plan'],
    metric_name=metric,
    metric_value=value,
    metric_type=mtype)
  event = __add_context(event)J
  return event
```

Our new version needs to add variable telemetry from the metadata hash based on what is passed in on the fields array. Here, we loop through the fields passed in, and if the metadata hash has any of the fields, they're added as context. Listing 12.2 shows the rewritten __do_metric function from listing 12.1, but all other code remains the same.

Listing 12.2   Revising __do_metric to accept variable telemetry

```
[...]
def __do_metric(metric, value, mtype, metadata = [], fields = []):
  event = logger.bind(
    metric_name=metric,
    metric_value=value,
    metric_type=mtype)                        Creates an empty context_fields
  context_fields = {}            ◁――――――――     hash to populate
  for f in fields:
    if f in metadata:                          Loops through fields and
      context_fields[f]=metadata[f]            adds to context_fields any
                                               metadata values that match

  event = event.bind(**context_fields)    ◁――┐  Applies context_fields
  event = __add_context(event)                │  to the telemetry
  return event
```

Now that we have __do_metric() updated, we should be able to see how telemetry handling has changed. Let's see what we get when we feed in the following calls to our revised metrics logger:

```
metadata1 = {'payment_plan': 'alpha', 'account_id': '1121'}
metadata2 = {'payment_plan': 'thunderdome', 'account_id': '23b9c1'}
metadata3 = {'payment_plan': 'skyfall', 'account_id': 'a3953021'}

counter('pdf_pages', 3, metadata1, ['payment_plan'])
counter('pdf_pages', 19, metadata2, ['payment_plan', 'account_id'])
timer('page_convert_time', 0.92, metadata3, ['account_id'])
timer('page_convert_time', 1.22)
```

Four different calls, each specifying slightly different fields. The last call to `timer()` specifies no telemetry at all, so the emitted telemetry for that call should have no `payment_plan` or `account_id`. To help, I've bolded the variable telemetry fields that were emitted:

```
timestamp='2020-09-24T00:43:37.659549Z' metric_name='pdf_pages'
➥ metric_type='c' metric_value=3 payment_plan='alpha' hostname='k8s-
➥ 14.euc1.prod.internal' pid=19661 release_id='0.7.1' commit='f0d00b1'
➥ level='info'
timestamp='2023-02-19T00:43:37.659707Z' metric_name='pdf_pages'
➥ metric_type='c' metric_value=19 payment_plan='thunderdome'
➥ account_id='23b9c1' hostname='k8s-14.euc1.prod.internal' pid=19661
➥ release_id='0.7.1' commit='f0d00b1' level='info'
timestamp='2023-02-19T00:43:37.659833Z' metric_name='page_convert_time'
➥ metric_type='t' metric_value=0.92 account_id='a3953021' hostname='k8s-
➥ 14.euc1.prod.internal' pid=19661 release_id='0.7.1' commit='f0d00b1'
➥ level='info'
timestamp='2023-02-19T00:43:37.659954Z' metric_name='page_convert_time'
➥ metric_type='t' metric_value=1.22 hostname='k8s-14.euc1.prod.internal'
➥ pid=19661 release_id='0.7.1' commit='f0d00b1' level='info'
```

Success! Now software engineers can add arbitrary context to their metrics! Empowerment!

How can we rewrite this to be a generic logger rather than a metrics emitter? To start, we need to get rid of the function defines for `counter()` and `timer()` because we don't need them anymore. In their place, we need to add new functions to handle different log levels, but we want to keep the idea that software engineers can add custom context to each log they create:

```
def counter(msg, value, metadata = [], fields = []):
  [...]

def timer(msg, value, metadata = [], fields = []):
  [...]

def info(event, metadata=[], fields=[]):
  [...]

def warning(event, metadata=[], fields=[]):
  [...]

def error(event, metadata=[], fields=[]):
  [...]
```

This gives us three different log levels to expose to the rest of the application: info, warning, and error. We are still using the same arbitrary context method from the metrics logger, accepting a hash and a list of fields in the hash as parameters to these functions. What we want is to take inputs such as this

```
metadata = {
  'account_id': '1515323',
  'payment_plan': 'Enterprise Plus',
```

```
    'region': 'euc1',
    'feature_flags': { 'new_login': True, 'new_profile': False }
  }

info("Profile image updated", metadata, ["account_id", "feature_flags"])
```

and turn it into a JSON hash like this, with the dynamic context boldfaced:

```
{"hostname": "k8s-14.euc1.prod.internal", "pid": 23030, "release": "0.7.1",
➡ "commit": "f0d00b1", "account_id": "1515323", "feature_flags":
➡ {"new_login":
➡ true, "new_profile": false}, "event": "Profile image updated", "timestamp":
➡ "2023-02-19T14:41:22.918238Z", "level": "info"}
```

Listing 12.3 shows the changes from listing 12.2 to make this work.

Listing 12.3   A general logger allowing arbitrary context-related telemetry to be added

```
[...]
configure(
  processors=[
    TimeStamper(fmt="iso"),
    UnicodeDecoder(),
    add_log_level,
    JSONRenderer(),
  ],
  context_class=dict,
  logger_factory=LoggerFactory(),
  wrapper_class=BoundLogger,
  cache_logger_on_first_use=False
)

logger = get_logger()                    ⎤  __add_context() is unchanged
                                         ⎦  from listings 12.1 and 12.1.
def __add_context():        ◁────┘
  context = {
    'hostname': socket.gethostname(),
    'pid': os.getpid(),
    'release': __release__,
    'commit': __commit__
  }
  return context

def __filter_metadata(metadata, fields):
  fcontext = {}                               Pulls the requested fields
  for f in fields:                            from the metadata hash and
    if f in metadata:                         returns them in a new hash
      fcontext[f] = metadata[f]

  return fcontext
                                              Merges context fetched from
                                              _add_context() to the context
def __merge_context(metadata, fields):  ◁──┘ from __filter_metadata()
  base_context = __add_context()
  filter_context = __filter_metadata(metadata, fields)
  merged_context = {**base_context, **filter_context}  ◁──── Merges the two hashes
  return merged_context
```

```
def info(eventdata, metadata=[], fields=[]):
    event = logger.bind(**__merge_context(
        metadata, fields))
    event.info(eventdata)
```

Emits the event at 'info' level, with
context added in the previous line

Binds all
context
to a new
logger

```
def warning(eventdata, metadata=[], fields=[]):
    event = logger.bind(**__merge_context(metadata, fields))
    event.warning(eventdata)

def error(eventdata, metadata=[], fields=[]):
    event = logger.bind(**__merge_context(metadata, fields))
    event.error(eventdata)
```

Let's follow the telemetry execution flow, shown in figure 12.4.

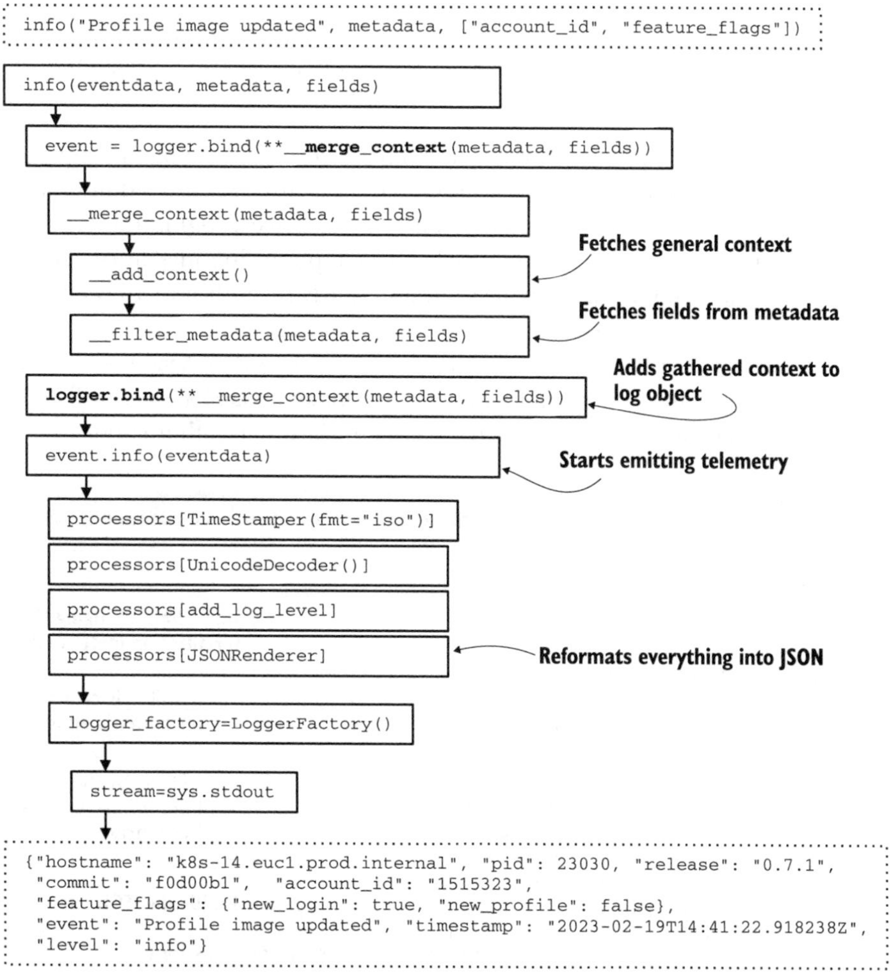

```
info("Profile image updated", metadata, ["account_id", "feature_flags"])
```

```
info(eventdata, metadata, fields)
```

```
event = logger.bind(**__merge_context(metadata, fields))
```

```
__merge_context(metadata, fields)
```

```
__add_context()
```
Fetches general context

```
__filter_metadata(metadata, fields)
```
Fetches fields from metadata

```
logger.bind(**__merge_context(metadata, fields))
```
Adds gathered context to
log object

```
event.info(eventdata)
```
Starts emitting telemetry

```
processors[TimeStamper(fmt="iso")]
```

```
processors[UnicodeDecoder()]
```

```
processors[add_log_level]
```

```
processors[JSONRenderer]
```
Reformats everything into JSON

```
logger_factory=LoggerFactory()
```

```
stream=sys.stdout
```

```
{"hostname": "k8s-14.euc1.prod.internal", "pid": 23030, "release": "0.7.1",
 "commit": "f0d00b1", "account_id": "1515323",
 "feature_flags": {"new_login": true, "new_profile": false},
 "event": "Profile image updated", "timestamp": "2023-02-19T14:41:22.918238Z",
 "level": "info"}
```

Figure 12.4 The flow of execution from listing 12.4, a logger function with three priorities that accepts arbitrary context-related telemetry. Our metadata hash and field list are handled as part of __add_context, which we see in the final JSON.

Figure 12.4 shows how execution flows through the stack and how context-related telemetry is gathered. When the context is added to the logging object, our emitted string, `"Profile image uploaded"`, is run through four processors. The final `JSON-Renderer` processor formats the telemetry and the context-related telemetry as a JSON hash, which is emitted to the standard output by way of the `LoggerFactory()`.

So far, we've seen standard key-value and JSON-formatted telemetry, but the standards-negotiation process sometimes produces strange results due to the technical (and political) requirements of everyone involved. This next format we'll look at is the product of just such a balancing act. Let's take a look at a sample, using the same inputs we diagramed above but with a new format that puts the timestamp and the logged statement outside the JSON string:

```
2023-02-19T14:41:22.918238Z Profile image updated -- {"hostname": "k8s-
14.euc1.prod.internal", "pid": 23030, "release": "0.7.1", "commit":
"f0d00b1", "account_id": "1515323", "feature_flags": {"new_login": true,
"new_profile": false}, "level": "info"}
```

On the surface, it's pretty clear: a timestamp, followed by the plain-language log statement, double dashes, and then a JSON data structure for any additional context. A strange format like this one makes sense if you have programming languages that aren't optimized for JSON; the initial timestamp and log line mirrored the state of centralized logging in this organization until fairly recently and are well supported by anything that can build strings.

In this case, we can't use the `KeyValueRenderer` or `JSONRenderer`, so we will need to make a custom processor. To do that, we make a class, shown in listing 12.4. We name this file `internalrenderer.py` to ease importing in other code.

Listing 12.4   Creating a custom processor class for Python structlog

`__init__` is called during the configure() block.

```
import json

class InternalRenderer(object):

    def __init__(self, serializer=json.dumps):
        self._dumps = serializer

    def __call__(self, logger, name, event_dict):
        timestamp = event_dict.pop('timestamp')
        event = event_dict.pop('event')
        context_json = self._dumps(event_dict)
        return timestamp + " " + event + " -- " +
        context_json
```

This allows changing the JSON serialization method, if desired.

`__call__` is called whenever telemetry is emitted.

Pulls out the timestamp and event hash-entries so they're not included in the JSON part

Builds the JSON part of the emission

Renders the entire string for emissions

This class has two functions. The first function, `__init__()`, is called during the configure() block that defines all the processors for our logger. Our function can accept the name of another JSON serializer in case the built-in one isn't good enough for some reason. This would be done as part of the configure() block.

The second function, __call__(), is called whenever telemetry is ready to emit. This function formats the emitted telemetry and is where our internal standard format is codified. Figure 12.5 shows how our new InternalRenderer class interacts with the logging framework we've been building in this chapter.

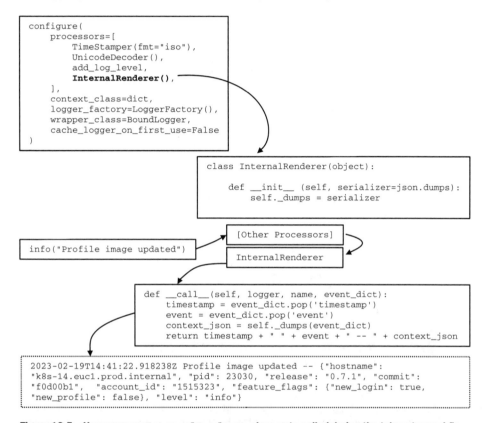

Figure 12.5   How our new `InternalRenderer` class gets called during the telemetry workflow. The `__init__`() function is called during the `configure()` block, near when the program starts up for the first time. The `__call__`() function is called whenever telemetry is emitted and performs the final formatting. This sort of create-early/call-late process is common.

Listing 12.5 updates listing 12.3 to use this InternalRenderer instead of the JSON-Renderer. To run this listing locally, put the code from listing 12.4 in a file named internalrenderer.py to get our custom formatter.

Listing 12.5   Updating the listing 12.3 code to use the `InternalRenderer`

```
import logging
import datetime
import sys
```

```
import socket
import os
from internalrenderer import (InternalRenderer)        ◁──┐  Imports our custom
from structlog import (                                    │  class into this scope
  get_logger,
  configure,
)
[...]
configure(
  processors=[
    TimeStamper(fmt="iso"),
    UnicodeDecoder(),              ┌─ Defines our InternalRenderer as the
    add_log_level,                 │  final processor, implementing our
    InternalRenderer(),        ◁───┘  standard format
  ],
  context_class=dict,
  logger_factory=LoggerFactory(),
  wrapper_class=BoundLogger,
  cache_logger_on_first_use=False
)
[...]
```

Listing 12.5 didn't require many updates to use the `InternalRenderer` from listing 12.4, merely two additional lines. With these changes, we get our desired telemetry emission:

```
2023-02-19T14:41:22.918238Z Profile image updated -- {"hostname": "k8s-
➡ 14.euc1.prod.internal", "pid": 23030, "release": "0.7.1", "commit":
➡ "f0d00b1", "account_id": "1515323", "feature_flags": {"new_login": true,
➡ "new_profile": false}, "level": "info"}
```

> ### Python is merely the example; think of the bigger picture
>
> I'm using Python for this dive into structured logging and standards because that's what I've been using for most of this book. These concepts are not unique to Python; the end of section 12.1 provides an abbreviated list of structured logging frameworks for a variety of languages. If Python isn't your choice, I hope that one of those frameworks will be suitable. Remember the base components of structured logging:
>
> - *Logger*—The entry point into the structured logger from your production code. In all these examples, it has been a function definition in our listings.
> - *Formatter*—Modifies telemetry to prepare it for the Shipping stage. In all these examples, this is the list of `processors` in the `configure()` block. All good structured loggers have an equivalent.
> - *Writer*—Ships fully formatted telemetry into the Shipping stage. In these examples, this is the base Python logger that structlog sits on top of and emits directly into the standard output.
>
> If you're not writing Python, consider looking up the structured logger for the language you're more familiar with and seeing whether you can build functionality equivalent to what I'm showing here.

> ### Exercise 12.1
> The previous two listings demonstrated how to add a new formatter (processor) to our structured logger. Listing 12.3 shows adding context to our telemetry as part of the logger (entry point for telemetry). How would you rewrite the listing to use a formatter to perform the context additions instead of doing it as part of the logger?

So far, we've been emitting only into the standard output. How about shipping into something more direct, such as a queue? The structlog module sits on top of the base Python logger, as we see at the beginning of listings 12.1 and 12.5:

```
logging.basicConfig(
    format="%(message)s",
    stream=sys.stdout,
    level=logging.INFO,
)
```

As it happens, we examined several methods for shipping to useful places in chapter 3. For now, let's focus on the changes needed to send telemetry into a Redis-based (https://redis.io) queue. Although the base logging module in Python doesn't ship with a `RedisHandler` or equivalent, a `RedisListHandler` extension is available as a module (https://github.com/lobziik/rlog). We can use this module to update our logger to send to a Redis list.

> **NOTE** To get this listing to compile, you need the rlog module installed (`pip3 install rlog`). To function, this listing needs a Redis server, which I do not expect you to set up. This implementation is an example.

Listing 12.6 Updating our logger to emit to a Redis-based list

```
[...]
from rlog import RedisListHandler          ◁──┐ Imports the RedisListHandler
[...]                                          └ we need from its module
redis_config = {
    'host': 'logqueue.euc1.prod.internal',     Hash needed to configure
    'port': 6379,                              RedisListHandler and tell it
}                                              where to find the Redis server

logging.basicConfig(
    format="%(message)s",
    handlers=[
        RedisListHandler(key='central_queue',   Configures RedisListHandler to tell it
        ⇨ **redis_config)                       which key to emit into and provides
    ],                                          the config hash
    level=logging.INFO,
)
[...]
```

We see in listing 12.6 that we're replacing `stream=sys.stdout` with the new `Redis-ListHandler()`, which is the only configuration change we're making in the entire script. With this one change, the telemetry we've been emitting to standard output will instead be sent to a Redis list.

Figure 12.6 shows the flow of telemetry now that we are using `RedisListHandler` in the basic Python logger. We see that telemetry is flowing over the network, rather than being sent to standard out in the hope that something else is configured to receive that stream and will send it somewhere useful.

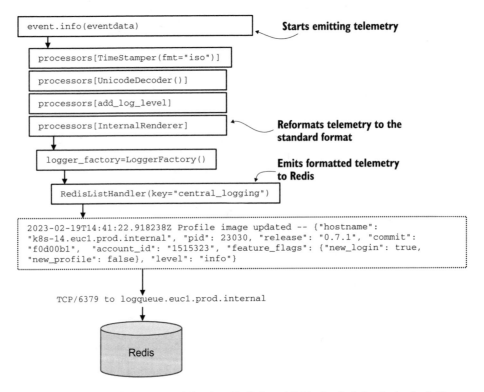

Figure 12.6 Our metrics logger emitting to a Redis-based list instead of standard output. The built-in Python logger is updated to use `RedisListHandler` instead of `sys.stdout`. The effect of this change is to redirect logging to a new place: across a TCP connection to a Redis server. Architectures like this one are discussed in chapter 3, but moving telemetry to a remote location from inside the production code itself means that fewer telemetry system components need to compete with the production code for resources.

There are trade-offs to make between emitting locally through stdout—requiring another telemetry system to move the telemetry further into the pipeline—and emitting remotely to a queue, stream, or API. Chapters 2 and 3 cover this topic extensively, but in brief:

- *Emitting locally,* such as to a file or standard out, is easy and lightweight on the production code itself. The cost of this ease is the need to have an additional Shipping-stage system, such as Fluentd or Elastic's Filebeat or Journalbeat, to receive this local telemetry and ship it onward.
- *Emitting remotely,* such as to a queue, stream, or API, means that the telemetry spends the least time on the box that generated it, giving attackers less time to modify it. When you use this method, you don't need additional software locally to move telemetry. But the production code must be able to handle telemetry network and service outages in a way that local emissions don't, which increases complexity in code.

Now that we've been through an entire structured logger, you can do a lot more things with one than implement your logging standards:

- Dig into emitting directly off the box, as we did with Redis. Chapter 13 covers techniques.
- If you care deeply about telemetry integrity, why not build a formatter (processor in the preceding examples) to compute the checksums of key fields and ship them alongside the telemetry? Chapter 15 covers telemetry integrity.
- If you're handling regulated information such as personally identifiable information (PII) or electronic personal health information (ePHI), the structured logger is your first point of defense to prevent such regulated data from entering your telemetry pipeline. Build a formatter that autoredacts (or outright rejects) regulated telemetry fields such as email or diagnosis code. Doing so as part of the Emitting stage will help you avoid the problem presented in chapter 16: what to do when such regulated information spills.
- Exceptions are among the highest-risk strings for containing regulated information because they often contain the parameter values passed to the function that failed. Consider building a second structured logger for exception logs that gets more thorough scrubbing than your regular centralized logging traffic.

> **Exercise 12.2**
> In the software you work with in your day-to-day life, how are exceptions tracked? How would your existing logging systems handle them? Given what you've learned here, how much work would it take to handle exceptions through a new path?

12.3 Implementing standards in the Shipping stage

This section is about parsing the telemetry we emitted in section 12.2 and seeing what it looks like in the Shipping stage. Parsing standard formats like JSON is a native, one-step operation in most modern languages, and all the open source Shipping-stage systems have easy ways to parse it:

- With Fluentd, `<parse> @type json </parse>` will do the job for inputs.
- With Logstash, using `codec => json` is all you need to do on an input.
- For Filebeat, which reads log files and isn't a general-purpose Shipping-stage package like the previous two, using the `decode_json_fields` processor will perform parsing before moving telemetry onward.

What is more interesting are non-JSON formats and how to build parsers for them. We will be looking at parsing key-value formatted telemetry (like what listing 12.1 emits) and the custom format we built in section 12.2 (listings 12.4 and 12.5). We will be looking at both a dedicated Shipping-stage framework like Logstash and a general-programming approach to parsing these formats. As a reminder, the custom format we built in section 12.2 looks like this for centralized logging:

```
2023-02-19T14:41:22.918238Z Profile image updated -- {"hostname": "k8s-
⮕ 14.euc1.prod.internal", "pid": 23030, "release": "0.7.1", "commit":
⮕ "f0d00b1", "account_id": "1515323", "feature_flags": {"new_login": true,
⮕ "new_profile": false}, "level": "info"}
```

The format is an ISO8601-formatted timestamp followed by a plain-text string, double dashes, and a JSON data structure. The key-value version of a metrics emitter looks like this:

```
timestamp='2023-02-19T14:41:22.918238Z' metric_name='pdf_pages'
⮕ metric_type='c' metric_value=3 payment_plan='alpha' hostname='k8s-
⮕ 14.euc1.prod.internal' pid=19661 release_id='0.7.1' commit='f0d00b1'
⮕ level='info'
```

First, we will look at the custom format and what parsing with Logstash would look like. Logstash is an open source, dedicated, Shipping-stage framework put out by Elastic.co, best known as the *L* in *ELK Stack* (the other two letters standing for Elasticsearch and Kibana). Logstash is written in a combination of JRuby (it started as a Ruby platform) and Java, and is slowly moving toward a straight Java implementation.

Listing 12.7 is a complete Logstash config file that will test parsing our standard formatted string. If you want to run it yourself, make sure to change the `path =>` value in the `file{}` output to be appropriate for your system.

Listing 12.7 Parsing the standard format with Logstash

```
input {
  generator {                                    ⟵  Generates our test string
    message => '2023-02-19T14:41:22.918238Z Profile    so we can test parsing
    ⮕ image updated -- {"hostname":
    ⮕ "k8s-14.euc1.prod.internal", "pid": 23030,
    ⮕ "release": "0.7.1", "commit": "f0d00b1",
    ⮕ "account_id": "1515323", "feature_flags":
    ⮕ {"new_login": true, "new_profile": false},
    ⮕ "level": "info"}'
    count => 10                                  ⟵  The number of times the
                                                     generator{} input will
                                                     generate a string
```

Our test string ⟶ (pointing to message lines)

```
    }
  }

  filter {
    if [message] =~ / -- / {          ◁── Makes sure we run the right
      dissect {                            field splitter on the string
        mapping => {
          "message" => "%{plain_part} -- %{json_part}"
        }
        remove_field => [ "message" ]
      }
    } else {
      mutate {
        copy => {
          "message" => "plain_part"
        }
        add_field => {
          "json_part" => ""
        }
        remove_field => [ "message" ]
      }
    }

    dissect {
      mapping => {
        "plain_part" => "%{timestamp} %{event}"
      }
      remove_field => [ "plain_part" ]
    }

    json {
      source => "json_part"
      remove_field => [ "json_part" ]
    }

    date { match => [ "timestamp", "ISO8601" ] }     ◁──
  }

  output {
    file {
      path => "/tmp/standard-format.log"
      codec => json_lines{}
    }
  }
```

Makes sure we run the right field splitter on the string

Splits the string into a plain_part and a json_part; will be further parsed later

If we're not field-splitting, rename the message field to plain_part.

Sets the json_part field to empty so the later parser won't barf on a missing field

Break the plain_part field into a timestamp and an event text, removing the plain_part field when done.

Parse the json_part field, and remove the json_part field when done.

Parse the timestamp field to change the date of the event to what is in the string.

As written, the code in listing 12.7 will create a file with ten lines of JSON-delimited strings. The output should look like this (the sequence and @timestamp fields are added by Logstash internally):

```
{"sequence":0,"feature_flags":{"new_login":true,"new_profile":false},"commit"
➥ :"f0d00b1","level":"info","@version":"1","@timestamp":"2023-02-
➥ 19T14:41:22.918Z","pid":23030,"account_id":"1515323","hostname":"k8s-
➥ 14.euc1.prod.internal","release":"0.7.1","event":"Profile image
➥ updated","timestamp":"2023-02-19T14:41:22.918238Z"}
```

```
{"sequence":1,"feature_flags":{"new_login":true,"new_profile":false},"commit"
  :"f0d00b1","level":"info","@version":"1","@timestamp":"2023-02-
  19T14:41:22.918Z","pid":23030,"account_id":"1515323","hostname":"k8s-
  14.euc1.prod.internal","release":"0.7.1","event":"Profile image
  updated","timestamp":"2023-02-19T14:41:22.918238Z"}
```

We're using a filter called dissect {} to break the string apart. Dissect uses delimiters to extract fields from strings, which makes it faster than regular expressions but also less flexible. This is why the if [message] =~ / -- / { conditional is there; we need to make sure that a delimiter is present before trying dissect {} on it. The first dissect {} creates the plain_part and json_part fields we will use later. If the conditional fails, we merely rename the message field to be plain_part and set a blank value for json_part. The second dissect {} breaks the plain_part field into the timestamp and event fields.

After that, we parse the json_part field with the json {} filter and the timestamp field with the date {} filter, and we're done parsing! We finish with the output {} section to send our fully parsed events somewhere interesting—a file in this case. Figure 12.7 diagrams this flow of execution.

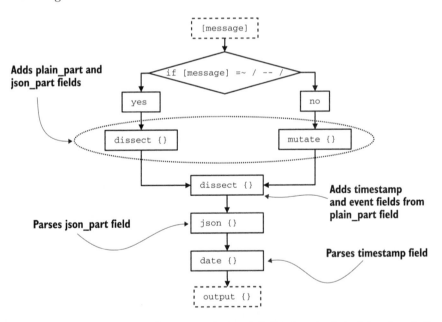

Figure 12.7   The Logstash parsing flow for listing 12.7. The first step is to determine whether we need to use dissect {} or mutate {} on the string. The second step creates the plain_part and json_part fields. The third part parses the plain_part field to create the timestamp and event fields. The fourth part parses the json_part field to add encoded fields to the object. The fifth part parses the timestamp field to set the timestamp of the object to be what the event's timestamp is. Finally, we move to the output {} block to send the parsed object somewhere interesting. This parser is relatively small to write and easy to understand for someone who is new to Logstash—a key maintainability feature.

Now that we've seen how Logstash parses our string, let's take a look at a Python parser. Listing 12.8 shows a complete Python parser that takes our test string and emits a JSON block to be consumed elsewhere in the Shipping stage. The flow of execution is similar to the Logstash version.

Listing 12.8   Parsing our logging-standard telemetry with straight Python

**If our delimiter string is present,
changes how we parse the string**

```
import json

test_string = '2023-02-19T14:41:22.918238Z Profile image updated --
   {"hostname": "k8s-14.euc1.prod.internal", "pid": 23030, "release":
   "0.7.1", "commit": "f0d00b1",  "account_id": "1515323", "feature_flags":
   {"new_login":  true, "new_profile": false}, "level": "info"}'

if ' -- ' in test_string:
    plain_part, json_part = test_string.split(' -- ', 1)
else:
    plain_part = test_string
    json_part = ''

timestamp, event = plain_part.split(' ', 1)
fields = json.loads(json_part)
fields['event'] = event
fields['timestamp'] = timestamp
print(json.dumps(fields))
```

Splits our string on the first occurrence of ' -- ', assigning plain_part and json_part

Splits our plain_part into timestamp and event variables by the first space in plain_part

Parses our json_part to create the fields hash

Adds the event and json variables to the fields hash

If our delimiter string is not present, assigns plain_ part as the whole string and json_part as empty

Execution flow in listing 12.8 is similar to what was shown in figure 12.7 and listing 12.7. The role `dissect {}` played with Logstash here is filled by `.split(pattern, 1)`. The only step missing is parsing the `timestamp` field, because Logstash keeps a separate `@timestamp` field that is considered to be authoritative for the event; we don't have `@timestamp` here, so we can safely avoid date parsing.

Exercise 12.3

We've seen two versions of building a parser for this logging standard format. How would you build a parser for this standard in your language of choice? Remember, it needs to handle the case where ' -- ' is not in the string.

```
2023-02-19T14:41:22.918238Z Profile image updated -- {"hostname": "k8s-
   14.euc1.prod.internal", "pid": 23030, "release": "0.7.1", "commit":
   "f0d00b1", "account_id": "1515323", "feature_flags": {"new_login": true,
   "new_profile": false}, "level": "info"}
```

Next, we will look at the key-value version of the telemetry, shown above in our metrics logger. As a reminder, this is what it looks like:

```
timestamp='2023-02-19T14:41:22.659549Z' metric_name='pdf_pages'
⇒ metric_type='c' metric_value=3 payment_plan='alpha' hostname='k8s-
⇒ 14.euc1.prod.internal' pid=19661 release_id='0.7.1' commit='f0d00b1'
⇒ level='info'
```

Logstash has a native filter for key-value-formatted telemetry, so we get to take fewer steps when building a Logstash config file that supports telemetry formatted this way. Listing 12.9 shows a complete Logstash pipeline configuration that will test our telemetry and parsing.

> **Listing 12.9   Parsing key-value-formatted telemetry with Logstash**

```
input {
  generator {
    message => "timestamp='2023-02-19T14:41:22.659549Z'
    ⇒ metric_name='pdf_pages' metric_type='c' metric_value=3
    ⇒ payment_plan='alpha' hostname='k8s-14.euc1.prod.internal'
    ⇒ pid=19661 release_id='0.7.1' commit='f0d00b1' level='info'"
    count => 10
  }
}

filter {
  kv {
    source => "message"              Tells Logstash to run the kv {} filter,
    remove_field => [ "message" ]    key-value, over the 'message' field,
  }                                  and remove the message field

  date {
    match => [ "timestamp", "ISO8601" ]   Parses the 'timestamp' field and populates
  }                                       the '@timestamp` field with that value
}

output {
  file {
    path => "/tmp/kv-format.log"
    codec => json_lines{}
  }
}
```

Listing 12.9 is much simpler than listing 12.7, which parsed the standard formatted telemetry! One filter, kv {}, does all the parsing. Handling the standard format telemetry required a conditional check followed by two parsing stages; for the key-value telemetry, we're doing a single parsing stage. Here are two lines of what this config creates:

```
{"release_id":"0.7.1","@timestamp":"2023-02-
⇒ 19T14:41:22.659Z","hostname":"k8s-14.euc1.prod.internal",
⇒ "payment_plan":"alpha","pid":"19661","commit":"f0d00b1","@version":"1",
⇒ "sequence":0,"level":"info","metric_value":"3","metric_type"
⇒ 14.euc1.prod.internal",:"c","timestamp":"2023-02-19T14:41:22.659549Z",
⇒ "metric_name":"pdf_pages"}
```

```
{"release_id":"0.7.1","@timestamp":"2023-02-19T14:41:22.659Z",
⇨ "hostname":"k8s-14.euc1.prod.internal",
⇨ "payment_plan":"alpha","pid":"19661","commit":"f0d00b1","@version":"1",
⇨ "sequence":1,"level":"info","metric_value":"3","metric_type"
⇨ :"c","timestamp":"2023-02-19T14:41:22.659549Z","metric_name":"pdf_pages"}
```

Having a premade filter for your telemetry format is a tremendous convenience. The key-value filter for Logstash is capable of handling quoted values, such as key="value with spaces", and changing your delimiters such as key:value. The code to handle such convenience is somewhat complex (http://mng.bz/ve1a), but that's the nature of convenience sometimes. Contrast this with the Python version of the parser, shown in listing 12.10. It gets the job done but isn't as flexible.

Listing 12.10   Parsing key-value delimited telemetry with Python

Uses quote character string to determine whether the first character in the value is a quote

```python
import re
import json

test_string="timestamp='2023-02-19T14:41:22.659549Z'
⇨ metric_name='pdf_pages' metric_type='c' metric_value=3
⇨ payment_plan='alpha' hostname='k8s-14.euc1.prod.internal' pid=19661
⇨ release_id='0.7.1' commit='f0d00b1' level='info'"

splitter = re.compile("(\S+)=(\S+)")     ⟵┐  Precompiles a regular expression
quote_chars = "'\""   ⟵                      to match key-value pairs
                     ┌─ A string of quote characters,
fields = {}          │  used for a conditional later   ┌─ Uses precompiled regex to produce a
for kv in splitter.findall(test_string):   ⟵───────────┘  list of key-value pairs to iterate over
⌐→  if kv[1][0] in quote_chars:
      trim_v = kv[1][0]                      ┌─ Removes quote characters from the
      value = kv[1].strip(trim_v).rstrip(trim_v) │  beginning and end of the string
    else:
      if '.' in kv[1]:              ┌─ Checks for existence of a period and
        value = float(kv[1])        │  then type-casts the value to float.
      else:
        value = int(kv[1])      ┌─ If no period, types cast to integer

  fields[kv[0]] = value

print(json.dumps(fields))
```

The output produced by listing 12.10 is somewhat different from the output produced by Logstash. Note the number types and the lack of the Logstash internal fields @timestamp and sequence:

```
{"timestamp": "2023-02-19T14:41:22.659549Z", "metric_name": "pdf_pages",
⇨ "metric_type": "c", "metric_value": 3, "payment_plan": "alpha",
⇨ "hostname": "k8s-14.euc1.prod.internal", "pid": 19661,
⇨ "release_id": "0.7.1", "commit": "f0d00b1", "level": "info"}
```

Figure 12.8 shows the processing flow of the Python parser in listing 12.10, using a much smaller test string than we did in the listing itself. The big capability difference between the Python in listing 12.10 and the Logstash config in listing 12.9 is the ability to handle quoted strings as values, such as the event field from our centralized logger examples, event="Profile image updated". The Python parser would need to be rather more complex to handle such values. But if the generated key-value pairs the metrics system produces never emits quoted strings with spaces, the inability to handle such strings doesn't matter.

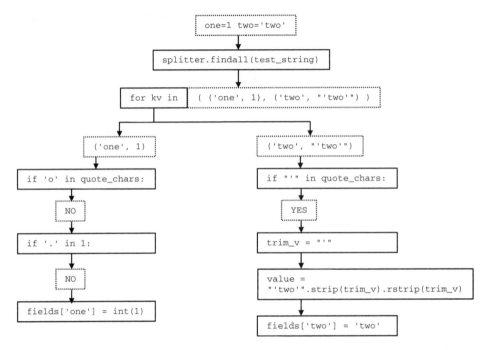

Figure 12.8   The processing flow for our Python key-value parsing script, showing two branches of execution. The left branch is an unquoted string, so it is tested for the presence of a period to determine whether it is an integer or float. The right branch is a quoted string, so the quotes are stripped from the value before being persisted in the `fields[]` hash. This parser is a simple one and would break down if the quoted string included a space. Fortunately, we don't expect to see that kind of value in this flow.

We have seen four ways to parse standardized telemetry emitted from a structured logger. Although these examples are specific to Logstash and Python, the techniques involved are generalizable:

- For the Shipping stage, the performance advantage of compiled languages versus interpreted languages can be significant.
- Building your logging standards around prebuilt parsers in your Shipping stage will make maintaining your telemetry pipeline easier for everyone involved.

- If you can trust that your inputs will be limited, you can reduce complexity in your parsers, thus improving maintainability.
- Although we didn't cover it here, string conversion between formats needs to happen in the Shipping stage. (Section 6.2.3 covers this topic specifically.) String conversion between EBCDIC and Unicode, for example, is something that your parsers will need to handle before deserializing your strings (unless you can deserialize directly from EBCDIC, in which case go for it).

Defending your telemetry system against dealing with toxic data spills matters in the Shipping stage as well as the Emitting stage. Section 12.2 ended with a suggestion for using the formatters in your structured logging system to filter out PII and ePHI from your logging system. The Shipping stage is capable of this filtering as well because it has even more awareness of the fields present in telemetry. Anything you can do to keep PII and ePHI from landing in a widely viewable database, you should do; your organization's lawyers will thank you.

Summary

- Standardizing the format of how telemetry emits from your production code makes your telemetry system easier to maintain overall.
- Your Emitting-stage systems encode your standardized telemetry, whereas your Shipping-stage systems decode it for further processing. This process is made easier when telemetry format standards are being used.
- A well-written set of telemetry event standards reduces your need for expensive regular expressions (see chapter 11) in your shipping stage.
- Structured logging frameworks make encoding into negotiated standard formats much easier, allowing emitting telemetry into novel formats such as TCP sockets and email.
- Structured logging is the first place you can start making your telemetry tamper-evident, such as adding checksum fields for key fields. (See chapter 15 for more on this topic.) Defending your telemetry from the point it enters the pipeline makes your telemetry more defensible in court.
- Structured logging frameworks have three components: loggers, formatters, and writers. Loggers are used by production code to emit telemetry. Formatters take that code and reformat it into standards for use in the Shipping stage. Writers send the formatted telemetry to the next step in the Shipping stage. Each structured logging framework likely calls these components by different names, but the concepts are the same.
- Most modern programming languages have structured logging built in or available as an add-on module. You should use structured loggers for your centralized logging needs instead of simply opening a file and writing to it.

- You are allowed to have more than one telemetry format standard! You want as many things to use a standard as possible, and sometimes, that means using more than one.
- During the format selection process, definitely test parsing speeds. Built-in parsers for JSON have seen radical improvement since 2010, but that doesn't mean other formats can't fill the need.
- Selecting a telemetry format has as much to do with the humans involved in the process as with the technical systems involved. The optimal technical solution sometimes isn't the optimal political one.
- Implementing your telemetry format in a structured logger requires modifying the formatter or writer components; which kind to update depends on the structured logger itself.
- Emitting telemetry locally, such as to stdout or to a file, is lightweight on the production code but requires additional telemetry components coexecuting with the code to move emitted telemetry further into the Shipping stage. These components compete with your production code for resources; you will need to decide whether this parasitic load is acceptable versus adding complexity to your production code.
- Emitting telemetry remotely—such as to a queue, stream, or API—reduces the need for additional telemetry software competing with your production code. But the added complexity of handling telemetry network and service outages will increase the complexity of telemetry-handling code in your production software. You will need to decide whether this complexity is acceptable versus using purpose-built shipping software like Filebeat and Fluentd.
- Beyond encoding your telemetry in a standard format, structured loggers support several other telemetry system goals. Writers can emit to novel targets such as a raw TCP socket. Formatters can add checksum fields to make your telemetry tamper-evident. Formatters are your first line of defense in keeping PII out of your telemetry.
- Dedicated Shipping-stage frameworks like Logstash and Fluentd have many prebuilt parsers for formats, making them convenient to use. Still test parsing performance, though! Convenience often has a cost.
- When parsing telemetry, consider the performance trade-off between the convenience of interpreted languages versus the deployment challenges of compiled languages. Interpreted languages like Ruby often perform worse than compiled languages like Go or Java.
- Building your logging standards around your most efficient parsers will pay technical dividends. (The political dividends are up to you.)

13
Using more nonfile emitting techniques

> **This chapter covers**
> - Sending telemetry using sockets/datagrams
> - Getting telemetry out of containers or FaaS
> - Encrypting telemetry over datagrams

In this chapter, we cover emitting telemetry using additional methods other than files (section 2.1.1) or the standard output (also known as the console or stdout; section 2.1.3). Chapters 2 and 3 covered emitting techniques that also aren't files or the standard output:

- The system logger, such as Syslog or Windows Event Log (section 2.1.2).
- Queues and streams (section 3.1.2), with chapter 8 giving complete sample architectures using queues and streams.
- SaaS APIs (section 3.1.3), useful for delegating Shipping- and Presentation-stage services to a third party. The same technique is useful for technical organizations that require use of API endpoints for everything rather than other techniques, such as queues.

- Directly into storage, bypassing the need for any further Shipping-stage systems (section 3.1.1).

This chapter will be adding more emitting techniques to our toolkit to handle additional cases. We will be looking at both container and FaaS (also known as serverless) environments, where writing files is a definite anti-pattern. Some serverless platforms lack a system logger, so that method is not available. Although the Kubernetes standard-output handler is highly featured, politics and telemetry formatting standards can make that telemetry delivery service less attractive than bypassing it.

Never forget the role that politics plays in telemetry system design! Section 10.3.2 described the telemetry systems in use for the Loyalty Programs department of a hypothetical global airline. This department operated a subsite on the airline's main website, which was maintained by a different department. Does Loyalty Programs use the built-in telemetry systems from this other department, which does things quite differently, or does it build its own, which is more compatible with the rest of the department's systems? Politics is the reason behind most seemingly strange technical choices.

Section 13.1 covers designing for socket (TCP)- and datagram (UDP)-based emitters. Section 13.2 dives into handling telemetry in container and serverless production code.

13.1 Designing for socket- and datagram-based emitters

This section covers building Shipping-stage components that use straight TCP or UDP, rather than an application protocol like HTTP, Redis, and Kafka. I'm using the Shipping stage for a component in production code in the way I did back in chapter 3, because moving telemetry off the box that generated it is the role of the Shipping stage. In light of the structured loggers we built in chapter 12, a writer that writes to the network is a Shipping-stage component, even though the logger and formatter parts of the structured logger are definitely Emitting-stage components. We saw this split in figure 12.1, reproduced here as figure 13.1.

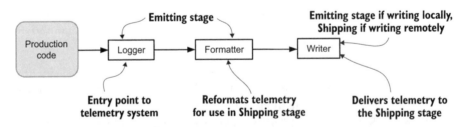

Figure 13.1   Elements of a structured logger: logger, formatter, and writer. The logger is the entry point into the structured logger, called from production code. The formatter reformats telemetry to be acceptable to the Shipping stage. The writer is part of the Emitting stage if it emits locally, such as to a file or the system log. The writer is part of the Shipping stage if it emits remotely over the network, such as to a Redis server, Kafka cluster, or HTTP API.

Making your writer use a raw TCP socket or UDP datagram makes it part of the Shipping stage, even though it is attached to the Emitting stage. This leads to a question: Why use TCP or UDP when application protocols likely have better handling for network problems? Application protocols do have better handling of network problems, which is why I cover them in most of the part 1 chapters. But modern infrastructures often have many containers, virtual machines, logical partitions, slices, and zones running on the same physical computing hardware. Under such conditions, networking problems such as packet loss, out-of-order arrival, routing flops, and switch resets are much, much less likely to occur. Simpler networks allow simpler networking protocols to work, which means that

- Your production software will have less code dedicated to telemetry system use, making it easier to ship.
- For microservices, not having to use an expensive (and expansive) library like Kafka makes for a much smaller deliverable binary.
- Not having to support a telemetry system application protocol means that you have one fewer module to include in your production software—one fewer module to keep track of dependencies, one fewer module to handle for security vulnerabilities, and less overall code to contain bugs.

The benefits of using TCP or UDP for telemetry delivery are felt less in large monolithic codebases that already have expansive software dependencies and more in mini- and microservices systems that are built to do a few things well. Simpler software has fewer edge cases to debug (in theory). Figure 13.2 shows how using simple networking for telemetry shipping can work in practice with Kubernetes and UDP.

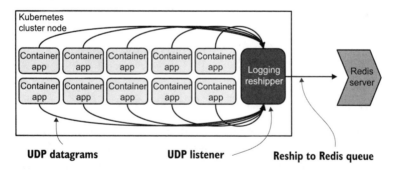

Figure 13.2   Ten containerized apps on a Kubernetes cluster node send UDP datagrams to a logging reshipper running on the same node. Then the reshipper delivers telemetry to a Redis server as part of a queue. This pattern, having a dedicated app for a specific metafunction like logging, is sometimes called the sidecar pattern.

Figure 13.2 shows a Kubernetes cluster node with a group of container applications, and a single container called a logging reshipper. The application containers send UDP packets to the logging reshipper over the internal Kubernetes network. Then the logging reshipper repackages telemetry and sends it out to a Redis server and the greater Shipping stage. The pattern of having a dedicated container for a utility or proxy, such as a logging function like this one, is called the *sidecar pattern*.

The service that performs the reshipping doesn't have to be another container, however. The reshipper can be a process on the Kubernetes node itself. Either will work, because both a process and another container have access to the same internal network. Use whatever works best for your service discovery systems. This pattern also works for the logical partitions (LPARs) on mainframes, as well as virtual machines on a VMware ESX host.

To demonstrate how the network in figure 13.2 works, we will look at a pair of listings. Listing 13.1 is a simple echo server that receives data through UDP and prints it to the console. We will use this echo server for testing listing 13.2.

Listing 13.1   A simple Python UDP echo server to use for testing

```
import socket

host = "127.0.1.2"        Imports socket library, and
port = 9201               sets our server and port

telemetry_in = socket.socket(     Creates our socket object
    socket.AF_INET,               using IPv4 and UDP
    socket.SOCK_DGRAM)

telemetry_in.bind((host, port))    ◁──  Starts our script listening on
                                         the given address and port
while 1:
    data, addr = telemetry_in.recvfrom(8192)   ◁──  Sets the receive buffer
    try:                                             to 8 KB, setting a data
        value = data.decode('utf8')   ◁──           and address variable
        print(value)
    except:                          Decodes the data as UTF-8
        print("Invalid data received.")


telemetry_in.close()
```

Listing 13.1 is a simple UDP echo server. All it does is print what it receives to the console, after making sure that the data it received is UTF-8 formatted. Using 127.0.1.2 as an address means that the server will listen on your computer's localhost network. Port 9201 is high enough that it isn't considered to be privileged (privilege ports are 1 through 1024), so unprivileged users can use it. If you have netcat installed (the nc command), you can test with

```
echo -n "Hello there!" | nc -u 127.0.1.2 9201
```

This code should cause "Hello there!" to be printed by the listing 13.1 script. Using -n for echo means to not send a line feed, and -u for nc tells it to use UDP instead of TCP.

Now that we have a way to see UDP output, we need to look at listing 13.2. Listing 13.2 is listing 12.6 rewritten to include emitting telemetry by way of UDP. Listing 12.6 demonstrates how structured loggers work and can be updated to emit arbitrary context-related telemetry. For more on what listing 12.6 is doing, see section 12.2. Listing 13.6 contains a few changes from 12.6, which are boldfaced.

> **NOTE** To run listing 13.2, you need to save listing 12.4 as a file named `internalrenderer.py` in the same directory in which you run this script and also install the `structlog` Python module. The full version of listing 13.2 is in the code repository.

Listing 13.2 The structured logger change to emit through UDP

```python
import logging
import datetime
import sys
import socket                                              Imports the socket library
import os                                                  so we can use UDP
import json
from internalrenderer import (InternalRenderer)            Imports the InternalRenderer
from structlog import (                                    (listing 12.4) for custom log
  get_logger,                                              formatting
  configure,
)
from structlog.stdlib import (
  LoggerFactory,
  BoundLogger,
  add_log_level,
)
from structlog.processors import (
  JSONRenderer,
  UnicodeDecoder,
  TimeStamper
)
from logging.handlers import (              Imports the DatagramHandler
  DatagramHandler,                          from structlog so we can modify it
)

class PlainDatagramHandler(DatagramHandler):      Overrides the emit() function in
  def emit(self, record):                          DatagramHandler to not pickle output
    try:
      s = record.msg                               Extracts the telemetry to export
      self.send(s.encode('utf8'))                  from the Python LogRecord
    except Exception:
      self.handleError(record)

logging.basicConfig(
  format="%(message)s",                            Tells the writer to use
  handlers=[                                       our overridden class
    PlainDatagramHandler('127.0.1.2', 9201)        for emitting
  ],
  level=logging.INFO,
```

Sends the telemetry over UDP, encoded in UTF-8

```
    )

    __release__ = "0.7.1"
    __commit__ = "f0d00b1"

    configure(
      processors=[
        TimeStamper(fmt="iso"),
        UnicodeDecoder(),
        add_log_level,
        InternalRenderer(),
      ],
      context_class=dict,
      logger_factory=LoggerFactory(),
      wrapper_class=BoundLogger,
      cache_logger_on_first_use=False
    )

    logger = get_logger()

    [... functions defining the logger ...]
```

The list of formatters our logger will use, including our internal format

Object to use in logger functions; instantiates all the previous configuration

If everything goes to plan, running listing 13.2 like info("*Profile image updated*", metadata, ["*account_id*", "*feature_flags*"]) when you have listing 13.1 running on the same machine should get output like this in the window running the listing 13.1 script:

```
2023-02-19T01:01:24.251261Z Profile image updated -- {"hostname": "k8s-
➡ 14.euc1.prod.internal", "pid": 11321, "release": "0.7.1", "commit":
➡ "f0d00b1", "account_id": "1515323", "feature_flags": {"new_login": true,
➡ "new_profile": false}, "level": "info"}
```

To show how we get from info("*Profile image updated*", metadata, ["*account_id*", "*feature_flags*"]) to the preceding result requires understanding how structured loggers work. This topic was covered in detail in chapter 12, but the logger, formatter, and writer components are all present in this listing. Figure 13.3 shows those components and the logical flow.

We are overriding the DatagramHandler that ships with Python's structlog module to make our UDP emitter because of a Pythonism. The stock DatagramHandler emits telemetry *pickled*, which is a Python-specific serialized format for passing objects that few other systems support. The PlainDatagramHandler I built in listing 13.2 skips the pickling step and instead emits strings. I'm doing this because a system that emits plain strings is more interoperable with other systems that aren't running Python themselves.

Also note that the UDP emissions here aren't encrypted in any way in transit, so they are best suited to emit over fully trusted networks. The sidecar pattern, in which the emissions occur entirely over the internal network of a hypervisor or host machine, is a good use case.

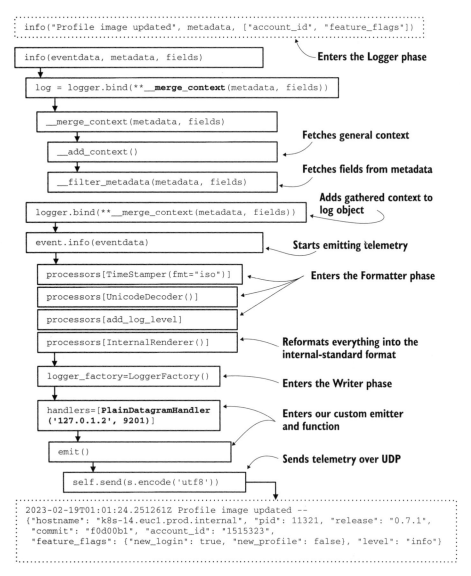

Figure 13.3 Logical flow of our emitted telemetry from where it enters the logger to when it emits over UDP. During the logger phase, the `__add_context()` and `__filter_metadata()` functions provide additional context. During the formatter phase, the Timestamper processor adds a timestamp in ISO-8601 format, ensures that strings are encoded correctly, adds the log level (`Info`), and finally reformats the telemetry into the internal standard. In the writer phase, the string is moved into our custom handler, where it is sent over a UDP socket to 127.0.1.2. port 9201. Section 12.2 goes deeper into the formatter phase of this execution.

It's worth our while to look at ways to receive streams of UDP events, so let's take a look at how Logstash and Fluentd are configured to consume UDP inputs. First up is

Elastic's Logstash. In Logstash, inbound telemetry is configured in `input {}` blocks; telemetry enrichment happens later in `filter {}` stages and is covered more in part 1:

```
input {
  udp {
    host  => "172.28.5.128"
    port  => 9201
    type  => "metrics"
    codec => plain {
      charset => "UTF8"
    }
  }

  udp {
    host  => "172.28.5.128"
    port  => 9202
    type  => "exceptions"
    codec => plain {
      charset => "UTF8"
    }
  }
}
```

We see two separate listeners set up here—one named metrics on port 9201 and a second named exceptions on port 9202. As with the simple UDP echo server from listing 13.1, we are configuring these listeners to expect UTF8-encoded data. We accomplish this task through the codec definition on both listeners. Open source Fluentd handles the inputs similarly:

```
<source>
  @type udp
  tag metrics
  bind 172.28.5.128
  port 9201
</source>

<source>
  @type udp
  tag exceptions
  bind 172.28.5.128
  port 9202
</source>
```

Fluentd doesn't have an expectation for UTF-8 the way Logstash does, but we do see two listeners set up. When we use an extremely lightweight shipper to move telemetry to a sidecar, the sidecar can use heavier shipping technologies (in terms of code complexity) to shield the simple functions and containers from that burden. Figure 13.4 reframes figure 13.2, talking to Kafka streams instead of a Redis queue.

The Kafka client is a fairly complex chunk of code. Although that complexity might not matter in a large monolith that already has a lot of code complexity, adding the

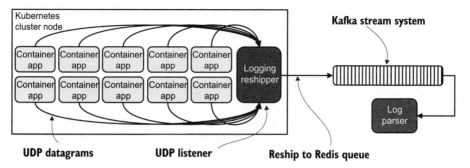

Figure 13.4   Moving telemetry from simple containerized applications and into the Shipping stage. The first leg of travel happens over UDP on the internal network of the Kubernetes cluster node, delivering to a logging reshipper sidecar. Then the sidecar reships telemetry to Kafka topics, where a log parser box in the Shipping stage subscribes to topics to further enrich telemetry. This architecture allows the containerized applications to avoid having the complex Kafka client library installed on each of them.

Kafka client as part of the logging system can add substantially to the size of a micro-service. A transport like UDP will require loading a sockets library into the microservice, which is likely already loaded due to the API-driven nature of many microservices architectures (telemetry without more libraries!).

Use of UDP for sending logging data goes back decades. Internet Engineering Task Force RFC 3164, defined in August 2001, formalized the de facto Syslog standard and set UDP/514 as the official Syslog port. Syslog had been using UDP/514 for many years before the standardization effort. As mentioned in chapter 2, hardware vendors often emit in Syslog format because it is a standardized format and therefore unlikely to change. Using UDP for your telemetry has a deep history behind it. Besides, after HTTP/3 gains widespread adoption, HTTP APIs will be using UDP as well.

Straight TCP sockets can also be used similarly to how figure 13.4 uses UDP datagrams. TCP is somewhat heavier in terms of effect on processing, because unless care is taken, the act of setting up a TCP connection can block production code while the telemetry is sent. UDP is connectionless, so it can be safely fired and forgotten, and therefore nonblocking. A portion of the heaviness in application protocols such as AMQP (RabbitMQ) and Kafka is due to the networking stack TCP brings with it.

As with UDP, if your telemetry is emitting across the in-memory network of a hypervisor, kernel, or mainframe, the chance that network problems will slow your TCP connections is greatly reduced. Because of this simplicity, a TCP-based emitter is less likely to need additional code to handle retries in case of a reset connection, among other issues.

One thing TCP has that UDP lacks (easily) is the ability to use Transport Layer Security (TLS): encryption. If your telemetry system has even the possibility of handling regulated information such as privacy or health information, regulation requires encryption of such regulated information in transit. Adding a TLS negotiation to your telemetry will slow things down, but it will also make your TCP telemetry transmission technique easier to justify to external auditors.

Exercise 13.1

Pair protocols from column A with attributes in column B.

Protocols:	Attributes:
TCP	Connectionless: fire and forget
TCP	Connection-oriented: tracks connection state
TCP	Will retry if the network glitches
TCP	Useful on fully private in-memory networks
UDP	The basis of application protocols like AQMP and Kafka
UDP	The basis of server protocols like Syslog and SNMP
UDP	Relies on the operating system to handle retries
UDP	Relies on the application to handle retries

Exercise 13.2

Which of the following is the most correct *definition* for the Sidecar Pattern in a Kubernetes system?

a A service on the cluster host that reships all output to containerd logs to a Kafka stream

b A container that serves as a log forwarder for all containers in a cluster node

c A network endpoint that serves a utility purpose, such as a proxy, relay, or service discovery

d A container that serves a utility purpose, such as a proxy, relay, or local service endpoint for all containers in a cluster node

13.2 *Emitting and shipping for container- and serverless-based code*

This section is about handling telemetry for platforms that don't have the full suite of operating system assumptions available to them: Kubernetes and other container-management frameworks, and FaaS (also known as serverless). *Serverless* is a style of computing popularized by AWS Lambda; since then, Azure Functions and Google Cloud Functions have emerged in the major public clouds. Serverless runs functions on cloud-provider managed servers and allocation, so all the developer has to worry about is triggering the function and consuming the output.

Container and serverless both consider small, targeted applications that do one thing well to be the ideal thing to run on either platform. Small applications are easier to understand and, therefore, to debug. Small applications limit the fault domain, so bugs don't spread when something goes wrong. As discussed in section 13.1, small applications need to consider their telemetry needs, and requiring heavy clients like the Kafka client can make the small application look more like a medium-size application. Getting telemetry out of container- and serverless-based systems is a little different from large applications running on servers and virtual machines.

Section 13.2.1 dives into Kubernetes and containerd, as well as the many ways to get telemetry out of there. Section 13.2.2 looks into serverless systems and the challenges those systems face for telemetry.

13.2.1 Emitting and shipping from containerd-based code

This section is about getting telemetry out of Kubernetes-based applications. Kubernetes has a lot working in its favor in the form of the capabilities of the containerd and Kubernetes platforms. We talked a little about this topic in section 4.2, noting that containerd is able to ship the standard output (stdout) to the host's journald system (if the host is a Linux system) by way of Kubernetes. But Kubernetes is able to direct stdout to many places:

- `json-file`—The default; stores telemetry in files on the host. (See chapter 3 for moving telemetry in log files into the rest of the telemetry system.)
- `syslog`—Sends telemetry to Syslog on the host but not across the network. (See chapters 2–4 for more about Syslog and telemetry.)
- `journald`—Works only if the host is a Linux machine, but sends telemetry to the journald process. journald is part of the systemd family of programs.
- `etwlogs`—Uses Event Tracing for Windows to send telemetry, which requires the host to be running Windows.
- `fluentd`—Sends telemetry to a Fluentd daemon running on the host.
- `gelf`—Sends Graylog Extended Formatted telemetry to a network endpoint, which can be Graylog, Fluentd, Logstash, or others.
- `splunk`—Sends telemetry to a Splunk endpoint, which can be a self-hosted or cloud-hosted Splunk.
- `awslogs`—Sends telemetry to Amazon's CloudWatch Logs service.
- `gcplogs`—Sends telemetry to Google's Cloud Platform Logging service.

All the methods in the preceding list require the application running in Docker (for development environments) or Kubernetes (for production environments) to send telemetry out through the standard output. (See section 2.1.3 for details on emitting to stdout.) If stdout is the only method to send centralized logging, metrics, and observability telemetry, your telemetry format standard will need to be able to encode all three styles. Figure 13.5 slightly updates figure 7.7.

The routing topology shown in figure 13.5 is made possible because the format of the telemetry—context-related telemetry encoded by the production systems themselves—allows the router to quickly determine what kind of telemetry it is looking at. If the telemetry format is pure JSON, it could be that a top-level field named `style`—

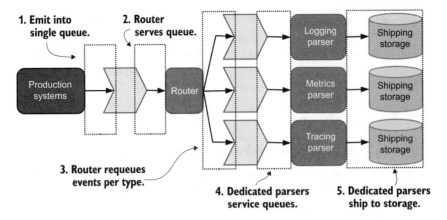

1. Emit into single queue.

2. Router serves queue.

Production systems

Router

Logging parser

Metrics parser

Tracing parser

Shipping storage

Shipping storage

Shipping storage

3. Router requeues events per type.

4. Dedicated parsers service queues.

5. Dedicated parsers ship to storage.

Figure 13.5 How a unified telemetry format ends up with appropriate systems parsing each style of telemetry. Telemetry leaves the production systems in a single stream. Then a router looks at each item of telemetry and determines how to route the telemetry based on details in the telemetry. After routing, telemetry is parsed and stored.

an example follows—is required to be set to one of three values (logs, metrics, or traces—the three Pillars of Observability).

```
{
  "style": "metrics",
  "metric_name": "pdf_pages",
  "metric_value": 3
}
```

Our router deserializes the JSON and looks for a single field, ignoring the rest. Then the router decides where to send that telemetry based on the contents of that field. If our container-based application emits both metrics and logging through the same channel, so long as the application sets the style field correctly, telemetry will end up in the right places. Using a router in this way requires any program emitting into the telemetry pipeline to do so with a common format (or one of a few common formats; human politics often require compromise).

Kubernetes doesn't strictly require telemetry to be emitted through stdout, however. Most distributed tracing systems in use in the early 2020s have a strong preference for emitting to an API—often, a SaaS provider's API—over encoding into a string and parsing later. Distributed tracing systems are an interesting case for telemetry and small services, because tracing needs to run alongside the production code to do the work it needs to do. The code-complexity charge has already been paid by the time telemetry needs to be emitted. Figure 13.6 shows a split of this nature, with tracing telemetry going over API to Honeycomb.io, and the rest going through stdout and into the Kubernetes system.

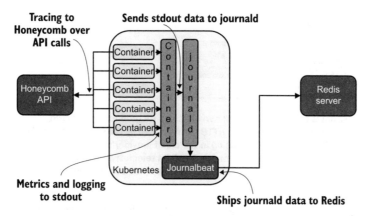

Figure 13.6   Here, containerd applications split their telemetry delivery. Tracing is sent to an API at Honeycomb.io, where metrics and logging telemetry emit through standard out. Standard out is gathered by containerd and Kafka and then sent into journald on the Kubernetes host (a Linux system). Journalbeat, a program from Elastic, reads journald and sends telemetry into a Redis server for processing later. Even tiny containers can follow this pattern and not significantly increase code complexity.

13.2.2 *Emitting and shipping from serverless-based code*

This section is about getting telemetry out of serverless, also known as FaaS-based code. Serverless as a style of computing took off with the introduction of AWS's Lambda service, which offers API-driven ways to trigger execution of code. Unlike container platforms like Kubernetes, serverless systems are running in platforms built by cloud providers and inherit the provider's logging capabilities and preferences. The three major serverless systems send their logs to:

- AWS Lambda logs stdout into CloudWatch logs, an API- and S3 (file object)-based service.
- Azure Functions logs stdout into a Storage Account or the Monitor Logs service, based on Log Analytics.
- Google Functions logs stdout into a Cloud Console, where you can query logs.

These default log targets are designed to be flexible enough for many needs, but *many needs* often doesn't overlap with *your needs.* For a startup looking to avoid the complexity of maintaining Kubernetes clusters, serverless looks like an amazing way to focus on what the company does best: write code that makes money. Such a startup is likely to be using the latest software development techniques, which means adopting distributed tracing. Both Azure (Application Insights) and Amazon AWS (X-Ray) now have API-driven tracing solutions. That serverless-using startup is almost definitely embracing HTTP APIs for its tracing system. Further, such a startup is likely to be using distributed tracing as its primary telemetry method, bundling metrics and centralized logging. Figure 13.7 shows this pattern.

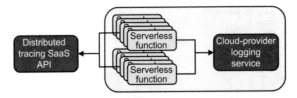

Figure 13.7 Telemetry flows for a startup using serverless as its production platform. Distributed-tracing telemetry flows directly to an HTTP API managed by the distributed tracing vendor. Everything else (what there is of it) ends up in the cloud provider's logging service. A startup of this nature is likely using distributed tracing for all its telemetry needs and may use the logging service more as a place to look up exceptions that killed computation early.

Contrast this latest and greatest startup with a much older company looking to adopt new techniques for doing what it does. A company of this type—old—has long-established patterns of computing and telemetry. Rather than radically reinvent everything, including telemetry, a company like this one will seek to speed adoption of the new technology by integrating what it can into existing telemetry services. Whereas the startup paid other people to handle telemetry, this older company can use existing infrastructure.

This older company also faces the code-complexity problem I've spoken about a few times in this chapter. The existing systems, which aren't serverless, can safely assume that the system logger is there and configured to centralize whatever is sent to it. The system logger for serverless platforms looks nothing like the Windows, Linux, or Kubernetes system loggers, which presents a challenge if their existing telemetry systems assume that Event Log (Windows) or Syslog (Linux) are in use. This company is in better shape if it engineered around the system logger by using other techniques, such as queues, streams, and APIs:

- If it built telemetry assuming that the system logger is present, adopting serverless will require the company to create novel telemetry delivery methods or engineer a new solution for consuming the cloud provider's logging store for serverless logs.
- If it built telemetry by using techniques such as streams, queues, and APIs, it will need to consider code complexity in serverless functions.

The simpler the function, the more onerous it becomes to have a thick set of libraries just to emit an event describing the successful transaction. Deciding whether to keep that library or add an abstraction layer to simplify the overall code is made easier by the fact that serverless is a cloud-provider offering. All the major cloud providers have easy-to-use ways to submit jobs to queues (and in some cases, streams as well). Figure 13.8 shows one way to embrace the convenience of provider-based queues.

Figure 13.8 shows two telemetry flows, one using traditional computing and the other using serverless. To address the code-complexity problem of putting the RabbitMQ client in every serverless function, this company instead uses the simple-to-use queue

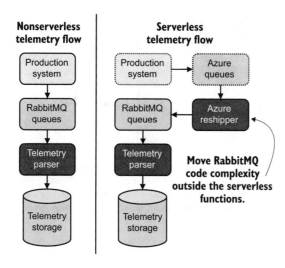

Figure 13.8 Two forms of telemetry delivery, one using traditional computing (left) and the other using serverless (right). Cloud-provider services have dotted borders. This architecture shields the serverless-based production systems from having to load the complex RabbitMQ client to ship telemetry; instead, it uses the much simpler cloud-provider hooks.

system that's native to the cloud provider. It also built a new Shipping-stage system that pops telemetry off the native cloud-provider queuing system and pushes events into the RabbitMQ system. From there, telemetry flows as it does for the traditional computing flows. The extra step in the telemetry pipeline adds latency—it takes data longer to hit storage and be searchable versus traditional computing—but enables the same Presentation-stage systems to support both traditional and serverless systems.

This architecture is not without risk. The job-size limit for the native cloud-provider queuing system, for example, is likely much, much smaller than the payload size of RabbitMQ (which can go up to 512 MB). Azure Queues limits jobs to 64 KB, and AWS's Simple Queuing Service limits them to 256 KB. If the events that our example company produces sometimes exceed the size limit of the cloud-provider native queues, the reshipper is going to have to deal with reassembly of events from multiple jobs (or possibly compression/decompression cycles).

Although serverless lacks a system logger that looks like what Linux and Windows run, the Syslog protocol works over a network. Section 2.1.2 focused on emitting to the system logger in detail, but as a reminder, Syslog classes in programming frameworks allow sending Syslog messages to remote servers. Because Syslog works over UDP, it doesn't require loading a complex client that performs service discovery to detect the architecture of a target service, the way that Kafka and RabbitMQ do. Syslog is small. If our older company is already using Syslog, its conversion to serverless can be pretty easy. Figure 13.9 shows how Syslog-based serverless could integrate with an existing Syslog-based telemetry shipping system.

Interestingly, a company that is based on something as constrained as Syslog has an easier time integrating a radically new computing technology than a company that uses direct-to-stream or direct-to-queue telemetry techniques. Because the Syslog RFCs do not uniformly describe how encryption is supported, Syslog-based telemetry will be sent unencrypted. This plain-text transmission is a major problem if the telemetry system has

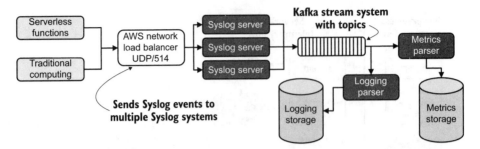

Figure 13.9   A Syslog-based telemetry system involving both traditional and serverless computing. Both techniques emit telemetry over UDP port 514. They also have metrics and logging parsers listening to dedicated topics that parse metrics and logging telemetry, respectively, to store in dedicated storage. For this company, serverless doesn't present much of a telemetry challenge.

even the possibility of containing regulated information, such as privacy and health information, because regulation governing such protected information often requires end-to-end encryption.

Exercise 13.3

In the following list, which are constraints facing telemetry flow in FaaS (serverless) environments?

- Complete reliance on emitting telemetry through stdout
- The cloud provider's opinionated storage system for telemetry emitted through stdout
- Lack of queue or stream support
- Lack of system logger support
- The size limit of jobs in the cloud provider's queues

13.3   *Encrypting UDP-based telemetry*

Taking a page from section 13.1, how would we build a UDP-based telemetry emitter that would be secure when used over an untrusted (for regulatory values of untrusted) network? Socket libraries are relatively cheap, in terms of code complexity, and cryptographic libraries are often already loaded if the function performs any API work. Listing 13.3 is a Python formatter class (see section 12.2 for far more on the role of formatters in structured logging) that we can use with the structured logger we worked with in section 13.1.

NOTE   This listing uses an encryption key directly in the code, which is clearly a bad idea. I use it here to demonstrate the concept. It is a best practice to deliver secrets through a channel other than code, such as environmental variables or a system like Hashicorp's Vault. To run this code, you need to install the cryptography Python module, which includes fernet.

Listing 13.3 A formatter named `Encrypter`, written in Python

```python
from cryptography.fernet import Fernet
import json
import base64


class Encrypter(object):

    def __init__(self):
        bkey = b'this is a bad key -- do not use.'
        self._key = base64.b64encode(bkey)
        self._key_version = '1.0'

    def __call__(self, logger, name, event_dict):
        enc_event = { 'kver': self._key_version }
        cipher = Fernet(self._key)
        safe_event = cipher.encrypt(
            event_dict.encode('utf8'))
        enc_event['event'] =
            base64.b64encode(safe_event).decode('utf8')
        return json.dumps(enc_event)
```

Imports the symmetric encryption helper from the cryptography module

The encryption key to use. Don't use this one.

Sets the Fernet key by base64-encoding the binary key; runs on program start

Sets the key version, used by the decrypter

Creates the Fernet cipher, using the key set during program start

Encrypts our telemetry, using the Fernet cipher, and sets the 'event' attribute

JSON serializes our telemetry.

Telemetry passing through this formatter will get encrypted and should look like this,

```
{"kver": "1.0", "event": "Z0FBQUFBQmZ[...cut for space...]MswzA"}
```

returning a two-element JSON hash, with kver setting the key version and event containing the base64-encoded encrypted hash. Updating the script in listing 13.2 to use this new formatter requires changing two lines of code, shown in listing 13.4. Changes are boldfaced. I used the Fernet helper for symmetric cryptography that Python provides because it uses safe defaults; this saves me from potentially making a security-breaking mistake in my selection of encryption algorithm, cipher, key lengths, and initialization vectors. (Fernet uses AES in CBC mode with a 128-bit key, AES256 for HMAC, and random Initialization Vector; reasonably safe, for early-2020s values of "safe.") To make sure that this listing will import our encrypter module, rename listing 13.3 encrypter.py in the same directory as listing 13.4.

Listing 13.4 Updating listing 13.2 to use the Encrypter

```python
[...]
from internalrenderer import (InternalRenderer)
from encrypter import (Encrypter)
from structlog import (
    get_logger,
    configure,
)
[...]
configure(
    processors=[
        TimeStamper(fmt="iso"),
```

```
      UnicodeDecoder(),          ┐   Appends Encrypter() to the
      add_log_level,             │   processors, encrypting the
      InternalRenderer(),        │   InternalRenderer() format
      Encrypter(),          ◄────┘
   ],
[...]
```

If you run the UDP echo server from listing 13.1 and then run listing 13.4, you will see our encrypted output with kver and event values. Encrypting in this way, at the Application layer rather than the Transport layer, will make telemetry that might contain private or health information easier to pass auditorial scrutiny. Because this listing does not use recognizable TLS (sometimes known as HTTPS), you should expect more questions about your encryption methods. But as long as you get your key management right, use correct key sizes, and select a correct cipher, you should have little trouble convincing your auditors that this path is secure. Figure 13.10 shows how the new formatter fits into the structured logger.

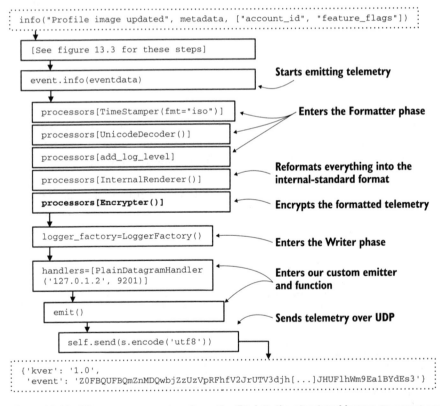

Figure 13.10 Where our `Encrypter` formatter fits into the structured logger. `Encrypter` follows `InternalRenderer`, so the `Encrypter` will be encrypting the formatted telemetry. As we see at the bottom, we have our kver key version and event crypt-text hash encoded as JSON. The UDP receiver uses the kver value to select the key to use to decrypt the telemetry.

To provide decryption, let's update our simple UDP echo server to decrypt and echo back our telemetry. Listing 13.5 updates listing 13.1 to decrypt the telemetry we are producing in listing 13.4. As with listing 13.3, you will need to install the `cryptography` Python module, which includes `fernet`.

Listing 13.5   A decrypting UDP echo server

```
from cryptography.fernet import Fernet
import socket
import json
import base64

host = "127.0.1.2"
port = 9201

badkey = b'this is a bad key -- do not use.'       Sets up the Fernet decryption object
decrypter = Fernet(base64.b64encode(badkey))        for use; runs at program start
telemetry_in = socket.socket(
  socket.AF_INET,
  socket.SOCK_DGRAM)

telemetry_in.bind((host, port))

while 1:
  data, addr = telemetry_in.recvfrom(8192)
  try:                                        Load the JSON from the
    value = data.decode('utf8')               UDP packet into a hash.
    print('Encrypted text: %s ' % value)
    enc_event = json.loads(value)                 Base64-decode the 'event'
    b64event = base64.b64decode(enc_event['event'])   attribute from the hash.
    try:
      event =                                     Attempt decrypting
        decrypter.decrypt(b64event).decode('utf8')   the event attribute.
    except:
      print('Failed decryption')
    print('Clear text: %s' % event)
  except:
    print("Invalid data received.")

telemetry_in.close()
```

To test the pair of programs, launch the listing 13.5 code first so that you have a UDP listener running. Second, run the listing 13.4 code. You should get output similar to this:

```
Encrypted text: {"kver": "1.0", "event":
  "Z0FBQUFBQmZnMUZvbVlMZEVTcE5qTExVbTJLb2w4UHc3XzZVdEZ66MHVKNFI5cnBobVBKTD
  hVY3ZVcWc0SUZ2eWprdFZsbm90d0tKaHo4WlRick9xR29rU1pVWWdPeG1ORG05UnJ0UmN5d
  VE4enllTGZVaVFYZ2JCcFN0N2hFQWUwS08tUUhGQU0yaFItSjZ6anphcTBPLU1lZWYyLWZ4
  TXlDDNDQ5N2dMcTNaTnRNaEw5TElXbHVlX2hBOGhHVTNvTTQ1MWStMGdRQ2d6U1Z2UUZSYjg
  0V09hd0ZEYUFYWWQ2YVpFaU53eWh2cCDMSФlЕZUFNUmJ3bm81VWhjNVVvvZ2YydDHhDMGg2R0
```

➥ dXYk1WZ18yektfdmRGRG"}
Clear text: 2023-02-19T18:39:36.090158Z Profile image updated -- {"hostname":
➥ "k8s-14.euc1.prod.internal", "pid": 15815, "release": "0.7.1",
➥ "commit": "f0d00b1", "account_id": "1515323", "feature_flags":
➥ {"new_login": true, "new_profile": false}, "level": "info"}

Because cryptographic functions are increasingly the cost of doing business over a network, they should be present in the runtime you are using for your serverless functions. Interpreted languages like Python have them shipping with the main language without having to import more modules. For compiled languages like Go, adding cryptographic functions will increase the final binary size somewhat, but the functions themselves are part of the base language.

> **WARNING**   I used Python's Fernet for a reason: it gives me an easy-to-use interface with safe defaults, so I didn't have to do a ton of research about what specific encryption options are safe today. I certainly could have encoded the Fernet defaults by using base encryption functions, but that approach would merely increase the surface area for bugs. If you decide to attempt encryption in your own code, it's preferable to use any similar safe-defaults interfaces present in your languages.

If you want more information about the role that encryption can play in telemetry systems, not just at the emitting stage, section 15.2 goes into more detail.

Summary

- A structured logger writer that emits to a remote location is part of the Shipping stage because it is involved in moving telemetry to a new location.
- Application protocols such as Kafka, AMQP (for RabbitMQ), and other distributed system applications often require large libraries and clients to be loaded into your production code, which increases the code complexity of your production code.
- Microservices are especially sensitive to code complexity. Their job is to be a small, maintainable piece of code; adding a heavy client for telemetry can create a serious increase in complexity.
- Monoliths can be quite complex with respect to code, so they are far less affected when a heavy application protocol is picked to move telemetry.
- Containers, virtual machines, logical partitions, slices, and zones have in-memory networks based in their hypervisor, kernel, or mainframe. These networks are far more reliable than cloud or hardware networks, allowing you to use simpler protocols safely to move telemetry.
- Transmitting telemetry over in-memory networks to a dedicated container (or equivalent), which is responsible for reshipping telemetry over heavy protocols, is called the sidecar pattern and is an effective way to shield your small containers and functions from complexity.

- Transmitting telemetry over TCP sockets or UDP datagrams over in-memory networks is far safer than using general networks and allows the use of simpler code in your containers and functions.
- If you are using a structured logger in your telemetry (see chapter 12), use a writer to build your TCP- or UDP-based logger. Some logging frameworks have a socket (TCP) or datagram (UDP) writer built in or available for you to customize.
- UDP-based writers don't have easy access to TLS, so they are best suited for in-memory network emissions to limit the "in the clear" exposure they experience.
- TCP-based writers do have access to TLS, which makes them more suitable for use over general networks.
- The Syslog protocol uses UDP port 514 by standard (RFC 3164 August 2001), so there is a long history of using UDP for telemetry.
- The HTTP/3 protocol is based on UDP, so expect increasing sophistication with UDP networking during the 2020s.
- Kubernetes offers a wide variety of ways to reship the standard output from containers to somewhere more interesting, such as Syslog, Event Tracing for Windows, and SaaS products like Splunk.
- Even though Kubernetes has a lot of shipping capabilities, the telemetry styles you use sometimes require another method. This requirement results in split telemetry flows, such as stdout for logging and a Datadog API call for metrics.
- Distributed tracing systems (at least in the early 2020s) have strong preferences for API-driven telemetry. Fortunately, using distributed tracing means that the code-complexity charge is already paid when it comes time to emit.
- If multiple telemetry styles are emitting through the Kubernetes logger, you need to encode ways to tell each style apart into the telemetry format itself. This approach enables a Shipping-stage component to route each item of telemetry to the correct parsers.
- All serverless frameworks emit logs into vendor-specific log-searching frameworks, which isn't suitable for all telemetry needs but is still better than digging through files by hand.
- As with Kubernetes, serverless leads to split telemetry flows for specific needs due to the limits of the default loggers. Some organizations will forgo using the default logger and will instead use a SaaS platform.
- When older organizations with established computing patterns adopt serverless, they often try to integrate serverless into their existing telemetry flows. If those flows are based on logging to files or using the system logger, these organizations will need to come up with new ways to get telemetry into their existing systems.

- Because serverless frameworks are made by cloud providers, they often provide easy ways to get data into other provider systems such as queues, which helps the code-complexity problem.
- The old Syslog protocol, based on UDP port 514, still works over networks. An older company that is still using Syslog can continue to use Syslog in serverless, so long as it pays attention to what telemetry requires encryption.
- Although using TLS with UDP is tricky, you can still use encryption to wrap telemetry. Some cryptography modules in programming languages have convenience methods that make this process less fraught with peril; use these methods. When used correctly, they will solve the auditor problem with respect to handling and safely transmitting regulated information.

Managing
cardinality in telemetry

This chapter covers

- How cardinality affects telemetry performance
- Ways to identify cardinality problems
- Techniques for managing cardinality

This chapter dives deep into one of the maintenance headaches of managing telemetry systems: cardinality in your storage systems. Here is the definition of cardinality from chapter 1:

> **DEFINITION** *Cardinality* is the term for index complexity—specifically, the number of unique combinations the fields in the index may produce. If you have fields A and B, where A has two possible values and B has three possible values, the cardinality of that index is A * B, or 2 * 3 = 6. Cardinality significantly affects search performance no matter what data storage system is being used.

All telemetry styles have searching telemetry as a key feature; searching is made faster through indexing, and indexing cardinality affects search performance.

Search performance is affected by many things besides indexing, such as search frequency and the shape of the data. Cardinality of the data and indices, however, is the problem that forces compromise by database makers. Because of this compromise, each storage system handles indexing and cardinality differently. Also different for each storage system is the degree of impact cardinality has on search performance and other maintenance operations. Section 14.1 goes into detail about how cardinality affects common storage systems used for telemetry. To demonstrate cardinality concepts, let's take a look at an example metrics table (table 14.1).

Table 14.1   An example metrics table with field definitions

Field name	Field type	Indexed
account_id	long-int	*
subscription_id	long-int	*
timestamp	long-int	*
metric_name	string(32 char)	*
metric_value	double-float	

Table 14.1 is a simple table with five fields, four of them indexed. As a metrics table, it has a small amount of context-related telemetry in the form of the account_id and subscription_id fields. We also index metric_name to ease searching but do not index metric_value. To compute the cardinality of this table, first we need to look at how many unique values exist in each field in table 14.2.

Table 14.2   An example metrics table with field definitions and uniqueness

Field name	Field type	Indexed	Unique count
account_id	long-int	*	256,121
subscription_id	int	*	132
timestamp	long-int	*	One per row
metric_name	string(32 char)	*	1251
metric_value	double-float		

Right away, we see in table 14.2 that the timestamp field will be a problem due to how many unique values it has. Timestamp columns often get a dedicated index specifically for this problem, especially in a metrics systems, where time-based searches happen on just about every query. So if we have one index for the timestamp column, how much cardinality do we have for the other indexed columns?

```
256,121 accounts * 132 subscriptions * 1251 metric_names = 42,293,772,972
➥ potential combinations
```

That 42 billion is an incredibly large number, but it is a theoretical maximum of a compound (multifield) index. Because every account doesn't have every subscription, and because in this hypothetical case each account uses only 70% of the total metric_name values possible on average, we can rephrase our cardinality computation. If you know through other sources that accounts have on average 4.8 subscriptions associated with them over time, the math turns into

```
256,121 accounts * 4.8 subscriptions * (1251 * .7) metric_names =
➥ 1,076,568,767 actual combinations
```

One billion is a far better number but still quite high. How much cardinality is a problem, though? The answer depends on your storage systems. For a relational database like MS-SQL or Postgres, indexes like these are perfectly fine; the "account" table that has account_id as a primary key likely is as highly cardinal as this metrics table. For the time-series databases InfluxDB and Prometheus, this cardinality is crippling. For a SaaS provider like Honeycomb.io, you don't care about this cardinality, because it is the provider's problem (and if cardinality is a problem for the provider, it will make you care about it through its billing structure).

Search performance is a complex balancing act among indexes, data, use patterns, and the shape of the data being searched. If you are maintaining Presentation-stage systems for telemetry, you care about search performance. Although I can't go over every telemetry storage engine out there and describe how it reacts to cardinality (more are made every month), I can give you the tools to identify whether you are in trouble (section 14.1), as well as techniques for getting out of and avoiding trouble (section 14.2).

14.1 Identifying cardinality problems

This section is about identifying a cardinality problem in your telemetry storage systems. The broadest measure that you might have a cardinality problem is slow search performance, but that can be caused by many things. Symptoms of cardinality problems depend on your storage system, but include the following:

- *Slow search performance*—This symptom is the one that most people notice, because search performance is a primary feature of Presentation-stage systems. Unfortunately, many things other than a cardinality problem can cause slow search, but slow performance is a sign to look for that problem.
- *Increased memory use for normal operations*—Many storage systems keep indexes in memory. As those indexes grow, so does memory use. Most of these storage systems allow reading indexes from disk if they won't fit in memory, which greatly slows search performance. Relational databases like MySQL are famous for this pattern.
- *Increased memory use for routine scheduled operations*—Scheduled optimization procedures in some storage systems are affected by cardinality. InfluxDB (as of version 2.0) performs compaction operations regularly, and high cardinality leads to increased (often much increased) memory use compared with the rest of the time.

- *Decreases in ability to insert new data*—As indexes get larger, they need to be updated. Indexing efficiency varies by storage engine, and not all storage engines are good at it. The overhead of handling inserting new values into the indexes can, for some systems, scale up as the unique-value count increases, which in turn reduces the ability to insert new data into the system.
- *Increased time to allow querying after starting the database*—Some storage systems need to load indexes into memory before being able to query. The larger the indexes are, the longer this process takes. Because stateful systems like these may not be restarted often, this problem can surprise you at a bad time.
- *Increases in consumed disk space that scales higher than your ingestion rate*—Some storage systems keep indexes in separate files from table data. Each time you insert new data with a new unique value, the storage system needs to update the table data with the new value, as well as update any indexes and their files. In other systems, such as Elasticsearch, every new piece of data gets all fields, even if those fields have a null value. Therefore, if you have 10,000 fields, and a new event is inserted with 15 fields, that new event will have 9,985 nulled fields on it.

In this section, we will go over two broad types of storage system and the ways in which cardinality affects each type. Cardinality in time-series databases is covered in section 14.1.1, and cardinality in logging databases is covered in section 14.1.2. The third Pillar of Observability—traces—is currently dominated by SaaS platforms. The dominant self-hosted platform is Jaeger, which sits on top of Cassandra or Elasticsearch and inherits the cardinality problems of those platforms (which are covered here).

14.1.1 *Cardinality in time-series databases*

Time-series databases are optimized for serving data organized by time, which is why time-series databases form the foundation of many metrics-style telemetry systems. The common design goals of time-series databases are to enable fast searches of recent data (the most common type of search in a metrics presentation system) and to make aggregating data over time easier (chapter 17). The four time-series databases I will be covering here are

- OpenTSDB, the first time-series database to really break out, which was created by StumbleUpon and based on Hadoop
- KairosDB, an open source time-series database based on Cassandra
- Prometheus, which was part of a larger monitoring platform, was made famous by SoundCloud, and is a member of the Cloud Native Computing Foundation
- InfluxDB, another stand-alone metrics datastore that is now part of a suite of utilities put out by InfluxData

OpenTSDB has a strict cardinality limit per field of 16 million unique values. Although this limit is generous, using a field to store highly unique information such as IP address or the container ID in a Kubernetes pod will quickly run your key out of space. You will notice this happening when you don't get new values in your metrics.

The other area where cardinality comes into play with OpenTSDB is the queries themselves. Queries that require a lot of fields, or that involve fields with a lot of cardinality, will be slower than queries involving little cardinality. You can speed things by using multiple region servers (a Hadoop concept) in your OpenTSDB cluster, which allows OpenTSDB to partition or shard data across the many region servers. When they're split up this way, queries will be submitted to each region, processed in parallel, and then reassembled. Parallel processing makes the query much faster, and most distributed databases make use of this pattern. Figure 14.1 demonstrates this process.

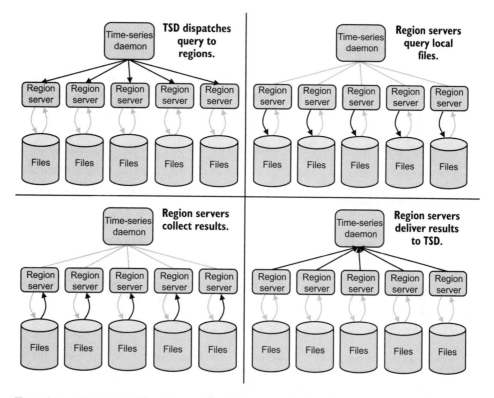

Figure 14.1 How OpenTSDB splits queries for high-cardinality data. The time-series daemon receives the query from the client and then redistributes it to the region servers. The region servers query their local storage and deliver any local results to the daemon. Then the daemon reassembles all the results to return to the client. A slow-performing high-cardinality query is made faster through parallel processing.

KairosDB doesn't have any explicit cardinality limits, but how it operates does provide some de facto limits to cardinality. There are four main pieces of data for a metric:

- The metric name
- The timestamp
- The value
- Any key-value pairs associated with the metric

A critical thing to understand with KairosDB is that the key-value pairs *are not indexed.* Using them in a query will slow your query, and the more unique values you have in a specific key, the slower your query gets. To use an SQL example of what is happening, let us look at how KairosDB returns results for a metric named `pdf_pages` and with the tag `datacenter=euc1` set. The SQL-like first query that KairosDB performs when processing a user query is

```
SELECT metric_value, tags
FROM metrics_table
WHERE
    metric_name = 'pdf_pages' AND
    timestamp > abc AND
    timestamp < xyz
```

which returns a list of all metrics with the name `pdf_pages` in it. Then KairosDB walks through the entire result set, looking for `tags` fields that contain `datacenter=euc1`. The more unique values are in the tags fields, the more data KairosDB has to throw away before returning results, which in turn means that queries cause a lot of storage I/O for few results. Figure 14.2 shows this process.

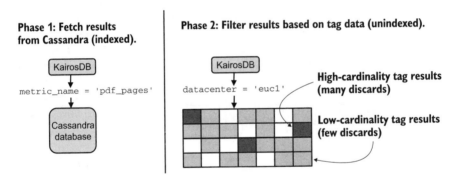

Figure 14.2   The two passes KairosDB makes when responding to a query using tags. The first pass, which uses Cassandra and its indexing, is pretty fast. The second pass goes over the result set one by one, looking for rows with the right tags. For tags with high cardinality (high uniqueness), most of the result set will be discarded, and few rows will match. For tags with low cardinality, a large percentage of the returned rows will match. The storage charge for the query is the same for high- and low-cardinality queries, but high-cardinality queries will require more I/O capacity to resolve.

If your KairosDB infrastructure is consuming a lot of storage I/O capacity and feels slow, you likely have a cardinality problem in your tags. In general, use tags only to indicate low-cardinality data. Our example uses `datacenter` as a tag; this tag has fewer than 10 values for this example company. Keep in mind that the first phase of the query, done on Cassandra, has its own cardinality issues; too many metrics slow that query as well. How much is too much? Keeping an eye on your query performance is the only way to tell.

Prometheus says in its documentation that you shouldn't put too many metrics in it, and the limiting factor is memory on the Prometheus server. Right now (2021), a Prometheus server with two million time series (metric name multiplied by each key value) needs 8 GB of memory to ingest and process queries. If you find that your Prometheus server is running out of memory, you likely have a cardinality problem.

InfluxDB (up to version 2.0) has an explicit cardinality limit that must be set, and this limit applies per database. When this cardinality limit is reached, InfluxDB will not accept metrics that attempt to increase cardinality. You will notice that this limit has been reached when you aren't seeing new data in the affected database. Setting the limit high will work to a point, but when InfluxDB performs shard compaction (a *shard* is the metrics data for a regular length of time), the amount of memory this takes is related directly to cardinality in the database.

InfluxDB will let you declare multiple databases, which is one way to get around the cardinality problems. Keep in mind that shard compaction needs to happen for each database, and when those events overlap, significant memory can be required to complete. You can tell that you have exceeded a database server's ability to support the InfluxDB databases when the InfluxDB process runs out of memory. On Linux systems, the OOMKiller will terminate the InfluxDB process unless you've configured the kernel to avoid the process.

Exercise 14.1

The following table shows the indexed fields for a time-series database table that is used as part of a metrics system supporting a Kubernetes environment. (Field values are not indexed.) The `metric` field is the metric name; the other fields are used for context-related details. Cardinality on this table is more than 12 million, which is causing problems with the database. To get table cardinality under 1 million and still keep maximum context-related details, which field should we drop?

Field name	Unique values	Use
metric	309	Name of the metric
host	19	Hostname of the node where it emitted
pod	78	Kubernetes pod where it emitted
service	15	The service that emitted the metric (could be from multiple applications)
environment	2	The deploy environment: prod or uat here

Pick which field to drop:

   a host
   b pod
   c service
   d environment

14.1.2 *Cardinality in logging databases*

This section is about the databases used to host centralized logging data. The most famous of these databases is the *E* in *ELK Stack*: Elasticsearch. Another document-oriented database that sees a lot of use for centralized logging is MongoDB. We will look at both databases to show the similarities.

Cardinality in Elasticsearch behaves rather differently from the time-series databases in section 14.1.1. An index in Elasticsearch contains a list of fields, and Elasticsearch further indexes each field to enable searching. Because Elasticsearch was initially built for searching plain language, making for highly unique fields, it is less bothered by individual field cardinality than the time-series databases are. Also, Elasticsearch shards its database by default, so you get parallelization working for you when you're resolving queries. (See figure 14.1 for that process.) Elasticsearch experiences cardinality pressure in two areas:

- *Disk-space consumption by field indexes*—The indexes for each field take up space. Depending on the mapping type set for each field and the text-analysis settings you chose, the amount of storage consumed can be quite variable. Large files slow search performance due to the need to sift through lots of disk to assemble results.
- *Average document size*—Every field in an index is present in every document, so if an index has 15,000 fields, and a document only has 15 fields defined, there will be 14,985 fields set to null. Such a small record—only 15 fields—likely has most of its space consumed by all those nulled fields. Large document sizes slow search performance, as Elasticsearch has to move large documents.

When it comes to Elasticsearch, there are two metrics to pay attention to in terms of cardinality:

- *Average document size*—Take the total size of the index, and divide it by the number of documents in the index. The result is the size per document. A slowly increasing value, even though you're not increasing the size of the documents being fed in, is a sign that you have a creeping index problem.
- *Count of fields*—This metric is a direct measure of cardinality, and the best case for your index is that all documents have all fields defined in them. If you find that the count of fields is steadily increasing, however, check your inputs to see whether someone is using something with high cardinality as a field *key* rather than a field *value.*

When Elasticsearch is used with time-based indexes—such as one index per day or week, which is common with centralized logging telemetry systems—you can easily track both of these metrics over time. Search performance generally scales with the size of the shards inside an index, so track that as well. Time-based indexes also let you see the progress you've made in fixing problems.

> ## How Elasticsearch field count affected my telemetry systems
>
> We adopted Spinnaker (https://spinnaker.io) to assess how it could be used in our application deployments. Spinnaker is a group of Java-based microservices with a different logging pattern from the rest of our systems, but we threw the log stream into our Elasticsearch-based telemetry systems anyway. Spinnaker used a JSON-based log format, which we dutifully ingested.
>
> What we hadn't noticed, however, was how many fields that process introduced to the Elasticseach index we sent those logs to. Before we hooked Spinnaker up, we ran between 500 and 700 fields in the index. After we hooked Spinnaker up, the field count ballooned to around 3,000. At the same time, average document size in the index went up significantly. Whereas Spinnaker was about 0.05% of overall traffic to that index, the other 99.95% of the documents in the index had an extra 2,500 nulled fields. Those fields accounted for nearly all the increase in average document size. If you're sharing an index, it only takes a tiny system with bad habits to create big headaches. Section 14.2 shows how we fixed this problem.

MongoDB is another document-oriented database. Unlike Elasticsearch, which provides an index for every field, MongoDB relies on externally defined indexes. The implication of having to define your own indexes is that all the data going into a given collection (similar to an index in Elasticsearch) looks about the same. This design makes MongoDB less flexible in the face of variable inputs but gives you more direct control of search performance. As with relational databases, searching for things in unindexed fields kills search performance.

All is not lost, though. MongoDB supports creating a single index for every string-type field in the collection. This design more closely matches the design of Elasticsearch in that all text searches will be done through the index. Using this feature for centralized logging will make the index of the collection significantly larger than the collection itself. This large index is not always a bad thing—it certainly improves search performance—but it does change where you look for problems.

MongoDB supports *sharding*, splitting a collection onto different database servers. This sort of splitting is a great way to allow more write capacity and also reduces the absolute sizes of your index and data files on each given shard server. Sharding allows MongoDB to take advantage of search parallelization, similar to how OpenTSDB (see figure 14.1) and Elasticsearch handle searches.

NOTE If you are setting up a new telemetry system and are looking to use MongoDB, make sure that you shard your databases from the beginning. This approach will make scaling horizontally far easier. Adding sharding after you've built your system is much more complex than doing it from the start. You can select a shard count of 1 to start with.

Exercise 14.2

Which of the following are symptoms of a telemetry system experiencing cardinality problems?

   a Increased disk use
   b Increased memory use
   c Increased CPU use
   d Increased query rates
   e Increased storage I/O
   f Increased search times
   g Decreased event ingestion rates
   h Decreased CPU use

14.2 Lowering the cost of cardinality

This section addresses what to do when you've identified that you have a cardinality problem or want to avoid having one in the future. Managing cardinality is good practice generally, so these techniques should serve most telemetry systems well. Definitely review the warning signs of cardinality problems in section 14.1, which should serve both to warn you of problems you already have and give you guidance on how your planned or existing systems can experience cardinality problems. This section covers three key concepts in managing cardinality costs:

- Section 14.2.1 describes how logging and telemetry standards are useful in reducing cardinality of produced telemetry.
- Section 14.2.2 covers two storage-side methods for reducing the cardinality penalty.
- Section 14.2.3 shows when it is a good idea to make cardinality someone else's problem.

14.2.1 Use logging standards to contain cardinality

This section is about how your logging and telemetry formatting standards help you reduce cardinality. Logging standards are more useful for software you develop in-house, because third-party applications and hardware are inflexible producers of telemetry. We will cover cardinality that affects centralized logging (and by extension SIEM systems) and metrics telemetry. Distributed tracing is currently dominated by inflexible formats, so cardinality there is better tackled on the storage side (section 14.2.2) or by someone else who's paid to handle it (section 14.2.3).

USING LOGGING STANDARDS TO TAME CARDINALITY IN CENTRALIZED LOGGING

We've covered logging standards in several places in this book—first in section 4.2, again in section 6.1, and with another long look in chapter 12. Those standards embraced flexibility, showing how you can add arbitrary context-related details to telemetry to improve its utility when it comes time to analyze what's going on in your production systems. This section is about what happens when *arbitrary* goes too far. Section 14.1.2 described how two commonly used data stores for centralized logging, Elasticsearch and MongoDB, react to cardinality problems.

Let's look at the hypothetical case of a centralized logging system that embraced JSON as its telemetry transmission format and required only three fields in its schema: app, level, and message. Any other fields would be added as context. Here is a sample, with the field keys boldfaced:

```
{ "application": "framulator", "level": "info", "message": "Retrieved profile
➡ pictures", "acct_id": 1121, "subs_id": 137, "team_id": 734,
➡ "retrieval_time": 2.1, "file_type": "svg", "file_count": 1,
➡ "file_size": 17232 }
```

We see the three required fields and seven additional pieces of context-related telemetry. All this code looks great; the context is relevant to what the message said happened. Now let's look at another sample:

```
{ "application": "framulator", "level": "info", "message": "Uploaded profile
➡ image", "account": 6823, "subscription": 96, "team": 612, "upload_time":
➡ 0.982, "upload_type": "png", "upload_count": 1, "upload_size": 9257 }
```

We see the same three required fields, but we're looking at an uploaded profile image instead of a retrieved one. If you look at the differences between the first and second samples, however, you will see similar concepts encoded in different ways. Although the line for the retrieved profile image uses file_type, file_count, and file_size, the one for the uploaded profile image uses upload_type, upload_count, and upload_size. Also, these two lines encode account-id, subscription-id, and team-id but use different field names for each—the same telemetry ideas, worded differently. This sort of thing happens all the time in codebases with more than one developer (also more often than you'd like for codebases with a single developer) and is completely terrible when it comes to cardinality.

What we need here is a schema for telemetry. Figure 14.3 shows how we can rewrite the two examples to bring down our field count.

Figure 14.3 demonstrates how our field-count cardinality (important for Elasticsearch) changes by rephrasing our example telemetry emissions to be more standardized. Most important, commonly added context-related telemetry must have standardized field names, which make searching for that data far easier and improve your search performance. The figure also shows us unifying retrieval_time and upload_time into transfer_time as a general concept. Although retrieval and upload describe the function, they hurt us in cardinality. The figure also shows turning file_type and upload_type (and their _count and _size siblings) into object_type, showing that providing ways to encode common concepts will also save in field-count cardinality.

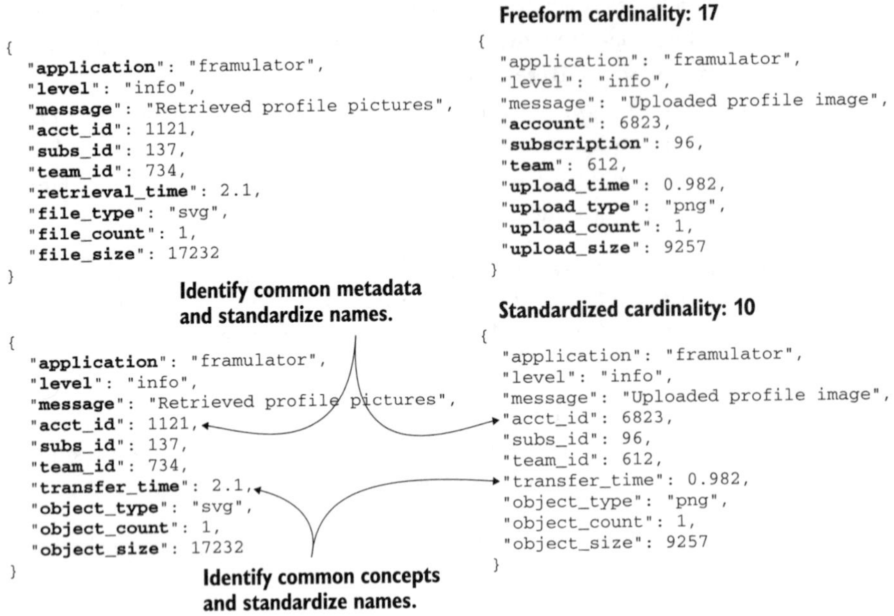

Freeform cardinality: 17

```
{
    "application": "framulator",
    "level": "info",
    "message": "Retrieved profile pictures",
    "acct_id": 1121,
    "subs_id": 137,
    "team_id": 734,
    "retrieval_time": 2.1,
    "file_type": "svg",
    "file_count": 1,
    "file_size": 17232
}
```

```
{
    "application": "framulator",
    "level": "info",
    "message": "Uploaded profile image",
    "account": 6823,
    "subscription": 96,
    "team": 612,
    "upload_time": 0.982,
    "upload_type": "png",
    "upload_count": 1,
    "upload_size": 9257
}
```

Identify common metadata and standardize names.

Standardized cardinality: 10

```
{
    "application": "framulator",
    "level": "info",
    "message": "Retrieved profile pictures",
    "acct_id": 1121,
    "subs_id": 137,
    "team_id": 734,
    "transfer_time": 2.1,
    "object_type": "svg",
    "object_count": 1,
    "object_size": 17232
}
```

```
{
    "application": "framulator",
    "level": "info",
    "message": "Uploaded profile image",
    "acct_id": 6823,
    "subs_id": 96,
    "team_id": 612,
    "transfer_time": 0.982,
    "object_type": "png",
    "object_count": 1,
    "object_size": 9257
}
```

Identify common concepts and standardize names.

Figure 14.3   **The effect on cardinality of freeform field names and standardized field names. The top pair of statements have freeform field names, and the bottom pair have standardized ones; boldfaced field names count toward cardinality. You can achieve substantial savings in field counts by standardizing commonly added context-related details (acct_id, subs_id, and team_id). You can find more by providing a way to encode common concepts—in this case, object type, count, and size.**

If you are facing a codebase with a lot of natural-language field names leading to a sprawl of cardinality, you have a few paths forward to try to urge people to a standard. The hard part is agreeing to the standard in the first place; that negotiation must be done with the owners of the code. When you have a standard, here are a few options to nudge people toward compliance:

- *Create a mandatory code review step that reviews all logging statements to ensure that they comply with the agreed-on schema.* This option is your automation-free option; it relies on humans to remember to do the code review. But you can do this review immediately after deciding on your standard.

- *Update your continuous integration (CI) jobs to check to make sure that new logging statements use only fields from the allowed list.* This option requires writing the automation for your CI pipeline but is more reliable than trusting code review and humans. When builds that include not-allowed field names fail, people will get the message.

- *Provide new logger interfaces that enforce schema, and move all your logging and metrics emissions to the new interface.* If you have a large codebase, it will take some time to get all the changes smoked out, but this option is the most long-term-maintainable option in this list.

I demonstrated another reliable technique in section 12.2: passing a hash of metadata around with execution, and passing the metadata hash and an array of field names as part of your telemetry emissions. In your production code, that technique looks like this:

```
context_fields = ['team_id', 'acct_id', 'region', 'datacenter']
counter('pdf_pages', 3, metadata, context_fields)
```

Here, we see a metrics function called `counter()` called with a metric name, a metric value, a metadata object, and an array. The metadata object is a hash that contains any amount of metadata and contains common fields like `acct_id` and `team_id` from our examples above. Execution can add more items to the hash. The important part is that the `counter()` function is built with the allowed list of fields in it, so it will reject attempts to emit fields that aren't allowed.

This production code looks fairly innocent; it contains no regulated information, such as email address, people's names, diagnosis codes, or phone numbers. The beauty of the logger-based filtering system is that if a software engineer writes the following, it won't cause a data cleanup incident:

```
context_fields = ['team_id', 'email_address', 'region', 'datacenter']
counter('pdf_pages', 3, metadata, context_fields)
```

The produced telemetry will not have the `email_address` field in it or will have a placeholder that looks like an email address, such as redacted@redacted.local. Figure 14.4 shows what you want to end up with.

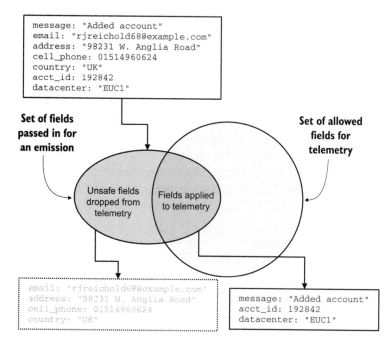

Figure 14.4 Using an allowed list of fields for telemetry with incoming telemetry emissions. When new telemetry emissions come in, their fields are checked against the list. Only fields on the allow list will be moved into the Shipping stage. This approach prevents unsafe fields, such as those containing personal or health-related information, from entering the telemetry system and risk being leaked.

Figure 14.4 shows a pure filter; fields that aren't on the allowed list are dropped without placeholders being put in place. Sanitized telemetry moves into the telemetry pipeline, entering the Shipping stage. Doing this filtering as part of your logger saves your storage systems cardinality, but also provides significant defenses against leaking regulated information.

USING LOGGING STANDARDS TO TAME CARDINALITY IN METRICS SYSTEMS

Metrics as a telemetry style emerged in the early 2010s as a way to provide long-term searchability for numbers-based telemetry. Centralized logging is incredibly expensive to keep online and searchable for years, which is why most organizations don't do things that way. Metrics systems and their numbers-based format made for vastly cheaper storage per item of telemetry, which made multiyear online searching economical for the first time. To get this flexibility, metrics systems of the early 2010s deliberately did not have high cardinality. Unfortunately, as the decade wore on, the utility of high-cardinality metrics became obvious. This section is for organizations that are already operating metrics systems and are looking for methods to tame their cardinality problems.

As we saw in section 14.1.1, cardinality in most time-series databases relates to index cardinality rather than the field-count cardinality we saw in the logging databases. A single field with 14,000 unique values is mostly no big deal for the logging databases, but it will blow up the database in a time-series database.

> **WARNING** A metrics system that is bursting at the seams for cardinality is a symptom of a technical organization that should take a serious look at distributed tracing. Software engineers looking to get tracing out of a metrics system will steadily increase cardinality to learn the exact circumstances (or frequency of a specific set of circumstances) under which an interesting event happens. Troubleshooting of this nature is far easier in distributed tracing systems. Metrics systems can be bent to do an approximation of this work, but the fit is bad, and the overall cost is hard to pay.

Due to how sensitive time-series databases are to cardinality in general, the centralized logging pattern of throwing a bunch of context-related telemetry on each telemetry emission is an antipattern. You want some context-related telemetry, but most metrics systems can't afford the sort of telemetry that will allow a searcher to isolate the metrics coming from a specific execution of a function. Metrics systems are meant to provide a *broad, systemwide view* of how the production systems are operating, not *fine, detailed views* of specific executions.

What sort of context-related information do we need to have beyond metric name and metric value to get the benefit of context-related information without killing the database with cardinality? Let's look at a few examples:

- *Application name*—In a production system running more than one application, storing application names is quite viable. The total unique count is likely to be small, and it will be used in nearly every query.

- *Application version*—Version is an interesting one when paired with retention periods, because the total unique values in the field will be the number of unique versions stored in the retention period. (For more on retention periods, see chapter 17.) If you can afford the cardinality hit, application version will let you track how metrics change versus their application version.
- *Class name*—This concept is more of a tracing concept, but if you have a `metric_name` that is used in more than one class for more than one purpose, having the class name as a metric will help you separate the two. Putting a class name on every piece of metric is an antipattern, however because most `metric_names` likely don't need this disambiguation, and using class names will explode your cardinality. A better pattern for separating two otherwise-identical `metric_name` uses is to use different `metric_name` values (`class1_pdf_pages` instead of `class2_pdf_pages`).
- *Cluster*—This word means different things to different organizations, but if you need to correlate error rates or something equivalent to a given group of machines/instances/nodes, *cluster* is quite useful.
- *Hostname*—For some organizations, especially those running on physical hardware, hostname is a small enough set of unique values to be as useful as `cluster` is for correlating behaviors. For other organizations, such as those running in a public cloud and using lots of autoscaling systems, hostname can be highly unique and a clear antipattern.
- *Data center or region*—If your organization is operating in more than one computing facility, having a split for those facilities is useful, especially because this value is not likely to have many unique values.

NOTE In most metrics systems, the `metric_name` value will end up with the highest cardinality. You want any associated context-related telemetry to be as low-cardinality as possible to maximize your metric volume.

Some of the fields in this list are clearly valuable, such as application name. Others, such as class name, have very limited utility in a metrics systems. As you review the fields in your metrics system, ask yourself these questions:

- Is this field used to get a broad sense of how the system is operating, or is it there to isolate execution in some way? If it is to isolate execution, you should be using a tracing system in addition to your metrics.
- Is the uniqueness in this field still useful? Time changes patterns, and it could be that sheer growth has turned a once-useful field into noise.

How growth changed our use of metrics telemetry

When my company first adopted the metrics style of telemetry, we were still small. For that reason, we decided to use hostname as one of the interesting fields to put on metrics. We were running few servers at that point, so knowing whether a host was bad in some way was useful information. Many people built dashboards to split metrics by hosts.

(continued)

Fast-forward a few years and we were much bigger. Whereas we used to be running a handful of servers, we were running many servers, and the lifetimes of those servers were much shorter. When the metrics system began, it was common for a server to last several days before being recycled. After a lot of growth, our average server lifetime was measured in hours.

That hostname field we picked at the beginning? No one used it anymore. The only time it got used was when someone needed to see a per-host split to identify whether we had a bad server in the mix. Otherwise, it was noise that added a lot of cardinality to our time-series database.

I dropped hostname from our list of fields. After enough time had passed for our database to be fully on the new field names, cardinality had dropped 86%. That one field alone had more cardinality than `metric_name` did!

When it comes to logging formats, you want the classes you write as the entry point to your metrics systems to limit the amount of context-related telemetry put on each emission. You don't necessarily want to follow the metadata pattern from the centralized logging example; instead, rely on adding a few pieces of context-related telemetry as part of the call from the production software, and add the rest as part of the metrics class. To demonstrate, here is an example entry point:

```
counter('pdf_pages', 19)
```

No context-related details are being added in this call! The telemetry possibilities from the list two paragraphs ago would be added after execution enters the `counter()` function and would add general context. The `counter()` function and the functions it calls run in the same process as the production code that started the call stack, so they share all the preceding telemetry. Here is another example, which is a little different from what you've seen before:

```
EXAM_LOG.info('metrics: converters c pdf_pages=19')
```

This example uses a centralized logging emission! Somewhere in the Shipping stage will be a parser looking for strings beginning with `metrics:` that will treat those as metrics statements. We see an application name, `converters`, a metrics type (`c` for counters), and a metric name-value pair. This emission would reach the Shipping-stage metrics parser with all the additional context-related telemetry of a centralized logging telemetry event, but the parser knows to strip out everything but the interesting fields. (For more on enrichment of this type, see chapter 6.) This sort of telemetry is easy on production systems and leaves the complexity to the Shipping stage.

> **Exercise 14.3**
>
> Which of the following types of context-related telemetry would be a bad choice for use in a time-series database?
>
> a Application name
> b Process ID
> c Application version
> d Account ID
> e Data center or region
> f Function or class name

14.2.2 Using storage-side methods to tame cardinality

Cardinality issues can be addressed at the opposite end of the telemetry pipeline from where the logging standards are applied: in the storage systems themselves at the end of the Shipping stage. This section is about techniques you can use to handle a cardinality problem by modifying your approach to storage. Many of the cardinality problems we've discussed so far come about because of too much cardinality in one place. Depending on what kind of database you are using, you have several options for shifting cardinality around.

You have two main ways to address cardinality problems by changing your storage systems:

- *Partitioning*—Create additional storage pools (databases, indexes, or even servers) and send different telemetry to everything. This approach keeps highly cardinal data narrowed to its own problematic pool while letting other data perform fast.
- *Sharding*—Spread your high cardinality data over multiple storage pools. Not every storage system supports this technique, but if yours does, this method is powerful.

PARTITIONING STORAGE TO ADDRESS CARDINALITY ISSUES

This section is about using partitioning to address your cardinality issues in storage. If your storage system has no support for sharding, such as with Prometheus, partitioning is your biggest tool. Partitioning is viable in most storage systems, though some storage systems do require you to create entire new systems to use it.

Consider the example of a growing startup. In the beginning, the company threw all its logs into a single centralized logging system. This approach worked well because the company was small and had a single log-producing product. As the company grew, its product grew in complexity. (Whether this complexity is a single monolith or a pack of microservices doesn't matter for this example.) The production systems are producing far more telemetry than they did when the company was three people with a big idea.

Figure 14.5 shows how this company's single centralized logging database grew with the organization to store the logging data for six applications. This approach can work fine if all six applications produce similar telemetry in terms of field names and contents; perhaps the company had a strong logging standardization effort in the past. But this architecture begins to fail when the logging needs of the applications drift apart, perhaps because each application is produced by different software teams. When that happens, this singular logging database can experience cardinality problems.

Six applications, one logging database

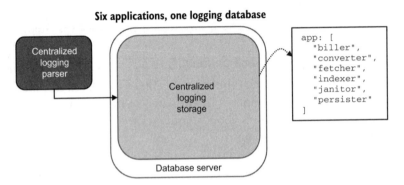

Figure 14.5   Our example company has six production applications sending centralized logging telemetry to a single database. This approach works so long as the logging produced by all six applications is similar in terms of fields and field contents, but it becomes a cardinality problem when logging needs change between the applications.

This company could address its cardinality problems by following the advice in section 14.2.1 and enforcing logging standards as a way of reducing the cardinality hitting the database. But politics sometimes makes that sort of standardization effort far more challenging than finding a technical solution in the storage systems. To solve the problem without engaging in heated political debates, the company needs to adopt partitioning. Figure 14.6 shows how this solution could look.

We see in figure 14.6 that our company split its storage system into five databases for the six applications. Two applications—the fetcher and the persister—are sharing a database because they perform similar functions and generate highly similar logging. No changes needed to be made in production code to make this change in the storage systems, which prevents a potentially lengthy political argument about logging standards. The centralized logging parser needed an update to route telemetry (chapter 7) to the correct database rather than simply throw everything into a single database.

Making this change took some work, but the project wasn't a major one. To support a centralized logging system, most telemetry systems operate some kind of retention policy to expire old logs out of the system to keep costs under control. (See section 17.1.1 for details on setting retention policies for centralized logging.) Our company is no different in this respect; all that new databases mean is that the company needs to

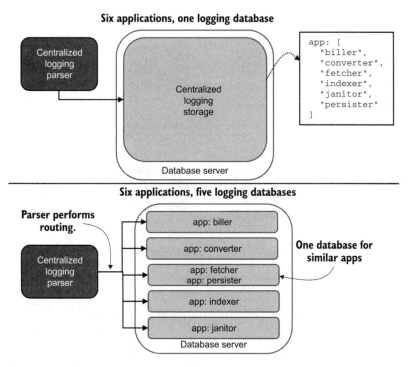

Figure 14.6 Our example company that has six logging-producing applications rebuilt its centralized logging storage to address a cardinality problem. To make this approach work, the centralized logging parser performs routing (chapter 7) to send telemetry to the correct database.

extend the expiration logic to those databases. Because the systems are highly available, the company also needs to add the new databases to any data backup strategies in play. Here are the project phases for moving to the new architecture (illustrated in figure 14.7):

1. Create the new databases.
2. Extend the expiration logic to the new databases.
3. Extend the backup system to include the new databases.
4. Update the Presentation-stage systems to include the new databases.
5. Update the centralized logging parser to send data to the new databases. At this point, the new databases are live.
6. Wait until the expiration logic has fully emptied the old database. Depending on the expiration policies in place, this process can take days, weeks, or months.
7. Remove the old database from the Presentation-stage systems.
8. Remove the old database from the backup system.
9. Remove the old database from the expiration logic.
10. Remove the old database.

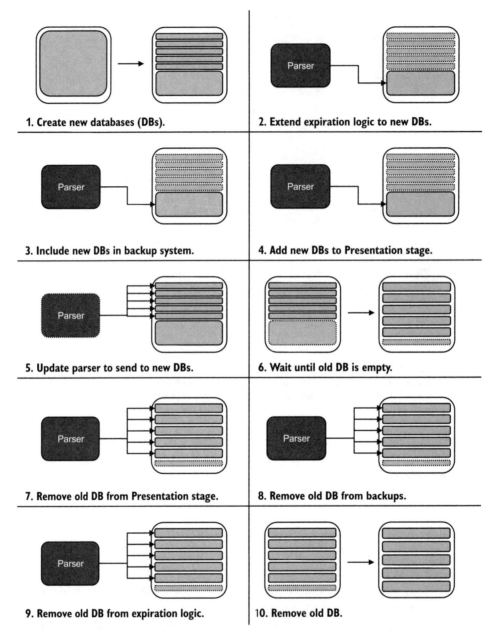

1. Create new databases (DBs).

2. Extend expiration logic to new DBs.

3. Include new DBs in backup system.

4. Add new DBs to Presentation stage.

5. Update parser to send to new DBs.

6. Wait until old DB is empty.

7. Remove old DB from Presentation stage.

8. Remove old DB from backups.

9. Remove old DB from expiration logic.

10. Remove old DB.

Figure 14.7   The 10-step process our example company followed to partition its single logging database into five databases. The dark box is the centralized logging parser, with dark arrows indicating where it is routing telemetry to. Dotted boxes are databases affected by that step's change. Sometimes, a technical process is easier to bring about than a political process among separate software teams.

Partitioning is an effective tool when your telemetry data provides easy separation points. What happens when you don't have an attribute as convenient as application, as in our example company? We need to look into sharding.

How partitioning saved us from a cardinality crisis

The sidebar in section 14.1.2 talked about how adding an application (Spinnaker) to our centralized logging exploded a cardinality problem in our centralized logging. Although this new application was 0.05% of our overall logging, it exploded the field count in our Elasticsearch index from between 500 and 700 to 3,000. Average document size ballooned because of all the nulled fields in each document, and the disk space consumed by the cluster grew incredibly.

The fix for this crisis was to look at how we were using the index. After investigating, I found out that one application was responsible for 98% of the events in that database and that those log entries created a small set of fields (fewer than 200). The solution seemed to be obvious: send all that application's events to a dedicated index.

We split the application's telemetry into a new index and updated our Presentation-stage systems to point to that index by default. The tiny application responsible for 0.05% of our logging traffic went into the "everything else" index, where the field explosion was far less harmful due to how small that index was now. Overall disk consumption in the Elasticsearch cluster dropped by a lot. Whew!

We should have sent that one application to its own index years before we did, but this example is life in a growing company. We didn't notice the lurking problem until we researched why disk consumption spiked as much as it did. Partitioning saved us!

SHARDING STORAGE TO ADDRESS CARDINALITY ISSUES

Sharding is a form of partitioning supported directly in the database rather than relying on an external process (such as a centralized log parser in figures 14.6–14.7). For databases that support sharding directly, such as KairosDB/Cassandra and MongoDB, you have a built-in way to address cardinality issues. This section is about using this capability to improve the performance of your searches.

There are many ways that sharding is supported in databases that support distributed (many-node) operation, but a common way is to select one field (or a group of fields) to act as a sharding key. This sharding key is hashed and used to determine which physical database server to write to or request from. This way, all data with the same sharding-key values end up on the same server. Alternately, if you pick the timestamp as your sharding key, reads and writes will be evenly spread across your group of database servers. Being careful in selecting your sharding key is critical to designing a system for scale. Here is some advice for picking a sharding key:

- If you are using MongoDB for metrics-style telemetry, using the timestamp field as your shard key will even out reads and writes across your servers.

- If you are using KairosDB for metrics, that database handles the sharding setup for Cassandra for you.
- If you are using MongoDB for a centralized logging system, using timestamp as the shard key will still even out reads and writes across servers. Using a compound shard key such as application plus year/month/day, however, will ensure that all application writes on a given day will be written to the same node, potentially reducing the cardinality in that shard versus truly even writes.
- If you are using Cassandra or MongoDB for a centralized logging system, using application as your shard key is functionally equivalent to partitioning (see the preceding section) but does not give you the benefit of horizontal scale.

The primary way that sharding helps your cardinality problem is by providing horizontal scale; the problem is cut into smaller pieces. If your indexes are getting too large, or if search results are too slow, adding more servers to your cluster should make your per-server indexes smaller and improve search performance. Figure 14.8 shows this process.

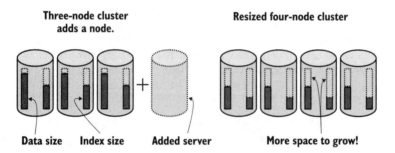

Figure 14.8   What happens when a sharded database adds a server. After the fourth node is added, the database rebalances data and indexes across all the nodes in the cluster. Although this rebalancing operation costs network, storage, and CPU resources, it reduces the total data and index size on each node, creating more room to grow.

Sharding, however, provides diminishing returns the larger your database cluster gets. Each new server you add provides steadily less new headroom in each existing shard. But if your ingestion rate is constant, adding shards makes the headroom each shard still has last longer due to fewer writes landing on each shard.

Don't overlook the possibilities of combining partitioning and sharding. Sharding a database makes it tempting to use a single database and keep adding servers to it. Partitioning into multiple databases will reduce cardinality for all the reasons mentioned in the preceding section. Pairing that with sharding will further reduce the performance hit of high cardinality.

How many shards is too many?

Sharding does not provide infinite scale, though some datasets and databases can get you close. Unfortunately, the answer to the question "How many shards is too many?" is "It depends." I've heard of an Elasticsearch cluster configured to provide an index per day, with 200 shards. If any one shard server failed, recovery provided enough disruption to slow ingestion across the whole cluster. This setup worked fine for the organization involved.

Sharding is a great way to scale up your ability to handle writes. More servers means more separate storage pools, which means more capacity to write things. For truly large telemetry systems—ones that ingest 1 million events a second—massively sharded storage is the only way to keep up.

Sharding is not a one-size-fits-all solution, though. The biggest warning sign that you need to take another look at your sharding configuration is when search doesn't improve after you add shards. If you find that search doesn't improve:

- Check your query endpoints for load.
- Consider increasing database/index size to reduce shard counts.

Consider this trade-off when the count of shards adds to query time. Picking a remediation will require testing, but the performance hit of large per-shard databases/indexes sometimes is less than the hit from having to coalesce results from a large number of shards. Large scale is tricky that way.

14.2.3 *Make cardinality someone else's problem*

This section is about what happens when all else fails. You have the option of making your cardinality problem go away by throwing money at it (paying someone else to deal with it). A wide variety of telemetry SaaS vendors out there will happily ingest your events and handle all the bother of managing storage cardinality so that you don't have to do it. Most small startups these days go for SaaS vendors by preference and bring telemetry handling inside only when they grow enough. (See chapter 8 for an example of this progression.) Data handling of this type is an expensive business, and most SaaS vendors charge by volume of data handled.

I mentioned this before, but it bears repeating: if you are facing a large cardinality problem in your metrics telemetry systems, that problem is a sign that you need to look into adopting distributed tracing. You can get some of the benefits of distributed tracing by adding cardinality to your metrics telemetry, but that approach is still a poor solution to the problem that engineers are trying to solve. Distributed tracing is currently dominated by SaaS providers, and adopting a new telemetry style is a prime place to consider going outside to solve the problem.

If you've followed the guidance here and are still facing cardinality problems in telemetry systems, you clearly need to make a change somewhere else. Perhaps your problems are in this list:

- Maybe the people who built your telemetry systems left the company a few years ago, and no one understands how it works, which means that all the steps in this chapter will require consultants.
- Maybe the person who built your telemetry systems is now in management and doesn't have time for a major rebuild project.
- Maybe the software used in your telemetry systems is so old that extending the cluster or reworking your logging patterns feels like making the same mistake all over again.
- Maybe you're the one who built the current systems and are tired of dealing with it.

Whatever the reason, the current solution isn't working now, and it doesn't look as though you can make it work. This circumstance makes throwing out your existing systems for a SaaS provider tempting. The major challenge with moving telemetry handling to an outside party is the same as for any project that moves something handled internally to something handled externally:

- The cost of employees maintaining your current system is often hard to assign a monetary value to, which makes comparing the costs of a SaaS option harder. When you're costing out an external solution, those unhidden costs will feel larger until you add the hidden people costs to the current solution.
- The cost of hardware or cloud-provider resources involved in your current system is amortized with the rest of your infrastructure costs, so those costs feel hidden. As with the people costs, if you don't factor in the hosting costs of your current system, you won't get a true comparison with the external solution's cost.
- Moving from open source tools to a per-month-cost provider feels like giving up. This reaction is an emotional one (the humans who make the decision are emotional creatures; ignore this fact at your peril), but it's no less of a barrier to decision-making than costs are. Focus on the rational costs and business value to get over the emotional reaction.

As with any significant business-process change, getting budget approval and management backing is an entirely political process. You want to demonstrate that a SaaS provider will be better able to deliver the service and do so in a way that is either cost-neutral or enables business growth in a new way. If you aren't a manager, get a manager on your side to help make the pitch. Generally speaking, SaaS providers consider their Presentation-stage systems to be the things that sell the product, so they are often higher quality than open source or in-house systems.

Summary

- All telemetry styles (centralized logging, metrics, SIEM, and distributed tracing) have searching as a core feature, which makes search performance a core performance metric.

- Cardinality is the number of unique values in an index. Different storage systems react in different ways when cardinality gets high.
- Cardinality affects search performance, which is the main feature of Presentation-stage systems, so if you manage telemetry systems, you have to pay attention to cardinality.
- Each data-storage system reacts to cardinality in different ways, so I have no one-size-fits-all pieces of advice to give.
- The most obvious way that cardinality problems show up in your Presentation-stage systems is poor search performance.
- Increases in cardinality usually cause an increase in key system resources, such as memory and disk space. Some of that use may occur only during maintenance operations.
- Time-series databases are optimized to provide fast searches for time-based data but less optimized for other kinds of cardinality, such as the kind that comes from context-related telemetry like `account_id`.
- OpenTSDB experiences cardinality problems when you have too many unique values per field (more than the hard limit of 16 million). Do not use fields with highly unique values if you are using OpenTSDB.
- KairosDB experiences cardinality problems when you use tags with highly unique values. The Cassandra database on which KairosDB runs also shows cardinality problems when too many metrics are in the system, but the only way to tell is when search performance gets bad. When you use tags, use only tags that have a low number of unique values.
- Prometheus experiences cardinality problems by requiring more memory for each unique value. If you have a memory problem on your Prometheus server, you likely have a cardinality problem too. Do not use fields with high numbers of unique values or use too many fields. If those approaches aren't feasible, consider partitioning.
- InfluxDB has a configurable explicit cardinality limit and experiences cardinality problems during routine background maintenance that can run your InfluxDB server out of memory. As with Prometheus, don't use fields with high numbers of unique values, or use too many fields. If those approaches aren't feasible, consider partitioning.
- Elasticsearch experiences cardinality problems when there are too many fields in an index, which takes up more disk space and makes searching slower as a result. Try to store telemetry data that looks similar in each index, and separate telemetry data that is formatted differently.
- MongoDB experiences cardinality problems in the size of its indexes, which can exceed the size of the data being indexed. When you're tracking resource use in MongoDB, be sure to track index size as well.

- Using your logging standard to enforce a schema for telemetry field names is powerful for dealing with a field-count cardinality problem. Standardizing common values is (depressingly) useful in reducing field sprawl.
- Code review and automation in CI systems are two places to enforce your telemetry standards in ways that urge software engineers to change their habits.
- Providing (or updating) logger libraries to encode your revised standards is a high-impact way to reduce field sprawl.
- Using an allowed list of telemetry fields, enforced in your structured logging formatter or the Shipping stage, is effective for both reducing cardinality and keeping regulated information out of your telemetry systems.
- Metrics databases experience cardinality problems mostly due to index sizes, rather than the field-count cardinality experienced by the centralized logging databases.
- A metric system experiencing lots of cardinality problems is a symptom that your technical organization should look into adopting distributed tracing. Metrics can stand in for tracing, but the fit is poor, and the cost is high. Tracing solves the base need better.
- Metrics systems are designed to provide a broad, systemwide view of the production system, unlike centralized logging, which looks at specific events in the context in which they happened.
- In metrics systems, the field representing the name of the metric should be the highest-cardinality field in the system after the timestamp field. This approach maximizes the amount of metrics you can store in a given database.
- Due to how cardinality-sensitive metrics systems are, you want to seriously limit how much context-related telemetry gets added to each metric when it is emitted. Do not treat metrics systems like centralized logging events.
- Partitioning is a database technique where different telemetry is sent to additional storage pools, which reduces the telemetry cardinality in each pool.
- Sharding is another database technique that spreads telemetry over multiple storage pools, reducing the data and index sizes for each. This technique is paired with distributed queries, so searching is generally faster than one giant database.
- Partitioning allows you to wall off problematic telemetry sources into their own pool, which lets the rest of your telemetry systems operate more efficiently.
- When using a database that supports sharding, selecting an appropriate shard key is critical. For most telemetry systems, using the timestamp field as the shard key will spread telemetry evenly across your storage pools.
- Using another telemetry field, such as application, for your shard key is functionally equivalent to partitioning.

- Combining partitioning and sharding is absolutely something you can do. The combination is powerful for speeding search performance and managing cardinality.
- If fixing your cardinality problem is more hassle than you want to put up with, moving your telemetry to a SaaS provider makes cardinality the provider's problem instead of yours.
- The distributed tracing space is currently dominated by SaaS vendors, so if your internal metrics systems are bursting at the seams with cardinality, adopting a SaaS-based tracing product will help take pressure off your metrics systems (if not outright replace it).
- Moving telemetry to a SaaS provider requires making the business case for investing in a new platform versus maintaining and upgrading the existing platforms.

15
Ensuring telemetry integrity

This chapter covers

- Understanding why you should defend telemetry integrity
- Defending telemetry against outside attackers
- Defending telemetry against malicious insiders
- Making telemetry tamper-evident

This chapter is about security. Your telemetry systems provide details about how your production systems are operating, which includes a whole host of details that an attacker looking to hide their tracks would rather not be present. Outside attackers seek to prevent telemetry that shows their presence from entering the system. Inside attackers (evil insiders) remove or alter telemetry to hide their activities. Your telemetry systems need to be resilient to both kinds of attacks, which requires multiple defense techniques.

Your goal as a system defender is to prevent alteration wherever possible, and if you can't do that, make it harder to perform alteration and slow the attacker down. By forcing an attacker to take more time or perform more steps, you increase your chance to catch them before they get too far. When you make alteration harder, attackers leave more traces that they have to modify, which increases the chances that they will miss one. That missed trace may be the key to detecting the attack.

Regulatory and compliance frameworks often have targeted requirements for the integrity of telemetry systems. One common requirement is that the design must ensure that someone who has access to the telemetry system can't alter the traces of their use of that system. That requirement is a mouthful, but it's why centralized logging systems often share telemetry with SIEM systems. Because access traces are also persisted in the SIEM systems, telemetry operators can still modify the centralized logging system (and operators can tell what security is doing inside the centralized logging system). Organizations that are not subject to regulation or compliance frameworks rarely go to the effort to defend their telemetry systems in this way, which is a major reason why attempting to achieve compliance forces such radical changes in telemetry systems.

It is not feasible to list all possible attacks on telemetry, but I feel that I need to share a few to get you thinking about ways to attack telemetry systems (and, by extension, think about ways to defend against these attacks):

- Force the production code to use an HTTP POST to dump out environment variables, including the API keys for the SaaS-based telemetry system.
- With remote code execution, dump the application's config file, including authentication details for the telemetry systems.
- With remote code execution, update the log-shipping software to monitor a different log file, allowing the attacker to filter the real application's log before it hits the one that enters the Shipping stage.
- Access a Presentation-stage system, such as Kibana, that had access control set up incorrectly.
- Access a public cloud storage system, such as AWS S3, that had access control set up incorrectly.
- Using an operator's credentials, live-patch the telemetry parsers (so that there is no Git or other VCS commit trace) to drop telemetry from a specific program, allowing the operator to run a program on production systems that leaves no traces.
- Deliberately add a bug that sends the SaaS provider's API token as an HTTP header on API callbacks.

Security is a dense topic, but if you read nothing else in this chapter, you must take these two major points to heart:

- *Production systems should emit telemetry using write-only methods.* If the production systems can read what they wrote—or, worse, delete what they wrote—you have a vulnerability. Section 15.1 covers methods to make write-only telemetry a reality.
- *Once emitted, all access to telemetry (including operator/root/admin access) must be traceable, and modifications must be made obvious.* This method ensures that telemetry that has already been emitted remains a true record of what happened in your production systems and makes later tampering evident. Section 15.2 covers these methods.

15.1   *Getting telemetry out of reach of an attacker*

Outside attackers have limited resources when trying to modify telemetry that might reveal their presence; your job is to make it as hard as possible for them to do that. One of the best techniques for making the job of hiding their tracks harder is to move the telemetry out of the system that produced it quickly. That process is what this section is about. Attackers can enter your production systems from many points, but the production code is one area you can robustly defend. When it comes to telemetry movement, you should be concerned about two zones:

- *The production code itself*—When a remote code execution or server-side-request forgery attack happens, the production code is the attacker's entry point.
- *The server running the production code*—The server may be inside the container for Kubernetes or inside the virtual machine for VM and cloud services. An insider with legitimate access looking to perform malicious actions uses this access as the entry point for an attack.

The direct-to-storage (section 3.1.1), direct-to-queue (section 3.1.2), direct-to-stream (also section 3.1.2), and direct-to-SaaS (section 3.2) methods all involve the production code emitting telemetry directly to somewhere off the place it is executing. This technique gives attackers minimal chance to modify telemetry before it enters the rest of the Shipping stage. These methods of defending against a local attacker are robust, but section 15.2 discusses their integrity problems.

Using direct-emissions methods isn't always possible, however. Emitting telemetry locally, as we examined in chapter 2 (log files in section 2.1.1, the system logger in section 2.1.2, and the standard output in section 2.1.3), gives attackers a better chance to modify or remove telemetry before it fully enters the Shipping stage. This section covers three broad methods for reducing the risk of locally emitted telemetry:

- Section 15.1.1 covers how a local shipper, such as a Filebeat process ingesting application log files, should be configured to defend against attacks.
- Section 15.1.2 covers how using operating system access control techniques, such as SELinux and NTFS permissions, allows you to create write-only methods of telemetry emission.
- Section 15.1.3 covers threats targeting SaaS-based telemetry systems and discusses what you should look for in a telemetry provider if you are concerned about telemetry integrity.

15.1.1   *Move telemetry too fast to catch*

This section covers the race between an attacker looking to hide their tracks and the Shipping-stage systems looking to move telemetry from where it was emitted to the greater Shipping stage. When you are using one of the techniques from chapter 2 for emitting telemetry locally and relying on a Shipping-stage component to move it on (chapter 4), you have a race on your hands. Ideally, as soon as your production systems emit something into a log file, the system logger, the standard output (stdout), or the Shipping-stage component—which can be many things, such as Logstash or Fluentd—immediately picks it up and moves it somewhere else. Figure 4.1, reproduced here as figure 15.1, demonstrates this architecture for log files and Filebeat.

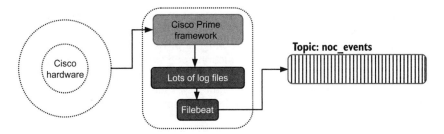

Figure 15.1 **An example of locally emitted telemetry from the Cisco Prime software, relying on a local Shipping-stage component, Filebeat, to move telemetry into a stream topic. An attacker gaining access to this server needs to race Filebeat to modify log files before it ships the telemetry inside the log files to the stream.**

We need to talk about log files because they are the most exposed of the three local emission methods. Keep in mind that some organizations configure their Syslog to emit into a local log file, so for these organizations, emitting to the system logger is equivalent to emitting directly to a log file. Emitting to stdout is how frameworks such as Kubernetes, containerd, and serverless work, and in those frameworks, telemetry enters the Shipping stage after it leaves the container or function. In other systems, such as those running under Systemd on Linux, emitting to stdout is functionally equivalent to emitting to the system logger, which can still result in the creation of a log file.

Section 4.1.1 generally discusses shipping telemetry from log files. But if integrity is one of your telemetry system design targets, you need to do a few more things than that section talks about:

- *Telemetry needs to be shipped continually.* Some telemetry systems rely on a Cron or Windows Scheduler task to copy log files from a server to a central NFS or shared drive. The long lag between when telemetry is emitted and when the log file leaves the box is a huge window for an attacker.
- *Telemetry needs to have low lag between when the emission happens and when it is shipped into the rest of the Shipping stage.* Low lag further reduces the window an attacker has to modify telemetry. Shipping continually is not enough; you need to be shipping recently as well. If telemetry integrity is highly important for your organization, creating an alarm for excessive shipping lag is called for.

How we experienced shipping lag

A few years ago, my company performed an experiment to see how our production code behaved on larger cloud-provider instances. It turned out that we had great vertical scalability; more processors didn't slow us much at all! It took us a while to notice that not everything scaled up as well as we hoped.

It turned out that our log file shipping was tremendously lagging. After handling a day of prod-like load, some of our shippers were more than an hour and a half behind. As daytime load reduced, they eventually caught up. We traced the problem to a single-thread issue in our shipper. The production code was running on 16 cores, and all those cores were writing to the same set of log files. Our log file shipper, on the other hand, had a single thread to monitor changes to that small group of files. The 16:1 ratio was high enough to saturate the log file shipper.

This information identified our scaling ceiling for our production code, and the problem wasn't the production code itself; it was the telemetry components. We down-sized the instance type one level, which got us fewer cores, and our log shipper behaved fine.

Could we have optimized our log file shipper to perform better? Definitely. But we were exploring options, so we didn't have any urgency about addressing the issue. We went with more, smaller instances, and everything worked fine.

The techniques you need to use to speed your shipper depend on what you are using for shipping. Here are tips on some of the most popular packages for shipping log files:

- *Filebeat* is based on threads. Each - input block handles multiple harvesters, so splitting files between - input blocks will improve parallelism.
- *Fluentd* has a multiprocess worker feature that allows spawning multiple workers. Although multiple workers can't track the same file, if you have a group of files, you can specifically assign workers to files to provide parallelism.
- *Logstash* is also based on threads. Each input {} block gets a thread. So if you have the thread-blocking we saw (see sidebar), move file inputs into many input {} blocks to maximize parallelism.
- *Syslog-ng* runs multithreaded by default. If you are performing any filters, ensure that they aren't relying on information in the MSG field.

Tracking your ingestion lag takes some work, but if you are tracking a hostname value in your telemetry, a simple query to figure lag out is to ask, *per host,* how old the most recently received telemetry is. If that value is increasing steadily, you have an ingestion problem in your log shippers.

15.1.2 Use ACLs to enforce write-only telemetry

If your production code is allowed to modify or delete emitted telemetry, an attacker's job is much easier. Using write-only techniques to emit telemetry defends against modification attacks from local attackers and makes attackers work harder to access queue and stream systems. This section covers the techniques you need to follow to defend against these sorts of attacks. It covers two areas:

- Using ACLs to create write-only areas for log files
- Using ACLs for write-only access to queues and streams

USING ACLS TO CREATE WRITE-ONLY AREAS FOR LOG FILES

Access control lists (ACLs) are nothing new to operating systems, and building defensible systems means that you need to understand the ACL systems available to you. Windows, UNIX, and Linux have different ways of providing ACLs, but the general techniques are similar. This section is about providing those techniques.

Let's start with Windows, which has a richly featured permissions system. This complexity makes for a readily accessible way to make write-only places to put log files. Granting `Write` permission without also granting `Modify` or `Read-only` permission on a directory allows a program to create a file and then write to it. If the program closes and reopens the file for writing, the ACL will allow it to do so. Figure 15.2 provides an example of configuring a write-only directory by using the icacls utility.

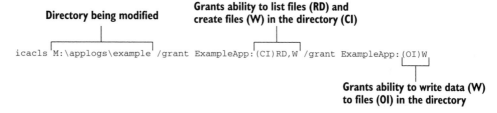

Figure 15.2   Using the `icacls` command to create a write-only directory for the example application. The first `/grant` parameter allows the ExampleApp user to read the list of files and create files in the directory. The second `/grant` parameter allows ExampleApp to write to files in the directory. (`create-files` does not imply the ability to write to them.) These permissions do not allow reading or deleting files in the directory.

This example grants the ExampleApp user the ability to list files in the M:\applogs\ example directory (`/grant ExampleApp:(CI)RD`) and create files for writing in M:\applogs\example (`/grant ExampleApp:(OI)W`). Because we used CI (container inherit) to set the list files permission (RD), created files (which are objects, not containers) will not inherit the RD permission. When the RD permission is set on a file, it grants the ability to read the file. We also set the W permission at the same time; in container context, W allows creating files within the directory.

To allow writing to created files, the second /grant is needed. This parameter gives created log files the W (write) permission, which allows writing to the files. Created files do not inherit a right allowing reading of files. We grant with OI (object inherit) to ensure that write is inherited on new files in the directory.

When it comes to UNIX, the access control landscape is both far simpler and more complex. It's simpler in that the standard ACL system is easy and more complex in that (for Linux, anyway) several optional ACL systems provide more refinement. Whereas Windows allows setting many access control statements on a given directory or file, UNIX systems allow one (unless you're using one of the optional systems; more on those later). Figure 15.3 shows how the standard ACL system works for Linux and UNIX systems.

This says:
Grant write(w), view-file-list(x) to User (exampleapp),
Grant read(r), view-file-list(x) to Group (adm), and no permissions to All.

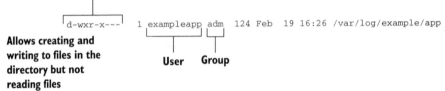

Figure 15.3   Example of using the built-in ACL system for UNIX systems, creating a write-only directory in which to put logs for an example application. No global access is granted (at the end of the ACL). To ensure that the exampleapp user can't read files, that user must not be in the adm group.

Setting an ACL to allow only write and execute on the directory (on directories, the execute bit allows listing directory contents) for the user of our example application lets that user create files in the directory and write to them. But any created file will get the default ACL for that user, which almost always includes the ability to read the file. Unlike Windows systems, in which the system operator can set permissions in a way that is secure by default, UNIX systems using the default ACL system require the production code to create the log file with secure settings.

The open() syscall in UNIX and Linux allows setting the permissions of the created file, but not all programming languages expose this feature; the concept isn't cross-platform, so why would they? This difficulty in creating write-only locations is part of why UNIX and Linux systems have additional, optional ACL systems. Here are the most common of those systems in Linux:

- *POSIX ACL*—This extension to the default ACL system allows Windows-like specification of multiple permissions on a directory or file. It requires filesystem support, however, and a specific mount option to enable it, Because remounting is a simple operation and you can remount with different parameters, removing POSIX ACL support from a volume is easy. Because ACL enforcement can be turned off so easily, most security teams don't consider POSIX ACLs to be truly viable.

- *SELinux*—Security Enhanced Linux is a Mandatory Access Control (MAC) system that is compiled into the Linux kernel. Unlike POSIX ACLs, SELinux can be enforced everywhere. SELinux works by giving every file, object, process, and everything else a label and defining how each label can interact with other labels. This setup allows defining relationships such as permitting exampleapp to access sockets created by logging_platform without having to specify file-level permissions. Red Hat and SLES support SELinux out of the box.

- *AppArmor*—This MAC system is also compiled into the Linux kernel. It was developed after SELinux as a way to provide most of the benefits of SELinux, but with a much easier method for managing the interface. When processes launch, they are assigned an AppArmor profile. Because the UNIX philosophy is to treat everything like a file, AppArmor profiles define which files each profile can access and what operations the profile is allowed to perform on them. Ubuntu and SLES support AppArmor out of the box.

SELinux and AppArmor work in conjunction with default permissions. If the default permissions allow access, SELinux or AppArmor can still deny access. At the same time, if SELinux and AppArmor permit access, the default ACL will still deny access. Let's take a look at SELinux and AppArmor versions of creating a write-only log file. First up is SELinux (figure 15.4).

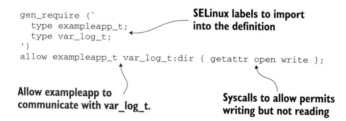

```
gen_require (`                    SELinux labels to import
   type exampleapp_t;            into the definition
   type var_log_t;
')
allow exampleapp_t var_log_t:dir { getattr open write };
```

Allow exampleapp to communicate with var_log_t.

Syscalls to allow permits writing but not reading

Figure 15.4 An example SELinux type-enforcement file that allows our example application to create and write to files in /var/log but not read from them. This example presumes that you already have a type defined for exampleapp. Even if the file is flagged to allow reading, SELinux will prevent reads!

We see a short, one-line definition that allows the `exampleapp_t` type (defined elsewhere) to communicate with the `var_log_t` type, using one of three syscalls. Note that the syscalls do not include read! This type enforcement policy allows our example application to write to /var/log, but not read it or delete it (the unlink syscall). This policy works in coordination with the default ACL policies. A file in /var/log/otherapp still can't be read by our example application, because the default ACL policies deny it. But

if /var/log/exampleapp/error.log is flagged to allow users to read it, SELinux will prevent attempts by our application to read the file. Next, let's look at the AppArmor equivalent (figure 15.5).

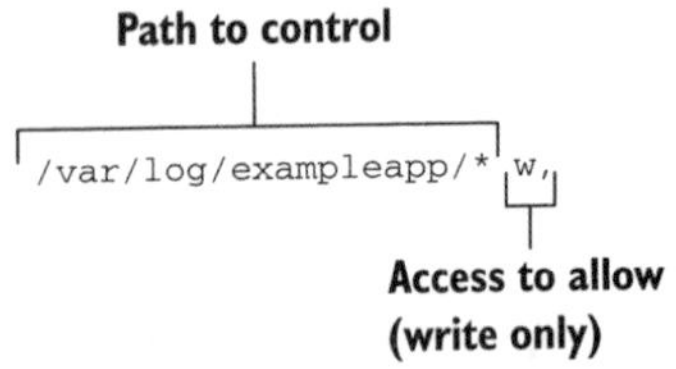

Path to control

```
/var/log/exampleapp/* w,
```

**Access to allow
(write only)**

The AppArmor version is shorter than the SELinux version, in part because this figure is merely a component of the larger exampleapp policy. This single line would be added to the ExampleApp AppArmor policy to enforce the write-only nature of files in the logging location. With our SELinux example, even if the file were flagged to allow the Example App user to read, AppArmor would prevent that from happening.

Figure 15.5 AppArmor policy statement in the exampleapp policy. This example grants the profile the ability to write to files in /var/log/exampleapp but not read or execute them. Even if the default ACLs allow the application user to read the file, AppArmor will prevent reading.

There is another benefit to using one of the MAC systems: auditing. If you are enforcing SELinux or AppArmor, the kernel will report attempts to read outside the allowed areas, which is a potential sign that an attacker is probing the boundaries. I encourage you to ingest these events into your system telemetry streams and take reports of out-of-bound access seriously. Most of the time, the access will be a developer adding a feature without consulting the platform teams, but when it isn't, you will be incredibly glad that you captured those events.

USING ACLS FOR WRITE-ONLY ACCESS TO QUEUES AND STREAMS

If your production systems are emitting directly into queues and streams, chances are good that they are already authenticating against the queue/stream service to publish telemetry. This section is about the techniques you need to follow to ensure that an attacker who gains access to your production code is unable to modify telemetry that's already in the queue or stream system.

If your production code also uses queue/stream systems as part of its operation, it is quite easy to use the same credentials for your telemetry system that you do for production operations. *This pattern is a clear antipattern* because your production access almost definitely includes read/write access and often also includes configure access to provide dynamic queues or stream topics. Think of a telemetry queue/stream as being owned by another team: you are granted the ability to publish events but not modify them.

> **WARNING** If your production system uses queues or streams, always provide different credentials for production and telemetry use. The production credential almost definitely has more access than write-only, which makes it unsuitable for telemetry use. The telemetry credential should allow only publishing events, and the production operation credential must be specifically denied access to the telemetry queues/streams. This separation makes telemetry more resistant to attack, and the audit logs from the queue/stream system will be able to discriminate between production and telemetry operations.

Redis added an access control system in version 6 in May 2020; earlier versions had a single password for entry that granted global access. If you are using Redis as a stream or queue system (it supports both), I strongly encourage you to use the ACL system. Create different users for production and telemetry use, and restrict the telemetry user to the telemetry keys. Here, we define the rights of two users:

```
ACL setuser telemetry_user ~appevents:*

ACL setuser prodops_user ~sessions:*
ACL setuser prodops_user ~locks:*
ACL setuser prodops_user ~shadowbans*
```

Here, we are allowing the `telemetry_user` access to any key beginning with `app-events:`, and adding access to three key prefixes for the `prodops_user`. This snippet works only in Redis 6 and later, but it is an example of setting different ACLs for Redis-based access.

The same guidance holds for AMQP-based systems such as RabbitMQ and Azure Event Hubs. Use one well-privileged credential for production operations and a second reduced-privilege credential for telemetry operations. Certain systems, such as RabbitMQ, allow the creation of virtual hosts in the AMQP cluster, which allows more logical separation between production operations and telemetry operations. Better yet, use separate clusters for production and telemetry use! Keep those failure domains separate.

15.1.3 *Durable telemetry when using SaaS providers*

If your telemetry is handled entirely by SaaS providers, you are not immune to the write-only requirement of durable telemetry. This section covers the features you want from your telemetry SaaS providers and the use patterns you should follow to use a SaaS provider safely. Most providers are aware of these risks and enable safe use.

When selecting a SaaS provider for telemetry, you want to know whether you can send events to that provider by using a method or authentication token that can't do anything else. This approach minimizes the impact if an attacker gets into your application (or your API key follows former employees out the door). Write-only endpoints leaking to attackers still enable an attacker to send garbage to your endpoints, potentially hiding their true attacks behind a sea of misdirection. For convenience, here are several common telemetry SaaS providers and their approaches to API key and ingestion-endpoint handling:

- *Datadog* has a dual-key model, requiring both an API key and an application key to read data. If you have only an API key, you can only write data. Be careful, though; you can still write data with an API+application key, which would give an attacker quite a bit more access in Datadog.
- *Honeycomb.io* allows the creation of multiple API keys and can assign different duties to each key. This design is somewhat unsafe, because it is easy to create a

key that can do everything and use that key in your application. For safety, create one API key to use the Events API (to insert telemetry), and use different API keys for additional API features.

- *New Relic* provides five kinds of API keys. One type is an insert key, which you use to submit telemetry. Most important, New Relic does not provide a "does everything" key! When they don't have such a key, software engineers have to make a conscious choice about what kind of operations they will be performing and which keys to use for them.

- *Splunk* has an HTTP event collector that requires authentication with a token dedicated to the collector. This token is used only to send events into Splunk; it can't be used for anything else.

- *Sumo Logic* provides write-only webhook endpoints to submit telemetry, which does not support authentication (security through obscurity). An application sending webhooks to Sumo Logic has no access to Sumo beyond the ability to insert events.

If you are using a SaaS provider for your telemetry, build your production code to use only the provider's ingestion API endpoints and API keys wherever possible. Mixing API keys in an application, to provide both ingestion and more advanced API use, is dangerous but unavoidable in some cases, such as providing an admin portal that exposes the ability to search telemetry. As with all security, understand the risks that your applications face when you pick your SaaS-provider access methods. Least privilege is best.

> **Exercise 15.2**
> If your production systems are using a SaaS platform for telemetry in any way, are they using a write-only key, or are they using an admin credential for convenience? What changes do you need to make to use a write-only key for sending telemetry?

15.2 *Making telemetry harder to mess with*

Whereas section 15.1 covered techniques to make telemetry harder to tamper with from the point of view of an outside attacker, this section is all about defending against inside attackers. Remember that an outside attacker that manages to impersonate a trusted internal resource is considered to be an inside attacker, the same as a malicious insider employee. The attacks I talk about defending against here are on the telemetry pipeline and storage itself.

> **REMINDER**   Once emitted, all access to telemetry (including operator/root/admin access) must be traceable, and modifications must be made obvious.

Prevent changes where possible, increase the effort of making changes everywhere else, make tampering obvious, and ensure that all telemetry access is tracked and traced to enable reconstruction of events after the fact. Telemetry systems are core parts of any organization's security infrastructure and should be treated that way. Attackers looking to change telemetry by using insider access can do so in several places. Figure 15.6 shows an example of attacking a centralized logging telemetry pipeline.

Attacking a centralized logging system

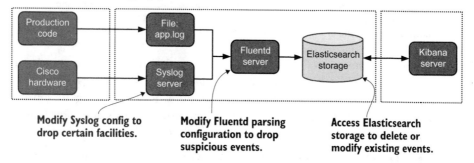

Figure 15.6 **Three ways to attack an example centralized logging pipeline to hide suspicious events. The Syslog server in front of the Cisco hardware can be modified to drop firewall events, hiding probing activity. The Fluentd server parsing all centralized logging events can be modified to drop suspicious events. Finally, suspicious events can be removed from the Elasticsearch storage system. If an authorized user is making these changes, the best defense is tracing the change and ensuring that hand-updated changes are overwritten quickly by the authorized configuration.**

We cover three broad techniques to defend against attacks:

- Examining the roles of authentication and access control in providing barriers, and enabling tracing of activities (section 15.2.1)
- Defending the integrity of your telemetry system configuration (section 15.2.2)
- Making modifications to telemetry obvious (section 15.2.3)

15.2.1 Using access control requirements to defend against attacks

We took a look at operating system and queue/stream level access control techniques in section 15.1.2; this section takes a more systemic view of the role that ACLs play in defense. These concepts are central to maintaining the security of *any* computer system, not only telemetry systems. If you take nothing else from this section, know two things:

- All systems must support authentication, if possible, and be configured to require it.
- The logs that show those authentication attempts must also be tracked (and likely forked into your security team's SIEM systems).

To help frame the concepts, we need to look at a generic telemetry pipeline in figure 15.7.

Generic telemetry pipeline

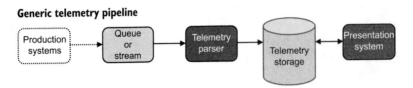

Figure 15.7   A generic telemetry pipeline. Anything with a solid line is potentially attackable. The dotted box and line were addressed in section 15.1. Solid lines and boxes represent vulnerable attack areas in telemetry pipelines in general. It's important to note that each solid arrow represents a different access control system or need.

As we see in the figure, we have telemetry flowing into a queue or stream, getting parsed by a parser, and injected into storage. From there, a presentation system consumes storage to display telemetry for people who are looking to solve problems. We've spent most of this book looking at event flows like this one. Now let's look at the areas where authentication should be happening:

- The telemetry parser needs to authenticate to the queue or stream to fetch events for processing. It needs to pop events off the queue or read events from the stream, which requires authentication and authorization to perform those actions.
- The telemetry parser needs to authenticate to telemetry storage to insert new telemetry.
- The presentation system needs to authenticate to telemetry storage to fetch telemetry for display.
- If the telemetry parser is anything other than a container or serverless system, it likely permits login by operators through SSH or other remote means.
- If the telemetry storage is not a cloud-provider system such as Amazon Elastic search Service, its highly stateful nature means that it also likely permits operator login through SSH or other remote means.

Each solid arrow in figure 15.7 is a different authentication with different permissions. These authentication and permission sets are functionally application users, similar to application users on operating systems that your applications run under. The users used by the telemetry applications *must not* be reused by telemetry system operators for purposes such as building monitoring infrastructure or by operators themselves. Monitoring and operator use should be done through different credentials. Structuring your credential use in this way—creating separate credentials for separate use cases—ensures that the audit log correctly describes who performed which activities.

In an ideal world, each telemetry system operator will get their own personal account in each area they might need to access. If you don't use shared admin accounts, you provide the most details to security teams that are attempting to reassemble events from audit-log traces. This approach is a best practice, though it isn't practical in some cases.

Also, telemetry system operators should not routinely be given accounts that can modify telemetry data. Yes, we sometimes need to modify telemetry data directly as part of cleaning up after toxic data spills (see chapter 16 for more on that topic), but that access should be temporary and targeted. Again, this approach isn't practical in every case, but it is a best practice.

15.2.2 Ensuring configuration integrity in your telemetry systems

As we saw in figure 15.6 at the start of section 15.2, some of the attacks are on the code involved in the telemetry pipeline. The problem faced by telemetry systems is the same problem faced by production code: how to defend against unauthorized changes. For technical organizations that have undergone the process of achieving a compliance framework certification, one of the biggest challenges is dealing with one of the big dictums of compliance:

If you wrote it, you can't edit it in production.

The big idea is that you create a change for production; it goes through a series of automated and manual tests and approvals, and only then is deployed to production. To ensure that what is running in production is what is approved to be running in production, everyone is locked out of the production systems except for the disaster response team. Connecting directly to a server and hand-updating code violates all this careful work, which is why deploying production code is defended as solidly as it is. (All that agility-destroying "useless overhead" is there for a reason.)

Unfortunately, telemetry system code often doesn't get the same rigorous attention to change control as production code, in part because significantly different teams may be producing the code running inside the telemetry systems. But team *cultural* differences are also partly responsible. Teams with a lot of operations background may not think about full testing suites for their "mere scripts."

If your organization is having trouble getting the telemetry system code under a full software development life cycle policy, you can use a few other techniques to make ad hoc changes harder. The first of these techniques is the concept of *configuration management*; the second, which is a competing philosophy, is *immutability*.

Configuration management was made famous through tools such as CFEngine, Puppet, and Chef. Since the first generation of tools, we've seen products like Salt, Ansible, and Rudder expand the space. You define a system state you want on your computing infrastructure, and the configuration management system enforces that state. If someone changed something manually, that change will be reverted automatically the next time state is enforced. Because hand changes do not persist, people get out of the habit of making hand changes, and the overall system becomes more consistent. Figure 15.8 shows the steps.

The first box in figure 15.8 is the configured state. We have a specific code version running in production, and Filebeat has its configuration file enforced. Then a telemetry operator comes in and makes two manual changes: updating production code a point and making a hand update to the Filebeat configuration. When Puppet runs

Figure 15.8 Example configuration-management workflow. After an operator makes manual changes to the code version and Filebeat, on its next enforcement run, Puppet reverts the manual changes. This approach ensures that what is running in production is what is approved to be running in production.

next, it downgrades production code to the approved version and reverts the hand updates to the Filebeat configuration. For organizations that are sensitive to production changes, the fact that Puppet made changes can raise alarms.

Immutability is a somewhat related concept, but it assumes that no one is permitted to make local changes. For Linux servers, this concept means that SSH is turned off. Docker and FaaS are famous applications of immutability principles, but the same technique can also be applied to servers. Immutability assumes that configuration management is *not run at all* or run only for operating-system-level components because configuration management that pushes a change violates the immutable state of the server.

An attacker who is looking to make changes to a telemetry pipeline following immutability principles won't be making local changes; they will be making changes upstream in the deployment pipeline. If a local attacker can push out a hacked version of a telemetry package and then hide the traces of their deploy, that's a vulnerability you need to address.

Keep in mind that immutability works best on stateless systems such as telemetry parsers and routers, where the amount of locally stored state is measured in seconds. For systems that hold a lot of state, such as the stream and storage systems in the Shipping stage, immutability is best achieved by delegating management of those systems to your cloud provider. If you can't delegate to your cloud provider, configuration management principles are better at managing stateful systems. Figure 15.9 shows the difference between the stateless and stateful components of your Shipping stage.

There is one exception to the guidance that stateful systems should be managed with configuration management: when the stateful system is already built to be a fully distributed database. Elasticsearch and MongoDB are two such distributed databases, built in such a way that the loss of a single state-holding server will not cause much disruption. Systems such as these are more able to be managed by immutable principles, but there is a trade-off:

- If you manage these systems by using immutable principles, every time you make a change, you have to remove a server and add a new one, so you need to recopy the full server's worth of data to that server. During this recopy period, the overall system is less resilient to additional failures.
- If you manage these systems by using configuration management, every time you make a change, the state is still on the system; the amount of data to recopy is limited to the changes made while the system undergoing change was unavailable.

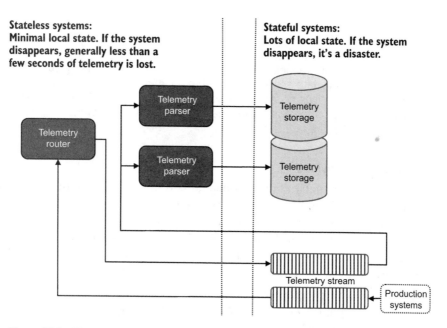

Figure 15.9 The stateful and stateless components of a generic telemetry pipeline. Stateful systems include telemetry storage and the stream systems used to pass data. Stream systems are considered to be stateful because they store stream data over long periods of time. Our telemetry router and parsers are stateless because they merely transact telemetry data and move it along; local state is held for at most a few seconds.

You need to decide which is more important to you: immutability and the security it brings, or minimizing the risk of data loss whenever you make a change. The answer will be different for each organization.

When telemetry isn't immutable

It's easy to look at what I'm talking about here and decide that telemetry should be written once and then carved into digital stone. Entire telemetry systems are built with immutability of telemetry itself in mind. The sorts of telemetry handled by security teams as part of SIEM systems may be of this type.

There is a major case against immutable logging, though. If your production systems handle regulated information such as privacy- or health-related information, the chance that regulated information will leak into your telemetry systems is not zero. For that reason, telemetry systems supporting production systems that handle regulated information must be built with toxic-data cleanup in mind. Cleanup means deleting wrongly logged data or redacting information inside logged data.

Systems such as Grafana Labs' Loki centralized logging system have immutability as a base assumption (at least as of 2021), and their entire architecture is built with that assumption in mind.

(continued)

Going back to remove or modify telemetry is a major problem. Chapter 16 goes into far more detail about redacting (section 16.2) and reprocessing (section 16.3) logging as part of toxic-data spills, but I need to bring up the implications of immutable logging here. If your logging system needs to clean up after spills occasionally, using immutable logging patterns is a bad idea—at least until your defenses of logging regulated information are far more reliable.

15.2.3 *Making changes obvious*

The third leg of telemetry defense is making any changes in telemetry obvious. This section is about techniques to digitally sign, checksum, encrypt, and otherwise make telemetry modifications evident. Open source Presentation-stage systems are not commonly built with support for these sorts of validation models in mind, as of 2021, but if you are developing Presentation-stage systems for your organization, you have the opportunity to advance the field. I cover two broad topics in this section:

- The role of cryptographic hashing in telemetry
- How encryption works with telemetry and the challenges facing encryption-based assurance systems

THE ROLE OF CRYPTOGRAPHIC HASHING IN TELEMETRY

This section is about the use of cryptographic hashes in telemetry. Hashes gives you a method to check whether telemetry was changed since the hash was generated. One somewhat common pattern of making telemetry tamper-evident is to provide a cryptographic hash of a given field, and if the hash doesn't match the field contents, to mark that mismatch somehow. This next snippet shows the `message` field accompanied by a `message_256` field containing the `sha256` hash of the `message` field:

```
message: "This is telemetry"
message_256: "82ca206123ed9fddaf0574e6992d827ac51acf88ed2ec68e854b6469b5e722ed"
```

As mentioned in the introduction to this section, open source presentation systems currently don't have out-of-the-box ways to indicate when a field fails its hash check. If that's the case, why is adding a hash a common pattern? There are two big reasons:

- When you're doing a security investigation, having hashed fields makes it far easier to detect events that were tampered with.
- Because the job of the Shipping stage is to modify telemetry (see chapters 3, 4, and 6), it is in a prime place to validate the hash coming from a production system (or another Shipping-stage component) and alarm in real time if it catches a hash failure.

Figure 15.10 shows how this process works when a structured logger creates a hash of the telemetry, which is checked by a parser in the Shipping stage.

As with all markup and enrichment (see chapter 6), hashes can be applied in the Emitting and Shipping stages. When hashing is done as part of the Emitting stage, as

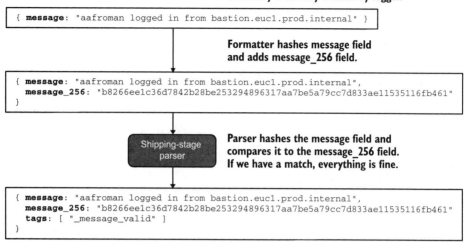

Telemetry is initially created by logger.

```
{ message: "aafroman logged in from bastion.euc1.prod.internal" }
```

**Formatter hashes message field
and adds message_256 field.**

```
{ message: "aafroman logged in from bastion.euc1.prod.internal",
  message_256: "b8266ee1c36d7842b28be253294896317aa7be5a79cc7d833ae11535116fb461"
}
```

Shipping-stage
parser

**Parser hashes the message field and
compares it to the message_256 field.
If we have a match, everything is fine.**

```
{ message: "aafroman logged in from bastion.euc1.prod.internal",
  message_256: "b8266ee1c36d7842b28be253294896317aa7be5a79cc7d833ae11535116fb461"
  tags: [ "_message_valid" ]
}
```

**Figure 15.10 How a hash added by a structured logger formatter is checked by the Shipping stage.
Telemetry enters the logger, and a formatter adds a new field with the `sha256` hash of the message
field. Telemetry with the hash is sent into the Shipping stage. The Shipping-stage parser validates
the telemetry by hashing the message field and comparing it with the `message_256` field. If the
computed hash matches the `message_256` field, it adds a tag to the message indicating that it
found the telemetry hash to be valid. If later investigation shows that the hashes do not match, the
presence of the tag suggests that the telemetry was modified after the Shipping-stage parser saw it.**

we saw in figure 15.10, it is considered to be markup. (The structured logger we investigated in chapter 12 would add hash fields as part of a formatter, the same way that we
added a timestamp field.) If the Shipping stage is adding a hash, that's more of an
Enrichment step, because the telemetry may have been modified legitimately. In fact,
the Shipping stage can add more hash fields based on telemetry it enriches from what
it received from the Emitting stage!

> **WARNING** Be careful of string encoding when hashing fields. To the human
> eye, a string encoded in UTF-16 looks identical to a string encoded in UTF-8,
> but their computed hashes will be different. When you are working in a plat-
> form with a preference for UTF-16 strings, such as Java, make sure that you
> are explicit about string encoding and that all stages of the telemetry pipeline
> will preserve your standard format. Unless told otherwise, platforms like Log-
> stash will quietly reconvert to UTF-8, which will break hashes generated on
> strings of different encodings.

To give you a brief example of this process, let's take a look at a synthetic example. Listings 15.1 and 15.2 go together to demonstrate the hash-creation and verification process, using Logstash and a Ruby script. Listing 15.1 is the Logstash config, which creates
three events. Each of these events has a hash of the message field applied to it; a mutate
filter alters one of the events so that the message field doesn't match the hash; the Ruby
script is called to validate the hash; and finally, the events are sent to a log file.

Listing 15.1   Logstash config demonstrating hash generation and checking

```
input {
  generator {
    lines => [
      "This is an event",
      "Another event",
      "Changed event"  ]
    count => 1
  }
}

filter {
  fingerprint {
    source => message
    target => message_256
    method => "SHA256"
  }

  mutate {
    gsub => [ "message", "Changed", "Altered" ]
  }

  ruby {
    path => "/etc/logstash/hash_check.rb"
  }
}

output {
  file {
    path => "/tmp/filtered.log"
    codec => "json_lines"
  }
}
```

Fingerprint {} generates the hash we will test.

Event generator, used for testing, creates three events.

The hash is generated from the contents of the message field, created by generator {}.

The hash function used is SHA256.

The resulting hash is put into the message_256 field.

The mutate {} filter modifies one event, to test a hash-match failure. Array is field, text to replace, replacement text.

Calls the listed ruby script (see listing 15.2) to validate the hash matches

When this code is run, the filtered.log file should look like this:

```
{"message_valid":true,"@timestamp":"2023-02-19T00:18:13.939Z","message":"This
  is an event","message_256":"b39d2a3411ed3575023b912a05f85172571022d93f65ad
  2b335450dcc5edc55e","host":"parser.euc1.prod.internal",
  "sequence":0,"@version":"1"}
{"message_valid":true,"@timestamp":"2023-02-19T00:18:13.940Z","message":
  "Another event","message_256":"57fd7fd1e61b532b820e10dd315957d76a9ebe416a8
  c190885a8b1effd57370e","host":"parser.euc1.prod.internal","sequence":0,
  "@version":"1"}
{"message_valid":false,"@timestamp":"2023-02-19T00:18:13.943Z","message":
  "Altered event","message_256":"ef95a48a219c20cc432772ddd50bc21610093d886
  cc48958ec08f51e52dd93e5","host":"parser.euc1.prod.internal",
  "sequence":0,"@version":"1"}
```

We see two events with message_valid set to true and one set to false. The message_256 field is created by the fingerprint {} filter, which is the technique you would use to add assurance inside the Shipping stage. The event that the mutate {} filter changed—turning Changed event into Altered event—was flagged as false by the ruby {} filter. To see how we did this, let's look at the Ruby script (in listing 15.2) that the ruby {} filter calls. Any script called by the ruby {} filter needs a filter() function that is called for each event and performs filtering.

Listing 15.2   Ruby helper script for Logstash config in listing 15.1

Required function filter(),
called for each event

```
def filter(event)
  msg  = event.get('message')
  hmsg = event.get('message_256')
  Thread.current['message_check'] ||=
    OpenSSL::Digest::SHA256.new
  hasher = Thread.current['message_check']
  test = hasher.hexdigest(msg.to_s)
  if hmsg == test
    event.set('message_valid', true)
  else
    event.set('message_valid', false)
  end
  return [event]
end
```

Fetches the message and
message_256 fields for testing

Thread safely creates a hash-check
function, if it hasn't been created yet.

Generates a SHA256 hash of
the current message field

Tests whether the generated hash
matches the stored hash and sets
message_valid appropriately

The meat of the filter is quite simple. We fetch the message and message_256 values out of the event, compute the SHA256 sum of the contents of the message field, and then check whether the computed hash equals the contents of the message_256 field. If so, flag the event as valid. If not, flag the event as false. We see this flow in figure 15.11.

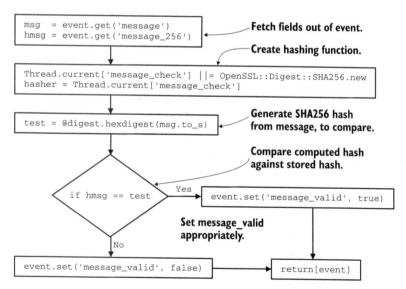

Figure 15.11   The flow of execution when validating a field hash in the Logstash pipeline from listing 15.1. This execution is from listing 15.2. If the contents of the message field have changed between when the stored hash was computed and when we try to validate it, this function will set the message_valid field to false, indicating potential tampering.

This example shows validating a hash inside the pipeline. I'm using Logstash because it is a general-purpose Shipping stage built for the task of moving telemetry, but this method comes with some performance and maintainability warnings. Using the `ruby {}` filter in Logstash generally slows things, so if performance is important, try to minimize how often you use that filter. Switching between a domain-specific language like Logstash configuration files and a language like Ruby means that anyone who's charged with maintaining this pipeline has to be fluent enough in both languages to maintain both. The `ruby {}` filter is powerful, but it increases the base knowledge a team needs to maintain it successfully. If you have to use the `ruby {}` filter, here are a few tips:

- Keep the functions simple to reduce the cognitive load of people who aren't you when it comes to maintainability.
- These plugins run inside the Ruby-language plugin context of Logstash (most plugins are Ruby-language plugins as of version 7.13), which is multithreaded, so build your scripts with thread safety in mind.
- Try not to use it at all. The built-in plugins are solidly optimized, so if you can use them, do.
- As we talked about with regular expressions in chapter 11, format your conditionals to run the `ruby {}` filter only on telemetry that definitely needs it. This approach will improve performance.

When it comes to applying a hash to fields, Logstash isn't the only Shipping-stage tool that comes with that function out of the box. Here are a few common ones:

- Elastic's Logstash comes with the `fingerprint {}` filter-stage plugin, which can create hashes of arbitrary telemetry fields.
- Elastic's Beat suite of tools (Filebeat, Journalbeat, and Auditbeat being the most significant for this book) has a `fingerprint` processor that works similarly to the Logstash fingerprinter.
- fluent-plugin-genhashvalue (http://mng.bz/2z7a) is a plugin for Fluentd that will create a hash value for a given set to keys. Unlike `fingerprint {}` for the Elastic products, this plugin can run on an event only once.

The examples so far have been simple hashes—ways to tell that telemetry has been tampered with. What if we wanted to use something stronger, such as providing a digital signature on telemetry to verify that it was created by a trusted party? For that task, we need to talk about encryption.

HOW ENCRYPTION WORKS WITH TELEMETRY

Any time you bring encryption into a process, you also bring in all the maintainability problems encryption comes with. This section gives you guidance on how to avoid the major pitfalls. This warning applies to both full encryption and cryptographic digital signatures.

Why would you use encryption or digital signatures in a telemetry system? Here are a few reasons:

- Encrypting the originally emitted telemetry side by side with unencrypted telemetry gives security-incident responders hints about what telemetry was changed.
- Encryption provides a safer way to handle toxic information, such as privacy- and health-related information.
- Compared with hashing (see the preceding subsection), digitally signing telemetry provides far stronger assurance that telemetry was last modified by a trusted party.
- Digital signatures provide all the benefits of hashing by making changes tamper-evident.

The biggest challenge for encryption in telemetry systems is supporting the retention periods required. The SIEM systems used by security teams often have retention periods measured in years, with seven years being a common period inherited from financial accounting regulation. Centralized logging systems often have similar retention periods, though most of their period is spent in offline storage. The threshold separating broken encryption from good-enough encryption is changing constantly, and seven years is long enough to likely include one such move. Encryption systems are fragile by design—you want encryption or validation to fail if someone changed something—so you must accommodate that fragility in your telemetry system design. To explore how encryption techniques support telemetry systems, I will describe two different models of encryption use:

- Using public-key cryptography to allow a structured logger in an Emitting stage to encrypt emitted telemetry right at the source
- Using public-key cryptography in the Shipping stage to validate that received telemetry was last modified by a trusted party

Let's look at encrypting telemetry right at the source. Here, public keys are shipped to production systems to allow them to encrypt telemetry securely. This method permits shipping an encrypted version of the emitted telemetry alongside a plain-text version that the Shipping stage will mark up and enrich. Figure 15.12 shows an example.

The process in figure 15.12 creates parallel telemetry: the plain text that will be modified by the Shipping stage and be searchable in the Presentation stage, and the encrypted version of the original telemetry that only someone with the private key can read. It's important to note that the encrypted data in this model is used by only a few people. This method is relatively easy to build, because only encryption operations are performed in the pipeline, which means that decryption, signature verification, and the hassles of safely handling private keys don't need to be automated.

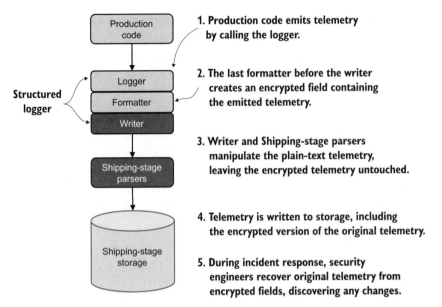

Structured logger

1. **Production code emits telemetry by calling the logger.**

2. **The last formatter before the writer creates an encrypted field containing the emitted telemetry.**

3. **Writer and Shipping-stage parsers manipulate the plain-text telemetry, leaving the encrypted telemetry untouched.**

4. **Telemetry is written to storage, including the encrypted version of the original telemetry.**

5. **During incident response, security engineers recover original telemetry from encrypted fields, discovering any changes.**

Figure 15.12   Encrypting originally emitted telemetry to support later security investigations. These five steps result in fully marked-up/enriched telemetry that is stored alongside the fully encrypted original telemetry. To a security investigator with the private key, decrypting the original telemetry reveals what changes were made to the telemetry since the original encryption.

Things get quite a bit more complicated (and more defensibly secure) when we look at using digital signatures inside a telemetry pipeline. Here, each process that creates or modifies telemetry cryptographically signs telemetry as it finishes with it. We see that process in figure 15.13.

The process in figure 15.13 is far more complicated than the one in figure 15.12, because far more encryption operations are taking place. We see digital signatures being applied in three separate places:

- In step 3, when the last formatter of the structured logger signs the telemetry emission with the Emitter key
- In step 6, when the router signs marked-up telemetry with the Router key
- In step 8, when the billing-platform parser signs enriched telemetry with the Parser key just before telemetry is stored for searching

Because signing something digitally requires access to the private key, this telemetry pipeline requires shipping private keys to three places in the system, including the most at-risk location: the edge of the network, where the production code is running. Securely distributing private keys is a process with many pitfalls that reduce security. This telemetry method provides a high degree of assurance that any telemetry tampering will be detected immediately in flight and offers the possibility of detecting tampering after telemetry is stored.

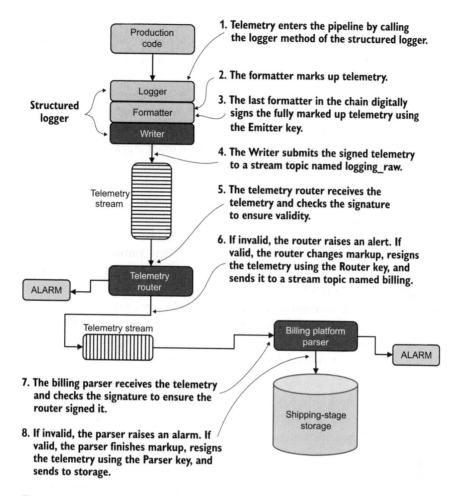

Figure 15.13 A centralized logging pipeline using three separate signing keys to provide assurance at multiple stages of the pipeline. In these eight steps, telemetry is signed three times: by the emitter that generated it, by the router that forwarded it to a parser, and finally by the parser. If any step fails signature verification, an alarm is raised.

Encryption is a deliberately fragile process, which makes a telemetry pipeline that depends on encryption/decryption cycles more fragile. This fragility means that the off-the-shelf Shipping stage engines such as Logstash and Fluentd don't have native support for digital signatures and encryption, because the encryption edge cases are so varied that writing a general-purpose framework is problematic. The method from figure 15.12, which encrypts only the raw telemetry as part of the Emitting stage, is supportable because no decryption or validation operations happen during the Shipping stage. The method in figure 15.13, with multiple sign/verify/sign cycles, requires custom code of some kind to build. If you want to build a system of strong assurance like the method shown in figure 15.13, here are pain points you want to address:

- If the writer of the structured logger silently recodes strings, such as ASCII to UTF-8, any digital signature created by a formatter will break. Make sure that the formatter and writer components of your structured logger are crystal-clear with regard to string encoding.
- If your queues, streams, or other telemetry transport methods silently recode strings, any digital signatures will break. Make sure that you build your system to handle those string conversions.
- If your storage system silently recodes strings or changes the precision of floating-point numbers, the last digital signature will break.
- Key expiration will break your telemetry system the same way that forgetting to renew the SSL certificates on your website breaks your website. To avoid that kind of outage, you need to create a system to safely renew signing/encryption keys. Also, you need to communicate the key renewals to the validation stages so that they know to expect the change. Using public key cryptography that chains up to a certificate authority will help but moves the problem to expiring certificate authorities.
- Any failure in distributing private and public keys will create at least a partial telemetry outage. Build this failure case into your service offering (modify your service-level agreements, to use the SRE term) so that your telemetry users have a better understanding of your availability promise.

Encrypting or signing telemetry digitally isn't something that every organization needs to do, but you should have a conversation about these techniques when considering updates to your telemetry systems. You pick these methods when you need strong assurance that telemetry hasn't been tampered with. Startup companies likely don't yet have the risk exposure to make this step necessary, whereas companies entering the healthcare market can find themselves suddenly having to put these techniques to use. Because these techniques require at least some custom coding, they're more for medium-size and large organizations. (See part 2 for a breakdown of organization by size and type.)

Exercise 15.3

What are the two key principles of defending telemetry from attackers?

a Production systems should emit using write-only methods.

b Telemetry must be transmitted over encrypted channels.

c Once emitted, all access to telemetry must be traceable, and modifications must be made obvious.

d Avoid using log files, because attackers can change them.

Summary

- Telemetry systems are incredibly useful in a security incident, which is why attackers try to break or subvert them to hide their tracks.

- Your goal as a telemetry system defender is to prevent telemetry alteration wherever possible and to increase the effort of making changes everywhere else. This approach makes the attacker's job harder and increases the chance that you will be able to trace their movements afterward.

- Compliance and regulatory frameworks often require system design that makes alteration by an insider harder. Because most growing organizations encounter these frameworks after their products (and telemetry systems) are created, they have to add assurance features to existing systems.

- Production systems should emit telemetry by using write-only methods, which make it harder for attackers to bend the production system to change telemetry.

- Once emitted, all access to telemetry (including operator/admin/root access) must be traceable, and modifications must be made obvious to ensure that recorded telemetry remains a true record of what happened in production.

- Emitting to log files gives attackers more of a chance to change telemetry than other methods, so plan to ingest and ship your log file contents as fast as possible.

- Telemetry needs to be shipped from log files continually, rather than in batches, which greatly reduces exposure to attackers.

- Telemetry needs to have low lag between when the emission happens and when it is shipped to the rest of the Shipping stage, further reducing the time that an attacker has to make changes.

- Creating a write-only place to put log files often can be done with operating system permissions. Grant the write permission, but not read.

- Creating a write-only directory is easiest on Windows systems because the access control system allows complexity that UNIX/Linux systems generally lack.

- SELinux and AppArmor are Mandatory Access Control systems for Linux that allow complex rights definitions, enabling the creation of true write-only directories for applications.

- When you're using a queue or stream system for both telemetry and production access, do not use the same credentials for production work and telemetry work. Instead, use separate credentials: make the telemetry credential write-only, and deny the production credential access to the telemetry channels.

- When you're selecting a telemetry SaaS provider, make sure that the provider offers a way to submit telemetry through a write-only API token or method. At all costs avoid using the admin token (if one is offered) to send telemetry.

- All telemetry systems—such as queues, streams, and APIs—must support authentication, and if possible, must be configured to require it. The logs showing those authentication requests must also be tracked and likely streamed into your SIEM systems as well. This approach provides security a way to trace events during an incident.

- Ideally, telemetry system operators will have individual accounts on each system they need to access instead of using a shared account. This approach gives security teams the highest-resolution details when they reassemble events during an incident.

- Code inside the telemetry system needs to be subjected to the same change-control techniques that production code undergoes, for many of the same reasons.

- Configuration management tools such as CFEngine, Puppet, and Chef are useful for enforcing the approved state of telemetry configuration, which makes ad hoc changes harder to bring about.

- Immutability is a related concept; you design your systems so that no one can make changes. Docker and FaaS are famous examples of this pattern, but servers and virtual machines can be made immutable as well.

- Attacking immutable systems likely requires attacking the deployment method for the immutable systems, so defend those systems as well.

- Cryptographic hashing of telemetry is useful for making changes to telemetry obvious; the stored hash and the newly computed hashes don't match.

- Security teams can use hashes in telemetry to isolate telemetry that potentially was modified by an attacker.

- Hashes can be used by Shipping-stage components to ensure that incoming telemetry has not been modified and send an alarm if it has been.

- String encodings are land mines if you are using hashes. Many systems silently recode strings, such as from UTF-16 to UTF-8, which will silently break a hash generated using the previous encoding. You need to be explicit with string encoding at every step to be sure that your hashes will continue to validate telemetry.

- Encryption and digital signatures are valuable in a telemetry system because they provide strong assurance that telemetry was last modified by a trusted party, not by some hacker who figured out that you're using unsalted SHA256 hashes as a checksum.

- The biggest problem facing encryption in telemetry systems is the retention period; in some cases, you legitimately need to be able to verify signatures or decrypt data that is up to seven years old.

- Using digital signatures inside a telemetry pipeline to validate that changes were made by a trusted party requires securely distributing private keys, which is easy to get wrong.

Redacting and reprocessing telemetry

This chapter covers

- Identifying toxic data and where it comes from
- Cleaning up after toxic data spills
- Reducing the scope of toxic data spills
- Reprocessing cold storage to improve restorability

There are two big reasons why you might want to rewrite stored telemetry:

- Regulated information—such as privacy- and health-related information, and sometimes financial information—somehow got into your telemetry systems and needs to be removed before your organization has to notify customers and users of the breach (*redaction*). I call information like this *toxic data* because information of these kinds require special handling, and there are severe penalties for getting it wrong.
- Upgrading a telemetry storage system often means that backups or databases need to be reformatted to ensure restorability, or replacing one telemetry system with another means having to import your old telemetry into the new system (*reprocessing*).

This chapter is about handling both of these concerns, which certainly can happen at the same time! When upgrading/replacing your storage, you have a great opportunity to redact things you don't want in your telemetry systems. Although most of what I talk about in this chapter focuses on toxic-information cleanup—it is the more complicated problem—reprocessing matters as much for long-term maintenance of telemetry systems.

These maintenance tasks are easy to miss, especially in a small but growing company. Compliance and regulatory frameworks force you to pay attention to these problems, so many growing companies have to pay down years of technical debt when they attempt to achieve compliance. Although regulation about health information with stern penalties has been present for decades, privacy regulation with similar penalties is relatively new, with the European General Data Protection Regulation (GDPR) going into force only in 2018 and other laws coming into force since then. This recency of regulation means that safe-by-default handling of certain inputs—name, address, email, phone number, and so on—is not yet built into programming languages and frameworks.

Although safe defaults will improve over the 2020s, most of us will be working on systems that weren't built on platforms with safe handling of privacy/health information in mind. Telemetry systems are a major leak point for privacy and health information, so expect to see telemetry systems start picking up features to handle them better. Until then, learn how to redact and reprocess your telemetry for safety.

16.1 *Identifying toxic data and where it comes from*

Data toxicity is my term for data that requires special handling, notification of spills, requirements for cleanup, and severe penalties for not following those procedures. Much as environmental regulations largely didn't bother with regulating toxic substances until the 1970s or so, 50 years later, toxic data is beginning to enter the realm of regulation. This section is about what makes up toxic data and how it enters your telemetry systems. There are three major types of toxic information.

- *Financial information*—The first kind of toxic data has been treated as such by financial institutions and their regulators for decades, though it took the Payment Card Industry to provide and enforce handling standards outside banks. This standard is called the Payment Card Industry Data Security Standard (PCI/DSS).
- *Health information*—The second type of toxic data to gain broad acceptance, computerization of health records (and the ease of sharing that enables) drove health-privacy regulation such as the American Health Insurance Portability and Accountability Act (HIPAA). This information is also known as ePHI (electronic protected health information).
- *Personally identifiable information* (PII) —PII is the third type of toxic data to gain acceptance. The European Union's GDPR was the first comprehensive regulation to arrive, and it started a cascade of other regulations in states, provinces, and nations across the world.

The standards defining what qualifies as one of these three types of toxic data evolves over time, as the regulating bodies update standards based on better understanding of data use. Before the GDPR, for example, the IP address that a user used to access a service was not generally considered to be the same kind of private information as home address and phone number. If your organization handles one of the three regulated toxic data types, make sure that your telemetry systems aren't making it easy to gather and display newly classified information types. (For more on getting rid of newly classified information you're already handling, see section 16.2.)

There is a fourth type of toxic data, somewhat different from the other three: security information. Data of this type includes plain-text passwords, private encryption keys, password hashes, API keys, and anything else that would allow someone looking at telemetry to impersonate someone else or access something they're not authorized to see. A government agency won't make trouble for your organization for mishandling security information (unless you're working with government secrets; then you'll be in more trouble than you ever want to experience), but it needs to be treated as toxic data, the same as the other kinds. The risk that this type of toxic data represents is reputational; if the world finds out that you don't treat this kind of data safely, everyone will stop using your services.

If at all possible, don't display toxic data in your telemetry systems. The special handling rules for toxic data make accessing telemetry much harder, which makes your telemetry systems harder to use overall. When you make access to your telemetry systems difficult, people stop using them—or, worse, make their own telemetry systems that aren't subject to the defenses you built, which leads to leaks and official penalties.

Figure 16.1 shows the penalties for getting caught leaking toxic information, which are severe. The penalties come in five types:

- *Denial of handling that sort of information for a period of time*—Violate PCI/DSS hard enough, and the Payment Card Industry will ban you from processing credit and debit cards. This penalty puts nearly all young companies out of business or shunts them into niche markets that accept only direct bank transfers and cryptocurrencies.
- *Great big fines*—Regulators know that businesses understand money, so they make violations hurt monetarily. To make matters even worse, such fines are commonly made public information, so a major hit to the organization's reputation also happens.
- *Publicly admitting that the violation happened*—Mandatory disclosure laws force violating organizations to notify the affected people or make a public disclosure that the violation happened. No company enjoys admitting fault, which is why regulations force this step as a way to make the "Don't violate" lesson stick.
- *Explicitly assigning civil liability*—Regulation and laws make it clear that the parties affected by the leaked information are entitled to sue for damages, possibly as a class action.

The penalties for mishandling privacy- and health-related data

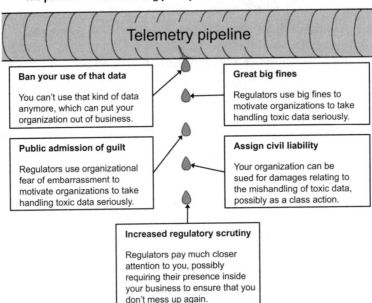

Figure 16.1   The penalties for mishandling toxic data are severe and can put your organization out of business.

- *Increased regulatory scrutiny*—Sometimes, violation means that regulators will be looking at your organization extra-hard for the next several years to ensure that no further violations happen. This extra attention often slows internal processes due to the need for the regulator to approve the change, and it sometimes forces internal process changes to appease the regulator well after the incident was resolved.

People absolutely do lose their jobs for violating (intentionally or not) data handling rules and regulations, and in certain cases, they can be held criminally liable. If your production systems handle toxic data, the chances that your telemetry systems will *unintentionally* handle toxic data are nonzero. You need to be scared of this stuff.

Toxic data enters telemetry systems in two big ways. The first way is programmatic exceptions. Every programming language throws exceptions, most of which allow emitting more than simply "crashed :(". Indeed, stack dumps are common. Unfortunately, so is emitting the parameters that caused the exception. Parameters are incredibly useful for diagnosing why the program died in that way, but they are absolutely evil when it comes to handling toxic data safely. Take the following exception example:

```
ExampleClass::VroomBoxFault at vroombox.vbr:192 with
[ speed = -999,
  firmware = "4.3.19.02",
```

```
    account_id = "0009121205",
    make = "Audi",
    model = "CRX-11",
    license = "US:NM:0000SU",
    owner = "John Rutherford",
    notification_email = "jruth73@example.com"
]
```

First, speed is a suspicious negative number and is likely why `VroomBoxFault` was thrown. But this exception also includes two pieces of privacy information: a full name and an email address. Why is that information there?

Sometimes, a programming language dumps these details by default, and it's up to the engineers to determine how much detail is included in exception dumps. At other times, engineers are unconditionally serializing function parameters and trusting that PII/ePHI won't be in there; worse, they don't understand that an email address has been considered to be PII ever since GDPR, as in this unconditional dump:

```
catch ExampleClass::VroomBoxFault
    logger.warn("Broke my toe sending an email notice. Params: " + toJson(params))
```

An engineer who is aware of the privileged nature of two of the fields could rewrite this code to be safer:

```
catch ExampleClass::VroomBoxFault
    safe_params = []
    safe_params.add(params["speed"])
    safe_params.add(params["firmware"])
    safe_params.add(params["account_id"])
    logger.warn("Broke my toe sending an email notice. Params: "
    ➡ + toJson(safe_params))
```

Including `account_id` but none of the identifying details of the car or owner urges our debugging engineer to use the production system—and all its access safeguards—to look up what the other parameters likely were. This method is a far safer way to log an exception, and you can do it immediately.

One safer pattern is not to serialize to string, as we're doing above, but pass in a hash to the logging function. This approach lets you create middleware in your logger to exclude toxic data automatically. Chapters 12 and 14 cover structured loggers (chapter 12) and methods of restricting the sorts of data that end up in logging streams (chapter 14) through using structured loggers. Section 16.4 discusses a second technique for safely handling high-risk telemetry when using a structured logger isn't possible.

Besides exceptions, the other big source of toxic data in telemetry streams is unconditionally echoing user-supplied input as part of telemetry. Similar to what I just talked about regarding exceptions, knowing what the user submitted greatly helps debugging what went wrong. If the user is submitting something that routinely includes PII, however, their bad values will likely include PII. To demonstrate, take this log statement:

```
logger.warn("Invalid payload for API call. Got: " + api_payload.to_string)
```

This statement is quite useful for figuring out bad API calls but ignores data safety. If the bad payload is a JSON block that had the final } cut from it, rendering the JSON invalid, the rest of the data structure is present and now in your telemetry stream. If the API call was submitting privacy- or health-related information, your telemetry system has that information in it (figure 16.2).

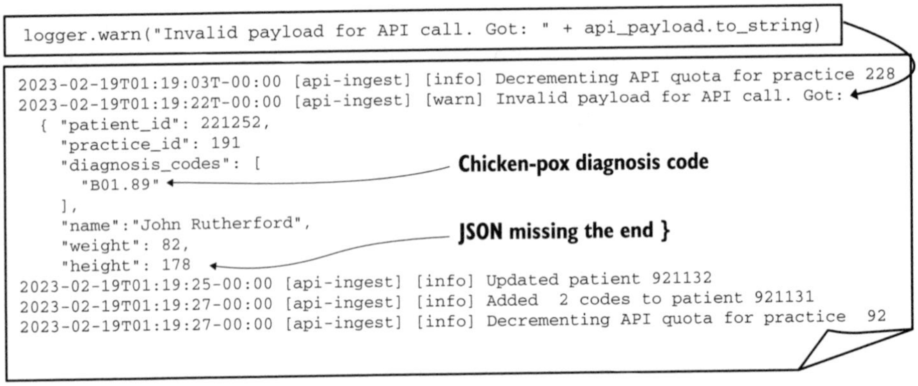

Figure 16.2   How an unconditional emission of a bad parameter leads to a leak of health information. The API call didn't have a valid JSON structure, which is sent directly into the logs, including all the troublesome health information. Don't do this.

There are safer ways of handling *bad-inputs* types of logging, and I talk about them in section 16.4. Now that we know how this stuff gets into the pipeline, let's talk about what to do about it.

> **Exercise 16.1**
> Which of the following is not one of the top two ways that toxic data enters telemetry streams?
>
>   a Engineers logging parameters as part of normal logging
>   b Exception logs including parameters
>   c Logging unredacted user-supplied input

16.2 *Redacting toxic information spills*

Section 16.1 describes what toxic data is, and what the penalties are for not handling it safely (fines, embarrassment for your organization, lawsuits, and sometimes criminal proceedings). This section describes what to do about toxic data that enters your telemetry system (other than hiding under your desk until the lawyers go away). Redaction is the process of removing or masking information, and it must be done if you have stored toxic data accidentally.

Before we get to redaction, we need to examine what happens when you find toxic data in your telemetry systems. Maybe someone else found it and came to you wondering what to do. Maybe you found it. Whatever the source, as a telemetry system operator, you have a duty to report the potential liability to the appropriate people:

1 *Report the spill to your security, compliance, or (if you have one) data control team.* This step starts the process, and the longer you wait to do this, the bigger the mess you will have to clean up later. For certain types of toxic data and under certain regulatory frameworks, not reporting a spill in a timely manner opens you personally to penalties.

2 *Work with the team to identify how widespread the problem is.* This step determines the scope of the problem. You will be acting as an expert on telemetry systems. The teams you are working with will be trying to determine how many people accessed the toxic data, assessing that risk, and judging whether it should trigger a more rigorous incident response. In most cases, this step goes fast, is quickly traced to a single line of code, and doesn't go much farther.

3 *Work with the team to determine an action plan.* Responses will vary, but this step is the first time you can be asked to remove the toxic data. The code that is leaking the data will be addressed through whatever hotfix or other urgent bugfix methods your organization uses to push code outside the regular development cycle. Depending on how long fixing the production code takes, you can end up performing the redaction steps several times.

4 *Perform a final redaction when the leak is plugged.* Now that the leak is fixed, you perform one last redaction to clean up all traces of the spill. Whether you need to go through your offline storage and redact there (reprocessing; see section 16.3) is a conversation you will have with your data control and security teams.

To demonstrate how this process works, let's look at an example that is all too common. Our example organization has a support widget on its site written in JavaScript, which communicates with an API on a server. We don't need to know more—only that the JavaScript sends things to a specific API. The code behind the API is wired into a centralized logging system, which we see in figure 16.3.

This support widget takes logged-in user-supplied data and sends it into the API. One of the fields in the API request is `username`. As on many websites, for our example organization, the username is an email address—something that is now considered to be PII per European standards.

One day, the support widget receives an update that changes how it constructs the API request. For whatever reason, email addresses with a plus sign in them, such as `jreichold63+techsupport@example.com`, now cause the format of the request to fail validation by the API server. We don't care why this happened; what we care about is how the API server reacts to an invalid request.

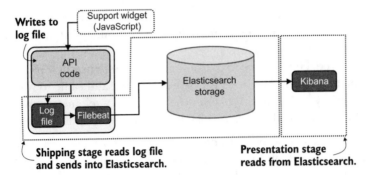

Figure 16.3   **The telemetry system for our redaction example. The code behind the API emits centralized logging telemetry into a log file, which is read by Filebeat and shipped into Elasticsearch. From there, Kibana is the Presentation stage and consumes Elasticsearch storage. The log file contains JSON-formatted lines, which Filebeat turns into a hash—the extent of the enrichment being performed here.**

Our API server has been there for a while, and the engineers who wrote it did so before realizing that email is a sensitive string that needs special handling. A previous incident revealed that the server was logging every event, similar to this code:

```
logger.info("Opening ticket for #{username}")
```

This code sent the email addresses into the logs for every API call. It was a bad day when security noticed what was happening, but engineering made a hotfix to log the account ID number instead. Engineering had to look up the ID from the username first, but the ID is a safe value to log and more useful for debugging (the primary key on the database table):

```
logger.info("Opening ticket for #{account_id}")
```

Engineering missed the exception handler, however. On the day the support widget received the breaking update, a slow trickle of API requests landed on a logging statement like this one:

```
logger.error("Invalid API payload received: #{payload.to_string}")
```

Nothing in this statement suggests that PII will be emitted when it is executed; all the details are hiding in whatever is lurking inside `payload`. On this day of the bug release, the logger statement produced a logging statement with the following in it (dangerous value in bold):

```
Invalid API payload received: {"date":"2023-02-19T01:55:32+0600",
"subject":"Why are my pajamas \"in holding \" in Ireland?",
"username":"jreichold63+"techsupport@example.com",
"details": "They're pajamas for Pete's sake!" }
```

We see that the support widget is inserting a double quote after the plus sign in the email address without escaping it, which renders this JSON block invalid. The important point is that we have an email address in our telemetry again.

Support calls engineering about angry customers who never got an email confirmation that their support requests were received. After digging into the logs, our engineer notices the email hiding in the exception trace. Their memory fresh from the earlier mini-crisis of removing email addresses from a large part of the logging, they know to contact their security team ("Help—it's happening again").

Security and engineering investigate and quickly identify both the exception log statement and the bug in the support widget as the cause. The bad support widget code has been in place for 22 hours, and new lines are being generated at a rate of three an hour—not a large leak, but still a leak, and leaks must be fixed. Engineering creates a hotfix for the exception logger to change how that event is handled:

```
logger.warn("Invalid API payload received: #{exception_name}")
```

Meanwhile, security sends a bug to the people who made the support widget to get them to fix the parsing and encoding bug they introduced in the release. So far, so normal. Our telemetry system operator is given the task of removing the PII from the Elasticsearch system. Luckily for our operator, Elasticsearch has a convenient API that they can use to remove the bad data in a single API call (listing 16.1).

Listing 16.1 Using Elasticsearch `delete_by_query` API

Uses the HTTP POST verb for the API

```
curl https://logger.es.prod:9200/filebeat-2023.02.19/
   _delete_by_query \
   -XPOST \
   -H'Content-Type: application/json' \        ← Sets the Content-Type header so
   -d'                                            Elasticsearch knows to expect JSON
{ "query": {
    "match": {
       "message": "Invalid API payload"          The body of the API call,
    }                                             removing all documents with
  }                                               'Invalid API payload' in them
}'
```

A single API will remove all the matching documents in the given index. Repeating the same call for the `filebeat-2023.02.18` index to pick up yesterday's bad records will finish the cleanup. This technique also removes all the exception traces for this function, including ones without PII in them. Sometimes, such collateral damage is acceptable; maybe engineering already reviewed two days of exceptions and doesn't need those logs anymore, or maybe the engineers simply don't care about them enough to be worried about rewriting instead of removing. In two calls, the problem is cleaned up, and everyone goes back to their planned work. There's no need for lawyers.

But what if there were thousands of these lines instead of fewer than a hundred? You can configure the `delete_by_query` API call to limit the number of delete requests per second that Elasticsearch attempts in the background. This technique is useful if the delete activity will slow ingestion of new events. Listing 16.2 shows the revised API call, with the change in boldface.

Listing 16.2   Using the Elasticsearch `delete_by_query` API with a rate limit

```
curl https://logger.es.prod:9200/filebeat-2023.02.19/
  _delete_by_query \
  -XPOST \
  -H'Content-Type: application/json' \          Limits the number of background
  -d'                                           deletes to 200 per second
{ "requests_per_second": 200,      ◁──────┘
  "query": {
    "match": {
      "message": "Invalid API payload"
    }
  }
}'
```

What if our engineering team wasn't fine with losing these logs? In that case, a simple `delete_by_query` is not viable, and we have to rewrite the given events, which takes more work. To resolve this problem, we need to write a short script to fetch the bad events, and then update them with the bad data removed. To handle cases with tens or hundreds of thousands of events to redact, we will use paginated search and bulk-update operations. The flow of our script will be

1 Set up a paginated search for our bad data, which will return a fresh block of documents each time the search is executed.
2 Iterate through the returned documents to build an update set, redacting the bad data.
3 When the size of our update set meets our arbitrary bulk-update threshold, send the update set to Elasticsearch as a bulk operation, and reset the update set to empty.
4 Repeat steps 2 and 3 until the paginated search stops giving us documents.

Listing 16.3 shows one method of fetching and rewriting events, based on scripts I've used in real life. This listing uses the paginated search and bulk-update techniques from figure 16.4. As of Elasticsearch 7.10, Elastic has added a new method for handling paginated search as part of its paid X-Pack extension. I'm using the free/OSS version here, as that version is more accessible. This listing is drawn from several versions I use in my own redaction processing.

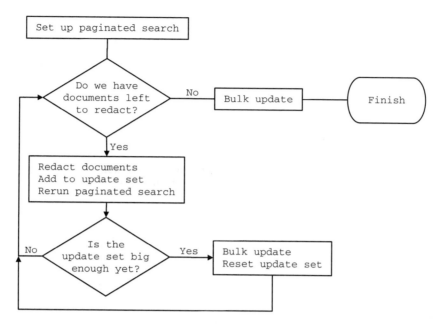

Figure 16.4 The process flow for redacting a large number of documents in Elasticsearch, using bulk updates. The paginated search returns zero documents when there are no more documents matching the search that have not yet been returned. We use a second loop to manage the size of the bulk updates to keep it reasonable, rather than throwing potentially hundreds of thousands of updates in a single call.

NOTE Listing 16.3 requires the elasticsearch gem. The version you install depends on the version of Elasticsearch you plan to talk to (gem install elasticsearch -v [version]). See the gem documentation for details.

Listing 16.3 Redacting our mistakenly logged PII in Ruby

Specifies the Elasticsearch index to search

```ruby
require 'elasticsearch'

ES_HOST = 'logger.es.prod'
BULK_SIZE = 1000

esclient = Elasticsearch::Client.new host: ES_HOST

result_set = esclient.search(
  index: 'filebeat-2023.02.19',
  search_type: 'scan',
  scroll: '2m',
  q: 'message:"Invalid API payload"
  AND message:"username"')

doc_count = 0
update_set = []
loop do
```

Creates a class to handle our Elasticsearch communication

Creates an object for our document search

Configures paginated search, keeping a snapshot of the results for two minutes

Our search query

Loops through our paginated search

```
result_set = esclient.scroll(                        Fetches a batch of documents
    scroll_id: result_set['_scroll_id'],             from our paginated search object
    scroll: '2m')
break if result_set['hits']['hits'].empty?           If we get no documents, break
result_set['hits']['hits'].each do |doc|             the loop! We're done.
    doc_count = doc_count + 1
    clean_mess = doc['fields']['message'][0]
    .split(':')                                       Splits the log line on the colons, which
    update_set.push( {                                is how we will redact the bad data
        update: {
            _index: doc['_index'],                    Pushes the Update object to the
            _id: doc['_id'],                          update_set array, with message
            data: {                                   set to 'Invalid API payload'
                message: clean_mess[0]
            }
    } } )
    end                                               Sends our updates in
    if doc_count >= BULK_SIZE                          batches of BULK_SIZE
        esclient.bulk body: update_set
        doc_count = 0
        update_set = []                               Submits the update set
    end                                               to the bulk updater
end
esclient.bulk body: update_set
```

If we have documents, loop through each.

But what about immutable logging?

Immutable logging—write once, read many style logging (WORM)—is a clear win in the fight to defend logging from later modification. In fact, certain regulatory frameworks (especially finance) mandate immutable logging in certain cases. But if PII or ePHI ends up in your immutable logs when it doesn't belong there, you have a real problem on your hands.

How this problem is allowed to be solved varies from organization to organization, but the main approach is simple: create a new immutable log set with the redactions performed, documenting the heck out of the need to perform that work and exactly what was done to make the new log set. Changing an immutable artifact must include a lot of paperwork and tracking.

All this is a long way of saying this: don't apply WORM techniques to application telemetry unless you have utter confidence that you've solved any potential leaks of regulated information or have the ability to live-redact queries.

Our example uses Elasticsearch as a data store, but other databases are in common use for centralized logging. Another popular option is MongoDB. Here are the MongoDB-equivalent Ruby and shell operations to the Elasticsearch Ruby and shell operations used in listings 16.1 through 16.4:

- The shell equivalent to the Elasticsearch `delete_by_query` is `db.collection.deleteMany()`, which also accepts a filter and will remove documents in a single call.

- Paginated search and update, demonstrated in figure 16.3, can be accomplished through a Ruby one-liner performing the `update_many` function after a `find` function. Then Mongo performs the looping in the background:

```
client = Mongo::Client.new(
  [logs.mongo.prod:27017]
)
documents = client.collection('documents')

documents.find({
  :message => "Invalid API Payload",
  :message => "username"
}).update_many({
  :message => "Invalid API Payload: [redacted]"
})
```

16.3 *Reprocessing telemetry to support upgrades*

Reprocessing is either rerunning your source telemetry through your pipeline (sometimes done for migrations to a new platform) or restoring old telemetry from offline storage to reformat, reorder, or modify every event. Not every storage system requires reprocessing for storage upgrades, but enough systems do that I want to cover the technique. This section is about reprocessing your telemetry to support storage system upgrades, migrations to new storage systems, and redactions of your cold/offline storage (section 16.2).

If you are using a SaaS provider for your telemetry, reprocessing applies only if you decide to migrate from the vendor and need to export all your telemetry. You can avoid this step by maintaining your SaaS-provider contract for the duration of your retention period and not sending any new telemetry to the provider. Most providers bill on ingestion rate anyway, so keeping a provider around for cold storage should be much cheaper than using it for active storage.

If you are maintaining the storage for your telemetry systems, consider reprocessing to be part of your telemetry system design. Periodic reprocessing is driven by a few things:

- Your telemetry storage system changes its format, requiring you to reprocess to update the storage format of telemetry already in the system.
- Your telemetry storage system changes its backup (offline) format, requiring you to reprocess to ensure that your backups (or offline storage) can be restored.
- Your presentation systems change their expectations for how telemetry is formatted, requiring you to reprocess old telemetry to match the new expectations.

Elasticsearch is famous for requiring reprocessing when used as part of a telemetry system. Elasticsearch supports snapshots—its method of making an offline copy of an index, used for both backup and offline storage purposes. Snapshots can be restored by the current and plus-one version of Elasticsearch. Because new Elasticsearch versions come out every 12 to 18 months, reprocessing your old snapshots every 12 to 18 months is required if you want to make sure that your old snapshots can be restored. Elastic and Open Search provide many tools to build automation for this process, but it is up to you to build the automation. One version of this process is presented later in this section. The need to reprocess your telemetry can also come from a variety of one-off reasons:

- A discovered PII leak has been leaking long enough that your offline storage contains the bad data too, requiring you to restore, clean, and re-offline your cold data.
- You move to a new telemetry storage system and want to restore your old telemetry into the new system so that you don't have to keep two storage systems around with one used only for restores.
- You change how you segregate telemetry—such as moving from one database per week to one database per day—and want to backport the change to your offline storage as well.
- You need to remove some technical debt present in your older offline data due to lack of understanding of how your storage system worked in the early days.

Figure 16.5 provides the broad steps of reprocessing.

Reprocessing is hard on the databases involved, because you're reinserting days or weeks of telemetry in a short period. When you restore a database, the load is light,

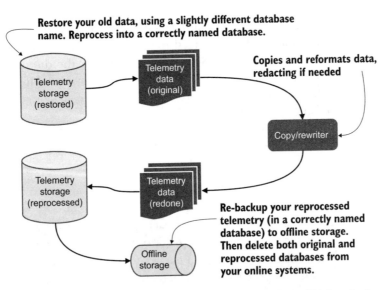

Figure 16.5 The broad steps of reprocessing telemetry. First, old telemetry is restored to the online system under a different database name. Second, telemetry is copied (and, if necessary, redacted) to a new database named what the original would have been named. Finally, when the copy is complete, you take a backup of the new database and delete both old and new databases. This approach allows future restores to continue to use expected database names.

because you're likely restoring the actual database files themselves. But for reprocessing, you're rebuilding the database through INSERTing and UPDATEing individual or bulk events, which requires building the database and index files from scratch.

When you set up to reprocess old telemetry, you need to understand the impact it will have on your systems. In the best case—which is much easier to do if your infrastructure is in a public cloud, where adding a new cluster means spending more money for a bit—you set up a new database cluster to do your restore/reprocess/backup procedures; this approach keeps reprocessing stress away from your production telemetry systems. If you have no choice but to use your production telemetry systems for reprocessing, definitely test reprocessing of a small part of your old data to judge the impact it will have on your telemetry operations. You want to know whether you have to keep that activity as an off-hours thing or whether it is safe for you to let it run 24/7 until done.

Let's take a look at a real-world concrete example: the procedure I used to reprocess telemetry stored in Elasticsearch 1.x for use in an Elasticsearch 2.x cluster. I open-sourced the framework (not that I know anyone else who has used it); you can find it at https://github.com/hellosign/logstash-reindexer. This framework was written in Ruby 2.x because that's what I was most familiar with at the time. The reprocessing framework I wrote has three components:

- A Redis server, used to support a Resque-based (https://github.com/resque/resque) queuing service.
- A Ruby-based worker named snapper, which is responsible for restoring and taking snapshots. In an Elasticsearch cluster, only one snapshot operation at a time is allowed, so this single worker governs that process.
- A Ruby-based worker named reindexer, which is responsible for copying events to the new index, performing any transformations needed, and triggering the restore of the next snapshot. You can have several of these workers running in parallel.

The queue hosts a list of snapshots yet to process, as well as the queues that the snapper and reindexer workers listen to. The snapshot list is primed through the gen_snaplist.rb script, which polls the snapshot repository for snapshots matching a given regular expression and pushes each into the queue. Figure 16.6 illustrates how a snapshot is restored, reprocessed, and retaken:

1. snapper restores an index and sends a job to the reindexer queue.
2. A reindexer worker picks up the job and performs any redactions or other modifications to the source and target indexes.
3. reindexer reprocesses, creating and populating a new index from the old.
4. reindexer pops a new snapshot off the snaplist queue.
5. reindexer sends a job to snapper to take a snapshot of the just-reprocessed index.
6. reindexer sends a job to Snapper to restore an index, using the snapshot popped from snaplist.
7. Go to 1 until snaplist is empty.

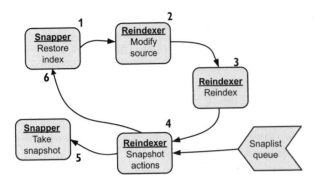

Figure 16.6   The flow of reprocessing an index. This flow iterates through the Snaplist queue until it's empty.

Only one Snapper worker should run, but multiple `reindexer` workers can run. For the Elasticsearch 1.x to 2.x reprocessing, reindexing speed was limited to CPU on the part of the nodes running the reindexer workers and write I/O performance on the Elasticsearch data nodes handling event ingestion.

Reprocessing rates and our Elasticsearch upgrade from 1.x to 2.x

When my company decided to upgrade our telemetry systems from Elasticsearch 1.x to 2.x, we had to reprocess our telemetry. This reprocessing wasn't due to snapshots/backup *format* incompatibility—all our snapshots were in ES 1.x format, which would theoretically run on ES 2.x just fine—but because Elasticsearch 2.x changed how schema management worked in ways that would break searching if we restored the old indexes. Because we were in a public cloud, we decided to spin up a second Elasticsearch cluster to handle all our reprocessing work.

It was a good thing that we did. At the time, our production centralized logging system was handling between 8,000 and 11,000 events a second. On the identically-sized reprocessing cluster, we hit our ingestion limit—the maximum rate at which our cluster could accept events—at between 20,000 and 25,000 events per second. To get that rate, we had to reprocess three to four indexes at the same time.

Even so, it took us almost three weeks to reprocess multiple years of history using that separate cluster. If we had to perform reprocessing on our production cluster, it would have taken us twice to three times as long to not affect regular telemetry processing and still get through everything.

Because reprocessing took us weeks of 24/7 processing, the reprocessing framework had to accommodate living in a production environment. This accommodation involved building in the ability to pause reprocessing so we could patch servers as part of our routine patching processes (the `pause_workers` and `unpause_workers` scripts in the logstash-reindexer repo), and additional scripts to trigger rerunning a reprocess against an index in case something broke (the `inject_reindexer` script in the repo).

When we reprocessed for the upgrade from 2.x to 5.x (Elasticsearch skipped versions 3 and 4 for branding reasons), we performed redactions (see section 16.2) during the reprocessing. We did this on the source (old format) index so that the created new-format index would be as optimized as possible. When we did the 5.x to 6.x reprocessing, we had significantly smaller snapshot sizes due to changes in Elasticsearch itself. This reprocessing also included redactions.

What if you want to reprocess to migrate to a new telemetry storage system, such as Grafana Labs' Loki? The redaction script we looked at in listing 16.3 (section 16.2) gave us much of the framework we need, so let's extend it to write to a Loki `promtail` server. We will need to make a few changes:

- Promtail expects the timestamp of each event to be newer than the previous one, so our search will need to be ordered by time.
- We won't be writing to another Elasticsearch service, so we will need to use HTTP POST instead to send events to Promtail.

These changes have little effect on the process flow we saw in figure 16.4. The few changes we see are in figure 16.7.

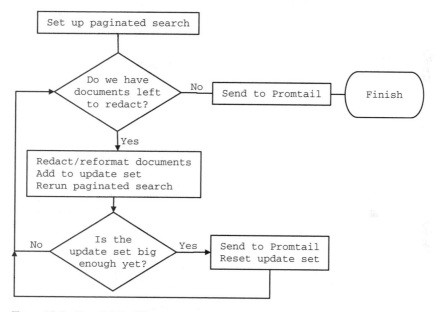

Figure 16.7   The slightly different reprocessing flow for migrating telemetry in an Elasticsearch index into Grafana Loki, by way of the Promtail client (part of Loki). This figure is similar to figure 16.4.

The code is about the same size, though it includes logic for handling the HTTP POST to Promtail, as we see in listing 16.4. The API call to ingest events in Promtail contains an ordered two-element array of events we will need to construct. The two elements of the inside array are a timestamp followed by the event text.

> **NOTE**   Like listing 16.3, listing 16.4 requires the `elasticsearch` gem. The version you install depends on the version of Elasticsearch you plan to talk to (`gem install elasticsearch -v [version]`). See the gem documentation for details. Also install the `rest-client` (for REST interfaces) and `json` gems.

Listing 16.4   Reprocessing an Elasticsearch index into Grafana Loki by way of Promtail

```ruby
require 'elasticsearch'
require 'rest-client'
require 'json'

ES_HOST = 'logger.es.prod'
PROMTAIL_HOST = 'logger.promtail.prod'
BULK_SIZE = 100                          ⟵——— Sets the bulk-update limit

esclient = Elasticsearch::Client.new host: ES_HOST

def reindex(source_idx)
  result_set = esclient.search(
    index: source_idx,                   Sets up the paginated
    search_type: 'scan',                 search, ordering results
    scroll: '2m',                        by _timestamp, ascending
    sort: ['_timestamp,asc'])
                                         As of version 2.1.0, Promtail
  uri = "http://#{PROMTAIL_HOST}:8080/   ⟵—— doesn't have HTTPS support.
➥    loki/api/v1/push"
  loki_base = { "streams": [ {           The base construct of
    "stream": { "label": "exampleapp" }, the Loki API call, to be
    "values": []                         completed later
  } ] }
  doc_count = 0
  update_set = []
  loop do
    result_set = esclient.scroll(
      scroll_id: result_set['_scroll_id'],   Fetches a new batch of
      scroll: '2m')                           documents from Elasticsearch
    break if result_set['hits']['hits'].empty?  ⟵———┐
    result_set['hits']['hits'].each do |doc|          If we get zero documents
      doc_count = doc_count + 1                        back, the search has found
      telemetry = doc['fields']                        everything; exit the loop.
      # Redactions, if any, go here
      update_set.push = [                     Builds the update set: an array
        doc['_timestamp'],                    of two-value arrays (timestamp
        JSON.dump(telemetry) ]                and a logging string)
    end
    if doc_count >= BULK_SIZE   ⟵——┐  If the update set is big enough,
      loki_update = loki_base          send the API call to Loki/Promtail.
      loki_update['streams'][0]['values'] = update_set
      RestClient.post(
        uri,                                  Sends JSON-formatted
        JSON.dump( loki_update ),             telemetry to Promtail
        :content_type => 'application/json' ) by way of HTTP POST
      update_set = []
      doc_count = 0
    end
  end
  loki_update = loki_base
  loki_update['streams'][0]['values'] = update_set    Sends the final batch of
  RestClient.post(                                    updates, if any are lingering
```

Builds the
API call
with our
update set

```
        uri,
        JSON.dump( loki_update ),
        :content_type => 'application/json' )
end
```

↑ **Sends the final batch of updates, if any are lingering**

The function in listing 16.5 would be called by

```
reindex('logstash-2019.08.21')
```

and would send documents in batches of 100 into the Promtail server. Depending on how Promtail's parsing performs, the batch size can be increased or decreased. Loki/Promtail uses a different method of telemetry markup (see chapter 6) from Elasticsearch, preferring to do more parsing at query time to take complexity out of the database. For this reason, Elasticsearch's extensive markup will be consumed at query time, and searchers will rely on a correctly set "label" here in the `loki_base` variable to speed searches.

How far back do you need to reprocess?

This sidebar touches on the topic of chapter 17, which is about retention and aggregation policies, but I can give you some guidance now.

- For telemetry that is more security- or compliance-focused, such as the kind of telemetry you use in a SIEM system, you want to reprocess your entire history. This history is likely seven or more years long, but it is important for your organization to comply with external regulation and compliance regimes.
- For application telemetry used by engineering, I find that requests to access telemetry more than 13 months old are extremely rare. Because application telemetry is likely the largest pool of telemetry in your system, reprocessing only 13 months' worth will save you money.

Exercise 16.2

For your telemetry storage systems, have you ever had to perform reprocessing? What drove the decision process? What will help you handle the process better next time?

16.4   *Isolating toxic data to reduce cleanup costs*

Redacting and reprocessing are expensive procedures: expensive in time, expensive in lost feature work, and expensive in direct costs if additional computing resources need to be spun up to accomplish it. If you know that you have leaks of toxic data (see section 16.1 for that definition) into your telemetry systems from your production systems, this section is about steps you can take to reduce the costs associated with cleanup activities. *Defense in depth* applies to more than security; when it comes to toxic data, it's about failing *safer*. If you take nothing else from this section, take these points:

- Isolating telemetry streams that are at risk of containing toxic data (such as API server events) from streams that definitely will not (such as networking hardware telemetry) will save you money and time when you need to deal with a spill.
- If your production systems handle toxic data, throwing all your centralized logging into a single system is a clear antipattern, which maximizes your cleanup zone.
- Use the access control list (ACL) features available in your Presentation-stage systems to limit access to potentially toxic data containing telemetry to the teams that specifically need that access. This policy reduces the impact of leaks.
- Because exceptions are among the highest-risk bits of telemetry for containing toxic data, take time to engineer separate handling for your exceptions. This policy gives you far better capabilities for *live redaction* (redacting toxic data as part of the emitting and shipping stages), allows you to have a different ACL for reviewing exceptions, and lets you grant wider access to your application logging.

Isolating access to telemetry that can contain toxic data is quite important for the safety of your organization. The more eyes that *potentially* could have viewed the toxic data, the more work the security, compliance, or data control teams have to do to judge the true risk of the spill, which increases the risk that a spill could become *notifiable*—an official breach under the law that requires public disclosure.

Why you should never, ever say "@security, I think I found a breach"

Well, you can say it if you're on the legal team in charge of determining whether a legal exposure is present; otherwise, never use the B word. Just about every reader of this book is not that kind of person. (If you are, I'm trying to help.) The problem with the word *breach* is that it now shows up in enough laws, with a legal definition, that using the word incorrectly can open your organization to legal liability. Start practicing not using the B word unless you're talking about breaches that are already declared or have happened to other organizations.

The problem comes from legal language that reads like this: "... shall notify the regulatory office within 48 hours of detection of the breach ..." The question boils down to when the breach was detected. Nearly every organization wants to put off the official notifications as long as possible, so not using the B word makes it easier to justify doing the official notifications only after the data controller, legal, or some other entity charged with managing data determines that a breach has officially occurred.

If you poke security in Slack with "I think I found a breach," that could, if cast in the right light, with the right judge, be viewed as starting the official notification clock, and the penalties for not performing the notices on time are *severe*. It doesn't matter how you interpret the rules; that's not your job. Don't open liability for your organization by using regulated language like the word *breach* unless you're talking about one that's already been declared.

Figure 16.8 shows the risk difference between managing a single large telemetry pool with everything in it versus telemetry pools isolated based on application and use. The big shared pool makes for a much higher potential impact for a spill, which can open the organization to legal liability. The isolated pools mean that a spill has a much smaller potential impact, and the organization reduces liability.

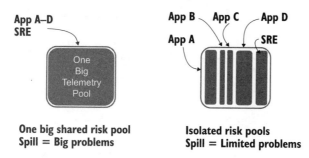

App A–D SRE

One Big Telemetry Pool

**One big shared risk pool
Spill = Big problems**

App B   App C   App D
App A   SRE

**Isolated risk pools
Spill = Limited problems**

Figure 16.8   The risk difference between shared versus isolated telemetry systems in light of the problems presented by a toxic data spill. The big shared pool is easy (and cheap) to manage; everyone sees everything. The isolated pool is trickier to manage (and likely more expensive), but the problem scope of a spill is much smaller as a result.

I've already talked about the biggest way to get this isolation: using ACLs in your Presentation-stage systems:

- Section 5.2.1 provided a feature list to qualify Presentation-stage systems to be used with centralized logging.
- Section 7.2.2 extended that list to support multitenancy, adding roles and ACL concepts. Multitenancy is about keeping telemetry out of the hands of teams that shouldn't see it, and protecting toxic data is much the same concept.

Managing ACL-based separation certainly is more work than letting everyone view everything, but if you are handling PII or ePHI, simplicity isn't a luxury you can afford for long. Centralized logging is the telemetry style most affected by PII and ePHI leaks, though organizations are increasingly using distributed tracing instead of (rather than in addition to) centralized logging and sending logging-like statements with their traces. Redaction tooling for distributed tracing systems is still developing; it's better to isolate where you can.

The other isolation technique is creating separate telemetry streams and handling those streams differently. In section 16.1, I talked about a way to handle bad-inputs-style logging, in which an engineer needs to know what the inputs to a function are to determine why it is failing. Separated telemetry is a great way to handle that use case. The same can be done for handling exceptions.

But also consider the different applications in your environment and their differing toxic data handling needs. To demonstrate separation, figure 16.9 shows two applications managed by the same team and their telemetry systems. One application handles PII directly, so it is at high risk of leaking toxic data into its telemetry feed. The other application supports the first but handles only anonymized data such as account IDs (not account names) and object paths to objects named with a globally unique identifier (GUID).

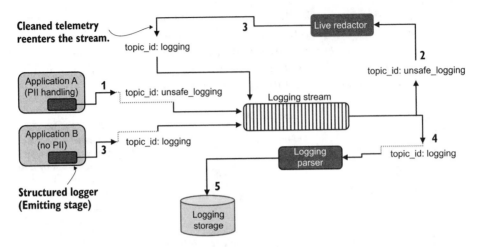

Figure 16.9 Separate telemetry handling for potentially PII-containing telemetry. Both applications emit to a stream for their telemetry, but on different topics. A live redactor listens to the stream from the risky application to act as a filter before resubmitting the cleaned telemetry for writing.

Let's follow the steps telemetry takes before getting stored:

1 Logging from application A (which handles PII) emits into the stream topic-id of unsafe_logging.
2 The live redactor subscribes to unsafe_logging and performs extensive detection and autoredaction of any toxic data.
3 The live redactor sends cleaned telemetry to the logging topic. Meanwhile, application B (not PII handling) sends directly to this topic.
4 The logging parser subscribes to the logging topic and performs telemetry enrichment.
5 The logging parser sends fully enriched telemetry to storage.

The method in figure 16.9 is one way to handle potentially toxic data, but there are other methods. If the unsafe_logging telemetry ended up in a different storage system, covered by a different (and more restrictive) ACL, you also get most of the benefits of isolation. Engineering your telemetry pipeline to include a live redactor like the one in figure 16.9 enables your organization to spend less time cleaning up spills. If you configure the live redactor to tag telemetry that required redaction, you have an easy way to indicate leaky code without having to go through all the trouble of a cleanup operation.

Because more and more organizations are using distributed tracing in the place of centralized logging, updating figure 16.9 for distributed tracing is similar, as we see in figure 16.10.

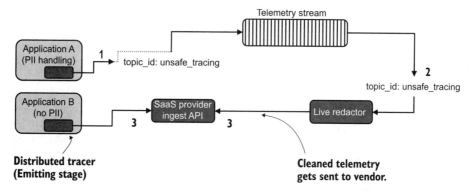

Figure 16.10 Separate telemetry handling for a distributed tracer. Traces emit from both applications, but only application B sends directly to the provider's API. Application A takes a tour through the live redactor before being sent to the provider!

Let's walk through the steps our unsafe tracing telemetry took:

1. Traces are emitted from application A, which handles PII; therefore, the traces might contain PII as well. These traces are sent to a stream system on the `unsafe_tracing` topic.

2. The live redactor subscribes to `unsafe_tracing` and performs extensive detection and redaction of PII on the tracing data.

3. The live redactor submits the cleaned tracing data to the SaaS provider's ingestion API. Meanwhile, application B (which does not handle PII at all) submits to the ingestion API directly without bothering with a stream.

The system we see in figure 16.10 is simpler than the one in figure 16.9 because we're using a SaaS vendor for telemetry, so application B doesn't need to pass through the stream first. This example provides the same benefits as the centralized logging framework shown in figure 16.9. Filters work!

As an industry, we are in the early stages of building generalized tooling for detecting toxic data in real time as part of a telemetry pipeline. This field is evolving rapidly, and there is a rush of mostly machine-learning-based products (open source and not) to fill this need. Any time you get a rush of new products, in five or ten years the field will be consolidated and quite different. Here are two tools put out by major public cloud providers, meaning that these tools are likely to still be around in 2025:

- *Microsoft Presidio* (https://github.com/microsoft/presidio)—An open source, standalone service that is extensible (needed if your PII could show up in different formats). Being a standalone service makes it horizontally scalable.

- *Amazon Comprehend* (https://aws.amazon.com/comprehend)—An API offered by AWS that accepts text and returns any detected toxic data. As an option, it auto-redacts detected toxic data so that you don't have to do it. Being an AWS product, it is definitely not free and charges based on the size of data being analyzed.

The Presentation-stage system features we need to defend against toxic data

Presentation-stage systems (see chapter 5) are where telemetry companies make their money. Open source frontends are increasingly the loss leaders for enterprise plans, but they're in wide use in organizations where reduced features are good enough. As an industry, however, we need to do more to deal with the increasing risk that toxic data presents to our organizations and our data-handling habits. *Presentation-stage systems such as Grafana, Jaeger, and Kibana need to start supporting live redaction in their interfaces, and they need to support it in their open source versions.*

Presentation-stage systems are the last stop before data enters the human eyeball, which means that these systems are the last chance to keep private data *private*. The modern web is full of sites using email addresses as usernames, and email addresses are now classified as PII. As a result, the modern web, from enterprise megasites to single-dev hobby sites, is full of sites handling PII. Making data safety features require an enterprise plan is disaster capitalism, ensuring that only enterprises will handle toxic data safely; startups and small organizations will continue to handle PII and ePHI unsafely. The profit motive makes the whole industry less safe overall when it comes to handling toxic data safely.

If you are developing a Presentation-stage system—perhaps it's for internal use, or maybe you're working on a new framework to challenge Grafana for the open source pie—please consider how toxic data is handled in your free tier. Do not treat that feature as an upsell opportunity; it isn't ethical.

To help systems designed to detect PII decrease their false-positive rate (and reduce the number of nuisance tickets you have to handle because of those false positives), figure 16.11 provides some application design tips to make your life easier:

- *Avoid using random 16-digit integers for things.* Credit card numbers are 16 digits. Although every 16-digit integer isn't a valid credit card number, if you are randomly generating enough of these integers, sheer probability will create numbers that pass the Luhn algorithm that defines the valid format of credit card numbers. A million monkeys banging on typewriters can turn out Shakespeare eventually, but a random-number generator can turn out a viable credit card number far faster. Save yourself some trouble; make those integers 15 or 17 digits instead. Better yet, make them hex and avoid integers entirely.

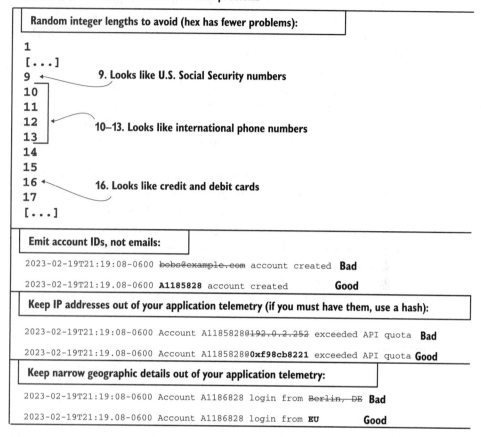

Figure 16.11   Four broad suggestions for avoiding PII/ePHI detections on your telemetry. Random-number generators are cool, but they sometimes spit out numbers that look like things they're not.

- *Avoid using random 10- to 13-digit integers for things.* Most phone numbers with country codes are in this range (or U.S. phone numbers with area code). If the first few numbers end up matching a country code, these integers can look like phone numbers and get flagged as PII by detectors.

- *Avoid using random 9-digit integers for things.* These integers are the same length as U.S. Social Security numbers. U.S. centrism in the tech industry means that PII detectors care about this fact, even if you aren't doing business in the United States. As for credit cards, a validation algorithm of sorts exists, and a random-number generator will make hits often enough to be annoying.

- *Emit account **numbers**, not account **names**.* All too often, the account name is an email address (or something that looks like an email address) and therefore gets flagged by detectors. It's better to emit telemetry in whatever the primary key of your account table is because that's probably a number. (Perhaps do it in another base to avoid the integer problems.)
- *Keep IP addresses in your networking, web server, API gateway, and load balancer logs, and out of your application telemetry.* IP addresses are now considered to be PII by many privacy regimes. Store IP addresses somewhere and provide a way to look them up in an admin portal easily, but keep the actual addresses out of your telemetry. If you still need IP-address tracing, use a hash or other proxy value instead.
- *Avoid emitting geographical IP data (GeoIP) with your application telemetry.* Several libraries and services will return a city, state, country, and continent if given an IP address. Paid services narrow GeoIP resolution even further, isolating IP addresses to neighborhoods or even specific buildings. As a result, privacy regulators consider such GeoIP data to be private data. These services are incredibly useful in fraud and malicious-use investigations, as well as complying with government-mandated sanctions against other countries, but putting this data on every single piece of application telemetry needlessly exposes your organization to legal risk. Keep GeoIP data to your web server and networking telemetry.

Summary

- Redacting (rewriting online telemetry) and reprocessing (rewriting offline telemetry) are done for two big reasons: to clean up after a spill of regulated information such as privacy- or health-related information, and to reformat telemetry to deal with a storage system upgrade or migration to a new storage system.
- Toxic data is data that has severe penalties for mishandling, including health information, privacy information, and financial information. The penalties come from regulatory frameworks such as HIPAA (United States) and GDPR (European Union). Handling toxic data makes your organization subject to these regulations and the effects on your telemetry systems that come with them.
- The penalties for mishandling toxic data are severe and often public. People get fired for it, so you should be scared of this stuff.
- What qualifies as toxic data changes as regulations change. When regulations change, your telemetry systems have to adapt. Sometimes, as happened with GDPR, you have to reprocess a lot of telemetry to get rid of newly toxic data types.
- You want to avoid displaying toxic data in your telemetry systems, because displaying it means that you have to encyst it in all the access control and overhead that come with toxic data handling. Restricting access to telemetry in this way reduces the ability of your technical organization to use their telemetry systems and degrades decision-making overall. Worse, it leads to shadow-telemetry sys-

tems (mostly in SaaS providers) that aren't cleared for handling your organization's data.

- Programs throwing exceptions are among the biggest risk points for leaking toxic data. Many exception handlers also emit the parameters that triggered the exception, which is where the leak happens. If your production system handles toxic data, ensure that exceptions do not emit parameters.

- Unconditionally emitting user-supplied data is the second biggest risk point for leaking toxic data. Although this information is incredibly useful for debugging, if there is any chance that the input data will be toxic, that data should not be emitted into your telemetry stream.

- Redacting telemetry comes in two types: removing the bad events and rewriting the events to remove the bad data selectively. Deleting is easier to write tooling for, whereas rewriting preserves more data but requires a case-by-case change to your tooling.

- The two most popular data stores for in-house hosting of centralized logging, Elasticsearch and MongoDB, have delete-by-query functions that allow you to make a single API call to remove all matching documents.

- When you have to rewrite hundreds of thousands of events or more, use the paginated search functions of your data store, and bulk-update where possible. This approach is easier on your data store and will block regular operations less.

- When you are designing your telemetry storage systems, consider the role that reprocessing will play in regular maintenance. Certain storage systems require reprocessing as part of version upgrades or whenever you change the database schema.

- Routine operations can force you to reprocess your telemetry (such as storage version upgrades). But less-routine events can force the need as well. You will need to reprocess your historical telemetry if a toxic data leak is bad enough that you need to scrub your cold storage, if you plan to move to a new storage system and need to import your historical telemetry, or if changes in how you separate telemetry need to be backported.

- Redaction and reprocessing are expensive operations in terms of time, money, and postponed feature work. You can limit the scale of the interruption by isolating telemetry that potentially contains toxic data to fewer people. This approach reduces the scope of the problem and often makes cleanup cheaper.

- If your production systems handle toxic data, throwing all your telemetry into a single datastore is an antipattern, which maximizes the cost of cleanup activities.

- Use ACL features in your Presentation-stage systems to isolate toxic data containing telemetry from telemetry that doesn't contain it. This approach reduces the exposure your organization faces when a leak happens.

- Build separate telemetry pipelines for telemetry that is at high risk of containing toxic data (such as exception traces and the application logs from applications that handle toxic data directly). This approach enables you to build live-redaction capabilities targeting the risky telemetry flows and ACL-based separation.
- Some organizations are using distributed tracing in the place of centralized logging for reporting text-based events. The redaction and reprocessing techniques here are less well supported with distributed tracing, so if your application handles toxic data, be certain of your ability to redact from your tracing systems.

Building policies
for telemetry retention
and aggregation

This chapter covers

- Creating retention policies for your telemetry
- Creating aggregation policies for your metrics
- Understanding the role sampling plays in telemetry and retention policies

Retention policies (how long to keep telemetry) and *aggregation policies* (how to summarize telemetry) are some of the most important policies you will set for your telemetry systems. Related to aggregation, the sampling technique uses statistical methods to summarize telemetry and is commonly used in distributed tracing. This chapter is about those policies and the trade-offs you need to consider when it comes time to set your own. For the most part, the trade-off is cost versus features—a familiar balancing act for business.

Your retention policy determines how long your telemetry is useful for people in supporting the decisions they need to make. Many organizations find the need for two retention periods: an online retention period, when everything is searchable, and an offline period (cold storage), when telemetry can be made online if needed but otherwise isn't searchable without bringing it online again. Retention policies are your most important policy for keeping the cost of your telemetry system reduced to something you're willing to pay.

Although retention policies are your most important policies for overall telemetry cost containment—especially in centralized logging and distributed tracing systems— aggregation policies are most important for containing metrics costs. The cost reductions come through summarization and loss of fine-grained resolution of events. Aggregation of metrics telemetry improves costs by reducing the amount of telemetry needed to be stored; it also improves performance by precomputing certain functions to make Presentation-stage activities faster. Aggregation as a technique chiefly helps metrics-style telemetry.

Whereas aggregation policies are the cost-containment policy for metrics systems, sampling is the cost-containment policy for distributed tracing. *Sampling* how your production systems are operating *as whole*, rather than diving into individual events, will allow you to store far less telemetry for a given period. Storing less telemetry allows you to keep telemetry online and searchable for longer than not sampling does. Sampling as a telemetry technique came into its own with the distributed tracing styles, though certain metrics implementations (such as StatsD) also used it. All three policies represent important decisions you need to make when building or updating a telemetry system.

- Section 17.1 addresses building retention policies and the trade-offs each telemetry style faces.
- Section 17.2 is about aggregation policies, mostly affecting metrics telemetry, and some of the hidden gotchas you will encounter.
- Section 17.3 covers sampling techniques (related to aggregation), which mostly affects distributed tracing systems.

17.1 Creating a retention policy

Retention policies determine how long you keep telemetry around and in what formats. Telemetry that is online and searchable is the most useful telemetry to have— and also the most expensive to retain. All retention polices, which is what this section covers, are careful balancing acts among

- The advantages to decision-makers of having online and searchable telemetry.
- The cost of keeping telemetry online and searchable.
- The ease of bringing offline telemetry online. The easier it is to do, the cheaper the telemetry system; your online set can be smaller if offline data can be brought online easily.
- The legal exposure brought about by telemetry that potentially contains privacy- or health-related information, or *toxic data*. See chapter 16 for more on managing that risk.

Retention policies are tightly linked with aggregation (section 17.2) and sampling (section 17.3), but I'm talking about retention policies first because the trade-off discussions you'll have about retention policies are similar to the discussions you'll have about aggregation and sampling. To demonstrate how linked these concepts are, figure 1.12, reproduced here as figure 17.1, shows the four telemetry styles in this book and their general online-and-searchable periods.

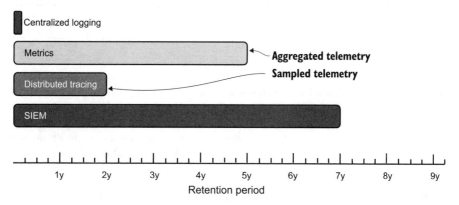

Figure 17.1   The four telemetry styles in this book and their general online and searchable retention periods. Also marked are their preferred methods of reducing cost (not applicable to SIEM and centralized logging).

We see in figure 17.1 that there is a high variation in general online retention periods! The period for centralized logging is smallest because it is the most expensive telemetry style to keep online and searchable; all that text is huge, and the indexes needed to search it are pretty big. The retention period for the Security Information Event Management (SIEM) systems used by security and compliance teams is the longest—seven years—because regulation and compliance frameworks often mandate a minimum retention period for certain kind of telemetry. Metrics and distributed tracing both use aggregation or sampling to reduce the amount of telemetry data being stored to save costs and increase their online retention periods (see sections 17.2 and 17.3).

Figure 17.1 shows the online-and-searchable retention period, but retention policies also include how long offline backups are kept just in case. If backups are easy to restore to the online system—or, better, easily automated so that humans don't have to do the restore tasks—the online retention period can be shorter. Figure 17.2 shows figure 17.1 revised to show the offline retention periods in addition to the online periods.

We see that centralized logging has as long an offline storage period as SIEM has an online storage period. Even though the two styles are technically similar, SIEM systems achieve this feat by being highly selective about the sort of telemetry stored in them. At the same time, metrics doesn't have an offline period at all! This lack of an offline period has more to do with the nature of most metrics databases than with anything else. In the time-series databases that metrics systems use, new telemetry is inserted into the same database as old telemetry is removed, whereas with centralized

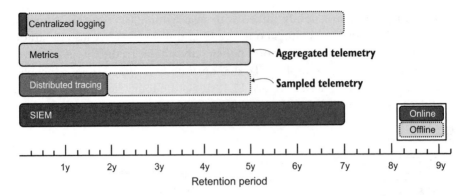

Figure 17.2   Online versus offline retention periods for the four telemetry styles covered in this book. Offline storage allows centralized logging to go much farther back in time.

logging, the most common pattern is a new database per day or week, and the databases are removed over time. Now let's look at the four telemetry styles and dig into the factors driving online storage cost for each:

- *Centralized logging* is not selective; it takes anything that's sent to it. Its primary format is strings and natural-language text. Indexing for strings and natural-language text is complex; therefore, the storage and presentation systems for this style are *expensive* due to the indexing and search capabilities required.
- *Metrics* is selective; it accepts only numbers and a small set of text-based tags. Its primary format is numbers. The small set of text-based tags makes indexing easy. Therefore, the storage and presentation systems for this style are *cheap* due to the simplicity of the databases. This cheapness is why metrics was the second telemetry type to break out after centralized logging.
- *Distributed tracing* is moderately selective; it needs telemetry to be in a specific format. Its primary format is a mix of numbers and text; it doesn't have to support natural-language search. The predefined format reduces indexing costs, but the allowance of arbitrary tags makes for a significant cardinality problem. (See chapter 14 for more on cardinality.) Distributed tracing performs extensive correlation work, which increases the complexity of storage systems. Therefore, the storage and presentation systems for this style are *expensive* due to the cardinality issues and indexing, as well as the added need to correlate events into process traces.
- *SIEM* systems are highly selective in the inputs they accept, and those inputs are often in well-understood formats to begin with. Although its primary format is text, and it does need to do natural-language processing to some extent, selectivity greatly reduces the raw amount of data that needs to be handled per day. Therefore, the storage and presentation systems for this style are probably a SaaS system that charges by ingestion rate due to the extensive correlation work that the Presentation-stage systems need.

NOTE All four styles can be SaaS services, but few open-source SIEM systems can stand up to the SaaS offerings in terms of features. My rankings of expense here also apply to the cost of SaaS providers; centralized logging providers like Splunk cost more to run per month than metrics providers like Datadog, in large part due to the differences in the size of data you send to them. Tracing providers are new enough that they're still working on their pricing models, so expect to see potentially significant changes over the 2020s.

17.1.1 *Building a policy for centralized logging*

In this section, we talk about the factors guiding your decisions in building a retention policy for centralized-logging-style telemetry systems. These systems are the largest and most expensive, and also some of the oldest in many organizations. Centralized logging systems also support the broadest array of decision-making in your organization, which makes them the hardest to pick a policy for. (I'm sorry.)

Every organization is different, but broad arrays of teams use centralized logging in slightly different ways. (See section 1.2 for the definitions of these teams.) Teams' uses are ranked by how general or specific the use is and how far back in time they like their telemetry to go:

- *Software engineering and SRE teams* write the logging statements that produce much of the data inside the centralized logging system; they use centralized logging to chase down errors, judge how the system is operating, and look for anomalies. They also need to compare with historical logging to dig up when bugs started and compare performance. Their use is both specific and general, and they need both recent and historical data. In general, software engineering teams like several release sprints' worth of telemetry to be online and searchable.
- *Operations, DevOps, and SRE teams* manage systems that produce logging, but for the most part, they don't control the logging statements themselves. Similar to how software engineering teams use telemetry, these teams use it to sniff out anomalies and chase errors. There is less drive to compare current and historical telemetry, though. Their use is both specific and general, but mostly over recent telemetry. In general, these teams like a few weeks' to months' worth of telemetry to be online and searchable.
- *Security and compliance teams* use centralized logging depending on whether they have a SIEM; if they lack a SIEM, the centralized logging system is their SIEM. Regardless of the presence of a SIEM system, these teams use centralized logging to handle audits, support security investigations, and reduce leaks of toxic data. Their use is specific and recent, but certain investigations will require old data, so a robust way to bring offline telemetry back online is needed.
  - For teams that have a SIEM system, the centralized logging system is merely a backup for that activity. Their use of centralized logging is mostly restricted to incident-response and toxic-data defense. In general, they like to have a month or two online and searchable.

- For teams that lack a SIEM system, the centralized logging system has to be their SIEM system. You need to give them a way to keep their security data separated in a way that allows you to keep potentially years' worth of it online and searchable. In general, they want to have multiple years online and searchable (or easily restorable if they can't).

- *Customer support teams* use centralized logging to troubleshoot problems reported by customers and users and to create bug reports for software engineering. Having your support teams use centralized logging is a major benefit for your organization, and you should do so if you haven't already. Their needs are specific and recent. In general, they want to have the last few weeks online and searchable.

Figure 17.3 illustrates these constraints.

Centralized logging – General retention guidance by team

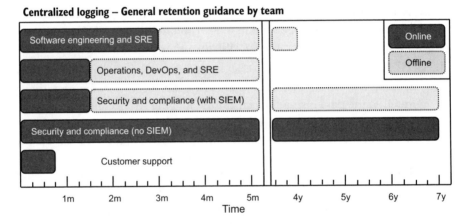

Figure 17.3   General guidance on retention period by team, showing a balance between recency of data and cost. Teams with a strong recency bias, such as customer support, don't need long offline retention periods. Meanwhile, teams such as security and compliance need many years' worth of data online and searchable if they don't have a separate SIEM system.

Software engineering and security will be the biggest drivers of long-term online retention periods. Only you can determine how expensive it is to keep longer periods online, but both groups will happily accept *all of time* for their retention period. Only companies like Google have a chance of supporting indefinite retention, and even they push back sometimes.

Offline retention periods are different, because they are rather cheaper to keep around. Ease of restoration and the toil of having to keep your offline telemetry restorable (see section 16.3) will guide you on how long you want to keep that stuff around.

> **But what about Loki?**
>
> Grafana Labs' Loki challenges some of the assumptions I make here, specifically because it was written to be cloud-native (using cloud storage and cloud databases). Not only that, Loki's design means that it isn't creating fast indexes the way historic centralized logging databases do (mostly Elasticsearch and MongoDB).
>
> Loki is new; it came to market only in 2018. But Loki embraced a feature more common among SaaS providers such as Sumo Logic and Splunk, in that it does quite a bit more query-time processing than Elasticsearch- and MongoDB-based systems do. The storage systems behind Loki are simple, but the trade-off is far more power needed in the presentation systems, and a willingness to read orders of magnitude more data from your storage to supply queries. That said, the march of technical progress means that the trade-off is beginning to make sense. Watch this space over the 2020s to see what happens!

17.1.2 Building a policy for metrics

In this section, we talk about building a retention policy for metrics-style telemetry. This style is heavily influenced by your aggregation policy, of course (see section 17.2). Even so, in the 2020s, metrics-style telemetry is likely the cheapest telemetry style you will support, so you have a lot of latitude here. The biggest pushback in terms of retention is less about space and more about managing cardinality (see chapter 14), although time-series databases that are emerging at the dawn of the 2020s are taking a lot of steps to reduce the impact of cardinality.

For the most part, metrics systems (or *monitoring systems*, to use the name familiar to sysadmins and pre-2010 environments) already support multiyear retention, though they do so through aggregation. Metrics is the second-most-widely-used telemetry style, second only to centralized logging. For this reason, two retention policies are key when it comes to metrics:

- *Full-resolution metric retention*—Full-resolution metrics retains every data point as it was received. This kind of metrics is the most useful to have around, but it is also expensive to keep for long periods due to slowdowns in queries.
- *Aggregated metrics retention* (see section 17.2)—Aggregation summarizes full-resolution metrics and is much smaller. It enables multiple years of retention for most systems, and it greatly reduces the amount of data that needs to be stored and sorted during queries.

The cost of each policy depends on your specific circumstances. To help, figure 17.4 shows a metrics-retention policy that I've used.

In my example retention period, the full-resolution data was kept for one week and still was the slowest-performance database in our metrics system. But one week is enough for "state of the system" and "Did that release just break production?" dashboards. Longer-term research on the performance of certain activities happened in the aggregated datasets, with reducing resolution over time. We'll talk about this topic

Metrics – Example retention policy by aggregation interval

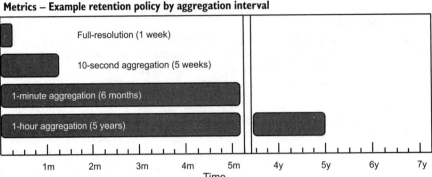

Figure 17.4   **An example metrics retention policy split by aggregation interval. I've used this policy, and the key drivers were search performance in each interval. Even at one week, searches on the full-resolution data performed slowest—in my experience, anyway. Your experience may be different.**

more in section 17.2, but the data in the aggregated sets were derived directly from the full-resolution data.

Most databases that support metrics also support changing your mind with regard to retention. The 10-second retention in figure 17.4 shows a five-week retention period; that period was 28 days until engineering management asked to be able to search a full month to support end-of-month reporting. Supporting that request cost more in backup time and space, but we did it because of the benefits it brought to the organization.

Also consider the benefits of using dedicated databases. SRE could use a dedicated database to store SLO metrics over time and not aggregate at all. The retention on that database could effectively be infinite!

17.1.3 *Building a policy for distributed tracing*

This section covers building a retention policy for distributed tracing style telemetry systems, which tend to be used only by software engineering (and sometimes SRE). Having fewer teams involved eases your decision process for retention. This space is dominated by SaaS providers, so chances are that the biggest factor in your retention-policy decision will be SaaS costs.

Software engineering teams use distributed tracing systems to compare how process behavior changes after code releases and isolating bugs, and generally learn how their production systems operate as a whole. Distributed tracing specifically helps individual teams track problems in a large system in which no one team manages the whole product.

In general, for tracing you will find that longer retention periods are better, but the benefits of longer retention fade over time. There is a big difference between 15-day retention and 30-day retention, but moving from four months to eight months isn't as significant. Tracing benefits from sampling (see section 17.3) to reduce the amount of data you have to pay to ingest and retain. Here are two points on the relationship between retention policy and sampling policy:

- A retention period long enough to compare several software release periods lets you watch how behavior changes across releases.
- Sampling lets you cut ingestion costs but risks missing errors. Tracing systems generally assume that if an error happened once, it'll happen more often, so the sample will catch it.

For those of you using OpenTelemetry-compliant databases, I don't have a lot to say yet. OpenTelemetry is still being developed in early 2021 as I write this chapter, so we don't yet have a lot of industry experience with how those systems are actually used. For this reason, I offer my generic advice for setting a retention policy:

- Search performance is a key detail for any telemetry system, tracing included. When search performance slows, people get cranky, and cranky people aren't having a good experience. Cranky users are a sign that you need to shorten your retention period.
- The cost of offline backups matters as much as the cost of online storage, so consider both costs in your calculations.

17.1.4 *Building a policy for SIEM systems*

This section covers the process of selecting a retention policy for SIEM systems. These systems are rarely used by teams other than security and compliance, and they are often subject to external compliance and regulation regarding how long certain kinds of data need to be retained. As a result, building a policy for a SIEM system is pretty easy; most of the work has already been done for you.

The seven-year retention period is inherited from certain long-standing financial accounting practices and shows up in several compliance frameworks as a result. For SIEM systems and retention policies, the bigger challenge is qualifying SIEM vendor products against the retention goals set by your organization (set in response to compliance and regulation). Budget absolutely plays a role in these negotiations.

Every organization is different, as are the compliance and regulation frameworks your organization is subjected to, which makes generalized guidance tricky to provide. Even so:

- Plan for a retention period measured in years.
- To contain costs, be highly selective in the telemetry you send to the SIEM.

Exercise 17.1

Match the telemetry styles with their method of handling long retention policies.

Centrallized logging	Aggregation
Metrics	Rewrites telemOffline archives that can quickly be brought online
Distributed tracing	Being highly selective about what is stored
SIEM	Statistical sampling

17.2 Creating an aggregation policy

Aggregation policies define how you summarize your metrics-style telemetry and are the biggest cost-containment tools available for that style of telemetry. This section describes how aggregation policies work and how to keep the aggregated metrics in your system statistically valid. These considerations are important if you want to preserve metrics across three, five, or even seven years.

> **NOTE** If you haven't encountered aggregation functions before, I strongly recommend reviewing sections 5.1.2 and 5.1.3, which walk through several aggregation functions and the kinds of stories they tell about your telemetry data. That material will make the concepts in this section far more clear.

An aggregation policy defines what sort of precomputed aggregation-function output you want to keep. Aggregation lets you store far less data in your metrics databases, which makes storing long time scales much cheaper. We saw an example of the time scales in figure 17.4, reproduced here as figure 17.5.

Metrics – Example retention policy by aggregation interval

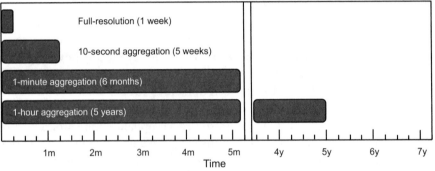

Figure 17.5   An example retention policy for a metrics system, showing four aggregation series: a full-resolution series that has no aggregations performed on it, a series aggregated on 10-second buckets, a series aggregated on 1-minute buckets, and finally a series aggregated on 1-hour buckets. The larger the time bucket, the longer the aggregation series can be kept.

Figure 17.5 shows one of the key concepts of aggregation policies: use of time buckets. We see four buckets in use. The first is the full-resolution bucket, which has no aggregations and contains every data point received from the telemetry system. The second is aggregated from the full-resolution bucket for all data in each 10-second interval, which could reduce thousands of data points to a single data point. The same thing is done for a 1-minute interval and a 1-hour interval.

To understand the aggregations themselves, let's look at a SQL statement that mimics what happens in these systems. This statement is aggregating a range of `pdf_pages` and `docx_pages` metrics on six functions:

```
SELECT metric_name,
  min(metric_value)    AS min,
  mean(metric_value)   AS mean,
  median(metric_value) AS median,
  max(metric_value)    AS max,
  sum(metric_value)    AS sum,
  count(metric_value)  AS count
FROM metrics_fullresoltuion
WHERE
  (timestamp >  "2023-02-19T16:44:20.000") AND
  (timestamp <= "2023-02-19T16:44:30.000")
GROUP BY metric_name
```

This statement returns rows that look something like this:

```
------------------------------------------------------------
| metric_name | min | mean | median | max | sum | count |
------------------------------------------------------------
| pdf_pages   |   1 | 1.2  |      2 |  19 | 392 |   157 |
| docx_pages  |   1 | 1.4  |      3 |  28 | 451 |    93 |
------------------------------------------------------------
```

This example uses common aggregation functions, but there are many more (and I go over several of them in section 5.1.3). What aggregation functions you pick depends on the type of data you are working on. You can find a good overview of metrics types on the StatsD metrics type page at http://mng.bz/PaRR. Here are the most relevant to metrics:

- *Counters*—These metrics track how many times a thing happens. `pdf_pages` is an example of a counter. Metrics of this type are most often added to get a single number but can also be subjected to population metrics such as percentiles.
- *Timers*—These metrics report how long something took. Metrics of this type often get aggregations breaking down the population, such as figuring out percentiles and standard deviations. The `pdf_pages` metric could easily be paired with a `pdf_convert_time` metric tracking how long those pages took to manage.
- *Gauges*—These metrics are the state of a thing at a given point in time, such as a water level or instantaneous RAM use value. Gauges are different from counters because adding them does not give you useful information. These metrics generally are not aggregated by means of numerical methods and are more likely to use a selection function, such as `first`, `median`, or `last`. Fancy aggregation functions such as `derivative` are needed to get a rate of change from these metrics.

My recommendation is to separate telemetry of different types to ease your aggregation work, but separation is not required. The problem with aggregations like these is that you need to know what kinds of questions you want to ask of your data weeks, months, and even years before you ask it. If you have the full-resolution telemetry available, you can run whatever functions you want on it, and it will still be statistically valid. That isn't the case for functions that have already been aggregated.

Suppose that we have timing metrics that gather min, mean, median, and max values, as well as a group of percentiles: 2nd percentile (p2), 10th percentile (p10), 25th percentile (p25), 75th percentile (p75), 90th percentile (p90), and 98th percentile (p98). Remember that min is equivalent to the p0 value, median is equivalent to the p50 value, and max is equivalent to the p100 value.

A year passes, and SRE wants to know whether changing the target for a service-level objective from the p98 value to the p95 will be a better fit for availability targets. SRE's ability to judge fitness will go back only as far as you have full-resolution data, because that's the only data that will provide a correct p95 value.

Because SLOs are moving targets, you add p95 to the list of percentiles you generate with your aggregations and then wait a couple of months. Two months later, SRE checks whether its hypothesis for fit makes sense. Lots of organizations aren't great with "Set it and check in a few months" workflows, but aggregations are one area in which you kind of have to make changes.

This example is a great case for splitting metrics! If you're using metrics to determine SLO compliance, sending the service-level indicators—metrics that tell you whether you are meeting your SLO—to a dedicated database for SLO stuff is a viable strategy. This split keeps the full-resolution metrics available longer, so SRE has an easier time testing different models for fit.

You need to be aware of a major problem with building an aggregation policy, and it has to do with how you build your larger time buckets. Figures 17.4 and 17.5 showed three buckets beyond the full-resolution one:

- One aggregating on 10-second buckets, kept for five weeks
- One aggregating on 1-minute buckets, kept for six months
- One aggregating on 1-hour buckets, kept for five years

I said earlier that these buckets need to be generated directly from the full-resolution bucket (one-week retention in my example), and now I need to explain why. Do not generate the larger-bucket aggregations from the next-smaller bucket, because you will get lies. Chapter 5 included this warning:

> **WARNING**   Beware of further aggregating aggregated data, because that technique almost always leads to lies. Wherever possible, work on raw values, because they will tell you accurate things. If the data you're working with has already been aggregated once, unless you take care to pick an appropriate function, subsequent functions turn what you see into lies. A sum function on data that has already had a sum run on it will be accurate, but running a sum on data that has been run through a mean function will be lies. If you are working with preaggregated data, a least-harm approach is to use the same aggregation function for data that has already been through an aggregation function. Summing your sums is safe, but anything else will be lies—lies that will look kind of like your data but not be statistically valid. I've lost count of the number of charts I've had to fix because they used a mean function on a sum, and the person who asked for help wondered why expanding the chart to one month from one week didn't increase the charted numbers. Section 17.2 covers this problem in more detail.

I will show the lies visually. The next two figures show the same 24-hour period for website response time, but with metrics derived from the four buckets listed above. The charts were built with Grafana, which applied a second aggregation after the hidden aggregation performed by the metrics systems. Figure 17.6 shows four versions of the mean, or average, response time. Note how the numbers vary.

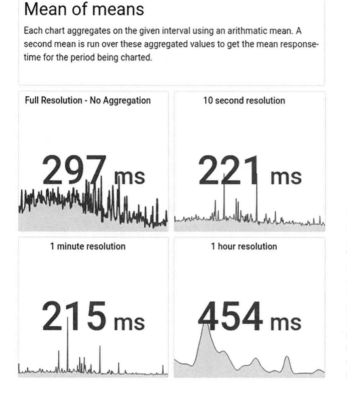

Mean of means

Each chart aggregates on the given interval using an arithmatic mean. A second mean is run over these aggregated values to get the mean response-time for the period being charted.

Full Resolution - No Aggregation

297 ms

10 second resolution

221 ms

1 minute resolution

215 ms

1 hour resolution

454 ms

Figure 17.6 The results of asking "What is the average response time for this site over the past 24 hours?" and the answers that four different metrics buckets give you. Full-resolution is the most accurate answer; it has all the data points. The other three charts show the average of the 10-second, 1-minute, and 1-hour averages, which give different numbers.

The difference is quite significant! The full-resolution, no-aggregation number is the real number, because it was computed against the full dataset of response times, and the only aggregation performed was done by Grafana when it built the chart. Notice how different the 10-second, 1-minute, and 1-hour aggregation answers are. The 10-second aggregation number is closest to the true one, but even it is off by 25%.

The explanation of this result has to do with populations. Each chart has a line showing the numbers in the interval. This chart is a website response time chart over a full day, with the left half of the curve tracking high-use time and the right half tracking low-use time. The 10-second, 1-minute, and especially 1-hour buckets are aggregating far more data points during the peak period than in the overnight trough. Yet when we try to aggregate the aggregated data points, Grafana treats a peak hour with the same weight as a trough hour. Treating each hour as identical in terms of population is lying with statistics, because the 03:00 data point aggregating 1,000 hits weighs the same as the 13:00 data point aggregating 10,000 hits in the averaging computation.

To compute a means value that is far more statistically correct, we would need to include the count of data points for each bucket in the interval and include it in a *weighted average*. Grafana has no support for this style of computation (yet), so getting this value requires running the numbers yourself in a script. Table 17.1 shows this computation for the 1-hour aggregation series, using example values:

- Weight factor is the total hits in the hour divided by the total hits in the day (114,300).
- Weighted response is the mean response time multiplied by the weight factor.
- Raw average is the *unweighted average* of the mean response column.
- Weighted average is the *sum* of the weighted response column.

Table 17.1   Deriving a true(ish) mean response time from the 1-hour aggregation series

Hour	Hits	Mean response	Weight factor	Weighted response
0–1	1200	150	0.010498687664042	1.5748031496063
1–2	1100	155	0.009623797025372	1.49168853893263
2–3	1000	145	0.008748906386702	1.26859142607174
3–4	1000	150	0.008748906386702	1.31233595800525
4–5	1000	150	0.008748906386702	1.31233595800525
5–6	1100	150	0.009623797025372	1.44356955380577
6–7	1200	150	0.010498687664042	1.5748031496063
7–8	1800	160	0.015748031496063	2.51968503937008
8–9	2500	165	0.021872265966754	3.60892388451444
9–10	4500	172	0.039370078740158	6.77165354330709
10–11	5700	199	0.0498687664042	9.9238845144357
11–12	8000	230	0.069991251093613	16.0979877515311
12–13	9100	250	0.079615048118985	19.9037620297463
13–14	10000	275	0.087489063867017	24.0594925634296
14–15	11000	275	0.096237970253718	26.4654418197725
15–16	10000	275	0.087489063867017	24.0594925634296
16v17	9700	250	0.084864391951006	21.2160979877515
17–18	8500	240	0.074365704286964	17.8477690288714
18–19	7700	210	0.067366579177603	14.1469816272966
19–20	6200	160	0.05424321959755	8.67891513560805

Table 17.1 Deriving a true(ish) mean response time from the 1-hour aggregation series *(continued)*

Hour	Hits	Mean response	Weight factor	Weighted response
20–21	4900	155	0.042869641294838	6.64479440069991
21–22	3200	150	0.027996500437445	4.1994750656168
22–23	2200	150	0.019247594050744	2.88713910761155
23–24	1700	140	0.014873140857393	2.082239720035
Hits	114300			
Raw average	187.75			
Weighted average	221			

We see a significant difference between raw average and weighted average. If you look down the weighted-response column, you can see that the 14–15 hour had the largest input into the weighted average by far and that the 2–3 hour had barely any input. In the raw average, which takes the average of the mean response column, both hours have the same weight. This is why an unweighted mean-of-means makes a lie—a lie that looks close to where the truth is on a chart but not a number you want to be taking as highly truthful.

The next chart of site response time computes the median, or 50th percentile from the same data we saw in figure 17.6. The median has different problems from the mean (figure 17.7):

- We can see the day/night split in the chart lines, whereas we couldn't see it with the means chart.
- Our median values are well below our means, telling us that we have a lot of high-latency somewhere. (For more about using aggregations to learn about the shape of data, see section 5.1.3.)
- We see that the 10-second aggregation chart got pretty darn close to the real result in the full-resolution chart.

Explaining why the variance here is less significant than it is with means is due to the nature of the median. The median is the exact middle value of the sorted values in the period, so it isn't too sensitive to the number of values in the period, the way that a mean is. Over a 24-hour period, the 10-second bucket series will have 8,640 values (6 per minute, 60 minutes per hour, 24 hours), which is a nicely large set and also fine-grained (lots of values) and evenly distributed across the period.

Explaining why the 1-minute aggregation is less than any of the others has to do with the nature of this particular data, which includes API traffic. API traffic is often driven by cron jobs, so the API gets hits at the top of the minute. The :00- to :09-second bucket gets a lot of hits, with higher response times, whereas the rest of the minute gets lower response times. Where the 10-second aggregation would produce one high value and

Median of medians

Each chart aggregates on the given interval using an arithmatic median (middle-value). A second median is run over these aggregated values to get the median response-time in the period being charted.

Full Resolution - No Aggregation

63.5 ms

10 second resolution

62.3 ms

1 minute resolution

55.9 ms

1 hour resolution

66.5 ms

Figure 17.7   Four ways of finding the median response time for a website during a 24-hour period. The true answer is the full-resolution, no-aggregation number because it is computing the median on the whole dataset. Although the differences in the other three charts aren't as profound as the means version of this chart (figure 17.6), they are clear.

five lower values in a 1-minute period, the 1-minute aggregation produces a generally lower value because over 60 seconds, more hits land in the 50 seconds of lower response time than in the 10 seconds of higher response time.

The 1-hour bucket is highest of the lot for a similar reason: populations. Because a day has only 24 hours, the higher-traffic slow hours count the same as the lower-traffic fast hours, skewing the results higher. The 1-minute bucket didn't have this problem as much because there are 1,440 minutes in a day—two orders of magnitude more data points to sort and compute a median with.

That's enough scaring you. Now for some recommendations:

- *Always make sure that the precomputed aggregations your metrics system performs are done against full-resolution data.* Because of how most Presentation-stage systems work (they need to get a single value per pixel, and if more data points exist in a pixel, they need to reduce it to one), double aggregations are hard to avoid. For this reason, you want the first aggregation to be as statistically valid as possible.

- *If possible, keep your full-resolution data for at least seven days.* This retention period allows telemetry users to build dashboards that show "the past week" and be able to use the full suite of statistical methods without fear of hidden aggregation-based accuracy problems.

- *When you plan your aggregations, find out what intervals people are interested in.* Intervals of 10 seconds and 1 minute are popular for tracking fast-moving changes, but 1-hour and 1-day intervals are popular for tracking changes across months and years. Intervals of 1-hour and 1-day aggregations are cheap to store, but performing the aggregation itself can be expensive.

- *Percentiles are great, except when you don't have enough data.* A p98 value in a 10-second bucket means something only when that bucket holds a lot of values. A p98 value for a bucket in which only two events happened isn't a p98 value. Fine-grained percentiles mean something only when there are more than 100 points of data to summarize. When you're picking percentiles to aggregate, understand the frequency of your events; you may need to increase your aggregation interval to collect enough data.

- *Know how your metrics database reacts to cardinality, and plan your aggregations accordingly.* Chapter 14 talks about cardinality directly, but this topic needs another mention. Although newer metrics databases are starting to tackle the cardinality problem, well-established metrics databases (such as Prometheus and InfluxDB) generally don't tolerate cardinality well. For this reason, don't plan aggregations based on frequently changing data. If you are in a public cloud and do a lot of autoscaling, for example, or if you operate Docker swarms, don't aggregate on Hostname or Docker-ID.

- *Build training on how to get valid data out of longer-time-range dashboards by using aggregated data.* I've lost count of the number of times I've seen graphs using the presentation system's `mean()` function on data that our metrics system used `sum()` on and then gotten questions about why zooming out to a full year shows much less volume than people were expecting. I've also found graphs that use the presentation system's percentile functions aggregating over a minute for 10-second aggregated data, meaning that the percentile function is operating on six values. Helping other people understand how to handle aggregated data correctly will help your organization achieve its missions.

But what about StatsD?

For those of you who haven't heard of it, StatsD is a metrics-gathering process made popular by Etsy and adopted widely after it made waves. The big cool factor of StatsD is the fact that it performs aggregations live so that the metrics storage system doesn't have to. Also, it can use UDP to keep your metrics logger from blocking when reporting metrics. It provides a fast, nonblocking, accurate-enough metrics system, which was important in the 2011–13 era when it broke out.

I'm not a fan, even though I ran it for several years. The trauma I experienced from running StatsD allowed me to write the past several pages. I find StatsD-style metrics to be problematic for two reasons:

(continued)

- You don't have the option of full-resolution metrics, which means that users of metrics systems need to understand what they're getting, and most of them don't. This lack of understanding leads to dashboards full of hidden lies, and I got tired of correcting them.
- If you have low-frequency metrics, such as events that fire only once or twice a minute, you need to set up different StatsD endpoints that aggregate on 1-minute or longer intervals. These StatsD instances carry a lot of local state, and when they restart, that state is lost, along with the metrics they were holding.

These two points were serious enough that I got fed up dealing with them and replaced our StatsD-based metrics with a different system that used a short full-resolution pool of metrics as the basis of our aggregations. Our dashboards became far more accurate after that work, especially our longer-time-frame items. The trade-off was more CPU spent deriving our aggregation buckets, but technology has advanced far enough by 2021 that "Throw more compute at it" was a viable choice for us.

My opinion is that preaggregating metrics before they enter storage was a viable trade-off in the 2010–15 era, but the state of metrics databases has advanced enough since then that we don't need to do that anymore. The time-series databases on the horizon at the dawn of the 2020s look to be doing away with the need to aggregate and are beginning to tackle the cardinality problem as well.

The only time I see preaggregation as being a good idea is when you are operating a truly large infrastructure, such as 20,000 servers, each producing 200 metrics a second, meaning that the metrics database has to ingest 4 million data points a second. Preaggregation is one method of taking some of the write burden off that database.

Another, somewhat novel approach is to use a top-of-rack metrics database (or a metrics database sidecar in your Kubernetes cluster) that hosts full-resolution metrics for that rack/cluster, which then submits aggregated data to the central metrics store. This approach allows you to safely produce longer time buckets, such as 1 hour and 1 day, which you can't do with a service such as StatsD. Most people don't work on truly large infrastructures, though. For smaller operators, a central full-resolution bucket is completely viable and makes your metrics more useful than preaggregation.

Exercise 17.2

I made the charts in figures 17.6 and 17.7 by using Grafana and an aggregated metrics database. If you are using Grafana in your organization, reproduce the mean and median charts, using your own aggregated data. How different do the aggregation intervals look? How many dashboards are relying on similar summarization?

17.3   *Using sampling to reduce costs and increase retention*

Sampling is a statistical technique for examining a representative subset of data to find truth about the whole. When it comes to telemetry systems, distributed tracing benefits most from sampling. Sampling gives you two big benefits: it allows you to keep more data online for less money, and it still lets you track population-level changes over long time frames. This section is about how to do sampling correctly and ways to work around some of the problems that sampling brings to your telemetry systems.

On the surface, sampling is easy to explain: send a randomized percentage of your traces or metrics into storage. This percentage could be 1%, 10%, or even 50%. The smaller the percentage, the more time you can keep your metrics in your storage systems. Randomization is key, because that's what makes your metrics statistically useful. So long as you also store your sample rate, you can extrapolate what the 100% version would look like.

The key concept with selecting sample rates is that you're allowed to have more than one. Your technical systems are not a uniform population, but a messy population full of buggy processes, nearly bulletproof processes that never fail, processes that are entering production for the first time, processes that have been unchanged in production for two years, processes that run only a few times an hour, processes that run hundreds of times a minute, and processes that happen only when internal users press a button. Real data is messy, and one sample rate will not unite it all.

Good distributed tracing systems let you attach different sample rates to different processes. Take two different API endpoints:

```
/v2/upload_document
/v3/upload_document
```

The `v2/upload_document` endpoint is well-established, but the `v3/upload_document` endpoint is new with this release. The v3 endpoint has never seen production, so no one trusts it yet. A good tracing system will let you set a low sample rate for the old and battle-tested v2 endpoint (perhaps as low as 0.1%), and a fairly high one for the new endpoint (perhaps even 100% for a short time). The old endpoint is likely still in heavy use anyway, so a low sample rate will save you money on ingest, and the new v3 endpoint may be getting only beta traffic while the feature gets tested.

Picking a sample rate depends on several factors:

- The more you understand a process, the lower the sample rate. You don't need to monitor it heavily if you understand it.
- The less you understand a process, the higher the sample rate. You need to build trust (and understanding) by observing the process under many conditions.
- The more frequently a process occurs, the lower the sample rate. If your population is large, you can get away with sample rates like 0.0001%. Imagine if Twitter attempted to trace every single tweet.

- If you've identified a low-frequency error that you need to capture, increasing the sample rate for a short time will help you catch it in the act.
- Production-system sample rates are allowed to be different from load-testing and continuous-integration sample rates. Yes, sampling your load-testing and pre-production environments lets you compare with production to see whether those tools are valid tests.
- A sample rate of 100% gives you the highest-quality data for the most cost.

Sample rates are a lot like feature flags—in fact, many distributed-tracing SDKs make setting the sample rate gateable by a feature flag—in that they let you perform experiments on your production code. So a customer calls in to say that the code breaks when they do this weird thing? Crank up the sample rate via feature flag when the customer's data goes through. This is some seriously powerful stuff.

That said, there are two opposing use cases for distributed tracing systems:

- Learn how the whole system reacts to changes.
- Learn why this one trace went wrong.

I call these use cases *opposing* because the first case benefits greatly from sampling, whereas the second case is mostly destroyed by it. The whole-system use case is about generality, whereas the error-tracking use case is about specificity. Sampling is about generality. Remember the thing I said about having to increase your sample rate to catch low-frequency errors? You do that in reaction to noticing the errors. If support comes to you and asks why this one thing failed—the customer is cranky and is a top-20 customer by contract value—not being able to pull up the bad process will make you break out in a sweat.

To know why getting the erroring trace is such a good thing, let's take another look at figures 5.19 and 5.20, combined here as figure 17.8. This figure shows two traces: a successful execution and one with an error.

The top trace shows a successful execution of upload_document, which calls a couple of other things that leads into a bunch of processes before ultimately returning successfully. The bottom trace, on the other hand, looks different. We see that we recorded exceptions in both file_type and docx_to_pdf. Looking into the file_type trace, we find that the exception is related to an inability to determine the type of a file, so the trace returned a default type: docx. When the docx_to_pdf process ran, it hit a fatal exception because the file it was working on was definitely not a .docx file. The upload_document process retried the docx_to_pdf process three more times just in case there was a glitch. Looking at this trace helps engineering determine that the default file-type behavior is not safe and revise how file_type handles bad detections.

Errors are interesting. If your distributed-tracing system allows it, making the sample rate for errors high will improve the lives of your production engineers. Better for you, the telemetry system operator, you won't have to crank up the sample rate for everything just to capture those pesky rare errors and end up spending a lot of money.

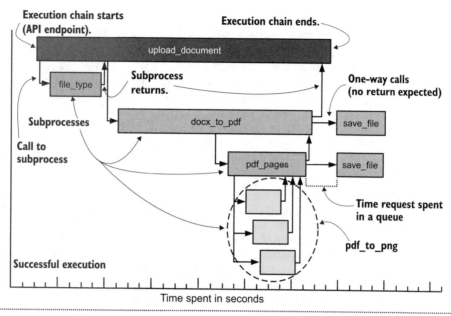

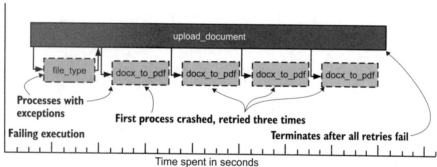

Figure 17.8 Two versions of `upload_document`. The top trace shows a successful execution. The bottom trace shows an execution that errored out. Dashed boxes are processes that recorded an exception. We see in the bottom trace that `upload_document` never received a return from `docx_to_pdf` and retried three times before finishing. We also see that `file_type` threw an exception but returned a value anyway. Could this behavior be related to the `docx_to_pdf` behavior?

If your tracing platform supports arbitrary sample rates, it will safely handle variable sample rates for the same process.

If your tracing system doesn't support changing sample rates, a centralized logging system can step in to help. Throw exceptions into a centralized logging pipeline. This technique isn't the same as having the error in your traces, but it's far better than not capturing the error at all. Telemetry systems support one another.

Metrics are numbers; statistics is about numbers; therefore, you can sample metrics. QED.

This statement is true! In fact, StatsD from Etsy has sampling built right into the protocol, and it was there from the beginning. You configure your metrics emitter to emit only a certain sample rate and put that sample rate into the metric. Here is the StatsD line protocol, which includes a sample rate. Translated, `pdf_pages:5|c|@0.1` means that the metric name (`pdf_pages`) is a counter (`c`) with a value of 5 and is running a 10% sample (`@0.1`). StatsD will do the right thing with this information when it reports summarized metrics back to the metrics database, so it looks as though you didn't sample your data.

That said, I haven't run into many metrics systems besides StatsD that offer sampling-support at ingestion. StatsD was built at a time when databases were tiny, space was precious, and write I/O still depended on spinning disks rather than solid-state ones. In short, StatsD is optimized to minimize writes. As I mentioned in the sidebar at the end of section 17.2, this sort of write reduction isn't needed anymore except in the largest organizations; technology has advanced enough that most organizations don't need to optimize that deeply. If you are working in a truly planet-scale metrics system, however, sampling is a great way to reduce write loading in addition to aggregations.

Exercise 17.3

Order the telemetry styles from longest default online retention period to shortest.

   a Centralized logging
   b Metrics
   c Distributed tracing
   d SIEM

Summary

- Retention policies define how long you keep telemetry data and in what form. The costs of your telemetry systems relate directly to how much telemetry you need to keep online. Long periods give decision-makers more advantages; shorter periods save money.
- Aggregation policies define how you numerically summarize telemetry data and greatly reduce the amount of data you need to keep online and searchable. These policies make storing telemetry cheaper.
- Sampling is a statistical technique used with distributed tracing systems (and sometimes metrics) to preserve the ability to learn about the system as a whole without keeping every single data point, reducing the costs of storage and SaaS-provider bills.
- The ability to restore data quickly from offline storage can reduce your need to keep telemetry online and searchable, and reduces overall costs.

- Long retention periods expose your organization to legal risk if your toxic-data handling (see chapter 16) is not sufficient.

- Centralized logging has the shortest default online retention period, because that data is both large and complex to index, making it the most expensive per day to keep online and searchable.

- SIEM systems have the longest default online retention period due to regulation and compliance frameworks that require the longer time range.

- Metrics has the second-longest default online retention period because the main data type, numbers, is cheap to store and index. When paired with an aggregation policy, retention periods of multiple years are economical.

- Distributed tracing is not as expensive per day as centralized logging but more expensive than SIEM and metrics. Longer retention periods are achieved through the use of sampling to make storage costs manageable.

- SIEM systems are most often SaaS systems, making their key scaling problem the annual or monthly subscription cost.

- Setting a retention policy for centralized logging systems is complicated by the fact that these systems are used by every team in a technical organization. Keep at least a few weeks online for support to help engineering, make it easy to restore offline telemetry, and accommodate engineering decision cycles such as monthly reporting.

- In the 2020s, cardinality is a bigger scaling problem for metrics systems than space is, which affects search performance. Longer time frames tend to make for more cardinality in your indexes. Consider search performance when you're setting your retention period for metrics.

- Keep a short full-resolution pool of metrics (not summarized/aggregated) from which you can derive your aggregated pools. Using seven days for your full-resolution pool allows your technical organization to build "over the past week" dashboards with top accuracy.

- Distributed tracing systems are typically used by software engineering and SRE. Longer time frames allow comparison of performance across multiple releases of code, which is quite valuable for engineering.

- An aggregation policy defines the sorts of precomputed aggregations you keep in your metrics storage, which lets you store orders of magnitude less data in your storage. This policy keeps costs down and improves search performance.

- Aggregation policies often define multiple series of data, aggregated on different intervals, such as a series aggregated over 10-second buckets, another on 1-minute buckets, and a third on 1-hour buckets. The larger the bucket is, the cheaper it is to store and chart long periods of time.

- Having a short full-resolution pool of metrics lets you compute the full array of aggregations in your aggregation series while maintaining statistical validity.

- The drawback to aggregation series is that you need to know which aggregations you're interested in well in advance of your need. When you've lost your full-resolution metrics pool, computing a 75th percentile when you didn't have it before is not possible. Adding one to new aggregations is easy, though.

- Splitting aggregation policies based on use case is entirely possible! If your SRE team needs to keep SLO-related information online and searchable for long periods, you can send those (much smaller than the rest of your system) metrics to a dedicated retention policy.

- When you're working with preaggregated data in a Presentation-stage system like Grafana, you have to understand how the aggregation functions that the Presentation-stage system uses interact with your data. Doing things wrong leads to dashboards full of lies. Figures 17.6 and 17.7 provide visual descriptions of the sorts of lies that come from reaggregating an aggregated metrics series.

- Sampling is a statistical technique for examining a representative subset of data to find truth about the whole, which makes sampling a key cost-saving technique for distributed tracing.

- A sampling rate is a percentage of events that will be sent on to the distributed tracing provider and often can be set at both function and program levels.

- Good distributed tracing systems natively support variable sample rates in a given program, which lets you use a higher rate for catching exceptions and a lower rate for well-understood processes that are known to be highly reliable.

- Using sampling in your load testing and other pre-production systems lets you compare performance with production to determine whether tests of those pre-production systems are useful.

- Many distributed tracing SDKs let you set a sample rate based on feature flags, a useful feature that allows you to use a higher sample rate for highly valuable customers.

- Errors are usually more interesting than regular operation, so build your sampling so that captured errors are always sent to the distributed tracing provider. This approach guarantees that you will have interesting events to review.

Surviving legal processes 18

This chapter covers

- The process of legal discovery
- The role telemetry plays in legal eDiscovery
- How to work with lawyers successfully

This chapter is unlike any other in this book because it isn't about dispassionate technology or the virtual arm wrestling of setting internal policies. This chapter is about an event that most technologists won't encounter in their careers—legal processes that make them the expert on the spot—so they're horribly unprepared when it happens to them. I want to prepare you for this event so if the unlikely happens, you will respond from a place of competence rather than shocked and reactive surprise.

> **WARNING** This chapter is not about turning you into a lawyer; this chapter is about helping you support your organization's lawyers. Your legal opinion doesn't matter; that's not what you were hired for. This chapter is about working with legal *processes*, which are far better documented than legal *opinion*.

The sorts of legal trouble that organizations can get into is infinite, but only a subset of that infinite could potentially put your telemetry systems in the crosshairs of the other side's lawyers. This brings me to the first of many definitions: eDiscovery.

> **DEFINITION** *eDiscovery* (noun): The short form of *electronic discovery*. Like email, it is no longer hyphenated. Discovery is the pretrial process of obtaining evidence from parties to the lawsuit and bears the weight of a court order. eDiscovery uses computer files instead of paper. If a party is ordered to produce documents, that party (your organization) must do so unless certain conditions are met—conditions that your lawyers will figure out for you.

eDiscovery is the legal procedure that affects telemetry systems, and this chapter gives you a primer on what it is, what you can expect if you have to participate in it, and how to talk to the lawyers involved. If your telemetry systems are relevant to a legal matter, something must have happened to make the operating telemetry of your production systems relevant to the case. Here are a few examples, both hypothetical and drawn from real life, to spur your imagination, along with the questions that eDiscovery hopes to answer:

- Your organization was caught leaking health information on a publicly accessible API.
  - How did the open API get there? How long has it been available? How many people had their information stolen? Two years ago, an engineering manager backlogged a ticket that would have fixed this problem; why?
- Members of your customer success team were caught selling private information to dark-web brokers for big payouts.
  - When did the payouts start? How many people had their information sold? Are other people participating in the same scheme? Was remote access granted to ease the transfer of private information?
- One of your top customers had an information leak because of a highly publicized vulnerability that supposedly was fixed six months ago, contradicting your compliance audit reports.
  - Why was the vulnerability management process not followed in this case? Why was this vulnerability not detected? What is the patching history for the affected system?
- A member of your software engineering organization was paid to pin a NodeJS module to a specific version that contained a back door placed by a hostile country.
  - Who wrote the code that pinned the version? Who approved the code? Why did the library vulnerability-scanning process not identify the vulnerable module? Were any other implants placed? Over the past three years, what did the bribed engineer do, when did they do it, and how did they do it?

- Your organization wants to bring a gross-negligence lawsuit against one of your SaaS suppliers after a series of recent outages not only blew way past its service-level agreement, but also caused your organization to lose massive revenue.
  - What specific problems did the outages cause? What workarounds were proposed by the SaaS provider's support, and how did they perform once deployed? How did your organization's users suffer as these mitigations and workarounds were deployed?

All organizations have some legal risk, but certain types of organizations have higher ones. All telemetry system operators should consider—on paper at minimum—how they could respond to eDiscovery requests for telemetry data. By keeping your deliberations hypothetical, similar to the tabletop exercises that disaster planners use, you can smoke out the most obvious problems. You should have a plan for the following two major requests:

- *A demand to preserve documents*—You can't delete anything that could be related to the case, even if your retention policy (chapter 17) says it should be deleted or you would otherwise redact it (chapter 16). This request comes first in a legal case, and the *legal hold* (what this demand is) can last years. We'll talk more about this topic in section 18.2.
- *A demand to provide documents*—You work with your lawyers to bundle up telemetry data that is relevant to the case. You have several ways to deal with this kind of thing; I go over them in section 18.3.

I talk about four different styles of telemetry in this book, but each style has different exposure to legal processes. Here is how they rank for exposure:

1. *SIEM systems*—These systems are built from the start to support security investigations and handle information safely enough to survive trials and prosecutions.
2. *Centralized logging systems*—The next-most-exposed after SIEM systems, centralized logging systems contain vast details about the events that happened in your production systems, which makes them big targets for legal processes.
3. *Distributed tracing systems*—If you have a centralized logging system, distributed tracing systems are less vulnerable. But if you are using your distributed tracing systems *in place of* a centralized logging system, they are just as exposed as centralized logging systems: you are likely tracking more than simple function states in these systems if you lack a centralized logging system, and those extras are often relevant to legal matters.
4. *Metrics systems*—These systems are the least exposed telemetry you have, mostly because this style is all about numbers. If the legal matter relates to performance, and your performance numbers are in your metrics system, you can see requests for metrics telemetry. In extreme cases, the statistical validity of your aggregation policy (see section 17.2) can be challenged in court to try to throw out your telemetry as invalid.

WARNING   Unless you have already been through eDiscovery, I strongly recommend reading section 18.1 before any others in this chapter. That section defines the legal processes involved here and provides many definitions that I use in later sections. The word *production*, for example, has a specific meaning to lawyers; you want to know how it differs from what the word means in chapters 1–17.

18.1 Defining the eDiscovery process

eDiscovery is the legal process that parties to a lawsuit use to gather electronic evidence. Discovery in the general sense (paper) evolved out of English common law and followed the British empire to all its colonies (including the United States). As various countries gained independence, their need to harmonize contract law and other legal frameworks for doing business was great enough that keeping the concept of *discovery* made a whole bunch of sense—which is to say that the concept of discovery exists in most European countries and the countries that once were their colonies.

Figure 1.13 gave us the simplified stages of eDiscovery. Let's update it a bit in figure 18.1.

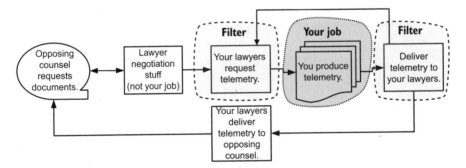

Figure 18.1   The eDiscovery life cycle and your role in it (unless you're a lawyer). Your job is to produce telemetry or enable telemetry to be produced by others—likely your organization's lawyers. Your lawyers may make repeated requests of you before they're ready to deliver telemetry to opposing counsel. Everything you do will be filtered through your organization's lawyers, which is safest for everyone involved.

Although figure 18.1 looks like an endless cycle (and can certainly feel like one if you're in the middle of it), it represents a form of agile iteration. When a matter starts, opposing counsel (the other side's lawyers) don't know much about the shape of the data they will be requesting. Their first requests will be broad and will be argued down by your organization's lawyers ("Your honor, this is a fishing expedition!", to use a cinematic example). As time passes, though, they begin to get a feel for how your data is shaped, so requests start getting extremely specific, which brings us to our next definition: *responsive*.

DEFINITION *Responsive* (adjective): A document (or telemetry event) that matches a discovery request is said to be *responsive*. Documents that are nonresponsive will not be delivered to opposing counsel. If a document is partially responsive, it will be redacted before delivering. Figuring out whether a document is responsive is the job of your organization's lawyers.

At its base, the discovery phase of a lawsuit is about discovering the responsive records, documents, and events that relate to the legal matter at hand. This phase, which can be extremely quick or can drag out over years, applies to all parties to the matter. When the responsive records are gathered, the matter—in theory, at least—can move forward to settlement negotiation or further legal wrangling.

This process does not begin when a lawsuit is filed, but when your organization's lawyers decide that a lawsuit is likely. That lawsuit might be threatened or planned. Your organization's lawyers are obligated to preserve (protect from any changes) records, documents, and events that could possibly be responsive and will order you to preserve telemetry. This order is called a *legal hold*, which is covered in detail in section 18.2.

DEFINITION *Legal hold* (noun): A requirement to protect business records (telemetry, in our case) from any deletion or modification. Records that are subject to a legal hold are exempted from retention policies, and if redaction is needed, that redaction will be made on a copy. Modifying or deleting records (or the metadata of the record) subjected to a legal hold can lead to sanction by the court and sanction by your organization. Mishandling this stuff can get you fired.

Legal holds can arrive at any time during the discovery phase. Record types and repositories that people didn't realize could contain potentially responsive records can be discovered and then subjected to a legal hold. Unless the matter obviously would involve telemetry systems from the outset, telemetry systems are more likely to be subject to these late-arriving hold orders. People who manage records systems (telemetry systems are records systems) are called *custodians* and are the people who implement the hold order.

DEFINITION *Custodian* (noun): People who are needed to provide records or otherwise manage record systems. *You*, in other words. Custodians are not legal professionals (usually). Examples of custodians include email administrators, Google-apps account administrators, and telemetry system administrators.

When the legal hold is in place, some organizations will start going through the process of *early case assessment* (ECA).

DEFINITION   *Early case assessment* (noun): When an organization expects a lawsuit, it reviews potentially responsive records to determine how much of a problem it has on its hands; this review is ECA. ECA drives formulation of legal strategy. It also applies to organizations that plan to file a lawsuit when the goal is to determine whether there is enough substance to support a legal matter.

ECA is the second place where you, the telemetry system operator, will be involved. Your organization's lawyers or their consultants will start diving through telemetry subjected to legal hold orders. A lot can happen in this phase, especially if the legal team is expecting to be able to export data out of your telemetry systems and into specialist document review systems. Or your legal team may rely on you and your team to search for and extract telemetry from your systems. Smaller organizations are more likely to expect you to be a key player in ECA; larger organizations are more likely to expect you to enable key players. The act of looking over potentially responsive documents is called *review*.

DEFINITION   *Review* (or *document review*) (noun): The phase in which records are assessed to determine whether they are responsive to the legal matter. Lawyers and paralegals perform review on data collected as part of a legal hold. You will hear *review* used by legal staff in phrases such as "Review has a production deadline of August 5" and "We are performing review for five requests."

When the lawsuit is filed, ECA can continue in the background, but your organization's lawyers will start fielding (and issuing) discovery requests. On the receiving end, discovery requests look a lot like ECA requests, but with a few differences:

- A different legal team may be making the requests. It's pretty common for organizations to retain outside counsel (consulting lawyers) to help with a case, so you'll probably be working with new people who don't understand your organization the way your organization's own lawyers do. Sometimes, these outside lawyers come with their own technical people (known as "legal support").
- You can be asked to provide records in a different format from the one used during ECA. Courts like to see records in specific formats (PDF and TIFF being the most common), and ideally, your lawyers will handle the re-encoding. Not all lawyers do, however.
- Unlike ECA requests, discovery requests come with deadlines that are set by the presiding judge and are not affected by your on-call, child-appointment, or athletic schedules. If you are unlucky, you will find out why lawyers (and their paralegals) often work weird and extended hours (see sidebar at the end of section of 18.3).

All the preceding points lead up to providing the requested documents to opposing counsel. The fully formatted bundle of records is called *document production*.

DEFINITION *Production* (noun): in the legal world, *production* is short for *document production* and is a singular noun. You might hear your legal team say, "We reviewed the January 29 production." In our world, *production* is an adjective, here modifying *systems* ("This chart diagrams our production systems"). A production is created by your organization's lawyers from telemetry data you provide.

Discovery requests typically come as a request for documents containing certain keywords. If the lawyers know what kind of record storage system you're using, the requests sometimes come as straight-up queries in whatever language your storage system supports. These keyword lists can be expansive, and as a matter drags on, the keywords have excludes and includes, and resemble some pretty gnarly logic statements.

Be careful about modifying records, though! Lawyers and the court care about both the data and the metadata, so you have to take care to preserve both. What counts as metadata depends on both your storage system and what your organization's lawyers decide counts as metadata, but it could include access logs for specific events in your telemetry. If you do end up changing data (perhaps because you dropped a field or accidentally redacted PII), you *spoliate* it.

DEFINITION *Spoliate* (verb): The act of modifying business records outside procedures. Telemetry data subject to a legal hold that was later modified is called *spoliated*. Spoliating data is a serious problem with potentially serious consequences to the legal matter and your job. If you feel that you need to change data inside the legal hold, consult your organization's lawyers before making changes—*any* changes.

18.2 Dealing with records-retention requests

The first time a legal matter is likely to affect your telemetry systems is when a request to retain records (a legal hold; see section 18.1) comes from your organization's legal team. This request is a demand to retain specific telemetry and shield it from further modification. Chapter 17 was about building retention and aggregation policies, and legal holds are the great big exceptions to all that nice work. This section is about adapting your procedures to deal with the potential for handling legal holds and some techniques to take some of the pain away.

The best way to deal with legal holds is to have a plan for them long before you have to handle them. Far too many telemetry system operators are caught with no plan at all when the legal team gives them a preservation request, which means that they react from a place of surprise and without awareness of how their answers will affect the organization's legal options. Section 18.4 is about working with lawyers in general, but you can save yourself and your team a lot of stress by having a plan for legal holds.

This plan doesn't have to be a fully fleshed-out and exercised runbook, with supporting automation that is actively maintained and refreshed. Such a runbook would be quite nice to have, but that's a lot of effort for what should be an extremely rare disaster for most organizations. What I'm talking about when I say "have a plan" is this: you have considered the possibility of legal holds in your telemetry system design and have a sketched-out procedure for handling one.

The best time to consider these problems is when you are planning on making a major change to your telemetry system. Perhaps you're thinking of upgrading a key component or migrating to something new. Whatever the cause, here are questions you need to have answers for:

- *If we get asked to save a part of our telemetry, is it easier to save that piece or to save everything from that time?* Knowing whether it's easier to store partial datasets or full datasets before you need to think about the issue will save everyone effort.

- *How will we shield the held data from routine redactions and reprocessing?* You need to be able to prevent changes to the legal-hold data. If your current systems make that task hard, spend time easing it.

- *How will we protect our unredacted/unreprocessed legal-hold data from our usual customers?* If you need to perform redactions, you need to keep the unredacted telemetry visible only to the lawyers. If the legal matter proceeds to discovery, the lawyers will perform any redactions. Also, if you need to run a second set of systems for the held data—systems that need to be exempted from your organization's patch policies—you can isolate access to the potentially vulnerable systems to the lawyers involved and the minimum number of telemetry system operators needed to keep the systems running.

- *How will we allow our lawyers to review our saved data?* Unless the hold order is for everything, chances are high that your organization's lawyers will want to make sure you're saving the right things. Let them. You will need to make this check anyway when ECA starts (section 18.1).

- *If the legal hold requires us to hold telemetry that is still being generated, what changes do we need to make to ensure that such telemetry is preserved?* Not all requests are solely for historic information; some holds may require you to hold some or all of your currently generated telemetry. Knowing what changes you need to make to support preserving live telemetry will make writing the changes much easier if you get asked to do so.

- *Is our oldest telemetry data viewable in our current software versions?* If part of your retention policy involves storing telemetry offline for a period of time, you need to know early whether your oldest telemetry can be restored into the current system or needs a second system for the restore. Setting up a second system requires resources, so knowing beforehand how much to request will save everyone time and worry.

- *If we have to upgrade our storage software during the hold period, will we need to avoid upgrading the legal hold systems?* Hold orders can last years as lawsuits grind their way through the process. Knowing whether it is safe to upgrade the resources involved in the hold order will help you stay compliant with whatever regulations you're subjected to. If upgrading is not safe, knowing early allows you to put exceptions in your patching and vulnerability management policies specifically for this edge case.

The next two sections examine two different centralized logging systems and answer the preceding questions. Section 18.2.1 shows a self-hosted, Elasticsearch-based centralized logging system; section 18.2.2 shows a SaaS hosted centralized logging system. Although your situation is likely different, one of these examples should be close enough to be useful as a jumping-off point for your own enquiries.

18.2.1 Examining an ELK-based centralized logging system

ELK is the de facto name for a centralized logging system that uses Logstash as a Shipping stage, Elasticsearch as Shipping-stage storage, and Kibana as the Presentation stage. ELK environments these days often include elements of Elastic.co's Beats framework of telemetry shippers, and you sometimes see Fluentd/Fluentbit instead of Logstash, but the details don't matter for our review in this section.

Figure 18.2 diagrams this architecture. Unlike similar figures in previous chapters, this figure includes retention-policy details on how long telemetry is retained online and offline. Remember that legal holds focus more on Shipping-stage storage than on markup and enrichment.

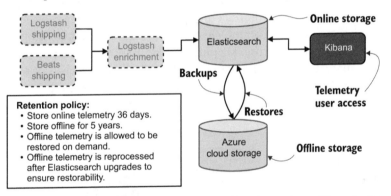

Figure 18.2 Our example ELK-based centralized logging system, with a retention policy. Dashed boxes are Shipping-stage elements that don't factor into our assessment of how suitable this system is for handling legal hold requests. We are most interested in the Elasticsearch (online) and Azure Cloud Storage (offline) telemetry storage systems.

Now that we have our architecture, let's ask the questions from section 18.2 how this system reacts to records-retention requests.

If we get asked to save a part of our telemetry, is it easier to save that piece or to save everything from that time?

Elasticsearch has many features, but one feature that's relevant to this question is the Reindex API. At its simplest, the Reindex API copies an entire index into another index, but it also supports using a query to restrict which documents get copied into the new index. You can perform this operation in a single command and simply wait for it to complete. If this system follows the usual pattern for ELK environments and creates indexes based on day, week, or month patterns, you can use the Reindex API to copy from multiple-source indexes into a single legal-hold one.

It looks as though in Elasticsearch, restoring everything and selective copying are similarly easy. To break the tie, pick the approach that's cheaper for resources!

How will we shield the held data from routine redactions and reprocessing?

Routine redactions of privacy and health-related data (toxic data) need to continue to happen in the regular indexes. That situation is not going to change. If you keep the legal-hold data in dedicated indexes that are not part of routine operations, however, you can shield them from modification. It looks as though shielding held data will be pretty easy.

How will we protect our unredacted/unreprocessed legal-hold data from our usual customers?

For this example, you're using Kibana. If you're using the enterprise or OpenSearch version, you have full access control support, which lets you write access control rules that keep regular users out of the legal-hold indices.

But if you're using the open source version of Kibana, which doesn't have robust access control support, not much prevents your regular users from accessing a separate index, which makes for a much more complicated answer. Resolving this matter likely requires using a separate Elasticsearch cluster for the legal-hold data, providing a second Kibana specifically for that use, keeping regular users out of that second Kibana.

Supporting that cluster isn't that bad except for the resource costs of setting it up. The Reindex API absolutely can copy documents to a different cluster. The difference is providing a target host in the API call. You see what a separate cluster could look like in figure 18.3.

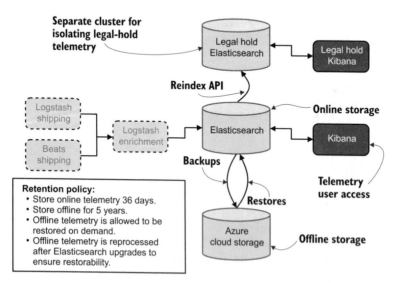

Figure 18.3 Adding a second Elasticsearch cluster because open source Kibana can't prevent regular users from accessing the legal-hold indices. Separating access matters if the legal-hold indexes contain unredacted information, such as privacy- or health-related information (toxic data) that your telemetry system was not designed to hold.

How will we allow our lawyers to review our saved data?

If you're using the paid version of Kibana, this process is as easy as creating a new ACL group for your lawyers and walking them through how to use the system. But if you're using the open source one, you have to set up a second Kibana. In this case, you have to set up network isolation or use a wrapping technique to shield the Kibana *server* inside a single sign-on (SSO) prompt. Then you would use your SSO system to grant only the lawyers (and telemetry system operators) access to this second Kibana.

If the legal hold requires us to hold telemetry that is still being generated, what changes do we need to make to ensure that such telemetry is preserved?

If current telemetry is subject to the hold order, you need a way to shield telemetry from redactions while providing a way to perform redactions. The dual-use nature of your telemetry—regular operations and legal hold—strongly suggests that your telemetry will be forking (see chapter 7 for forking and routing topics) into multiple indexes or multiple clusters, depending on the ACL features available in your version of Kibana. The Logstash enrichment box needs to get updated to handle the fork, as shown in figure 18.4.

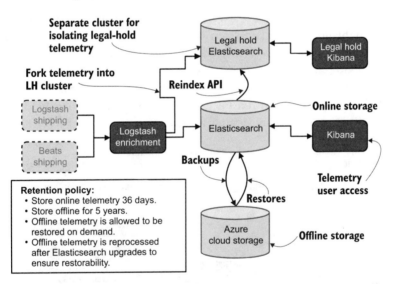

Figure 18.4 If live telemetry is subjected to a legal hold, you need a way to fork telemetry into both the regular cluster and the legal hold cluster. The Logstash enrichment system is updated to write the full telemetry stream to the regular Elasticsearch cluster and any telemetry subject to the hold order to the legal-hold cluster. This way, you can continue to redact toxic data from the regular cluster while providing unmodified telemetry to your legal team.

Is our oldest telemetry data viewable in our current software versions?

You see from your retention policy that offline storage is reprocessed to make sure that it is always restorable with the current cluster, so the answer is "By policy, yes." If data requested by a legal hold is up to five years old, you should have no trouble bringing it back online.

If we have to upgrade our storage software during the hold period, will we need to avoid upgrading the legal hold systems?

This question gets into the weeds a bit. If the amount of data subjected to hold is relatively small, chances are good that you are keeping separate indexes online just for that purpose. Elasticsearch will support indexes from the current and previous versions, so online index should be fine for (probably) up to 24 months. When you get to the +2 version, that index will need to be moved to a separate system or reprocessed into the newer format. Ask your lawyers whether reprocessing is permissible.

If the amount of held data is sizable, running a second cluster just for the legal-hold data makes sense. If you already do this because you're using open source Kibana, keeping the second cluster at the older version is easier. By keeping the second cluster you don't need to ask the lawyers to make a judgment about whether doing an index upgrade spoliates (section 18.1) the data.

18.2.2 *Examining a Sumo Logic-based centralized logging system*

This section is about examining the Sumo Logic SaaS offering for the kinds of changes you might need to make to accommodate a hold order coming from your lawyers. Although I examine a specific SaaS service here, this section is intended to guide your thinking about these questions in cases where a SaaS provider is your telemetry storage and presentation system. Figure 18.5 shows the example Sumo Logic-based telemetry system, with a bit more detail than we've had before because the SaaS provider's internal details matter for this analysis.

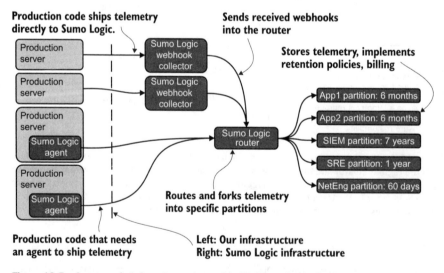

Figure 18.5   An example telemetry system using the Sumo Logic SaaS platform for centralized logging and SIEM work. Partitions are where telemetry is stored and retention policies are defined, and they are key to billing. Telemetry that lands in multiple partitions counts more than once for billing purposes.

The production environment sends all telemetry into Sumo Logic via either of two methods: sending direct to SaaS (section 3.1.3) or using a local agent to do the shipping into SaaS (section 4.1). From there, telemetry eventually enters a router that makes decisions about which partitions telemetry will end up in. Telemetry can land in more than one partition. Because billing is tied to ingestion rate in the partitions, telemetry that lands in more than one partition costs more per item of telemetry than single-partition telemetry does. Partitions are where we define our retention policies, as figure 18.5 shows. The figure shows five partitions in use: two for applications, one for security, and two more for SRE and network engineering.

Now that we have our architecture, let's answer the questions from section 18.2.

If we get asked to save a part of our telemetry, is it easier to save that piece or to save everything from that time?

Sumo Logic allows you to change the retention policy for a partition simply, so if you want to keep everything in a partition for longer, this job is easy to do (if more expensive). Partial saving takes more work, because Sumo Logic doesn't provide a single reindexing API, the way Elasticsearch does (section 18.2.1). What it does provide is an export API that lets you use a query and export the results into a CSV file. From there, it's up to you to do something with it.

If you want to keep your saved telemetry in Sumo Logic, here's one possible way:

1 Set up a new partition for your saved telemetry, and update the router with a rule to send your reprocessed telemetry into it.
2 Export the CSV.
3 Write a script to send each event back into Sumo Logic, where the router sends it into a partition.

All things considered, "save all" is definitely the easier option; simply increase the retention period. But if cost becomes a problem, you can use a more complex method to save money. That method looks like figure 18.6.

How will we shield the held data from routine redactions and reprocessing?

You're in good shape here; Sumo Logic doesn't require routine reprocessing, so reprocessing is not a concern. Redactions currently require a support case to be opened, in which case the details of redaction are out of your control. To make things easier on Sumo Logic support, making a dedicated partition should allow you to prove to the court that you are not making changes.

How will we protect our unredacted/unreprocessed legal-hold data from our usual customers?

As with the ELK system in section 18.2.1, if you've performed redactions on your regular telemetry, you will not be performing them on the held data, which means that you need to keep your held data from being accessed. If you know that the responsive telemetry is not subject to redactions, you can safely extend an existing partition's retention policy as needed and not worry about it. But if you are performing redactions, you will

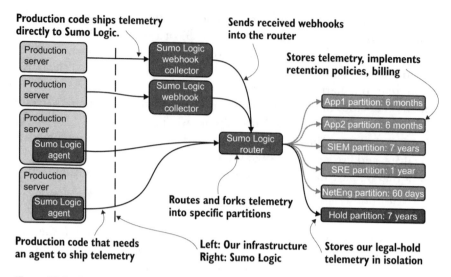

Figure 18.6   Showing how figure 18.5 changes when a legal-hold partition is added. Telemetry flows potentially involving responsive telemetry are dark lines with arrows; lighter lines show regular telemetry flows. This example also demonstrates telemetry routing; incoming telemetry that is potentially responsive is sent to both its usual partitions as well as to the hold partition.

need a dedicated legal hold partition, which enables you to build ACLs to prevent certain groups from querying the legal hold partition.

How will we allow our lawyers to review our saved data?

Sumo Logic is a SaaS telemetry platform, so it comes with an ACL system even in the lowest tiers. This system lets you create a role to allow our lawyers to read telemetry in as much or as little of the telemetry system as you want. This part is easy, fortunately.

If the legal hold requires us to hold telemetry that is still being generated, what changes do we need to make to ensure that such telemetry is preserved?

This is where you embrace the router. If you're keeping everything, you don't have to do anything; the partition's retention policy does all the work for you. But if you have to make a hold partition, you will need to update the rules in the router to send potentially responsive telemetry into both the legal-hold partition and its usual location. These changes are straightforward to set up in the Sumo Logic platform.

Is our oldest telemetry data viewable in our current software versions?

You are using a SaaS platform, so this problem does not apply!

If we have to upgrade our storage software during the hold period, will we need to avoid upgrading the legal hold systems?

Because you are using a SaaS platform, software versions are among the things you're paying the SaaS vendor to worry about. Where you potentially get into a problem is if your SaaS vendor makes a new product offering with better features. Will you move to that product, or will the requirements of a legal hold force you to keep your held data in the older platform? Only your organization's lawyers will be able to tell you which path is correct. Most SaaS vendors don't advertise breaking changes well in advance, so you'll have to put this problem down as a known risk and plan to deal with it when it happens.

18.3   *Dealing with document-production requests*

After the first legal holds are in place, lawyers start digging through your telemetry. First is ECA (see section 18.1), in which your organization's lawyers go through the telemetry to decide on a legal strategy. After ECA, when the legal matter has been filed, the matter enters the discovery phase which is when opposing counsel starts requesting records. This section is about handling document production requests from your own lawyers (ECA) and other lawyers (discovery). Figure 18.1 illustrated the discovery process. Let's look at it again as figure 18.7.

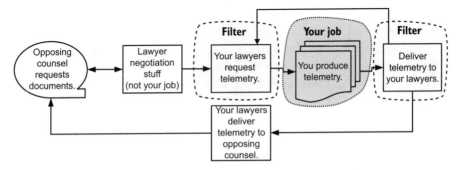

Figure 18.7   The eDiscovery life cycle and your role in it (unless you're a lawyer). Your job is to produce telemetry or enable telemetry to be produced by others—likely your organization's lawyers. This job can involve your lawyers making repeated requests of you before they're ready to deliver telemetry to opposing counsel. Everything you do will be filtered through your organization's lawyers, which is safest for everyone involved.

When ECA or discovery starts, you need to allow lawyers to look at the telemetry you've put aside as part of the legal hold. (Section 18.2 covers handling legal-hold orders.) Ideally, you can give the lawyers access to the Presentation-stage systems and they will handle the rest of the tasks, so you have to be concerned only with keeping them fed with telemetry. The first passes are likely to be done by your organization's lawyers, but retaining outside counsel is quite common in large cases, so later requests might come from lawyers who don't know your organization or you. Section 18.4 goes into more detail about working with lawyers, but in brief, when you have questions about what outside counsel is asking for, ask your organization's lawyers. The lawyers are your guides in this process and the parties responsible for translating needs and requirements to all sides. If you are entering ECA or discovery, it is an incredibly good idea to make friends with your organization's lawyers: you will be working together for a long time.

Any discovery request has three phases:

- *Collection*—Reviewing held data to see what *might* be responsive and extracting it into a new repository.
- *Review*—Lawyers and paralegals review each document to determine responsiveness and perform redactions on documents that are partially responsive.
- *Production*—All the responsive documents and their redactions are exported in a negotiated format to send to opposing counsel.

For small companies that are trying to save legal costs, doing review in place through native tooling instead of dedicated review software eases the costs of paying for a review platform. The cheap method means that you, the telemetry system operator, will likely be asked to write automation to turn responsive telemetry into court-standard formats (probably PDF or TIFF, but other formats are occasionally used). Full-service review platforms make reviewing large document sets easy and offer predefined ways to turn documents into court-standard formats. You won't use these systems but may be asked to produce exports for them.

In bad cases, you will be involved with all three phases, but the more resources your legal team (and its retained law firms) has, the less work you must do. In the next three sections, I'll go over each phase and explain how it might affect telemetry system operators.

18.3.1 *Telemetry in the collection phase*

The collection phase of a discovery request is when lawyers or their delegates identify potentially responsive document repositories and export them into a new repository. This phase is distinct from a legal hold because this new repository is no longer controlled by your organization. For nontelemetry records, these activities enable the legal teams to dig through and export telemetry in your legal-hold systems, which is what this section is about. *Important:* The collection phase starts the *chain of custody*.

> **DEFINITION**   *Chain of custody* (noun): The complete record of transfers and copies of records, including who performed the operation and any changes in who is possessing the records. Breaking the chain of custody by not documenting a copy or making changes risks spoliating the records, which could result in sanction by the court.

The best thing you can do to reduce the impact of the collection phase on you and your day-to-day work is to enable the lawyers to collect their own telemetry and to grant them API access. You and your organization's lawyers will have to work with your organization's security and IT teams to enable this collection, but you will save a lot of work by not being in the collection workflow. You may be asked to write automation to turn something like an Elasticsearch query into an archive full of JSON documents, but if you write the automation well enough, you won't have to be involved in every document collection. If you can manage to grant this access to your legal team, your role in collections is pretty much done.

If you can't grant this access for some reason, you will likely end up pairing with a lawyer or one of their delegates while they ask you to search for potentially responsive documents, using your credentials and access. This supervision is incredibly important in maintaining the chain of custody. You will be identifying queries that reveal potentially responsive telemetry, digging into them to see whether they lead to other potentially responsive telemetry. When you have those queries, you will be asked to export them. This process can take quite a lot of time and may be unavoidable for smaller organizations.

Granting API access to telemetry systems to people who are not directly employed by your organization (the retained outside counsel) is likely to be an unplanned exception to your normal access control policies. You will have to negotiate with whoever manages corporate identities, and likely with your organization's security team, to build a framework to grant this access. If you meet strenuous resistance, providing this access can require you to build a fully isolated network to host these legal-matter-related telemetry systems. Building an isolated network will feel like a lot of work, but if the legal matter is likely to last a long time (ask your organization's lawyers), the front-loaded work will mean that your day-to-day work for the rest of the matter will look more usual instead of unusually legal. Figure 18.8 shows one possible isolated-network diagram.

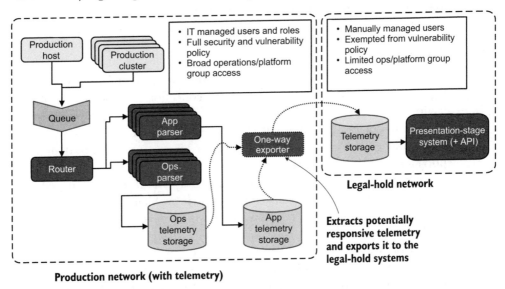

Figure 18.8 Two isolated networks; one production network with a full telemetry system, and a legal-hold network containing only telemetry storage and a Presentation-stage system. Regular telemetry flows are diagramed with straight lines with arrows. A one-way exporter extracts potentially responsive telemetry from the production network's telemetry storage and injects it into the legal-hold network's telemetry storage. Extraction flows are diagramed with dotted lines with arrows. By limiting authorized access in the legal-hold network much more tightly than in the production network, you make the relaxed security policies—such as exempting the legal-hold telemetry systems from the vulnerability management policy—easier to justify to your security team. Also, granting outside access to these legal-hold systems is much easier to justify to your security team: the granted access is extremely narrow.

The fully isolated network in figure 18.8 gives you a much better chance of persuading your security and IT teams to allow outsiders to access organizational systems. Having an isolated network is especially important for teams that are unused to working with lawyers and don't quite know what the rules are or when they can safely say no. Having this option in your pocket will make those negotiations easier on everyone.

If you have to perform the document collections, you will do so under supervision, and your lawyers will tell you what formats they will accept. The most common format by far is PDF, but TIFF is also common. These formats may seem *unusual,* considering that most telemetry systems these days happily spit out JSON data structures that don't turn into pages in any kind of pretty way. The review systems your lawyers will use, however, have their own list of acceptable formats, which will almost definitely be broader than PDF or TIFF.

If you have to perform the document collection yourself, you will need to write a utility to take whatever your telemetry system produces and translate it into whatever your lawyers need. Think of this process as being a kind of batch mode and ad hoc Shipping stage, because you will be translating a format much as your telemetry systems do in their Shipping stage. In some cases, your lawyers may already have such a tool.

Doing the document collection means that you are involved in the chain of custody. Make sure that your organization's lawyers train you in correct handling procedures, and follow those procedures strictly. You don't want to spoliate the records.

18.3.2   *Telemetry in the review phase*

The review phase of a discovery request is when your organization's lawyers and paralegals review telemetry collected during the collection (section 18.3.1) phase. The collection phase identified any telemetry that *potentially* was responsive; during the review phase, each piece of telemetry is *specifically determined* to be responsive or not. Some poor paralegal is likely looking at events one by one (usually with deduplication support) and marking each one as responsive or nonresponsive.

In the best case, you won't need to worry about this phase. If you've managed to get collection delegated to the legal teams, review is their problem now. Review is happening in systems your organization doesn't manage, which makes it blessedly not your problem.

For smaller matters, or in an organization that is trying to save money, you may have to support review. You won't be doing review yourself, but you will be enabling the people who are involved in it. As I talked about in the collection phase (section 18.3.1), you will be required to provide access to the telemetry systems that hold the potentially responsive telemetry. The big difference between the collection and review phases is the reviewers will be looking for specific events rather than groups of events.

Doing manual review extends the chain of custody to the telemetry systems themselves, not just the gathered documents. The extension limits the changes you are allowed to make in those systems, including routine changes such as patching and vulnerability remediation. You will need to work with the legal team involved to identify safe actions.

The person who does manual review will then store records. Likely, this task involves print-to-PDF or something much like it. You are not likely to be involved in this phase other than providing tech support. Lawyers working with electronic data often employ technical specialists, so you will become one of those people for your lawyer or work with them.

18.3.3 Telemetry in the production phase

The production phase of a discovery request is when your organization's lawyers package all the responsive documents and deliver them to opposing counsel. In the first decade of the 2000s, this task often required FedExing a hard drive to the other party's lawyers. In the second decade, as Internet speeds grew, this delivery process increasingly happened online through secure upload portals. As SaaS offerings get more market share, this sharing increasingly involves granting access to the production to another user on the system.

In the best case, you won't even know that productions are happening because you aren't involved in any way. If you've managed to get yourself out of the review process, you've gotten yourself out of the production process as well. Purpose-built review systems come with ways to build productions, so your legal team won't have to involve you.

If you are involved, production looks much like the collection phase, but with tighter restrictions on format. Telemetry system operators should be involved in the production phase only for small matters or reduced sets of documents. This process is a key part of the chain of custody, so if you are building the productions, you simply must be trained. Ideally, your organization's lawyers will have technical specialists to help you extract the responsive events and turn them into the correct formats. This area is not one you can spend ten minutes researching on Google and then decide that you know what you're doing; your lawyers need to help you determine what the acceptable formats are. If the lawyers are not helpful, tell someone who might have leverage.

Discovery and the life of a paralegal

"Be a lawyer," they said. "Make lots of money," they said. Instead, I'm reviewing documents at 9:30 p.m. on a Saturday to meet a 9 a.m. Monday production deadline because the lawyers annoyed the judge for playing games.

Before electronic discovery was ruled to be admissible, you had to perform discovery on paper. In the 1980s, when CBS News announced that Chrysler responded to a lawsuit with umpty-million pages of documents, those pages were actual paper and likely took more than one semi-truck to ship to opposing counsel. Then lawyers and paralegals had to review each and every page, one by one, for responsiveness. As you can well imagine, this process took many, many months. Burying the other side in paper is a long-standing legal tradition.

In the late 1990s, after office automation had advanced to the point that most offices had a file server full of Microsoft Office (or, less frequently, WordPerfect or Lotus 1-2-3) files, courts still required paper.

(continued)

This electronically stored information (ESI) wasn't admissible, so lawyers responding to discovery requests had to print it out (a process called *blowing*, named after the high-speed printers used for this purpose). Because law firms performing review charged by the page, and because it's a good idea to make the other side pay more for legal costs, each printed email had the full reply chain printed with it. Reviewers had to check to make sure that no one edited the chain along the way. It was a terrible job.

After electronic discovery was allowed, the process of review increasingly moved online. eDiscovery was late to the SaaS game because the problem is incredibly complex: you legitimately need to handle any office file format used since 1985 correctly, in multiple languages, and also render the fonts correctly; there are so many edge cases (such as pre-Unicode mid-1990s Japanese business systems). *When trying to make a SaaS product for eDiscovery, the V in MVP is a much higher bar, so you didn't get startups going straight to SaaS (not successfully, at least); you saw established players moving into SaaS.*

I worked for one of these companies from 2011–2013, and I can attest to the sheer complexity of handling that many document types. But we brought a product to market that did the job, though getting the interface right took some work. (That job was the most interesting distributed-processing job I've ever had.) Artificial Intelligence has been a hot topic in legal tech spaces since 2012, long before it became a trendy word in the rest of the industry. AI is more often called *predictive coding* in legal circles; it's yet another tool that cuts down on the toil of doing review.

These days, the poor paralegal doing review at 9:30 p.m. on a Saturday to meet a 9 a.m. Monday production deadline is likely doing it at home rather than the office (or, before eDiscovery, in a warehouse full of paper) and has the benefit of autotagging to speed the process of tagging responsive documents.

18.4 *Working with lawyers*

This section is about a skill that few technologists need to develop: working effectively with lawyers. I hope that *other people* will do all this work so that you don't have to, but if you do have to, the advice in this section will serve you well. Lawyers are professionals with their own specialty, one that a lot of people seem to think they can do well enough after a bit of Internet searching. You know how that goes in *our* specialty.

The first thing to understand about lawyers is that they come in many different types. The sort of lawyer you go to unpick the mess your parents made of their estate is not the same kind of lawyer you'd use to handle a real-estate transaction. The sort of lawyer whom software engineers are most likely to encounter is the one we need to consult when asking this question: "I'd like to use this software module in our product, but it's GPL3-licensed. Can we use it?"

Lawyers who answer questions like this one are for the most part not scary. It's their job to assess the legal risks of new licenses and end-user agreements, which does mean that they will tell you no from time to time.

The next-most-common type of lawyer we software-handling people encounter works more with senior ICs and managers as part of contract negotiations with new service and product providers. Enterprise agreements have a lot of moving parts, and legal needs to be involved in the process. Your role depends on how central you are to the negotiation process. These lawyers generally are not scary because they're pointed at the other side.

The lawyers who get involved in the sorts of matters that lead to discovery requests are a quite different type. To explain how, I need to put a mirror in front of software engineers. Our job involves understanding the minute details of the languages we work with to produce the products we're paid to produce. The "Pay attention to the details" feature of our jobs mean that some of us have a hard time turning it off; we always sweat the details.

We've all met the engineer who needs to dig into the details of everything and calls out any imprecision as being unworkable ambiguity. Pedantism is a great thing when you're doing code reviews; it's less great when you're trying to plan a vacation for a family of five. This person isn't all of us, but they're enough of us.

Lawyers—trial lawyers specifically—have a similar trait. There's a reason for the term *arguing in court*. Whereas we sweat the details, trial lawyers learned early that you always ask for the moon when all you need is low orbit. Just as we get overly detailed when planning vacations, trial lawyers sometimes have trouble turning off their "ask for the moon" mindset. They ask for everything to get a feel for what's possible, *and they fully expect you to push back*. Given that fact, here are a few tips on working with the trial lawyers who are involved in your organization's matter:

- *Your own organization's lawyers speak lawyer better than you do.* If you're uncertain what the trial team is talking about, ask your organization's lawyers to clarify. (This tip applies to interpreting happenings in the matter, by the way, even if the events don't affect you.) Unlike outside counsel, your organization's lawyers are likely salaried and not billing by the minute.

- *Cost management is a key responsibility of your organization's lawyers.* Outside counsel costs money; they charge for every interaction and find ways to bill for any time when their attention is on your case. If you think that a request is too broad (that is, possibly too expensive), ask your organization's lawyers to advise. Advice is what they're there to provide.

- *Outside trial lawyers usually come with technical specialists. Use them.* If you're not clear about what a request means, even after asking your own lawyers, the trial lawyers' technical people likely can translate the request from lawyer to engineer. Their billing rate is far lower than that of actual lawyers too.

- *If you have to push back on technical details, do that with the technical specialists.* The outside team's specialists are much better versed in discovery procedure than you are, so they are valuable for determining what is feasible. They're also much less likely to be "ask for the moon" types.

If you read that list and are thinking "I really shouldn't ever talk to trial lawyers," you've made the right choice. Your reflexes aren't right for that job; you are merely a small technician in a large machine. A whole legal team is there to support you. Make friends with your organization's lawyers as early as you can; you'll be much happier.

Summary

- The one legal process that could affect telemetry systems is pretrial discovery. If records in the telemetry system are identified as being potentially responsive to the trial, your telemetry system will be subject to legal holds, and outsiders may start digging through your records.

- Discovery can be triggered by an outside threat of a lawsuit or your organization's decision to file suit against another organization. Both events could affect your telemetry system.

- During the discovery process, your organization's lawyers will be your interface to the whole process, which is safest for everyone involved. If you build a good relationship with your lawyers, your job during the legal matter will be much easier.

- Legal holds mean that you must not exercise your retention and redaction policies on telemetry that is subject to the hold. You need a plan (preferably made well in advance) to exempt held telemetry from these routine processes. By creating at least a rough plan before a hold order arrives, you will save time and grief dealing with the order.

- It is quite common for organizations to hire outside lawyers (retain outside counsel) to help in litigation, which means that you likely will be working with unfamiliar people and nonemployees during the discovery phase.

- Allowing nonemployees to view organizational telemetry is going to cause concern on the security team, and I strongly advise you to argue in favor of granting that access. When the lawyers can access held telemetry on their own, your role in the discovery process is greatly reduced.

- When the legal matter reaches the point at which discovery requests are issued, your ability to make routine changes (such as patching and routine software version upgrades) to the system holding the held data is not guaranteed. Always consult your organization's lawyers before proceeding, because you may need to support running old and insecure software for a time.

- Legal matters often take years to resolve and may enter and exit discovery multiple times. No one enjoys this process, but you still need to be ready to avoid spoliating records during the entire matter.

- Discovery requests have three phases: collection, review, and production. Collection gathers potentially responsive telemetry and starts the chain of custody. Review is performed by legal professionals to determine exact responsiveness (and make redactions). Production is when responsive telemetry is delivered to opposing counsel. Your role in these three phases depends on the choices your lawyers make and how successful you are in getting the lawyers direct access to the legal-hold telemetry.

- If your security group is unhappy with granting outsiders access to telemetry systems, or if you need to isolate the legal-hold telemetry systems from the vulnerability management program, one effective method is to put the legal-hold telemetry systems in an isolated network. This isolated network will be accessed only by the legal team and telemetry system operators—no one else. Because this approach reduces the blast radius in the event of a security incident, you may be able to persuade security to grant direct access to the legal team.

- Granting direct access to the legal-hold telemetry systems allows the legal team to perform its own collections, which means you don't have to worry about the chain of custody. If you can't grant this access, you will be responsible for building collections and will have to be supervised by someone who is trained in the chain of custody.

- If the legal team can perform its own collections, you won't be involved in the review process. For small matters, your legal team will be performing review directly from your telemetry systems. Your job will be tech support, helping the lawyers navigate the telemetry system and helping them build ways to mark responsive telemetry.

- If the legal team can perform its own collections, you won't be involved in the production process either. For small matters on which your legal team is performing direct review, you may be asked to build export utilities to move telemetry from your native system to a format specified by your lawyers (likely PDF).

- When working with lawyers, remember that your organization's lawyers understand your organization and are on your side. They are your best resource for resolving conflicts with the matter's legal team, which can include outside counsel. Their opinions are the only ones that matter in your organization.

- Outside counsel almost always comes with technical professionals (legal support) who are deeply familiar with legal procedure. They are quite useful in translating lawyer to engineer, and their hourly rate is better than lawyers'.

appendix A
Telemetry storage systems

Storage systems compete with the Presentation-stage systems for being the most important technical component of a telemetry system. If you don't elect to use a SaaS platform for your telemetry, picking and specifying your storage system should be one of your top priorities when setting up or updating a telemetry system. In this appendix, I give you guidance on what each of these storage systems is good at and finds challenging. Although chapter 14, which covers cardinality, touched on several storage systems, there is more to consider than simply how well each handles cardinality.

If you are using Kubernetes, you have some well-qualified default systems to choose from. If your production systems are small to medium-size, these options will take you far. The systems in this list have plenty of documentation for integrating with a Kubernetes-based infrastructure:

- *Use Prometheus for metrics.* This Cloud Native Computing Foundation product is the de facto standard for Kubernetes deployments.
- *Use Grafana Labs' Loki or Elasticsearch for logs.* Grafana Labs is attempting to make Loki the Prometheus of logging and might pull it off! Elasticsearch has been used for centralized logging for close to a decade, so there is a lot of documentation for that use case.
- *Use FluentD or Fluentbit as the Shipping-stage log mover.* This system isn't a storage system, but Kubernetes deployments have a strong preference for this platform because it is also a Cloud Native Computing Foundation product. It has native support for shipping into Elasticsearch, and Grafana Labs offers a plugin to ship to Loki.
- *Use Jaeger (which sits on top of Elasticsearch or Cassandra) for tracing.* This Cloud Native Computing Foundation product will likely be the first product to fully support the emerging OpenTelemetry standard when that process is complete.

In this appendix, I cover these systems, as well as a few others that are used outside containerized environments. No matter what product you pick, you need to understand three concepts to discuss telemetry storage systems. These concepts are familiar from general-purpose database talks but are equally relevant for telemetry systems:

- *Ingestion rate*—The number of events (individual metrics, log lines, or traces) a storage system has to write in a given period, usually specified in seconds. This rate defines your write throughput. I discuss factors that affect a given system's ingestion rate.
- *Query rate*—Queries coming from Presentation-stage systems. The more queries you have to support, the more your storage systems need to be optimized for read-only workflows as well as writing a lot of telemetry. This rate defines your read throughput.
- *Cardinality*—The topic of chapter 14, so I won't be going into detail here.

No matter which storage system you use, all of them perform better if you can batch your writes. Instead of sending each log, metric, or trace as an individual insert, bundling them up into a group will get you a higher ingestion rate before you run into problems, as shown in figure 3.4, reproduced here as figure A.1.

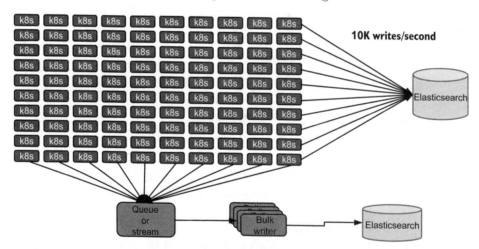

Figure A.1   The benefits of bulk writing versus everything writing on its own. Both Elasticsearch clusters handle the same number of events per second (ingestion rate), but the one being written to by the bulk writer has fewer write transactions in-flight at any given time. The bulk writer Elasticsearch cluster will be able to handle a higher ingestion rate as a result.

A.1   *Analyzing Elasticsearch*

Elasticsearch is perhaps the most famous telemetry storage system, having grown to prominence as part of the ELK Stack—which stands for Elasticsearch (storage), Logstash (shipping automation), and Kibana (presentation)—a centralized logging system that arose in the early 2010s and improved throughout the decade. The Jaeger tracing platform can use Elasticsearch as its storage system, and other lesser-known telemetry systems are built on top of Elasticsearch.

Elasticsearch was built to optimize for one thing: extremely fast searches of text. This speed makes Elasticsearch excellent for use as a centralized logging system. Over the years, Elasticsearch has had more capabilities bolted on, which make it a viable platform for distributed tracing and even metrics telemetry. Elastic.co's X-Pack add-on allows you to use Elasticsearch for all three Pillars of Observability: logs, metrics, and tracing.

Elasticsearch is a distributed database, sharding by default. This horizontal scale allows Elasticsearch to scale to high ingestion rates and storage volumes. Elasticsearch has features that allow you to optimize your cluster for tiers of service, with one tier optimized for ingesting high rates of data and another tier that holds a lot of data optimized to support searching. This flexibility allows Elasticsearch to scale from 2 data nodes to 500.

In early 2021, the maker of Elasticsearch, Elastic.co, changed the license for Elasticsearch in an attempt to prevent cloud service providers from reselling Elasticsearch services. AWS, which had been doing that for years, responded by forking Elasticsearch into OpenSearch and promised to keep the Apache 2.0 license that the Elastic.co version left behind. This fight is ongoing, and only the future will tell us which company will gain de facto control of Elasticsearch (or OpenSearch).

A.1.1   *What Elasticsearch is good at*

Elasticsearch is one of the best databases for storing centralized logging telemetry. A lot of centralized logging is strings, and string processing is what Elasticsearch does best. Elasticsearch easily handles highly enriched telemetry that has many fields defined on each event. This field flexibility makes Elasticsearch a useful platform on which to build a distributed tracing system.

Two important Elasticsearch concepts are tokenizers and analyzers. *Tokenizers* identify parts of a field, such as which parts of the string are words, to speed searches for those components. *Analyzers* go a step further, performing deeper analysis of strings to provide language-specific (human language, not computer language) indexing of strings. Tokenizers and analyzers allow a high degree of customizability of searching.

For *ingestion rate*, Elasticsearch scales horizontally pretty well through sharding. The more shards an index has, the more write capacity it has. The number of fields in the index plays a role, though. If you have a lot of fields (thousands) that aren't on every event, you will see more write I/O because you are writing a lot of nulled fields instead of event content.

For *query rate*, Elasticsearch was designed to offer search for production applications, so it is built to handle a lot of simultaneous queries. Even so, you want to keep your shard sizes at 50 GB or smaller to maximize your query performance. The number of shards per data node plays a role as well, because too many shards in one place will put memory pressure on the JVM and slow queries.

A.1.2   What is challenging for Elasticsearch

Because Elasticsearch was written to provide a search engine for text hosted in another system, it wasn't written to have a high degree of write integrity; you could always reload it from primary storage. It will drop writes in some circumstances, so if you need 100% of your telemetry in your storage, you will need to work harder to ensure that Elasticsearch doesn't reach the conditions at which it will drop writes.

Although Elasticsearch does support large shard counts (I've heard of a cluster of 200 shards in the version 2.4 era), changing the sharding of an index isn't supported. For telemetry use cases, this lack of support is not a major problem, because most telemetry systems use time-based indexes based on day, week, or month; wait for the next period to get your new shard count. If you need to reshard an existing index, you will have to re-create the entire index into a new one with new shard settings—an I/O- and CPU-intensive process.

Elasticsearch has some support as a metrics database, but the purpose-built time-series databases such as Prometheus and InfluxDB have a wider array of the statistical and analytic functions needed for a truly first-class metrics system.

A.2   Analyzing Apache Cassandra

Apache Cassandra is a database designed to be horizontally scalable to a high degree and not be rigid about schema. Cassandra has an interesting feature that allows you to select the level of consistency of writes from the highest ("Don't confirm the write until all nodes have confirmed that the write is flushed"), to the most permissive ("Always confirm writes"). As a telemetry data store, it can be used for

- Metrics by being the backing store for KairosDB
- Metrics again through bespoke metrics systems at a multinational company
- Tracing by being one possible backing store for Jaeger
- Centralized logging for a bespoke logging system

Cassandra allows a high degree of horizontal scale, which is why the preceding list mentions bespoke systems. Large software-producing companies (see chapter 8) often have enough engineering talent on hand to justify building their own telemetry pipelines instead of assembling them from open source parts.

A.2.1   What Cassandra is good at

The number one thing Cassandra is good at? Scale. You pick Cassandra because you are expecting to store and ingest high volumes of telemetry. If you expect to reach a petabyte of storage, Cassandra can handle it; simply add more nodes to the cluster.

For *ingestion rate*, Cassandra scales linearly with the number of nodes in the cluster, which is why global-scale companies use Cassandra for datasets that span multiple data centers. If you're in a growing company where ingestion rate is doubling every 18 months, Cassandra can carry you through the growth curve without forcing you to redesign your entire telemetry system.

For *query rate*, Cassandra scales linearly, like the ingestion rate.

A.2.2 *What is challenging for Cassandra*

Although Cassandra brings a lot of scale to your infrastructure, it finds rich searching to be a challenge. The query language for Cassandra is a *query* language, in that it is good at supporting queries for exact field contents. What it doesn't do easily is search for *parts* of fields. For this reason, Cassandra gets a lot of use for metrics and tracing but little for logging. Metrics and tracing have a schema and rarely use subfield searching; whereas for logging, subfield searching is extremely nice to have. Elasticsearch was built for subfield searching (with all those tokenizers) and does it fantastically well, but Cassandra wasn't built for that task and doesn't perform it well.

When you do see Cassandra used for centralized logging, it's on logging data that has been rigidly formatted. In the part 3 chapters, I presented a method for using structured logging to handle leaks of privacy- and health-related information that uses a static string, with an array of context details. Here is one example, sending a static string and a hash of context:

```
logger.info("Added account to team", {"team": 1597682, "account_id":
➥ "A881821"})
```

A structure like this one could work on a Cassandra database because searchers would look for the exact string "Added account to team" and pair it with some context details. The more typical log statement often wouldn't work well:

```
logger.info("Added account A881821 to team 1597682")
```

With Elasticsearch, you could phrase a search like this one and get everything you want:

```
"Added account" AND "1597682"
```

With Cassandra, getting the list of added accounts for team 1598682 will require highly inefficient searches. Cassandra benefits greatly from structure.

A.3 *Analyzing Grafana Labs' Loki*

Grafana Labs' Loki is quite new as a centralized logging system, announced only in 2018. Its youth means that it is still being assembled in 2021, so expect many changes in coming years. I mention Loki because Grafana Labs is directly targeting the Kubernetes and Cloud Native Computing Foundation market, and its goal is to make a highly scalable centralized logging system—something that the foundation is missing, something like Cassandra but good for the centralized logging use case.

Loki has two major components when it comes to storage:

- *The service hosting the key-value chunks*, which can be several things, such as AWS DynamoDB, AWS S3, Cassandra, Google Cloud Storage, or Google Bigtable.
- *The service hosting the index of key-value chunks*, which can be AWS DynamoDB, Cassandra, or Google Bigtable.

Loki also embraces the postprocessing concept used by some SaaS logging vendors, such as Splunk and Sumo Logic, in which the Presentation-stage system performs a lot of enrichment while a user is making queries. Whereas Elasticsearch is indexing and tokenizing every field it encounters as that field is ingested into storage, Loki does those things only for major fields that you already know you need (called *labels*) and relies on the Presentation stage to handle the smaller fields. This approach takes some of the load off your Shipping-stage components. The following query finds a specific application's telemetry and then uses Presentation-stage enrichment to further drill down into the telemetry from a specific team:

```
{datacenter="euc1",app="account-maint"} | json | team="A881821"
```

This query pulls telemetry from the EU Central 1 data center—specifically from the account-maint application—and runs the fetched telemetry (a lot of it) through a JSON deserializer to bring more fields into the query. Finally, it returns any telemetry with a team attribute of A881821. In the kind of telemetry system that relies on pre-processing, the Shipping stage would perform the JSON deserialization and create the team field before the Presentation stage got involved.

The key innovation that Loki brings to a data store like Cassandra is the query frontends. Those frontends perform the kind of searches that Cassandra is bad at, which makes this product more competitive with Elasticsearch as a centralized logging system.

Finally, like Elasticsearch (Elastic.co version), MongoDB, and InfluxDB, Loki is an open core product.

A.3.1 *What Loki is good at*

Loki was made for one thing: handling logs at scale. By using cloud provider storage buckets like AWS S3 and Google Cloud Storage, you take the thought out of scaling your storage. When you use technologies such as Cassandra and DynamoDB (which Cassandra was inspired by) for the index, the main technological problem is reduced to keeping the indexes happy instead of keeping petabytes of storage servers happy.

Ingestion rate is linearly scalable by expanding distributor nodes to increase their ability to accept incoming telemetry and by expanding ingester nodes to handle writing chunks to storage and indexing. You can run into bottlenecks from the indexer service if you haven't provisioned enough capacity.

For *query rate*, Loki relies on a tier of query frontend nodes to handle queuing queries, distribute queries across the cluster, and perform transforms (such as the JSON transform from the earlier example). User queries can bottleneck again on the indexer service when it runs out of capacity.

A.3.2 *What is challenging for Loki*

Loki is young, and it has young problems. That said, it is being actively developed, so these problems might not exist much longer. The three big problems are

- *No support for out-of-order arrival*—Each log should have a more recent timestamp than the previous one. If your telemetry workflows include processing old sets once in a while—maybe your business involves mobile telemetry that sometimes arrives hours late due to airplane mode—Loki may be a bad fit.
- *No support for targeted deletions*—Retention policies are set globally; everything gets a single policy, with no chance for different policies for different systems. Also, if you need to delete a specific set of telemetry for some reason (perhaps you have a spill of privacy- or health-related information to clean up), that deletion is better done in storage than in Loki directly.
- *No support for redaction*—If your logging might contain privacy- or health-related information, Loki does not support rewriting. To deal with spills of such data, you will need to remove the old streams and reprocess the entire set.

A.4 *Analyzing MongoDB*

MongoDB was one of the first NoSQL storage engines to get a lot of mindshare. The project made some controversial design decisions in the early years, earning MongoDB a lot of scorn among people who didn't pay attention to the nuances and got burned. Twelve years later, MongoDB versions 4 and later have done away with those controversial design choices and removed many of the hidden gotchas that vexed early adopters.

MongoDB is the top document storage engine, which is subtly different from the search engine that is Elasticsearch. MongoDB was designed to be a primary storage system; Elasticsearch was not. This difference matters when it comes to maintaining the system and defending it from failure.

MongoDB is sometimes used as a centralized logging storage system due to how it handles text-based data. It isn't as laser-focused on text-based search as Elasticsearch, but it has much better text-search features than Cassandra and is already being used for in-application search in many places. Because of these features, some companies pick MongoDB as the foundation of a bespoke centralized logging system.

Similarly to Elasticsearch, MongoDB embraces a shard-and-replica approach to scaling out storage. Sharding splits the database into smaller parts, allowing you to scale your storage performance. Replicas duplicate shards, allowing you to better survive outages.

Unlike with Elasticsearch, you have to specifically define what indexes you want to have in place, so you need to know what your data looks like as you are designing your MongoDB system. For an existing production system, you already have those details, so the task shouldn't be too hard. But when you're setting up a new system, expect to have to redo things several times before you get a good fit.

Finally, MongoDB is an open core product, like Elasticsearch (Elastic.co variant) and InfluxDB. Although you can do a lot with the free version, including contribute code, you may need a paid license to use certain features.

A.4.1   *What MongoDB is good at*

MongoDB is great at centralized logging with a high guarantee of write fidelity. Elasticsearch drops writes in certain rare circumstance, but MongoDB doesn't (or can be configured not to). Unlike Loki, MongoDB was not built as a dedicated telemetry engine, but the fact that it is a document store makes it a great fit for telemetry use cases. If you're already using MongoDB in your production systems, using MongoDB for telemetry should be quite easy for you.

For *ingestion rate*, MongoDB scales based on the ability of shards to keep up with write volume, so if writes are getting highly latent, add more shards. Also, you want to use many collections (a database; think of it like partitioning) to further enhance your ability to scale horizontally. MongoDB also is aware of locality (called *zones*), such as data center or cloud-provider region, which enhances performance by directing reads and writes to local shards.

For *query rate*, MongoDB is governed by the presence of indexes, but it also benefits from query optimization in Presentation-stage systems. Unlike with Elasticsearch, you have to specifically define the indexes you want. MongoDB can have up to 64 indexes in a collection, so if you need more indexes, consider splitting your collection into multiple collections.

A.4.2   *What is challenging for MongoDB*

The biggest challenges in using MongoDB as a telemetry storage system are how complex it is to manage and the lack of off-the-shelf Presentation-stage systems that support it. You need to actively manage how MongoDB stores telemetry to a greater extent than you do with most of the other logging storage systems discussed in this appendix. If you're already doing this management for your production systems, this extra management should not be an impediment.

A.5   *Analyzing Prometheus*

Prometheus is a time-series database and metrics system that is the default platform for Kubernetes environments. This Cloud Native Computing Foundation project is fully open source. Prometheus provides a query interface specially designed for working with time-series data and includes a wide array of transformation and summarization functions—incredibly important for gaining value from metrics.

Prometheus can operate as a standalone, single-node system, which is easy to set up and get going. The popularity of Prometheus in the Kubernetes space makes the Prometheus protocol a de facto standard for transmitting metrics. Prometheus the product embraces this popularity by allowing the use of other storage systems (such as InfluxDB, as well as various cloud-provider-specific systems) as the main storage of Prometheus while still providing the same interface to consumers.

The swappable nature of the Prometheus storage layer makes it trickier to discuss storage performance, but if you are reaching the limits of the native storage engine, evaluate the possibility of moving to a new engine. In this section, I'll be examining the native storage engine.

A.5.1 What Prometheus is good at

Prometheus is good at metrics, and anything (assuming that it's running in a containerized environment) is likely built to assume that it will talk to Prometheus. Organizations that are beginning to outgrow Prometheus will create several Prometheus servers rather than consider a different platform.

Unlike the other storage systems discussed in this appendix, Prometheus embraces a hierarchical approach to scaling. Rather than sharding a single data store horizontally, the way Elasticsearch, Cassandra, MongoDB, and InfluxDB (paid) do, Prometheus creates a tree to roll up metrics (figure A.2).

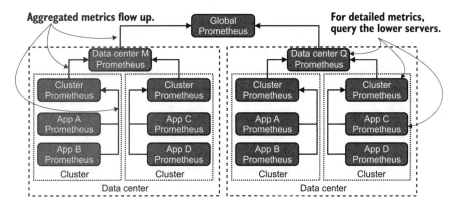

Figure A.2   The Prometheus scaling model. Unlike most of the other storage systems discussed in this appendix, Prometheus does not provide a single wide-scale storage system. Instead, it relies on rolling aggregations up the tree and querying area-specific (data center, cluster, application, and so on) Prometheus servers for detailed metrics.

Prometheus uses aggregations (see sections 5.1.1 and 17.2) to provide a view of what is happening in wider scopes. Presentation-stage systems (likely Grafana) will be configured with multiple data sources: use top-level Prometheus for aggregated views and use lower-level Prometheus for detailed views in narrow areas. This approach allows Prometheus to scale up to a high degree.

For *ingestion rate*, individual Prometheus servers scale based on the storage performance of the server itself but are limited by cardinality in the database. As a Prometheus ecosystem, ingestion depends entirely on your ability to route metrics into individual servers and configure the aggregation rollups—not as easy as adding a shard, but more scalable than setting up a single server.

For *query rate*, the split nature of Prometheus means that your top-level aggregated servers will be seeing a lot of traffic, probably from alerting systems running automated queries to feed on-call rotations in addition to the usual dashboarding traffic. Lower-level, narrow scoped servers will see traffic from engineering looking for details and queries will be mostly infrequent. Prometheus also limits query rate on the cardinality of the database, which makes queries more expensive for RAM.

A.5.2   *What is challenging for Prometheus*

Prometheus becomes a challenging platform to adopt in two situations:

- *Large environment or large monolithic product*—In this case, Prometheus's scaling technique will require more effort to deploy than a shardable data store like InfluxDB or Cassandra. Prometheus grew up in the container and microservices space, where it's far easier to hand-shard metrics telemetry into different Prometheus servers. As always with a popular open source product, many SaaS offerings and consulting services are available to handle the complexity for you.
- *Cardinality*—I talked about this topic in chapter 14. Time-series databases in general have a problem handling high cardinality, and Prometheus is no different. Prometheus's documentation is clear that you need to pay attention to cardinality and that the cost of not paying attention to cardinality is slow queries and high RAM use.

A.6   *Analyzing InfluxDB*

InfluxDB is another time-series database, which makes it a great place to store metrics. InfluxData, the creator of InfluxDB, has made this data store the core of an entire metrics pipeline as a way to compete with the Prometheus and Grafana combination. As a data store, InfluxDB and Prometheus have a lot in common, but the *commercial version* of InfluxDB offers the ability to shard the database for horizontal scale and cardinality reasons.

The commercial version of InfluxDB, InfluxDB Enterprise, lets you create a cluster of multiple data and metadata servers. Clusters allow replication between nodes to tolerate failures (and routine operations like patching cycles) and a configurable level of write consistency. Sharding within the cluster increases the effective cardinality limit for a database by spreading the costs of cardinality across multiple data servers.

A.6.1   *What InfluxDB is good at*

Low cardinality metrics is what InfluxDB was designed to handle well. InfluxData knows that Prometheus is the dominant player in the self-hosted metrics market, so InfluxDB has a Prometheus-compatible API endpoint as well as several less-popular metrics transports, including StatsD and Graphite. InfluxDB represents a paid self-hosted option, one that comes with the kind of support contracts that large, old enterprises consider to be the minimum requirement for a mission-critical component.

For *ingestion rate*, InfluxDB is mostly limited by storage performance (not a major concern if solid state drives are used) and the CPU required to update indexes. That said, InfluxDB enforces maximum cardinality per database and rejects writes that increase cardinality.

For *query rate*, InfluxDB is limited by CPU and memory to hold indexes, because increased CPU and memory use are the manifestations of the cardinality problem. Prometheus has a similar issue with cardinality of queries.

A.6.2   *What is challenging for InfluxDB*

The chief problem for InfluxDB is scaling up in the free version: you have to follow the Prometheus model and create a tree of discrete servers that aggregates metrics from lower-tier servers into higher-tier ones. Scaling up with a single database is an Enterprise-plan feature, so if your organization is already large, plan to budget for sharding and clustering features.

Like most time-series databases, InfluxDB has a problem with high cardinality metrics. The company has plans to address that problem over the lifetime of the 2.x series, so keep an eye out for advances in coming years. The industry as a whole has a deep need for high cardinality metrics, which is a fundamentally difficult problem.

A.7   *Analyzing Jaeger*

Jaeger is a self-hosted tracing system, which makes it stand out in a market dominated by SaaS players. Jaeger is also a member of the Cloud Native Computing Foundation, so it is fully open source. Jaeger is likely to be the first self-hosted tracing data store to fully support the emerging OpenTelemetry tracing standard (also a CNCF project) when it is finalized.

Like Grafana Labs' Loki, Jaeger sits on top of other storage systems to provide its data store. In Jaeger's case, you can use either Elasticsearch or Cassandra to provide the storage layer. The rest of Jaeger sits on top, ingesting traces coming from the Shipping stage and providing a query layer for the Presentation stage. Because Jaeger sits on top of other storage technologies, scaling Jaeger out relies as much on Cassandra or Elasticsearch as it does on its own components.

Jaeger can use Kafka (a streaming service) as part of its internal operations. It does so for many of the reasons I talked about in part 1: to make telemetry operations asynchronous, to improve resilience in the face of errors, and to handle back pressure if telemetry processing gets backed up.

A.7.1   *What Jaeger is good at*

Jaeger is the dominant player in the self-hosted distributed tracing space and was built to scale out. When used on top of Elasticsearch, Jaeger can let Elasticsearch take some of the indexing load and write more telemetry per ingestion worker. If you're already using Elasticsearch for centralized logging or as part of your production applications, Jaeger is an easier product to deploy.

For *ingestion rate,* Jaeger scales horizontally pretty well. It requires an ingester worker to insert telemetry into the storage systems, but this ingester can scale horizontally far enough to saturate the storage system. Jaeger recommends running Elasticsearch over Cassandra because Elasticsearch can take on some of the indexing work.

For *query rate,* Jaeger provides a UI and API for fetching traces and spans. Performance depends on storage performance and CPU available for the query service. Due to the nature of tracing, storage will be handling far more writes than reads. The UI and API services are horizontally scalable, though they don't necessarily support browser session storage across discrete query services. Other services, such as Grafana, will use the API for queries.

A.7.2   *What is challenging for Jaeger*

Jaeger was designed to run in Kubernetes, and if you are not a Kubernetes shop, Jaeger will be challenging for you to deploy. Some organizations are beginning to use their distributed tracing system in place of a centralized logging system, which Jaeger has some support for. You will still be better served by a purpose-built centralized logging system.

appendix B
Recommendation
checklist reference

Over the 18 chapters of this book, I made many recommendations on any number of things. This appendix collates those recommendation lists into a single reference that you can look up as you work on improving your telemetry systems. Perhaps these lists will be helpful for you in your efforts to persuade management to make the changes you're pushing for.

B.1 Telemetry standards, structure, and setting policies

These lists cover the topics of telemetry format and standards, as well as policies related to telemetry, such as retention and sampling policies.

Section 4.2.2: Setting standardized telemetry formats

Section 4.2.2 was a walk-through of setting telemetry format standards for a multinational logistics company. This process is as much political as it is technical. You should keep a few things in mind while having your standards-setting meetings:

- *The goal is to get people using the new telemetry systems.* Wrong use is generally better than no use; wrong can be corrected later.
- *Simple is relative to the observer.* What is simple for you can be quite complex for another team; the converse is also true. Have empathy for everyone involved.
- *Shared understanding of goals and constraints helps everyone toward consensus.* Teach, guide, and then direct the conversation.
- *You're allowed to use more than one telemetry shipping format.* You want people using the standards, and allowing more than one format lowers the barrier to adoption facing telemetry producers.

Section 4.2.4: Designing telemetry formats with cardinality in mind

Section 4.2.4 was the first time I gave specific advice on handling cardinality in telemetry. The list was mostly a pointer to chapter 14, but the summary bullets are useful:

- If your traffic is dominated by a single generator of telemetry, such as more than half your overall events, your telemetry storage systems will likely behave better if telemetry emitted by that generator is sent to a separate index that's not shared with other telemetry. (See section 14.2.2 for more on this method.) Telemetry will be stored efficiently for both the high-rate system and the rest, and you will save money and space.

- If you have the ability to modify telemetry fields within the Shipping stage, taking steps to ensure that different telemetry formats overlap on fields will create some efficiencies. (See section 14.2.1 for more on this method.) Many logging formats have a field for `priority`, so if you can get all the priority fields into the same data type, you will save field counts.

- If you have a telemetry generator that produces huge numbers of fields, perhaps because it emits in an object-encoding format, sending that telemetry to a single index will isolate the performance hit to that specific production system. (See section 14.2.2.)

- If your large telemetry-producing systems are software that your organization develops, taking the time to work with the software engineering teams for your organization's software to teach them how to optimize their telemetry systems can help reduce field sprawl. (Chapter 12 and section 14.2.1 address this topic in detail.)

Section 6.4.1: When and where to mark up or enrich telemetry in centralized logging systems

Section 6.4.1 was a discussion on how markup (adding context-related telemetry) and enrichment (pulling details out of existing telemetry) affect centralized logging. Centralized logging benefits greatly from both techniques, so the following list is longer:

- If the Emitting stage can't do context-related markup (see section 6.2.1), such as for hardware systems, the Shipping stage may be used to extract and enrich telemetry based on the logged strings, as demonstrated in listings 6.4 and 6.5.

- If software is emitting telemetry, it has the best context for adding context-related markup right at the time telemetry is emitted, just before or during the Emitting stage. Markup can be added directly to the event right at emission.

- If hardware is emitting telemetry, it often includes context-related telemetry in the logged string. The Shipping stage can extract the context-related telemetry and enrich the telemetry event for the Presentation stage, as was done in section 6.2.2.

- Timestamps and other date/time structures are critical for making centralized logging systems work well. The Shipping stage should transform various date/time strings from their source format to the format that the Presentation-stage systems need.
- Syslog's protocol deliberately leaves the year off its timestamp because it should be obvious when a line was emitted. If you are dealing with Syslog-formatted telemetry in any capacity, consider adding a timestamp in the logged line if possible or making rules for how to add a year.
- Regular expressions may be needed to extract interesting telemetry from strings—a function done mostly by the Shipping stage.
- Object-encoding formats such as JSON, YAML, and XML are one way to ship telemetry objects in strings, to be converted back to objects (enriched) by the Shipping stage.

Section 6.4.3: When and where to mark up or enrich telemetry in metrics systems

Metrics systems don't benefit as greatly from markup and enrichment as centralized logging systems do. That said, due to the cardinality sensitivity of most time-series databases, the concerns for markup and enrichment with metrics are different:

- Emitting-stage systems add context-related telemetry, such as a class path, hostname, program name, or other broad details, as shown in listing 6.1.
- Shipping-stage systems transform emitted telemetry into numbers and deliver them to a metrics database, as shown in listing 6.7.
- Shipping-stage systems may generate metrics on their own, based on telemetry observed in the pipeline, such as a count of telemetry with priority set to WARN.
- Emitter/shipper functions, the direct-to-storage pattern from section 3.1.1, do all these things in one place.
- Metrics databases often have limits on cardinality, so be selective when picking context-related telemetry.
- Presentation systems use aggregation functions to enrich displayed telemetry, as covered in-depth in section 5.1.

Section 7.2.1: How parasitic is that parasitic load?

The sidebar in section 7.2.1 lists the sorts of parasitic load (load that takes resources away from your production operations) that telemetry systems running on the same server/VM/container/partition/function as your production systems can incur. The following things are important to understand when you make telemetry system decisions:

- *CPU costs*—If the only thing you're doing with your telemetry is reshipping it, with no other changes, this area is not likely to be significant. If you do perform changes, however (perhaps one of the chapter 15 techniques to ensure telemetry integrity), this charge can be significant. In large hardware instances, you may not notice these costs. But in container or FaaS environments, the increased run time of the container or function can be noticeable.
- *RAM costs*—Depending on how your shipping software works, you need RAM to perform your change operations and to batch up events for sending downstream. On large hardware instances or virtual machines, this change may not be significant. For containers or FaaS, where RAM usage is metered, these effects can be noticeable.
- *I/O costs*—Writing a whole bunch of telemetry to disk is an I/O charge; so is reading it by your telemetry software. If your storage is slow, telemetry I/O absolutely will compete with production I/O. If you're running slow storage, you will be better off if you put your logs on separate disks from your production operations. Or maybe you can redesign your telemetry systems to use one of the chapter 13 techniques and avoid files altogether. In my career, I've seen cases in which telemetry I/O dwarfs I/O generated by production operations!

Chapter 11: Making regular expressions fast

Chapter 11 was one giant checklist for making regular expressions (regexes) fast. Although the chapter had a checklist (which I'll get to below), there wasn't one that summarized the entire chapter. This new checklist provides the summary:

- *The best way to make regular expressions fast is to not use them.* Regular expressions are computationally expensive, and putting them in your telemetry pipeline will slow the pipeline. Avoid using them where you can.
- *The best regular expression is one that stops trying matches fast.* Regular expression engines try hard to find matches in a given string, so you will gain efficiencies by phrasing your regexes in a way that tells the regex engine to stop trying to match a string. Fail fast for faster performance.
- *If you are matching the whole string, using the anchor tags will speed everything.* The ^ tag (for beginning of string) and $ tag (for end of string) tell the regex engine where to start trying matches. Anchors are powerful for getting the regex engine to stop trying to match a string that will never match.
- *You gain speed by specifying narrow character sets and match lengths.* If you know that a given field in a string is between four and eight characters long, writing your regex to specify that length rather than a lazy operator like + means that the regex engine has to make fewer comparisons while testing for a match. This approach improves match speeds.

- *Beware of overoptimization; long regexes can perform worse than shorter expressions.* Although narrow character sets and match lengths reduce the number of match attempts the regex engine attempts, some programming languages perform worse with long and precise regexes versus short and general ones. When optimizing your expressions, always test them with real data to validate your performance assumptions.

- *You will gain telemetry speed by taking the time to rewrite your logging statements to be regex-friendly.* Not every organization has the option of using a structured logger. If your organization is one of those, taking the time to rewrite your logging statements to make them efficient to parse with regexes will gain you a lot of telemetry performance.

- *Well-specified regular expressions often perform better than lazy versions but are harder to maintain.* Regexes are not easy for humans to parse visually, and complex expressions force even regex experts to stop to figure out what those expressions are saying. This cognitive load reduces the number of people who will feel comfortable maintaining a given regex.

Section 11.4: The project phases for optimizing your logging statements for regular expressions

Section 11.4 walked through how you could turn a program that had been using natural language logging statements into one that used easily regexed grammar in the name of increasing telemetry throughput. This is the list of the major project phases:

1 Agree to a set of prepended strings.
2 Agree to a regexable grammar with your team.
3 Update your telemetry system to handle prepended and not-prepended log data.
4 Add your unified regexes for each prepend-string to your telemetry system.
5 Convert existing log emissions to the new grammar.
6 Once all log emissions are converted, remove support for the old grammar from your telemetry system.

Chapter 12: The benefits of using a structured logger

Chapter 12 was about structured logging, and that chapter's introduction included a list of the benefits of structured logging. Use this list if you need to make the case for converting to a structured logger in your projects:

- A well-written set of standards reduces your need to include regular expressions in your Shipping-stage systems, which will make your telemetry system more efficient overall. (See chapter 11 for the impact of regular-expression use.)

- Embracing structured logging techniques—mentioned in part in chapter 2 but explored in depth in section 12.1—gives your Emitting stage far more options regarding where it sends telemetry data and enables multiple streams of telemetry. Structured logging emitters allow sending data over novel channels like TCP sockets directly, as discussed in chapter 13.

- Taking a systematic look at logging standards gives you tools to fight the problem of index cardinality in your centralized logging and metrics data stores. Chapter 14 is your deep dive into managing the cardinality problem.

- Structured logging formatters (more on this topic in section 12.1) are where you can start making your telemetry tamper-evident, providing resistance to attackers meddling with telemetry. Chapter 15 examines more of the topic of making telemetry durable in the face of attack.

- By providing a systematic way to add context-related details (markup) as part of the Emitting stage, telemetry in your Presentation stage will be far more detailed about *when and how* an event happened, improving your ability to plug leaks of regulated information. (See chapter 16 for more on cleaning up after data spills.)

Section 13.1: In-memory networking and how it eases telemetry

Chapter 13 was about nonfile emitting techniques, and section 13.1 was about using TCP and UDP transports for telemetry. When you are using Kubernetes or another technology in which containers or virtual machines communicate over an in-memory network, you can use simpler (and smaller) networking technologies. Using in-memory networks provides several advantages:

- Your production software will have less code dedicated to telemetry system use, making it easier to ship.

- For microservices, not having to use an expensive (and expansive) library like Kafka makes for a much smaller deliverable binary.

- Not having to support a telemetry system application protocol means that you have one fewer module to include in your production software—one fewer module to keep track of dependencies, one fewer module to handle for security vulnerabilities, and less overall code to contain bugs.

Section 14.2.1: Enforcing logging standards through development process

Chapter 14 was about cardinality, and section 14.2.1 was about using logging standards to contain cardinality problems. Moving to a new standard is a political process, and you can ease the transition by making a few updates to your software development practices:

- *Create a mandatory code review step that reviews all logging statements to ensure that they comply with the agreed-on schema.* This option is your automation-free option; it relies on humans to remember to do the code review. But you can do this review immediately after deciding on your standard.

- *Update your continuous integration (CI) jobs to check to make sure that new logging statements use only fields from the allowed list.* This option requires writing the automation for your CI pipeline but is more reliable than trusting code review and humans. When builds that include not-allowed field names fail, people will get the message.

- *Provide new logger interfaces that enforce schema, and move all your logging and metrics emissions to the new interface.* If you have a large codebase, it will take some time to get all the changes smoked out, but this option is the most long-term-maintainable option in this list.

Section 17.1.3: Recommendations on setting a tracing retention policy

Chapter 17 was about setting retention, aggregation, and sampling policies for telemetry. Section 17.1 was about retention policies, and it had two checklists. This one is for distributed tracing, which benefits from sampling:

- Search performance is a key detail for any telemetry system, tracing included. When search performance slows, people get cranky, and cranky people aren't having a good experience. Cranky users are a sign that you need to shorten your retention period.
- The cost of offline backups matters as much as the cost of online storage, so consider both costs in your calculations.

Section 17.1.4: Recommendations on setting a SIEM retention policy

SIEM systems have unique constraints on their telemetry and retention policies:

- Plan for a retention period measured in years.
- To contain costs, be highly selective in the telemetry you send to the SIEM.

Section 17.3: Considerations when picking a sampling rate

Distributed tracing (and to a lesser extent metrics) benefits from statistical sampling as a way to keep telemetry costs down. Picking the right sample rate is tricky, and I provided a list of considerations:

- The more you understand a process, the lower the sample rate. You don't need to monitor it heavily if you understand it.
- The less you understand a process, the higher the sample rate. You need to build trust (and understanding) by observing the process under many conditions.
- The more frequently a process occurs, the lower the sample rate. If your population is large, you can get away with sample rates like 0.0001%. Imagine if Twitter attempted to trace every single tweet.
- If you've identified a low-frequency error that you need to capture, increasing the sample rate for a short time will help you catch it in the act.
- Production-system sample rates are allowed to be different from load-testing and continuous-integration sample rates. Yes, sampling your load-testing and pre-production environments lets you compare with production to see whether those tools are valid tests.
- A sample rate of 100% gives you the highest-quality data for the most cost.

B.2   Presentation-stage recommendations

Chapter 5 gave you several recommendations on what a good Presentation-stage system needs to have for each of the telemetry styles in this book. Later chapters added to those recommendations in certain circumstances. Here they are in one place for easy reference.

Section 5.1.1: The features of a good metrics system

Metrics systems are the backbone of so many things—from SLO/SLA compliance auditing to seeing if the latest deploy is performing right. You want a good one, which will have these features:

- *They allow a wide variety of users to create charts and graphs,* enabling decision support or troubleshooting for any team that needs it.
- *They have guided user interfaces for building the queries behind charts and graphs,* so users don't have to memorize query syntax and can build complex queries easily.
- *They have the ability to organize collections of charts and graphs,* often called dashboards, to provide at-a-glance views of a decision point that a team needs.
- *They have the ability to organize dashboards,* making locating the right ones easy. Otherwise, you get a big pile of dashboards that's hard to work with.
- *They allow the creation of ad hoc dashboards without saving,* permitting a user to investigate something immediately without having to clutter the dashboard listings with a dashboard that will be used once.

Section 5.1.1: Considerations for building dashboards

Dashboards and graphs are how metrics presentation systems operate, so I gave you a few tips on doing it right. That said, effective visualizations are a broad topic, and there is a lot of work out there better than mine on how to do it right or beautifully. Here are three points to keep in mind when building dashboards:

- *Beware of how dark-/light-mode themes affect contrast.* If the presentation system supports changing background colors, pick colors so that users with dark and light backgrounds will be able to see the lines. Yellow pops on black but is nearly invisible on white, for example, and dark blues show up beautifully on white but disappear on black.
- *For dashboards with multiple charts, put the most important charts at the top.* People don't like to scroll.
- *Beware of information density.* If you have too many charts on a page, users who are unfamiliar with what the dashboard is displaying won't know what to look at.

Section 5.2.1: The features of a good centralized logging system

Centralized logging systems overlap in many ways with SIEM systems but are still the largest physical telemetry systems in terms of space consumed. The presentation system for your centralized logging has to support robust, complicated searches as people diagnose what happened in their production systems. To perform these duties effectively, a good centralized logging system should have these abilities:

- *Ability to search by field contents*—All centralized logging systems I've interacted with have the concept of fields and allow users to build queries by using those fields. Use of field (searching for `priority:"high"` versus `"high"`) content will greatly speed the performance of searches.
- *Ability to support complex search logic*—Sometimes, all you need is a single string. At other times, getting what you need requires a complex "If this, then that, except for these other things, but do include this one thing" kind of statement.
- *Ability to customize field display*—Events in centralized logging systems may include tens or even hundreds of fields, displaying each one in a table that often shows information the searcher doesn't care about. The ability to customize a result table to show specific fields allows the searcher to scan the table for interesting events.
- *Ability to save searches and table layouts for later*—If you wanted to know something enough to build a search and table layout, chances are good that you might need it again. The ability to save the layout for later will save you work in the future.
- *Ability to share saved searches/layouts between users*—Sharing searches among users of the telemetry system allows sharing analysis tools to improve the organization's ability to respond to problems instead of relying on a few skilled searchers to do the work.
- *Ability to share URLs of searches and have the same search and layout come up*—Related to sharing saved searches, sharing improvised or ad hoc searches is critical during problem response. If the URL of the telemetry display system doesn't re-create the search, other responders will have to do more work to see the interesting results. A good display system will ease this effort.
- *Require a login to use*—Centralized logging systems often contain company-sensitive information and sometimes contain regulated information such as personally identifiable information (PII). The absolute minimum requirement is to require authentication and authorization before using the display system. Chapter 15 covers this security topic in detail.

Section 5.3: Extending centralized logging to SIEM work

SIEM systems need a few extra features beyond what I specified in section 5.2.1 to support the mission of security teams:

- *Ability to define alerts*—Whereas centralized logging systems are about asking questions you may not have thought to ask before, SIEM systems function as part of a monitoring system. Therefore, the ability to create alerts to notify humans of problems is a critical feature, whereas in centralized logging systems, it is merely optional.

- *Ability to define alert priorities*—Automatically triaging alarms by priority levels allows responding humans to defer lower-priority alarms safely, leading to better sleep and greater workplace enjoyment.

Section 7.2.2: Adding multitenancy

When your telemetry systems grow enough, you eventually need to isolate telemetry to specific groups. This isolation is multitenancy. This list extends the feature list you need for your presentation systems:

- *Ability to define roles*—The core of any access control system is the ability to define roles or groups with permissions.
- *Ability to use single-sign-on* (SSO) *frameworks such as SAML and OpenID Connect* (OIDC)—The Presentation system can hook into an existing authentication framework maintained by the technical organization.
- *Ability to restrict access to data sources by role*—You can keep members of different roles from accessing databases they shouldn't, which reduces the cleanup area of leaks of regulated data.
- *Ability to assign users to multiple roles*—Users should be able to serve in multiple roles, such as engineering managers who need to be in several team roles.
- *Ability to restrict access to dashboards by role*—Not every dashboard is intended for use by every member of the system, so limiting access applies to accessing dashboards, making for a less-crowded experience for everyone.
- *Ability to restrict who can create or modify dashboards by role*—View-only users can find existing dashboards to be quite powerful, and restricting edit access reduces dashboard sprawl.

B.3   *Cardinality management*

Cardinality is one of the most important constraints on telemetry storage, which is why I spent chapter 14 on it and why it's getting its own section in this appendix.

Section 4.2.4: Designing telemetry formats with cardinality in mind

Section 4.2.4 was the first time I gave specific advice for handling cardinality in telemetry. The list was mostly a pointer to chapter 14, but the summary bullets are useful.

- If your traffic is dominated by a single generator of telemetry, such as more than half your overall events, your telemetry storage systems will likely behave better if telemetry emitted by that generator is sent to a separate index not shared with other telemetry (see section 14.2.2 for more on this method). Telemetry will be efficiently stored for both the high-rate system and the rest, and you will save money and space.
- If you have the ability to modify telemetry fields within the Shipping stage, taking steps to ensure different telemetry formats overlap on fields will make some efficiencies (see section 14.2.1 for more on this method). Many logging formats have a field for priority, if you can get all the priority fields into the same data-type, you will save field counts.

- If you have a telemetry generator that produces huge numbers of fields, perhaps because it emits in an object-encoding format, sending that telemetry to a single index will isolate the performance hit to that specific production system (see section 14.2.2 for more).
- If your larger telemetry producing systems are software your organization develops, taking time to work with the Software Engineering teams for your organization's software to teach them how to optimize their telemetry systems can help reduce field-sprawl. Chapter 12 and section 14.2.1 address this topic in detail.

Section 14.1: The symptoms of high cardinality

While not a list of recommendations, the following is a list of signs telling you that you need to take steps to address a creeping cardinality problem in your telemetry systems:

- *Slow search performance*—This symptom is the one that most people notice, because search performance is a primary feature of Presentation-stage systems. Unfortunately, many things other than a cardinality problem can cause slow search, but slow performance is a sign to look for that problem.
- *Increased memory use for normal operations*—Many storage systems keep indexes in memory. As those indexes grow, so does memory use. Most of these storage systems allow reading indexes from disk if they won't fit in memory, which greatly slows search performance. Relational databases like MySQL are famous for this pattern.
- *Increased memory use for routine scheduled operations*—Scheduled optimization procedures in some storage systems are affected by cardinality. InfluxDB (as of version 2.0) performs compaction operations regularly, and high cardinality leads to increased (often much increased) memory use compared with the rest of the time.
- *Decreases in ability to insert new data*—As indexes get larger, they need to be updated. Indexing efficiency varies by storage engine, and not all storage engines are good at it. The overhead of handling inserting new values into the indexes can, for some systems, scale up as the unique-value count increases, which in turn reduces the ability to insert new data into the system.
- *Increased time to allow querying after starting the database*—Some storage systems need to load indexes into memory before being able to query. The larger the indexes are, the longer this process takes. Because stateful systems like these may not be restarted often, this problem can surprise you at a bad time.
- *Increases in consumed disk space that scales higher than your ingestion rate*—Some storage systems keep indexes in separate files from table data. Each time you insert new data with a new unique value, the storage system needs to update the table data with the new value, as well as update any indexes and their files. In other systems, such as Elasticsearch, every new piece of data gets all fields, even if those fields have a null value. Therefore, if you have 10,000 fields, and a new event is inserted with 15 fields, that new event will have 9,985 nulled fields on it.

Section 14.2.1: Healthy low-cardinality context-related telemetry

Context-related telemetry (markup) is incredibly important for telling people what happened in their production systems. At the same time, context-related telemetry is one of the chief drivers of cardinality. Although systems like Elasticsearch are generally fine with many unique values per field, time-series databases are incredibly sensitive. Even so, some common context-related telemetry options are usually helpful for metrics telemetry:

- *Application name*—In a production system running more than one application, storing application names is quite viable. The total unique count is likely to be small, and it will be used in nearly every query.
- *Application version*—Version is an interesting one when paired with retention periods, because the total unique values in the field will be the number of unique versions stored in the retention period. (For more on retention periods, see chapter 17.) If you can afford the cardinality hit, application version will let you track how metrics change versus their application version.
- *Class name*—This concept is more of a tracing concept, but if you have a `metric_name` that is used in more than one class for more than one purpose, having the class name as a metric will help you separate the two. Putting a class name on every piece of metric is an antipattern, however because most `metric_names` likely don't need this disambiguation, and using class names will explode your cardinality. A better pattern for separating two otherwise-identical `metric_name` uses is to use different `metric_name` values (`class1_pdf_pages` instead of `class2_pdf_pages`).
- *Cluster*—This word means different things to different organizations, but if you need to correlate error rates or something equivalent to a given group of machines/instances/nodes, *cluster* is quite useful.
- *Hostname*—For some organizations, especially those running on physical hardware, hostname is a small enough set of unique values to be as useful as `cluster` is for correlating behaviors. For other organizations, such as those running in a public cloud and using lots of autoscaling systems, hostname can be highly unique and a clear antipattern.
- *Data center or region*—If your organization is operating in more than one computing facility, having a split for those facilities is useful, especially because this value is not likely to have many unique values.

Section 14.2.2: How sharding affects cardinality management

Section 14.2 discusses a pair of storage-side techniques that are useful in the fight against excessive cardinality. Section 14.3.2 talks about *sharding*, a common feature of distributed databases to spread read and write loading. Sharding impacts cardinality management in several ways, depending on the data store you are using:

- If you are using MongoDB for metrics-style telemetry, using the timestamp field as your shard key will even out reads and writes across your servers.

- If you are using KairosDB for metrics, that database handles the sharding setup for Cassandra for you.
- If you are using MongoDB for a centralized logging system, using timestamp as the shard key will still even out reads and writes across servers. Using a compound shard key such as application plus year/month/day, however, will ensure that all application writes on a given day will be written to the same node, potentially reducing the cardinality in that shard versus truly even writes.
- If you are using Cassandra or MongoDB for a centralized logging system, using application as your shard key is functionally equivalent to partitioning (see the preceding section) but does not give you the benefit of horizontal scale.

Section 14.2.3: When to make cardinality someone else's problem

Section 14.2.3 is about what happens when you decide to stop managing telemetry yourself and pay someone else to do it by picking up a SaaS platform. This choice is not an easy one to make, and such a fundamental shift in how everything works will create disruption on your teams. I provided a list of challenges to consider when you are planning your pitch to management to change your practices:

- The cost of employees maintaining your current system is often hard to assign a monetary value to, which makes comparing the costs of a SaaS option harder. When you're costing out an external solution, those unhidden costs will feel larger until you add the hidden people costs to the current solution.
- The cost of hardware or cloud-provider resources involved in your current system is amortized with the rest of your infrastructure costs, so those costs feel hidden. As with the people costs, if you don't factor in the hosting costs of your current system, you won't get a true comparison with the external solution's cost.
- Moving from open source tools to a per-month-cost provider feels like giving up. This reaction is an emotional one (the humans who make the decision are emotional creatures; ignore this fact at your peril), but it's no less of a barrier to decision-making than costs are. Focus on the rational costs and business value to get over the emotional reaction.

B.4 Telemetry safety and effects

Telemetry safety covers both protecting it from attackers who are looking to hide their tracks and from spills of regulated data such as data related to finances, privacy, and health (what I call *toxic data*). Chapter 15 and 16 covered both topics and provided many recommendation lists on these two topics.

Chapter 15: The two principles of secure telemetry

Chapter 15 is about securing your telemetry systems against internal and external attack. You need to follow two broad principles in planning your defenses:

- *Production systems should emit telemetry using write-only methods.* If the production systems can read what they wrote—or, worse, delete what they wrote—you have a vulnerability. Section 15.1 covers methods to make write-only telemetry a reality.
- *Once emitted, all access to telemetry (including operator/root/admin access) must be traceable, and modifications must be made obvious.* This method ensures that telemetry that has already been emitted remains a true record of what happened in your production systems and makes later tampering evident. Section 15.2 covers these methods.

Section 15.1.1: Moving telemetry too fast to catch

The defense technique I talked about in section 15.1.1 was moving telemetry off the production server/VM/instance/container/partition faster than an attacker could change it. I gave two design goals for this process:

- *Telemetry needs to be shipped continually.* Some telemetry systems rely on a Cron or Windows Scheduler task to copy log files from a server to a central NFS or shared drive. The long lag between when telemetry is emitted and when the log file leaves the box is a huge window for an attacker.
- *Telemetry needs to have low lag between when the emission happens and when it is shipped into the rest of the Shipping stage.* Low lag further reduces the window an attacker has to modify telemetry. Shipping continually is not enough; you need to be shipping recently as well. If telemetry integrity is highly important for your organization, creating an alarm for excessive shipping lag is called for.

Section 15.2.1: The three Linux Mandatory Access Control systems

Section 15.2.1 talked about using access control systems to create write-only places to put log files. Windows is easy, but Linux has a complex set of options for creating a write-only directory. I provided a list of the three mandatory ACL systems Linux has available and advice on where they're better used:

- *POSIX ACL*—This extension to the default ACL system allows Windows-like specification of multiple permissions on a directory or file. It requires filesystem support, however, and a specific mount option to enable it, Because remounting is a simple operation and you can remount with different parameters, removing POSIX ACL support from a volume is easy. Because ACL enforcement can be turned off so easily, most security teams don't consider POSIX ACLs to be truly viable.
- *SELinux*—Security Enhanced Linux is a Mandatory Access Control (MAC) system that is compiled into the Linux kernel. Unlike POSIX ACLs, SELinux can be enforced everywhere. SELinux works by giving every file, object, process, and everything else a label and defining how each label can interact with other labels. This setup allows defining relationships such as permitting exampleapp to access sockets created by logging_platform without having to specify file-level permissions. Red Hat and SLES support SELinux out of the box.

- *AppArmor*—This MAC system is also compiled into the Linux kernel. It was developed after SELinux as a way to provide most of the benefits of SELinux, but with a much easier method for managing the interface. When processes launch, they are assigned an AppArmor profile. Because the UNIX philosophy is to treat everything like a file, AppArmor profiles define which files each profile can access and what operations the profile is allowed to perform on them. Ubuntu and SLES support AppArmor out of the box.

Section 15.2.1: Places to use ACLs in a telemetry pipeline

Section 15.2 examined the Shipping stage and the areas an inside attacker can exploit to modify telemetry. Two guiding principles are involved:

- All systems must support authentication, if possible, and be configured to require it.
- The logs that show those authentication attempts must also be tracked (and likely forked into your security team's SIEM systems).

Section 15.2.3: How encryption and digital signatures support telemetry

This section had two recommendation lists. The first list defined how digital signatures (a way to verify that something hasn't been tampered with) help the goals of telemetry:

- When you're doing a security investigation, having hashed fields makes it far easier to detect events that were tampered with.
- Because the job of the Shipping stage is to modify telemetry (see chapters 3, 4, and 6), it is in a prime place to validate the hash coming from a production system (or another Shipping-stage component) and alarm in real time if it catches a hash failure.

The second list extended the first list to address the role of encryption in a telemetry pipeline:

- Encrypting the originally emitted telemetry side by side with unencrypted telemetry gives security-incident responders hints about what telemetry was changed.
- Encryption provides a safer way to handle toxic information, such as privacy- and health-related information.
- Compared with hashing (see the preceding subsection), digitally signing telemetry provides far stronger assurance that telemetry was last modified by a trusted party.
- Digital signatures provide all the benefits of hashing by making changes tamper-evident.

Section 15.2.3: How encryption and digital signatures make telemetry more fragile

Encryption is the best way to prove that telemetry hasn't been tampered with, but it also makes your telemetry more fragile—a trade-off that you have to make. If you want to add encryption or digital signatures to your telemetry, here is a list of pain points to consider before you embark on your project:

- If the writer of the structured logger silently recodes strings, such as ASCII to UTF-8, any digital signature created by a formatter will break. Make sure that the formatter and writer components of your structured logger are crystal-clear with regard to string encoding.
- If your queues, streams, or other telemetry transport methods silently recode strings, any digital signatures will break. Make sure that you build your system to handle those string conversions.
- If your storage system silently recodes strings or changes the precision of floating-point numbers, the last digital signature will break.
- Key expiration will break your telemetry system the same way that forgetting to renew the SSL certificates on your website breaks your website. To avoid that kind of outage, you need to create a system to safely renew signing/encryption keys. Also, you need to communicate the key renewals to the validation stages so that they know to expect the change. Using public key cryptography that chains up to a certificate authority will help but moves the problem to expiring certificate authorities.
- Any failure in distributing private and public keys will create at least a partial telemetry outage. Build this failure case into your service offering (modify your service-level agreements, to use the SRE term) so that your telemetry users have a better understanding of your availability promise.

Section 16.1: The three types of toxic data

Toxic data is data subject to regulations mandating safe handling procedures, and there are penalties for not getting those procedures correct. If your production systems handle toxic data, your telemetry systems can inadvertently contain it as well. Here are the biggest categories of toxic data:

- *Financial information*—The first kind of toxic data has been treated as such by financial institutions and their regulators for decades, though it took the Payment Card Industry to provide and enforce handling standards outside banks. This standard is called the Payment Card Industry Data Security Standard (PCI/DSS).
- *Health information*—The second type of toxic data to gain broad acceptance, computerization of health records (and the ease of sharing that enables) drove health-privacy regulation such as the American Health Insurance Portability and Accountability Act (HIPAA). This information is also known as ePHI (electronic protected health information).

- *Personally identifiable information* (PII)—PII is the third type of toxic data to gain acceptance. The European Union's GDPR was the first comprehensive regulation to arrive, and it started a cascade of other regulations in states, provinces, and nations across the world.

Section 16.1: The penalties for mishandling toxic data

Getting toxic data handling wrong will put your organization in legal jeopardy. The impacts are variable, but I provided a list of possible penalties. Use this list to scare people into taking this threat seriously:

- *Denial of handling that sort of information for a period of time*—Violate PCI/DSS hard enough, and the Payment Card Industry will ban you from processing credit and debit cards. This penalty puts nearly all young companies out of business or shunts them into niche markets that accept only direct bank transfers and cryptocurrencies.
- *Great big fines*—Regulators know that businesses understand money, so they make violations hurt monetarily. To make matters even worse, such fines are commonly made public information, so a major hit to the organization's reputation also happens.
- *Publicly admitting that the violation happened*—Mandatory disclosure laws force violating organizations to notify the affected people or make a public disclosure that the violation happened. No company enjoys admitting fault, which is why regulations force this step as a way to make the "Don't violate" lesson stick.
- *Explicitly assigning civil liability*—Regulation and laws make it clear that the parties affected by the leaked information are entitled to sue for damages, possibly as a class action.
- *Increased regulatory scrutiny*—Sometimes, violation means that regulators will be looking at your organization extra-hard for the next several years to ensure that no further violations happen. This extra attention often slows internal processes due to the need for the regulator to approve the change, and it sometimes forces internal process changes to appease the regulator well after the incident was resolved.

Section 16.3: What drives periodic reprocessing

Reprocessing is a telemetry procedure in which you have to rewrite all your telemetry for some reason. This process can be driven by a few things:

- Your telemetry storage system changes its format, requiring you to reprocess to update the storage format of telemetry already in the system.
- Your telemetry storage system changes its backup (offline) format, requiring you to reprocess to ensure that your backups (or offline storage) can be restored.
- Your presentation systems change their expectations for how telemetry is formatted, requiring you to reprocess old telemetry to match the new expectations.

Section 16.4: Why isolating telemetry helps you

Section 16.4 opened with a list of principles explaining why isolating your telemetry ultimately reduces the impact of toxic data spills. Reducing impact reduces all the bother of spill cleanup.

- Isolating telemetry streams that are at risk of containing toxic data (such as API server events) from streams that definitely will not (such as networking hardware telemetry) will save you money and time when you need to deal with a spill.
- If your production systems handle toxic data, throwing all your centralized logging into a single system is a clear antipattern, which maximizes your cleanup zone.
- Use the access control list (ACL) features available in your Presentation-stage systems to limit access to potentially toxic data containing telemetry to the teams that specifically need that access. This policy reduces the impact of leaks.
- Because exceptions are among the highest-risk bits of telemetry for containing toxic data, take time to engineer separate handling for your exceptions. This policy gives you far better capabilities for live redaction (redacting toxic data as part of the emitting and shipping stages), allows you to have a different ACL for reviewing exceptions, and lets you grant wider access to your application logging.

Section 16.4: Tips to avoid false-positive toxic-data detections

Section 16.4 ended with advice on writing your applications to avoid false-positive detections when the telemetry is scanned with a toxic-data detector, such as the PII detectors available from Amazon and Microsoft:

- *Avoid using random 16-digit integers for things.* Credit card numbers are 16 digits. Although every 16-digit integer isn't a valid credit card number, if you are randomly generating enough of these integers, sheer probability will create numbers that pass the Luhn algorithm that defines the valid format of credit card numbers. A million monkeys banging on typewriters can turn out Shakespeare eventually, but a random-number generator can turn out a viable credit card number far faster. Save yourself some trouble; make those integers 15 or 17 digits instead. Better yet, make them hex and avoid integers entirely.
- *Avoid using random 10- to 13-digit integers for things.* Most phone numbers with country codes are in this range (or U.S. phone numbers with area code). If the first few numbers end up matching a country code, these integers can look like phone numbers and get flagged as PII by detectors.
- *Avoid using random 9-digit integers for things.* These integers are the same length as U.S. Social Security numbers. U.S. centrism in the tech industry means that PII detectors care about this fact, even if you aren't doing business in the United States. As for credit cards, a validation algorithm of sorts exists, and a random-number generator will make hits often enough to be annoying.

- *Emit account **numbers**, not account **names**.* All too often, the account name is an email address (or something that looks like an email address) and therefore gets flagged by detectors. It's better to emit telemetry in whatever the primary key of your account table is because that's probably a number. (Perhaps do it in another base to avoid the integer problems.)

- *Keep IP addresses in your networking, web server, API gateway, and load balancer logs, and out of your application telemetry.* IP addresses are now considered to be PII by many privacy regimes. Store IP addresses somewhere and provide a way to look them up in an admin portal easily, but keep the actual addresses out of your telemetry. If you still need IP-address tracing, use a hash or other proxy value instead.

- *Avoid emitting geographical IP data (GeoIP) with your application telemetry.* Several libraries and services will return a city, state, country, and continent if given an IP address. Paid services narrow GeoIP resolution even further, isolating IP addresses to neighborhoods or even specific buildings. As a result, privacy regulators consider such GeoIP data to be private data. These services are incredibly useful in fraud and malicious-use investigations, as well as complying with government-mandated sanctions against other countries, but putting this data on every single piece of application telemetry needlessly exposes your organization to legal risk. Keep GeoIP data to your web server and networking telemetry.

B.5 Legal topics

Chapter 18 was unique in this book, because it talked about something that gets little coverage in technical books: how to work with lawyers. This chapter had two lists that need to be repeated.

Section 18.2: Questions to ask when assessing a telemetry system to handle legal hold orders

The first step in responding to a potential legal matter is when your organization's legal department issues a *legal hold* on records that might be relevant to whatever legal matter is brewing. This hold can include your telemetry systems. You will be much happier with the whole process if you have already thought about what happens during this process. Here are the questions you should ask yourself as you assess telemetry design:

- *If we get asked to save a part of our telemetry, is it easier to save that piece or to save everything from that time?* Knowing whether it's easier to store partial datasets or full datasets before you need to think about the issue will save everyone effort.

- *How will we shield the held data from routine redactions and reprocessing?* You need to be able to prevent changes to the legal-hold data. If your current systems make that task hard, spend time easing it.

- *How will we protect our unredacted/unreprocessed legal-hold data from our usual customers?* If you need to perform redactions, you need to keep the unredacted telemetry visible only to the lawyers. If the legal matter proceeds to discovery, the lawyers will perform any redactions. Also, if you need to run a second set of systems for the held data—systems that need to be exempted from your organization's patch policies—you can isolate access to the potentially vulnerable systems to the lawyers involved and the minimum number of telemetry system operators needed to keep the systems running.

- *How will we allow our lawyers to review our saved data?* Unless the hold order is for everything, chances are high that your organization's lawyers will want to make sure you're saving the right things. Let them. You will need to make this check anyway when ECA starts (section 18.1).

- *If the legal hold requires us to hold telemetry that is still being generated, what changes do we need to make to ensure that such telemetry is preserved?* Not all requests are solely for historic information; some holds may require you to hold some or all of your currently generated telemetry. Knowing what changes you need to make to support preserving live telemetry will make writing the changes much easier if you get asked to do so.

- *Is our oldest telemetry data viewable in our current software versions?* If part of your retention policy involves storing telemetry offline for a period of time, you need to know early whether your oldest telemetry can be restored into the current system or needs a second system for the restore. Setting up a second system requires resources, so knowing beforehand how much to request will save everyone time and worry.

- *If we have to upgrade our storage software during the hold period, will we need to avoid upgrading the legal hold systems?* Hold orders can last years as lawsuits grind their way through the process. Knowing whether it is safe to upgrade the resources involved in the hold order will help you stay compliant with whatever regulations you're subjected to. If upgrading is not safe, knowing early allows you to put exceptions in your patching and vulnerability management policies specifically for this edge case.

Section 18.4: How to work with lawyers

Working with lawyers can be scary if you've never done it before! Remember that lawyers are different kinds of technicians. Better, you can have your organization's lawyers talk to the extra-scary lawyers for you. If you are required to work with lawyers, keep these points in mind:

- *Your own organization's lawyers speak lawyer better than you do.* If you're uncertain what the trial team is talking about, ask your organization's lawyers to clarify. (This tip applies to interpreting happenings in the matter, by the way, even if the events don't affect you.) Unlike outside counsel, your organization's lawyers are likely salaried and not billing by the minute.

- *Cost management is a key responsibility of your organization's lawyers.* Outside counsel costs money; they charge for every interaction and find ways to bill for any time when their attention is on your case. If you think that a request is too broad (that is, possibly too expensive), ask your organization's lawyers to advise. Advice is what they're there to provide.

- *Outside trial lawyers usually come with technical specialists. Use them.* If you're not clear about what a request means, even after asking your own lawyers, the trial lawyers' technical people likely can translate the request from lawyer to engineer. Their billing rate is far lower than that of actual lawyers too.

- *If you have to push back on technical details, do that with the technical specialists.* The outside team's specialists are much better versed in discovery procedure than you are, so they are valuable for determining what is feasible. They're also much less likely to be "ask for the moon" types.

appendix C
Exercise answers

This appendix contains the answers to exercises that have a correct answer. Open-ended exercises are omitted.

EXERCISE 2.1
The correct answer is C. The `docker logs` command reviews output sent to the standard out.

EXERCISE 2.2
The correct associations are

- Logger —> Entry point into the structured logger
- Formatter —> Rewrites telemetry to fit the Shipping stage
- Writer —> Delivers telemetry to the Shipping stage

EXERCISE 2.3
The correct answer is B; both protocols emit over UDP. Syslog can often be configured to use TCP, but I don't talk about that topic in this book.

EXERCISE 3.1
The correct answer is B: shipping through a queue or stream. Apache Kafka made streaming famous.

EXERCISE 3.2
Looking to the future and working to address problems before they arise is the sort of work that can get you promoted.

EXERCISE 4.1
The correct answer is A: log files. Log files were among the first types of telemetry created, and files are ubiquitous. Off-the-shelf software often has the option of using the system logger, but log files are the first choice of most off-the-shelf and open source software.

EXERCISE 11.1
Several answers will match correctly. Here is one:

```
^\[(?<log_level>\w+?)\] (?<action>.+?) to APPID (?<app_id>\d+?), response
➥ (?<response_code>\d{3})$
```

Remember that +? means a lazy match. Watch what happens to the number of steps when you remove the ? characters. Use the regex debugger to watch how matching flow changes between the greedy and nongreedy versions.

EXERCISE 11.3
Multiple answers will work. Here is one example

```
Converted type:pdf size:0.192 time:0.89
Signed type:pdf size:0.192 time:1.2
Successful Upload type:pdf size:192 time:0.019
```

that matches the regular expression:

```
^(?<action>.+?) type:(?<file_type>\w{0,6}) size:(?<file_size>[\d.]+?)
➥ time:(?<op_time>[\d.]+)$
```

The `^(?<action>.*+?)` expression matches the first everything at the beginning of the string before " type:". The `type:(?<file_type>\w{0,6})` expression matches file types, which are allowed to be zero to six characters. The `(?<file_size>[\d.]+?)` expression matches numbers with a single decimal, such as 12.3.

EXERCISE 12.1
There are several ways to answer this question, but the broad strokes of one answer are

1 Remove the __add_context function from the main file (or make it return an empty hash).
2 Create a new file named addcontext.py.
3 Define a class in addcontext.py named AddContext.
4 In the main file, add from addcontext import (AddContext), which puts our class (and the context-adding features) back into scope.
5 In the processors list, add AddContext before the final processor.

The Python in addcontext.py doesn't have to be that complex and in fact could be mostly the removed code from the __add_context function:

```
import socket
import os

__release__ = "deadbeef"
__commit__  = "abcd1234"

class AddContext(object):
```

```
def __init__(self):
  self.context = {
      'hostname': socket.gethostname(),
      'pid': os.getpid(),
      'release': __release__,
      'commit': __commit__
  }

def __call__(self, logger, name, event_dict):
  return {**event_dict, **self.context}
```

> Defining context in __init__ means we have to run this code only once.

> Returns the merged hash of context and the keys already added

EXERCISE 13.1

The correct associations are

- TCP
  - Connection-oriented, tracks connection state
  - Will retry if the network glitches
  - The basis of application protocols such as AQMP and Kafka
  - Relies on the operating system to handle retries
- UDP
  - Connectionless: fire and forget
  - Useful on fully private in-memory networks
  - The basis of server protocols such as Syslog and SNMP
  - Relies on the application to handle retries

HTTP/3 is based on UDP and deliberately moves TCP concepts such as flow control, transmission window sizing, and retransmits into the browser and away from the base operating system.

EXERCISE 13.2

The correct answer is D: a container that serves a utility purpose, such as a proxy, relay, or local service endpoint for all containers in a cluster node.

A is an example of the direct-to-standard-out telemetry method because containers emit logs to stdout and rely on something on the cluster server to reship.

B is an example use of the sidecar pattern for logs, not the definition of the sidecar pattern.

C is an example of a conventional network service and could exist outside Kubernetes or service mesh environments.

EXERCISE 13.3

The correct constraints are

- The cloud provider's opinionated storage system for telemetry emitted through stdout
- Lack of system-logger support

Complete reliance on emitting telemetry through stdout is incorrect because each cloud provider captures stdout for display in its opinionated storage.

Lack of queue or stream support is incorrect because each cloud provider has some native queue available for programmers to use.

The size limit of jobs in the cloud provider's queues is not a constraint of the FaaS system; it is a constraint on the native queues provided by the cloud provider.

EXERCISE 14.1

The correct answer is A: host.

- Dropping host (A) changes cardinality to 723,060 (309 * 78 * 15 * 2). This environment is Kubernetes, and host is rarely used in Kubernetes environments, making it a good piece of context to lose.
- Dropping pod (B) would change cardinality to 139,050 (309 * 19 * 15 * 2), which is quite nice. But pod is a key piece of context-related telemetry in Kubernetes environments, so losing it also drops a lot of key context.
- Dropping service (C) would change cardinality to 915,876 (309 * 19 * 78 * 2), but service tells you what code generated the metric, so it is highly useful.
- Dropping environment (D) would change cardinality to 6,869,070, which is above the required 1,000,000 threshold.

EXERCISE 14.2

The correct answers are

- *Increased disk use*—As indexes grow, so does the disk to contain them.
- *Increased memory use*—Most databases hold indexes in memory. As those indexes grow, so does the memory use of the database. Also, certain databases spike memory use during maintenance activities.
- *Increased storage I/O*—As cardinality increases, the database has to store more data per index. Larger indexes manifest as high I/O during query operations, as cardinality is managed during query and high I/O during maintenance operations.
- *Increased search times*—This symptom is the most visible consequence of cardinality!
- *Decreased ingestion rates*—As indexes grow more complex, the overhead of inserting data becomes bigger with each new event, slowing performance.

The incorrect answers are wrong because

- *Increased CPU use*—The impact here is slight and dwarfed by the other impacts.
- *Increased query rates*—This impact is caused more by sharding a database (Elasticsearch, Cassandra, and InfluxDB) than by increasing cardinality.
- *Decreased CPU use*—If the CPU is waiting for storage to come back with index contents, those cycles can be used for other queries.

EXERCISE 14.3

The correct answers are

- *Process ID*—Identifies a specific execution; metrics systems are all about generalities. Process ID is also highly unique, making it a poor choice for metrics telemetry.

- *Account ID*—Unless the production systems have few accounts, this detail will have too many unique values to make it a good fit for a metrics system.
- *Function or class name*—This attribute is useful only if you're using the same metric name in different places and need disambiguation. As a general key, it has too many unique values to be useful in a metrics system. On the other hand, it highly useful in a centralized logging system!

EXERCISE 15.3
The correct answers are

- Production systems should emit using write-only methods.
- Once emitted, all access to telemetry must be traceable, and modifications must be made obvious

EXERCISE 16.1
The correct answer is A: engineers logging parameters as part of normal logging. A is definitely one leak, and I've seen it happen more than once, but it is not one of the top two.

EXERCISE 17.1
The correct associations are

- Centralized logging = Offline archives that can quickly be brought online
- Metrics = Aggregation
- Distributed tracing = Sampling
- SIEM = Being highly selective about what is stored

EXERCISE 17.3
The correct order is

- SIEM
- Metrics
- Distributed tracing
- Centralized logging

index

RELATED MANNING TITLES

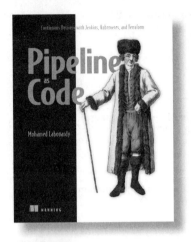

Pipeline as Code
by Mohamed Labouardy

ISBN 9781617297540
385 pages (estimated), $59.99
Fall 2021 (estimated)

Data Engineering on Azure
by Vlad Riscutia

ISBN 9781617298929
336 pages, $49.99
July 2021

Securing DevOps
by Julien Vehent

ISBN 9781617294136
384 pages, $49.99
August 2018

For ordering information go to www.manning.com